Color Figure 2

Part a

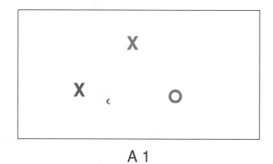

A 1

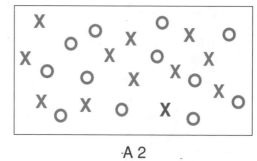

A 2

Part b

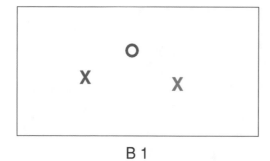

B 1

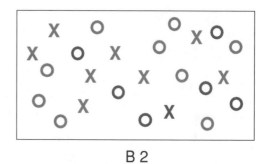

B 2

FOURTH EDITION

COGNITION

Margaret W. Matlin
State University of New York, Geneseo

FOURTH EDITION

COGNITION

Margaret W. Matlin

State University of New York, Geneseo

Harcourt Brace College Publishers

Fort Worth   Philadelphia   San Diego   New York   Orlando   Austin   San Antonio
Toronto   Montreal   London   Sydney   Tokyo

Publisher   Christopher P. Klein
Acquisitions Editor   Earl McPeek
te Acquisitions Editor   Lisa D. Hensley
oduct Manager   Don Grainger
Developmental Editor   Amy Hester/Van Strength
Project Editor   Tamara Neff Vardy
Production Manager   Eddie Dawson/Andrea A. Johnson
Art Director   Don Fujimoto

Cover image: © H. Okamoto/Photonica

Address editorial correspondence to:
Harcourt Brace College Publishers
301 Commerce Street, Suite 3700
Fort Worth, TX 76102

Address orders to:
Harcourt Brace & Company
6277 Sea Harbor Drive
Orlando, FL 32887-6777
1-800-782-4479

Harcourt Brace may provide complimentary instructional aids and supplements or supplement packages to those adopters qualified under our adoption policy. Please contact your sales representative for more information. If as an adopter or potential user you receive supplements you do not need, please return them to your sales representative or send them to:
Attn: Returns Department
Troy Warehouse
465 South Lincoln Drive
Troy, MO 63379

Printed in the United States of America

ISBN: 0-15-504081-2

Library of Congress Catalog Card Number: 96-79969

7 8 9 0 1 2 3 4 5 6 039 9 8 7 6 5 4 3 2

*T*his
book
is
dedicated
to
Helen and Donald White
and
Clare and Harry Matlin

As I write the preface for this fourth edition of *Cognition,* I'm reminded of the impressive advances in our discipline since the first edition was published in 1983. Cognitive psychologists have explored topics that were not even mentioned in the first edition—topics such as bilingualism, working memory, and children's eyewitness testimony. They have also developed new theoretical approaches. For example, parallel distributed processing was not even mentioned in the first edition, and the topic was discussed in only a paragraph of the second edition. New research techniques have also opened new pathways for exploration; neuroscience research allows us to investigate the biological basis for attention, mental imagery, and language. Cognitive psychologists are increasingly creative in developing their research techniques, so it's exciting to contemplate how the field of cognition will expand during the 21st century.

This research continues to emphasize the astonishing competence of our cognitive processes. We manage to recall the names of classmates from elementary school, details of an event that occurred a decade ago, and even the meaning of foreign language vocabulary we haven't contemplated since high school. Infants who are 14 months old can remember information about a trivial event from three months earlier, and 6-year-olds know about 14,000 words, which they use to construct sentences that are both unique and accurate.

Still, many cognitive psychology textbooks are written in such a dry academic style that they fail to capture these inherently interesting capabilities. Over the years, I've received letters and comments from hundreds of students and professors, telling me how much they enjoyed reading this textbook. Using their feedback, I have tried to write this fourth edition so that the features readers most appreciate are even stronger than in previous editions.

FEATURES OF THE TEXTBOOK

I have now taught the Cognitive Psychology course at SUNY Geneseo approximately 25 times. In writing *Cognition,* I have continually kept in mind students like those in my classes. Here are some of the ways in which I consider this textbook to be student-oriented:

1. The writing style is clear and interesting, with numerous examples.
2. The text demonstrates how our cognitive processes are relevant to our everyday, real-world experiences.
3. The book frequently examines how cognition can be applied to other disciplines, such as education, communication, clinical psychology, medicine, law, and consumer psychology.
4. The first chapter introduces five major themes that are then traced throughout the book, providing students with a sense of continuity across many diverse topics.

5. Many easy-to-perform demonstrations illustrate important experiments in cognition and clarify central concepts in the discipline.

6. Each new term is introduced in ***boldface and italic print*** and is accompanied by a concise definition that appears in the same sentence; pronunciation guides are included for new terms with potentially ambiguous pronunciation.

7. An outline and a preview introduce the chapters, providing an appropriate framework for new material.

8. Each major section in a chapter concludes with a summary. This feature enables students to review and consolidate material before moving to the next section, rather than waiting until the chapter's end for a single, lengthy summary.

9. Each chapter includes review questions and a list of new terms.

10. Each chapter concludes with a list of recommended readings and a brief description of each resource.

THE TEXTBOOK'S ORGANIZATION

A textbook must be interesting and helpful. It must also reflect current developments in the discipline, and it must allow instructors to adapt its structure to their own teaching plans. Instructors will therefore find the following features appealing.

1. *Cognition* offers a comprehensive overview of the field, including chapters on perception, memory, imagery, general knowledge, language, problem solving and creativity, reasoning and decision making, and cognitive development.

2. Each chapter is a self-contained unit. For example, terms such as *heuristics* or *schema* are defined in every chapter in which they are used. This feature allows instructors considerable flexibility in the sequence of chapter coverage. For example, some instructors may wish to cover the topic of imagery prior to the three chapters on memory.

3. Each section of a chapter is a discrete unit, particularly because every section concludes with a section summary. Instructors may choose to cover individual sections in a different order. For example, one instructor may decide to cover the section on schemas prior to the chapter on long-term memory. Another instructor might prefer to subdivide Chapter 12, on cognitive development, so that the first section of this chapter follows Chapter 5, the second section follows Chapter 7, and the third section follows Chapter 9.

4. Chapters 2 through 12 each include an in-depth section, which focuses on recent research about selected topics in cognitive psychology and provides details on research methods. Five are new to this fourth edition, and the remaining six have been substantially updated and revised.

5. In all, the bibliography contains 1,623 references, 820 of them from the 1990s. As a consequence, the textbook provides a very current overview of the discipline.

HIGHLIGHTS OF THE FOURTH EDITION

As I emphasized earlier, the discipline of cognitive psychology has made tremendous advances since the third edition of this textbook was published in 1994. Research in the areas of memory and language has been especially ambitious, and theoretical approaches to the discipline have been greatly expanded. Feedback from people who have used the textbook suggested that the sequence of 12 chapters in the fourth edition should remain the same as in the third edition. However, every page of this textbook has been updated and rewritten. Some of the more noteworthy changes include the following:

- Chapter 1 features updated information on the history of cognitive psychology, more material on neuroscience techniques (including functional magnetic resonance imaging), new coverage of artificial intelligence, and more details on the parallel distributed processing approach.

- Chapter 2 now includes a new in-depth section on face perception, a new discussion of the cognitive unconscious, and updated coverage of divided attention, selective attention, feature integration theory, and the biological basis of attention.

- Chapter 3, on models of memory, now contains sections on the long-term recency effect and the generation effect, as well as expanded coverage of Tulving's model and parallel distributed processing.

- Chapter 4 now features an in-depth section on the working-memory approach to short-term memory, with an emphasis on this approach throughout the chapter; new material has also been added on sensory memory, the duration of short-term memory, and the code in short-term memory.

- In Chapter 5, the sections on determinants of accuracy, expertise, and memory improvement are rearranged and updated; the discussion of eyewitness testimony now examines the false memory controversy and the constructivist approach.

- Chapter 6 features a new in-depth section on imagery and interference; the discussion has been updated on rotation of mental images, ambiguous figures, and the neuropsychology of imagery.

- Chapter 7, on general knowledge, has shortened the coverage of semantic memory and updated the sections on schemas, the tip-of-the-tongue phenomenon, and metamemory.

- Chapter 8 is the most thoroughly revised chapter of this fourth edition. The chapter now begins with an introduction to the nature of language, and a new section on neurolinguistics has been added. New coverage is added to the sections on Chomsky's theory, ambiguity, speech perception, saccadic eye movements, word recognition, inferences in reading, and metacomprehension.

- In Chapter 9, new material has been added to the production process, narratives, and bilingualism; a new in-depth section focuses on the maintenance of first-language skills among immigrants.
- Chapter 10 features updated coverage on the means-ends heuristic, the analogy approach, expertise, problem solving and memory, mental set, verbalization and problem solving, and creativity.
- In response to comments from professors who used earlier editions, Chapter 11 has been significantly shortened, so that cognitive processing is examined for conditional reasoning but not for syllogisms. New material has been added on hypothesis confirmation, the small-sample fallacy, base rate, and overconfidence. The in-depth section now focuses on the framing effect.
- Chapter 12 features a new in-depth section on memory in children (including eyewitness testimony); also included is new research on infant memory, working memory in the elderly, children's language, and pragmatic mastery.

In preparing this new edition, I made every possible effort to include up-to-date research. I examined every relevant entry in *Psychological Abstracts* between 1992 and 1996; this investigation was supplemented by numerous specific *PsycLIT* searches. Furthermore, I examined every relevant book reviewed in *Contemporary Psychology*. In addition, I wrote to more than 200 researchers, requesting reprints and preprints. The research on cognition is expanding at an ever-increasing rate, and this textbook captures the excitement of the current research.

Professors should contact their Harcourt Brace & Company sales representative to obtain a copy of the Test Item File. This ancillary has been extensively revised for this fourth edition, with 240 new questions added. I have continued to emphasize conceptual knowledge in these questions, as well as applications to real-world situations. The testbank is now available in computerized formats.

ACKNOWLEDGMENTS

I have many individuals to thank for their impressive efforts on this book. First, I would like to praise the people at Harcourt Brace & Company. Earl McPeek, executive editor at Harcourt, helped to clarify the goals for this fourth edition, and he guided my writing during the preparation and revision of the manuscript. Amy Hester, who served as my developmental editor, arranged for a superb set of reviewers, organized the reviewers' feedback in an exemplary fashion, and helped to make decisions about the book's structure. I would also like to acknowledge the expertise of two individuals whose expertise was valuable during the final preparation of this book: Lisa Hensley, associate editor, and Van Strength, developmental editor.

I also want to thank many Harcourt people who worked on the production of this fourth edition. Tamara Vardy is a superb project editor. I truly appreciate her organizational skills, precision, and intelligence; it was reassuring to me that she genuinely cared about this book. Production managers Eddie Dawson and Andrea Johnson also coordinated the numerous decisions that needed to be made throughout the production of *Cognition.*

Florence Fujimoto deserves my genuine gratitude for her superb artwork on this edition; her careful work, creativity, and conscientiousness made this phase of the production problem-free. Don Fujimoto served as art director for the book; I'm very pleased with the clean and readable design of this edition. Carolyn Crabtree is a treasured copy editor who pointed out some inconsistencies, smoothed out ambiguities, and contributed her substantial expertise in all phases of the task. Sandra Lord served as photo editor, and Roberta Kirchhoff was the proofreader; their conscientious work is also appreciated. Once more, Linda Webster compiled both the subject index and the author index; I continue to be impressed with her intelligent and careful work on this important phase of the textbook. Finally, I would like to thank Don Grainger, the product manager, and the Harcourt Brace sales representatives for their good work and enthusiastic support.

During my undergraduate and graduate training, many professors kindled my enthusiasm for the growing field of cognition. I would like to thank Gordon Bower, Albert Hastorf, Leonard Horowitz, and Eleanor Maccoby of Stanford University, and Edwin Martin, Arthur Melton, Richard Pew, and Robert Zajonc of the University of Michigan.

Many others have contributed in important ways to this book. Tanya Charbonneau, Benjamin Griffin, Melissa Katter, Kristina Rodolico, and Rebecca Sitler are exemplary student assistants who helped locate references and prepare the bibliography. Also, Shirley Thompson, Mary Lou Perry, Carolyn Emmert, and Connie Ellis kept other aspects of my life running smoothly, allowing me more time to work on this writing project.

Others have helped in a variety of ways. Three members of Milne Library, SUNY Geneseo, deserve special thanks: Paula Henry ordered numerous books for me and kept me updated on interesting, relevant references. Judith Bushnell helped track down wayward references and elusive supplemental information. Harriet Sleggs efficiently ordered several hundred books and articles through interlibrary loan.

In addition, a number of students contributed to the book and provided useful suggestions after reading the first three editions: Mary Jane Brennan, Miriam Dowd, Elizabeth Einemann, Michelle Fischer, Benjamin Griffin, Don Hudson, Jay Kleinman, Mary Kroll, Kelly Lim, Pamela Mead, Pamela Mino, Michelle Morante, Judith Rickey, Mary Riley, Margery Schemmel, Richard Slocum, John Tanchak, Dan Vance, Heather Wallach, and Rachelle Yablin. Several students at Stanford University's Casa Zapata provided insights about bilingualism: Laura Aizpuru, Sven Halstenburg, Rodrigo Liong, Jean Lu, Edwardo Martinez, Sally Matlin, Dorin Parasca, and Laura Uribarri. Other students provided information about useful cognitive psychology articles: Ned Abbott, Patricia Kramer, Leslie Lauer, Sally Matlin, Christopher Piersante, Laura Segovia, and Nancy Tomassino. Thanks also to colleagues Drew Appleby, Ada Azodo, Hugh Foley, Ken Kallio, Lisbet Nielsen, Lori Van Wallendael, and Alan Welsh for making suggestions about references and improved wording for passages in the text.

I would also like to express my continuing appreciation to the textbook's reviewers. The reviewers who helped on the first edition included Mark Ashcraft, Cleveland State University; Randolph Easton, Boston College; Barbara Goldman, University of Michigan-Dearborn; Harold Hawkins, University of Oregon; Joseph Hellige, University of Southern California; Richard High, Lehigh University; James Juola, University of Kansas; Richard Kasschau, University of Houston; and R. A. Kinchla, Princeton University.

The reviewers who gave assistance on the second edition were: Harriett Amster, University of Texas at Arlington; Francis T. Durso, University of Oklahoma; Susan E. Dutch, Westfield State College; Sallie Gordon, University of Utah; Richard Gottwald, University of Indiana at South Bend; Kenneth R. Graham, Muhlenberg College; Morton A. Heller, Winston-Salem State University; Michael W. O'Boyle, Iowa State University; David G. Payne, SUNY Binghamton; Louisa M. Slowiaczek, Loyola University at Chicago; Donald A. Smith, Northern Illinois University; Patricia Snyder, Albright College; and Richard K. Wagner, Florida State University.

The third-edition reviewers included: Ira Fischler, University of Florida; John Flowers, University of Nebraska; Nancy Franklin, SUNY Stony Brook; Joanne Gallivan, University College of Cape Breton; Margaret Intons-Peterson, Indiana University, Christine Lofgren, University of California, Irvine; Bill McKeachie, University of Michigan; William Oliver, Florida State University; Andrea Richards, University of California, Los Angeles; Jonathan Schooler, University of Pittsburgh; and Jyotsna Vaid, Texas A & M University. The excellent advice from the reviewers on these three earlier editions continued to guide me as I prepared this most recent version.

Reviewers for this fourth edition provided superb advice on both the empirical and theoretical portions of this book, and they recommended some extremely helpful additional resources. They also gave useful guidance on the organizational and syntactic aspects of the manuscript. Finally, they advised me about sections that needed expansion or shortening. I would like to thank the following psychologists for their careful, thoughtful work: Lucinda DeWitt, Concordia College; Susan Dutch, Westfield State College; Kathleen Flannery, Saint Anselm College; Linda Gerard, Michigan State University; Catherine Hale, University of Puget Sound; Timothy Jay, North Adams State College; W. Daniel Phillips, Trenton State College; Dana Plude, University of Maryland; Jonathan Schooler, University of Pittsburgh; Matthew Sharps, California State University-Fresno; Greg Simpson, University of Kansas; Margaret Thompson, University of Central Florida; and Paul Zelhart, East Texas State University.

The final words of thanks belong to my family members. My husband, Arnie Matlin, encouraged me to write the first edition of this book during the early 1980s. His continuing enthusiasm and loving support always bring joy to my writing—and to my life! Our daughters, Beth and Sally, now live in other parts of the world. However, their ongoing pride in my accomplishments makes it even more rewarding to be an author! Last, I would like to express my gratitude to four other important people who have shaped my life, my parents by birth and my parents by marriage: Helen and Donald White, and Clare and Harry Matlin.

Margaret W. Matlin
Geneseo, New York

CONTENTS

CHAPTER 1
INTRODUCTION 1

A BRIEF HISTORY OF THE COGNITIVE APPROACH 3
The Origins of Cognitive Psychology 3
The Emergence of Contemporary Cognitive Psychology 6
Section Summary: A Brief History of the Cognitive Approach 8

CURRENT ISSUES RELATED TO COGNITIVE PSYCHOLOGY 9
Cognitive Science 10
Cognitive Neuroscience 11
Artificial Intelligence 13
The Parallel Distributed Processing Approach 15
Section Summary: Current Issues Related to Cognitive Psychology 17

AN OVERVIEW OF THE BOOK 18
A Preview of the Chapters 18
Themes in the Book 20
How to Use the Book 21
Chapter Review Questions 23
New Terms 24
Recommended Readings 24

CHAPTER 2
PERCEPTUAL PROCESSES 26

PREVIEW 27

INTRODUCTION 27

PATTERN RECOGNITION 28
Theories of Pattern Recognition 29
Top-Down Processing and Pattern Recognition 35
In Depth: Face Perception 40
Section Summary: Pattern Recognition 42

ATTENTION 43
Divided Attention 44
Selective Attention 45
Theories of Attention 48

The Biological Basis of Attention 54
Consciousness 57
Section Summary: Attention 61
Chapter Review Questions 61
New Terms 63
Recommended Readings 63

CHAPTER 3
MODELS OF MEMORY 64

PREVIEW 65

INTRODUCTION 65

THE ATKINSON-SHIFFRIN MODEL 67
    Description of the Atkinson-Shiffrin Model 67
    Research on the Atkinson-Shiffrin Model 70
    The Current Status of the Atkinson-Shiffrin Model 74
    Section Summary: The Atkinson-Shiffrin Model 76

THE LEVELS-OF-PROCESSING APPROACH 76
    Description of the Levels-of-Processing Approach 76
    Research on the Levels-of-Processing Approach 78
    In Depth: The Self-Reference Effect 81
    The Current Status of the Levels-of-Processing Approach 86
    Section Summary: The Levels-of-Processing Approach 87

TULVING'S MODEL: EPISODIC, SEMANTIC, AND PROCEDURAL MEMORY 87
    Description of Tulving's Model 87
    Research on Tulving's Model 91
    The Current Status of Tulving's Model 93
    Section Summary: Tulving's Model of Episodic, Semantic, and Procedural Memory 93

THE PARALLEL DISTRIBUTED PROCESSING APPROACH 94
    Description of the Parallel Distributed Processing Approach 94
    The Current Status of the Parallel Distributed Processing Approach 98
    Section Summary: The Parallel Distributed Processing Approach 99
    Chapter Review Questions 100
    New Terms 101
    Recommended Readings 101

CHAPTER 4
SENSORY MEMORY AND SHORT-TERM MEMORY (WORKING MEMORY) 103

PREVIEW 104

INTRODUCTION 104

SENSORY MEMORY 105
  Iconic Memory 107
  Echoic Memory 111
  Section Summary: Sensory Memory 114

SHORT-TERM MEMORY (WORKING MEMORY) 115
  The Methodology in Classic Short-Term Memory Research 116
  The Size of Short-Term Memory 118
  The Duration of Short-Term Memory 122
  The Code in Short-Term Memory 122
  In Depth: The Working-Memory View of Short-Term Memory 126
  Section Summary: Short-Term Memory 131
  Chapter Review Questions 132
  New Terms 133
  Recommended Readings 133

CHAPTER 5
LONG-TERM MEMORY 135

PREVIEW 136

INTRODUCTION 136

DETERMINANTS OF ACCURACY 137
  The Effects of Context: Encoding Specificity 140
  Mood 143
  In Depth: Explicit Versus Implicit Measures of Memory 145
  Expertise 151
  Section Summary: Determinants of Accuracy 154

AUTOBIOGRAPHICAL MEMORY 154
  Flashbulb Memories 155
  Schemas and Autobiographical Memory 157
  Memory for Action 159
  Eyewitness Testimony 162

Ecological Validity and Autobiographical Memory Research 168
Section Summary: Autobiographical Memory 169

MEMORY IMPROVEMENT 169
Mnemonics Using Imagery 170
Mnemonics Using Organization 174
Practice 176
External Memory Aids 177
The Multimodal Approach 177
Metamemory 178
Section Summary: Memory Improvement 179
Chapter Review Questions 179
New Terms 180
Recommended Readings 181

CHAPTER 6
IMAGERY 182

PREVIEW 183

INTRODUCTION 183

THE CHARACTERISTICS OF MENTAL IMAGES 184
Imagery and Rotation 186
Imagery and Size 188
Imagery and Shape 193
In Depth: Imagery and Interference 196
Imagery and Ambiguous Figures 200
Imagery and Other Vision-Like Processes 203
Neuropsychological Evidence for the Similarity Between Imagery and Perception 204
The Imagery Controversy, Revisited 205
Section Summary: The Characteristics of Mental Images 207

COGNITIVE MAPS 208
Cognitive Maps and Distance 209
Cognitive Maps and Shapes 212
Cognitive Maps and Relative Positions 213
Using Verbal Descriptions to Create Mental Models 217
Section Summary: Cognitive Maps 219
Chapter Review Questions 220
New Terms 221
Recommended Readings 221

CHAPTER 7
GENERAL KNOWLEDGE 222

PREVIEW 223

INTRODUCTION 223

THE STRUCTURE OF SEMANTIC MEMORY 224
The Feature Comparison Model 225
Network Models 228
The Prototype Approach 233
Section Summary: The Structure of Semantic Memory 241

SCHEMAS 242
Scripts 243
Schemas and Memory Selection 245
Schemas and Memory Abstraction 250
Schemas and Inferences in Memory 252
Schemas and Integration in Memory 254
Conclusions About Schemas 255
Section Summary: Schemas 255

METACOGNITION 256
The Tip-of-the-Tongue Phenomenon 257
In Depth: Metamemory 260
Section Summary: Metacognition 266
Chapter Review Questions 266
New Terms 267
Recommended Readings 268

CHAPTER 8
LANGUAGE COMPREHENSION: LISTENING AND READING 269

PREVIEW 270

INTRODUCTION 270

THE NATURE OF LANGUAGE 271
Phrase Structure 272
Transformational Grammar 274
Factors Affecting Comprehension 276
Neurolinguistics 278
Section Summary: The Nature of Language 283

SPEECH PERCEPTION 283
    Characteristics of Speech Perception 283
    Theories of Speech Perception 288
    Section Summary: Speech Perception 289

BASIC READING PROCESSES 290
    Perceptual Processes in Reading 291
    Discovering the Meaning of an Unfamiliar Word 292
    Reading and Working Memory 294
    Theories About the Role of Sound in Word Recognition 295
    Section Summary: Basic Reading Processes 299

UNDERSTANDING DISCOURSE 300
    Forming a Coherent Representation of the Text 300
    In Depth: Inferences in Reading 301
    Artificial Intelligence and Reading 306
    Metacomprehension 308
    Section Summary: Understanding Discourse 311
    Chapter Review Questions 312
    New Terms 312
    Recommended Readings 313

CHAPTER 9
LANGUAGE PRODUCTION: SPEAKING, WRITING, AND BILINGUALISM 314

PREVIEW 315

INTRODUCTION 315

SPEAKING 316
    The Production Process 316
    Selecting the Active or the Passive Voice 317
    Speech Errors 317
    Producing Discourse 320
    The Social Context of Speech 322
    Section Summary: Speaking 327

WRITING 327
    Planning 328
    Sentence Generation 328
    Revision 329
    Section Summary: Writing 330

BILINGUALISM 331
    Advantages of Bilingualism 333
    In Depth: Maintenance of the First Language Among Immigrants 334
    Second-Language Proficiency as a Function of Age of Acquisition 336
    Section Summary: Bilingualism 338
    Chapter Review Questions 338
    New Terms 339
    Recommended Readings 339

CHAPTER 10
PROBLEM SOLVING AND CREATIVITY 340

PREVIEW 341

INTRODUCTION 341

UNDERSTANDING THE PROBLEM 343
    The Requirements for Problem Understanding 343
    Paying Attention to Important Information 345
    Methods of Representing the Problem 346
    Section Summary: Understanding the Problem 353

PROBLEM-SOLVING APPROACHES 354
    The Means-Ends Heuristic 355
    In Depth: The Analogy Approach 358
    Section Summary: Problem-Solving Approaches 362

FACTORS THAT INFLUENCE PROBLEM SOLVING 363
    Expertise 363
    Mental Set 366
    Functional Fixedness 368
    Insight and Noninsight Problems 369
    Section Summary: Factors That Influence Problem Solving 372

CREATIVITY 372
    Definitions 373
    Approaches to Creativity 373
    Factors Influencing Creativity 377
    Section Summary: Creativity 379
    Chapter Review Questions 379
    New Terms 380
    Recommended Readings 381

CHAPTER 11
DEDUCTIVE REASONING AND DECISION MAKING 384

PREVIEW 385

INTRODUCTION 385

DEDUCTIVE REASONING 386
  An Overview of Conditional Reasoning 387
  Difficulties With Negative Information 390
  Difficulties With Abstract Reasoning Problems 391
  The Belief-Bias Effect 391
  Constructing Only One Model of the Premises 392
  Making an Illicit Conversion 393
  Trying to Confirm a Hypothesis, Rather Than Trying to Disprove It 394
  Failing to Transfer Knowledge to a New Task 396
  Section Summary: Deductive Reasoning 396

DECISION MAKING 397
  The Representativeness Heuristic 398
  The Availability Heuristic 406
  The Anchoring and Adjustment Heuristic 414
  In Depth: The Framing Effect 420
  Overconfidence in Decisions 425
  New Developments in Decision Making: The Optimists versus the Pessimists 429
  Section Summary: Decision Making 430
  Chapter Review Questions 430
  New Terms 432
  Recommended Readings 432

CHAPTER 12
COGNITIVE DEVELOPMENT 434

PREVIEW 435

INTRODUCTION 435

THE DEVELOPMENT OF MEMORY 436
  Memory in Infants 436
  In Depth: Memory in Children 441
  Memory in Elderly People 449
  Section Summary: The Development of Memory 453

THE DEVELOPMENT OF METACOGNITION 454
  Metacognition in Children 454
  Metacognition in Elderly People 459
  Section Summary: The Development of Metacognition 460

THE DEVELOPMENT OF LANGUAGE 460
  Language in Infants 461
  Language in Children 466
  Section Summary: The Development of Language 473
  Chapter Review Questions 473
  New Terms 474
  Recommended Readings 475
  One Last Task 475

  References 476
  Photo Credits 535
  Literary Acknowledgments 536
  Name Index 538
  Subject Index 549

INTRODUCTION

A BRIEF HISTORY OF THE COGNITIVE APPROACH

The Origins of Cognitive Psychology
The Emergence of Contemporary Cognitive Psychology

CURRENT ISSUES RELATED TO COGNITIVE PSYCHOLOGY

Cognitive Science
Cognitive Neuroscience
Artificial Intelligence
The Parallel Distributed Processing Approach

AN OVERVIEW OF THE BOOK

A Preview of the Chapters
Themes in the Book
How to Use the Book

If you are like most students who have just begun to read this textbook, you will not yet feel qualified to offer a definition of the term *cognition*. Nevertheless, you have already performed a variety of cognitive processes in order to reach the second sentence in the first paragraph! For example, you used pattern recognition to interpret the assorted squiggles and lines that form the letters and words on this page. You consulted your memory to search for word meanings and to link together ideas in this paragraph. Right now, as you contemplate your own thought processes, you are engaging in another component of cognition called *metacognition*. You may also have used decision making—another cognitive process—if you tried to estimate how long you would take to read this first chapter.

Cognition, or mental activity, involves the acquisition, storage, transformation, and use of knowledge. As you might imagine, cognition includes a wide range of mental processes if cognition operates every time we acquire some information, place it in storage, transform that knowledge, and use it. This textbook will explore a variety of mental processes, including perception, memory, imagery, language, problem solving, reasoning, and decision making.

A related term, **cognitive psychology,** has two meanings: (1) Sometimes it is a synonym for the word *cognition,* and it therefore refers to the variety of mental activities we just listed and (2) sometimes it refers to a particular theoretical approach to psychology. The **cognitive approach** is a theoretical orientation that emphasizes mental structures and processes (Craik, 1991). For example, a cognitive psychology explanation of stereotypes would emphasize how cognitive processes such as perception, memory, and decision making help to create and preserve stereotypical beliefs. The cognitive approach is often contrasted with several other current psychological approaches. For example, the behaviorist approach emphasizes observable behaviors; the psychodynamic approach focuses on unconscious emotions; and the humanistic approach emphasizes personal growth and interpersonal relationships. To explain stereotypes, these three approaches would describe behaviors, emotions, and personal growth—rather than cognitive processes.

Why should psychology students learn about cognition? One reason is that cognition occupies a major portion of the study of human psychology. What have you done in the past hour that did *not* require perception, memory, language, or some other higher mental process?

A second reason to study cognition is that the cognitive approach has widespread influence on other areas of psychology. For instance, social psychology has been deeply affected by cognitive psychology (e.g., Fiske & Taylor, 1991; Wyer & Srull, 1994). The cognitive approach has also influenced educational psychology (e.g., Schneider & Graham, 1992), developmental psychology (e.g., Golombok & Fivush, 1994; Simon, 1990), and health psychology (e.g., Clark, 1994). Cognitive psychology has also influenced interdisciplinary areas. For example, a journal called *Political Psychology* emphasizes how cognitive factors can contribute to political situations. In summary, an appreciation of cognitive psychology will help you understand many other areas of psychology.

The final reason for studying cognition is more personal. You own an impressive piece of equipment—your mind—and you use this equipment every minute of the day. When you purchase a car, you typically receive a booklet that describes how it works. However, no one issued you an owner's manual for your mind when you were born. In a sense, this book is an owner's manual, describing what is known about how your mind works. This book—like a car manual—also contains hints on how to improve performance.

The remainder of this introductory chapter focuses on three topics. First, we'll briefly consider the history of cognitive psychology, and then we'll outline some important current issues. The final part of the chapter describes this textbook, including its content and major themes, as well as suggestions for using the book effectively.

A BRIEF HISTORY OF THE COGNITIVE APPROACH

The cognitive approach to psychology traces its origins to the classical Greek philosophers and to developments in nineteenth- and twentieth-century psychology. As we will also see in this section, however, the contemporary version of cognitive psychology emerged within the last 50 years.

The Origins of Cognitive Psychology

Human thought processes have intrigued philosophers and other theorists for at least 2,000 years. For example, the Greek philosopher Aristotle proposed laws for learning and memory, and he emphasized the importance of mental imagery (Mayer, 1983). As Hearnshaw (1987) notes, cognitive psychology is both the oldest and the newest component in the history of psychology.

The Nineteenth Century. Theorists in the history of psychology often celebrate 1879 as the birth of scientific psychology. It was then that Wilhelm Wundt (pronounced "voont") opened his laboratory in a small lecture room in Leipzig, Germany, Thus, psychology emerged as a new discipline that was separate from philosophy and physiology. Within several years, students flocked from around the world to study with Wundt, who eventually sponsored 186 PhD dissertations in psychology (Hearst, 1979).

Wundt proposed that psychology should study mental processes, using a technique called introspection. *Introspection,* in this case, meant that trained observers paid careful attention to their own sensations, made precise discriminations among these sensations, and reported them as objectively as possible (Gardner, 1985; Posner, 1986; Rachlin, 1994). For example, observers might be asked to report their reactions to a specific musical chord. These observers were encouraged to describe the sensations they felt, rather than the stimuli that produced the sensations. They were also instructed to report thoughts and images without attempting to give them meaning.

Wundt's program was not simply stated once and then forgotten. Instead, Wundt worked continuously for 50 years to promote the introspective technique through journals and conferences (Gardner, 1985). His work emphasized careful training of observers and the use of relevant controls. These techniques have been incorporated in twentieth-century research on cognitive processes. Wundt also pointed out the importance of *replications,* which are experiments in which a phenomenon is tested under different conditions. Most of the research discussed in this book has been replicated several times.

In many ways, Wundt's careful, rigorous methods were similar to present-day cognitive research. Wundt specifically wrote, however, that higher mental processes such as thinking, language, and problem solving could not be appropriately investigated with the introspective technique (Rachlin, 1994).

Not all of Wundt's colleagues adopted the introspective technique, however. Another German psychologist named Hermann Ebbinghaus (1885/1913), for example, devised his own methods for studying human memory. He constructed more than 2,000 nonsense syllables (for instance, DAP) and tested his own ability to learn these stimuli. Ebbinghaus examined a variety of factors that might influence performance, such as the amount of time between list presentations. He specifically chose nonsense syllables rather than meaningful material so that the stimuli would not have previous associations with past experiences. Meanwhile, in the United States, similar memory research was being conducted by psychologists such as Mary Whiton Calkins (1894), who was the first woman to be president of the American Psychological Association. For example, Calkins reported a phenomenon called the *recency effect* (Madigan & O'Hara, 1992); as we will see in Chapter 3, our recall is especially accurate for the final items in a long series of stimuli.

Ebbinghaus, Calkins, and other memory researchers had greater influence on cognitive psychology and on other areas of experimental psychology than did Wundt and his introspection technique. For instance, later researchers were more likely to conduct experiments testing how selected variables influenced memory than to ask observers to report the sensations produced by a stimulus. However, Ebbinghaus's methods encouraged decades of experimental psychologists to use meaningless material to study memory. Unfortunately, they avoided investigating the very different approach that humans adopt when they must recall meaningful material.

Another crucial figure in the history of cognitive psychology is William James, an American whose theories became especially prominent at the end of the nineteenth century. James was not much impressed with Wundt's introspection technique or Ebbinghaus's research with nonsense words. Instead, James preferred a more informal approach, emphasizing the kinds of psychological questions encountered in daily life. He is best known for his textbook, *Principles of Psychology,* published in 1890, which has been described as "probably the most significant psychological treatise ever written in America" (Evans, 1990, p. 11).

Principles of Psychology provides detailed descriptions about the stream of human experience and emphasizes that the human mind is active and inquiring. The book foreshadows numerous topics that currently fascinate cognitive psychologists, such as perception (Dember, 1990), attention (LaBerge, 1990), reasoning (Nickerson,

1990), and the tip-of-the-tongue phenomenon (Brown, 1990). Consider, for example, a portion of James's description of the tip-of-the-tongue experience:

> Suppose we try to recall a forgotten name. The state of our consciousness is peculiar. There is a gap therein but no mere gap. It is a gap that is intensely active. A sort of wraith of the name is in it, beckoning us in a given direction, making us at moments tingle with the sense of our closeness and then letting us sink back without the longed-for term. (1890, p. 251)

Perhaps James's most significant contributions to the field of cognitive psychology were his theories about memory. He proposed two different kinds of memory and distinguished between memory structure and memory processing. This framework foreshadowed the important memory model proposed about 80 years later by Atkinson and Shiffrin (1968), which we will examine in detail in Chapter 3.

The Twentieth Century. In 1924, the American psychologist John B. Watson initiated a major new force in psychology known as behaviorism. ***Behaviorism*** is an approach that relies only on objective, observable reactions; it emphasizes the environmental determinants of behavior, rather than mental processes (Hineline, 1992). The behaviorists believed that introspection was far too subjective and unscientific, and that consciousness was far too vague to be investigated properly. In fact, their emphasis on observable behavior led them to reject any terms referring to mental events, such as *image, idea,* or *thought.* Many behaviorists classified thinking as simply subvocal speech. Presumably, appropriate equipment could detect the tiny movements made by the tongue (observable behaviors) during thinking. In other words, if you are thinking as you read this sentence, some early behaviorists would have said that you are really just talking to yourself, but so quietly that you cannot be heard. Behaviorists did not believe that vague, invisible constructs such as *thought* were necessary. Significantly, behaviorists were likely to avoid the human research participants favored by Wundt and Ebbinghaus, preferring instead the laboratory rat.

The study of mental activity was certainly hampered by behaviorists' refusal to study hidden processes. However, behaviorism still contributed significantly to the methods of current cognitive psychology (Simon, 1992a). Behaviorists stressed that concepts should be carefully and precisely defined. For example, *performance* might be defined as the number of trials that a rat required to complete a maze without error. Current cognitive psychology research also emphasizes precise definitions. For example, a cognitive researcher must use a precise definition for *memory.* In addition, behaviorism stressed experimental control. As a result, research psychologists primarily studied animals other than humans, because animals can be reared under far more carefully specified conditions than humans. Clearly, then, behaviorists rarely studied the kinds of human higher mental processes that interest contemporary cognitive psychologists.

Behaviorism thrived in the United States for several decades, but it had less influence on European psychology. An important new development in Europe at the turn of the century was Gestalt psychology. ***Gestalt psychology*** is an approach that emphasizes that humans have basic tendencies to organize what they see and that the whole is greater than the sum of its parts. Consider, for example, the first seven notes of the Alphabet Song ("AB-CD-EFG . . ."). The melody that results is more than simply seven tones strung together; it seems to have unity and organization. It has a Gestalt, or overall quality that transcends the individual elements (Gardner, 1985).

The Gestalt psychologists strongly objected to the introspective technique of analyzing experiences into separate components, because they stressed that the whole experience is inherently organized. The Gestalt psychologists constructed a number of laws that explain why certain components of a pattern seem to belong together. For example, the law of proximity or nearness states that items tend to be grouped together when they are physically close to one another.

Gestalt psychologists also emphasized the importance of insight in problem solving (Holyoak & Spellman, 1993). When you are trying to solve a problem, the parts of the problem initially seem unrelated to each other. However, with a sudden flash of insight, the parts fit together into a solution. Most of the early research in problem solving was conducted by Gestalt psychologists; their work represents an important contribution to cognitive psychology.

In the first part of this century, the behaviorists were dominant in the United States, and the Gestalt psychologists were influential in Continental Europe. Meanwhile, a British psychologist named Frederick C. Bartlett conducted his research on human memory. His important book, *Remembering: An Experimental and Social Study* (Bartlett, 1932), rejected the experimental methods of Ebbinghaus. Instead, Bartlett used meaningful materials, such as lengthy stories, and he examined how people's mental set influenced their later recall of the material. He proposed that memory is a reconstructive process involving interpretations and transformations of the original material (Kendler, 1987).

Bartlett's work was largely ignored in the United States during the 1930s, because American psychologists were so devoted to the experimental methods of behaviorism. However, American cognitive psychologists later discovered his work and appreciated his naturalistic material, in contrast to Ebbinghaus's artificial nonsense syllables and rigorous control (Bransford & Johnson, 1972; Hintzman, 1993). Bartlett's emphasis on a schema-based approach to memory foreshadowed some of the research we will explore in Chapters 5 and 7 (Mandler, 1985).

The Emergence of Contemporary Cognitive Psychology

We have briefly traced the historical roots of cognitive psychology, but when was this new approach actually "born"? Cognitive psychologists generally agree that the birth of cognitive psychology should be listed as 1956 (Eysenck, 1990a; Gardner, 1985; Simon, 1981). During this prolific year, a large number of researchers published influential books and articles on attention, memory, language, concept formation, and problem solving. Some psychologists even specify a single *day* on which cognitive psychology was born. On September 11, 1956, many of the important researchers attended a symposium at the Massachusetts Institute of Technology. As George Miller recalled the event:

> I went away from the Symposium with a strong conviction, more intuitive than rational, that human experimental psychology, theoretical linguistics, and computer simulation of cognitive processes were all pieces of a larger whole, and that the future would see progressive elaboration and coordination of their shared concerns. (1979, p. 9)

Enthusiasm for the cognitive approach grew rapidly, so that by about 1960, the methodology, approach, and attitudes had changed substantially (Mandler, 1985). Another important turning point was the publication of Ulric Neisser's book *Cognitive Psychology* (Neisser, 1967). In fact, the increasing enthusiasm for the cognitive approach has sometimes been called the "cognitive revolution." Although some researchers are skeptical that the current approach is substantially different from the "pre-revolutionary" framework (Hintzman, 1993), others claim that the transition resembled an explosion. For example, Sperry (1993) wrote, "It was as if the floodgates holding back the many pressures of consciousness and subjectivity were suddenly opened" (p. 881). Several factors contributed to the dramatic rise in popularity of cognitive psychology:

1. Psychologists were becoming increasingly disappointed with the behaviorist outlook that had dominated American psychology. Complex human behavior could not readily be explained using only the terms and concepts from traditional behaviorist theory, such as stimuli, responses, and reinforcement. Because behaviorists limited themselves only to observable responses, many psychological activities could not be examined. For example, suppose we present an individual with a difficult problem (the stimulus). We wait 20 minutes until he or she produces the solution (the response). This exclusive focus on observable stimuli and responses tells us nothing about psychologically interesting processes, such as the thoughts and strategies used solving the problem (Eysenck & Keane, 1990).

2. Linguists, such as Noam Chomsky (1957), rejected the behaviorist approach to language acquisition and emphasized the mental processes we need for language. These linguists convinced many psychologists that the structure of language was too complex to be explained in behaviorist terms (Barsalou, 1992a). Many linguists argued that humans have an inborn ability to master language, an idea that clearly contradicted the behaviorists' emphasis on learning in the acquisition of language.

3. Research in human memory began to blossom at the end of the 1950s. Researchers explored the possibility of different kinds of memory, examined the organization of memory, and proposed memory models. Behavioral terms could not be easily applied to memory phenomena.

4. Jean Piaget, a Swiss theorist, had been constructing a new theory of developmental psychology that emphasized how children develop an appreciation of concepts, such as object permanence. Piaget's books began to be admired by American psychologists and educators toward the end of the 1950s.

5. One of the most important developments, the information-processing approach, evolved from computer science and communication science. Two important components of the *information-processing approach* are that (a) a mental process can best be understood by comparing it with the operations of a computer, and (b) a mental process can be interpreted as information progressing through the system in a series of stages, from stimuli to response (Eysenck, 1993; Massaro & Cowan, 1993).

Because the information-processing approach is so central to the development of cognitive psychology, we need to examine this approach in more detail. Consider, for example, the flow of information that occurs when you want to determine whether a particular bus goes to your desired destination in an unfamiliar city. First, the stimuli are received by the senses (the form of a large vehicle is registered on your retina). These data are then compared with information stored in memory (the retinal image matches the information you have stored about buses). Next, you seek additional information (you ask the driver about the destination), and these data are compared with information stored in memory (the driver's reply matches the destination you have stored). You then make your decision (you plan to board the bus), and finally, you execute the response (you step into the bus). Notice that the information-processing approach can examine the flow of information both within the organism and between the organism and the environment (Mandler, 1985).

Furthermore, the information-processing approach often attempts to understand a very sophisticated computer—the human brain (Evans, 1983). Computers are human-made tools that capture some of our cognitive flexibility (Sanford, 1985), a feature that interests psychologists. In addition, the information-processing approach argues that a number of simple mental operations can be grouped together to produce complex cognitive behavior, in the same way that complex tasks can be accomplished with the computer by stringing together a series of simple operations (Posner & McLeod, 1982).

For many years, the information-processing approach dominated cognitive psychology, and many people still favor this framework. However, in the past decade an increasing number of cognitive psychologists have abandoned the information-processing approach. Many favor the parallel distributed processing approach, which we will discuss in the next section. Still others no longer maintain loyalty to the information-processing approach, but they do not have a clear theoretical framework within cognitive psychology. As noted researchers in the field have remarked, the discipline currently lacks a clear theoretical direction for the future (Neisser, 1994; Sperry, 1993). Throughout this book, we will consider a number of small-scale theoretical viewpoints as we examine the research in cognitive psychology.

SECTION SUMMARY: A BRIEF HISTORY OF THE COGNITIVE APPROACH

1. The term *cognition* refers to the acquisition, storage, transformation, and use of knowledge; *cognitive psychology* is sometimes used as a synonym for

cognition and sometimes as a term referring to a theoretical approach to psychology.

2. Scientific psychology is often traced to Wilhelm Wundt, who developed the introspection technique.

3. Hermann Ebbinghaus studied human memory for nonsense syllables; his experimental methods were adopted by later researchers.

4. William James, in the United States, examined everyday psychological processes; he stressed the active nature of the human mind.

5. Beginning in the 1920s, behaviorists such as John B. Watson rejected the study of cognitive processes; however, behaviorist methodology had an important influence on current research techniques in cognitive psychology.

6. Gestalt psychology emphasized organization in pattern perception and insight in problem solving.

7. Cognitive psychology began to emerge in the mid-1950s; this new approach was encouraged by a disenchantment with behaviorism and also by a growth of interest in linguistics, human memory, Piagetian psychology, and the information-processing approach.

8. According to the information-processing approach, mental processes can best be understood by comparison with a computer, and a particular cognitive process can be represented by information flowing through a series of stages. Although many still favor this approach, others now endorse the parallel distributed processing approach, and still others have no specific theoretical preference within cognitive psychology.

CURRENT ISSUES RELATED TO COGNITIVE PSYCHOLOGY

Cognitive psychology has had an enormous influence on the discipline of psychology. For example, almost all researchers recognize the importance of *mental representations,* a term that would have been forbidden by behaviorists several decades earlier (Gardner, 1985). In fact, examples of "pure behaviorism" are now difficult to locate. For instance, a recent convention of the Association for Advancement of Behavior Therapy featured such presentations as "Cognitive Processing in Body Image and Eating Disorders" and "Vulnerability to Depression: Recent Advances in Cognitive Mechanisms."

The cognitive approach has also permeated most areas of psychology that had not previously emphasized thought processes. For example, the cognitive approach has had a revolutionary impact on the field of social psychology (Ostrom, 1994). In fact, a survey of psychologists in U.S. colleges and universities reported that more than 75% classified themselves as cognitive psychologists (Eysenck & Keane, 1990).

The discipline of cognitive psychology has its critics, however. Some claim that many subspecialists within cognitive psychology often do not communicate with one another. For example, a researcher in visual perception may have little contact with someone conducting research on understanding stories (Gardner, 1985).

One of the most common complaints in recent years concerns the issue of ecological validity. *Ecological validity* means that the results obtained in research should also apply to naturally occurring behavior in the real world (Cohen, 1989). Consider an experiment in which participants must memorize pairs of unrelated words, presented at 10-second intervals on a blank screen in a barren laboratory room. The results of this experiment might tell us something about the way memory operates. However, this task may have limited ecological validity, because real-life situations seldom involve this kind of controlled, context-free memorization. Furthermore, people may perform more competently in familiar environments than in laboratory settings (Rogoff, 1984).

Indeed, most cognitive psychologists prior to the 1980s did tend to conduct research in artificial laboratory environments, often using tasks that differed from daily cognitive activities. However, current researchers are much more likely to emphasize ecological validity. Psychologists interested in memory, for example, are currently studying real-life issues, such as eyewitness testimony, absent-mindedness, and memory for songs (e.g., Cohen, 1989; Rubin, 1995). However, an important drawback to these real-life memory tasks is that they cannot be as rigorously controlled as in the laboratory. This issue of ecological validity will be discussed in more detail in Chapter 5. In general, most cognitive psychologists acknowledge that the discipline must advance by conducting *both* ecologically valid and laboratory-based research (Tulving, 1991; Winograd, 1993).

Several topics are important to our discussion of current cognitive psychology. First, we need to introduce the interdisciplinary field of cognitive science. Then we will look at two areas within cognitive science that have contributed most to cognitive psychology—neuroscience and artificial intelligence. Our final topic is the new approach to cognitive psychology called parallel distributed processing.

Cognitive Science

Cognitive psychology is part of a broader field known as cognitive science. *Cognitive science* is a contemporary field that tries to answer questions about the mind. It examines the nature of knowledge, its components, its development, and its use (Gardner, 1985).

Cognitive science includes within its scope the disciplines of psychology, philosophy, linguistics, anthropology, artificial intelligence, and neuroscience (Gardner, 1985; Hunt, 1989). Some scholars also add sociology and economics to the list (Gardner, 1985). Because the field is both young and interdisciplinary, participants have not yet reached a consensus about either its content or its methods (Luger, 1994).

Theorists within the broad field of cognitive science propose that thinking involves the manipulation of internal representations of the external world (Hunt, 1989). Cognitive scientists focus on these internal representations, also called *mental models.* As a consequence, this perspective clearly differs from the behaviorist approach.

Cognitive scientists generally do not emphasize such factors as emotions or the differences among individuals (Gardner, 1985). They do tend to value interdisciplinary studies. Unfortunately, scientists in this field have not yet reached the point where they engage in many fruitful interactions with individuals from other disciplines (Keil, 1991; McTear, 1988). However, psychologists are likely to interact with researchers in two disciplines—cognitive neuroscience and artificial intelligence. Let us turn our attention to these two topics.

Cognitive Neuroscience

Cognitive neuroscience examines how the structure and function of the brain explain cognitive processes (Kosslyn & Koenig, 1992). The field began to flourish in the 1980s, when cognitive psychologists and neuroscientists began to use brain-imaging techniques to record brain activity during cognitive tasks (Waldrop, 1993). In recent years, researchers have increased their efforts to build a bridge between cognitive psychology and the neurosciences.

However, neurological explanations for complex higher mental processes are often elusive. As Gardner (1985) notes, it is a cognitive challenge to build explanatory bridges between the level of the neuron and the level of the cognitive concept. Furthermore, the neuroscience approach is more likely to determine *where* a process takes place, rather than *how* that process works (Banks & Krajicek, 1991).

Let's examine some neuroscience techniques that have provided particularly useful information for cognitive psychologists. We will begin with a method that examines individuals who have experienced brain damage, next consider three methods used with normal humans, and then, examine one method used with animals.

Brain Lesions. Brain lesions involve the destruction of tissue, most often by strokes, tumors, or accidents. The study of lesions is one of the oldest techniques that neuroscientists have used to examine cognitive processes, with research first beginning in the 1860s. Some major advances were made following World War II, because many people with war-related injuries showed very specific language disorders. The laboratory researchers in New York, Oxford, Paris, Berlin, and Moscow began to share their findings with one another. These researchers noticed similar cognitive disorders, even though the victims came from different cultures and spoke different languages (Gardner, 1985).

The study of brain lesions has greatly increased our understanding of the organization of the brain (Farah, 1990; Goodglass & Butters, 1988). Fortunately, individuals with brain lesions can often compensate for their deficits within a short time. However, this compensation sometimes makes research findings less conclusive (Robinson & Petersen, 1986).

Positron Emission Tomography (PET Scan). At any particular moment, the brain has the greatest energy demands in the regions where it is most active. As a consequence, the blood flow to these active regions increases dramatically.

Neuroscientists can obtain a picture of brain activity by measuring this blood flow pattern with a technique called *positron emission tomography,* or a *PET scan* (Roland et al., 1995). A research participant can be asked to perform a cognitive task for about 40 seconds—for example, to read a specific word naming an item and to think of a use for that item. The researchers note a correspondence between the cognitive activity and the blood flow pattern (Posner & Raichle, 1995; Thompson, 1993). PET scans can be used to study such cognitive processes as attention, mental imagery, and reading (Posner & Raichle, 1994). Color Figure 3 (inside the front cover) shows a series of PET scans. In Chapter 8 we'll discuss how they can be used in neuroscience investigations of reading.

Magnetic Resonance Imaging (MRI). When using *magnetic resonance imaging,* or *MRI,* techniques, researchers pass a strong (but harmless) magnetic field through a person's head. The MRI scanner picks up radiation from certain molecules, which are present in different concentrations in different tissues. The technique provides detailed images of brain anatomy (Posner & Raichle, 1994).

During the 1990s, neuroscientists developed an important modification of the MRI technique. In *functional magnetic resonance imaging,* or *fMRI,* the MRI technique is used to gather a series of brain images; it can make an image of blood flow changes across a 5-second period, whereas an MRI requires 90 seconds (Raichle, 1994; Schneider, 1995). The fMRI also produces more highly detailed images than the PET scan at much lower cost. This technique will allow researchers to provide far more refined accounts of the biological underpinnings of cognitive processes.

Event-Related Potential. PET scans and the fMRI technique provide maps of brain activity, but they are still too slow to provide precise information about the *timing* of brain activity. In contrast, the *event-related potential technique (ERP)* records the tiny fluctuations (lasting less than one second) in the electrical activity of the brain in response to a stimulus (Rugg, 1995). The technique is also called the *evoked-response potential technique.*

To use the event-related potential technique, researchers place electrodes on a person's scalp to record electrical signals generated from a large number of neurons located underneath the electrodes. This technique cannot identify the response of a single neuron. However, it can identify electrical changes over very brief periods. The event-related potential responds in different ways to different cognitive tasks. In Chapter 2 we will discuss how this technique is used to study the shifts in people's attention patterns when they listen to an unexpected tone; this shift in attention appears on the researcher's record of the brain's electrical signals.

Single-Cell Recording Technique. So far, we have examined four techniques that neuroscientists can use to study humans. In the *single-cell recording technique*—a technique that cannot safely be used on humans—researchers study characteristics of the brain and nervous system in animals by inserting a tiny electrode next to (or even into) a single *neuron,* the basic cell in the nervous system. For example, a neuroscientist might insert an electrode into a neuron of a cat's visual cortex.

When Hubel and Wiesel (1965, 1979) used this classic technique, they found that some kinds of cells in the visual cortex respond vigorously only when lines are presented in a particular orientation. Other kinds of cells are even more specific in their "preferences"; the visual stimulus must have not only a particular orientation, but also a specific shape and direction of movement. More details on this technique can be found elsewhere (e.g., Coren et al., 1994; Hubel, 1982; Matlin & Foley, 1997). Clearly, this research has important implications for visual pattern recognition, because the cells provide a mechanism for recognizing specific patterns, such as letters of the alphabet. We will examine this research further in Chapter 2.

A detailed investigation of cognitive neuroscience techniques is beyond the scope of this book. However, these techniques will be mentioned further in the chapters on perception, memory, and language. More information can also be obtained from other resources (e.g., Gazzaniga, 1995; Posner & Raichle, 1994).

Artificial Intelligence

Artificial intelligence (AI) is the branch of computer science concerned with creating computer programs capable of exhibiting the kind of "intelligent" behavior typically associated only with humans (Luger, 1994). Two topics that are often studied by researchers in artificial intelligence are language and problem solving; we will consider AI work in these areas in Chapters 8 and 10.

The Machine Metaphor. In recent years, many cognitive psychologists have adopted the computer as a machine metaphor for the human mind. Different kinds of machine metaphors have intrigued theorists for centuries. As early as 430 B.C., philosophers compared the human mind to a machine (Marshall, 1977). The activity of the brain has also been compared to a telephone exchange and to weaving on a loom. Thus, the computational (or computer) metaphor—represented in artificial intelligence—is only one of the latest in a long list of machine metaphors. In the next section of this chapter, we'll consider an even newer machine metaphor; the parallel distributed processing approach is modeled after the most complicated "machine"—the human brain.

According to the *computational metaphor,* the human brain works like a computer—a complex, multipurpose machine that processes information quickly and accurately. Researchers acknowledge obvious differences in physical structure between the computer and the human brain. However, they point out that both may operate according to similar general principles (Crevier, 1993; Luger, 1994). Like humans, computers feature a variety of internal mechanisms. Computers have a central-processing mechanism with a limited capacity. This resembles the limited attention capacity found in humans. (As we'll discuss in the next chapter, we cannot pay attention to everything at once.)

Another similarity is that computer systems distinguish between an active processor and a large-capacity information storage system. Likewise, cognitive psychologists often make a similar distinction between short-term and long-term memory in humans. Furthermore, both computers and humans can compare symbols and can make choices according to the results of the comparison. Researchers who favor the computational approach try to design the appropriate "software." With the right computer program, researchers hope to mimic the adaptability and the fluidity of human thought processes (McClelland et al., 1986).

AI researchers favor the analogy between the human mind and the computer because computer programs must be detailed, precise, unambiguous, and logical. Researchers can represent the functions of a computer with a flowchart that shows the sequence of stages in processing. The flowchart also illustrates the relationships among various internal functions. Suppose that the computer and the human show equivalent performance on a particular task. Then the researchers can speculate that the program that directed the computer represents an appropriate theory for describing the human's mental operations (Jacquette, 1993; Lewandowsky, 1993).

A problem arises, however, in deciding what constitutes "equivalent performance." For example, a computer program may perform a series of mathematical calculations as accurately as a human. However, the computer is much faster.

Furthermore, humans have more complex and fluid goals. For instance, people playing a game of chess may be concerned about how long the game lasts, about other social obligations, or about interpersonal interactions with their opponent. In contrast, the computer's goals are simple and rigid; the computer deals only with the outcome of the chess game (Eysenck, 1984; Neisser, 1963). In many respects, then, the performance patterns may *not* be equivalent. Every metaphor has its limitations, and the computer cannot precisely duplicate human cognitive processes.

Another issue that intrigues many AI researchers is whether a machine can think. Can a machine have conscious thoughts in the same sense that you and I have? This topic is beyond the scope of a cognition book, but if the question interests you, you can consult other resources (e.g., Churchland & Churchland, 1990; Crevier, 1993; Dennett, 1991; Searle, 1990a, 1990b).

Computer Simulation. We need to draw a distinction between "pure AI" and computer simulation. ***Pure AI*** is an approach that seeks to accomplish a task as efficiently as possible. For example, the most successful computer programs for chess evaluate as many potential moves as possible in as little time as possible. A program that considers a larger number of moves is more likely to win the game. However, the strategies employed in these computer programs show little resemblance to the strategies humans use when they play chess. In contrast, ***computer simulation*** attempts to take human limitations into account. For example, most human chess players do not have the ability to evaluate several dozen potential moves at the same time. Therefore, a computer simulation should show similar limitations in its strategies.

Computer-simulation research has been most active in such areas as basic visual processing, language processing, and problem solving. However, some tasks that humans accomplish quite easily seem to defy computer simulation. For example, any 10-year-old child can quickly search the living room for a clock, read the pattern on the clock's face, and announce the time. However, a computer cannot yet simulate this task. Computers also cannot match humans' sophistication in learning language, identifying objects in everyday scenes, or solving problems by drawing analogies with other situations (Stillings et al., 1987).

Computers have clear limitations. Nevertheless, the classic artificial intelligence approach—based on serial processing—has certainly influenced both research and theory in cognitive psychology (Harder & Togeby, 1993). These contributions will be noted throughout this textbook. However, a more recent development called the *parallel distributed processing approach* has captured the imagination of many cognitive psychologists, thereby reducing the appeal of the classic AI approach. Let us now consider this new development.

The Parallel Distributed Processing Approach

In 1986, James McClelland, David Rumelhart, and their colleagues at the University of California, San Diego, published an enormously influential two-volume book called *Parallel Distributed Processing*. Palmer's (1987) review of these volumes captures the enthusiasm with which this new approach has been greeted: "These two volumes may turn out to be among the handful of most important books yet written for cognitive psychology" (p. 925).

The *parallel distributed processing approach* proposes that cognitive processes can be understood in terms of networks that link together neuron-like units. The parallel distributed processing approach is often referred to by its initials, the *PDP approach,* or by its alternate names, *connectionism* and *neural networks.*

An undergraduate textbook in cognition cannot examine this elaborate theory or its application in detail. However, in this section we can outline its origins, its basic principles, and reactions to the PDP approach. The PDP approach will also be covered in some detail as a model of memory (Chapter 3), and it will be mentioned in several additional chapters.

Origins of the PDP Approach. Some psychologists have traced the origins of the PDP approach to William James's (1890) *Principles of Psychology* (e.g., Crovitz, 1990). We will begin with the more recent past, noting developments in both neuroscience and artificial intelligence—the two topics we have just discussed.

With the development of more sophisticated research techniques during the 1970s, neuroscientists were able to explore the structure of the *cerebral cortex,* the outer layer of the brain that is most responsible for cognitive processes. One important discovery was the numerous connections among neurons (e.g., Mountcastle, 1979). In fact, this pattern of interconnections resembled many elaborate networks.

In other words, many cognitive processes could not be localized in a particular pinpoint-sized portion of the brain. Instead, the neural activity for a particular cognitive process seems to be distributed throughout a section of the brain. For example, we cannot pinpoint one small portion of your brain in which the name of your cognitive psychology professor is stored. Instead, that information is probably distributed throughout thousands of neurons in a region of your cerebral cortex. Those who developed the PDP approach proposed a model that simulated the important features of the brain. Naturally, the model captures only a fraction of the brain's complexity. However, it includes simplified neuron-like units, numerous interconnections, and distributed neural activity (Schneider & Graham, 1992).

At the same time that theorists were learning about the features of the brain, they were becoming discouraged about the limits of the classical artificial intelligence approach favored by information-processing psychologists (e.g., Lupker, 1990). According to some classical AI models, processing was viewed as a series of discrete operations; one step must be completed before the system could go on to the next step in the flowchart (McClelland, 1988). This one-step-at-a-time approach may capture the leisurely series of operations you conduct when solving a long-division problem. However, it cannot explain how you can instantaneously perceive a visual scene (Churchland & Churchland, 1990; Martindale, 1991). When you look at a visual scene, the retina presents input to your cortex in the form of close to a million distinct signals—all at the same time.

In other words, many cognitive activities seem to involve *parallel processing,* with many signals handled at the same time, rather than *serial processing,* when only one item is handled at a given time. In short, processing appears to be both parallel and distributed, explaining the name *parallel distributed processing.*

Basic Characteristics of the PDP Approach. The parallel distributed processing approach includes several important principles. Let us begin with the two principles we have just discussed and add other major points.

1. Many cognitive processes are based on parallel operations, not serial operations.
2. The neural activity underlying a particular cognitive action (for example, remembering a word) is typically distributed across a relatively broad area of the cerebral cortex, rather than being limited to a single, pinpoint-sized location. These locations of neural activity are called *nodes,* and the nodes are interconnected.
3. When a node reaches a critical level of activation, it can affect another node to which it is connected, either by exciting it or inhibiting it (Martindale, 1991).
4. When two nodes are activated at the same time, the connection between the nodes is strengthened; thus, learning is defined as a strengthening of connections (Martindale, 1991).
5. If information is incomplete or faulty, you can still carry out most cognitive processes. For example, you can still recognize a friend's face, even if a scarf is covering her hair and forehead. Similarly, suppose that a friend is describing Dr. Brown, noting that this individual is a short, very bright professor in the chemistry department, who is very politically active. You might say, "Oh, I think you mean Dr. Black in the physics department." Our pattern recognition, memory, and other cognitive processes are extremely flexible, tolerating cues that are less than perfect (Churchland & Churchland, 1990; Luger, 1994).

The PDP approach has been widely applied throughout cognitive psychology; it has been used to explain such processes as pattern recognition, the structure of memory, dyslexia, and problem solving. Chapter 3, on models of memory, will explore in more details how the PDP approach accounts for the intricacy, flexibility, and accuracy of human memory. However, the most important characteristic of the PDP approach is that it is designed with the human brain as the basic model, rather than the serial computer (Schneider & Graham, 1992).

Reactions to the PDP Approach. Because the PDP approach is relatively new, we cannot assess its long-term impact. However, many cognitive scientists have welcomed the PDP approach as a ground-breaking new framework (e.g., Bechtel & Abrahamsen, 1991; Palmer, 1987; Schneider & Graham, 1992). Some scientists have even suggested that the PDP approach will transform the field as dramatically as did the "cognitive revolution," which replaced the earlier behaviorist approach.

Naturally, some PDP models may fail to account fully for humans' performance on cognitive tasks (Schneider & Graham, 1992). Furthermore, some cognitive scientists reject the basic framework of PDP models (e.g., Besner et al., 1990; Fodor & Pylyshyn, 1988; Pinker & Mehler, 1988). However, numerous psychologists have endorsed parallel distributed processing, developing models in areas as unrelated to each other as unconscious processing (Kihlstrom, 1987), slips of the tongue (Dell, 1986), children's cognitive development (Bates & Elman, 1993), impression formation (Kunda & Thagard, 1996), and attitude change (Eiser, 1994). With additional research, cognitive scientists should be able to determine whether the PDP approach can account for the broad range of skills represented by our cognitive processes.

SECTION SUMMARY: CURRENT ISSUES RELATED TO COGNITIVE PSYCHOLOGY

1. Cognitive psychology has gained widespread support throughout the broader field of psychology. Still, the discipline has been criticized on such issues as ecological validity.
2. Cognitive science includes several disciplines: psychology, philosophy, linguistics, anthropology, artificial intelligence, and neuroscience; cognitive scientists emphasize internal representations of the external world.
3. Cognitive neuroscientists search for brain-based explanations for cognitive processes, using such techniques as brain lesions, positron emission tomography, magnetic resonance imaging, event-related potentials, and single-cell recording.
4. Artificial intelligence approaches to cognition can involve designing computer programs that accomplish cognitive tasks as efficiently as possible (pure AI) or programs that accomplish these tasks in a human-like fashion (computer simulation).
5. In contrast to the serial processing approach of classical AI, the parallel distributed processing approach argues that the human brain provides the

ideal model. The PDP approach emphasizes that cognitive processes operate in parallel, that neural activity is distributed across a relatively broad region of the brain, and that cognitive processes can be executed even when the information is incomplete or faulty.

AN OVERVIEW OF THE BOOK

This textbook covers many different kinds of mental processes. We'll begin with perception and memory—two processes that are involved in virtually every other aspect of cognition. Later chapters discuss "higher order" processes. As the name suggests, these higher order cognitive processes depend upon the more basic processes introduced at the beginning of the book. The final chapter examines cognition across the life span. Let's preview Chapters 2 through 12.

A Preview of the Chapters

Perceptual processes *(Chapter 2)* involve the use of previous knowledge to interpret the stimuli that are registered by our senses. For example, pattern recognition allows you to recognize each of the letters on this page. Another perceptual process is attention. If you have ever tried to follow two conversations at the same time, you have probably noticed the limits of your attention!

Memory is the process of maintaining information over time. Memory is such an important part of cognition that it requires three chapters. *Chapter 3* examines four models of memory. One model emphasizes the difference between short-term and long-term memory, whereas the second model stresses that the accuracy of recall depends upon how deeply that information was processed. The third model focuses on the nature of the material stored in memory, and the fourth model is the parallel distributed processing approach, which we have just discussed.

Chapter 4, the second of the memory chapters, describes sensory and short-term memory. Have you ever heard a large clock chiming out the time when you were not really paying attention? Sensory memory makes the chimes seem to still ring inside your head for a couple of seconds after the physical stimulus has stopped. In the section on short-term memory, we will explore another phenomenon, which occurs when you forget someone's name that you heard just 30 seconds ago!

Chapter 5, the last memory chapter, focuses on long-term memory. We'll examine several factors, such as mood and expertise, that are related to people's ability to remember material for a long period of time. The section on autobiographical memory is concerned with our everyday memory experiences. For example, do you seem to have particularly vivid recall for the clothes you were wearing when an important event occurred? The final section of this chapter provides suggestions for memory improvement.

Chapter 6 examines imagery, which is the mental representation of things that are not physically present. An important controversy is whether mental images truly resemble perceptual images. For example, does your mental image of a clock resemble the visual image formed when you actually look at a clock? Another important topic concerns the mental representations we have for physical settings, such as the cognitive map you developed for your college campus.

Chapter 7 concerns general knowledge. One area of general knowledge is semantic memory, which includes factual knowledge about the world as well as knowledge about word meanings. General knowledge also includes schemas, which are generalized kinds of information about situations. For example, you have a schema for what happens during a child's birthday party. A final topic in this chapter is metacognition, which is your knowledge about your own cognitive processes. For instance, do you know whether you could remember the definition for *metacognition* if you were to be tested tomorrow morning?

Chapter 8 is the first of two chapters on language, and it examines language comprehension. One component of language comprehension is perceiving spoken language. A friend can mumble a sentence, and yet you can easily perceive the speech sounds. A second component of language comprehension is reading; you recognize words and figure out the meaning of unfamiliar words. You can also understand discourse, or long passages of spoken or written language.

Chapter 9, the second language chapter, investigates language production. When we speak, we need to select the content that we want to express, but we are also attuned to the social context of speech. For example, we make certain that the person with whom we are speaking has the appropriate background knowledge. Psychologists are just beginning to examine writing as a form of language production, but writing clearly involves different processes than speaking. The final topic is bilingualism; even though learning a single language is challenging, some people master two or more languages with fluency.

Chapter 10 considers problem solving. Suppose you want to solve a problem, such as how to cook some soup when the electricity has gone out. You'll need to represent the problem, perhaps in terms of a list, a mental image, or symbols. You can solve the problem by several strategies, such as dividing the problem into several smaller problems. Several factors that influence problem solving include expertise and whether the problem solver has a mental set that blocks alternative approaches to the problem. Our final topic is creativity. Some research demonstrates, for example, that creativity can be squelched by telling people that they will be graded for their creative efforts.

Chapter 11 addresses logical reasoning and decision making. Reasoning involves drawing conclusions from several known facts. In many cases, a person's background knowledge interferes with accurate conclusions for reasoning problems. When we make decisions, we supply judgments about uncertain events. For example, people may cancel a trip to Europe after reading about a recent terrorist attack, even though statistics might show that chances of danger are small.

Chapter 12 examines cognitive processes in infants, children, and elderly adults. People in these three age groups are more competent than you might guess. For example, 6-month-old infants can recall an event that occurred 2 weeks earlier. Young children are also quite accurate in recognizing whether they have seen something before. Finally, elderly people are very competent on many memory tasks, such as recognizing whether they have seen something before.

Themes in the Book

This book will stress certain themes and consistencies in cognitive processes. These themes can guide you, offering a framework for understanding many of the complexities of our mental abilities.

Theme 1 *The cognitive processes are active, rather than passive.* The behaviorists viewed humans as passive organisms; humans wait until a stimulus arrives from the environment, and then they respond. In contrast, the cognitive approach proposes that people are eager to acquire information. Furthermore, memory is a lively process, involving active synthesis, rather than passive storage. When you read, you actively draw inferences that were never directly stated. In summary, your mind is not a sponge that passively absorbs information leaking out from the environment. Instead, you continually search and synthesize.

Theme 2 *The cognitive processes are remarkably efficient and accurate.* The amount of material in your memory is awe-inspiring. Language development is similarly impressive because of the large number of new words and complex language structures that must be mastered. Naturally, humans make mistakes. However, these mistakes can often be traced to the use of a rational strategy. For instance, people frequently base their decisions on the ease with which examples spring to mind. This strategy often leads to a correct decision, but it can occasionally produce an error. Furthermore, many of the limitations in human information processing may actually be helpful. For instance, you may sometimes regret that you cannot

---

DEMONSTRATION 1.1

LOOKING AT UNUSUAL PARAGRAPHS

How fast can you spot what is unusual about this paragraph? It looks so ordinary that you might think nothing was wrong with it at all, and, in fact, nothing is. But it is atypical. Why? Study its various parts, think about its curious wording, and you may hit upon a solution. But you must do it without aid; my plan is not to allow any scandalous misconduct in this psychological study. No doubt, if you work hard on this possibly frustrating task, its abnormality will soon dawn upon you. You cannot know until you try. But it is commonly a hard nut to crack. So, good luck!

I trust a solution is conspicuous now. Was it dramatic and fair, although odd? *Author's hint:* I cannot add my autograph to this communication and maintain its basic harmony.

remember information for more than a few seconds. However, if you retained all information forever, your memory would be hopelessly cluttered with facts that are no longer useful. Before you read further, try Demonstration 1.1, which is based on a demonstration by Hearst (1991).

Theme 3 *The cognitive processes handle positive information better than negative information.* We understand sentences better if they are worded in the affirmative, for example, "Mary is honest," rather than in the negative, "Mary is not dishonest." Reasoning tasks are also easier with positive than with negative information. Furthermore, we have trouble noticing when something is missing, as illustrated in Demonstration 1.1. (Hearst, 1991). Incidentally, if you are still puzzled, check the end of this chapter for the answer to the demonstration. We also tend to perform better on a variety of different tasks if the information is emotionally positive (that is, pleasant), rather than emotionally negative (unpleasant). In short, our cognitive processes are designed to handle *what is,* rather than *what is not* (Hearst, 1991).

Theme 4 *The cognitive processes are interrelated with one another; they do not operate in isolation.* This textbook discusses each cognitive process in one or more separate chapters. However, this organizational plan does not imply that each process can function by itself, without input from other processes. For example, decision making relies on perception, memory, general knowledge, and language. In fact, all higher mental processes require careful integration of the more basic cognitive processes. Consequently, such tasks as problem solving, logical reasoning, and decision making are impressively complex.

Theme 5 *Many cognitive processes rely on both bottom-up and top-down processing.* **Bottom-up processing** stresses the importance of information from the stimuli, whereas **top-down processing** stresses the influence of concepts, expectations, and memory upon the cognitive processes. Both factors work simultaneously to ensure that our cognitive processes are typically fast and accurate.

Consider pattern recognition. You recognize the professor for your cognitive psychology course partly because of the specific information from the stimulus— information about this person's face, height, shape, and so forth; bottom-up processing is important. At the same time, top-down processing operates because you have come to expect that the person standing in front of your classroom is that professor. Similarly, research by Brewer and Treyens (1981) shows that students who were asked to recall everything they saw in a college professor's office indeed recalled many of the stimuli they saw (bottom-up processing). However, they also "recalled" many objects —such as books—that could be expected but were not actually present in that particular office (top-down processing).

How to Use the Book

This textbook includes several features that are designed to help you understand and remember the material. I would like to describe how you can use each of these features most effectively.

Notice that each chapter begins with an outline. When you start to read a new chapter, first examine the outline so that you can appreciate the general structure of a topic. For example, you can see that Chapter 2 contains two major sections, labeled *Pattern Recognition* and *Attention.*

Another feature in the next 11 chapters is a chapter preview, which is a short description of the material to be covered. This preview builds upon the framework provided in the outline and also defines some important new terms.

As you read the actual chapters, notice the numerous applications of cognitive psychology. The recent emphasis on ecological validity has produced many studies that describe our everyday cognitive activity. In addition, research in cognition has important applications in such areas as education, medicine, and clinical psychology. These examples provide concrete illustrations of psychological principles. As research on memory has demonstrated, people recall material better if it is concrete, rather than abstract, and if they try to determine whether it applies to themselves. Finally, a third kind of application in this book is the informal experiments or "demonstrations." Each demonstration requires little or no equipment, and you can perform most demonstrations by yourself. Students have reported that these demonstrations help make the material more memorable. Incidentally, more tips on improving memory will be discussed in Chapter 5.

Notice also that each new term appears in boldface and italic type (for example, *cognition*) when it is first discussed. I have included the definition in the same sentence as the term, so you do not need to search an entire paragraph to discover the term's meaning. A phonetic pronunciation is provided for words that are often mispronounced by undergraduates; the accented syllable appears in italics. These pronunciation guides are not intended to insult your intelligence, but to aid your learning. Also, some important terms appear in several different chapters. These terms will be defined each time they occur, so that the chapters can be read in any order.

Chapters 2 through 12 each contain an "In Depth" section, which examines recent research on a selected topic relevant to the chapter. These sections focus on experimental methodology and the outcome of the studies.

A unique feature of this textbook is a summary at the end of each major section in a chapter, rather than at the end of the entire chapter. For example, Chapter 2 includes two section summaries. This feature allows you to review the material more frequently and to master small manageable chunks before you move on to new material. When you reach the end of a section, test yourself to see whether you can remember the important points. Next, read the section summary and notice which items you omitted or remembered incorrectly. Then test yourself again and recheck your accuracy. You may also find that you learn the material more efficiently if you read only one section—rather than an entire chapter—at a time.

A set of review questions and a list of new terms appear at the end of each chapter. Many review questions ask you to apply your knowledge to a practical problem. Other review questions encourage you to integrate information from several parts of a chapter. Notice that the new terms are listed in order of their appearance in the chapter. Check whether you can supply a definition and an example for each new term. You can locate the definition by checking the subject index at the end of the book.

The final feature of each chapter is a list of recommended readings. This list can supply you with resources if you want to write a paper on a particular topic or if an area is personally interesting. In general, I tried to locate books, chapters, and articles that provide more than an overview of the subject but are not overly technical.

One unusual aspect of cognition is that you are actually using cognition to learn about cognition! These suggestions may help you use your cognitive processes even more efficiently.

CHAPTER REVIEW QUESTIONS

1. Define the terms *cognition* and *cognitive psychology*. Think about a career that you have selected and suggest several ways in which the information from cognitive psychology may be relevant to your career.

2. Compare the following approaches to psychology with respect to their emphasis on higher mental processes: (a) Wundt's introspective technique, (b) William James's approach, (c) behaviorism, (d) Gestalt psychology, and (e) the cognitive approach.

3. The concept of ecological validity was introduced in this chapter. Define the term and compare the following approaches in terms of the ecological validity of their contributions: (a) Ebbinghaus's approach to memory, (b) James's approach to psychological processes, (c) Bartlett's approach to memory, (d) the cognitive psychology research from several decades ago, and (e) the more recent cognitive psychology research.

4. List several reasons for the increased interest in cognitive psychology and the decline of the behaviorist approach. In addition, describe the field of cognitive science, noting the disciplines that are included in this field.

5. The section on cognitive neuroscience described five different research techniques. Answer the following questions for each technique.
   a. Can it be used with humans?
   b. Can it be used with minimal interference with normal brain functions?
   c. How precise is the information it yields?
   d. What kind of research questions can it answer?

6. What is artificial intelligence, and how is the information-processing approach relevant to this topic? Think of a human cognitive process that might interest researchers in artificial intelligence, and give examples of how the pure AI and the computer simulation investigations of this cognitive process might differ.

7. How does parallel distributed processing differ from the classical artificial intelligence approach? How is this new approach based on discoveries in cognitive neuroscience? What are the basic characteristics of the PDP approach?

8. According to Theme 2 of this book, our cognitive processes are impressively efficient and accurate. However, we often tend to downplay our cognitive strengths and emphasize our errors. Think about several occasions on which you have forgotten something. Contrast the number of those events with the numerous occasions when you have accurately recalled material—for example, the names of people, vegetables, countries, popular songs, and movies.

9. Theme 4 argues that the cognitive processes are interrelated. Think about a problem you have solved recently, and point out how the solution to that problem depended upon perceptual processes, memory, language, and any other relevant processes mentioned in the "Preview of the Chapters" section.

10. Review each of the five themes of this book. Which of them seem consistent with your own experiences, and which seem surprising?

New Terms

cognition
cognitive psychology
cognitive approach
introspection
replications
behaviorism
Gestalt psychology
information-processing
  approach
ecological validity
cognitive science
mental models
cognitive neuroscience
brain lesions
positron emission tomography (PET scan)

magnetic resonance
  imaging (MRI)
functional magnetic resonance imaging (fMRI)
event-related potential
  technique (ERP)
evoked-response potential
  technique
single-cell recording
  technique
neuron
artificial intelligence (AI)
computational metaphor
pure AI
computer simulation

parallel distributed
  processing approach
PDP approach
connectionism
neural networks
cerebral cortex
parallel processing
serial processing
nodes
Theme 1
Theme 2
Theme 3
Theme 4
Theme 5
bottom-up processing
top-down processing

Recommended Readings

Gardner, H. (1985). *The mind's new science: A history of the cognitive revolution.* New York: Basic Books. Howard Gardner's introduction to cognitive science remains the best historical overview of the discipline. Cognitive psychology receives special treatment, but the book also includes excellent descriptions of the other disciplines within cognitive science.

Gazzaniga, M. S. (Ed.). (1995). *The cognitive neurosciences.* Cambridge, MA: MIT Press. Michael Gazzaniga, a pioneer in the discipline of cognitive neuroscience, has brought together challenging chapters on various neuroscience techniques as well as reviews of the literature on biological bases underlying various cognitive processes.

McClelland, J. L. (1988). Connectionist models and psychological evidence. *Journal of Memory and Language, 27,* 107–123. The parallel distributed processing approach is complex and challenging; this article provides a brief overview, written by one of the founders of the PDP approach.

Stillings, N. A., Weisler, S. E., Chase, C. H., Feinstein, M. H., Garfield, J. L., & Rissland, E. L. (1995). *Cognitive science: An introduction* (2nd ed.). Cambridge, MA: MIT Press. Although the discipline of cognitive science is inherently complex, this undergraduate textbook provides a fairly readable introduction to the field.

Thompson, R. F. (1993). *The brain: A neuroscience primer* (2nd ed.). New York: Freeman. Intended for undergraduates, Thompson's textbook is clearly written, with useful diagrams and interesting background on some of the pioneering research.

ANSWER TO DEMONSTRATION 1.1

The letter *e* is missing from this passage. The letter *e* is the most frequent letter in the English language. Therefore, a passage this long—without the letter *e*—is highly unusual. The exercise demonstrates the difficulty of searching for something that is *not* there.

PERCEPTUAL PROCESSES

INTRODUCTION

PATTERN RECOGNITION

Theories of Pattern Recognition
Top-Down Processing and Pattern Recognition
In Depth: Face Perception

ATTENTION

Divided Attention
Selective Attention
Theories of Attention
The Biological Basis of Attention
Consciousness

=============================== **Preview** ===============================

Perception is a process that uses our previous knowledge to gather and interpret the stimuli that our senses register. Two aspects of perception that are most relevant for cognitive psychology are pattern recognition and attention.

Pattern recognition involves identifying a complex arrangement of sensory stimuli, such as a letter of the alphabet, a human face, or a complex scene. We will examine four theories of pattern recognition and then discuss how pattern recognition is influenced by both context and past experience. We'll also explore how people process human faces differently from other visual stimuli.

If you have ever tried to study while a friend is talking, you can appreciate the limits of attention. Research demonstrates that performance usually suffers if attention must be divided between two or more tasks. Furthermore, when we selectively attend to one task, we recall very little about other, irrelevant tasks. This chapter will discuss several theories of attention, as well as the biological basis of attention. Finally, we consider the topic of consciousness, including awareness about cognitive processes, thought suppression, and the cognitive unconscious.

INTRODUCTION

Perception seems so effortless that you may be tempted to ignore this important cognitive process. For example, you turn your head, and your visual system immediately registers a wastebasket next to a book bag. Your attention shifts to a sound in the hall, and you instantly recognize the footsteps of a friend. Admittedly, perception requires less skill than such cognitive tasks as problem solving or decision making. Still, even the most sophisticated computers cannot rival a 3-year-old child in their ability to perceive stimuli (Pinker, 1984).

Perception uses previous knowledge to gather and interpret the stimuli registered by the senses. For example, you used perception to interpret each of the letters on this page. Consider how you managed to perceive the letter *n* at the end of the word *perception*. You combined information registered by your eyes with your previous knowledge about the shape of the letters of the alphabet, as well as your previous knowledge about what to expect when your visual system has already processed *perceptio-*. Notice that perception combines aspects of both the outside world (the visual stimuli) and your own inner world (your previous knowledge). In other words, this process of pattern recognition is a good example of the fifth theme of this book, because it combines bottom-up and top-down processing.

Most colleges offer an entire course on the topic of perception, so we cannot do justice to this discipline in just a single chapter. More details are available in other books (e.g., Coren et al., 1994; Goldstein, 1996; Matlin & Foley, 1997). Our discussion of perceptual processes will address two topics that are particularly relevant to cognition: pattern recognition and attention. These processes are important because they prepare the "raw" sensory information so that it can be used in the more complex mental processes, which are discussed in later chapters of this book. Pattern recognition allows us to perceive a shape in a stimulus, and attention allows us to process some information more completely, while other information is ignored.

PATTERN RECOGNITION

To illustrate your own ability to recognize patterns, try Demonstration 2.1. Within a fraction of a second, you can recognize meaningful patterns on the television set. *Pattern recognition* is the identification of a complex arrangement of sensory stimuli. When you recognize a pattern, your sensory processes transform and organize the raw information provided by your sensory receptors. You also compare the sensory stimuli with information in other memory storage. In some cases, pattern recognition simply involves realizing that you have seen a particular pattern before. For example, a minor character in a movie may look familiar, even though you cannot recall her name. In other cases, pattern recognition involves applying a label to a particular arrangement of stimuli. For example, you recognize the letter Z, you recognize your Aunt Angela, and you recognize Beethoven's Fifth Symphony. In each of these examples, you match a particular set of stimuli with a label stored in memory.

Our examination of pattern recognition focuses on vision; auditory pattern recognition will be discussed in Chapter 8 in connection with speech perception.

DEMONSTRATION 2.1

THE IMMEDIATE RECOGNITION OF PATTERNS

Turn on a television set and adjust the sound to "mute." Now change the channels with your eyes closed. Open your eyes and then immediately shut them. Repeat this exercise several times. Notice how you can instantly identify and interpret the image on the TV screen, even though you did not expect that image and have never previously seen it in that exact form. In less than a second—and without major effort—you can identify colors, textures, contours, objects, and people. This demonstration was originally suggested by Irving Biederman (1990), who noted that people can usually interpret the meaning of a new scene in $\frac{1}{10}$ of a second. Incidentally, you can also recognize the rapidly presented images on MTV, even though they may be shown at a rate of five per second. Consistent with Theme 1, humans are impressively efficient in recognizing patterns.

We'll begin with the major theories of pattern recognition. Then we will see how pattern recognition is facilitated both by the context in which the stimulus occurs and by a person's previous experience with that stimulus. Finally, an in-depth section will explore the complex topic of face perception.

Theories of Pattern Recognition

Researchers have proposed many different theories of pattern recognition, but we will look at only four of them. The first theory, template matching, is now generally acknowledged to be inadequate. Nevertheless, this section begins with template matching because it was the first modern explanation for pattern recognition. The three other theories represent more sophisticated developments. As you read about these three current theories, keep in mind that we don't need to decide that only one theory is correct. Humans are flexible creatures, and we may use different approaches for different pattern-recognition tasks.

Template-Matching Theory. You look at a letter *Z* and you immediately recognize it. According to the *template-matching theory,* you compare a stimulus to a set of *templates*—specific patterns that you have stored in memory. After comparing the stimulus to a number of templates, you note the template that matches most closely. You've probably had the experience of trying to find a piece of a jigsaw puzzle that will complete part of the puzzle. The piece must fit precisely, or else it won't work. Similarly, the stimulus must fit the template precisely. Thus, the letter *Q* will not fit the template for the letter *O* because of the extra line on the bottom.

Some nonhuman pattern recognition systems are based on templates. For example, if you have a checking account, look at one of your checks. Notice the numbers at the bottom of the check, which are specially designed to be recognized by check-sorting computers. Each number has a constant, standardized shape. Furthermore, each number is distinctly different from the others. Humans sometimes write a number 4 that looks like a 9. The 4 on your check, however, looks very different from the 9, so the computer will not make errors in pattern recognition when the patterns are compared with the templates.

A template system may work well for computers that are provided with a standardized set of numbers. However, notice why templates are totally inadequate for explaining the complex process of pattern recognition in humans. One problem with the template-matching theory is that it is extremely inflexible. For example, if a letter differs from the appropriate template even slightly, the pattern would not be recognized. However, every day we succeed in recognizing letters that differ substantially from the classic version of a letter. Notice, for example, how all the *Z*'s in Figure 2.1 differ from one another. The print types vary and the sizes vary. Some *Z*'s are fragmented, blurry, or rotated. Still, all of these patterns are recognizable *Z*'s. Our pattern recognition procedure must therefore involve a more flexible system than matching a pattern against a specific template.

Even if we could devise a modified template theory, we would still have difficulty with patterns viewed from nonstandard angles. If you rotate Figure 2.1, or view it

Figure 2.1

VERSIONS OF THE LETTER Z.

from a slant, the shape of the image on your retina changes drastically for each Z. Nonetheless, you still recognize the letters (Treisman, 1992). In fact, Jolicoeur and Landau (1984) estimate that humans require as little as 15 milliseconds* of additional processing time to recognize a letter that has been rotated a complete 180°. A template theory would need to suggest a different template for each rotation of a figure, a clearly unwieldy proposal for a task we accomplish so quickly.

Finally, template models only work for isolated letters and other simple objects presented in their complete form (Pinker, 1984). Look up from your textbook right now and notice the complex array of fragmented objects registered on your retina. Perhaps these include a lower edge of a lamp, a corner of a desk, and a part of a book. Nonetheless, you can sort out this jumble and recognize the shapes. How could the visual system include templates for lower edges of lamps and other fragments? Clearly, then, the template theory cannot account for the complexity of human visual processing.

Prototype Models. Prototype models are more flexible versions of template-matching theories. According to **prototype models,** we store abstract, idealized patterns (or **prototypes**) in memory. When we see a stimulus, we compare it with a prototype. The match does not need to be exact; minor variations are allowed. If the match is close enough, we identify the stimulus. If the match is inadequate, we compare the stimulus with other prototypes until we locate a match.

For example, think about the prototype you have developed for your best friend. This abstract, idealized pattern includes certain characteristic facial features, body build, and height. The prototype does not include a specific set of clothing or a specific facial expression. After all, your memory stores a prototype, not an exact template. Thus, you can recognize your friend even when the stimulus pattern differs from the prototype on features such as facial expression, hair length, and clothing style.

A number of studies have demonstrated that prototypes are useful in perceiving geometric designs, letters of the alphabet, and cartoon-like drawings (Franks & Bransford, 1971; Posner et al., 1967; Reed, 1972; Rhodes et al., 1987), but other researchers are more skeptical (e.g., Shin & Nosofsky, 1992).

Prototype-matching theory is an appealing approach to the problem of pattern recognition. It describes how shapes can be easily recognized despite the variety of

---

*A millisecond is $\frac{1}{1000}$ of a second.

representations of the same shape, the variety of orientations of the shape, and the fragmented view we often have of those shapes. However, the details of this approach have not been developed. For example, do we have templates for these prototypes (Spoehr & Lehmkuhle, 1982)? The next approach that we will consider is based on distinctive features. This approach offers more neurological details, although it has other, different problems.

Incidentally, we consider prototypes again in Chapter 7, when we focus on the research of Eleanor Rosch and her colleagues. That chapter will consider how real-life categories—such as birds, tools, and vehicles—are conceptually organized in terms of prototypes or best examples.

Distinctive-Features Models. The ***distinctive-features models*** state that we make discriminations among stimuli on the basis of a small number of characteristics. These characteristics that differentiate one stimulus from another are called ***distinctive features.*** When distinctive-features theorists try to explain how we recognize letters of the alphabet, they argue that we store a list of feature components for each letter. For example, the letter *G* has a curved component and a horizontal line in the middle. When we see a new letter, we compare that letter with the list of distinctive features that we have stored in memory. In contrast, those who favor the prototype model of pattern recognition would argue that we store an abstract, idealized version of each alphabet letter in our memory.

Try Demonstration 2.2, which is based on a chart developed by Eleanor Gibson (1969). Distinctive-features models propose that the distinctive features of alphabet letters remain constant, whether the letter is handwritten, printed, or typed. These models can explain how we perceive a wide variety of two-dimension patterns, such as figures in a painting, designs on fabric, and illustrations in books. However, most of the research in this area focuses on our ability to recognize letters and numbers.

Distinctive-features models are consistent with both psychological and physiological research. For example, studies by Eleanor Gibson (1969) demonstrated that people require a relatively long time to decide whether some letters are different from one another when those letters share a large number of critical features. Note that the table in Demonstration 2.2 shows that the letters *P* and *R* share many critical features; research participants made slow decisions about whether these two letters were different. In contrast, *G* and *M* differ from each other on many distinctive features; people decided relatively quickly whether letter pairs like these were different from each other. Research by Garner (1979) confirmed that decision speed depends upon the number of shared distinctive features.

An important advantage of distinctive-features models is that they are compatible with some evidence from biological research. As discussed in Chapter 1, the research team of Hubel and Wiesel inserted small wires, called microelectrodes, into a series of neurons in the visual cortex of anesthetized animals (Hubel, 1982; Hubel & Wiesel, 1965, 1979). Then they presented a simple visual stimulus—such as a vertical bar of light—directly in front of each animal's eyes.

The researcher's results showed that each neuron responded especially vigorously to a bar in a particular orientation. Thus, one neuron might respond strongly

DEMONSTRATION 2.2

A DISTINCTIVE-FEATURES APPROACH.   SOURCE: GIBSON, 1969.

Eleanor Gibson proposed that letters differ from each other with respect to their distinctive features. She proposed the table that is reproduced below. Notice the top three kinds of features—straight, curve, and intersection. Notice that *P* and *R* share many features. However, *Z* and *O* have none of these kinds of features in common. Compare the following pairs of letters to determine the number of distinctive features they share: *E* and *F*; *K* and *M*; *Z* and *B*; *N* and *M*.

Features	A	E	F	H	I	L	T	K	M	N	V	W	X	Y	Z	B	C	D	G	J	O	P	R	Q	S	U
Straight																										
horizontal	+	+	+	+		+	+								+				+							
vertical		+	+	+	+	+	+	+	+	+	+			+		+		+				+	+			
diagonal /	+							+	+		+	+	+	+	+											
diagonal \	+							+	+	+	+	+	+	+									+	+		
Curve																										
closed																+		+			+	+	+	+		
open V																			+							+
open H																	+		+	+			+			
Intersection	+	+	+	+		+	+				+					+						+	+	+		
Redundancy																										
cyclic change		+						+		+						+							+			
symmetry	+	+		+	+	+	+	+	+	+	+	+				+	+	+			+					+
Discontinuity																										
vertical	+		+	+	+	+	+	+	+		+											+	+			
horizontal		+	+			+	+								+											

to a vertical bar of light. Another neuron, just a hairbreadth away, might respond most vigorously to a bar rotated about 10° from the vertical. One small patch of the visual cortex could contain a variety of neurons, some especially responsive to vertical lines, some to horizontal lines, and some to specific diagonal lines. The visual system seems to contain special feature detectors "wired in," which help us recognize certain features of letters and simple patterns.

We need to consider some basic problems with the distinctive-features approach. First, a theory of pattern recognition should not simply list the features found in a stimulus; it must also describe the physical relationship among those features (Bruce, 1988). For example, in the letter T, the vertical line *supports* the horizontal line. In contrast, the letter L consists of a vertical line resting at the side of the horizontal line. Also, as you might guess, some features are more important than others.

Furthermore, Pinker (1984) points out that the distinctive-features models were constructed to explain the relatively simple recognition of letters. However, the shapes that occur in nature are much more complex. How can you recognize a horse? Do you analyze the stimulus into features such as its mane, its hooves, and its head? A horse contains far too many lines and curved segments, and the task is far more complicated than letter recognition. The final approach to pattern recognition specifically addresses how people recognize more complex kinds of stimuli found in everyday life.

The Computational Approach. The ***computational approach*** contains components of both the prototype approach and the distinctive-features approach. However, its emphasis is different. The major aim of the computational approach is to develop computer-based theories that can perform some of the cognitive tasks accomplished by humans, such as the rapid, accurate recognition of three-dimensional objects (Biederman, 1987, 1990; Marr, 1982). The use of computers to simulate human perceptual processes is known as ***machine vision.***

Several computational approaches to pattern recognition have been developed. For example, Irving Biederman has explored the categorization of 3-D shapes in a theory called recognition-by-components (Biederman, 1987, 1990). The basic assumption of ***recognition-by-components theory*** is that a given view of an object can be represented as an arrangement of simple 3-D shapes. Biederman calls these 3-D shapes ***geons,*** a name that stands for *geometrical ions*. Like letters of the alphabet, geons can be combined to form something meaningful.

Five of the proposed geons are shown in Figure 2.2, together with various objects that can be constructed from the geons. As you know, letters of the alphabet can be combined to form different meanings, depending upon the specific arrangements of the letters; *no* has a different meaning from *on*. Similarly, geons 3 and 5 from Figure 2.2 can be combined to form different meaningful objects; a cup is different from a pail. In general, an arrangement of three geons gives people enough information to classify any object. Notice, then, that Biederman's geon theory is essentially a distinctive-features theory for the recognition of 3-D objects (Oliver, 1992).

The recognition-by-components model has not yet been extensively tested. Some early reports on normal humans and on people with specific visual deficits are compatible with the model (Banks & Krajicek, 1991). However, other research by Cave and Kosslyn (1993) asked observers to identify sketches of objects that were either

===== Figure 2.2 =====

FIVE OF THE BASIC GEONS (a) AND REPRESENTATIVE OBJECTS THAT CAN BE CONSTRUCTED FROM THE GEONS (b). SOURCE: BIEDERMAN, 1990.

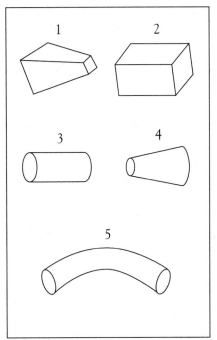 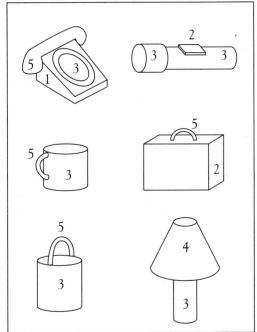

a.   b.

broken into "natural" parts (consistent with geons) or broken into "unnatural" parts. (See Figure 2.3.) The observers were equally quick and accurate in the two conditions. These results suggest that people encode the overall shape first and analyze the parts afterwards—the reverse of the recognition-by-components model.

Additional work must be done to test whether people typically recognize the components before they identify the overall shape. Researchers must also explore whether the model can account for pattern recognition of objects that are more complicated than isolated cups and pails—for example, the complex stimuli we identify when we glance quickly at a TV screen.

The astonishing talents of the visual system, emphasized by Theme 2 of the book, may be partially described by the prototype, distinctive-features, and computational approaches. However, even a combination of these three approaches cannot completely explain how you can glance at a scene and instantly recognize dozens of complex objects and their relationships with one another.

Figure 2.3

AN EXAMPLE OF STIMULI USED IN RESEARCH BY CAVE AND KOSSLYN (1993).
Notice that panel a shows a pair of scissors broken into "natural," geon-consistent parts; panel b shows the same pair of scissors broken into "unnatural" parts.

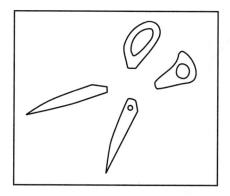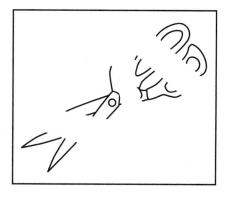

a.   b.

Top-Down Processing and Pattern Recognition

The theories of pattern recognition discussed so far have emphasized how people perceive isolated objects. We have not mentioned how knowledge and expectations might aid recognition. A perceiver tries to decipher a hastily written letter of the alphabet, without the benefit of the surrounding letters in the word. Another perceiver tries to identify an object that consists of a narrow, curved geon, attached to the side of a wider, cylindrical geon, without the reminder that the object resembles the coffee cup from breakfast.

Theme 5 emphasizes the difference between two kinds of processing. Let's review that distinction and see how these kinds of processes work together in a complementary fashion in pattern recognition. So far, our discussion of pattern recognition has emphasized *bottom-up processing,* or *data-driven processing,* which stresses the importance of the stimulus in pattern recognition. Information about the stimulus arrives from the sensory receptors (from the bottom level in processing). The arrival of the information sets the pattern-recognition process into motion. The combination of simple, bottom-level features allows us to recognize more complex, whole patterns.

The other important process in pattern recognition is called *top-down processing* or *conceptually driven processing.* This approach stresses how a person's concepts and higher-level processes influence pattern recognition. According to this approach, our knowledge about how the world is organized helps in identifying patterns. We expect certain shapes to be found in certain locations, and we expect to encounter certain shapes because of past experiences. These expectations help us recognize patterns rapidly.

DEMONSTRATION 2.3

CONTEXT AND PATTERN RECOGNITION. CAN YOU READ THE FOLLOWING SENTENCE?

THE MAN RAN.

Cognitive psychologists propose that both bottom-up and top-down processing are necessary to explain the complexities of pattern recognition. As Palmer (1975a) notes, it is impossible to believe *only* in one or the other kind of processing; we cannot ask whether perceivers first interpret the whole or first interpret the parts. For example, a face is recognized because of two simultaneous processes: (a) when each shape—such as a pink oval representing the mouth—is placed in the context of a face, it becomes recognizable because of top-down processing and (b) bottom-up processing forces us to combine the component features into the perception of a face. Futhermore, top-down and bottom-up processing work smoothly together in seamless interaction to allow us to recognize patterns quickly and accurately (Hoffman, 1986).

Let's turn our attention to top-down processing. We will see how pattern recognition is facilitated by the context in which the stimulus appears and by past experience with the stimulus.

Context and Pattern Recognition. Before you read further, try Demonstration 2.3. As you can see, the same shape—an ambiguous letter—is sometimes perceived as an *H* and sometimes as an *A*. In this demonstration, you began to identify the whole word *THE,* and your tentative knowledge of that word helped to identify the second letter as an *H.* In other words, context facilitates pattern recognition.

Some of the research on context and pattern recognition focuses on identifying ambigious objects. For example, Palmer (1975b) found that people were more likely to recognize an ambiguous figure when it was located in an appropriate context. Thus, in a kitchen scene, a loaf of bread was recognized more readily than a mailbox.

Most of the research on this topic examines how context enhances the recognition of letters of the alphabet. Psychologists who study reading realized that a theory of pattern recognition would be inadequate if it were based only on stimulus information. For example, suppose that we do identify each letter in terms of its distinctive features. In addition, suppose that each letter contains four distinctive features, a conservative guess. This would mean that a typical reader would need to make about 5,000 feature detections each minute, a ridiculously high estimate. Furthermore, do you have the impression that you really see and identify each letter in every sentence? You probably could read most sentences fairly well even if only half the letters were present. F-r -x--pl-, -t's e-s- t- r--d t--s s--t-n--.

One of the most widely demonstrated phenomena in pattern recognition is the word superiority effect. According to the *word superiority effect,* we can identify a single letter more accurately and more rapidly when it appears in a word than when it appears in a string of unrelated letters. The word superiority effect was first reported more than a century ago by James Cattell (1886), an American psychologist who studied with Wilhelm Wundt. During the current century, Reicher (1969) renewed psychologists' interest in the effect when he demonstrated that recognition accuracy was significantly higher when a letter appeared in a word, such as *work,* rather than in a nonword, such as *orwk.* Since then, dozens of studies have confirmed the importance of top-down processing in letter recognition (e.g., Chastain, 1981, 1986; Jordan & Bevan, 1994; Krueger, 1992; Pollatsek & Rayner, 1989; Taylor & Taylor, 1983; Wheeler, 1970). The word superiority effect operates even when the target letter is silent in the word in which it is embedded. For example, the letter *s* is quickly recognized in the word *island,* even though the *s* is not pronounced (Krueger, 1992).

One likely explanation for the word superiority effect involves an interaction between top-down and bottom-up processing (McClelland & Rumelhart, 1981; Richman & Simon, 1989; Rumelhart & McClelland, 1982). This model is based on *parallel distributed processing,* the approach introduced in Chapter 1 that proposes that complex cognitive processes can be understood in terms of networks that link together related units. According to this connectionist model, when a person sees fragments of features in a word, these features activate letter units. These letter units then activate a word unit in the person's mental dictionary for that combination of letters. Once that word unit is activated, excitatory neural feedback helps in identifying individual letters. As a result, people can identify letters more quickly than if no word context provided excitatory feedback.

So far, we have seen that objects and letters can be more readily recognized when context is provided, demonstrating the importance of top-down processing. An additional way in which context can aid pattern recognition is that the context of a sentence can facilitate recognition of a word in a sentence. Many experiments have demonstrated that the context of a sentence, such as "Mary drank her orange _____ ," makes it easier to recognize a word, in this case, *juice.* In contrast, *juice* would take longer to recognize if it appeared alone or in an inappropriate context (Forster, 1981; Stanovich & West, 1981, 1983).

Let's discuss an interesting variant of these words-in-sentences studies. Rueckl and Oden (1986) demonstrated that both the features of the stimulus and the nature of the context influence word recognition; that is, bottom-up and top-down processing occur. These researchers used stimuli that were letters and letter-like characters. For example, one set of stimuli consisted of a perfectly formed letter *r,* a perfectly formed letter *n,* and three symbols that were intermediate between those two letters. Notice these stimuli arranged along the bottom of Figure 2.4. In each case, the letter pattern was embedded in the letter string "bea-s" so that there were five stimuli that ranged between "beans" and "bears."

=== **Figure 2.4** ===

THE INFLUENCE OF STIMULUS FEATURES AND SENTENCE CONTEXT ON WORD IDENTIFI-CATION. BASED ON RUECKL & ODEN, 1986.

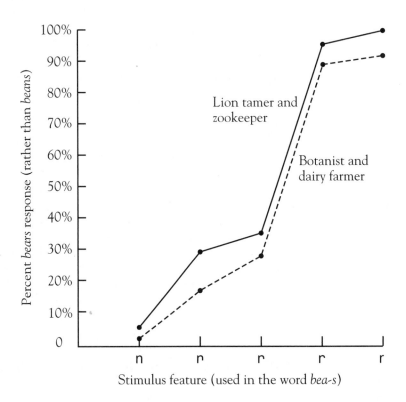

Stimulus feature (used in the word *bea-s*)

The nature of the context was also varied by using the sentence frame, "The _____ raised (bears/beans) to supplement his income." The words chosen to fill the blank were carefully selected: "lion tamer," "zookeeper," "botanist," and "dairy farmer." You'll notice that a lion tamer and a zookeeper are more likely to raise bears, whereas the botanist and the dairy farmer are more likely to raise beans. Other similar ambiguous letters and sentence frames were also constructed, each using four different nouns or noun phrases.

On each trial, the participant saw one sentence for one second. Then the two test words were presented in uppercase letters (for example, *BEANS* and *BEARS*). People were told to select the word they had seen.

Figure 2.4 shows the results. As you can see, people were increasingly likely to choose the "bears" response when the segment on the right side of the letter was short, rather than long: The features of the stimulus are extremely important because pattern recognition operates in a bottom-up fashion. However, you'll also notice that people were consistently more likely to choose the "bears" response in the lion tamer and zookeeper sentences than in the botanist and dairy farmer sentences: The context is important because pattern recognition also operates in a top-down fashion. Specifically, our knowledge about the world leads us to expect that lion tamers and zookeepers would be more likely to raise bears than beans.

Think about how these context effects can influence the speed of reading. The previous letters in a word help you identify the remaining letters more quickly. Furthermore, the other words in a sentence help you identify the individual words more quickly. Without context to help you read more quickly, you might still be reading the introduction to this chapter!

Past Experience and Pattern Recognition. We have seen that pattern recognition is facilitated by context. Pattern recognition is also facilitated when a person has had previous experience with an object. You can recognize a coffee cup more readily because you are familiar with this object. In contrast, people from another culture unaccustomed to coffee cups might have difficulty recognizing that distinctive shape if a blurry slide were quickly presented.

Research by Daniel Schacter and his colleagues (1991) shows that previous experience with objects can indeed aid recognition. These researchers showed drawings of three-dimensional objects to the participants in their study. Some of these objects are structurally possible in the real world (for example, Figure 2.5a). Other objects in their study are known as "impossible figures" (for example, Figure 2.5b). That is, these impossible figures contain structural violations; they could not really exist in three dimensions. The participants were not told that they would be

Figure 2.5

REPRESENTATIVE EXAMPLES OF POSSIBLE (a) AND IMPOSSIBLE (b) FIGURES USED IN THE PATTERN RECOGNITION STUDIES OF SCHACTER AND HIS COLLEAGUES (1991).

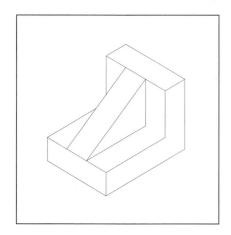 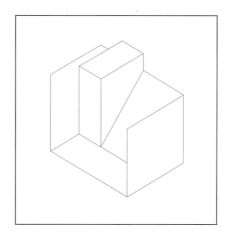

a. A possible figure   b. An impossible figure

expected to remember the figures. Instead, they were simply instructed to judge whether the figure was facing primarily to the right or primarily to the left.

Later, the participants were shown these figures again, together with figures they had not previously seen. They were instructed to judge whether each figure could really exist in three dimensions or whether it was an impossible figure. The results showed that, in the case of the possible figures, people made these judgments much faster about the items they had previously seen; judgments were relatively slow for the possible figures that were new. In the case of the impossible figures, judgments were equally fast for the old and new figures. These results have been replicated several times in other research (Cooper & Schacter, 1992; Schacter & Cooper, 1993; Schacter et al., 1995).

This research implies that we can store the structure of possible figures so that past experience encourages relatively rapid, top-down processes. However, our perceptual system cannot figure out a consistent interpretation of an impossible figure. As a result, we cannot store the structure of impossible figures; past experience offers no top-down advantages.

IN DEPTH: Face Perception

One of the most active research areas within the topic of pattern recognition involves the perception of faces. On some kinds of face recognition tasks, people are remarkably accurate. For example, humans are very skilled in judging whether a face is female or male. In one study, for instance, Vicki Bruce and her colleagues (1993) took photos of 88 adult females and 91 adult males. Each individual wore a swimming cap to conceal the hair. Furthermore, females wore no makeup and the males had just shaved. Even with these faces relatively free of gender cues, a group of judges was 96% accurate in sorting the photos into male and female piles.

Bruce and her coworkers speculated that people recognize the sex of faces primarily because of the relationships between important features of the face. If this is true, then subjects would have great difficulty making discriminations if the faces were presented upside down. In fact, this prediction was correct. For example, when judging the sex of profile faces, people made errors only 5% of the time for faces in the normal, upright position. However, when the faces were inverted, the error rate rose to 21%.

You might argue, however, that it's relatively easy to tell whether a face is male or female. The real challenge comes in identifying the name associated with someone who seems to know *you*—but whose face looks completely unfamiliar! This kind of face recognition is especially challenging because you may have originally seen that face from a different viewing angle, and with different lighting. That face may also have changed in age, expression, and hairstyle—as well as other important cues that help us identify individuals (Bruce, 1994).

One of the central theoretical issues in the face recognition research is whether we recognize faces on the basis of their component features or on a more *holistic*

=== **Figure 2.6** ===

RECOGNITION ACCURACY FOR ISOLATED PARTS VERSUS PARTS EMBEDDED IN WHOLE OBJECTS, FOR SKETCHES OF FACES AND HOUSES. SOURCE: TANAKA & FARAH, 1993.

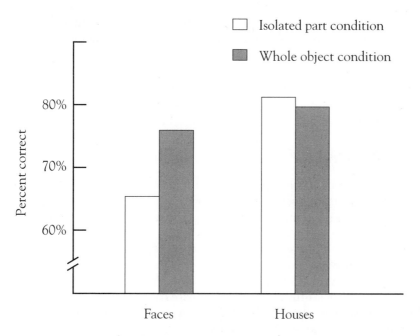

basis, that is, in terms of the overall shape. In other words, do we concentrate on the individual parts, or on the whole face? Furthermore, does our perceptual system process human faces differently than it processes other visual stimuli?

James Tanaka and Martha Farah (1993) devised sketches of two kinds of stimuli, faces and houses. The participants were told that they would see a face accompanied by a name (or else a house accompanied by the owner's name), six items in all. After learning these items, the participants were tested. On some trials, they were asked to choose which of two face parts they had seen before, for example, two noses. On other trials, they were asked to choose which of two whole faces they had seen before; here, the participants might choose between two faces that were identical except for the nose. (When judging houses, the corresponding house part might be a large window.)

Figure 2.6 shows the results. As you can see, people were significantly more accurate in recognizing facial features when they appeared within the context of a whole face, rather than in isolation. In contrast, when they judged houses, they were just as accurate for the isolated house-features as for the house-features within the context of a whole house.

In other words, we seem to process faces in a different fashion from other stimuli; faces apparently have special, privileged status in our perceptual system. This conclusion is consistent with recent research on the biological explanations for face perception. Specifically, researchers have discovered that specific neurons—located in the temporal lobe of monkeys—respond selectively to monkey faces (Desimone et al., 1984; Gross, 1992; Rolls, 1992). Damage to this same region of the cortex in humans leads to great difficulty in recognizing human faces (Farah, 1990; Farah, 1992; Sergent & Signoret, 1992). Because of this special system, we use a different series of operations when we process faces, as opposed to other, more ordinary stimuli. Furthermore, face perception is governed by different laws. As we have seen in the research by Tanaka and Farah, face perception emphasizes the organization of component parts into a cohesive overall pattern—rather than a simple arrangement of isolated features.

◀◀

SECTION SUMMARY: PATTERN RECOGNITION

1. Perception uses previous knowledge to gather and interpret the stimuli registered by the senses.
2. Pattern recognition involves identifying a complex arrangement of sensory stimuli.
3. Four theories of pattern recognition have been proposed. Of these, the template-matching theory can be rejected because it cannot account for the complexity and flexibility of pattern recognition.
4. Prototype models propose that we compare each stimulus with a prototype. Experiments have demonstrated that people can form prototypes based on similar—but not identical—examples.
5. Distinctive-features models are supported by research showing that people require more time to make decisions about letters when the letters share distinctive features.
6. The computational approach, which attempts to develop computer-based theories, is represented by Biederman's recognition-by-components theory, involving the arrangement of geons.
7. In bottom-up processing, pattern recognition begins with the arrival of the stimulus. Top-down processing emphasizes the role of context and expectations in identifying a pattern. Both processes are necessary to explain pattern recognition.
8. Research using figures, letters in words, and words in sentences has demonstrated that context facilitates pattern recognition.
9. Research by Schacter and his colleagues demonstrates that previous exposure also enhances pattern recognition, at least when the stimuli are ones we could encounter in real life.
10. People can accurately identify the gender of a face, even when important cues are removed; we seem to process faces in terms of features within the context of the entire face, rather than in isolation.

ATTENTION

Take a moment to pay attention to your attention processes. Close your eyes and try to notice every sound that is reaching your auditory system. Now continue to pay attention to those sounds and keep your eyes open, simultaneously expanding your attention to include visual stimuli. If you can manage these combined tasks, continue to include additional stimuli, specifically those that involve touch, smell, and taste. You'll discover that you cannot attend to everything at once.

In everyday speech, we use the word *attention* to include several kinds of mental activity. Psychologists also use the word in many different contexts. Attention can refer to the kind of concentration on a mental task in which you select certain kinds of perceptual stimuli for further processing, while trying to exclude other interfering stimuli (Shapiro, 1994). For example, when you take an examination, you concentrate on the visual stimuli contained in the exam, excluding all other sensory information. Attention can also refer to being prepared to receive further information. For instance, someone may tell you to pay attention to an important announcement. It also refers to receiving several messages at once and ignoring all but one. For example, you may focus on one conversation at a noisy party.

We will use a general definition of attention that applies to all these kinds of attention. Specifically, *attention* is a concentration of mental activity.

The topic of attention has varied in its popularity throughout the history of psychology. It intrigued the introspectionists in Europe, for example. In the United States, William James (1890) speculated about the number of ideas that could be attended to at one time—a speculation that still intrigues psychologists more than a century later. With the arrival of behaviorism, however, speculation about attention was considered inappropriate. Attention was regarded as such a hidden process that it was not a legitimate area for scientific study (Hirst, 1986). As recently as 1953, a major textbook on experimental psychology did not even mention attention (Eysenck, 1982; Osgood, 1953). However, in recent decades, attention has become a "hot topic." Attention has finally begun to receive the attention it deserves!

Attention is an important topic in its own right, and it is also important for other cognitive processes discussed in this book. For example, attention is an important factor in problem solving. As Chapter 10 describes, when people read a description of a problem, they inspect certain important sentences several times and disregard other sentences that seem trivial. Also, Chapter 11 explains how people make incorrect decisions when they pay attention to relatively unimportant information.

We will begin our discussion by considering two interrelated cognitive tasks—divided attention and selective attention. We will then examine explanations for attention, both theoretical and biological. Our final topic, consciousness, is closely related to attention.

Divided Attention

Imagine a busy executive, talking on her cellular phone as she drives to an important appointment. The telephone conversation captures her attention so completely that she misses the correct turnoff and wastes 15 minutes backtracking. However, the consequences of divided attention can also be much more significant. For example, in the former Yugoslavia in 1976, two airplanes collided and all 176 passengers and crew members were killed. The air-traffic controller had been working without an assistant, and he was monitoring 11 aircraft simultaneously! In the preceding minutes, he had transmitted 8 messages and received 11 (Barber, 1988). Humans are extremely competent, yet they cannot pay attention to everything at the same time.

Research on Divided Attention. In *divided-attention tasks,* people must attend to several simultaneous messages, responding to each as needed (Hawkins & Presson, 1986). In the laboratory, divided attention is typically studied by instructing participants to perform two tasks at the same time. For example, Duncan (1993) asked participants to make judgments about a single object. They could make two simultaneous judgments about this object—*what* it was, as well as *where* it was located—without any loss in accuracy. However, they made many errors when asked to make two simultaneous judgments about two different objects, for example, where both objects were located. In other words, our perceptual system can handle some divided-attention tasks, but we fail when the tasks become too demanding.

When our attention is divided, we often fail to perceive stimuli accurately. Mark Reinitz and his colleagues (1994) asked their research participants to look at sketches of faces, with dots across each face. People in the full-attention condition received no instructions about the dots, whereas people in the divided-attention condition were instructed to count the dots. Later, everyone was asked to judge whether each face in a series was old or new. Some of these faces were indeed old, because these exact faces had been shown during the first phase of the study. Other faces were actually new, because they had not been presented before. However, these new, or conjunction, faces consisted of new combinations of old features, perhaps combining a mouth from one figure with a nose from another figure.

Reinitz and his coworkers found that people in the full-attention condition said "old" to the truly old faces much more than to the conjunction faces, as Table 2.1 shows. In contrast, you can see that people in the divided-attention condition answered "old" to the conjunction faces almost as often as to the truly old faces. With divided attention, they were unable to recognize these previously presented faces.

Divided Attention and Practice. "Practice makes perfect," according to the familiar saying. The research on practice and divided attention confirms the wisdom of that saying. For example, in two classic studies, college students were trained to read stories silently at the same time that they copied down irrelevant words dictated by the experimenter (Hirst et al., 1980; Spelke et al., 1976). At first, the

TABLE 2.1

PROPORTION OF RESPONSES THAT WERE "OLD" FOR EACH OF TWO STUDY CONDITIONS AND TWO TEST CONDITIONS. BASED ON REINITZ ET AL., 1994.

	Study conditions	
Test condition	*Full attention*	*Divided attention*
Old Faces	.81	.48
Conjunction Faces	.48	.42

students had trouble combining the two tasks; their reading speed decreased substantially, and their handwriting was illegible. However, after six weeks of training, they could read as quickly while taking dictation as when they were only reading. Their handwriting also improved.

Still, even at this well-practiced stage, the students were not really attending to the dictated words. In fact, they were able to recall only 35 of the several thousand words they had written down. However, with more extensive training, they became so accomplished at this divided-attention task that they could even categorize the dictated word (for example, by writing *fruit* when they heard the word *apple*) without any decline in their reading rate. As Hirst (1986) argues, practice apparently alters the limits of attentional capacity. Humans do not seem to have a built-in, fixed limit to the number of tasks they can perform simultaneously (Allport, 1989).

Selective Attention

Selective attention is closely related to divided attention. In divided attention, people are instructed to pay equal attention to several tasks. In **selective-attention tasks,** people are confronted with two or more simultaneous tasks and are required to focus their attention on one while disregarding the others (Hawkins & Presson, 1986). Selective-attention studies often show that people notice little about the irrelevant tasks. You have probably noticed that you can usually follow closely only one conversation at a noisy party; the content of the other conversations is generally not processed. You may have also experienced selective attention when picking up two stations on your radio. If you listen closely to one program, you notice only the superficial characteristics of the other.

At times, you might wish that attention were *not* so selective. Wouldn't it be wonderful to participate in one conversation, yet notice the details of all the other conversations going on around you? On the other hand, think how confusing this would be. Perhaps you would start talking about baseball—the topic of a neighboring conversation—when you had originally been talking about a friend's new job prospect. Furthermore, imagine the chaos you would experience if you

simultaneously paid attention to all the information your senses register. You would notice hundreds of sights, sounds, smells, tastes, and touch sensations. It would be extremely difficult to focus your mental activity enough to respond appropriately to just a
few of these sensations. Fortunately, selective attention can simplify our lives. As Theme
2 suggests, our cognitive apparatus is impressively well designed. Features such as selective attention—which may initially seem to be drawbacks—may really be beneficial.

In general, the research on selective attention falls into two basic categories.
Some studies examine dichotic listening, whereas others assess selective attention
through a visual task called the Stroop effect.

Dichotic Listening. Have you ever held a phone to one ear, while your other ear
registers a message from a nearby radio? If so, you have created a situation known
as dichotic listening (pronounced "die-*kot*-ick"). In the laboratory, ***dichotic listening*** is studied by asking people to wear earphones; each ear is presented with a different message. Typically, the research participant is asked to shadow the message
in one ear, by listening to the message and repeating it after the speaker.

In the classic research, people noticed very little about the unattended, second
message (Cherry, 1953). For example, the second message sometimes was switched
from English words to German words. However, people reported that they assumed
this unattended message was in English. In other words, their attention was so concentrated upon the attended message that they failed to notice the switch to a foreign language! People did notice, however, when the voice of the unattended
message was switched from male to female. Therefore, some characteristics of the
unattended message can be detected.

If people can notice the gender—or, more likely, the pitch of the speaker's
voice—what else do they notice? Moray (1959) reported that people notice their
own name if it is inserted in the unattended message. You may have noticed this
phenomenon. Even if you are paying close attention to one conversation at a party,
you can often notice when your name is mentioned in a nearby conversation. Wood
and Cowan (1995) repeated the research under more controlled conditions than
Moray had used, and they found that 35% of the participants recalled hearing their
name in the channel that they were supposed to ignore. Notice, then, that the so-
called cocktail party phenomenon can sometimes operate, but we ignore even our
own name about two-thirds of the time.

In some cases, people can follow the meaning of a message in the unattended
ear. For example, Treisman (1960) presented two messages to the participants in
her study. As Figure 2.7 illustrates, people were instructed to shadow one message
and to leave the other message unattended. However, after a few words, the meaningful sentence in the shadowed ear was suddenly interrupted by a string of unrelated words. Simultaneously, that same sentence continued in the "unattended" ear.
Treisman found that people sometimes followed the meaningful sentence and
began to shadow the message that they were supposed to ignore. Thus, they might
say, "In a picnic basket, she had peanut butter sandwiches and chocolate brownies."
Interestingly, the participants in Treisman's study reported that they were unaware
that the meaningful sentence had shifted to the unattended ear.

=== **Figure 2.7** ===

AN ILLUSTRATION OF TREISMAN'S (1960) SHADOWING STUDY

To what extent do people notice semantic aspects of the unattended message? This topic is controversial, because some studies suggest that people can notice the meaning of the unattended message, but other studies suggest they cannot (e.g., Corteen & Wood, 1972; Hirst, 1986; Johnston & Dark, 1986; Wardlaw & Kroll, 1976). The answer probably depends upon task characteristics. Still, meaning is less noticeable than characteristics such as pitch (Allport, 1989).

In summary, when people's auditory attention is divided, they can notice some characteristics of the unattended message, such as the gender of the speaker and whether their own name is mentioned. On the other hand, they may be unaware of whether the unattended message is in English or in a foreign language. Finally, people can sometimes notice the meaning of the unattended message, but in some conditions, they do not.

The Stroop Effect. So far, we have examined selective attention on auditory tasks; people are instructed to shadow the message presented to one ear and ignore the message to the other ear. However, researchers have conducted a greater number of studies on selective visual attention. Try Demonstration 2.4, which illustrates the famous Stroop effect. The ***Stroop effect*** refers to the observation that people take much longer to name the color of a stimulus when it is used in printing an incongruent word than when it appears as a solid patch of color. For example, they have trouble saying "blue" when blue ink is used in printing the word *red.* Note that the Stroop effect demonstrates the effects of selective attention because people take

---

DEMONSTRATION 2.4

THE STROOP EFFECT

For this demonstration, you will need a watch with a second hand. Turn to the colored page inside the front cover called Demonstration 2.4. First, measure how long it takes to name the colors in part a. Your task is to say out loud the names of the ink colors, ignoring the meaning of the words. Measure the amount of time it takes to go through this list *five* times. (Keep a tally of the number of repetitions.) Record that time.

   Now you will try a second color-naming task. Measure how long it takes to name the colors in the rectangular patches in part b. Measure the amount of time it takes to go through this list five times. (Again, keep a tally of the number of repetitions.) Record the time. Does the Stroop effect operate for you? Are your times similar to those obtained in Stroop's original study?

---

longer to name a color when they are distracted by another feature of the stimulus, namely, the meaning of the words themselves.

   The effect was first demonstrated by J. R. Stroop (1935), who found that people required an average of 110 seconds to name the ink color of 100 words that were incongruent color names (for example, blue ink used in writing the word *red*). In contrast, people required an average of only 63 seconds to name the ink color of 100 solid color squares.

   Since the original experiment, more than 400 additional studies have examined variations of the Stroop effect (e.g., MacLeod, 1991; Richards et al., 1992; Sugg & McDonald, 1994). Incidentally, we will emphasize in Chapter 12 that older adults perform as well as younger adults on many cognitive tasks. However, older adults find the Stroop task to be even more difficult than do younger adults (Hartley, 1993).

   A review article by MacLeod (1991) examines a variety of explanations for the Stroop effect. MacLeod believes that the most promising account is provided by a parallel distributed processing approach (e.g., Cohen et al., 1990). According to this explanation, the Stroop task activates two pathways at the same time. One pathway is activated by the task of naming the ink color, and the other pathway is activated by the task of reading the word. Interference occurs when two competing pathways are active at the same time. As a result, task performance suffers.

Theories of Attention

Let us first consider some early theories of attention and then discuss Schneider and Shiffrin's theory of automatic versus controlled processing. The final portion of this section examines Treisman's feature-integration theory.

Early Theories of Attention. The first theories of attention emphasized that people are extremely limited in the amount of information that they can process at any given time. A common metaphor in these theories was the concept of a bottleneck. Just as the neck of a bottle restricts the flow into or out of the bottle, *bottleneck theories* proposed a similar narrow passageway in human information processing. In other words, this bottleneck limits the quantity of information to which we can pay attention. Thus, when one message is currently flowing through a bottleneck, the other messages must be left behind. Many variations of this bottleneck theory were proposed (e.g., Broadbent, 1958; De Jong, 1993; Deutsch & Deutsch, 1963; Moray, 1993; Treisman, 1964).

You'll recall from the section on theories of pattern recognition that the template theory was rejected because it was not flexible enough. Similarly, the bottleneck theories lost popularity because they underestimated the flexibility of human attention (Eysenck, 1982). As Chapter 1 pointed out, no metaphor based on a simple machine or a simple structure can successfully account for the sophistication of human cognitive processes. The next two theories point out how the nature of the task, the amount of practice, and the stage in processing can all change the way people use attention.

Automatic Versus Controlled Processing. Walter Schneider and Richard Shiffrin have proposed two levels of processing relevant to attention. *Automatic processing* can be used on easy tasks involving highly familiar items. In contrast, *controlled processing* must be used on difficult tasks or tasks involving unfamiliar items. Furthermore, automatic processing is *parallel;* that is, you can handle two or more items at the same time. In contrast, controlled processing is *serial;* only one item can be handled at a time.

Automatic and controlled processing can be related to other topics discussed earlier in this chapter. We mentioned that people can use automatic processing on easy tasks with familiar items. Therefore, on a selective-attention task in which people use automatic processing, it should be relatively easy to pick up features of the unattended message. On a divided-attention task where both tasks require automatic processing, it should also be relatively easy to perform two tasks simultaneously. In addition, consider the relationship between practice and automatic processing. Tasks that have been extensively practiced will tend to involve automatic processing.

Now consider difficult tasks with unfamiliar items, which typically require controlled processing. On a selective-attention task in which people use controlled processing, very few features of the unattended message will be noticed. On a divided-attention task, it will be difficult to perform two tasks simultaneously. In addition, tasks that have *not* been extensively practiced will usually require controlled processing. To help you distinguish between these two terms, try thinking of examples of tasks that require either automatic or controlled processing.

The research by Schneider and Shiffrin examined the difference between automatic and controlled processing (Schneider & Shiffrin, 1977; Shiffrin & Schneider, 1977). Participants in these studies saw a rapid series of 20 pictures, or frames, on each trial. Each of four locations in a particular frame could be occupied by a number, a letter, or a set of dots. The numbers and letters could occupy one, two, or all four locations on a frame. Figure 2.8 shows a typical frame. Before seeing the 20 pictures, each participant was instructed to remember and look for either one or four targets. For example, a typical person might have been told to search the pictures for the four targets, *B, P, Q,* and *Y.* Notice, then, that both the number of items in a frame and the size of the target set were varied.

This study included two other important variables. The exposure time for each frame varied between 40 and 800 milliseconds. Finally, the difficulty of the task was varied. In the "consistent-mapping condition," the target-set items and the irrelevant items were from different categories. For example, a person might search for numbers, with the irrelevant items on a frame being letters. The "varied-mapping condition" was much more difficult. First of all, the target-set items and the irrelevant items were all from the same category. For example, a person might search for certain letters, with the irrelevant items also being letters. Furthermore, target-set items on one trial could become irrelevant items on the next trial. (For example, on Trial 1, you might search for an *E,* with irrelevant items being *A, C, N, S,* and so forth; on Trial 2, you might search for an *S,* with irrelevant items being *E, A, C, N,* and so forth.) This varied-mapping condition basically resembled a card game in which the rules keep changing!

Let's consider the results of this study. The factors affecting accuracy were different for the two mapping conditions. In the easier, consistent-mapping condition, frame-exposure time was the only variable that influenced accuracy; people were more accurate when they saw each frame for a long time. However, neither target-set size nor frame size influenced accuracy; that is, people were just as accurate

---

Figure 2.8

A TYPICAL FRAME IN THE STUDIES BY SCHNEIDER AND SHIFFRIN (1977)

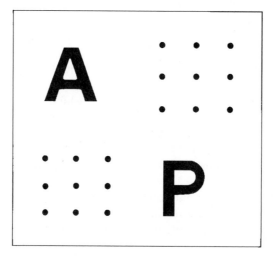

when they were searching for four items as for one. People were also just as accurate when there were four letters or numbers on each frame as when there was only one letter or number. This consistent-mapping condition was so easy that people used *automatic processing*, even with a large number of target-set items and irrelevant items. People apparently conducted a parallel search, looking for all four targets in all four positions at the same time.

The varied-mapping conditions produced different results. Exposure time influenced accuracy; as in the consistent-mapping condition, people were more accurate when the frames were exposed longer. However, the other two variables also influenced accuracy. People were more accurate when searching for one target than for four. They were also more accurate when there was only one letter or number on each frame than when there were four. In the varied-mapping condition, people were forced to use *controlled processing*, because the task could not be performed automatically. People in this condition apparently conducted a serial search, looking for each target—one at a time—through all items in a frame.

Schneider and Shiffrin's research inspired further research and theoretical debate (e.g., Cheng, 1985; Corballis, 1986; Fisher, 1984; Jonides et al., 1985; Ryan, 1983; Schneider & Shiffrin, 1985; Shiffrin & Schneider, 1984). For example, Fisher (1984) argued that we have clear limits to the amount of information that we can process simultaneously. After all, Schneider and Shiffrin showed a maximum number of only four items on each frame. Perhaps the limit for parallel search is slightly beyond four items. However, people probably cannot look at a frame of 10 items and search them all simultaneously and automatically.

Feature Integration Theory. Anne Treisman has developed an elaborate theory of attention and perceptual processing. Her original theory, proposed in 1980, was elegantly simple (Treisman & Gelade, 1980). However, as she emphasized in a more recent article, "simple stories never stay that way" (Treisman, 1993, p. 5). Let's look at the current version of feature integration theory (Treisman, 1992, 1993; Treisman & Sato, 1990).

According to Treisman's ***feature-integration theory***, we sometimes process a scene using divided attention, with all parts of the scene processed at the same time; on other occasions, we use focused attention, with each item in the scene processed one at a time. Furthermore, divided attention and focused attention form a continuum, so that you frequently use a kind of attention that is somewhere between the two extremes of divided and focused attention.

Let's consider these two kinds of processing in more detail before considering other components of Treisman's theory. The first stage of the theory involves *divided attention*, a concept we have already discussed. Divided attention allows the automatic registration of features, using parallel processing across the field. Divided attention, the relatively low-level kind of processing, is therefore roughly equivalent to Schneider and Shiffrin's automatic processing. This kind of processing is so effortless that we are not even aware when it happens.

The second stage of Treisman's theory, ***focused attention,*** involves serial processing, in which objects are identified one at a time. Focused attention, the more

---

DEMONSTRATION 2.5

DIVIDED ATTENTION VERSUS FOCUSED ATTENTION

After reading this paragraph, turn to the colored figures marked Demonstration 2.5 inside the front cover. First, look at the two figures marked part a. In each case, search for a blue *X*. Notice whether you take about the same amount of time on these two tasks. After trying part a, return to this page and read the additional instructions.

Additional instructions: For the second part of this demonstration, return to part b inside the front cover. Look for the blue *X* in each of the two figures in part b. Notice whether you take the same amount of time on these two tasks or whether one takes slightly longer.

---

demanding kind of processing, is required when the objects are more complex. Thus, focused attention is roughly equivalent to Schneider and Shiffrin's controlled search. Focused attention selects which features belong together—for example, which shape goes with which color.

Treisman and Gelade (1980) examined these two kinds of processing approaches by studying two different stimulus situations, one that used isolated features (and therefore involved divided attention) and one that used combinations of features (and therefore involved focused attention). Let's first consider the details of the research on divided attention. Treisman and Gelade proposed that if isolated features are processed automatically in divided attention, then people should be able to rapidly locate a target among its neighboring, irrelevant items. That target should seem to "pop out" of the display automatically, no matter how many items are in the display.

To test their hypothesis about divided attention, Treisman and Gelade conducted a series of studies. They discovered that if the target differed from the irrelevant items in the display with respect to a simple feature such as color or orientation, observers could detect the target just as fast when it was presented in an array of 30 items as when it was presented in an array of only 3 items (Treisman, 1986; Treisman & Gelade, 1980). If you try Part a of Demonstration 2.5, you'll find that the blue *X* seems to "pop out," whether the display contains 2 or 23 irrelevant items. Divided attention can be accomplished in a parallel fashion and relatively automatically.

In contrast, consider the details of the research on focused attention. Part b of Demonstration 2.5 requires you to search for a target that is an object—that is, a conjunction (or combination) of properties. When you search for a blue *X* among red *X*'s, red *O*'s, and blue *X*'s, you must use focused attention because you are forced to focus attention on one item at a time, using serial processing. You are searching at the object level, rather than the feature level. This task is more complex, and the

SEARCHING FOR FEATURES THAT ARE PRESENT OR ABSENT (FROM TREISMAN & SOUTHER, 1985)

In part a, search for the circle with the line. Then, in part b, search for the circle *without* the line.

a.

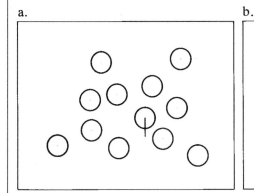

b.

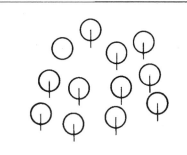

time taken to find the target increases dramatically as the number of distractors increases. In Demonstration 2.5, Figure b2 required a more time–consuming search.

Theme 3 of this book states that our cognitive processes handle positive information better than negative information. Turn back to Demonstration 1.1 on page 20 to remind yourself about this theme. The research of Treisman and Souther (1985) provides additional support for that theme, as you can see from Demonstration 2.6.

Notice, in part a of this demonstration, that the circle with the line seems to "pop out" from the display. In contrast, you must search part b more closely to determine that it indeed contains the target. Treisman and Souther (1985) found that people performed rapid searches for a feature that was present (as in part a), whether the display contained zero or 11 irrelevant items. People who are searching for a feature that is *present* can use divided attention efficiently. In contrast, when searching for a feature that was missing (as in part b), the search time increased dramatically as the number of irrelevant items increased. People who are searching for a feature that is *absent* must use focused attention. This task is substantially more challenging (Treisman, 1991).

Treisman and her colleagues have also demonstrated an interesting effect that can occur when attention is either overloaded or distracted. Specifically, when attention demands are high, we may form an illusory conjunction (Treisman &

Schmidt, 1982; Treisman & Souther, 1986). An *illusory conjunction* is an inappropriate combination of features, perhaps combining one object's shape with a nearby object's color. For example, a person whose attention is distracted might be presented with two nonsense words, *dax* and *kay*. This observer may report seeing the English word *day*. When nonsense words are presented so quickly that the items do not receive focused attention, we form illusory conjunctions that are consistent with our expectations. Top-down processing helps us screen out inappropriate combinations (Treisman, 1990).

Treisman's work on illusory conjunctions should remind you of two topics discussed earlier in this chapter. Her discovery that people perceive English words, rather than nonsense words, is similar to the word superiority effect. Furthermore, you'll recall from Table 2.1 on page 45 that people in a divided-attention condition "recognized" conjunction faces almost as often as they recognized the faces they had actually seen (Reinitz et al., 1994).

The basic elements of feature-integration theory were proposed almost 20 years ago. Since that time, dozens of additional studies have been conducted, and the original, straightforward theory has been modified. For example, Treisman and her colleagues (1992) have found that when participants have extensive practice in searching for conjunction targets that initially required focused attention, the targets can be located very rapidly. For example, after 9,000 trials, participants were able to locate a target that was blue and X-shaped as quickly as they had located—prior to practice—a target that was simply blue.

To explain how people can sometimes search very efficiently under divided attention conditions, some researchers have proposed that the visual system manages to extract enough information during this challenging situation to guide further attention (e.g., Wolfe, 1992). Treisman and Sato (1990) have introduced a new component to feature-integration theory. Specifically, they suggest that a *feature inhibition mechanism* can simultaneously inhibit all irrelevant distractor features. When these irrelevant features are very different from the target for which you are searching, you may be able to search very quickly for objects that are conjunctions of two properties. For example, if you're looking at a group of kindergartners and their mothers and fathers on a field trip, you can easily disregard all the children if you are searching for the conjunction-target, "adult males."

As we will see throughout Chapter 3, researchers often propose a theory that initially draws a clear-cut distinction between two or more psychological processes. With extensive research, however, theorists frequently conclude that reality is much more complex. Rather than two clear-cut categories, we find that, in some conditions, divided attention can occasionally resemble focused attention. Similarly, in Chapter 3, we will see that distinctions among different kinds of memory systems may actually become quite blurry.

The Biological Basis of Attention

During the past 20 years, researchers have developed a variety of sophisticated techniques for examining the biological basis of behavior. Research using these

Figure 2.9

REGIONS OF THE CEREBRAL CORTEX THAT ARE INVOLVED IN PATTERN RECOGNITION, VISUAL-SEARCH ATTENTION, AND WORD-MEANING ATTENTION (VIEW OF THE LEFT HEMISPHERE, FROM THE SIDE).

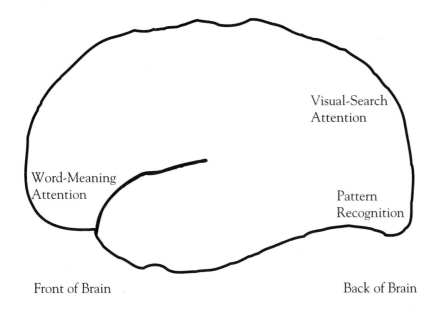

Front of Brain   Back of Brain

techniques has identified a network of areas throughout the brain that accomplish various attention tasks (Posner & Raichle, 1994; Posner & Rothbart, 1991; van Zomeren & Brouwer, 1994; Vecera & Farah, 1994).

Figure 2.9 shows the left hemisphere of the cerebral cortex. Notice that pattern recognition, which we discussed in the first part of this chapter, is a process that takes place mostly in the lower portion of the back of the cerebral cortex. This area is therefore activated when you recognize the letters within this sentence.

As you can see, attention involves different regions of the brain. Michael Posner and his colleagues at the University of Oregon have examined the kind of attention required for visual search. For example, imagine that you are searching the area around a bathroom sink for a lost contact lens. When you are attending to a location in space, the posterior attention network is activated. The *posterior attention network,* which is responsible for the kind of attention involving visual search, includes part of the outer covering of the brain called the parietal cortex (where the label "Visual-Search Attention" is located in Figure 2.9), as well as structures buried deep in the center of the brain (Posner, 1992; Posner & Raichle, 1994).

How was the parietal cortex identified as a region of the brain involved in attention? Much of the research uses the *positron emission tomography scan,* which traces the chemical activity of various parts of the living brain. A tiny amount of a radioactive chemical is injected into blood vessels that carry the chemical to the brain, and the active regions in the brain temporarily accumulate this chemical. A machine then passes X-ray beams through the head. Positron emission tomography, also known as a **PET scan,** therefore allows us to measure the blood flow in various regions of the brain (Posner, 1992). According to PET-scan research, the parietal cortex shows increased blood flow when people pay attention to spatial locations (e.g., Corbetta et al., 1991; Posner et al., 1991).

Another important method used to determine the biological basis of attention involves clinical studies on people with *lesions,* or specific brain damage caused by strokes, accidents, or other traumas. People who have brain damage in the parietal region of the right hemisphere of the brain have trouble noticing a new visual stimulus that appears on the left side of their visual field. Those with damage in the left parietal region have trouble noticing a visual stimulus on the right side (Posner, 1991).

The German artist Anton Raderscheidt provides a particularly vivid example of the importance of the parietal cortex. The self-portraits he painted prior to suffering a stroke are full and complete. After he suffered a stroke that damaged the right parietal cortex, his painting underwent a startling change. The first self-portrait painted after the stroke is reasonably complete on the right side of the paper, but the left side is completely blank! The artist seemed unable to attend to visual stimuli appearing in the left visual field. His later self-portraits showed greater development on the left side of the paper, but the detail was never as complete as on the right side (Wurtz et al., 1982).

Figure 2.9 also shows that an area in the frontal lobe of the cortex performs the kind of attention tasks involving word meaning. The **anterior attention network** is active when people try the Stroop task, in which word meaning interferes with color identification (Posner & Raichle, 1994). It is also active when people are asked to listen to a list of nouns and to state the use of each word (e.g., listening to the word *needle* and responding *sew*).

Chapter 1 also described the event-related potential technique, which records electrical signals generated from a large number of neurons located underneath an electrode. Whereas the PET scan identifies the region of the brain that is most active during various attention tasks, the **event-related potential technique (ERP)** records the tiny fluctuations in the electrical activity of the brain during attention. For example, a research group in Finland instructed people to listen to a series of tones. Most were tones of a particular pitch, but sometimes a higher-pitched tone was included (e.g., Näätänen, 1982, 1985; Sams et al., 1985; Tiitinen et al., 1993). In some conditions, the participants were instructed to press a response key whenever they heard this unexpected tone. In these conditions, the pattern of electrical activity showed a new component. However, this component was absent when participants were tested in other conditions, where they had been instructed to ignore the higher-pitched tone. This series of studies therefore identifies a clear-cut neurological correlate of attention.

In summary, research on the biological basis of attention has used PET scans as well as case studies of people with lesions to identify regions of the brain, such as the parietal cortex, that are responsible for attention. In addition, the event-related potential technique has documented neuronal activity that corresponds to attention processes. Future researchers will continue to combine the results of various neuroscience techniques to help us understand the biological explanations of attention.

Consciousness

Our final topic—consciousness—is extremely controversial. One reason for the controversy is the variety of different definitions for the term (Farthing, 1992). For example, some resources on consciousness list as many as seven different definitions (e.g., Natsoulas, 1993a; Wallace & Fisher, 1983). I prefer a broad definition of the term: *consciousness* means the awareness people have of the outside world and of their perceptions, images, and feelings (Hirst, 1995; Posner, 1994).

Consciousness is closely related to attention, but the processes are not identical. After all, we are not aware or conscious of the tasks we are performing with automatic processing or divided attention. For example, when you are driving, you may use automatic processing to put your foot on the brake in response to a red light. However, you may not be at all *conscious* that you performed this motor action.

As Chapter 1 noted, the behaviorists considered topics such as consciousness to be inappropriate for scientific study. By the 1950s, the study of consciousness had essentially vanished from psychology (Baars, 1992; Nelson, 1996). However, spurred by the enthusiasm about cognitive psychology in the 1960s, consciousness edged back into favor. Since the mid-1980s, consciousness has become a popular topic for books and review articles (e.g., Farthing, 1992; Gardner, 1988; Hirst, 1995; Natsoulas, 1993b; Searle, 1992; Tulving, 1993a).

In recent years, cognitive psychologists have been especially interested in three interrelated issues concerned with consciousness. The first topic explores our ability to bring thoughts into consciousness, and the second emphasizes our *inability* to let thoughts escape from consciousness. The final topic examines cognitive psychologists' perspectives on the unconscious.

DEMONSTRATION 2.7

THOUGHT SUPPRESSION

This demonstration requires you to take a break from your reading and just relax for five minutes. Take a sheet of paper and a pen or pencil to record your thoughts as you simply let your mind wander. Your thoughts can include cognitive psychology, but they do not need to. Just jot down a brief note about each topic you think about as your mind wanders. One final instruction: During this exercise, *do not think about a white bear!*

Consciousness About Our Higher Mental Processes. To what extent do we have access to our higher mental processes? For example, answer the following question: "What is your mother's maiden name?" Now answer this second question: "How did you arrive at the answer to the first question?" If you are like most people, the answer appeared swiftly in your consciousness, but you probably cannot explain your thought process (Miller, 1962). The name seemed to simply "pop" into your memory.

According to a classic article by Richard Nisbett and Timothy Wilson (1977), we have little direct access to our thought processes. We may be fully conscious of the *products* of our thought processes (such as our mother's maiden name), but we are usually not conscious of the *processes* that created these products. For example, Nisbett and Wilson discuss the early research by Maier (1931). In this study, two cords hung down from a ceiling, and participants in the study were told to tie the two ends of the cord together. (The cords were so far apart that people could not hold one end and reach for the other end simultaneously.) The correct solution required swinging one cord like a pendulum. When Maier casually swung a cord during the study, people typically reached the solution in less than a minute. However, when asked how they solved the problem, their answers usually showed no consciousness of the thought process. A typical response was, "It just dawned on me."

Nisbett and Wilson's (1977) article stimulated discussion about the accuracy of our introspections. However, many researchers misinterpreted their claim. Nisbett and Wilson had said that we do not necessarily have access to our thought processes. Bowers (1984) notes, though, that several theorists mistakenly thought that they had said we *never* have access to thought processes.

The truth is clearly somewhere in between the two extremes (Nelson, 1996). Except for the strictest behaviorists, no one argues that verbal reports are absolutely worthless (Wilson, 1994). Also, no one argues that we are perfectly accurate in describing how information—such as our mother's maiden name—first enters into consciousness (Hirst, 1995). As we'll see in Chapter 7, we do have relatively complete access to some thought processes (e.g., how likely we are to remember the English translation of a French vocabulary word). However, we have only limited access to some other thought processes (e.g., how well we understand the information in an essay). Furthermore, our reports may be fairly accurate for some cognitive task we are currently doing, but fairly *inaccurate* for some task we completed many days earlier (Ericsson & Simon, 1993).

Our thought processes are hidden, rather than overt. Psychologists therefore have difficulty designing an experiment to measure these covert, private thoughts. Sometimes experiments yield different results. Furthermore, different interpretations of these experiments yield different models. We saw, for example, that some psychologists prefer distinctive-features models of pattern recognition, whereas others prefer a computational approach. This controversy thrives because we cannot trust verbal reports about pattern recognition and because we cannot directly observe people recognizing patterns. Instead, we must examine the research that has been conducted and decide which explanations are most consistent with the data.

In this chapter on perceptual processes and in the chapters that follow, we will examine some processes for which we have rival explanations and some for which we have insufficient explanations. This uncertainty is an inevitable result in an area as complex, covert, and inaccessible as human cognition.

Thought Suppression. Before you read further, try Demonstration 2.7 on page 57. Notice whether you have difficulty carrying out the instructions.

The original source for the white bear study is literary, rather than scientific. Apparently, when the Russian novelist Tolstoy was young, his older brother tormented him by instructing him to stand in a corner and *not* think about a white bear (Wegner et al., 1987; Wegner, 1996). Similarly, if you have ever tried to avoid thinking about food when on a diet, you know the difficulty of trying to chase these undesired thoughts out of consciousness. Smokers trying to give up cigarettes and depressed people trying to cheer themselves can also verify that thought suppression is a difficult assignment. As Wegner and his colleagues (1987) point out, this process of ***thought suppression*** includes two components: (1) planning to eliminate a thought from consciousness and (2) carrying out that plan by suppressing all evidence of the thought, including the original plan.

To test the difficulty of Tolstoy's task scientifically, Wegner and his coauthors instructed a group of students *not* to think about a white bear during a 5-minute period. Whenever they did think about a white bear, they rang a bell. They rang the bell an average of more than three times during the first minute in which they were supposed to be avoiding thoughts about the white bear, though they managed to limit their thoughts to about one instance per minute during the remainder of the 5-minute period. After this session, they were instructed to spend the next 5 minutes freely thinking about a white bear. This time, the white bears overpopulated consciousness, with close to five instances each minute. In contrast, another group of students who were instructed to think freely about a white bear—without a previous thought suppression session—thought about white bears an average of only three times each minute. In other words, initial suppression had produced a rebound effect in the first group.

In his more recent work, Wegner (1992) has related the components of thought suppression to the concepts of controlled and automatic processing, which we introduced earlier in the chapter. Wegner proposes that when you try to suppress a thought, you engage in a controlled search for thoughts that are *not* the unwanted thought. For example, when you are on a diet, you consciously, systematically search for items other than food to think about—a friend, a movie, exercise. At the same time, you also engage in an automatic search for any signs of the unwanted thought; this process demands little attention and it occurs automatically. On a diet, this automatic search effortlessly produces thoughts about rich pastries and other caloric treats. When you stop trying to suppress a thought, you discard the controlled search for irrelevant items, but the automatic search continues. Consequently, you experience a rebound effect, with thoughts about the previously forbidden topic now overpopulating your consciousness!

Many studies have replicated the rebound effect following thought suppression (e.g., Clark et al., 1993; Wegner, 1989). However, some research shows that the rebound effect is less common when you are trying to suppress your own, self-generated intrusive thoughts, rather than white bears and other ideas suggested by the researchers (Kelly & Kahn, 1994). For example, when asked to think about an unpleasant topic, many people spontaneously thought about death or injury. After a period of thought suppression, they were no more likely to show the rebound effect (i.e., think about death or injury) than were people in a control group. It's not clear why this study did not demonstrate the typical rebound phenomenon.

The rebound effect is not limited to suppressing thoughts about white bears and other relatively trivial kinds of ideas. Wegner (1994) summarizes a wide variety of other areas in which our efforts not to think about something can actually backfire. For example, when people are instructed not to feel sad (meanwhile trying to remember some irrelevant material), they became still sadder. Similar ironic effects—which occur when we try to suppress our thoughts—have been documented when people try to concentrate, relax, control pain, and avoid movement.

The Cognitive Unconscious. For many decades, research psychologists were extremely skeptical about a psychodynamic concept called the unconscious (Greenwald, 1992). We noted earlier that psychologists have constructed numerous definitions for consciousness. You won't be surprised to learn that they have even more difficulty defining the unconscious—especially because the term has been used most often in connection with theories inspired by Sigmund Freud, rather than by mainstream cognitive psychologists. However, we will use a definition proposed by Kihlstrom and his colleagues (1992): The ***cognitive unconscious*** refers to "information processing outside of conscious awareness" (p. 788).

We should stress, however, that the conscious and the unconscious are not divided into two clear-cut categories. Instead, a continuum connects these two kinds of processes (Erdelyi, 1992). As we discussed earlier in the chapter, clear-cut dichotomies are seldom found in cognitive psychology.

What kind of evidence do we have for the cognitive unconscious? As Greenwald (1992) notes, the most persuasive evidence comes from research on such topics as the ability to perceive a single word when it is presented as an unattended second message in a dichotic listening study. Also, as we will see in Chapter 5, people often show signs of having learned material when they fail to recall any of this material. However, our cognitive unconscious is not exactly brilliant (Loftus & Klinger, 1992). Instead, its talents are limited to such modest accomplishments as analyzing the meaning of a single word (Greenwald, 1992).

In summary, we have seen in this section on consciousness that we have difficulty bringing some information about our higher mental processes into consciousness. The discussion of thought suppression suggests another concern: We often have difficulty *eliminating* some information from consciousness. Finally, the section on the cognitive unconscious suggests that our higher mental processes may sometimes process information beyond the boundaries of conscious awareness.

SECTION SUMMARY: ATTENTION

1. Attention is a concentration of mental activity.
2. Research on divided attention shows that performance often suffers when people must attend to several stimuli simultaneously. However, with extensive practice, performance on some divided-attention tasks can improve.
3. Selective-attention studies using the dichotic listening technique show that people may notice little about the irrelevant message. They may notice the gender of the speaker and (occasionally) whether their own name is mentioned, but they may not notice whether the irrelevant message is in English; semantic aspects of the irrelevant message are occasionally processed, as well.
4. The Stroop effect is an example of a visual selective-attention task; the task is especially difficult for older adults.
5. Early theories of attention emphasized a "bottleneck" that limits attention. Somewhat later, Schneider and Shiffrin suggested that automatic processing is parallel, and it can be used on easy tasks with highly familiar items. In contrast, controlled processing is serial, and it must be used with difficult or unfamiliar tasks.
6. Treisman proposed a feature-integration theory that contains two components: (a) divided attention, which can be used to register single features automatically, and (b) focused attention, which is used to search for combinations of features and for a feature that is missing. Illusory conjunctions may arise when attention is overloaded.
7. Biological research on attention has used the PET scan to establish that visual search is handled by the posterior attention network, located in the parietal cortex. In contrast, tasks involving word meaning are handled by the anterior attention network, located in the frontal region of the brain. In addition, the event-related potential technique has documented neuronal activity during attention.
8. Consciousness, or awareness, is a currently popular topic. One issue is the extent to which we can be aware of our higher mental processes. Research on thought suppression illustrates the difficulty of eliminating some thoughts from consciousness. Finally, psychologists have begun to explore how some higher mental processes may occur in the cognitive unconscious.

CHAPTER REVIEW QUESTIONS

1. How would you describe perception to a friend who has never had a cognitive psychology course? Point out five different perceptual tasks that you have accomplished in the past 5 minutes.
2. Imagine that you are trying to read a sloppily written number that appears in a friend's class notes. You conclude that it is an 8, rather than a 6 or a 3. Explain how you recognized that number, using template-matching theory, prototype models, and distinctive-features models.

3. What is the goal of the computational approach to pattern recognition? Look up from your book and identify two nearby objects; how would Biederman's recognition-by-components theory describe how you recognize these objects?

4. Distinguish between bottom-up and top-down processing. Explain how top-down processing can help us recognize a variety of patterns; be sure to cite relevant studies. The chapter emphasized visual pattern recognition; provide examples of how top-down processing could help you recognize sounds, tastes, odors, and touch sensations.

5. According to the in-depth section on face recognition, "faces apparently have special privileged status in our perceptual system." Discuss this statement, mentioning research on identifying the gender of faces and on the comparison between faces and other visual stimuli.

6. What is divided attention? Give several examples of divided-attention tasks you have performed within the past 24 hours. What does the research show about the effects of practice on divided attention? Can you think of some examples of your own experience with practice and divided-attention performance?

7. What is selective attention? Give several examples of selective-attention tasks—both auditory and visual—that you have performed within the past 24 hours. Based on the discussion of practice and *divided* attention, what predictions would you make about the effects of practice on noticing information about the irrelevant task in a selective-attention situation?

8. Imagine that you are trying to carry on a conversation with a friend at the same time you are reading an interesting article in a magazine. Describe how the bottleneck theories and automatic versus controlled processing would explain your performance. Then describe Treisman's feature-integration theory and think of an example of this theory, based on your previous experiences.

9. Imagine that you are searching page 55 for the bold-faced phrase *posterior attention network*. What part of your brain is activated during this task? Now suppose that you are trying to pay attention to the meaning of the word *posterior*. What part of your brain is activated during this task? Describe how research has clarified the biological basis of attention.

10. Describe Nisbett and Wilson's argument that we do not typically have access to our thought processes. Think of an example of each of the following tasks, and describe whether you can arrive at an answer without being conscious of your thought process: (a.) speaking a sentence, (b.) remembering information about a word's meaning, (c.) remembering where you last left your Cognition textbook. Now try to think of examples of occasions when thought suppression was difficult. Finally, can you think of examples of occasions where unconscious thoughts seemed to influence your actions?

NEW TERMS

perception
pattern recognition
template-matching theory
templates
prototype models
prototypes
distinctive-features models
distinctive features
computational approach
machine vision
recognition-by-components
  theory
geons
bottom-up processing
data-driven processing
top-down processing

conceptually driven
  processing
word superiority effect
parallel distributed
  processing
holistic (processing)
attention
divided-attention tasks
selective-attention tasks
dichotic listening
Stroop effect
bottleneck theories
automatic processing
controlled processing
parallel (processing)
serial (processing)
feature-integration theory

focused attention
illusory conjunction
feature inhibition
  mechanism
posterior attention
  network
positron emission
  tomography scan
PET scan
lesions
anterior attention network
event-related potential
  technique (ERP)
consciousness
thought suppression
cognitive unconscious

RECOMMENDED READINGS

Bruce, V., Cowey, A., Ellis, A. W., & Perrett, D. I. (Eds.). (1992). *Processing the facial image.* Oxford, Great Britain: Clarendon Press. Topics included in this interesting book include neurophysiological mechanisms for face perception, facial expressions of emotion, and lipreading.

Farthing, G. W. (1992). *The psychology of consciousness.* Englewood Cliffs, NJ: Prentice Hall. Farthing's textbook discusses various components of consciousness, including such interesting topics as introspection and the mind-body problem. I also recommend his chapters on altered states of consciousness, such as daydreaming, sleep, and dreams.

Goldstein, E. B. (1996). *Sensation and perception* (4th ed.). Pacific Grove, CA: Brooks/Cole. Goldstein's textbook emphasizes a phsyiological approach to perception; the chapter on perceiving objects is most relevant to pattern perception.

Matlin, M. W., & Foley, H. J. (1997). *Sensation and perception* (4th ed.). Boston: Allyn and Bacon. This textbook emphasizes a top-down approach to perception, exploring in some detail pattern recognition and other aspects of perceptual processing.

Posner, M. I., & Raichle, M. E. (1994). *Images of mind.* New York: Freeman. This book was written for well-educated laypeople, so its style is more accessible than that of most books on the biological basis of cognition. It also includes numerous full-color illustrations and examples of PET scans.

Wegner, D. M. (1994). Ironic processes of mental control. *Psychological Review, 101,* 34–52. Daniel Wegner was the first psychologist to conduct systematic research on thought suppression; this article reviews thought suppression and other situations in which our mental operations produce an effect that is the opposite of our intentions.

MODELS OF MEMORY

INTRODUCTION

THE ATKINSON-SHIFFRIN MODEL

Description of the Atkinson-Shiffrin Model
Research on the Atkinson-Shiffrin Model
The Current Status of the Atkinson-Shiffrin Model

THE LEVELS-OF-PROCESSING APPROACH

Description of the Levels-of-Processing Approach
Research on the Levels-of-Processing Approach
In Depth: The Self-Reference Effect
The Current Status of the Levels-of-Processing Approach

TULVING'S MODEL: EPISODIC, SEMANTIC, AND PROCEDURAL MEMORY

Description of Tulving's Model
Research on Tulving's Model
The Current Status of Tulving's Model

THE PARALLEL DISTRIBUTED PROCESSING APPROACH

Description of the Parallel Distributed Processing Approach
The Current Status of the Parallel Distributed Processing Approach

Preview

Memory is a critical part of all cognitive processes, because we use memory whenever we maintain information over time. Chapter 3 is the first of three chapters about memory; it explores four important models of memory. As we will emphasize, these four approaches represent four different perspectives on memory—often focusing on different attributes of memory. Thus, they are not really in competition with one another.

The Atkinson-Shiffrin model proposes that memory consists of three memory stores: sensory memory, short-term memory, and long-term memory. The model also includes control processes, such as the strategy of repeating information to maintain it in memory. A controversial feature is the model's proposal that short-term memory and long-term memory constitute two separate stores.

The levels-of-processing approach proposes that the way we process material influences how well we recall it. Deep processing (for example, making judgments about a word's meaning) produces more permanent retention than shallow levels of processing (for example, making judgments about a word's physical appearance). Two kinds of tasks create especially strong retention: One produces the generation effect, in which you create material yourself, and the other produces the self-reference effect, in which you determine whether a target item refers to yourself.

According to Tulving's model, episodic memory handles information about events, semantic memory deals with organized knowledge about the world, and procedural memory involves knowing how to do something. Tulving assembled theoretical and research evidence for these distinctions, but skeptics have argued that the evidence is not convincing.

A new, extremely influential approach to cognition is called parallel distributed processing (PDP), which proposes that networks link together neuron-like units. The PDP approach accounts for some important features of memory. For example, when a person mentions a word or a name, we spontaneously recall numerous related items. The PDP approach also explains how we can often retrieve correct information from a variety of clues, even when one of the clues is incorrect. This approach has won the enthusiasm of many supporters, but it is too new to draw conclusions about whether it can account for a wide variety of memory phenomena.

INTRODUCTION

Imagine that your memory were to fail right in the middle of the next sentence. You could not continue to read the sentence because you would be unable to recognize any letters or understand the meaning of any words. In fact, you wouldn't even be able to recall why the book was lying in front of you. You wouldn't remember your name or your age, let alone the name of your cousin's girlfriend. Good friends would not look familiar. Furthermore, you wouldn't even be able to recall what you were thinking about just a minute ago.

Memory involves maintaining information over time. You can maintain this information for less than a second or as long as a lifetime. For example, you use memory to store the beginning of a word until you hear the end of the word. You also use memory to recall your own name, which you probably learned when you were about a year old.

Memory is so central to cognitive processes that it influences almost every aspect of every topic in this book. Pattern recognition and attention, two topics from Chapter 2, are clearly affected by our memory for shapes and attentional strategies. Memory occupies center stage in Chapters 4 and 5, where we examine the research on sensory memory, short-term memory (also known as working memory), and long-term memory. In Chapter 6 we will discuss how images are stored in memory. Chapter 7 concentrates on memory for concepts and general knowledge. In Chapters 8 and 9, memory is an important part of both language understanding and language production. Clearly, memory is central in most of our cognitive activities. As Theme 4 emphasizes, the cognitive processes are strongly interrelated.

We will begin our examination of memory by introducing four influential models of memory. This chapter emphasizes the theoretical components of each approach; in several cases we'll postpone the discussion of relevant research until a later chapter. For example, short-term memory occupies more than half of Chapter 4, and semantic memory is relevant in nearly all of Chapter 7.

Before we begin, I need to emphasize that you should not view these four models as four rivals on a battlefield, all competing for the same patch of territory. Instead, these models represent four different perspectives, each offering a point of view that attempts to clarify different components of the complex memory processes. Rather than a battlefield metaphor, think of a scene from a movie, filmed by cameras placed at four different locations within a room.

The first theory we'll discuss in the current chapter was proposed by Atkinson and Shiffrin; it attempts to encompass all of memory, and it especially focuses on the distinction between short-term memory and long-term memory. The second approach stresses that we remember more material if we use a deep level of processing. The third model, proposed by Tulving, distinguishes among memory for events, memory for general information, and memory for procedures. Thus, these first three models focus on distinctions among different *kinds* of memory, though the distinction may emphasize the length of storage, how the material is processed, or the nature of that material. In contrast, the fourth model—parallel distributed processing—proposes that memory should be viewed in terms of the interactions within a network of basic neuron-like units; as you know from Chapter 1, the PDP approach attempts to explain not only memory, but also other cognitive processes such as perception, language, and problem solving.

Notice, then, that the four models differ tremendously in their scope—as well as in their focus. To continue the metaphor of making a movie, the Atkinson and Shiffrin model sweeps the camera around the whole room called "memory." The levels-of-processing approach and Tulving's approach each offer close-up examinations of very specific parts of the room. The parallel distributed approach, while also sweeping the camera around the entire room called "memory," explores many other rooms devoted to additional cognitive processes.

Students often wonder why psychologists emphasize models and theories. Why can't they be happy simply conducting research? Cognitive psychologists, like other psychologists, frequently develop theoretical explanations. For example, you encountered several theories of pattern recognition and several theories of attention in Chapter 2. Memory is such a major topic in cognitive psychology that we need to set aside this entire chapter to address theoretical issues. One value of these theories is that they attempt to simplify and organize all the diverse phenomena we call "memory" (Fischler, 1992). Otherwise, we simply have a collection of memory phenomena, with no understanding about how they might be related to one another. Another value is that they guide further research, helping to identify unexplored areas.

We also need to stress that theories are not necessarily mutually exclusive. In the discussion of theories of pattern recognition in Chapter 2, we saw that the various theories could account for different tasks. Similarly, each of the four memory theories we examine in this chapter may help us understand different components of memory.

THE ATKINSON-SHIFFRIN MODEL

During the 1960s, psychologists became increasingly excited about information-processing approaches to memory. A number of different models of memory were outlined that proposed separate memory stores for different kinds of memory (e.g., Waugh & Norman, 1965). These multistore models provided the first systematic account of the structures and processes that form the memory system (Eysenck & Keane, 1990).

The multistore model that is most often discussed is one proposed by Richard Atkinson and Richard Shiffrin (1968). This model soon became tremendously popular within the emerging field of cognitive psychology (Nadel, 1992; Squire et al., 1993). Because the Atkinson-Shiffrin theory quickly became the standard approach, it is sometimes called the "modal model." Figure 3.1 shows this model, with arrows to indicate that information is transferred from one storage area to another.

Let's first examine the components of this influential model. Then we'll look at the experimental research, as well as the case studies that neuroscientists have discussed. We will see that the model has some research support, but other results are not consistent with the model. We will conclude with an evaluation of the model's current status.

Description of the Atkinson-Shiffrin Model

At the top of Figure 3.1, you can see how external stimuli from the environment first enter sensory memory. *Sensory memory* is a large-capacity storage system that

Figure 3.1

ATKINSON AND SHIFFRIN'S MODEL OF MEMORY. BASED ON ATKINSON & SHIFFRIN, 1968.

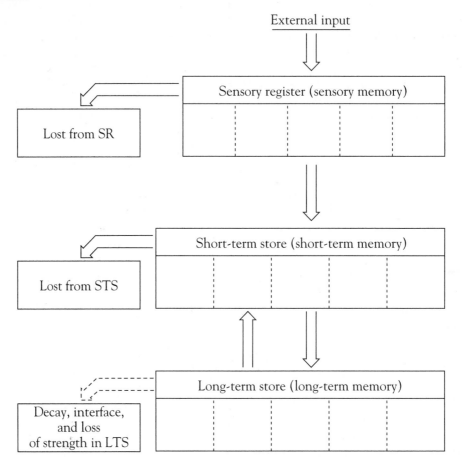

records information from each of the senses with reasonable accuracy. Psychologists are especially likely to study *iconic memory* (visual sensory memory) and *echoic memory* (auditory sensory memory). Touch, smell, and taste can also be represented in sensory memory, but these sensory modalities are studied much less often. In any case, information in sensory memory decays rapidly. Chapter 4 examines the research on sensory memory in much more detail.

Atkinson and Shiffrin's model proposes that material from sensory memory then passes on to short-term memory. *Short-term memory* (abbreviated *STM*) contains only the small amount of information that we are actively using. Atkinson and Shiffrin proposed that verbal information in STM is encoded acoustically, in terms of its sounds. Memories in STM are fragile—though not as fragile as those in sensory memory—and they can be lost from memory within about 30 seconds unless they are somehow repeated. Short-term memory is discussed in much more detail in the second part of Chapter 4.

According to the model, material that has been rehearsed passes from short-term memory to long-term memory. *Long-term memory* (abbreviated *LTM*) has a large capacity and contains memories that are decades old, in addition to memories that arrived several minutes ago. Atkinson and Shiffrin proposed that information in LTM is encoded semantically, in terms of its meaning. Memories in LTM are relatively permanent, and they are not likely to be lost. Chapter 5 examines the extensive research on long-term memory.

Suppose, for example, that a friend is reading a magazine article on food in China, and she relates to you an unusual fact:

> In Eastern China, a featured item on the menu is deep-fried scorpion.

In terms of Atkinson and Shiffrin's model, the words in that sentence would first be registered in the auditory store of your sensory memory. That information could then be lost, or it could be transferred to short-term memory. Suppose, for example, that the sentence about the deep-fried scorpion does arrive in short-term memory. One option is that this information may be lost from short-term memory. The other option is that it can pass on to long-term memory. If that information reaches long-term memory, it may be lost; however, the dotted arrow next to long-term memory suggests that loss from long-term memory is less likely than from the other two kinds of memory.

Notice that another arrow at the bottom of Figure 3.1 indicates that information in long-term memory can pass back into short-term memory when we want to actively work with that information again. Suppose, for example, that an evening's conversation has drifted to the topic of deep-fried scorpions, and you wish to share your knowledge. You can retrieve this useful information from your relatively inactive long-term memory and bring it back to short-term memory.

So far, we have examined the model's *structural features,* which are the stable memory stores used during information processing. Atkinson and Shiffrin also proposed *control processes,* which are strategies that people use flexibly and voluntarily, depending upon the nature of the material and their own personal preferences. Chapter 7 examines these control processes in the section on metacognition. One important kind of control process is *rehearsal,* or the silent repetition of information that encourages it to recycle through short-term memory. For example, you may silently repeat information about deep-fried scorpions in order to recall it later. According to the model, information that is rehearsed frequently and kept for a long time in short-term memory is more likely to be transferred to long-term memory.

Control processes can operate in other ways in memory. For instance, people can decide whether they want to fill their short-term memory with material that needs to be remembered or to leave "work space" to think about something else. Furthermore, they can decide whether to use a particular memory strategy—such as a mental picture—to encode that sentence about deep-fried scorpions.

Research on the Atkinson-Shiffrin Model

Within the framework of the Atkinson-Shiffrin model, the concept of sensory memory has created some controversy. In Chapter 4 we will see that current evidence suggests the possibility of at least two kinds of iconic memory (visual sensory memory). Researchers have also proposed two kinds of echoic memory (auditory sensory memory). Furthermore, some theories have questioned whether the concept of iconic memory is even worth retaining.

However, any controversy surrounding sensory memory has been greatly overshadowed by the controversy about another distinction in Atkinson and Shiffrin's model: the proposed separation between short-term memory and long-term memory. Numerous articles and books have debated this question (e.g., Baddeley, 1984, 1989; Melton, 1963; Squire, 1987; Squire et al., 1993; Wickelgren, 1973). In general, some research shows that short-term memory really *is* different from long-term memory. However, the evidence is not overwhelming.

The issue, then, is whether we have enough evidence to support a model with two separate memory storages—a short-term memory that stores information for about 30 seconds or less and a long-term memory that stores material for long periods of time. Psychologists typically prefer simple models, if these models can explain the data. However, suppose that we can demonstrate that certain factors have one kind of effect on material stored for short periods, and a different effect on material stored for longer periods. Then we should support a **duplex model,** or a model featuring two separate kinds of memory. Let us examine some representative research.

Kintsch and Buschke's Research. In one influential study, Kintsch and Buschke (1969) asked people to learn 16 English words in order. They proposed that the words from the beginning of the list would be in LTM when recall was requested because so much time had passed since they were presented. On the other hand, the most recent items should still be in STM. Their research focused upon one distinction that duplex theorists had proposed: material in STM is coded in terms of its acoustic or sound characteristics, whereas material in LTM is coded in terms of its semantic or meaning characteristics. The first study examined whether items at the beginning of the list—which were presumably in LTM—would be influenced by semantic factors. The second study examined whether items at the end of the list—which were presumably in STM—would be influenced by acoustic factors. Table 3.1 shows lists that are similar to the ones used in Kintsch and Buschke's research.

Notice that the first list contains pairs of synonyms, which are words that are similar to each other in *meaning.* This list resembles Kintsch and Buschke's semantically similar list. After the material had been presented, the experimenters supplied one word from the list, for example, *pleased.* The participants were requested to supply the next word in the list. The correct answer would be *forest.* However, suppose that a person confuses the words *pleased* with its synonym *happy.* Then this person might supply the word *rug* as the answer, because *rug* follows *happy.* Kintsch and Buschke measured the number of instances of this kind of semantic confusion that occurred

---

TABLE 3.1

TWO LISTS SIMILAR TO THOSE USED BY KINTSCH AND BUSCHKE (1969)

List 1 (from study 1) (Semantically similar pairs)	List 2 (from study 2) (Acoustically similar pairs)
angry	tacks
pleased	so
forest	buy
sofa	owe
ocean	tied
woods	sew
carpet	their
sea	tax
happy	by
rug	there
mad	oh
couch	tide

---

for items in each part of the list. They found that items at the beginning of the list produced a greater number of semantic confusions than items at the end of the list. This result suggests that items at the beginning of the list, which should be in LTM, are coded in terms of their meaning.

The second list contains pairs of homonyms, which are words that are similar to each other in *sound*. This second list is comparable to Kintsch and Buschke's acoustically similar list. If a person confuses two words that sound the same, then he or she might see the word *so* and respond *their,* because *so* was confused with *sew,* which appeared before *their.* Kintsch and Buschke (1969) found that acoustic confusions were more likely at the end of the list than at the beginning of the list. This result suggests that items at the end of the list, which should be in STM, are coded in terms of their sound.

Rundus's Research. According to Atkinson and Shiffrin (1968), items that are frequently rehearsed would be most likely to be transferred to long-term memory. An experiment by Dewey Rundus (1971) tested this hypothesis and also provided evidence that seemed to support another part of the Atkinson-Shiffrin model.

Specifically, Rundus presented a list of 20 nouns to students, who were instructed to rehearse the words by saying out loud any word that they were currently reviewing. Rundus recorded the number of times each word was rehearsed, as well as the number of words the student later recalled.

First, let's explore the data on recall, shown in Figure 3.2 by the curve with the black dots. The term ***serial position effect*** is used to refer to the U-shaped relationship between a word's position in a list and its probability of recall. The serial position effect highlights two common findings—the **primacy effect** (better recall for items at the beginning of a list) and the **recency effect** (better recall for items at the end of a list).

Now shift your attention to the relationship between serial position and the number of times each word was rehearsed. As you can see, the words at the beginning of the list were rehearsed much more often than the later words. Atkinson and Shiffrin's theory proposes that these early words are rehearsed often enough to be passed on to long-term memory; they can easily be retrieved during recall. By the time the student sees the sixth word, however, he or she has such a backlog of earlier items that frequent rehearsal is impossible. Notice that the probability of recall decreases rapidly as a function of serial position, for the first part of the list. In other words, the primacy effect seems to be explained very efficiently by the frequency of rehearsal.

Figure 3.2

THE RELATIONSHIP BETWEEN THE AVERAGE NUMBER OF REHEARSALS AND THE PROBABILITY OF RECALL, AS A FUNCTION OF A WORD'S SERIAL POSITION. BASED ON RUNDUS, 1971.

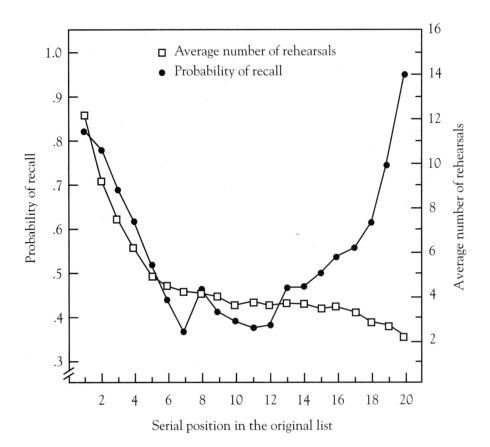

Serial position in the original list

But how does the Atkinson-Shiffrin theory account for the recency effect? Obviously, the high probability of recall for items 13–20 cannot be explained by rehearsal patterns. One explanation is that these items are still in short-term memory when the experimenter asks for recall. As you can imagine, people who are trying to recall a random list of words frequently begin by immediately "dumping out" the most recent ones. Thus, Rundus (1971) suggested that the recency effect can be explained by the concept of short-term memory.

Neuroscience Research. The neuroscience approach to memory has provided additional evidence for the Atkinson-Shiffrin model, especially through case studies of people with lesions. The most dramatic case is H.M., a man known only by his initials (Milner, 1966). In an attempt to cure H.M.'s serious epilepsy, neurosurgeons removed portions of his temporal lobes and his hippocampus. The operation successfully cured the epilepsy, but it left him with a severe kind of memory loss. H.M. can accurately recall events that occurred before his surgery, and his short-term memory is also normal. However, he cannot learn or retain any new information. For example, anyone H.M. meets on a Monday would not look familiar on a Tuesday. Furthermore, he cannot recall more than six numbers in order, suggesting that his short-term memory is normal but he lacks the ability to transfer material from short-term memory to long-term memory (Squire, 1987).

The case of a second man, known as K.F., suggests roughly the opposite symptoms. K.F. had been in a motorcycle accident, which damaged a portion of the left side of his cerebal cortex. His long-term retention is normal, but his short-term memory is severely limited (Shallice & Warrington, 1970). For example, Philip Johnson-Laird (1988) reports on his own interactions with K.F. First, Johnson-Laird asked K.F. to repeat the following sentence:

The dog bit the man and the man died.

K.F. repeated the sentence perfectly. Then Johnson-Laird asked him to repeat a second sentence:

The man the dog bit died.

This sentence was shorter but actually placed a greater burden on short-term memory; the subject, *the man,* needs to be held in short-term memory—while processing the next three words—until reaching the main verb, *died.* K.F. was unable to repeat this second sentence. These two case studies are often cited as evidence for the separation of short-term memory and long-term memory (Baddeley, 1990).

Evidence Against the Atkinson-Shiffrin Model. In psychology, distinctions often seem crisp when they are first proposed. As more research and theory are produced, however, the distinctions often seem to blur. For example, one crisp distinction used to be that short-term memory was acoustically coded, whereas long-term memory was semantically coded. We saw how this was illustrated in the study by Kintsch and Buschke (1969). However, more recent research has demonstrated that items in short-term memory can also be coded in terms of their meaning (Nilsson, 1992). We will discuss this aspect of short-term memory in more detail in Chapter 4. In addition, theorists pointed out that we often have a clear representation of the sound of an item in long-term memory; for example, you can probably recall the sound of a song you heard on the radio yesterday. In other words, STM may be *primarily* acoustic, and LTM may be *primarily* semantic, but the distinction is fuzzy.

What about the recency effect? Isn't that strong evidence for the role of short-term memory? Yes, it does seem to account quite convincingly for the results in Rundus's study. However, more recent researchers have also demonstrated a ***long-term recency effect,*** or better recall for items at the end of a list, when that list was learned long ago. If you ask some friends to recall the names of the presidents of the United States or the prime ministers of Canada, they will certainly show a recency effect. In other words, they will recall the names of Ronald Reagan or Brian Mulroney even though these names were certainly not stored in short-term memory before you asked for recall (Crowder, 1993). Perhaps both the standard recency effect and the long-term recency effect can really be explained by the same mechanism. This mechanism probably would *not* involve short-term memory (Thapar & Greene, 1993).

Now let's consider the neuroscience evidence. We noted that H.M. has normal STM and abnormal LTM, whereas K.F. has abnormal STM and normal LTM. This observation is often cited as strong evidence for the distinction between the two kinds of memory (e.g., Baddeley, 1990). However, the case of K.F. suggests a problem (Baddeley, 1990). The Atkinson-Shiffrin model proposes that information must pass through short-term memory before long-term learning can occur. If K.F. has abnormal short-term memory, then how could his long-term memory be normal?

In Chapter 4, the discussion of working memory will point out another problem with the Atkinson-Shiffrin model. Specifically, short-term memory does *not* have the strict size limitations that Atkinson and Shiffrin proposed (Baddeley & Hitch, 1974).

The Current Status of the Atkinson-Shiffrin Model

The research on the distinction between short-term memory and long-term memory reveals mixed results. Some studies support the distinction, and many current cognitive theories still separate short-term memory and long-term memory (Estes, 1991; Searleman & Herrmann, 1994). However, 25 years after the original model was proposed, even Richard Shiffrin concludes that the Atkinson-Shiffrin model was too simple (Shiffrin, 1993). As we'll see in Chapter 4, short-term memory does not seem to be a single storehouse with a limited capacity. Instead, it may involve three separate processes.

Despite the controversy over the distinction, however, most textbooks on memory or cognitive psychology discuss the research on short-term memory and long-term memory in different sections of the book (Searleman & Herrmann, 1994). The rationale is that the studies in these two areas explore different issues. For example, research on information stored in memory for brief periods frequently focuses on the limits of memory. In contrast, research on information stored in memory for longer periods usually examines such topics as autobiographical memory, encoding, and mnemonics.

Like most books in cognitive psychology, this book considers short-term memory and long-term memory in two separate chapters. However, this division reflects the

---

DEMONSTRATION 3.1

LEVELS OF PROCESSING.

Read each of the following questions and answer "yes" or "no" with respect to the word that follows.

1. Is the word in capital letters?	BOOK
2. Would the word fit the sentence: "I saw a _____ in a pond"?	duck
3. Does the word rhyme with BLUE?	safe
4. Would the word fit the sentence: "The girl walked down the _____"?	house
5. Does the word rhyme with FREIGHT?	WEIGHT
6. Is the word in small letters?	snow
7. Would the word fit the sentence: "The _____ was reading a book"?	STUDENT
8. Does the word rhyme with TYPE?	color
9. Is the word in capital letters?	flower
10. Would the word fit the sentence: "Last spring we saw a _____"?	robin
11. Does the word rhyme with SMALL?	HALL
12. Is the word in small letters?	TREE
13. Would the word fit the sentence: "My _____ is six feet tall"?	TEXTBOOK
14. Does the word rhyme with SAY?	day
15. Is the word in capital letters?	FOX

Now, without looking back over the words, try to remember as many of them as you can. Count the number correct for each of the three kinds of tasks: physical appearance, rhyming, and meaning.

nature of the tasks, rather than an enthusiastic endorsement of the Atkinson-Shiffrin model.

At about the time that many psychologists were growing dissatisfied with the duplex model proposed by Atkinson and Shiffrin, other researchers proposed a new theory. This new levels-of-processing theory stressed other concepts, and the distinction between short-term memory and long-term memory was not emphasized.

SECTION SUMMARY: THE ATKINSON-SHIFFRIN MODEL

1. Memory requires maintaining information over time; memory is involved in almost every cognitive process.
2. The classic model of memory proposed by Atkinson and Shiffrin consists of three memory storage systems: sensory memory, short-term memory, and long-term memory.
3. The Atkinson-Shiffrin model also includes control processes, which are the strategies that people use voluntarily (for example, rehearsal).
4. Numerous studies have examined the proposed distinction between short-term memory and long-term memory. For example, some research shows that short-term memory is coded in terms of acoustics, whereas long-term memory is coded in terms of meaning.
5. The experimental research and the case studies do not consistently support the STM–LTM distinction.
6. Despite the mixed support, many contemporary cognitive theories distinguish between STM and LTM, though the theories are typically more complex than the Atkinson-Shiffrin model.

THE LEVELS-OF-PROCESSING APPROACH

Before you read further, try Demonstration 3.1. Which kind of task produced the best recall? Was it the task in which you judged physical appearance, rhyming, or suitability in a sentence? This demonstration is based on a classic study by Craik and Tulving (1975) that explored levels of processing. Let's begin the discussion of this second approach to memory by describing the levels-of-processing framework. Then we'll look at the research, including an in-depth examination of an especially deep level of processing called the "self-reference effect." We'll end with an evaluation of the current status of this approach.

Description of the Levels-of-Processing Approach

The *levels-of-processing approach* proposes that deep, meaningful kinds of information processing lead to more permanent retention than shallow, sensory kinds of processing (Craik, 1979). For example, this approach would predict that in Demonstration 3.1, you would recall more words when you judged a word's meaning (for example, whether the word would fit in a sentence), rather than its physical appearance (for example, whether it is typed in capital letters) or its sound (for example, whether it rhymes with a word). The theory is also called the *depth-of-processing approach* because it emphasizes whether the processing is deep or shallow. In general, then, people achieve a greater depth of processing when they extract more meaning from a stimulus.

The levels-of-processing approach was proposed by Craik and Lockhart in 1972. This approach was not intended to be an all-encompassing theory of memory, rivaling the Atkinson-Shiffrin model. Instead, it was designed as a framework for thinking of memory as a process of analyzing stimuli. In any event, Craik and Lockhart's paper was one of the most influential publications in the area of human memory. In fact, Roediger (1980) pointed out that, by 1980, at least 700 articles had quoted this paper.

Let us examine the levels-of-processing approach in more detail. Craik and Lockhart (1972) proposed that people can analyze stimuli at a number of different levels. The shallow levels involve analysis in terms of physical or sensory characteristics, such as brightness or pitch. The deep levels require analysis in terms of meaning. When you analyze for meaning, you may think of other associations, images, and past experiences related to the stimulus.

The by-product of all this analysis is a memory trace. If the stimulus is analyzed at a very shallow level (perhaps in terms of whether it had capital letters or whether it was printed in red), then that memory trace will be fragile and may be quickly forgotten. However, if the stimulus is analyzed at a very deep level (perhaps in terms of its semantic appropriateness in a sentence or in terms of the meaning category to which it belongs), then that memory trace will be durable: It will be remembered.

Craik and Lockhart also focused on rehearsal, the process of cycling information through memory, which we discussed in connection with the Atkinson-Shiffrin model. Craik and Lockhart proposed two kinds of rehearsal. *Maintenance rehearsal* merely repeats the kind of analysis that has already been carried out. In contrast, *elaborative rehearsal* involves a deeper, more meaningful analysis of the stimulus. Thus, if you see the word *book*, you could use maintenance rehearsal and simply repeat the sound of that word to yourself. On the other hand, you could use elaborative rehearsal by thinking of an image of a book or by relating the word *book* to another word on the list.

What will happen if you spend more time rehearsing? Craik and Lockhart (1972) predicted that the answer to this question depends on the kind of rehearsal you are using. If you are using shallow maintenance rehearsal, then increasing the rehearsal time will not influence later recall. Simply repeating the word *book* five more times will not make it any more memorable. However, if you are using deep elaborative rehearsal, then an increase in rehearsal time *will* be helpful. During that time, you can dig out all kinds of extra images, associations, and memories to enrich the stimulus, and your later recall will be more accurate.

Research on the Levels-of-Processing Approach

The major hypothesis emerging from Craik and Lockhart's (1972) paper was that deeper levels of processing should produce better recall. This hypothesis has been widely tested. For example, in an experiment similar to Demonstration 3.1, Craik and Tulving (1975) found that people were about three times as likely to recall a word if they had originally answered questions about its meaning than if they had originally answered questions about the word's physical appearance. Similarly, Parkin (1984) discovered that people who made semantic judgments about a word's category or its synonym performed much better on a surprise recall test than did people who made nonsemantic judgments (for example, about the number of vowels contained in a word or whether it had been printed only in capital letters).

Numerous reviews of the research conclude that deep processing generally produces better recall than shallow processing (Baddeley, 1990; Howard, 1995; Lockhart & Craik, 1990; Koriat & Melkman, 1987). Much of the research on this topic has focused on the generation effect, face recognition, the compatibility between encoding and retrieval, and the explanations for the effectiveness of deep processing. Let's examine these areas, and then we will turn to an in-depth discussion of the self-reference effect, an especially popular area of research.

The Generation Effect. According to the ***generation effect,*** we remember items better if we generate or make them up ourselves, rather than simply studying items that other people made up. In the classic study on the generation effect, Slamecka and Graf (1978) showed people a series of English words and gave them instructions on how to create a response for each word. For instance, they might be instructed to create a response for the word *sea* that was a synonym beginning with the letter *o.* In this example, the appropriate response would be *ocean.* A second group of people were simply asked to read the pairs of words out loud (for example, "sea–ocean"). The results showed that recall was consistently better in the generation condition.

Subsequent research, summarized by Greene (1992) and by Searleman and Herrmann (1994), replicated the generation effect. An obvious application of this research is that you should study by trying to rephrase the material you are reviewing for an examination. You should recall substantially more material than if you merely read someone's else's words. Consistent with the levels-of-processing approach, we recall more material when we process it more thoroughly.

Depth of Processing and Face Recognition. Most of us can recall embarrassing incidents where we failed to recognize someone with whom we had interacted for many hours. For instance, a student in my cognitive psychology class named Michelle recalled how she had taken dance lessons with another female student, totaling about 3 hours each week for 2 years. One day Michelle saw the other student in a shopping mall and did not recognize her. Michelle had apparently failed to use deep processing to encode her face; with different clothing, that face was now unrecognizable.

Research has shown that shallow processing of faces—like shallow processing of words—leads to poor recall. For instance, research participants recognize a greater number of photos of faces if they make judgments about whether a person is honest, rather than the gender of the person or the width of the person's nose (Sporer, 1991).

Bloom and Mudd (1991) have provided an appealing explanation. Their research demonstrated that people who had been instructed to judge whether a person was honest looked at the faces longer and made more eye movements compared to people who had been instructed to judge whether a person was male or female. These authors argue that deeper processing leads to encoding a greater number of features, and therefore to superior recall. Alternately, when people make character judgments, they may encode the faces holistically, rather than in terms of isolated features (Wells & Hryciw, 1984). As you may recall from Chapter 2, our everyday face perception tends to rely on holistic processing, rather than on isolated features. No matter which explanation is correct, you should emphasize deep processing the next time you want to remember somebody's face!

The Compatibility Between Encoding and Retrieval. Craik and Lockhart's (1972) original description of the levels-of-processing approach emphasized *encoding,* or how items are placed into memory. It did not mention details about *retrieval,* or how items are recovered from memory. In a later paper, Craik and another colleague proposed that people recall more material if the retrieval conditions match the encoding conditions (Moscovitch & Craik, 1976). In other words, shallow processing can sometimes be *more* effective than deep processing when the retrieval task emphasizes superficial information. Notice that this point is not consistent with the original formulation of the levels-of-processing approach.

Let us consider a study that stresses the importance of the similarity between encoding and retrieval conditions. Suppose that you performed the various encoding tasks in Demonstration 3.1. Imagine, however, that you were then tested in terms of rhyming patterns, rather than in terms of free recall. For example, you might be asked, "Was there a word on the list that rhymed with *toy?*" Bransford and his colleagues (1979) found that people performed better on this rhyming test if they had originally performed the rhyming-encoding task, rather than the meaning-encoding task.

This area of research demonstrates that deep semantic processing may not be ideal unless the retrieval conditions also emphasize these deeper, more meaningful features. This research also emphasizes that memory often involves problem solving; to determine how to store some information, you'll need to figure out the characteristics of the recall task (Phillips, 1995). Incidentally, we will again discuss the importance of the compatibility between encoding and retrieval when we consider encoding specificity in Chapter 5.

Explanation for the Effectiveness of Deep Processing. Craik and Lockhart (1986) believe that deep levels of processing encourage recall because of two factors: distinctiveness and elaboration. ***Distinctiveness*** means that a stimulus is different from all other memory traces (Craik, 1979). For example, I can vividly recall a scene I witnessed during the 1970s. A friend had arranged for us to tour a nearby salt mine. Hundreds of feet below the earth's surface, we were traveling in a little cart through absolute darkness—until we suddenly came to a brightly lit area where five workers were nonchalantly sitting at a picnic area eating their lunch. That surreal image is so distinctly different from any scene I've experienced above ground that I'm unlikely to forget it!

Researchers have supported the value of distinctiveness. For instance, people recall words with distinctive sequences of short and tall letters, such as *lymph, khaki,* and *afghan,* better than words with more common arrangements of letters, such as *leaky, kennel,* and *airway* (Hunt & Elliott, 1980). Distinctiveness is especially useful in enhancing memory when we want to emphasize differences among items that seem highly similar (Phillips, 1995).

The second factor that operates with deep levels of processing is **elaboration,** which involves rich processing in terms of meaning (Anderson & Reder, 1979; Cohen et al., 1986). Unlike distinctiveness, elaboration is especially useful in enhancing memory when we want to emphasize similarities and relationships among items. In other words, elaboration helps us synthesize information (Phillips, 1995).

Think about the way you processed the word *duck* in Demonstration 3.1, for example. Perhaps you thought about the fact that you had indeed seen ducks on ponds and that ducks paddle along on the surface of ponds. The semantic encoding encouraged rich processing. In contrast, if the instructions for that item had asked whether the word *duck* was printed in capital letters, you would simply answer yes or no; extensive elaboration would be very unlikely.

Let's consider research on the importance of elaboration. Craik and Tulving (1975) asked participants to read sentences and decide whether the words that followed were appropriate to the sentences. Some of the sentence frames were simple, such as "She cooked the _____." Other sentence frames were elaborate, such as "The great bird swooped down and carried off the struggling _____." The word that followed these sentences was either appropriate (for example, *rabbit*) or inappropriate (for example, *book*). You'll notice that both kinds of sentences required deep or semantic processing. However, the more elaborate sentence frame produced far more accurate recall. Thus, more extensive elaboration leads to enhanced memory of stimuli.

Other research on elaboration emphasizes a practical point: In studying for a test, you will recall more if you elaborate on the material (Palmere et al., 1983). Palmere and his coauthors used a 32-paragraph essay on a fictitious African nation. Each paragraph contained only one major idea and consisted of four sentences—one main-idea sentence and three other sentences that provided examples for the main-idea sentence. In these studies, 8 of the 32 paragraphs remained intact; 8 had one sentence removed; 8 had two sentences removed; and 8 had all three example sentences removed. After participants had read the essay, they were tested for recall of the main ideas.

Figure 3.3 combines the results of three studies, each of which involved minor variations in presenting the paragraphs. The message is clear: More extensive

=== Figure 3.3 ===

THE NUMBER OF MAIN IDEAS RECALLED, AS A FUNCTION OF ELABORATION. BASED ON PALMERE ET AL., 1983.

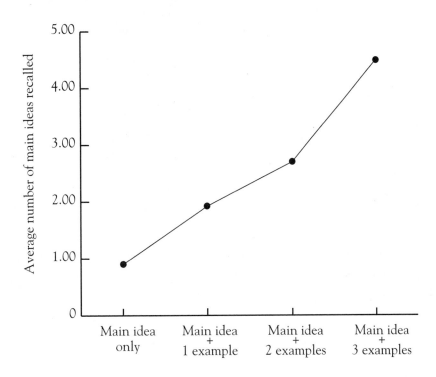

elaboration—via a large number of examples—promotes greater recall of the main ideas. Try applying the results of this experiment in reading your textbooks or reviewing your class notes. First identify the main ideas, and then think up examples that illustrate the main ideas. In psychology courses such as cognitive psychology, it is reasonably easy to think up examples, particularly examples from your own experience. As the following in-depth section demonstrates, a particularly deep level of processing occurs when you process information in terms of your personal experience.

▶▶ IN DEPTH: The Self-Reference Effect

We often deal with new information by relating it to ourselves. For example, students taking a course in abnormal psychology often suffer from "medical students' syndrome"—most psychological disorders seem to fit themselves! The professor describes how a depressed person feels pessimistic about the future, and suddenly dozens of students are wondering if their own pessimism means that they are clinically depressed.

This personal framework for new information is an important topic in the levels-of-processing approach. Specifically, the ***self-reference effect*** points out that people recall more information when they try to relate that information to themselves. In the classic demonstration of the self-reference effect, Rogers, Kuiper, and Kirker (1977) asked participants to process lists of words according to the kinds of instructions usually studied in levels-of-processing research, that is, in terms of the words' physical characteristics, their acoustic (sound) characteristics, or their semantic (meaning) characteristics. However, other words were to be processed in terms of self-reference. People were asked to decide whether a particular word could be applied to themselves.

As Figure 3.4 illustrates, the self-reference task produced the best recall. Apparently, when we think about a word in connection with ourselves, we develop a particularly memorable coding for that word. For example, suppose that you are trying to decide whether the word *generous* applies to yourself. You might remember how you loaned your notes to a friend who had missed class, and you shared a box of

---

Figure 3.4

NUMBER OF WORDS RECALLED, AS A FUNCTION OF LEVEL OF PROCESSING. BASED ON ROGERS ET AL., 1977.

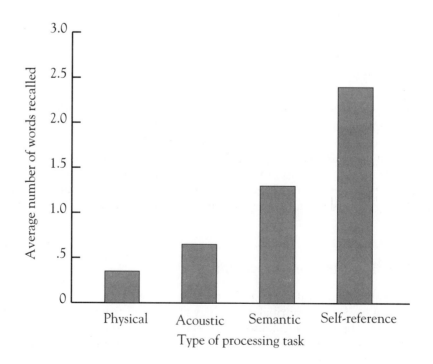

candy with the other people in the lounge—yes, *generous* does apply. The mental processes involved in the self-reference task seem to increase the chances that we will recall an item.

The self-reference effect has been demonstrated repeatedly, for example, with instructions to create mental imagery (Brown et al., 1986), with words related to creativity (Katz, 1987), and with paragraph-long prose passages (Reeder et al., 1987). The self-reference effect works with children as young as 10 years of age (Halpin et al., 1984), as well as elderly adults (Rogers, 1983).

The research on the self-reference effect has also produced a strong demonstration of one of the themes of this book. As Theme 3 proposes, our cognitive system handles positive instances more effectively than negative instances. In the self-reference studies, people are more likely to recall a word that *does* apply to themselves than a word that does not (Bellezza, 1992a; Bower & Gilligan, 1979; Ganellen & Carver, 1985; Mills, 1983). For example, the participants in Bellezza's (1992a) study recalled 46% of the adjectives that applied to themselves, compared with 34% of the adjectives that did not apply.

Explanations for the Self-Reference Effect. Why should we recall information especially well when we apply it to ourselves? Francis Bellezza suggests that the self is treated as an especially rich set of internal cues to which information can be associated. We can easily create these cues associated with the self, and we can easily link these cues with new information. These cues are also very discriminable from one another; your trait of *honesty* seems quite different from your trait of *intelligence* (Bellezza, 1984; Bellezza & Hoyt, 1992).

Before you read further, turn to the next page and try Demonstration 3.2, which focuses on an explanation for the self-reference effect.

According to Anthony Greenwald and Mahzarin Banaji (1989), the self is not unique in its ability to increase our memory accuracy. They argue that other similarly rich sources of ideas should also enhance recall. Their experiment resembled Demonstration 3.2; people produced names of friends and then constructed a sentence featuring each name, together with a concrete noun. People also constructed sentences using names supplied by the experimenter, just as you did.

The participants then completed a filler task in which they learned an assortment of trivial facts, and then they performed several recall tasks. Like you, they first provided free recall, listing the concrete nouns. For another task, called *cued recall,* they were given each of 20 names and were asked to supply the noun that had been paired with each name.

Figure 3.5 shows the results of this study. As you can see, people recalled nearly twice as many of the nouns that had been paired with their friends' names, compared to nouns paired with strangers' names. To check your own memory, count the number of odd-numbered words you recalled from the list in Demonstration 3.2 (the ones paired with strangers) and compare it with your recall for even-numbered words (previously paired with friends). Figure 3.5 also shows that the contrast in recall was even greater for the cued recall task.

DEMONSTRATION 3.2

CONSTRUCTING SENTENCES

Before you begin this demonstration, identify something that is enjoyable and interesting that you can do for a 5-minute break midway through this demonstration. Have that activity all set to go. Also, take out three sheets of paper.

On the first sheet of paper, write the numbers 1 through 20 on the left side. On the odd-numbered lines (1, 3, 5, . . .) write the last names of 10 current friends; on the even-numbered lines, copy the following last names: 2. Ziegler; 4. Dutton; 6. Gonzales; 8. McCrae; 10. Bunce; 12. Pletcher; 14. Wolter; 16. Henry; 18. Mann; 20. Burdett.

On the second sheet of paper, again write the numbers 1 through 20. Your task is to construct a sentence in which a name from the first sheet is linked with the corresponding word in the list below. For example, if the first name on your list were *Jones,* and the first word on this list were *refrigerator,* you might construct the following sentence: *Jones created a large sandwich out of leftovers that filled the refrigerator.* Here is the list of words, in order:

1. snow	6. map	11. photograph	16. door
2. chair	7. bicycle	12. soup	17. cookie
3. library	8. candle	13. coat	18. book
4. leaf	9. football	14. bird	19. horse
5. apple	10. rug	15. car	20. shirt

As soon as you have finished writing these sentences, take a 5-minute break. Please try not to think about any of this material during your break. When you are finished, place these two sheets of paper where you cannot see them. Then turn to Demonstration 3.3, and look at the bottom line for further instructions (page 89).

Clearly, the self is not the only source of rich, memorable ideas. In addition, the names of our friends can serve as a nucleus around which new knowledge can be readily gathered. Additional research by Bellezza and Hoyt (1992) confirmed that friends' names are especially likely to promote accurate recall.

Bellezza's explanation and the research by Greenwald and Banaji emphasize that the self-reference effect operates because each individual item is especially rich and useful in forming associations. A second explanation, proposed by Klein and Kihlstrom (1986), focuses on organization as an explanation for the self-reference effect. In particular, they suggest that when people think about whether words

Figure 3.5

FREE RECALL AND CUED RECALL FOR NOUNS, AS A FUNCTION OF WHETHER THE NOUNS WERE PAIRED WITH NAMES GENERATED BY THE EXPERIMENTER OR BY THE PARTICIPANT. FROM GREENWALD & BANAJI, 1989.

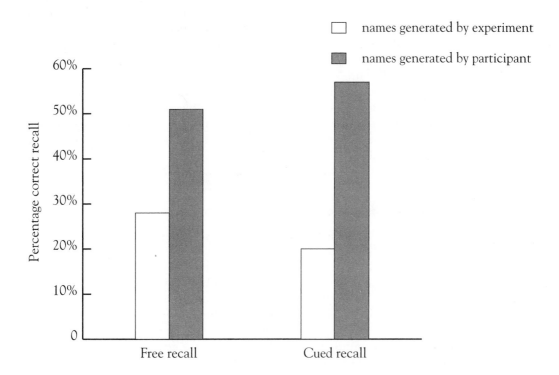

apply to themselves (the typical self-reference task), people also consider how some of these words are related to one another. After all, these words are all applied to the same person, so people might emphasize some interconnections. Klein and Kihlstrom (1986) then conducted a series of studies, and the results confirmed that self-reference instructions do encourage people to cluster related characteristics together.

Applications of the Self-Reference Effect. One important application of the self-reference effect is obvious: When you really want to remember material, try to relate it to your own experience—or to your friends. Reeder and his colleagues (1987) demonstrated that this technique works for prose passages, as well as isolated words. In fact, one effective way to learn the material in this textbook is to imagine yourself as a participant in each study you read about. You will find the material more memorable if you imagine how you might respond to the stimuli or situation. Furthermore, the demonstrations were specifically designed to use the self-reference effect.

The self-reference effect can also be applied to advertising. In one study, people made judgments about items that were pictured in advertisements (D'Ydewalle et al., 1985). A question about physical attributes might ask a person to judge a picture of a camera and answer the question, "Is there a red color in the picture?" A semantic question might ask, "Is it edible?" A self-reference question might ask, "Have you ever used this product?" The participants were later told to recall the brand names of the items. The self-reference instructions produced the best recall, followed by the semantic instructions. Performance was worst with the instructions on physical attributes.

As D'Ydewalle and his colleagues point out, advertisers make enormous efforts to construct a visually attractive ad. However, if they really want consumers to remember the brand name—presumably a major goal of an advertisement—they should invite consumers to process the picture at a deeper level, by considering how they themselves could use the product. Self-reference should encourage brand-name recall.

The Current Status of the Levels-of-Processing Approach

Let's now return from the specific issue of the self-reference effect to the more general issue of the levels-of-processing approach. One major contribution from this approach is that it emphasized the importance of the mental processes that occur when the material is being learned. Perhaps because of behaviorist influence, research in the 1950s and 1960s emphasized external variables—such as the number of times a stimulus had been exposed and the length of those exposures—rather than the hidden mental processes we use to learn the material.

A second contribution from the levels-of-processing approach is very practical. If we want to improve memory, we need to emphasize deep, meaningful processing.

However, the levels-of-processing approach also has drawbacks. The first problem is circularity: We have no independent assessment of depth (Nelson, 1977). Specifically, we say that if processing is deep, then retention will be better. Then we say that because the retention was better, the processing must have been deep. To avoid circularity, researchers need a measure of depth-of-processing *in advance* that can predict which conditions will produce the best retention.

A second problem is one we discussed earlier: Deep processing is not always better, because performance depends upon the way memory is tested. As we said earlier, shallow processing—in terms of sound—is more effective than deep processing when memory is tested by asking whether any words on the list rhymed with *toy.*

In summary, then, the levels-of-processing approach played an important role in the history of cognitive psychology, and all current and future theories of memory need to acknowledge its contribution. However, the two major problems with the approach have prevented psychologists from developing it into a more comprehensive theory.

SECTION SUMMARY: THE LEVELS-OF-PROCESSING APPROACH

1. The levels-of-processing approach suggests that deeper levels of processing produce more permanent retention than shallow levels of processing.
2. According to the generation effect, we remember material better if we construct it ourselves, an activity that encourages deeper processing.
3. Levels of processing can explain why we remember some faces, but not others.
4. Deep processing is only effective if the retrieval conditions emphasize meaning; shallow processing may be more useful if the retrieval conditions emphasize more superficial characteristics.
5. The self-reference task encourages especially deep levels of processing, resulting in enhanced memory. Self-reference seems to be effective because the self is a rich source of associations and because these instructions encourage greater organization among the items to be learned.
6. The self-reference task can be applied to improving memory, studying, and advertising.
7. The self-reference approach has been useful because it emphasizes the mental processes that occur during learning. However, psychologists criticize the circularity of the approach and the fact that "deeper is not always better."

TULVING'S MODEL: EPISODIC, SEMANTIC, AND PROCEDURAL MEMORY

So far, we have considered the Atkinson-Shiffrin model, which focuses on the length of time the material has been in memory, and the levels-of-processing approach, which focuses on how the material was processed during learning. In contrast, a model proposed by Endel Tulving in 1972 focuses on the *nature* of the material that is stored in memory. The original article was cited in other research publications more than 500 times between 1972 and 1984 (McKoon et al., 1986). In more recent publications, Tulving has expanded his original model and discussed the distinctions in more detail (e.g., Tulving, 1983, 1984, 1986, 1989, 1993a, 1993b; Tulving et al., 1994). Let us discuss the model, look at the research, and evaluate it.

Description of Tulving's Model

Tulving's original model distinguished between only two kinds of memory, episodic and semantic (Tulving, 1972). Since then, he has added another category called procedural memory, and he also emphasizes that short-term memory constitutes a separate memory system (Tulving, 1993a). Tulving's emphasis on a separation between short-term memory and other kinds of memory makes his current model compatible with the structure of the Atkinson-Shiffrin model.

Episodic memory stores information about when events happened and the relationship between those events. This information refers to your personal experiences—for example, *when* you saw or heard something. Here are some examples of episodic memory:

1. The telephone rang a short while ago, followed by a thud when the snow fell off the roof.
2. I saw a student faint in class yesterday during a movie about neurosurgery.
3. I have a dental appointment at 3:30 tomorrow.
4. The first word I saw on this memory test was *eyebrow.*

Notice, then, that episodic memory includes events that happened, events that will happen, and lists of items on a memory test.

Semantic memory is the organized knowledge about the world. Semantic memory involves a fairly constant knowledge structure, in contrast to the changing event registered in episodic memory. It includes knowledge about words—as the name *semantic* implies—but it also includes many things we know that cannot readily be expressed in words. Incidentally, Tulving (1983) admits that the name *semantic memory* is too narrow; terms such as *generic memory* are more descriptive (Hintzman, 1978). However, people are now accustomed to the less accurate term, which this textbook will also use. Here are some examples of semantic memory:

1. I know that the meaning of the word *semantic* is closer to the meaning of the word *vocabulary* than it is to the word *disarmament.*
2. I remember that the chemical formula for water is H_2O.
3. I know what a French angelfish looks like.
4. I know that the shortest day of the year is in December.

More recently, Tulving has added a third category of memory to his model, called procedural memory (e.g., Squire, 1987; Tulving, 1987). Whereas episodic and semantic memory focus on factual information, *procedural memory* involves knowing how to do something, or learning connections between stimuli and responses. Some examples of procedural memory might include:

1. I know how to ride a bicycle.
2. I know how to tip the frying pan just right when making *injera,* an Ethiopian pancake.
3. I can start my car and put it into reverse.
4. I can dial the operator on the telephone.

Interestingly, procedural knowledge is often difficult to describe verbally. For example, you could read a book about how to ride a bicycle, yet that verbal information is unlikely to keep you from falling. Also, Demonstration 3.3 illustrates how your procedural knowledge can sometimes be more complete than comparable semantic knowledge. Incidentally, Tulving (1993a) argues that procedural knowledge is the first system to develop during infancy, followed by semantic knowledge and—last of all—episodic memory.

DEMONSTRATION 3.3

COMPARING SEMANTIC AND PROCEDURAL KNOWLEDGE

Each of the following tasks requires you to first describe your semantic knowledge and then demonstrate your procedural knowledge.

Task A: Using a Keyboard

1. Without looking at a keyboard, draw a diagram that shows the four rows of letters and numbers. Then describe which fingers of which hand you would use to type each of the alphabet letters listed below. (See if you can hold your fingers still!) Also describe whether the finger must reach up, reach down, or remain in place on the second row from the bottom on the keyboard.

   a n y w h e r e y o u g o

2. Now sit down in front of an actual keyboard. Without looking at the letters on the keyboard, type the letters listed above.

If you are like most people, you will find that your knowledge of the positions of letters is minimal unless you are allowed to inspect the keyboard. Your semantic knowledge about keyboard positions is weak. In contrast, you can rapidly type those letters without a single error. Your procedural knowledge is superb.

Task B: Tying a Bow

1. Write out explicit, detailed instructions for tying a standard bow (for example, a bow on a gift).
2. Now take a piece of string or a ribbon and actually tie it around a box or around a book.

Once again, you should find that your procedural knowledge on this task is far superior to your semantic knowledge. (Task B of this demonstration is based on Waterstreet, 1995).

Demonstration 3.2 (continued). Now write on the third sheet of paper, in any order you like, the 20 words you learned in Demonstration 3.2.

In 1984, Endel Tulving received the Distinguished Scientific Contribution Award from the American Psychological Association. When receiving this award, he outlined why he supports a multiple-memory system (Tulving, 1985). Here are several reasons:

1. Profound generalizations cannot be made about all the different kinds of memory; a generalization about episodic memory may not apply to semantic memory.
2. Memory in humans has come about through a long evolutionary process, characterized by sudden twists, turns, and other irregularities. Human brain structures concerned with memory probably reflect these evolutionary quirks; they are likely to be complex (e.g., Sherry & Schacter, 1987).
3. The varieties of memory that seem so different cannot all involve the same underlying set of structures and processes. For example, consider the difference between (a) learning to adjust your motor movements when you

---

DEMONSTRATION 3.4

THE DISTINCTION BETWEEN EPISODIC AND SEMANTIC MEMORY

Review the definitions of episodic and semantic memory, together with the examples provided. Now think of at least three of your own examples of each kind of memory. The chart below lists some of the dimensions on which Tulving (1983) suggests that episodic memory differ from semantic memory. Test each of your examples to see whether it is consistent with the characteristics listed in the chart. For instance, do your examples of episodic memory seem to be derived from sensory experiences (for example, something you saw or heard), rather than comprehension (something you understood)?

Characteristic	Episodic memory	Semantic memory
1. Source of the information	Sensory experiences	Comprehension
2. Units of information	Episodes and events	Concepts, ideas, and facts
3. Organization	Time-related	Conceptual
4. Emotional content of the memory	More important	Less important
5. Likelihood of forgetting	Great	Small
6. Time required to remember the information	Relatively long time	Relatively short time
7. How tested in the laboratory	Recall of particular episodes	General knowledge
8. General usefulness	Less useful	More useful

wear eyeglasses that turn the world upside down and (b) answering *yes* to the question "Is Abraham Lincoln dead?"

Initially, Tulving distinguished between only two kinds of memory, episodic and semantic (Tulving, 1972), so his description of the distinctions between these two is more complete. Demonstration 3.4 lists some of these distinctions from his list of 28 different contrasts. Try to decide whether the distinction between episodic and semantic memory seems like a useful one to you.

Research on Tulving's Model

Several kinds of research approaches have been used to explore possible distinctions betwen episodic and semantic memory. Unfortunately, researchers have not turned their attention to the distinctions between procedural memory and the other two categories. Let's look at the neuroscience research, the correlational research, and other investigations.

Neuroscience Research. Tulving argues that some of the strongest support for his theory comes from neuroscience research studies. For example, consider some studies using the positron emission tomography (PET) technique, a brain-imaging method we discussed in Chapters 1 and 2. Tulving (1989) asked volunteers to perform a variety of semantic retrieval tasks in which they thought about general, impersonal knowledge. For instance, one professor recalled information about the history of astronomy. The PET results showed greatest activity in the back part of the cerebral cortex. These same volunteers were also instructed to perform a variety of episodic retrieval tasks, in which they thought about a particular personal experience. For example, this same professor recalled a Sunday afternoon excursion that had taken place a few days earlier. The PET scan showed greatest activity in the frontal lobe of the cerebral cortex.

More recent neuroscience research has refined the knowledge about the biological basis of episodic memory. Specifically, the left frontal lobe of the cortex is especially active when episodic information is encoded into memory. In contrast, the right frontal lobe is more active in retrieving episodic information from memory (Tulving et al., 1994; Tulving & Kroll, 1995).

We should note that critics of Tulving's theory are not convinced by these neurological studies (e.g., Baddeley, 1984; McKoon et al., 1986). They would argue, for example, that the professor—whom we mentioned earlier—might show different PET scan patterns for *any* two tasks, maybe even two similar semantic tasks.

Tulving also believes that his theory is supported by several studies with K.C., a Canadian man who had experienced brain lesions throughout both the left and right hemisphere of his cortex during a motorcycle accident. Tulving (1989) argues that K.C. has impressive semantic memory but poor episodic memory. For example, he knows many things about the world, including history, geography, politics, and music. He can also point out the location of his family's summer cottage in Ontario, using a map of Canada. However, he cannot retrieve from episodic memory any incident that occurred at this cottage.

Critics such as Eysenck and Keane (1990) argue that it isn't fair to compare amnesic individuals' semantic and episodic memory. After all, language and world information were typically acquired before the onset of amnesia. In contrast, the typical tests of episodic memory are based on information acquired after the onset of amnesia.

To address this problem, Tulving and his associates have conducted numerous sessions in which they attempted to teach new semantic information to K.C. (Hayman et al., 1993; Tulving, 1993c). In one task, for instance, K.C. learned new semantic definitions for selected words. For example, a parakeet was defined as "a talkative featherbrain." K.C. recalled about the same number of items as three control individuals without any signs of amnesia, when all four were tested more than a year after the material had been learned. Thus, K.C.'s normal semantic memory cannot be explained simply in terms of material learned prior to his motorcycle accident.

Correlational Research. Underwood and his colleagues (1978) took a very different approach in trying to determine whether episodic and semantic memory involve different processes. Specifically, they tested 200 college students on 28 diffeent measures of episodic memory and 5 different measures of semantic memory. The episodic memory tests included standard tasks such as free recall (which you tried in Demonstration 3.2) and serial learning (where people learn a list of words that must be recalled in the same order they originally appeared). The semantic memory tests mainly emphasized vocabulary.

In general, people's scores on the episodic memory tests were not closely correlated with their scores on the semantic memory tests. For example, a person who recalled a large number of words on a free recall test was not especially likely to have a superb vocabulary. If only one kind of memory were being assessed on these tasks, we would expect to find a high correlation among the tasks. The low correlations are consistent with a model in which episodic memory and semantic memory are separate.

Other Investigations of the Episodic/Semantic Distinction. Other research summarized by Shoben (1984) and Tulving (1983) also supports the distinction between episodic and semantic memory. For example, Shoben and his colleagues (1978) found that a variable related to semantic memory (sentence verification) influenced performance on a semantic memory task, whereas a variable related to episodic memory (sentence recognition) had no effect. In contrast, a variable related to episodic memory influenced performance on an episodic memory task, whereas a variable related to semantic memory had no effect.

However, other research does not support the episodic–semantic distinction. According to an experiment by Ratcliff and McKoon (1978), episodic memory emphasizes conceptual relationships, and not simply time-related organization (the third characteristic in Demonstration 3.4).

Other distinctions from the table in Demonstration 3.4 have also been questioned by researchers. For example, in a test of the sixth characteristic, McKoon and Ratcliff (1986) demonstrated experimentally that episodic information can be recalled very quickly. And we can all think of examples where semantic information requires many minutes before it is recalled (Hirst, 1984; McKoon et al., 1986). If you've ever played Trivial Pursuit—a game that relies on retrieving offbeat, trivial information from semantic memory—you know how long retrieval from semantic memory can take!

The Current Status of Tulving's Model

In general, reviews of the research on Tulving's model are skeptical about the distinction between episodic and semantic memory (e.g., Humphreys et al., 1989; Johnson & Hasher, 1987; Richardson-Klavehn & Bjork, 1988; Searleman & Herrmann, 1994). Tulving (1986) has pointed out that the evidence for this distinction is not strong. He has also suggested that episodic memory may be an important kind of semantic memory—in the way that apples are an important class within the category of fruit—rather than being an entirely separate system (Tulving, 1984, 1986).

At present, psychologists are more likely to agree that procedural memory—the third category—represents a separate system (Baddeley, 1990). They argue that knowing how to do something seems distinctly different from knowing or remembering information. However, this position is based more on an intuitive feeling than on empirical research.

In discussing the Atkinson-Shiffrin model, we emphasized the convenience of distinguishing between short-term memory and long-term memory for the purpose of organizing the research. This organizational framework is useful, even if we are not convinced that the distinction actually occurs in human memory. Similarly, psychologists often distinguish between episodic, semantic, and procedural memory, even when they are not committed to a separate-memories model (e.g., Snodgrass, 1987). Accordingly, Chapter 5 in this textbook emphasizes episodic memory, and it also mentions procedural memory. Chapter 7 explores semantic memory and the structure of our knowledge about the world.

SECTION SUMMARY: TULVING'S MODEL OF EPISODIC, SEMANTIC, AND PROCEDURAL MEMORY

1. Tulving proposed that episodic memory stores information about events, semantic memory stores organized knowledge about the world, and procedural memory involves knowing how to do something.
2. According to Tulving, episodic memory and semantic memory differ in terms of such characteristics as organization, likelihood of forgetting, and time required to remember the information.
3. Research on the distinctions among kinds of memory has involved neuroscience research using PET scans of normal individuals as well as case studies of brain-injured individuals, correlational research on individual differences, and experimental studies.
4. Researchers currently question the distinction between episodic memory and semantic memory, although they often consider procedural memory to be different from the other two.

THE PARALLEL DISTRIBUTED PROCESSING APPROACH

Chapters 1 and 2 introduced the parallel distributed processing approach to cognition. In this chapter, we will explore in somewhat more detail how this approach explains the organization of memory. As you will see, this model differs from the other three because it does not focus on distinctions among different kinds of memory. Instead, the *parallel distributed processing approach* argues that cognitive processes can be represented by a model in which activation flows through networks that link together neuron-like units (Rueckl, 1993). The parallel distributed processing approach is often abbreviated the *PDP approach.* Two other names, *connectionism* and *neural networks,* are often used interchangeably with the PDP approach. Because the PDP approach is new and not yet fully developed or tested, we will limit our discussion to a description of the model and an assessment of its current status.

Description of the Parallel Distributed Processing Approach

Before you read further, try Demonstration 3.5, which illustrates some features of the PDP approach.

Human memory has a remarkable ability so familiar to us that we usually take it for granted: One thing reminds us of another (Johnson-Laird, 1988). Each of the

---

DEMONSTRATION 3.5

PARALLEL DISTRIBUTED PROCESSING

For each of the two tasks below, read the set of clues and then guess as quickly as possible what thing is being described.

Task A

1. It is orange.
2. It grows below the ground.
3. It is a vegetable.
4. Rabbits characteristically like this item.

Task B

1. Its name starts with the letter *p.*
2. It inhabits barnyards.
3. It is typically yellow in color.
4. It says "oink."

clues in Task A of Demonstration 3.5 reminded you of several possible candidates. You probably thought of the correct answer after just a couple of clues, even though the description was not complete. Notice, however, that you did not conduct a complete search of all orange objects before beginning a second search of all below-ground objects, then all vegetables, then all rabbit-endorsed items. In other words, your search for *carrot* was not serial. Instead, your search considered all attributes simultaneously. You used a parallel search—consistent with the word *parallel* in the name parallel distributed processing.

Furthermore, notice that your memory can cope quite well, even if one of the clues is incorrect. In Task B, you searched for a barnyard-dwelling, oink-producing creature whose name starts with *p*. The word *pig* emerged, despite the misleading clues about the yellow color. Similarly, if someone describes a classmate from Saratoga Springs who is a tall male in your child development course, you can identify the appropriate student, even if he is from Poughkeepsie.

Before we proceed, note three characteristics of the memory searches you performed in Demonstration 3.5:

1. If a machine has one faulty part, it typically will not work, even if all other parts function well. If your car's battery is dead, the cooperative effort of all the functioning parts still cannot make your car move forward. Human memory is much more flexible, active, and remarkable, consistent with Themes 1 and 2 of this book. Memory can still work well, even with some inappropriate input.
2. Memory storage is **content addressable;** that is, we can use attributes (such as an object's color) to locate material in memory. PDP theory argues that, if we enter the network with an attribute such as a color, we'll activate the appropriate neural unit or units (Martindale, 1991).
3. Some clues are more effective than others in helping us locate material in memory. For example, in Task B, most people would find the information about "oink" noises to be more useful than information about the number of legs the animal has.

James McClelland is one of the major developers of the PDP approach. McClelland (1981) described how our knowledge about a group of individuals might be stored by connections that link these people with their personal characteristics. His original example portrayed members of two gangs of small-time criminals, the Jets and the Sharks. We'll use a simpler and presumably more familiar example that features five college students. Table 3.2 lists these students, together with their college majors, year in school, and political orientation. Figure 3.6 shows how this information could be represented in network form. Notice that the figure represents only a fraction of the number of people a college student is likely to know and also just a fraction of the characteristics associated with each student. Try to imagine how large a piece of paper you would need to represent all the people you know, together with all the characteristics you consider relevant.

According to the PDP approach, each individual's characteristics are connected in a mutually excitatory network. If the connections among the characteristics are

=== TABLE 3.2 ===

ATTRIBUTES OF REPRESENTATIVE INDIVIDUALS WHOM A COLLEGE STUDENT MIGHT KNOW.

Name	Major	Year	Political Orientation
1. Joe	Art	Junior	Liberal
2. Marti	Psychology	Sophomore	Liberal
3. Sam	Engineering	Senior	Conservative
4. Liz	Engineering	Sophomore	Conservative
5. Roberto	Psychology	Senior	Liberal

=== FIGURE 3.6 ===

A SAMPLE OF THE UNITS AND CONNECTIONS THAT REPRESENT THE INDIVIDUALS IN TABLE 3.2.

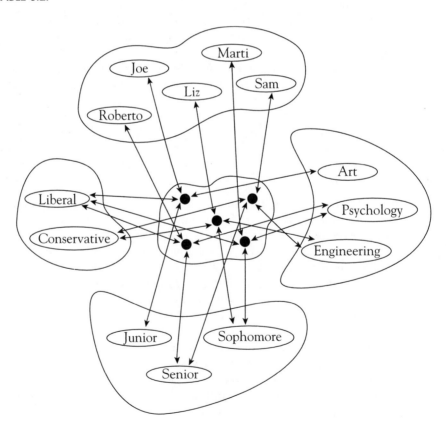

well established through extensive practice, then an appropriate clue allows you to locate the characteristics of a specified individual (McClelland, Rumelhart, & Hinton, 1986; Rumelhart et al., 1986).

Imagine that you want to locate the characteristics of Roberto, who is the only Roberto in the system. If you enter the system with the name *Roberto,* you can discover that he is a psychology major, a senior, and politically liberal. However, as we noted earlier, some clues are more effective than others. If you enter the system with the characteristic *psychology major,* your search produces ambiguity, because you would locate two names—Marti and Roberto.

One advantage of the PDP model is that it allows us to explain how human memory can help us when some information is missing. Specifically, people can make a ***spontaneous generalization,*** which involves making inferences about general information that they never learned in the first place (McClelland, Rumelhart, & Hinton, 1986).

For example, suppose that your memory stores the information in Figure 3.6 and similar information on other college students. Suppose, also, that someone were to ask you whether engineering students tend to be politically conservative. PDP theory suggests that the clue *engineering student* would activate information about all the engineering students you know, including information about their political orientation. You would reply that they do tend to be politically conservative, even though this factual statement is not directly stored in memory. (Our ability to make inferences will be discussed in more detail in Chapter 11.) Notice, then, that the structure of the PDP model makes some predictions about human cognitive processes, and these predictions can then be tested by researchers. As you can imagine, spontaneous generalization can help to explain stereotyping, a complex cognitive process that we'll discuss in more detail in Chapter 11.

Spontaneous generalization involves making inferences about a category (for example, the category called "engineering student"). PDP models also allow us to fill in missing information about a particular person or a particular object by making a best guess; we can make a ***default assignment*** based on information from similar people or objects. Suppose, for example, that you meet Christina, who happens to be an engineering student. Someone asks you about Christina's political preferences, but you have never discussed politics with her. This question will activate information about the political leanings of other engineers. Based on a default assignment, you will reply that she is probably conservative.

Incidentally, students sometimes confuse the terms *spontaneous generalization* and *default assignment.* Remember that spontaneous generalization involves making a judgment about a general category, whereas default assignment involves making a judgment about a specific member of a category.

Notice, however, that both spontaneous generalization and default assignment can produce errors. For example, Christina may really be the president of your university's chapter of the Democratic Socialists of America.

So far, our discussion of parallel distributed processing has been concrete and straightforward. In reality, the theory is extremely complex, sophisticated, and abstract (e.g., Crick, 1994; McClelland et al., 1986; Raaijmakers & Shiffrin, 1992;

Rueckl & Kosslyn, 1992; Rumelhart et al., 1986). Other general characteristics of the PDP approach include the following:

1. A network contains basic neuron-like units or **nodes,** which are connected together so that a specific unit has many links to other units (hence the alternate name for the theory, *connectionism*).
2. The connections between these neuron-like units are weighted, and the **connection weights** determine how much activation one unit can pass on to another unit.
3. When a unit reaches a critical level of activation, it may affect another unit, either by exciting it (if the connection weight is positive) or by inhibiting it (if the connection weight is negative).
4. Cognitive processes are based on parallel operations, rather than serial operations. Therefore, many patterns of activation may be proceeding simultaneously.
5. Knowledge is stored in the association of connections among the basic units, Notice that this view is very different from the common-sense idea that all the information you know about a particular person or object is stored in one specific location in the brain. In fact, the term *distributed processing* suggests that knowledge is distributed across many locations.
6. Every new event changes the strength of connections among relevant units by adjusting the connection weights. As a consequence, you are likely to respond differently the next time you experience a similar event. For example, while you have been reading about the PDP approach, you have been changing the strength of connections between the name *PDP approach* and such terms as *content addressable* and *spontanous generalization*. The next time you encounter the term *PDP approach,* all these related terms are likely to be activated.
7. Sometimes we have partial memory for some information, rather than complete, perfect memory. The brain's ability to provide partial memory is called **graceful degradation.** For example, Chapter 7 will discuss the **tip-of-the-tongue phenomenon,** which occurs when you know exactly which target you are seeking; you may even know the target's first letter and the number of syllables . . . but the word itself refuses to leap into memory.

The Current Status of the Parallel Distributed Processing Approach

The PDP approach is the most important shift in cognitive psychology in recent decades (Estes, 1991; Rueckl, 1993). Unfortunately, the approach is so new that we cannot yet evaluate whether this approach can accommodate actual data about a wide variety of cognitive processes (Rueckl & Kosslyn, 1992; Schacter, 1990a).

Some supporters are enthusiastic that the PDP approach seems generally consistent with the neurological design of neurons and the brain (Crick, 1994; Howard,

1995; Lewandowsky & Li, 1995). Many are therefore hopeful that PDP research may provide important links between psychology and neuroscience.

Theorists argue that the PDP approach works better for some kinds of cognitive tasks than for others (Crick, 1994; Rueckl, 1993). As you might expect, parallel distributed processing works better for tasks in which several processes tend to operate at the same time, as in pattern recognition, categorization, and memory search. However, other cognitive tasks demand primarily serial processing. Language use, problem solving, and reasoning—cognitive tasks we consider later in this book— seem to involve serial processing, rather than parallel operations. For these "higher mental processes," artificial intelligence models may be more effective (Crick, 1994; Rueckl, 1993).

So, what are some of the cognitive tasks that *can* be accounted for by the PDP approach? These include letter and word recognition (Rumelhart & McClelland, 1982), memory for serial position (Lewandowsky & Murdock, 1989), the reading problems experienced by people with dyslexia (Seidenberg, 1993), and cognitive difficulties experienced by people with schizophrenia (Cohen & Servan-Schreiber, 1992).

Researchers believe that the PDP approach works quite well for certain memory tasks, such as recovering from memory an item for which we have only partial information. Also, the current PDP models can explain situations where learning accumulates gradually across trials. However, these models cannot yet provide a satisfactory account for our memory of a single episode. Furthermore, the PDP approach has trouble explaining the rapid forgetting of extremely well learned information that occurs when we learn additional information (McCloskey & Cohen, 1989; Ratcliff, 1990). Finally, the models cannot account for our ability to recall earlier material when it has been replaced by more current material (Lewandowsky & Li, 1995).

Each of the first three theoretical approaches—the Atkinson-Shiffrin model, the levels-of-processing approach, and Tulving's model—also generated tremendous enthusiasm when they were first proposed. However, the PDP approach is much broader, addressing perception, language, and decision making, as well as numerous aspects of memory. Will the enthusiasm initially generated by this approach eventually fade as it did for the other three approaches? As Rueckl and Kosslyn (1992) point out, we must remember that "connectionism is a young field. We're still learning what networks can or can't do, and about how a variety of factors influence their behavior" (p. 256). One possibility is that the PDP approach will eventually become the standard framework for analyzing human memory.

SECTION SUMMARY: THE PARALLEL DISTRIBUTED PROCESSING APPROACH

1. According to the PDP approach, the cognitive processes can be explained by activation flowing through networks that link together neuron-like units.

2. The PDP approach explains some important characteristics of memory:
   (a) Memory can function even with some inappropriate input.
   (b) We can use attributes to locate material in memory.
   (c) Some clues are more effective than others in helping retrieve material from memory.
   (d) We can make spontaneous generalizations to construct general information about a category.
   (e) We can make default assignments to fill in missing information.
3. According to the PDP approach, memory consists of networks of units linked according to varying connection weights; these connections can involve excitation or inhibition.
4. Cognitive processes involve parallel operations; new events change the strength of the connections, but sometimes we have only partial memory for a target (graceful degradation).
5. The PDP approach has generated tremendous enthusiasm, though it works better for pattern recognition, categorization, and memory search than for higher mental processes that are more serial in nature; the approach is so new that it cannot yet be evaluated adequately.

CHAPTER REVIEW QUESTIONS

1. Two of the models discussed in this chapter emphasize the idea that humans have different kinds of memory. Discuss the evidence for and against the distinctions between short-term and long-term memory. Then do the same for the distinctions among episodic, semantic, and procedural memory.
2. What is rehearsal? How do the Atkinson-Shiffrin and levels-of-processing theories view its role in memory? If researchers favored a PDP approach, what feature would they use to explain how rehearsal improves memory?
3. Some theories stress the difference between structure and process. Compare the Atkinson-Shiffrin theory, the levels-of-processing approach, and Tulving's framework in terms of their relative emphasis on structure and process.
4. Suppose that a fourth-grade teacher asks his class to read a paragraph about mealtimes in the Bedouin culture. With respect to levels-of-processing theory, what *two* kinds of instructions should he use to encourage the greatest retention of material? What kind of instructions would be the least effective.
5. Discuss the self-reference effect, mentioning some of the research that has demonstrated this effect. What two explanations seem to account for this phenomenon?
6. At several points in the chapter, we discussed neuroscience research on the study of memory. Describe these research techniques, referring to Chapter 1 if necessary. Summarize the neuroscience findings about human

memory. Why is the PDP approach especially appealing to many theorists who emphasize neuroscience research?

7. Suppose that the Atkinson-Shiffrin theory and Tulving's theory were *both* correct. Ignoring sensory memory, what six kinds of memory would we have? Give examples from your own experience of each of those six memory categories.

8. Think of some kind of information that could be represented in a diagram similar to the one in Figure 3.6 (for example, American novelists, popular singers, people you know at your college). Provide an example of spontaneous generalization, as well as an example of default assignment, that could be applied to this body of information. How might the terms *content addressable* and *graceful degradation* be applied to this example?

9. Suppose that a friend is reading an introductory psychology textbook that briefly mentions the PDP approach. How would you describe the characteristics of this approach to your friend? Why is it called parallel distributed processing? What would you say about how this approach differs from traditional approaches?

10. Chapter 5 discusses suggestions for memory improvement in some detail. However, Chapter 3 also offers a number of suggestions for enhancing memory. List as many of them as possible.

NEW TERMS

memory
sensory memory
iconic memory
echoic memory
short-term memory (STM)
long-term memory (LTM)
structural features
control processes
rehearsal
duplex model
serial position effect
primacy effect
recency effect
long-term recency effect

levels-of-processing
   approach
depth-of-processing
   approach
maintenance rehearsal
elaborative rehearsal
generation effect
encoding
retrieval
distinctiveness
elaboration
self-reference effect
episodic memory
semantic memory
procedural memory

parallel distributed pro-
   cessing approach
PDP approach
connectionism
neural networks
content addressable
spontaneous
   generalization
default assignment
nodes
connection weights
graceful degradation
tip-of-the-tongue
   phenomenon

RECOMMENDED READINGS

Baddeley, A. (1990). *Human memory: Theory and practice*. Boston: Allyn and Bacon.

Baddeley is a key researcher in the area of human memory. His book discusses all four models of memory; however, it examines in greatest detail the Atkinson-Shiffrin model and the PDP approach.

Crick, F. (1994). *The astonishing hypothesis: The scientific search for the soul.* New York: Scribner's. Despite his exaggerated title, Nobel Laureate Francis Crick offers a clear and accessible description of the PDP approach.

Howard, R. W. (1995). *Learning and memory: Major ideas, principles, issues and applications.* Westport, CT: Praeger. This is a good advanced-level textbook, providing some more details on each of the memory theories explored in the current chapter.

Lockhart, R. S., & Craik, F. I. M. (1990). Levels of processing: A retrospective commentary on a framework for memory research. *Canadian Journal of Psychology, 44,* 87–112. In this article, the two creators of the levels-of-processing approach discuss the original purpose of their paper and address some of the criticisms that have been made about the theory.

Tulving, E. (1993a). Varieties of consciousness and levels of awareness in memory. In A. Baddeley & L. Weiskrantz (Eds.), *Attention: Selection, awareness, and control* (pp. 283–299). Oxford, England: Clarendon Press. This chapter is one of Tulving's more recent explanations of his theory; here, he examines how each kind of memory is related to consciousness.

SENSORY MEMORY AND SHORT-TERM MEMORY (WORKING MEMORY)

INTRODUCTION

SENSORY MEMORY

Iconic Memory
Echoic Memory

SHORT-TERM MEMORY (WORKING MEMORY)

The Methodology in Classic Short-Term Memory Research
The Size of Short-Term Memory
The Duration of Short-Term Memory
The Code in Short-Term Memory
In Depth: The Working Memory View of Short-Term Memory

=========================== **Preview** ===========================

In this chapter, we will explore the two briefest kinds of memory: sensory memory and short-term memory (also known as working memory). Both are limited in capacity and temporary in duration, in contrast to the long-term memory that we will examine in Chapter 5.

Sensory memory holds information in a relatively unprocessed form. Visual sensory memory, also called iconic memory, holds material for a fraction of a second. Iconic memory therefore allows time for that information to be processed after the stimulus has disappeared. Auditory sensory memory, also called echoic memory, holds material for 2 to 3 seconds after the stimulus has disappeared, so it is especially important when we process spoken language.

Short-term memory retains information for as long as 30 seconds. In contrast to sensory memory, information in short-term memory can be manipulated, for example, by recoding the items. Several decades ago, psychologists believed that short-term memory had a strict capacity, limited to between 5 and 9 items. We will see that the capacity of short-term memory is indeed limited, but many factors influence its limits. Furthermore, the information in short-term memory is often stored in terms of its sound, but it can also be stored in terms of its visual appearance or its meaning. Finally, the most recent interpretation of short-term memory is a more flexible view called *working memory*. According to this approach, working memory consists of three parts: an auditory component, a visuo-spatial component, and a central executive that coordinates information and plans strategies.

INTRODUCTION

During the past few minutes, dozens of items have entered your memory. The clear majority of those items were forgotten just moments later. This chapter focuses on those fleeting, fragile kinds of memory known as sensory memory and short-term memory. As we noted in Chapter 3, **sensory memory** is a large-capacity storage system that records information from each of the senses with reasonable accuracy. According to the Atkinson and Shiffrin (1968) model, material from sensory memory then passes on to **short-term memory** (which many now call *working memory*), which contains only the small amount of material we are actively using. Much of the information in short-term memory is forgotten, and only a fraction passes on to long-term memory. Chapters 5, 6, and 7 will explore these more permanent memories. During the current chapter, however, we will examine memories that last substantially less than one minute.

SENSORY MEMORY

Sensory memory, also known as *sensory storage* or the *sensory register,* holds information in a relatively raw, unprocessed form for a short time after the physical stimulus is no longer available. Thus, sensory memory permits some trace of a stimulus to remain after the stimulus has disappeared. Demonstration 4.1 illustrates several examples of sensory memory. Unfortunately, researchers have conducted only a few studies on sensory memory in the "minor" senses, such as touch, smell, and taste (e.g., Hill & Bliss, 1968). The vast majority of information concerns vision and hearing (Howard, 1995). Therefore, we will look at visual sensory memory (iconic memory) and auditory sensory memory (echoic memory).

Why do we need sensory memory? Psychologists propose that sensory memory serves three major purposes. First, the stimuli that surround your senses are constantly and rapidly changing. For example, consider what happens when you read the sentence "Why do we need sensory memory?" aloud to a friend. The *wh* sound from the *why* is long gone by the time you speak the *y* sound of the word *memory*. However, a listener needs to retain this information about the pitch of your voice at the beginning of the sentence and compare it with similar information at the end of the sentence. The rising pitch in your voice allows the listener to decide that this sentence was a question. Listeners also need to retain an entire sentence so that they can determine which word in the sentence is stressed. Notice, for example, how the meaning of the sentence "I wouldn't buy tickets to hear him sing" changes, depending upon whether you stress the *I,* the *buy,* the *him,* or the *sing.*

A second reason why we need sensory memory is that we need to keep an accurate record of the sensory stimulation for a brief time while we select the most

---

DEMONSTRATION 4.1

EXAMPLES OF SENSORY MEMORY

Visual Sensory Memory. Hold your hand in front of your eyes and quickly wave it back and forth. If your hand motion is quick enough, you will be able to "see" your hand in one position for a fraction of a second after it has moved on to a different position.

Auditory Sensory Memory. With your hands, beat a quick rhythm on the desk. Can you still hear the echo after the beating is finished?

Tactile (Touch) Sensory Memory. Quickly rub the palms of your hands along a horizontal edge of your desk, moving your hands so that the heels touch first and the fingertips touch last. Can you still feel the sharp edge, even after your hand is off the desk?

important stimuli for further processing (Cowan, 1995). For example, think about the rich variety of stimuli that are now entertaining your senses. You can see the words on the page in front of you and other details of the surrounding area in which you are reading. Maybe you hear the squeak of your marker as it underlines an important point, and you may also hear faint music in the background. You can feel the pressure of your chair against your back and can also sense that your body is slightly tilted. You may be somewhat aware of the pain from yesterday's paper cut, and you may also notice that the room is exactly the temperature you find comfortable. Perhaps you can barely taste the toothpaste you used several hours ago or smell the distant aroma of cookies baking. You would be overwhelmed if you noticed all the information from all of your senses all of the time. Instead, your sensory memory keeps a record of the stimuli for a few moments, and the stimuli are quickly examined to determine which ones will receive further processing.

A third function of sensory memory is that it allows us to integrate fragments of a stimulus into a single, unitary perception (Cowan, 1995). Demonstration 4.2 illustrates this principle. Similarly, a friend who passes by your almost-closed door appears to be intact—fortunately—rather than a series of longitudinal slices.

The second section of this chapter will consider short-term memory. Sensory memory differs from short-term memory in several respects:

1. Items generally remain in sensory memory for about 2 seconds or less, whereas they remain in short-term memory for as long as 30 seconds.
2. Information in sensory memory is relatively unprocessed, whereas information in short-term memory can be manipulated (for example, by rehearsing or comparing the items or by changing their order).
3. The information in sensory memory is a fairly accurate representation of the stimulus, whereas the information in short-term memory is more likely to be distorted and inaccurate.

DEMONSTRATION 4.2

HOW SENSORY MEMORY CREATES A UNITARY PERCEPTION FROM FRAGMENTS. BASED ON COWAN, 1995.

Take an index card and cut a narrow slit (about 1/8" wide) in the middle of the card, orienting the slit lengthwise and making it as long as possible. Then hold the slit in front of the cover of this textbook, at a distance that allows you to see both the top and the bottom edges of the book. Now, begin with the slit toward the left edge of the textbook and move it toward the right. In reality, you are seeing a sequence of fragmentary views of the photo. However, sensory memory allows you to incorporate these fragments into one single perception of the photo.

4. Information is passively registered in sensory memory, whereas the information is actively selected for entry into short-term memory (Estes, 1988).

Iconic Memory

Ulric Neisser, a major figure in the origins of cognitive psychology, proposed the name *iconic memory* to describe visual sensory memory. He wrote that iconic memory (pronounced "eye-*conn*-ick") involves the brief persistence of visual impressions that "makes them briefly available for processing even after the stimulus has terminated" (Neisser, 1967, p. 15). Whereas the term *iconic memory* refers to the memory process, the term *icon* refers to a particular visual impression, such as your impression of the letter *A*. You may have heard the words *icon* or *iconography* in an art class, referring to figures and the art of representing figures. Let's first look at Sperling's classic study on iconic memory and then consider more recent research.

Sperling's Research. George Sperling (1960) conducted one of the first demonstrations of iconic memory. His experiment cannot be illustrated without the use of special equipment. However, Demonstration 4.3 shows how experiments prior to Sperling's might have measured the size of iconic memory. If you are typical, you recalled only four or five letters in this demonstration (Gegenfurtner & Sperling, 1993). However, you may think you *saw* more than you were able to report. Perhaps you believe you saw about 10 items, rather than just 4 or 5. But does it seem that many of these 10 items faded during the time you took to report the earlier items?

DEMONSTRATION 4.3

THE WHOLE-REPORT TECHNIQUE

WITH YOUR HAND, COVER THE CHART AT THE BOTTOM OF THIS DEMONSTRATION AND DO NOT LOOK AT THE LETTERS UNTIL THE INSTRUCTIONS INDICATE TO DO SO! Find a room without outside light, and stand near the light switch. As soon as you have finished reading these instructions, turn off the lights, removing your hand from the chart. Quickly switch the light on and then off, keeping it on just a fraction of a second. Now try to recall as many of the letters as possible. OK, begin.

X	B	S	T
D	H	M	G
R	L	W	C

Sperling's objective was to measure the true size of iconic memory. To do this, he needed to overcome the long amount of time that participants required to report all the items in iconic memory. This problem plagued previous researchers, who had used the method illustrated in Demonstration 4.3. This **whole-report technique** instructs people to report everything they saw. In contrast, Sperling's **partial-report technique** instructs people to report only a specific portion of the display. The same chart of letters is exposed very briefly. After the chart has disappeared, participants hear a tone that indicates which portion of the display they must report. Specifically, if they hear a high tone, they report the letters in the top row; a middle tone indicates the middle row; and a low tone indicates the bottom row.

Imagine that you were a participant in Sperling's (1960) experiment. You would see the display flashed briefly; then it disappears. Then suppose that you hear a low tone, indicating that you should report as much as possible from the bottom line, for example, *R L W C*. Notice that while you were looking at the letters, you had no clue about which line in the display would be tested. Suppose that you manage to recall three of those letters, *R L C*. If you recalled three letters from the bottom row, we can assume that you could have also recalled three letters from the top row if you had heard a high tone, or three letters from the middle row if you had heard a middle tone. Thus, the number of items correct on any one line can be multiplied by three to obtain an estimate of the number of items the participant actually saw in the entire display.

Sperling found that people recalled slightly more than three items from one line when the partial-report technique was used. Therefore, he multiplied that figure by three and estimated that people actually saw between 9 and 10 items out of the 12 possible items. However, suppose that the whole-report technique is used, rather than the partial-report technique. In this situation, the image of these 9 or 10 items fades so rapidly that a person can report only about 4 of them before the remaining items have disappeared from iconic memory.

Sperling also varied the length of the delay between the disappearance of the stimulus display and the sounding of the tone that indicated which line was to be recalled. If this partial-report tone sounded just as soon as the display disappeared, then people saw an estimated 9 to 10 items in the display—as we just discussed. However, if the partial-report tone was delayed as little as half a second, then people saw only an estimated 4.5 items. In other words, the iconic memory fades so rapidly that it is gone in half a second, and recall performance deteriorates to the same unspectacular level as in the whole-report technique. Figure 4.1 illustrates both the estimated recall with the partial-report technique and the typical recall using the whole-report technique.

Sperling's results produced enthusiastic responses from cognitive psychologists. These findings were quite compatible with an information-processing approach, such as the Atkinson-Shiffrin (1968) model. The information-processing approach emphasizes that perception is not an instantaneous result of stimulation (Long, 1980). Instead, our visual experience is the product of a sequence of well-defined processes or stages, each requiring a measurable amount of time. Iconic storage permits a briefly presented stimulus to be prolonged, allowing for the next stage in information processing to begin.

=== **FIGURE 4.1** ===

NUMBER OF LETTERS RECALLED, AS A FUNCTION OF TECHNIQUE AND DELAY (TYPICAL RESULTS)

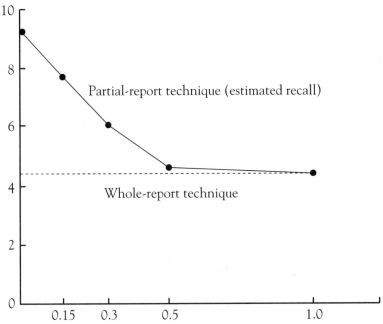

Delay between disappearance of stimuli and presentation of tone
(in seconds)

Following Sperling's classic study, hundreds of other researchers began to explore iconic memory, using a wide variety of research procedures (Cowan, 1995; Long, 1980). This research generally supported the concept of an icon that persisted 200 to 400 milliseconds—less than half a second—after the stimulus disappeared (van der Heijden, 1981). More recent research has focused on such topics as the location of the icon and the usefulness of the icon.

The Location of an Icon. At one point, several researchers argued that icons are stored in the rods—the black-and-white receptors—of the eye, rather than in a more central part of the brain (e.g., Long & Beaton, 1982; Sakitt & Long, 1979). However, others have demonstrated that iconic memory contains color information, as well as black-and-white cues (Adelson, 1978; Banks & Barber, 1977).

Furthermore, Di Lollo and his coworkers point out that if information is stored in the retinal receptors, then iconic memory should last longer when the stimulus is exposed for a longer time (Di Lollo, 1977, 1980; Di Lollo & Hogben, 1987). However, Di Lollo and his colleagues obtained a surprising and counterintuitive result. As they increased the stimulus duration beyond about 10 milliseconds, the duration of iconic memory became progressively *shorter!* As Di Lollo (1992) explains, iconic memory is based on a period of information-processing activity. This period has a fixed duration, and the clock starts ticking just as soon as the stimulus is presented. In short, Di Lollo's work suggests that the icon is stored in some more central part of the brain, rather than in the visual receptors of the eye.

The Usefulness of an Icon. One of the controversies about iconic memory involves its usefulness in everyday life, outside of the laboratory. Haber (1983a, 1983b, 1985) composed an "obituary" for the concept of the icon in a series of articles with such gloomy titles as "The icon is really dead." Haber claims that the concept of the icon might be useful if we frequently engaged in activities such as reading with only the brief flashes of light provided by lightning. Outside the laboratory, he argued, people spend most of their waking time viewing three-dimensional scenes featuring movement—not viewing briefly presented, two-dimensional letters of the alphabet.

In general, psychologists rushed to resuscitate the icon after Haber pronounced it dead. They have argued that the concept of the icon is actually very useful. For example, when we watch a movie, we need to integrate the brief flashes in order to perceive the images correctly. Furthermore, many people spend considerable time looking at two-dimensional displays on computer screens, and information about the icon can be useful in helping to build more effective video display systems (Loftus, 1985).

Even people living low-tech lives are aided by iconic memory. As Loftus (1985) emphasizes, when selective attention is combined with iconic memory's large storage capacity, we humans have a mechanism for retaining only a fraction of all the stimuli reaching our senses. Thus, iconic memory may not initially seem as useful as short-term or long-term memory, but it does help us sort out the stimuli in our environment.

Directions for Further Research. Research on iconic memory has decreased somewhat in recent years (Cowan, 1995). However, one important issue is that iconic memory does not seem to be unitary. Instead, two or more different kinds of brief visual memory may occur during the early stages of information processing (Coltheart, 1980; Cowan, 1988, 1995; Di Lollo & Dixon, 1988; Irwin & Yeomans, 1986). As we will note throughout this textbook, cognitive processes are seldom as simple as the earlier researchers proposed.

A second theoretical issue concerns how the visual information is actually acquired from the stimulus. Researchers are creating models to explore this important issue (Busey & Loftus, 1994). They are also exploring how the visual system combines information from both eyes to create a binocular representation in sensory memory (Cowan, 1995).

Another issue in future research will be to identify additional ways that we use iconic memory in our daily lives. For example, iconic memory may help keep our visual world stable, despite constant eye movement (Banks & Krajicek, 1991; Irwin et al., 1990). Notice how, as you are reading this sentence, your eyes are jumping forward along the page, an action called *saccadic movement.* Iconic memory may help you preserve one image long enough so that it can be compared with an image registered after your eyes have moved ahead. From this comparison, you can conclude that the words have *not* changed position relative to each other and that your visual world has remained stable.

Echoic Memory

Ulric Neisser (1967) coined the phrase *echoic memory* to serve as the auditory equivalent of iconic memory. **Echoic memory** refers to auditory sensory memory, or the brief auditory impressions that persist after the sound itself has disappeared. A particular auditory impression is called an **echo,** because of its similarity to the echo that sometimes persists after a sound has disappeared.

The name echoic *memory* seems particularly appropriate. Have you ever noticed how you can "hear" a loud crash echoing inside your head after the actual crashing sound has stopped? You may also have noticed that when your professor has been lecturing, his or her words will "echo" in your head for a few moments after they have been spoken—fortunately just long enough for you to write them down. By their very nature, auditory stimuli are much less permanent than visual stimuli. The soprano you are watching on television sings a few notes and they disappear as soon as they escape from her mouth, though the visual image remains on the screen. For this reason, echoic memory is even more useful than iconic memory (Cowan, 1995).

Let's first examine the classic research on echoic memory, conducted by Darwin and his colleagues (1972). Then we will consider more recent studies on this important topic.

Darwin's Research. An important demonstration of echoic memory was a study modeled on Sperling's (1960) partial-report technique. You will recall that Sperling presented a visual display to participants and used an auditory signal to indicate which part of the display was to be reported. Darwin, Turvey, and Crowder (1972) neatly reversed Sperling's study by presenting an auditory display and using a visual signal to cue the partial report. These authors used special headphones to present three different auditory messages to the participants. Figure 4.2 illustrates how this was done. One group of items (*J 4 T*) was presented to a person's right ear. A second group of items (*A 5 2*) was presented to the left ear. A third group of items (*3 M Z*) was prepared by recording the list on both the right and left channels; this list was presented in such a way that it seemed to come from in between the right and the left ears—in other words, right in the middle. All three sequences were presented at the same time.

After hearing the sequences, people saw a visual cue on a screen, indicating which of the three sequences they should report. Specifically, a bar on the left meant that the participant should report the sequence from the left ear, a bar in the middle indicated the middle sequence, and a bar on the right indicated the sequence from the right ear.

======================= **FIGURE 4.2** =======================

A PERSON PARTICIPATING IN AN ECHOIC MEMORY STUDY

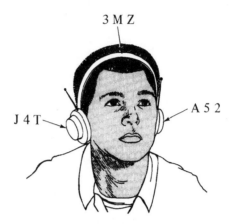

Darwin and his coauthors found that the partial-report technique allowed people to report a larger estimated number of items than did the whole-report technique, in which people tried to report all nine items. These results are similar to the results for iconic memory. Thus, sensory memory stores items for a brief time—so brief that this memory is gone before people can list all the items in their sensory memory.

However, Darwin's study also pointed out some potential differences between the two kinds of sensory memory. Specifically, the maximum number of items correctly recalled in echoic memory was estimated to be about 5, which is considerably fewer than the 9 to 10 items in iconic memory. Darwin and his coauthors speculated that their estimate of echoic memory was relatively small because people had difficulty separating the three different input channels. Another potential difference between echoic memory and iconic memory may be their duration. Darwin's study estimated that echoic memory could last as long as 2 seconds, in contrast to Sperling's estimate of a fraction of a second for iconic memory.

Other Characteristics of Echoic Memory. Robert Crowder (1982a) used a different technique to explore echoic memory. He presented two artificially produced vowel sounds, one after another. Sometimes, the vowels were highly similar to each other; for example, they might be two variants of the *a* sound in *cat*. Other times, the two vowels were identical. The two sounds were sometimes presented ½ second apart, and sometimes with longer gaps—ranging up to 5 seconds—between the two presentations. Participants were instructed to report for each trial whether the vowels were the same or different. Their responses were used to calculate an index of discrimination ability, that is, how accurately people reported whether the two sounds were different.

FIGURE 4.3

THE ABILITY TO DISCRIMINATE BETWEEN TWO SOUNDS. BASED ON CROWDER (1982A).

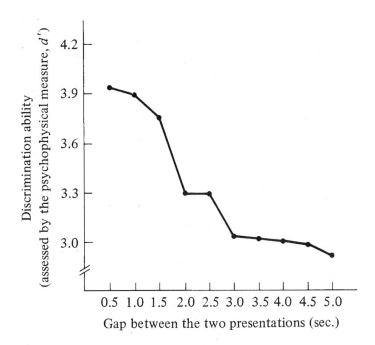

Figure 4.3 shows the results of Crowder's study. As you can see, performance is much more accurate when two vowels are presented less than a second apart. Performance seems to reach asymptote at about 3 seconds (that is, the curve remains essentially flat between 3 and 5 seconds). Crowder's study therefore identifies the upper limit of echoic memory to be about 3 seconds, slightly longer than the 2 seconds specified by Darwin and his coauthors (1972).

In discussing iconic memory, we noted that some theorists believe there is more than one kind of iconic memory. The evidence is even stronger that we have more than one kind of echoic memory (Cowan, 1984, 1988, 1995). One kind, **short auditory storage,** is a simple store that involves no analysis of the stimulus and decays less than one second after the auditory stimulus has disappeared. **Long auditory storage,** in contrast, lasts several seconds; the material in this storage may be partly analyzed and transformed. Cowan suggests that a model of memory requires this longer kind of storage to account for a common phenomenon in auditory perception. Often, a single word spoken in a noisy environment cannot be deciphered until the listener has heard additional cues several seconds later in the sentence. Long auditory storage may retain this "mystery word," allowing later analysis.

Cowan makes an excellent point about the complexity of human cognitive processes. He notes that psychologists are taught to use parsimony as a guiding principle in constructing theories. That is, theories are supposed to be as simple as possible and still account for all the data. In the case of echoic memory, the rule of parsimony would suggest only a single kind of auditory memory storage. However, Cowan (1984) writes, "Nature may not equal this degree of parsimony" (p. 341). As we emphasize throughout this textbook, the truth about cognitive processes is typically complex.

Directions for Further Research. Some of the current research on echoic memory examines topics that could have some practical implications. For example, Keller and his coauthors (1995) have discovered that people can silently rehearse musical tones, a strategy that slows the rate of decay for auditory information about tone pitch. This strategy could be helpful for musicians who want to duplicate a tone they heard a few seconds earlier (for example, in order to tune an instrument). It would also be helpful for people trying to master pronunciation in a foreign language.

An important new development in echoic memory is that neuroscientists are now exploring echoic memory. Näätänen and his colleagues in Finland used the event-related potential technique described in Chapter 1 (Mäntysalo & Näätänen, 1987; Näätänen, 1986). In this research, a participant is told to concentrate on reading a book while a tone of a particular pitch is repeatedly presented. On some trials, however, a tone of a slightly different pitch is presented. By examining the values from the electroencephalograms, researchers have noticed that the new tone produces a shift in the wave pattern about 200 milliseconds after this tone has been presented. The neuronal representation decays about 4 seconds later, an interval that is roughly consistent with other estimates of the length of echoic memory.

Researchers have also located a site in the primary auditory cortex that seems to generate the reported change in the electroencephalogram (Lu et al., 1992). With additional research, we may be able to draw confident conclusions about the site within the brain where one component of echoic memory operates.

SECTION SUMMARY: SENSORY MEMORY

1. Sensory memory holds information in a relatively unprocessed form; virtually all the research focuses on iconic memory and echoic memory.
2. Compared to short-term memory, sensory memory stores material for a shorter time; information is stored in a raw form that is fairly accurate, and registration is relatively passive.
3. Sperling's classic research on iconic memory has been replicated numerous times. Iconic memory lasts about 200 to 400 milliseconds.
4. The icon is processed in a location that is more central than the receptors of the eye.
5. Although some psychologists have questioned the usefulness of iconic memory in everyday life, others have pointed out its usefulness in viewing movies and computer displays, as well as helping us sort out visual stimuli in the environment.

6. Iconic memory may actually have two different components.

7. Echoic memory has been demonstrated using a variety of techniques; it seems to last about 2 to 3 seconds.

8. The evidence for two different components in echoic memory is even more persuasive than the evidence for iconic memory; a division between short auditory storage and long auditory storage seems likely.

9. New developments in research on echoic memory include topics such as the rehearsal of echoic memories and the location of echoic memory in the auditory cortex.

SHORT-TERM MEMORY (WORKING MEMORY)

You can probably recall a recent experience like this. You are standing in a telephone booth looking up a phone number. You find the number, repeat it to yourself, and close the phone book. You take out the coins, insert them, and raise your index finger to dial the number. Amazingly, you cannot remember it. The first digits were 586, and a 4 appeared somewhere, but you have no idea what the other numbers are!

This kind of forgetting occurs fairly often when you want to remember material for a short period of time. Perhaps 15 seconds pass while you close the phone book and insert the coins, yet some memories are so fragile that they evaporate before you can begin to use them. One characteristic of short-term memory specified in the Atkinson-Shiffrin (1968) model is that material is lost within 30 seconds unless it is somehow repeated.

Another characteristic of short-term memory described by Atkinson and Shiffrin is its clear-cut limits. You are certainly familiar with the strain you feel when you try to keep a list of items in short-term memory. Doesn't it seem that if one more item is added, one of the original items will need to be shoved out? These same limits are obvious when you try to learn how to do a new procedure that involves many rules or specifications (e.g., Carlson et al., 1989; Woltz, 1988). You also become aware of these limits when you try mental arithmetic, read complicated sentences, or solve reasoning problems that contain many elements (Holyoak & Spellman, 1993; Just & Carpenter, 1992; Waldrop, 1987). Demonstration 4.4, on page 116, illustrates the limits of short-term memory for two of these tasks; try each task before reading any further.

In Demonstration 4.4, you probably had no difficulty with the first mathematics and reading tasks. The second tasks may have seemed more challenging, but still manageable. The third tasks probably seemed beyond the limits of your short-term memory.

In discussing short-term memory, we need to repeat the point we made in Chapter 3: Some psychologists do not believe that short-term memory and long-term memory are different processes requiring different kinds of storage systems (e.g., Crowder, 1993). Another important point is that those who *do* believe that short-term memory is a different kind of memory may not all share the same theoretical

---

DEMONSTRATION 4.4

THE LIMITS OF SHORT-TERM MEMORY

A. Try each of the following mental multiplication tasks. Be sure not to write down any of your calculations; do them entirely "in your head."
   1. $7 \times 9 =$
   2. $74 \times 9 =$
   3. $74 \times 96 =$

B. Now read each of the following sentences, and construct a mental image of the action that is being described.
   1. The repairperson departed.
   2. The deliveryperson that the secretary met departed.
   3. The salesperson that the doctor that the nurse despised met departed.

---

explanation for this kind of memory (e.g., Atkinson & Shiffrin, 1968; Baddeley, 1986, 1990; Cowan, 1995; Shiffrin, 1993). For example, many psychologists now argue that short-term memory is not a simple storage place for lists of unrelated items. These psychologists prefer to use the phrase *working memory* to describe this more dynamic and flexible approach to short-term memory (e.g., Baddeley, 1986, 1990; Gathercole, 1992).

In this section, we will look at several topics: (1) the methodology in classic short-term memory research; (2) the size of short-term memory; (3) the duration of short-term memory; and (4) the code in short-term memory. Our fifth and final topic in this chapter is an in-depth exploration of the working memory approach to short-term memory.

The Methodology in Classic Short-Term Memory Research

Demonstration 4.5 shows a modified version of the Brown/Peterson & Peterson technique, a method that established much of our original information about short-term memory. John Brown (1958), a British psychologist, and Lloyd Peterson and Margaret Peterson (1959), two American psychologists, independently demonstrated that material held in memory for less than a minute is frequently forgotten. The technique therefore bears the names of both sets of researchers.

Peterson and Peterson, for example, asked people to study three letters. The participants then counted backward by threes for a short period and tried to recall the letters they had originally seen. On the first few trials, people recalled most of the letters. However, after several trials, the previous letters produced interference, and recall was poor. After a mere 5-second delay, people forgot approximately half of what they had seen. (See Figure 4.4 on page 118.)

DEMONSTRATION 4.5

A MODIFIED VERSION OF THE BROWN/PETERSON & PETERSON TECHNIQUE

Take out five index cards. On one side of each card write a group of three words, one underneath another. On the back of the card write the three-digit number. Set the cards aside for a few minutes and practice counting backwards by threes from the number 792. Then show yourself the first card, with the side containing the words toward you, for about 2 seconds. Then immediately turn over the card and count backward by threes from the three-digit number. Go as fast as possible for 15–20 seconds. (If you can, convince a friend to time you.) Then write down as many of the three words as you can remember. Continue this process with the remaining four cards.

1. appeal
   temper   687
   burden

2. sober
   persuade   254
   content

3. descend
   neglect   869
   elsewhere

4. flower
   classic   573
   predict

5. silken
   idle   433
   butcher

This dramatic demonstration of forgetting after a few seconds' delay had an important impact on memory research. Psychologists who had previously asked people to learn long lists of words—and recall them after lengthy delays—switched to investigating recall after just a few seconds' delay. The Brown/Peterson & Peterson technique was extremely popular during the 1960s and the early 1970s. As a consequence, psychologists conducted relatively little research on long-term memory during those years. Beginning in the late 1970s, researchers shifted their interest back to long-term memory, and this area of research is still more popular in the 1990s (Shiffrin, 1993). Nonetheless, the early research using the Brown/Peterson & Peterson technique yielded important information about the fragility of memory for material stored just a few seconds.

Another technique that has often been used to examine short-term memory makes use of the serial position effect, which we discussed in Chapter 3. Refresh your memory by looking at Figure 3.2 on page 72. As you can see, the curve shows a strong *recency effect,* with better recall for items at the end of the list. Although the interpretation is controversial, many researchers argue that this relatively accurate recall of the final words in a list can be attributed to the fact that these

=========================== FIGURE 4.4 ===========================

TYPICAL RESULTS FOR PERCENTAGE RECALLED WITH THE BROWN/PETERSON & PETERSON TECHNIQUE

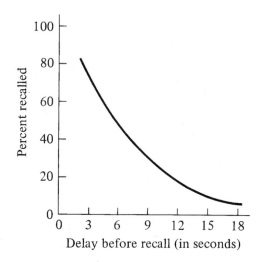

items were still in short-term memory at the time of recall. Thus, one way of measuring the size of short-term memory is to count the number of accurately recalled items at the end of the list (Cowan, 1994). Typically, the size of short-term memory is estimated to be two to seven items when the serial-position curve method is used.

More often, short-term memory size is measured in terms of *memory span,* or the number of items in a row that can be correctly recalled. Your ability to remember phone numbers is therefore a test of memory span. Your memory span is not highly correlated with most measures of intelligence (Baddeley, 1992a). However, several intelligence tests include a test of memory span.

The Size of Short-Term Memory

Suppose a friend told you his age: 19. You would have no trouble remembering that. Furthermore, you would have little trouble remembering a four-digit street address, such as 2614. However, a standard seven-digit phone number is more challenging: 346-3421. If you add an area code to make the phone number 212-346-3421, you are unlikely to remember the entire number correctly. One of the primary attributes of short-term memory is its limited capacity (Shiffrin, 1993).

During the early period of enthusiastic research on short-term memory, psychologists were convinced that we could precisely specify the number of items that could be stored in short-term memory. However, more recent research suggests that pronunciation time is another important determinant of short-term memory. We also know that the storage capacity of short-term memory is a complex issue; factors such as anxiety influence the number of items that can be held in temporary storage. Incidentally, the final section of this chapter—on working memory—raises additional questions about the size of short-term memory.

Miller's Magical Number. Researchers have been interested in the size of the memory span for more than a century. However, memory-span research gained particular importance in 1956 when George Miller wrote his famous article titled "The Magical Number Seven, Plus or Minus Two: Some Limits on Our Capacity for Processing Information." Miller proposed that we can hold only a limited number of items in short-term memory. Specifically, he suggested that people can remember about seven items (give or take two), or between five and nine items.

Miller used the term *chunk* to describe the basic unit in short-term memory. According to a more current definition, a chunk is "a well-learned cognitive unit made up of a small number of components representing a frequently occurring and consistent perceptual pattern" (Bellezza, 1994, p. 579). Miller suggested, therefore, that short-term memory holds about seven chunks. A chunk can be a single numeral or a single letter, because people can remember about seven numerals or letters if they are in random order. However, those numbers and letters can be organized into larger units. For example, perhaps your area code is 212 and all the phone numbers at your college begin with the same digits, 346. If 212 forms one chunk and 346 forms another chunk, then the phone number 212-346-3421 really contains only six chunks (that is, $1 + 1 + 4$). The entire number may be within your memory span.

Miller's (1956) article received major attention, and the magical number 7 ± 2 became a prominent concept known to almost all psychology students. However, many people argued that Miller's term *chunk* was not a well-defined concept. For example, Simon (1974) complained that a major problem was that chunks were defined in a circular fashion. That is, (1) there are seven chunks in short-term memory, and (2) a chunk is what there are seven of in short-term memory! In order for *chunk* to be a more meaningful term, the chunk should be related to a different psychological task, independent of short-term memory performance.

The different task that Simon chose to examine was performance on a long-term memory task. He reasoned that if the chunk is a real, legitimate concept, then the number of chunks in the stimulus list should be related to the amount of time that people take to commit a list to long-term memory. Simon then examined previous experiments that addressed this question. Indeed, the number of chunks in a stimulus showed a strong positive correlation with the amount of time required to learn that stimulus. He concluded that the chunk is a legitimate concept, because it is so closely related to learning time. Therefore, the chunk is not simply an arbitrary term describing the seven units in memory.

What is the status of Miller's magical number, several decades after it was originally proposed? According to Alan Baddeley (1994), the prominent theorist who has explored working memory, the concept is still magical. However, the magic does not arise primarily from the concept of a strict limit on memory capacity. Instead, the concept is important because—in an era when behaviorism dominated—Miller emphasized that the cognitive process of *recoding* was a vitally important factor in determining the amount of material that could be stored. The concept of chunking is important because it emphasizes the active nature of our cognitive processes.

Pronunciation Time. Other researchers have pointed out that pronunciation time may be even more important than the number of chunks formed by the items (Cowan, 1994, 1995). For example, Schweickert and Boruff (1986) tested memory span for a variety of materials, such as consonants, numbers, nouns, shapes, color names, and nonsense words. With impressive consistency, people tended to recall the number of items that could be pronounced in about 1.5 seconds. These authors propose that the capacity of short-term memory is not determined by a fixed number of items or chunks in memory; instead, it is determined by the limited time for which the verbal trace of the items endures. In the case of nonsense syllables, a person might be able to pronounce only four items in 1.5 seconds; therefore, only four items will be recalled. In the case of numbers in the English language, a person can typically pronounce six items in 1.5 seconds, and so recall is somewhat greater. Incidentally, the importance of pronunciation time makes sense in light of the discussion of acoustic coding in short-term memory in Chapter 3 and later in this chapter.

Researchers have also tested the pronunciation-time hypothesis for other kinds of items. Try Demonstration 4.6, which is a modification of a study by Baddeley and his colleagues (1975). These researchers found that people could accurately recall an average of 4.2 words from the list of countries with short names, but only 2.8 words from the list of countries with long names.

DEMONSTRATION 4.6

PRONUNCIATION TIME AND MEMORY SPAN

Read the following words. When you have finished, look away from the page and try to recall them.

England, Burma, Greece, Spain, Iceland, Malta, Laos

Now try the task again with a different list of words. Again, read the words, look away, and recall them.

Czechoslovakia, Switzerland, Nicaragua, Afghanistan,
Venezuela, Philippines, Madagascar

However, the most systematic research has been conducted on the recall of numbers in a variety of languages. Naveh-Benjamin and Ayres (1986) tested memory spans for people who spoke English, Spanish, Hebrew, and Arabic. The English numbers between one and ten can be spoken rapidly; most of them are one-syllable words. Spanish and Hebrew have a somewhat greater average number of syllables for the numbers one to ten, and Arabic numbers are even longer. As you can see from Figure 4.5, the memory span is significantly greater for people speaking English than for people speaking the other three languages. Furthermore, the dotted line shows the pronunciation rate for each of the four languages. As you can see, greater memory spans are associated with languages that can be spoken rapidly. Clearly, pronunciation rate—as well as number of chunks—needs to be considered when discussing the capacity of short-term memory.

Other Factors Affecting Memory Span. As you can imagine, numerous other variables also influence memory span. For example, one important factor is the nature of the distractor task, the task people perform between the time the stimulus is presented and the time when they must recall the stimulus. If the stimulus is visual and the distractor is visual—or if both are auditory—people recall fewer items (Greene, 1992).

═══════════════════════ **FIGURE 4.5** ═══════════════════════

MEMORY SPAN AND PRONUNCIATION RATE FOR NUMBERS IN FOUR DIFFERENT LANGUAGES. NAVEH-BENJAMIN & AYRES (1986).

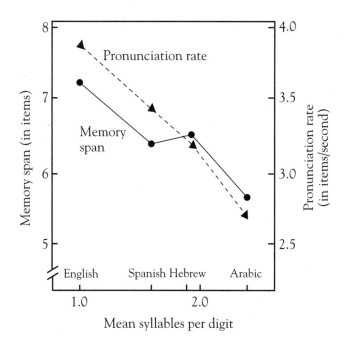

You won't be surprised to learn that individual differences also affect the size of short-term memory (e.g., Frensch & Miner, 1994; Jurden, 1995). For example, people vary widely in their ability to inhibit irrelevant information, and this irrelevant information can occupy part of short-term memory capacity (Conway & Engle, 1994). People who are highly anxious also seem to have more limited short-term memory capacities (Darke, 1988; MacLeod & Donnellan, 1993). In summary, short-term memory does not have a rigidly fixed capacity. Instead, characteristics of the task and individual differences can influence the number of items we remember.

The Duration of Short-Term Memory

Researchers have focused most of their attention on the important capacity limits of short-term memory. A second characteristic—the brief duration of short-term memory—has seldom been studied. Of course, the fragility of short-term memory is obvious to anyone who has quickly forgotten a telephone number, a person's name, or a crucial piece of information just seconds after hearing it. Also, research with the Brown/Peterson & Peterson technique emphasized that items can disappear from memory a mere 18 seconds after learning them, if rehearsal is prevented—as Figure 4.4 pointed out.

Some psychologists have attempted to assess the duration of an item in short-term memory (Cunningham et al., 1993; Muter, 1980; Sebrechts et al., 1989). For example, Marc Sebrechts and his colleagues (1989) assessed short-term memory, each time presenting three common English nouns. In one condition, the participants did not expect that they would be asked to recall the items. Furthermore, the researchers used a strict criterion for correct recall: All three words needed to be recalled in the correct order. In this condition, correct recall fell to 1% after only four seconds. When we are not making a concerted effort to retain material in short-term memory, information can vanish within a few seconds.

The Code in Short-Term Memory

We have seen that the size and duration of short-term memory are quite limited; these characteristics might encourage pessimism about human cognitive processes. However, research on the way information can be coded in short-term memory emphasizes the flexibility of these processes. As you will see, we often use an *acoustic code*—that is, storage in terms of the sound of an item. However, as Postman (1975) and Crowder (1982b) warn us, the acoustic code is certainly not the only code used in short-term memory. An item can also be coded in terms of a *visual code,* involving the physical appearance of the item, or in terms of a *semantic code,* focusing on the item's meaning.

Acoustic Coding in Short-Term Memory. Suppose that you have checked your address book to find the ZIP code for a friend in Portola Valley, California. You saw the number "94028." How do you keep *94028* in your short-term memory until you can write it down? If you are like most people, you'll note that the ZIP code seems to be coded in terms of its sound. Can you almost "hear" yourself repeating *94028* over and over to yourself as you rehearse it?

Numerous experiments have demonstrated the importance of acoustic coding in short-term memory. For example, the study by Kintsch and Buschke (1969), discussed in Chapter 3 in connection with the Atkinson-Shiffrin model, offers clear support for acoustic coding. Let's look at another representative study, performed by Wickelgren (1965). On each trial, Wickelgren presented a tape recording of an eight-item list, consisting of four letters and four digits in random order. Thus, a typical item might be *4NF9G27P*. As soon as the tape was finished, people tried to recall the list. Wickelgren was particularly interested in the kinds of substitutions people made. For example, if they did not correctly recall the *P* at the end of the list, what did they recall in its place? He found that people tended to substitute an item that was acoustically similar. For example, instead of the last *P*, they might substitute a *B, C, D, E, G, T,* or *V,* all letters with the "ee" sound. Furthermore, if they substituted a number for *P,* it would most likely be the similar-sounding number *3.*

Visual Coding in Short-Term Memory. Acoustic coding may be the standard mechanism for coding material in short-term memory. However, when that option is not available, items can be coded in terms of their visual characteristics. Let's consider the research conducted by M. A. Brandimonte and her colleagues (1992), which shows that people use visual coding when acoustic coding has been suppressed.

In particular, let's compare the performance for two groups of participants in one of Brandimonte's studies. In one condition, which we'll call the control group, people saw six pictures of objects, such as the ones labeled "original picture" in Figure 4.6. The series was repeated until they knew the pictures in order. On the second task, they were asked to create a mental image of each picture in the series, and to subtract a specified part from each image. They were told to name the resulting image. For example, if they had created a mental image of the piece of candy in Figure 4.6 and they then subtracted the specified part, they should end up describing the resulting image as a fish. Similarly, the pipe minus the specified part should be described as a bowl. The participants in this control condition succeeded in naming an average of 2.7 items correctly, out of a maximum of 6.0 items.

A second condition involved verbal suppression, in an attempt to suppress acoustic coding. Students performed the same tasks as in the control group—with one exception: While they were learning the original list of pictures, they were instructed to repeat an irrelevant sound (*la-la-la* . . .). Notice that this repetition would block the acoustic representation of each picture. You can't say *candy* or *pipe* to yourself if you are chanting *la-la-la* out loud! How well did these people do on the task of identifying the image that was created by subtracting the specified part? As it turned out, they performed significantly better than people in the control condition, naming an average of 3.8 items correctly. Because acoustic coding was difficult, they were probably more likely to use visual coding. In the picture subtraction task, they found it relatively simple to subtract a part from a visual image.

========= FIGURE 4.6 =========

TWO OF THE STIMULI USED IN THE STUDY BY BRANDIMONTE ET AL. (1992)

Original Picture   Specified Part to Be   Image that
                    Subtracted From the   Should Result
                    Mental Image   After Subtraction

1.

2.

In contrast, the people in the control condition were more likely to use acoustical encoding. Therefore, they had difficulty subtracting a part from a stimulus that had been coded as a word, such as *candy* or *pipe*, because they had not created a visual code.

The research by Brandimonte and her colleagues illustrates that people will use visual coding if they are deprived of auditory coding. In Chapter 6, visual coding will occupy the center stage when we see how people create visual images and manipulate those images.

Semantic Coding in Short-Term Memory. We also have substantial evidence that items in short-term memory can be coded in terms of their meaning. For example, consider a study by Wickens and his colleagues (1976). Their technique is based on a concept from memory called proactive inhibition. ***Proactive inhibition (PI)*** means that people have trouble learning new material because previously learned material keeps interfering with new learning. Suppose you had previously learned the items *XCJ*, *HBR*, and *TSV* in a Brown/Peterson & Peterson test of short-term memory. You will then have trouble remembering a fourth item *KRN*, because the three previous items keep interfering (Laming, 1992). However, if the experimenter shifts the category of the fourth item from letters to, say, numbers, your memory will improve. You will experience a ***release from proactive inhibition;*** performance on a new, different item (say, *529*) will be almost as high as it had been on the first item, *XCJ*.

Many experiments have demonstrated release from PI when the category of items is shifted, as from letters to numbers. However, Wickens and his coauthors

(1976) demonstrated that release from PI could also be obtained when the semantic class of items is shifted. They gave people three trials on the Brown/Peterson & Peterson test. Each trial consisted of three items, similar to those in Table 4.1. For example, as you can see, those in the "Professions" condition might begin with "lawyer, busdriver, teacher" on the first trial. Then the people in this condition saw lists of additional professions on Trials 2 and 3. Then on the fourth trial, they saw a list of three fruits—as did the people in the other four conditions. For all four trials and all five conditions, people were tested with the standard Brown/Peterson & Peterson test. That is, they saw a list of three words, followed by a three-digit number. After counting backward from this number for 18 seconds, they tried to recall the three words.

Look through the five conditions in Table 4.1. Wouldn't you expect the buildup of PI on Trial 4 to be the greatest for those in the "Fruits" (control) condition? After all, people's memories should be so full of other fruits that would be interfering with the three new fruits. However, if meaning is important in working memory, performance in the other four conditions should depend upon the semantic similarity between these items and fruit. For example, people who had seen vegetables on Trials 1–3 should do rather poorly, because fruits and vegetables are similar—they are both edible and grow in the ground. People who had seen either flowers

TABLE 4.1

THE SETUP FOR AN EXPERIMENT ON RELEASE FROM PI

Condition	Trial 1	Trial 2	Trial 3	Trial 4
Fruits (control)	banana peach apple	plum apricot lime	melon lemon grape	orange cherry pineapple
Vegetables	onion turnip corn	radish beans spinach	potato peas okra	orange cherry pineapple
Flowers	daisy rose iris	violet daffodil zinnia	tulip dahlia orchid	orange cherry pineapple
Meats	salami pork chicken	bacon hot dog beef	hamburger turkey veal	orange cherry pineapple
Professions	lawyer busdriver teacher	dancer minister executive	accountant doctor editor	orange cherry pineapple

=== FIGURE 4.7 ===

RELEASE FROM PI, AS A FUNCTION OF SEMANTIC SIMILARITY.   BASED ON WICKENS ET AL. (1976).

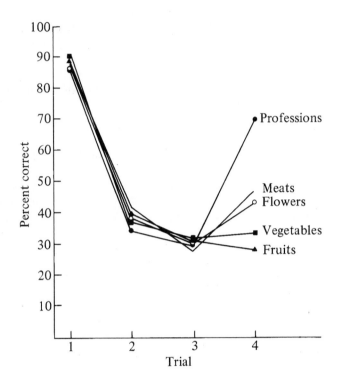

or meats should do somewhat better, because flowers and meats each share only one attribute with fruits. However, people who had seen professions should do the best of all, because professions are not edible and do not grow in the ground.

Figure 4.7 is an example of the kind of results every researcher hopes to find. Note that the results match the predictions perfectly. In summary, meaning is important in short-term memory because old words interfere with the recall of new words that are similar in meaning. Furthermore, the degree of semantic similarity is related to the amount of interference. Similar results have also been found for the short-term recall of sentences (Dempster, 1985).

In this section, we have explored the various ways in which information is stored in short-term memory. An auditory code seems to be most common. However, in certain situations, people can use either visual or semantic codes.

IN DEPTH: The Working-Memory View of Short-Term Memory

Earlier, we noted that many current researchers and theorists argue that neither iconic memory nor echoic memory is unitary. They propose, instead, that iconic memory and echoic memory each have at least two components. Therefore, you should not be surprised to learn that psychologists have also proposed several components for short-term memory. Our memory is extremely flexible, and multiple systems have evolved that are specialized for different tasks (Gathercole, 1992; Schneider, 1993). Alan Baddeley and his colleagues have developed the most complete description of a multicomponent interpretation of short-term memory, which they call working memory (Baddeley, 1986, 1992b; Gathercole & Baddeley, 1993).

According to Baddeley's approach, *working memory* is a three-part system that temporarily holds and manipulates information as we perform cognitive tasks. Notice that this view emphasizes that working memory is not simply a passive storehouse, with a number of shelves to hold partially processed information until it moves on to another location, presumably long-term memory (Smyth et al., 1994). Instead, the emphasis on the manipulation of information means that working memory is more like a workbench where material is constantly being handled, combined, and transformed. Furthermore, this workbench holds both new material and old material you have retrieved from storage.

Before we examine the three components of working memory, let's see why Baddeley felt compelled to conclude that working memory is not unitary. In a classic study, Baddeley and Hitch (1974) presented a string of random numbers and instructed people to rehearse them while performing a reasoning task. The sequence of numbers varied in length from zero to eight items. Thus, the longer list approached the upper limit of short-term memory, according to the 7 ± 2 proposal. The reasoning task required participants to judge whether certain statements about letter order were correct or incorrect. For example, when the two letters *BA* appeared, participants should respond to the statement "*A* follows *B*" by pressing a "*yes*" button. If *BA* was accompanied by the statement "*B* follows *A*," participants should press the "*no*" button.

Imagine yourself performing this task. Wouldn't you think you would take longer and make more errors on the reasoning task if you had to keep rehearsing eight numerals, instead of only one? Surprisingly, Baddeley and Hitch discovered that people required less than a second longer when instructed to rehearse eight numerals, in contrast to a task that required no rehearsal. Even more impressive, the error rate remained at about 5%, no matter how many numerals the participants rehearsed! These data clearly contradicted the view that temporary storage has only about seven slots. Instead, short-term memory or working memory seems to have several components, which can operate partially independently of each other.

Baddeley and his colleagues have proposed three components for working memory: a phonological loop, a visuo-spatial working memory, and a central executive (Baddeley, 1986, 1988, 1992a, 1992b; Gathercole & Baddeley, 1993; Logie, 1995). Let's examine each of these components and then briefly look at some new directions for research in this area.

Phonological Loop. According to the working-memory model, the ***phonological loop*** stores a limited number of sounds for a short period of time. The phonological loop contains two separate components (Gathercole & Baddeley, 1993). One component, the ***phonological store,*** maintains a limited amount of information in an acoustic code that decays after a few seconds. The second component, the *sub-vocal rehearsal process,* allows you to repeat the words in the phonological store silently to yourself. This process helps to maintain the items in the phonological store. It is also used to translate printed words, pictures, and other non-acoustic material into a phonological form, so that it can be maintained in the phonological store (Gathercole & Baddeley, 1993).

Susan Gathercole and Alan Baddeley (1993) argue that the pronunciation-time research you learned about in Demonstration 4.6 can be accounted for by the phonological loop. You can pronounce country names such as Burma and Greece fairly quickly, and you can rehearse a large number of them quickly. In contrast, names such as Switzerland and Nicaragua will be lost from the phonological store when you have a large number of these long names to rehearse.

Recent research by Martin (1993) provides neuropsychological evidence for a separate phonological loop. Martin tested a woman known as E.A., who demonstrated normal comprehension for English sentences. However, she showed a very specific deficit for remembering phonological information. For example, she could not retain words presented in Spanish, a language in which she had no expertise. Apparently, the phonological loop is not critical for comprehending spoken language in one's native tongue.

Visuo-Spatial Working Memory. A second component of the working-memory model is *visuo-spatial working memory,* which stores visual and spatial information, as well as verbal information that has been encoded into visual imagery (Gathercole & Baddeley, 1993; Logie, 1995). This component has been known by several different names, such as *visuospatial sketch pad* and *visuo-spatial scratchpad.* Following the example of Robert Logie's (1995) recent book on the subject, we will use the more generic name, visuo-spatial working memory. Incidentally, Chapter 6 examines the kind of mental manipulations we perform on the visuo-spatial information stored in this component of working memory. Furthermore, in the study by Brandimonte and her colleagues (1992), the people who were instructed to repeat *la-la-la* were presumably forced to use visuo-spatial working memory because their phonological loop was busy repeating the syllable.

Like the phonological loop, the capacity of visuo-spatial working memory is limited (Frick, 1988, 1990). If you try to solve a geometry problem on a small piece of paper, you will make some errors. Similarly, when too many items enter into visuo-spatial working memory, you cannot represent them accurately enough to be successfully recovered. Keep in mind, however, that the limits of the phonological loop and visuo-spatial working memory are independent. As Baddeley and Hitch (1974) discovered, you can rehearse numbers in the phonological loop while making decisions about the spatial arrangements of letters in visuo-spatial working memory.

At some point in the near future, ask several friends to try Demonstration 4.7. See whether the friends who closed their eyes construct the matrix more accurately.

Demonstration 4.7 is based on a study by Margaret Toms and her colleagues (1994). They asked the participants in their study to perform a spatial task like this, under four different kinds of conditions. Two of these conditions involved minimal

INTERFERENCE WITH VISUO-SPATIAL WORKING MEMORY

For this demonstration, you will need to recruit several friends, who can all be tested in one group. Begin by covering up these instructions. Show the group only the matrix of squares at the bottom of the demonstration. Point out the black star in the one square, and tell them that they must try to visualize this matrix, with its black star, while they follow your instructions. After you have shown them the matrix, tell them that you will read a list of sentences. They should try to visualize the matrix beginning with the square that has the black star, and then follow the instructions carefully. Instruct half the group to close their eyes and half to look at a specific object in the room. Then read aloud the following sentences:

In the square with the black star, put a 1.
In the next square to the right, put a 2.
In the next square to the right, put a 3.
In the next square down, put a 4.
In the next square to the left, put a 5.
In the next square down, put a 6.
In the next square to the left, put a 7.
In the next square up, put an 8.
In the next square to the left, put a 9.
In the next square down, put a 10.

Finally, hand each student a blank matrix (which you have xeroxed or drawn beforehand) and ask them all to place the appropriate number in the appropriate square.

When they are done, collect the papers and count the number of correctly placed numbers for the eyes-closed and for the eyes-open group. (You can find the answer at the end of the chapter.)

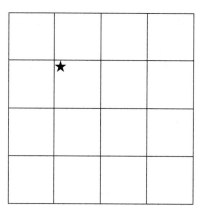

visual interference; participants either closed their eyes or looked at a blank monitor screen. The other two conditions did involve visual interference; they looked at either a white square on the screen or at a continuously shifting blue-and-white pattern on the screen. As you can see from Table 4.2, people performed substantially better in the two conditions where no visual input interfered with their visuo-spatial working memory.

Toms and her colleagues also asked their participants to perform a verbal task that involved remembering nonsense sentences that contained no spatial information. Here, the words *up, down, left,* and *right* were replaced by the words *good, bad, slow,* and *quick*. Thus, a sample sentence might be, "In the next square to the quick, put a 2." They listened to these nonsense sentences under the same four kinds of conditions that were used on the spatial task. However, because the spatial words were missing, their visuo-spatial working memory was presumably inactive. As Table 4.2 shows, the participants' recall performance on this verbal task was similar across all four conditions. This verbal task presumably involves the phonological loop, so visual input does not provide interference. As the working-memory approach emphasizes, visuo-spatial working memory and the phonological loop are independent; furthermore, visual input interferes with the first component without touching the second component.

Central Executive. According to the working-memory model, the ***central executive*** integrates information from the phonological loop and visuo-spatial working memory, as well as from long-term memory. The central executive also plays a major role in attention, planning, and coordinating behavior (Baddeley, 1988, 1992b; Gathercole & Baddeley, 1993; Morris & Jones, 1990). Compared to the other two systems, the central executive is more difficult to study using controlled research techniques. However, it plays a critical role in the overall functions of working memory. As Baddeley (1986) points out, if we concentrate on, say, the phonological loop, the situation would resemble a critical analysis of *Hamlet* that focuses on Polonius—a minor character—and completely ignores the prince of Denmark!

Baddeley proposes that the central executive works like a supervisor. The executive decides which issues deserve attention and which should be ignored. The

---

TABLE 4.2

THE EFFECT OF VISUAL CONDITION ON ACCURACY ON A VISUAL TASK AND ON A VERBAL TASK. BASED ON TOMS ET AL. (1994).

	Average percentage correct per trial in each condition			
	Eyes shut	*Blank screen*	*Square*	*Pattern*
Spatial Task	85%	84%	69%	69%
Verbal Task	77%	77%	73%	80%

executive also selects strategies, figuring out how to tackle a problem. We will examine this issue of strategy selection more completely in Chapter 7, in connection with metacognition.

Like any executive in an organization, the central executive has a limited capacity; our cognitive executive cannot make numerous decisions simultaneously. Furthermore, like any competent supervisor, the central executive gathers information from a variety of sources. To continue this metaphor, the central executive in working memory synthesizes the information from the two assistants, the phonological loop and visuo-spatial working memory, and also from the large library known as long-term memory. In the next chapter, we will examine the characteristics of this remarkable storehouse. In contrast to the restricted capacity of sensory memory and short-term memory, long-term memory has no limits.

New Directions for Research in Working Memory. In the 1980s and early 1990s, most of the research on working memory focused on the phonological loop. More recent research has examined visuo-spatial working memory and the central executive (e.g., Gathercole & Baddeley, 1993; Logie, 1995).

One of the recent developments in this area is that researchers are trying to examine working memory from the perspective of parallel distributed processing, the prominent new theory we introduced in Chapter 3 (e.g., Burgess & Hitch, 1992; Logie, 1995). Another avenue for research is to relate working memory to other cognitive systems. For example, Carlson and his colleagues have examined how information from working memory is coordinated with information from perception.

Other psychologists are attempting to expand the working-memory model. For example, Berz (1995) points out that the model does not account for musical memory; in some cases, we can listen to instrumental music without disrupting performance on other acoustical tasks. Furthermore, Ericsson and Kintsch (1995) emphasize that a complete model must include another component called long-term working memory. These authors feel that this new component is necessary to explain how highly skilled experts can directly access information from long-term memory, based on retrieval cues in working memory.

In short, the working-memory approach describes a more complex view of those memories we store for very brief periods. Instead of a simple storehouse, this working memory is both flexible and strategic.

SECTION SUMMARY: SHORT-TERM MEMORY

1. As the Brown/Peterson & Peterson technique shows, a large proportion of material is forgotten in short-term memory after just a few seconds' delay.
2. The size of short-term memory is small; according to Miller's classic article, it is limited to 7 ± 2 chunks.
3. Others argue that the size of short-term memory is most closely related to pronunciation time; that is, less material is remembered when words are

long. In addition, short-term memory is influenced by factors such as an individual's anxiety level.

4. The duration of short-term memory is short, especially when people do not expect to be tested for recall.

5. Information in short-term memory is usually stored in terms of an acoustical code; however, in some circumstances, semantic and visual cues can also be used.

6. According to the working-memory approach developed by Baddeley and his colleagues, the phonological loop consists of a phonological store and a subvocal rehearsal process; the phonological loop stores a limited number of sounds for a short period of time.

7. A second feature of the working-memory approach is visuo-spatial working memory, which stores visual and spatial information; its capacity is independent of the phonological loop, but this capacity is also limited.

8. The central executive integrates information from the phonological loop and visuo-spatial working memory, as well as from long-term memory; the central executive is also important in attention, planning, and coordinating behavior.

9. Research on working memory currently focuses on such topics as developing models based on the parallel distributed processing approach, relating working memory to other cognitive systems, and expanding the model.

CHAPTER REVIEW QUESTIONS

1. Think of an example of echoic memory and of short-term memory (one stored in terms of an auditory code). Try to recall the list of distinctions between sensory memory and short-term memory from the beginning of the chapter; point out how your two examples illustrate these distinctions.

2. We discussed sensory memory for sights and sounds. Sperling's (1960) method of examining iconic memory was modified to test echoic memory. How could this method be adapted to test sensory memory for touch? Describe both Sperling's study and the research on echoic memory.

3. Explain why sensory memory is necessary in vision and hearing. How is sensory memory related to the information about attention discussed in Chapter 2? Why is sensory memory necessary for pattern recognition—another topic we discussed in Chapter 2?

4. According to a quote by Cowan in this chapter, echoic memory may not be as simple as we once thought. Review Cowan's proposal about two kinds of echoic memory, and point out how one of these may share some characteristics with short-term memory.

5. Describe Miller's classic notion about the magical number 7. Why are chunks relevant to this notion, and what more recent evidence suggests that this number may not be as rigidly universal as we once thought?

6. What kinds of codes can be used for items stored in short-term memory? Review the research that has been conducted in this area.

7. A brief section in this chapter examined the duration of short-term memory. Review this information. In light of the newer working-memory approach, why might it be difficult to be very specific about the duration of short-term memory?

8. Which component of the working-memory approach is relevant for the research on pronunciation time? Discuss this research, and point out what the research suggests about the limits of this component of working memory.

9. Why did Baddeley reject the classic conception of a single storehouse for short-term memory? What did he suggest instead? Can you think of examples from your own experience where you have simultaneously used Baddeley's two proposed storehouses?

10. Recent theories of sensory memory have proposed dividing both iconic memory and echoic memory into two or more components. However, no one has suggested a concept similar to a central executive for sensory memory. Why is the concept of a central executive not necessary for sensory memory?

NEW TERMS

sensory memory	echo	release from proactive
short-term memory	short auditory storage	inhibition
sensory storage	long auditory storage	working memory
sensory register	recency effect	phonological loop
iconic memory	memory span	phonological store
icon	chunk	subvocal rehearsal process
whole-report technique	acoustic code	visuo-spatial working
partial-report technique	visual code	memory
saccadic movement	semantic code	central executive
echoic memory	proactive inhibition (PI)	

RECOMMENDED READINGS

Cowan, N. (1995). *Attention and memory: An integrated framework.* New York: Oxford University Press. Nelson Cowan is one of the major researchers in the area of sensory memory, so his overview of this topic is especially well informed; he also offers a somewhat different perspective of short-term memory from the working-memory approach.

Gathercole, S. E., & Baddeley, A. D. (1993). *Working memory and language.* Hove, Great Britain: Erlbaum. Two of the major proponents of the working-memory approach—Susan Gathercole and Alan Baddeley—provide a very readable summary of this approach, with special applications to reading, language comprehension, and other aspects of language.

Logie, R. H. (1995). *Visuo-spatial working memory*. Hove, Great Britain: Erlbaum. Logie's volume provides the ideal complement to Gathercole and Baddeley's book, because it emphasizes aspects of working memory that are not linguistic.

Memory & Cognition (1993). Volume 21, issue 2. Most of this special issue of the journal *Memory & Cognition* is devoted to short-term memory; it includes review articles and research-based reports by psychologists who are prominent in this area.

ANSWER TO DEMONSTRATION 4.7

	★ 1	2	3
9	8	5	4
10	7	6	

LONG-TERM MEMORY

INTRODUCTION

DETERMINANTS OF ACCURACY

The Effects of Context: Encoding Specificity
Mood
In Depth: Explicit Versus Implicit Measures of Memory
Expertise

AUTOBIOGRAPHICAL MEMORY

Flashbulb Memories
Schemas and Autobiographical Memory
Memory for Action
Eyewitness Testimony
Ecological Validity and Autobiographical Memory Research

MEMORY IMPROVEMENT

Mnemonics Using Imagery
Mnemonics Using Organization
Practice
External Memory Aids
The Multimodal Approach
Metamemory

========================= **Preview** =========================

Several factors can dramatically influence the accuracy of your long-term memory. For example, if you have ever returned to a once-familiar location and experienced a flood of long-lost memories, you know the importance of encoding specificity. Mood also affects recall; for example, you'll typically remember better when you are learning material with an emotional tone that matches your own mood. Memory accuracy can also be influenced by the way memory is assessed, as the In-Depth section on explicit versus implicit memory illustrates. Finally, people who have expert knowledge in an area recall more than novices, although their general intelligence may be similar.

One important topic in the research on autobiographical memory is flashbulb memories, or vivid memory about an emotionally arousing event. Because memory is influenced by our general knowledge about objects and events (schemas), we sometimes mistakenly "recall" events that never really happened. We may also have difficulty deciding whether we truly performed a particular action we had intended to do, or we may forget to perform an action in the future. The research on eyewitness testimony has implications for the courtroom, and the debate about ecological validity considers the relative merit of research on real-world topics such as eyewitness testimony versus laboratory-based research.

The third section of this chapter considers two mnemonic devices: visual imagery and organization. We will also examine four general strategies: practice, external memory aids (such as taking notes), the multimodal approach (which emphasizes the complexity of factors that influence memory), and metamemory, which is your knowledge about your memory.

INTRODUCTION

Chapter 4 emphasized the fragility of sensory and short-term memory. As we saw, information that we want to retain can disappear from memory—after less than a minute. In contrast, Chapter 5 demonstrates that material retained in long-term memory can be amazingly resistant to forgetting.

Think about the information stored in your own long-term memory. For example, can you recall the details about how you learned you had been accepted into the college you now attend? If you received a letter of acceptance, for instance, can you remember where you were standing when you opened the letter, what you were wearing, and whom you told first? Or perhaps you recognize a magazine advertisement, even though you originally saw that ad several years earlier. Indeed, Standing (1973) found that people who had seen 10,000 pictures later recognized most of them. People can also remember odors of items—such as bubble gum and baby shampoo—even when they have not smelled them since childhood (Goldman & Seamon, 1992).

We also have impressive memory for information learned in school. At some point while you are reading this chapter, try Demonstration 5.1, which illustrates the durability of foreign-language vocabulary. This demonstration is based on the research of Bahrick (1984), who tested retention of Spanish learned in high school or college. Participants in this study had learned the material between 0 and 50 years earlier, and their recall was far from perfect. However, even 50 years later, people still recalled about 40% of the vocabulary, idioms, and grammar they had originally learned. Bahrick proposed the name *permastore* to refer to this relatively permanent, very long-term form of memory.

Disciplines other than foreign language provide additional evidence of permastore. For example, Bahrick and Hall (1991) tested recall for algebra and geometry, subjects that people have had little opportunity to practice or rehearse since completing their education. These authors compared individuals from two groups. One group had taken a college-level course at or beyond the level of calculus. A second group had performed similarly in high-school math courses, but they had taken no advanced math courses in college. As Figure 5.1 shows, people in the "high math" group retained their mathematics knowledge remarkably well, decades afterward. However, the "low math" group showed a systematic decline.

How much do people remember from a subject of immediate relevance to those of you reading this book—cognitive psychology? Martin Conway and his colleagues (1991) tested students who had taken a course in cognitive psychology, examining their recall for the names of researchers and for technical concepts. These researchers found that recall declined during the first two years after taking the course, and it remained steady at about 25% ten years later. Fortunately, students' recall for general facts and research methods was much more impressive; they recalled about 70% of this information ten years later!

We do not yet have studies from enough disciplines to be able to predict what kind of information will be retained in very long-term memory and what will be forgotten. However, under ideal circumstances, people can recall substantial amounts of a discipline, more than a decade after acquisition.

Most of the research we'll discuss in this chapter examines much shorter retention intervals, from a few minutes to several hours. Let's begin by considering some factors that influence accuracy. Then we'll discuss autobiographical memory for events in people's everyday lives. The last section of the chapter suggests strategies for improving your memory.

DETERMINANTS OF ACCURACY

We have noted that long-term memory is typically robust. Individuals can remember a large number of words from a foreign language, even though a half-century has passed since they learned that *abajo* means *down*. As you might expect, accuracy is influenced by a number of factors; we will examine four of these factors in this section.

DEMONSTRATION 5.1

VERY LONG-TERM MEMORY

For this demonstration, you will need to locate at least one person who studied either Spanish or French but has not used the language in the last year. Ask the volunteer how many years have passed since studying the foreign language. Then hand him or her the appropriate list of vocabulary words (either in Spanish or French), with the instructions to take as long as necessary to supply the English translation. (The answers are at the end of the chapter.)

Spanish

1. ferrocarril _____
2. gato _____
3. hermana _____
4. cama _____
5. cabeza _____
6. manzana _____
7. corazón _____
8. zapato _____
9. silla _____
10. cocina _____

11. camino _____
12. diablo _____
13. naranja _____
14. pájaro _____
15. abuelo _____
16. brazo _____
17. falda _____
18. desayuno _____
19. ventana _____
20. luna _____

French

1. chemin de fer _____
2. chat _____
3. soeur _____
4. lit _____
5. tête _____
6. pomme _____
7. coeur _____
8. chaussure _____
9. chaise _____
10. cuisine _____

11. rue _____
12. satan _____
13. orange _____
14. oiseau _____
15. grand-père _____
16. bras _____
17. jupe _____
18. petit déjeuner _____
19. fenêtre _____
20. lune _____

You may wish to locate several individuals, so that you can determine whether recall decreases for longer retention intervals. (To provide a larger sample, your instructor may choose to gather the data from the entire class.) Incidentally, Bahrick (1984) found that recall for Spanish-English vocabulary declined rapidly in the initial years when people were no longer actively studying Spanish, but the decrease then leveled off after about three years.

═══════ FIGURE 5.1 ═══════

RECALL OF ALGEBRA BY STUDENTS WHO HAD TAKEN CALCULUS OR OTHER AD-VANCED MATH COURSES VERSUS STUDENTS WITH NO ADVANCED MATH. CONWAY ET AL. (1992). BASED ON BAHRICK AND HALL (1991).

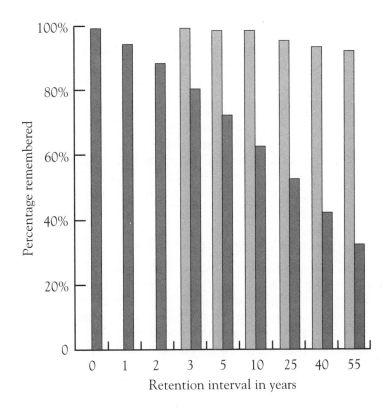

"High math" (Calculus or other advanced math)

"Low math" (No college math courses)

At first glance, these four factors may seem unrelated. However, each focuses on the importance of context; you will recall that Theme 5 emphasizes the role of contextual factors in top-down processing. This textbook first emphasized research on context in Chapter 2, when we saw how context facilitates pattern recognition. Then in Chapter 3, the discussion of levels of processing examined how memory depends upon context. We saw that recall is best when the context at the time of retrieval matches the context at the time of encoding. For example, you'll remember more about a word's sound if the encoding task emphasizes sound, rather than meaning.

In the current section on determinants of accuracy, context emerges once again as an important factor. We will begin by directly addressing the issue of context, elaborating on encoding specificity. The research on mood also underscores the importance of context. For example, people recall material more accurately if its emotional tone matches their mood. Furthermore, people often remember material better if their mood during encoding matches their mood during recall.

The in-depth section explores how memory can be measured either explicitly or implicitly. An explicit measure will emphasize top-down processing. When retrieval is assessed by an explicit measure, performance is better when encoding also emphasized top-down processing. In contrast, an implicit measure will emphasize bottom-up processing. When retrieval is assessed by an implicit measure, performance is better when encoding also emphasized bottom-up processing.

The final determinant of accuracy—expertise—is related to context in a different fashion. As you'll see in this section, a person's expertise is limited to a specific context. For example, someone who is an expert in chess may not be astonishingly talented in other domains.

The importance of context emphasizes the complexities of human long-term memory. People do not learn and remember in isolation, oblivious to the richness of contextual cues in the outside world. Instead, humans are situated within a broader framework, and they take their surroundings and social interactions into account (e.g., Kihlstrom, 1994; Lave, 1988). Let us begin our discussion of determinants of accuracy by exploring this context in more detail.

The Effects of Context: Encoding Specificity

Does this scenario sound familiar? You are in the bedroom and realize that you need something from the kitchen. Once you arrive in the kitchen, however, you have no idea why you made the trip. Without the context in which you encoded the item you wanted, you cannot retrieve this memory. You return to the bedroom, which is rich with contextual cues, and you immediately remember what you wanted. Similarly, an isolated question on an exam may look completely unfamiliar, although you would have remembered the answer in the correct context.

These examples illustrate the *encoding specificity principle,* which states that recall is better if the retrieval context is like the encoding context (Begg & White, 1985; Tulving, 1983). In contrast, forgetting occurs when the two contexts do not match. We introduced the concept of encoding specificity in our discussion of levels of processing in Chapter 3, when we examined research in which words could be encoded in terms of their meaning or their sound. Let's now consider this topic of encoding specificity in more detail.

Research on Encoding Specificity. In a representative study, Geiselman and Glenny (1977) presented words visually to the participants in their experiment. The participants were asked to imagine each of the words as being spoken by a familiar person; some were instructed to imagine a female voice, and others were

━━━━━━━━━━━━━ FIGURE 5.2 ━━━━━━━━━━━━━

PERCENTAGE OF PARTICIPANTS WHO CORRECTLY RECOGNIZED A WORD, AS A FUNCTION OF ENCODING CONDITION AND RETRIEVAL CONDITION. BASED ON GEISELMAN AND GLENNY (1977).

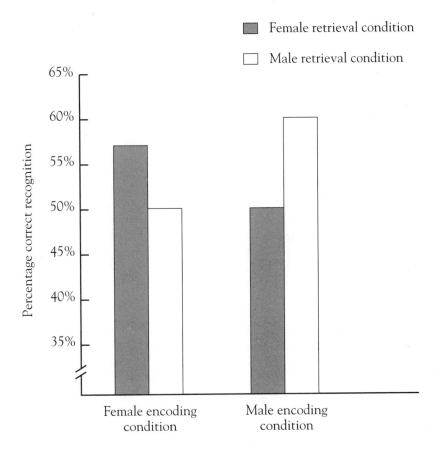

instructed to imagine a male voice. Later, recognition was tested by having a male or a female speaker say each word; the participants were instructed to indicate whether each word was old or new. For some people, the gender of the speaker matched the gender of the imagined voice; others had a mismatch between the encoding context and the retrieval context. As Figure 5.2 illustrates, recognition was substantially more likely when the contexts matched. This study also illustrates that "context" is not limited to physical locations; context can include other cues present during encoding and recall, such as a speaker's voice.

Everyone reading this book can readily recall real-life examples of the importance of context. Psychologists have also explained why context effects help us to function even more effectively in our daily lives. After all, we don't want to remember numerous details that were important in a previous context but are no longer relevant (Bjork & Bjork, 1988). For instance, you don't want your memory to be cluttered with details about your third-grade classroom or the class trip you took in high school.

However, we have a problem: Context effects are sometimes difficult to demonstrate reliably in the laboratory (Bjork & Richardson-Klavehn, 1987; Smith, 1988). An inspection of the 29 laboratory research studies on this topic found that 27 showed at least some evidence of context effects (Smith, 1988). However, psychologists have difficulty explaining why context effects may be important in one experiment (e.g., Smith et al., 1978), and yet context has absolutely no influence in a highly similar replication experiment (e.g., Bjork & Richardson-Klavehn, 1987).

One explanation for some of the inconsistencies is called the outshining hypothesis. This explanation is based on a principle from astronomy (Smith, 1988). Imagine that you are looking up in the sky on a moonless night, and you can just barely see a particular star. The star would be more difficult to see when the moon is full, and the star would be completely outshone by the sun in the daytime. Similarly, the *outshining hypothesis* proposes that context can trigger memory when better memory cues are absent; however, context can be completely outshone when other, better cues are present. In general, when the material to be recalled has been well learned, then the memory cues from that material should be strong enough to outshine the relatively weak context cues. When the material has *not* been well learned, context cues can help trigger memory (Smith, 1988). In short, context should be especially important when you have not yet mastered the material.

Other Illustrations of Context Effects. Let's consider two variations of the context-effects research that have practical implications. First, several psychologists have shown that the context in which human faces are observed can influence your ability to remember the faces (Davies, 1988). You can certainly remember occasions in which you have failed to recognize a classmate whom you see in a new setting.

The second variation is relevant to Chapter 6 on imagery. We can enhance memory by trying to *imagine* the context in which we originally encoded information (Smith, 1988). Have you ever tried to create a mental image of a page from a textbook, to help reconstruct the answer to a question on a test? Smith (1988) suggests an additional factor—in addition to the outshining hypothesis—to explain some of the inconsistencies in the research on context effects. Specifically, in the conditions where researchers do not reinstate the actual context cues, the participants may spontaneously reinstate their own imaginary versions. Sometimes you don't need to return to the bedroom to remember why you had departed for the kitchen; a mental image of the bedroom may trigger your memory.

In summary, then, memory is sometimes enhanced when the retrieval context resembles the encoding context, though the context effect may be outshone when stronger memory cues are present. Furthermore, the effects of context can be demonstrated for visual material such as human faces—as well as for verbal material—and also when context is created through mental imagery.

DEMONSTRATION 5.2

LISTS OF ITEMS

Take out a piece of paper and make three columns of numbers from 1 to 10. For the first set of numbers, list 10 colors in any order you wish. For the next set, list 10 desserts. Finally, list 10 professors from whom you have taken courses.

Now arrange each of the three lists in alphabetical order on a separate piece of paper, and set the original lists aside. Rank each item in the alphabetized list, with respect to the other members of the list. For example, give your favorite color a rank of 1 and your least favorite color a rank of 10. Finally, transfer each of those ranks back to the original list. At this point, each of the 10 items on each of the three lists should now have a rank next to it.

Mood

Try Demonstration 5.2 before you read farther. This demonstration illustrates one way in which mood or emotion can influence memory, through the emotional tone of the stimuli themselves. After examining this dimension of mood, we will discuss two topics that emphasize context. Specifically, memory is influenced by whether the emotional tone of the material matches your current mood. Furthermore, memory can be influenced by the match between your encoding mood and your retrieval mood.

Memory for Items Differing in Emotion. For nearly a century, psychologists have been interested in the way that emotional tone can influence memory (e.g., Hollingworth, 1910; Rychlak, 1994). In a typical study, people learn lists of words that are pleasant, neutral, or unpleasant. Then their recall is tested after a delay of several minutes to several months. In a review of the literature, we found that pleasant items are often recalled better than either negative or neutral items, particularly if the delay is long (Matlin & Stang, 1978). For example, in the 52 studies we located involving long-term memory, pleasant items were recalled significantly more accurately than unpleasant items in 39 of the studies. In a recent study, Walker and his colleagues (1996) reported a similar finding; people recalled pleasant events more accurately than unpleasant events.

We proposed that this selective recall of pleasant items is part of a more general Pollyanna Principle (Matlin & Stang, 1978). The ***Pollyanna Principle*** states that pleasant items are usually processed more efficiently and more accurately than less pleasant items. The principle holds true for a wide variety of phenomena in perception, language, and decision making.

Demonstration 5.2 illustrates another aspect of the Pollyanna Principle: We remember pleasant items *prior to* less pleasant items. Inspect your responses for Demonstration 5.2. Did you list the colors you like (those with ranks of 1, 2, and 3) prior to the colors you detest (those with ranks of 8, 9, and 10)? Are your favorite desserts first on the list? My colleagues and I found that when people made lists of fruits, vegetables, and professors, the pleasant items "tumbled out" of memory prior to neutral or unpleasant items (Matlin et al., 1979). For example, the correlation* between an item's pleasantness and its order in the list was + .87 for colors and + .69 for desserts; both of these correlations are highly significant.

Matlin and Stang (1978) proposed that pleasant items seem to be stored more accessibly in memory. As a result, they can be recalled quickly and accurately. The Pollyanna Principle is consistent with Theme 3 of this book: Positive information is processed more efficiently than negative information.

Mood Congruence. A second category of studies about mood and memory is called **mood congruence** or **mood congruity;** mood congruence means that memory is better when the material to be learned is congruent with a person's current mood (Bower, 1987, 1992). Thus, a person who is in a pleasant mood should remember pleasant material better than unpleasant material, whereas a person in an unpleasant mood should remember unpleasant material better.

As Blaney (1986) points out, psychologists have two major ways to examine mood congruence. One way is to study people who differ from each other in general mood. In these studies of individual differences, depressed people tend to recall more negative material (Gara et al., 1993; Gotlib, 1992; Haaga et al., 1991; Mineka & Sutton, 1992; Nasby, 1994; Ruiz-Caballero & González, 1994). These findings are important for clinical psychologists. If depressed people tend to forget the positive experiences they have had—recalling only the negative experiences—the depression could increase still further.

A second way to examine mood congruence is to manipulate people's moods—for example, by asking them to think about particularly happy or unhappy events from their past. Blaney (1986) reviewed 29 articles in which mood was experimentally induced. Of these articles, 25 demonstrated mood congruence, 3 showed no significant differences, and 1 showed mood *in*congruence in recall. Thus, mood has an important effect on memory for different kinds of material (Mayer, 1986).

Mood-State Dependence. According to **mood-state dependence,** your recall when you are in a particular mood depends partly on your mood when you originally learned the material. In this research, the emotional nature of the material doesn't matter. Instead, the important variable is whether the mood during encoding matches the mood during recall. Notice, then, that mood-state dependence is one

---

*A correlation is a statisical measure of the relationship between two variables, where .00 represents no relationship and +1.00 represents a strong positive relationship.

example of the encoding specificity principle, a concept we discussed at the beginning of the chapter.

The research on mood-state dependence is inconsistent (e.g., Blaney, 1986; Bower, 1987; Bower & Mayer, 1989), and mood-state dependence doesn't seem to be as reliable as mood congruence. Consider this study that *failed* to demonstrate mood-state dependence. Bower and Mayer (1985) hypnotized participants in their study. Then the participants were asked to recall either a happy or a sad event from their lives, thereby inducing either a happy or a sad mood. During this first mood state, the participants heard a list of English words. A second mood state (either happy or sad) was then induced, and participants heard a second list. After a break, a third mood state (again, either happy or sad) was induced, and the participants were instructed to recall the words from each of the lists.

If mood-state dependence were to operate successfully in this study, we would expect recall to be better when the mood during recall matched the mood during encoding. For example, a person who is happy during recall should remember more from the list encoded during a happy mood (rather than a sad mood). However, people in this study recalled 57% of material in the conditions where encoding matched recall mood and 56% in conditions where the moods did not match.

Fortunately, a new statistical technique allows us to draw conclusions where research results are inconsistent. The **meta-analysis technique** provides a statistical method for synthesizing numerous studies on a single topic. A meta-analysis can combine numerous previous studies into one enormous superstudy that can provide a general picture of the research. The increasing popularity of this technique can help us resolve some of the controversies in cognitive psychology.

Claudia Ucros (1989) conducted a meta-analysis on the research on mood-state dependence. She found a moderately strong relationship between matching mood states and amount of material recalled. Furthermore, a number of variables influenced the strength of that relationship. For example, mood-state dependence was especially likely to operate if the stimulus material was real-life events, rather than material such as sentences constructed by the researchers. Also, adults were more likely than children to show the effect. In ideal circumstances, the effects of mood-state dependence can be strong, but, like encoding specificity, it will not always operate.

IN DEPTH: Explicit Versus Implicit Measures of Memory

Imagine this scene. A young woman is walking aimlessly down the street, and she is eventually picked up by the police. She seems to be suffering from an extreme form of amnesia, because she has lost all memory of who she is. Unfortunately, she is carrying no identification. Then the police have a breakthrough idea—they ask her to begin dialing phone numbers. As it turns out, she dials her mother's number—though she is not aware whose number she is dialing.

Daniel Schacter tells this story to illustrate the difference between explicit and implicit measures of memory—a difference that can be demonstrated for people

DEMONSTRATION 5.3

EXPLICIT AND IMPLICIT MEMORY MEASURES

Take out a piece of scratch paper. Then read the following list of words:

picture commerce motion village vessel window number reindeer custom amount fellow advice dozen flower kitchen bookstore

Now cover up that list. Take a break for a few minutes and then try the following tasks:

A. Explicit Memory Measures
   1. Recall: On the piece of scratch paper, write down as many of those words as you can recall.

   2. Recognition: From the list below, circle the words that appeared on the original list:

woodpile fellow leaflet fitness number butter motion table people dozen napkin picture kitchen bookstore cradle advice

B. Implicit Memory Measures
   1. Word completion: From the word fragments below, provide an appropriate, complete word. You may choose any word you wish.

v_s_e_ l_t_e_ v_l_a_e p_a_t_c m_t_o_ m_n_a_ n_t_b_o_ c_m_e_c_ a_v_c_ t_b_e_ f_o_e_ c_r_o_ h_m_w_r_ b_o_s_o_e

   2. Repetition priming: Perform the following tasks:
      • Name three rooms in a typical house.
      • Name three items associated with Christmas.
      • Name three different kinds of stores.

with normal memory as well as for those who have amnesia (Adler, 1991). Let us clarify the basic concepts of this distinction and then look at some research.

Definitions and Examples. Demonstration 5.3 provides two examples of explicit memory measures and two examples of implicit memory measures. Try these examples before you read farther.

On ***explicit memory measures,*** the researcher instructs participants to remember information. Almost all the research we have discussed in Chapters 3, 4, and 5 has used explicit memory tests. The most common explicit memory measure is *recall,* in which the participant must reproduce items that have been learned earlier. Another explicit memory measure is *recognition,* in which the participant must identify which items on a list had appeared on a previous list.

In contrast, on *implicit memory measures,* the researcher asks participants to perform a perceptual task or a cognitive task (Schacter, 1992). The task typically seems unrelated to any previous material that has been learned, and words such as "remember" or "recall" are not mentioned (Roediger et al., 1992). In Schacter's anecdote about the woman with amnesia, dialing a phone number was a test of implicit memory. Implicit memory shows the effects of previous experience that creep out in our ongoing behavior, when we are not making a conscious effort to recall the past (Roediger, 1991).

Researchers have devised numerous measures of implicit memory; you tried two of these in Demonstration 5.3. If the words in the original list were stored in your memory, you would complete those words (for example, *commerce* and *village*) faster than words that had not been on the list (for example, *letter* and *plastic*). Furthermore, you would be likely to supply those words on a *repetition priming task,* in which a recent exposure to a word affects the likelihood that it will later come to mind, when you are given a cue that could evoke a number of different words. For example, on Task B2, you would be more likely to supply the words *kitchen, reindeer,* and *bookstore*—words you had seen at the beginning of the demonstration—than words you had not seen, such as *dining room, ornament,* and *drugstore*. So far, researchers have devised at least 25 different measures of implicit memory (Roediger et al., 1994).

One of the critical distinctions between explicit and implicit memory is that explicit memory tasks require conscious recollection of previous experiences (Graf & Schacter, 1985; Hirst, 1989). For example, you needed to make a conscious effort to remember the words on the original list in order to decide whether the word *fellow* had appeared there. In contrast, implicit memory tasks do not require conscious recollection of previous experiences. To complete the word *village* from the fragments, you did not need to recall having seen it on the original list. However, reading the word earlier enabled you to complete it rapidly, even if you were not able to recall it on the two explicit memory tasks.

You may recall that consciousness was discussed in Chapter 2 in connection with perceptual attention. In that chapter, we examined Nisbett and Wilson's (1977) argument that we often have little direct awareness of our thought processes. Lockhart (1989) points out that implicit memory may be the norm—especially if we include infants and nonhuman species. In contrast, explicit memory may be limited to some of the activities of the most highly evolved species.

Currently, implicit memory is one of the most heavily studied topics in research on memory (Greene, 1992; Mitchell, 1991). Psychologists are intrigued by paradoxes, and paradoxes are common when we compare performance on explicit and implicit memory tasks. For example, in some studies, amnesic patients perform disastrously on explicit memory tasks, but they score well on implicit memory tasks. In other studies involving people with normal memories, experimental variables have potent effects on explicit memory tests, but no effects (or even the opposite effect) on word-fragment tests or other measures of implicit memory (Schacter et al., 1989). Let's now consider the experimental research on explicit and implicit memory.

Research with Amnesic Patients. Some of the pioneering work on implicit memory in amnesics was conducted by Elizabeth Warrington and Lawrence Weiskrantz (1970). They examined four amnesics, one whose temporal lobe had been surgically removed and three with Korsakoff's syndrome, a disorder associated with severe alcoholism, which involves brain damage and amnesia. These researchers presented some English words and then gave the amnesics recall and recognition tasks. Compared to normal control group participants, the amnesics performed much poorer on both of these explicit memory tasks. So far, then, the results are not surprising.

Warrington and Weiskrantz (1970) also administered two implicit memory tasks. These were presented as word guessing games, though they actually assessed memory for words shown earlier. In one task, the previously presented English words were shown in a mutilated form that was difficult to read. Participants were told to guess which word was represented. Amazingly, the implicit memory scores of the amnesics and the control group participants were virtually identical; both groups correctly supplied the words from the previous list for about 45% of the mutilated stimuli. In the second implicit memory task, people saw the first few letters of a word, and they were instructed to produce the first word that came to mind. On this task, both groups correctly supplied the words from the previous list for about 65% of the word stems. These results have been replicated many times since the original research, with both visual and auditory tasks (e.g., MacLeod & Bassili, 1989; Roediger, 1990; Roediger et al., 1994; Schacter et al., 1994).

The research by Warrington and Weiskrantz (1970) is a good example of a concept called *dissociation*. A ***dissociation*** occurs when a variable has large effects on one kind of test, but little or no effects on another kind of test; a dissociation also occurs when a variable has one kind of effect if measured by Test A, and the opposite effect if measured by Test B (Roediger et al., 1989). Thus, the term, *dissociation* is similar to the concept of a statistical interaction, which you may already know from a course in statistics. In Warrington and Weiskrantz's data, the dissociation was evident because the variable of memory status (amnesic versus control) had a major effect when measured by explicit memory tests, but this same variable had no effect when measured by implicit memory tests.

Incidentally, you may wonder whether people with Alzheimer's disease may perform like people with amnesia. Unfortunately, they do not; these individuals show severe deficits on both explicit and implicit memory tests (Butters et al., 1990; Greene, 1992). Alzheimer's disease involves such pervasive cognitive problems that both forms of memory are affected.

The results on amnesics might have been dismissed as simply an interesting quirk, limited to a small number of people with a memory deficit. However, researchers then discovered similar dissociations in data collected on normal adults.

Research with Normal Adults. A variety of studies have demonstrated dissociations in adults who have no identified brain damage. For example, normal people may score higher on an explicit test when they had used deep levels of processing to learn the material, using semantic encoding rather than perceptual encoding. On an implicit test, however, semantic and perceptual encoding may produce similar memory scores, or people may even score higher with perceptual encoding (e.g., Jacoby, 1983; Schacter et al., 1993). These results demonstrate a dissociation because semantic encoding produces higher memory scores on Test A—compared to perceptual encoding—and similar (or lower) scores on Test B.

Let's look in more detail at an excellent example of dissociation, using normal college students. Mary Susan Weldon and Henry Roediger (1987) decided to examine a well-known phenomenon called the picture superiority effect. Research on the *picture superiority effect* shows that pictures are usually remembered better than words. In typical research, participants study either pictures that have obvious names (for example, a picture of an elephant) or names of concrete objects (for example, the word *elephant*). Later, they are asked to recall names of the items seen previously. They typically recall a significantly larger number of pictures than names.

Previous research had tested the picture superiority effect only with explicit memory measures, specifically, recall and recognition. What would happen if memory were assessed using implicit memory measures—in addition to explicit measures?

Weldon and Roediger (1987) showed students slides that contained either a simple black-on-white line drawing or the typed name of a concrete object. Later, the students either supplied recall (an explicit measure) or completed a word fragment, such as e_ep__n_ for the word *elephant* (an implicit measure). They were allowed 5 minutes for the recall task, and they were allowed to recall the words in any order they wished. For the word-fragment task, they were allowed 20 seconds for each item. They also completed word fragments for other, similar items that had not appeared on the slides, to provide a comparison with nonstudied items.

Figure 5.3 shows how recall depends upon the original method of processing. As you can see, the explicit memory task showed the usual picture superiority effect; participants recalled more of the items originally seen as pictures, rather than words. Notice, however, that the results are dramatically reversed for the implicit memory measure. On this word-fragment task, participants performed much better on the items originally seen as words, rather than pictures. In fact, their performance on the items originally seen as pictures was not much better than their performance on some items they had never seen before. In other words, Figure 5.3 clearly illustrates a dissociation, with different results for explicit memory measures than for implicit memory measures.

Roediger and his colleagues explain how these results resemble the encoding specificity principle examined at the beginning of this chapter (Roediger, 1990; Roediger et al., 1989). That is, test performance is better when the retrieval context is like the encoding context. These authors argue that when people saw a picture of an elephant, their encoding emphasized top-down processing, with the meaning of the elephant achieving special prominence. They argue that explicit

============================ FIGURE 5.3 ============================

**PERFORMANCE ON A RECALL TEST AND A WORD-COMPLETION TASK, AS A FUNC-
TION OF METHOD OF PRESENTATION (PICTURE OR NAME). BASED ON WELDON &
ROEDIGER (1987).**

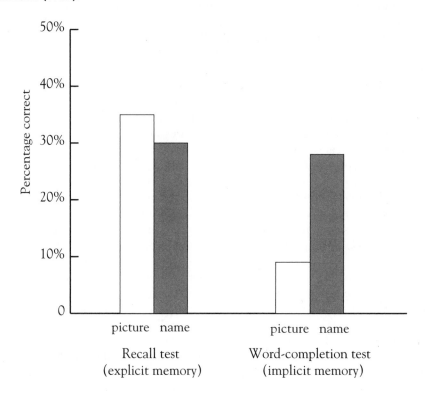

memory tests—such as free-recall tests—emphasize top-down processing. Therefore, performance is good because the retrieval conditions match the encoding
conditions. In contrast, when people saw the word *elephant,* they encoded the word
in terms of its letters (emphasizing bottom-up processing). Implicit memory tests—
such as a word-completion task—emphasize bottom-up processing. Once again,
performance is good because the two contexts match. However, you'll recall that
the encoding specificity principle states that retrieval is poor when the retrieval
context does not match the encoding context, and the data in Figure 5.3 certainly confirm this part of the principle. (Incidentally, subsequent research by
Church and Schacter, 1994, has confirmed the idea that explicit memory tests emphasize top-down processing, whereas implicit memory tasks emphasize bottom-up
processing.)

Current Status of Implicit Memory. The excitement about implicit memory is
still strong, as memory researchers explore these new ways of assessing memory.

One intriguing development is that patients who have been anesthetized during surgery show no evidence of memory for information transmitted under anesthesia when memory is assessed with explicit memory tasks. However, they do remember a substantial amount of information when memory is assessed with implicit memory tasks (Kihlstrom et al., 1990; Sebel et al., 1993).

Unfortunately, the theoretical explanation for implicit memory is not yet clear (Greene, 1992). Some psychologists emphasize context and the encoding specificity principle (e.g., Weldon & Roediger, 1987). Others propose that the results can best be explained in terms of multiple memory systems, such as Tulving's theory that we examined in Chapter 3 (e.g., Schacter, 1990b; Tulving & Schacter, 1990). Neuroscientists are currently working to establish the anatomical basis for implicit memory (Ostergaard & Jernigan, 1993; Paulsen, 1995).

Other researchers are trying to relate the new information about implicit memory to other areas, such as social psychology and developmental psychology (Roediger, 1990). Some have also speculated about the implications for education (Roediger, 1990). For example, educators may want to develop implicit memory tests—rather than explicit memory tests—to assess some forms of learning. Furthermore, researchers should examine how advertisers and the media influence our implicit memory and our actions when we buy products, vote for candidates, and make other decisions. The material on implicit memory has important implications for many disciplines within psychology because it illustrates that we often know more than we can reveal in actual recall.

Expertise

So far, we have examined how three important factors influence the amount of material people recall. We saw that memory performance is enhanced when the retrieval context resembles the encoding context. Memory performance is also influenced by the emotional tone of the material, by the match between the material and a person's mood, and by the match between the mood during learning and the mood during recall. We also saw that the advantage of matching contexts applies in both explicit and implicit memory tasks.

Expertise is a fourth factor that influences long-term memory. *Expertise* is defined as consistently superior performance on a set of tasks for a domain, achieved by deliberate practice over a period of at least 10 years (Ericsson & Lehmann, 1996). Once again, context plays an important role, though the nature of its role is different. Let's first consider how this expertise is context-specific. Next we'll consider two areas of specific memory expertise as we examine a waiter's memory and memory skills displayed by professional actors. Then we'll examine some of the ways in which experts and novices differ. Our final topic will examine how people can accurately identify individuals from their own ethnic background.

The Context-Specific Nature of Expertise. Interestingly, people who are expert in one area seldom display outstanding general memory skills (Ericsson &

Pennington, 1993; Ericsson & Smith, 1991a). For example, chess masters are outstanding in their memory for chess positions, but they do not differ from control subjects in their basic cognitive and perceptual abilities (Cranberg & Albert, 1988). Furthermore, men who are experts in remembering information at the horse races do not score especially high on standard IQ tests. For instance, one horse-race expert had an eighth-grade education and an IQ of 92 (Ceci & Liker, 1986). In other research, Bellezza and Buck (1988) found that experts in football scored high on a test of recall for a passage about a football game, whereas experts in knowledge about clothing scored high on a test of recall for a passage about clothing. Both groups' recall was low for the areas in which they were not expert. Incidentally, in Chapter 10, we'll see how this memory for specific areas of knowledge helps chess players.

An Expert Waiter. Let's now consider a classic case study of expertise, an expert restaurant waiter examined by K. Anders Ericsson (1985). This waiter, known by the initials J.C., was able to memorize up to 20 complete dinner orders in a typical restaurant situation. In a laboratory setting, Ericsson re-created the restaurant task by pairing a picture of a face with a dinner order, which could contain one of eight meat entrees, one of five meat temperatures (rare to well-done), one of five salad dressings, and one of three side dishes. In other words, there were 600 possible dinner orders! On this laboratory task, J.C. required dramatically less time to study the orders than did the college students who also participated in the study. Furthermore, J.C. made virtually no errors in recalling the orders for tables of three, five, and eight customers. A critical difference, too, was the difference in memory strategy between J.C. and the college students. Students tended to store the orders as a list and to recall the orders in the same order in which they had been presented. In contrast, J.C. recalled all information from one category together, usually using a memory strategy. For example, he recalled all salad dressings together, encoding them in terms of the first letters of their names (for example, Bleu cheese, Oil-and-vinegar, Oil-and-vinegar, Thousand Island became BOOT). Clearly, J.C.'s memory qualifies as a very specific kind of expertise.

Professional Actors. Have you ever watched an actor in a play, delivering an entire monologue flawlessly . . . and felt embarrassed that you can't even remember the first verse of "The Star-Spangled Banner" . . . or "O Canada"? Helga Noice (1992) began her investigation of expertise by asking seven professional actors to describe how they learned a theatrical script. All of them agreed that they specifically avoided rote memorization. Instead, they read the script numerous times, trying to determine the motivation for each line: Why did the character say those exact words? As one actor commented about memorization strategies, "What was the impulse that created the thought that created the words?" (Noice, 1992, p. 421).

In a follow-up study, Noice (1993) found that this kind of deep processing produces significantly greater verbatim recall than the strategy of simply repeating the lines, using rote rehearsal. She also discovered that professional actors are more likely than novices to try to relate their passage to earlier material in the play.

How Do Experts and Novices Differ? From the information we've discussed, as well as from other resources, we know that experts have several advantages over nonexperts (Bellezza, 1992b; Cohen, 1989; Ericsson, 1988; Ericsson & Kintsch, 1995; Ericsson & Lehmann, 1996; Ericsson & Pennington, 1993; Ericsson & Smith, 1991a; Intons-Peterson & Smyth, 1987). Let's consider these advantages:

1. Experts possess a well-organized, carefully learned knowledge structure. This may be stored in ***long-term working memory,*** which is a stable body of information that can be easily accessed via retrieval cues from "regular," short-term working memory.
2. Experts typically have more vivid visual images for the items they must recall. If you know more about clothing than football, you can visualize an epaulet better than a scrimmage.
3. Experts can rapidly access their knowledge, whereas novices require more time.
4. Experts are more likely to reorganize the material they must recall, forming meaningful chunks that group related material together. In contrast, those of us with no experience in remembering restaurant orders would be unlikely to regroup the customers' orders so that salad dressings were separate from side dishes.
5. Experts rehearse in a different fashion. For example, an actor may rehearse his or her lines by focusing on words that are likely to trigger recall.
6. Experts are better at reconstructing missing portions of information from material that is partially remembered.

Throughout this book, we have emphasized that our cognitive processes are active, efficient, and accurate (Theme 2). Our cognitive processes also employ top-down as well as bottom-up strategies (Theme 5). As we have seen in this list, each of these characteristics is even more elaborately developed for someone with memory expertise in a given area.

Own-Race Bias. The information on expertise has a practical application for eyewitness testimony, a topic we will examine more thoroughly in the next section. Specifically, people are more accurate in identifying members of their own ethnic group than members of another ethnic group, a phenomenon called ***own-race bias*** (Brigham & Malpass, 1985; Ng & Lindsay, 1994; O'Toole et al., 1994). This effect is also known as the *other-race* effect or the *cross-race* effect.

For example, reviews of the literature show that both Black and White individuals were substantially more accurate in recognizing faces of people of their own ethnic group (Anthony et al., 1992; Bothwell et al., 1989). Similar findings were reported for White and Asian individuals (Ng & Lindsay, 1994). In some cases, the own-race bias is somewhat decreased when people have greater contact with members of the other ethnic group (Brigham & Malpass, 1985). Thus, we might expect that a White college student with many Black friends will develop expertise in recognizing the facial features of Black individuals.

SECTION SUMMARY: DETERMINANTS OF ACCURACY

1. Long-term memory can store an impressive amount of material for an impressive length of time; research on very long-term memory or permastore shows that retention can be excellent, even more than a decade after the material was originally learned.
2. Context is relevant in many of the mechanisms by which various factors influence long-term memory. For example, the encoding specificity principle states that recall is better if the retrieval context resembles the encoding context. The encoding specificity principle often operates, but it is reduced when better cues than context are available.
3. In general, people recall pleasant material more accurately than less pleasant material. People also recall material more accurately when that material is consistent with their mood (mood congruence). Although exceptions often occur, people also tend to remember material better if their mood during encoding matches their mood during recall.
4. Explicit memory tasks instruct participants to remember information, whereas implicit memory tasks ask participants to perform a perceptual or cognitive task. Amnesics perform worse than people with intact memories on explicit memory tasks, but similarly on implicit memory tasks. Also, research with normal college students shows that pictures are remembered better than words on explicit memory tasks, but the reverse is true for implicit memory tasks. The data can be interpreted in light of the encoding specificity principle.
5. Expertise has an important effect on long-term memory, although expertise is context-specific. Research on memory expertise shows that experts have advantages such as well-organized knowledge structure, vivid visual images, rapid access to knowledge, reorganizing during learning, rehearsal strategies, and reconstruction. The own-race bias is one important example of the effects of expertise.

AUTOBIOGRAPHICAL MEMORY

Autobiographical memory is memory for events and issues related to yourself (Conway & Rubin, 1993). In general, the research on autobiographical or *everyday memory* examines recall for naturally occurring events that happen outside the laboratory. Your autobiographical memory is a vital part of your identity, shaping your personal history and your sense of who you are (Robinson, 1992).

Interest in autobiographical memory has grown rapidly during the last 20 years (Herrmann & Gruneberg, 1993; Robinson, 1992). A glance through some of the recent studies in this area suggests the wide variety of topics within autobiographical memory: estimating the dates of personal events, academic lectures, and recent political events (Brown, 1990; Friedman, 1993; Rubin & Baddeley, 1989; Thompson et al., 1993; Thompson et al., 1996); recognizing faces at a 25th high school reunion (Bruck et al., 1991); remembering grades from college courses (Bahrick et al., 1993); professors' memory for students' names (Seamon & Travis, 1993); women students' recall of their first menstrual period (Pillemer et al., 1987); and recall for comments focusing on sexual activity (Pezdek & Prull, 1993).

In this section on autobiographical memory, we'll first examine especially vivid memories and then see how autobiographical memories can become schematized when they are not especially vivid. We'll then see what kinds of errors occur when we are trying to remember to do something. The next section focuses on eyewitness testimony, a topic that has obvious applications in the courtroom. Our final topic concerns the debate about ecological validity and the value of research on autobiographical memory.

Several important themes are interwoven throughout this material on autobiographical memory:

1. Although we sometimes make errors, memory is typically accurate across many different situations (Theme 2). In a typical study on memory accuracy, Howes and Katz (1992) found that middle-aged adults showed accurate recall for public events 98% of the time.
2. When people do make mistakes, they generally concern peripheral details and specific information about commonplace events, rather than central information about important events (Johnson & Sherman, 1990; Schacter, 1995).
3. When new information is added about an event, our memories often blend together information, actively constructing a new representation of that event—as Theme 1 emphasizes (Kihlstrom & Barnhardt, 1993; Ross & Buehler, 1994).

Flashbulb Memories

At some point in the near future, try Demonstration 5.4 on flashbulb memory. *Flashbulb memory* is the memory for the situation in which you first learned of a very surprising and emotionally arousing event (Brown & Kulik, 1977).

DEMONSTRATION 5.4

FLASHBULB MEMORY

Ask several acquaintances whether they can identify any memories of a very surprising event. Tell them, for example, that many people can recall in vivid detail the circumstances in which they learned about the death of President Kennedy, the fall of the Berlin Wall, the *Challenger* disaster, or the verdict in the O. J. Simpson criminal trial. Also tell them that other vivid memories focus on more personal important events. Ask them to tell you about one or more memories, particularly noting any small details that they recall.

My clearest flashbulb memory, like many of my generation, is of learning that President John Kennedy had been shot. I was a sophomore at Stanford University, just ready for a midday class in German. I had entered the classroom from the right, and I was just about to sit down at a long table on the right-hand side of the classroom. The sun was streaming in from the left. There was only one other person seated in the classroom, a blond fellow named Dewey. He turned around and said, "Did you hear that President Kennedy has been shot?" I also recall my reaction and the reactions of others as they entered the class. Kennedy was shot more than 30 years ago, yet trivial details of that news are stunningly clear to many today. You can probably think of personal events in your own life that triggered flashbulb memories—the death of a relative, a piece of important good news, or an amazing surprise.

The Classic Research. In the first description of this controversial topic, Roger Brown and James Kulik (1977) pointed out that these flashbulb memories are definitely not as accurate as a photograph in which a true flashbulb has been fired. For example, I don't remember what books I was carrying or what Dewey was wearing. Nonetheless, flashbulb memories do include details that would be missing from the memory of a neutral event from the same period.

To examine flashbulb memories, Brown and Kulik questioned people to see whether various national events triggered these memories. Six kinds of information were most likely to be listed in these flashbulb memories: the place, the ongoing event that was interrupted by the news, the person who gave them the news, their own feelings, the emotions in others, and the aftermath. Check the responses to Demonstration 5.4 to see if these items were included in the recall.

Brown and Kulik concluded that the two main determinants of flashbulb memory were a high level of surprise and a high level of emotional arousal or perceived importance. These authors also proposed that these surprising, arousing events were more likely to be rehearsed, either silently or in conversation. Consequently, the memory of these events is more elaborate than that of more ordinary daily events.

These vivid memories may capture highly positive as well as tragic events. For example, an Indian friend of mine recalls in detail the circumstances in which Mohandas Gandhi, the nonviolent political leader, spoke to a crowd of people in Gauhati, India. My friend was only 5 years old, yet he vividly recalls Gandhi, wearing a white outfit and accompanied by two women. He can recall that his aunt, who was with him, was wearing a white sari with a gold and red border, and he can distinctly remember how the heat of the day had made him very thirsty. Rubin and Kozin (1984) studied similar vivid memories for events in people's lives. These vivid memories had to meet the criteria of being clear and detailed, and almost lifelike, in order to be included in the study. However, they were not required to be caused by surprising or consequential events. The participants in this study were asked to describe the three clearest memories from their past.

What kind of events did people supply? Of these memories, 18% concerned injuries or accidents to the participants or their friends. Other frequent categories included sports, love relationships, animals, and events from the first week of college. Interestingly, however, only 3% of the events were judged to have any national importance. In general, people reported that their vivid memories were consequential and surprising, and they also reported rehearsing the memories frequently. Rubin and Kozin conclude that almost all important autobiographical memories have flashbulb-like clarity immediately after they occur. However, flashbulb memories and vivid memories—which may really be equivalent—maintain this clarity for a longer time than more ordinary memories, because they are rehearsed more often.

More Recent Research. Most of the research conducted during the late 1980s and the 1990s has focused on whether these memories are somehow special. Alternately, do they simply represent the more impressive end of normal memory? In a typical study, Weaver (1993) found that students in the United States had similarly vivid memories for President Bush's decision to bomb Iraq and for a much less important event, meeting a friend. However, as Conway (1995) points out, Weaver did not obtain measures on the "surprisingness" of the bombing; perhaps the bombing was not sufficiently surprising to qualify as a flashbulb memory. Conway's own research, in contrast, showed that British students had very clear memories for the unexpected resignation of the British prime minister, Margaret Thatcher (Conway et al., 1994).

Conway is perhaps one of the strongest supporters of the "pro-flashbulb memory" viewpoint. In a book on flashbulb memory, he argues that true flashbulb memories are most likely to be formed when an event is surprising, important, and emotional, and when that event has important consequences for the individual (Conway, 1995).

However, Conway seems to be in the minority. For example, Neisser and Harsch (1992) argue that people made too many errors in recalling details about the *Challenger* disaster; memories for important events like this do not seem to be unusually strong. Indeed, people do *claim* that their memories for these events are very vivid and accurate, but in fact the memories are far from perfect (Brewer, 1992; McCloskey, 1992; Weaver, 1993).

Future research will have to demonstrate more consistently that the events being tested are indeed surprising, important, emotional, and consequential. At present, however, the skeptical, "anti-flashbulb memory" position seems more justified. As McCloskey and his colleagues (1988) conclude, "flashbulb memories are neither uniformly accurate nor immune to forgetting" (p. 177). The ordinary mechanisms, which serve us well in our everyday life (Theme 2), are powerful enough to produce even more accurate (though not perfect) recall when we experience a surprising event of great importance.

Schemas and Autobiographical Memory

Whereas the section of flashbulb memories emphasized memory for unusually important events, this section on schemas emphasizes memory for common, ordinary

---

DEMONSTRATION 5.5

THE SCHEMATIZATION OF MEMORY

Describe what you ate for lunch exactly one week ago. Also note where you sat and with whom you ate. What time did you eat lunch? What did you carry with you to lunch? What foods did you finish, and what did you leave on your plate? What did you talk about?

---

events. Try Demonstration 5.5 on memory schemas before you read farther. A *schema* is our general knowledge about an object or an event that has been acquired from past experience (Cohen, 1989). Schemas are abstracted from a large number of specific examples of events in our lives, and these schemas summarize the important characteristics contained in the events. For example, you have probably developed a schema for "eating lunch." You tend to sit in a particular area with a constant group of people. Conversation topics may also be reasonably standardized.

As Barclay (1986) writes, you notice common features through repeated exposure to similar kinds of activities. Thus, for autobiographical material, schemas lead to the organized storage in memory of everyday information about yourself. Typically, memory capacity limitations prevent us from remembering precise details about our daily life (Did that green salad contain carrot shreds?). However, schemas allow us to process large amounts of material because we can summarize the regularities in our lives. After some time, any single event is not distinguishable from other, similar events. Therefore, when you were asked to recall the details of last week's lunch, you probably reconstructed a plausible, "generic" memory based on many similar events.

The concept of schemas also suggests that we may mistakenly "recall" events that never really happened, as long as they are conceptually similar to the schemas we have developed. Furthermore, the generic aspects of events may become blended as time passes, particularly because you continue to experience similar events. Inaccuracy should also increase as time passes. Neisser (1988) calls this kind of inaccuracy *repisodic memory* (note the pun with *episodic memory*), meaning the recall of a supposed event that is really the blending of details over repeated and related episodes. The schematization of memory is an example of Theme 1 of the book: The cognitive processes actively reshape and categorize our memories. It also illustrates part of Theme 2 of this book: Errors in cognitive processing can often be traced to logical strategies, such as mistakenly recalling an event similar to one that had actually happened.

Craig Barclay and his colleagues have provided research evidence for the importance of schemas in memory (Barclay, 1986; Barclay & Wellman, 1986). Three students kept records of memorable daily events for a period of 4 months. Then, 2 ½ years later, they were asked to read an item and decide whether it was exactly what they had originally written or an item that was unfamiliar. The students correctly recognized about 85% of the original items, a testimony to their accuracy. However, they also said that they recognized about 50% of the items that were actually schematic versions, rather than the true originals. For example, a student originally wrote:

> I went shopping downtown looking for an anniversary present for my parents but couldn't find a thing. I get so frustrated when I can't find what I want.

About half the time, this same student might say, "Yes, I recognize it" to a version that read:

> I went shopping downtown. I must have gone to 10 stores before giving up and going home. I get so frustrated when I can't find what I want.

This research illustrates that our general schemas for events in memory are likely to provoke "false alarms" reasonably often. That is, we are likely to think we recognize something that is really not familiar. However, we are persuaded because it matches quite nicely our more generalized schema. Perhaps one reason that our flashbulb memories seem so vivid is that each of these memories is unique and unrepeated, in sharp contrast to the more pedestrian, generic quality of the more abundant memory schemas. Incidentally, Chapter 7 will examine schemas in more detail.

Memory for Action

In the section on memory schemas, we saw that people can mistakenly "recall" events that never really happened, if they resemble the schema for similar events. In this section, we will see that people can mistakenly "recall" events that never really happened, as long as they *imagined* a similar event.

Something like this has certainly happened to you: You borrowed a book from a friend, and you distinctly remember returning it to him or her. However, the next day, you find that the book is still on your desk. Apparently, you simply imagined returning the book. This process of trying to discriminate between memories of real and imagined events is called *reality monitoring* (Johnson, 1988; Johnson et al., 1994). This section on memory for action examines two issues: (1) reality monitoring, or memory about actions that have been performed in the past, and (2) remembering to do actions in the future.

Reality Monitoring. We should be able to distinguish quite readily between real actions that are derived from perception and imagined actions—ones we generated only in our thoughts. For example, it should be easy to tell the difference between giving a book to a friend and merely *thinking* that you gave the book to a friend. In truth, however, this decision is often difficult. For example, Anderson (1984) found that people had trouble remembering whether they had really traced a pen along a specified outline, or whether they had simply imagined themselves doing so. Similarly, Buehler and Ross (1993) found that people had trouble remembering whether or not they had actually made particular statements.

How do we make decisions about whether an action is real or imagined? According to Marcia Johnson, we use two processes (Johnson, 1995; Johnson et al., 1993; Johnson & Raye, 1981). The first process involves a quick rule of thumb. We decide that an event really happened if the memory we are judging is rich in perceptual detail and if it requires little cognitive effort to reconstruct that memory. In contrast, we decide that we merely imagined performing the action if the memory lacks perceptual details and if reconstruction requires great cognitive effort.

Consider the following example, which illustrates this first process. You are trying to recall whether you took an antibiotic that was prescribed for an illness. You examine your memory and realize that you can readily "see" the pill in your hand and "feel" the glass of water at your lips. The memory is rich with perceptual detail, and that memory came readily to mind—without any of the cognitive effort that would have been necessary to construct an imagined experience. As a consequence, you conclude that, yes, you really *did* take the pill.

The first decision-making process is rapid, but the second process is much more leisurely. During this second process, you retrieve additional knowledge to help you decide whether the action occurred. For example, you might realize that you couldn't have told a friend a story about your skiing trip because he had left for his brother's wedding before you returned.

According to Johnson and her colleagues, these two processes act as potential checks on each other. As a consequence, we usually make a correct decision about whether we performed an action. As you'll notice, Johnson's approach offers support for Theme 4, that the cognitive processes are interrelated. In fact, memory requires a substantial amount of decision making, a cognitive process we will explore in more detail in Chapter 11.

Prospective Memory. Some time today, try Demonstration 5.6, which involves *prospective memory,* or remembering to do things. Prospective memory requires memory for intentions; we must remember that we want to perform some action in the future (Morris, 1992). Throughout this textbook's four chapters on memory, the major focus is on *retrospective memory,* or recalling information that has been previously learned. Prospective memory is studied much less often, but most people rank prospective memory errors among the most embarrassing of memory lapses (Morris, 1992) and also among the most common (Pollina et al., 1992; Sellen, 1994).

Some typical prospective memory tasks might include remembering to pick up a friend at work, to mail a letter, to let the dog out before you leave the house, and to keep your office-hour appointment with a professor. In many cases, the primary

---

DEMONSTRATION 5.6

REMEMBERING TO DO THINGS

Take 10 index cards and hand them out to 10 acquaintances. Instruct five of the acquaintances to return the cards to you tomorrow at approximately the same time of day. (You may want to specify that they can return the cards by slipping them under your door, noting the time at which they do so.) Instruct the other five to return the cards 7 days from now, at approximately the same time. In each case, make note of the number who successfully return the cards on time. You may also wish to question them about the memory strategies they used.

---

challenge is to remember to perform an action in the future. However, sometimes the primary challenge is to remember the content of that action. You've probably experienced the feeling that you are supposed to do something, but you cannot remember *what* it was (Koriat et al., 1990).

One intriguing component of prospective memory is absentmindedness (e.g., Reason, 1984; Reason & Mycielska, 1982; Sellen, 1994). Most people do not publicly reveal their slips. So you may want to read some of the publications on this topic if you feel that you are the only person who gets into bed with your slippers on, who dials Chris's phone number when you want to speak to Alex, or forgets why you walked from one room in your house to another.

Absentminded behavior is especially likely when the action requires disrupting the customary schema surrounding an action (Morris, 1992). These slips are more likely in highly familiar surroundings when you are performing tasks automatically. Slips are also more likely if you are preoccupied, distracted, or feeling time pressure. In most cases, absentmindedness is simply irritating. However, sometimes these slips can produce an airplane collision, such as the disastrous Tenerife accident of 1977, or the nuclear accident at Three Mile Island in 1979.

Most of the research on prospective memory involves laboratory research that is designed to be naturalistic. In a representative study, students received eight postcards to mail back to the experimenter, one a week for 8 weeks (Meacham, 1982; Meacham & Singer, 1977). Some students were instructed to mail them once a week on a specified different day of each week, whereas others were instructed to mail them every Wednesday. Furthermore, some students were told that they would receive up to $5.00 payment for conscientiously mailing the cards; others received no payment. Meacham and Singer found that people in the "every Wednesday" condition were no more likely to mail the cards than those in the random-day condition. However, monetary reward was an effective motivator. The average participant in the paid condition returned only 1.4 cards late, in contrast to 2.1 late cards in the unpaid condition.

In this section, we have examined memory for your own actions, either for past events or future events. Now let us turn to memory for other people's actions, specifically eyewitness testimony.

Eyewitness Testimony

In 1979, a Catholic priest awaited trial for several armed robberies in Delaware. Seven witnesses had identified him as the "gentleman bandit," referring to the robber's polite manners and elegant clothes. During the trial, many witnesses identified the priest as the one who had committed the robberies. Suddenly, however, the trial was halted; another man had confessed to the robberies (Loftus & Ketcham, 1991).

Reports like this one have led psychologists to question the reliability of eyewitness testimony. However, in close to 80,000 cases each year in the United States, the only critical evidence against a person who has been arrested is eyewitness identification (Goldstein et al., 1989). By some estimates, between 2,000 and 10,000 people are wrongfully convicted each year in the United States on the basis of faulty eyewitness testimony (Cutler & Penrod, 1995; Fruzzetti et al., 1992; Loftus & Ketcham, 1991).

Throughout our discussion of memory, we have emphasized that human memory is reasonably accurate, but it is not flawless. Eyewitness testimonies, like other memories, are generally accurate, but the reports can contain errors (Schacter, 1995). Similar to other kinds of memory, eyewitness testimony can be influenced by pre-existing schemas (List, 1986). When eyewitness testimony is inaccurate, the wrong person may go to jail or—in the worst cases—be put to death (Loftus & Ketcham, 1991). Let us consider how inaccuracies can arise when people identify faces, when they are given misleading information after the event that they had witnessed, and when they create false memories for events that never occurred.

Identifying Faces. Think about the factors that might influence how accurate you would be in identifying faces in an eyewitness situation. Fortunately, we have extensive information on this topic. For example, Shapiro and Penrod (1986) located 128 research studies about facial recognition, which involved 960 experimental conditions and a total of 16,950 participants. With the data from these studies, they conducted a meta-analysis, the statistical analysis we discussed earlier. This meta-analysis confirmed the own-race bias that we mentioned in connection with expertise; people indeed remember faces better when those faces are of their own race. Let us discuss other factors that influence identification accuracy, based on Shapiro and Penrod's analysis as well as other research.

In general, as you might expect, identification accuracy is better when people devote greater time and attention to looking at the face (Ellis, 1984; Shapiro & Penrod, 1986). Furthermore, people are less accurate when something distracts attention away from the face. For example, if a robber is holding a gun, eyewitnesses are likely to focus on the gun rather than the details of the robber's face (Cutler et al., 1987; Egeth, 1994; Ellis, 1984).

The length of the retention interval also influences facial recognition (Fruzzetti et al., 1992; Shapiro & Penrod, 1986). Still, as Ellis (1984) concludes, "delay intervals even as long as weeks or months do not automatically reduce recognition accuracy" (p. 25). However, accuracy is substantially reduced if pictures of other faces—such as misleading composite faces—are shown during the delay interval (Davies & Jenkins, 1985; Jenkins & Davies, 1985). Obviously, all these factors that influence the accuracy of facial identification have important practical implications in the courtroom.

Misleading Post-Event Information. Errors in eyewitness testimony can arise not only from misleading pictures of faces, but also from misleading information. According to the ***misinformation effect,*** people may make errors in an eyewitness account if they are given misleading information after viewing an event (Weingardt et al., 1995).

In Chapter 4, we discussed ***proactive inhibition,*** which means that people have trouble recalling new material because previously learned material keeps interfering with new memories. The misinformation effect resembles another kind of interference called retroactive inhibition (Titcomb & Reyna, 1995). In ***retroactive inhibition,*** people have trouble recalling old material because recently learned, new material keeps interfering with old memories. For example, a witness may be unable to accurately recall a detail from the scene of a crime because the lawyer supplied some incorrect information during a question several minutes earlier.

In the classic experiment on the misinformation effect, Loftus and her coauthors (1978) showed participants a series of slides. In this sequence, a sports car stopped at an intersection, and then it turned and hit a pedestrian. Half the participants saw a slide with a yield sign at the intersection; the other half saw a stop sign. Twenty minutes to 1 week after the slides had been shown, the participants answered questions about the details of the accident. A critical question contained information that was either consistent or inconsistent with a detail in the original slide series, or else did not mention the detail. For example, some people who had seen the yield sign were asked, "Did another car pass the red Datsun while it was stopped at the yield sign?" (consistent). Other people were asked, "Did another car pass the red Datsun while it was stopped at the stop sign?" (inconsistent). For still other people, the sign was not mentioned (neutral). The participants were shown two slides, one with a stop sign and one with a yield sign. They were asked to select which slide they had previously seen.

As Figure 5.4 shows, people who saw the inconsistent information were much less accurate than people in the other two conditions. Their selections were based on the information in the questionnaire, rather than the original slide. Several studies have replicated the detrimental effects of misleading post-event information (e.g., Cutler & Penrod, 1995; Garry & Loftus, 1994; Lindsay, 1990; Loftus, 1992; Weingardt et al., 1995).

Interestingly, participants are often as confident about the accuracy of these new memories as they are about their genuinely correct memories (Cutler & Penrod, 1995; Fruzzetti et al., 1992; Loftus et al., 1989; Loftus & Hoffman, 1989). However,

=== FIGURE 5.4 ===

THE EFFECT OF TYPE OF INFORMATION AND DELAY ON PROPORTION OF CORRECT ANSWERS. LOFTUS ET AL. (1978).

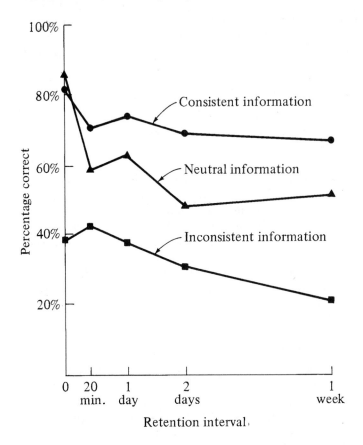

the descriptions of these two kinds of memory are actually somewhat different. Schooler and his coauthors (1986) asked the participants in their study to describe in detail what they had seen in a previous series of slides. Those who had actually seen a stop sign were likely to emphasize perceptual details of the scene; these details were rarely mentioned by those who had been told misleading information about the stop sign.

Notice that these findings are consistent with Marcia Johnson's (1995) explanation of reality monitoring. If an event really happened, the scene is more likely to have rich perceptual detail than if we had merely imagined the event. Jurors in a court case who are trying to decide whether an eyewitness really saw an event should base their decision on the level of perceptual detail, rather than the level of the eyewitness's confidence about the memory.

DEMONSTRATION 5.7

REMEMBERING LISTS OF WORDS

For this demonstration, you must learn and recall two lists of words. Before beginning, take out two pieces of paper. Next, read List 1, then close the book and try to write down as many of the words as possible. Then do the same for List 2. After you have recalled both sets of words, check your accuracy. How many items did you correctly recall?

List 1	*List 2*
bed	water
rest	stream
awake	lake
tired	Mississippi
dream	boat
wake	tide
snooze	swim
blanket	flow
doze	run
slumber	barge
snore	creek
nap	brook
peace	fish
yawn	bridge
drowsy	winding

The information on the misinformation effect emphasizes the active, constructive nature of memory. As Theme 1 points out, cognitive processes are active, rather than passive. The **constructivist approach** to memory argues that "recollections change as people revise the past to satisfy their present concerns and reflect their current knowledge" (Ross & Buehler, 1994, p. 207). In short, memory does not consist of a list of facts, all stored in intact form; instead, memory combines, blends, and replaces the information we have stored about events we have witnessed (Kihlstrom & Barnhardt, 1993).

The False Memory Controversy. If you scan popular magazines such as *Newsweek, People,* and *Ms. Magazine,* you seldom come across articles on iconic memory, the encoding specificity principle, or reality monitoring. However, one topic from cognitive psychology *has* become popular—the issue of false memory. Before you read farther, be sure that you have tried Demonstration 5.7.

Most of the discussion about false memory focuses on child sexual abuse. According to one group of researchers, many individuals who experienced sexual abuse during childhood managed to repress that memory for many years. *Repressed memory* means that a person presumably excluded a painful experience from consciousness (Briere & Conte, 1993; Ceci & Loftus, 1994). At a later time, often prompted by a specific event or by encouragement from a therapist, this presumably repressed memory comes flooding back into consciousness.

A second group of researchers interprets phenomena like this in a different light. We must emphasize that this second group does *not* deny that child sexual abuse often occurs. Instead, they deny the accuracy of many reports that individuals supply about repressed memory and the sudden recovery of those early memories. Specifically, they argue that many of these recovered memories are actually *false memories,* or constructed stories about events that never occurred (Loftus, 1993a; Loftus & Ketcham, 1994; Pressley & Grossman, 1994). These researchers also argue that repression is a psychodynamic concept for which we have no empirical evidence.

Our discussion throughout this section on autobiographical memory should convince you that memory is less than perfect. For example, people cannot recall with absolute accuracy whether they performed an action or merely imagined performing it. People also cannot consistently remember to do something. We also saw that eyewitness testimony can be flawed, especially when misinformation has been provided. Similar problems arise in recalling memories from childhood. For instance, some psychotherapists provide suggestions that could easily be blended with reality to create a false memory (Lindsay & Read, 1994). For example, one therapist typically approached clients with the following comment, "You know, in my experience, a lot of people who are struggling with many of the same problems you are, have often had some kind of really painful things happen to them as kids—maybe they were beaten or molested. And I wonder if anything like this ever happened to you?" (Forward & Buck, 1988, p. 161). As you can imagine, this statement invites the client to invent a false memory.

We cannot easily determine whether or not a memory of childhood abuse is correct. After all, the situation is far from controlled, and other, independent witnesses can rarely be found (Schooler, 1994). Research is much more straightforward when people are simply asked to remember a list of words, and accuracy can be objectively measured. For example, Demonstration 5.7 asked you to memorize and recall a list of words, and then you checked your accuracy. Take a moment now to check something else. On List 1, did you write down the word *sleep?* Did you write *river* on List 2? If you check the textbook, you'll discover that neither word was listed. In research with lists of words like these, Roediger and McDermott (1995) found a false recall rate of 55%; people created false memories of words that did not appear on the lists. Intrusions are common on these lists because each word that *does* appear on a list is commonly associated with the missing word. Similar intrusions could occur with respect to childhood memories. People may falsely recall events related to their actual experiences. (Before you read further, try Demonstration 5.8.)

In reality, both the "repressed memory" and the "false memory" positions are probably at least partially correct (Schooler, 1994). Indeed, memories of traumatic

DEMONSTRATION 5.8

INSTRUCTIONS AND MEMORY

Learn the following list of pairs by repeating the members of each pair several times. For example, if the pair is CAT–WINDOW, say over and over to yourself, "CAT–WINDOW, CAT–WINDOW, CAT–WINDOW." Just repeat the words, and do not use any other study method. Allow yourself one minute for this list.

CUSTARD–LUMBER   IVY–MOTHER
JAIL–CLOWN   LIZARD–PAPER
ENVELOPE–SLIPPER   SCISSORS–BEAR
SHEEPSKIN–CANDLE   CANDY–MOUNTAIN
FRECKLES–APPLE   BOOK–PAINT
HAMMER–STAR   TREE–OCEAN

Now, cover up the pairs above. Try to recall as many responses as possible.

ENVELOPE	_____	JAIL	_____
FRECKLES	_____	IVY	_____
TREE	_____	SHEEPSKIN	_____
CANDY	_____	BOOK	_____
SCISSORS	_____	LIZARD	_____
CUSTARD	_____	HAMMER	_____

Learn the following list of pairs by visualizing a mental picture in which the two objects in each pair are in some kind of vivid interaction. For example, if the pair is CAT–WINDOW, you might make up a picture of a cat jumping through a closed window, with the glass shattering all about. Just make up a picture and do not use any other study method. Allow yourself one minute for this list.

SOAP–MERMAID   MIRROR–RABBIT
FOOTBALL–LAKE   HOUSE–DIAMOND
PENCIL–LETTUCE   LAMB–MOON
CAR–HONEY   BREAD–GLASS
CANDLE–DANCER   LIPS–MONKEY
DANDELION–FLEA   DOLLAR–ELEPHANT

Now, cover up the pairs above. Try to recall as many responses as possible.

CANDLE	_____	DOLLAR	_____
DANDELION	_____	CAR	_____
BREAD	_____	LIPS	_____
MIRROR	_____	PENCIL	_____
LAMB	_____	SOAP	_____
FOOTBALL	_____	HOUSE	_____

Now, count the number of correct responses on each list. Did you recall a greater number of words with the imagery instructions? Incidentally, you may have found it very difficult to *avoid* using imagery on the first list, because you are reading a section about memory improvement. In that case, your recall scores were probably similar for the two lists. You may wish to test a friend, instead.

experiences can vary in their accessibility, sometimes being not available to consciousness and sometimes being painfully present (Schooler, 1994). On the other hand, some individuals have indeed been encouraged to "remember" events that never really occurred (Loftus, 1993a). One clear message from this controversy is that therapists must be meticulously careful not to ask leading questions that might create a misinformation effect.

Ecological Validity and Autobiographical Memory Research

In Chapter 1, we introduced the concept of *ecological validity*, which means that the results obtained in research should also hold true in "real life." More than any other area of cognition, the research on long-term memory has embraced the concept of ecological validity. This section on autobiographical memory has examined such real-world phenomena as flashbulb memories, schematic memories for everyday events, absentmindedness in our daily lives, eyewitness testimonies in the courtroom, and memories of childhood sexual abuse. This emphasis on real-life applications is a dramatic departure from the controlled laboratory settings used for memory research during the 1960s and 1970s (Morris, 1988). Now that you have read about some of the research in real-world settings, you are in a better position to appreciate the debate about ecological validity.

In 1989, an article by Banaji and Crowder appeared in a prominent psychology journal. The title of the article, "The Bankruptcy of Everyday Memory," made the authors' position quite clear. Banaji and Crowder claimed that the research methods used to explore everyday memory were unsophisticated. They also argued that the kind of well-controlled memory research conducted in the laboratory could indeed have important implications for our daily memory tasks. For example, they would probably point out that Roediger and McDermott's (1995) laboratory-based study with English words—which you tried in Demonstration 5.7—could help us understand how people can create false memories.

Many researchers rushed to the aid of the everyday memory approach. For example, Ceci and Bronfenbrenner (1991) pointed out that the laboratory and the real-world setting often yield different results. Their research showed how young children used a much different strategy to remember to check a clock when they were in a real kitchen, rather than in a lab setting. Other researchers complained that Banaji and Crowder had not examined some of the better developed examples of everyday memory (Conway, 1991). Enthusiastic supporters of the everyday memory approach would probably argue that Roediger and McDermott's study was conducted with bland stimuli in a context-deprived room in a university. We could not safely generalize these results to such an emotional topic as child sexual abuse.

Probably the wisest conclusion about this controversy is that *both* the laboratory and the real-world approaches can advance our understanding of human memory (Winograd, 1992, 1993). Endel Tulving (1991), whose memory research has spanned several decades, provided a wise resolution to the controversy about research approaches:

There is no law that says that good facts or ideas can come out of one type of approach only if some other approach is suppressed. As in other fields of science, there is room for many different kinds of facts and ideas about memory and for many approaches. (p. 42)

SECTION SUMMARY: AUTOBIOGRAPHICAL MEMORY

1. Research on autobiographical memory has increased rapidly in recent years.
2. Flashbulb memories and other vivid memories are rich with information, but specific details seem to fade as time passes; recall is not perfectly accurate.
3. Memory schemas encourage us to mistakenly recall events that never really occurred, as long as those events are similar to a schema.
4. According to the work on reality monitoring, we decide whether we really did perform an action on the basis of perceptual details and cognitive effort; we may also conduct a more leisurely decision-making process, based on additional information.
5. The research on prospective memory demonstrates that we are most likely to forget to do something when we are automatically performing routine tasks, and if there are no special rewards for remembering to do the task.
6. Factors that influence eyewitness testimony for faces include time and attention in looking at the face, the own-race bias effect, length of the retention interval, and misleading information.
7. The misinformation effect can occur when misleading information is introduced after an event that a witness has seen; although people may be confident about these incorrect memories, the memories lack perceptual detail.
8. We have no clear-cut resolution to the false memory controversy; perhaps some people can recover repressed memories, but other people appear to have created false memories.
9. The controversy over the value of research in everyday memory is best resolved by emphasizing that both laboratory research and research in the real world can help us understand human memory.

MEMORY IMPROVEMENT

Our discussion of memory has already emphasized a particularly important suggestion for improving your memory. As you know from the discussion of levels of processing in Chapter 3, you will recall more information if you process it at a deep level. Therefore, whenever you need to learn some information, concentrate on its meaning and try to develop rich, elaborate encodings (Pressley & El-Dinary, 1992). Also, try to relate the material to your own experiences because the self-reference effect demonstrates that this kind of encoding is particularly helpful.

In this section, we will consider six additional methods for improving memory. The first two methods emphasize mnemonics (pronounced ni-*mon*-icks, with a silent *m*). **Mnemonics** is the use of a strategy to help memory; we will discuss two strategies, imagery and organization. Memory can also be enhanced by four more general approaches, which include practice, external memory aids, the multimodal approach, and—perhaps most important—metamemory. Notice as you read this section that each of these methods employs familiar concepts; we remember more effectively if we pay attention, use deep levels of processing and distinctive cues, and emphasize effective retrieval strategies (Fischler, 1992).

Mnemonics Using Imagery

When we use *imagery,* we mentally represent objects or actions that are not physically present. Chapter 6 examines the nature of these mental images; in this chapter, we'll focus on how imagery can enhance memory.

Be sure you tried Demonstration 5.8 on page 167 before you read further. Which set of instructions produced the highest recall, the repetition or the imagery instructions? This demonstration is a simplified version of a study by Bower and Winzenz (1970). They used concrete nouns in their study and tested participants in four different conditions: (1) repetition, in which people repeated the pairs silently to themselves; (2) sentence reading, in which people read sentences devised by the experimenters, and each pair was included in one sentence; (3) sentence generation, in which people made up a sentence about each pair and said it aloud; and (4) imagery, in which people tried to construct a mental picture of the two words in vivid interaction with each other.

After learning several lists of words, the participants saw the first word of each pair and were asked to supply the second word. The results were quite remarkable. Out of a possible 15 items, people in the repetition condition recalled only 5.2 pairs. In contrast, people in the imagery condition recalled 12.7 words—more than twice as many!

Research shows that visual imagery is a powerful strategy for enhancing memory (Bellezza, 1986, 1996; McDaniel & Pressley, 1987; Paivio, 1995). In some cultures within North America—and in many cultures throughout the world—people memorize long poems or ballads. Most of these pieces contain extremely vivid imagery, which certainly facilitates memorization (Rubin, 1995).

Perhaps you have read an article in a popular magazine that suggested you should create an unusual or bizarre image. In reality, the research on imagery shows that bizarre images are not consistently more effective than ordinary images in enhancing memory (Bellezza, 1996; Einstein & McDaniel, 1987; Einstein et al., 1989; McDaniel et al., 1995).

However, the research consistently shows that imagery is most effective when the items that must be recalled are shown interacting with each other (Begg, 1982; Bellezza, 1992a; McKelvie et al., 1994). For example, if you want to remember the pair *elephant* and *dollar bill,* try to visualize an elephant holding the bill in its trunk, rather than these two items separated from each other.

As you might imagine, one of the tricks to remembering more effectively is to make the task interesting and enjoyable. Higbee (1994) argues that imagery mnemonics are more entertaining than rote rehearsal, and this factor is an important part of their effectiveness. Let's now consider two specific mnemonic devices that employ mental imagery, the keyword method and the method of loci.

The Keyword Method. If you need to remember unfamiliar vocabulary items, the keyword method is especially helpful. In the ***keyword method,*** you identify an English word (the keyword) that sounds similar to the new word you want to learn, and then you create an image that links the keyword with the meaning of the new word (Bellezza, 1996). For example, imagine that you are learning Spanish, and you want to remember that the unfamiliar Spanish word *rodilla* means *knee* in English. From the word *rodilla* (pronounced roe-<u>dee</u>-ya), you could derive a similar-sounding English word, *rodeo.* Then imagine a cowboy at a rodeo with his knees conspicuously protruding, as in Figure 5.5.

The early research on the keyword method showed that it seemed to help students who were trying to learn new English vocabulary words or foreign-language vocabulary (Desrochers & Begg, 1987; Kasper & Glass, 1988; McDaniel et al., 1987; Searleman & Herrmann, 1994). The keyword method has also been used to help

=== FIGURE 5.5 ===

THE KEYWORD REPRESENTATION FOR THE PAIR OF WORDS *RODILLA–KNEE*

DEMONSTRATION 5.9

CHUNKING

Read this list of letters and then cover them up. Try to recall them as accurately as possible.

YMC   AJF   KFB   INB   CLS   DTV

Now read this list of letters and then cover them up. Try to recall them as accurately as possible.

AMA   PHD   TWA   VCR   XKE   SDI

Finally, read this list of letters and then cover them up. Try to recall them as accurately as possible.

N Z K L E Q B N P I J W U Y H R T M

---

individuals with Alzheimer's disease learn people's names (Hill et al., 1987). This research matches my own personal experience with learning Spanish vocabulary over a period of several years. (Try Demonstration 5.9 before you read further.)

The more recent research on the keyword method is more pessimistic, however. Specifically, a series of studies by Margaret Thomas and Alvin Wang suggests that the keyword method does produce superior recall immediately after learning. However—without repeated testing, pictures of the keyword, and repeated rehearsal—the keyword-based memories are fragile (Thomas & Wang, 1996; Wang & Thomas, 1995; Wang et al., 1992). Because so many academic disciplines require students to learn new vocabulary, we can hope that future researchers will identify the conditions in which the keyword method effectively improves long-term recall.

The Method of Loci. If you want to use the ***method of loci,*** you must associate items to be learned with a series of physical locations. The method of loci (pronounced low-sigh) is one of the oldest mnemonic devices (Searleman & Herrmann, 1994). The basic rules for using this method involve (1) visualizing a series of places that you know well, arranged in a specific sequence; (2) making up an image to represent each item you want to remember; and (3) associating the items, one by one, with the corresponding location in memory. The method of loci is especially useful when you want to memorize a list of items in a specific order (Bellezza, 1996). A clear strength of the method of loci is that it takes advantage of the encoding specificity principle discussed earlier in the chapter; the material is

FIGURE 5.6

PERCENTAGE OF WORDS RECALLED IN THE CORRECT ORDER, AS A FUNCTION OF CONDITION AND DELAY.   BASED ON GRONINGER (1971).

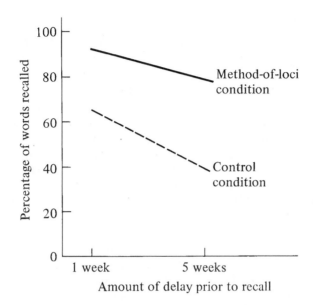

encoded together with memory cues that are so familiar that they are virtually guaranteed to be available at the time of recall (Oliver, 1992).

Gordon Bower (1970) describes how we might use the method of loci for a familiar sequence of loci associated with a home, such as the driveway, the garage, the front door, the coat closet, and the kitchen sink. If you need to remember a grocery shopping list (for example, hot dogs, cat food, tomatoes, bananas, and orange juice), you could make up a vivid image for each item. Then imagine each item in its appropriate place. You could imagine giant *hot dogs* rolling down the *driveway,* a monstrous *cat eating food* in the *garage,* ripe *tomatoes* splattering all over the *front door,* and a quart of *orange juice* gurgling down the *kitchen sink.* When you enter the supermarket, you can mentally walk the route from the driveway to the kitchen sink, recalling the items in order.

The method sounds unlikely, but does it work? In a representative experiment by Groninger (1971), participants in one condition were told to think of 25 locations that could be placed in order. Then they mentally pictured items on a 25-word list, using the method of loci. Participants in the control condition simply learned the 25 words in order, using any method they wanted. Everyone was instructed not to rehearse the material any further. Then everyone returned for testing 1 week and 5 weeks later, and those people who said they had rehearsed the material during the retention period were eliminated from the study. Figure 5.6 shows the results of the study. As you can see, the method of loci was particularly effective—relative to the control group—when recall was measured 5 weeks after learning.

Mnemonics Using Organization

Organization is the attempt to bring systematic order to the material we learn. Chapter 4 discussed an organizational strategy called **chunking,** in which we combine several small units into larger units. For instance, Demonstration 5.9 is a modification of a study by Bower and Springston (1970). These researchers found that people recalled much more material when a string of letters was grouped according to meaningful, familiar units, rather than in arbitrary groups of three. In Demonstration 5.9, you probably recalled a greater number of items on the second list, which was organized according to familiar chunks, than on either the list where the letters were grouped in arbitrary units or the ungrouped list.

Another effective way to organize material is to construct a hierarchy. A **hierarchy** is a system in which items are arranged in a series of classes, from the most general classes to the most specific. For example, Figure 5.7 presents part of a hierarchy for animals.

Gordon Bower and his colleagues (1969) asked people to learn words that belonged to four hierarchies similar to the one in Figure 5.7. Some people learned the words in an organized fashion, and the words were presented in the format of the upside-down trees you see in Figure 5.7. Other people saw the same words, but the words were randomly scattered throughout the different positions in each tree. Thus, there was no pattern for the words. The group who had learned the organized structure performed much better. For instance, on the first trial, the group who learned the organized structure recalled an average of 73 words, in comparison to only 21 for the group who learned the random structure. Other studies (e.g., Wittrock, 1974) have shown that hierarchical organization is useful even for recalling words chosen at random from a dictionary. Structure and organization clearly enhance recall (Hirst, 1988).

A hierarchy is a form of outline. An outline is valuable because it provides organization and structure for concepts that you learn in a particular discipline. Naturally, the material is usually not as simple as a list of individual words, but the ideas can still be arranged into a series of classes. For example, this chapter is divided into three general areas: determinants of accuracy, autobiographical memory, and memory improvement. See if you can construct a hierarchy similar to Figure 5.7 that includes more specific topics for this chapter. Then check the outline at the beginning of the chapter to see whether you omitted anything. If you study the outline of each chapter, you will have an organized structure that can help your recall on an examination.

Another popular mnemonic that makes use of organization is the **first letter technique,** which involves taking the first letter of each word you want to remember and composing a word or a sentence from these letters (Herrmann, 1991). Maybe you learned the colors of the rainbow by using the mediator ROY G. BIV to recall

=========== **FIGURE 5.7** ===========

AN EXAMPLE OF A HIERARCHY

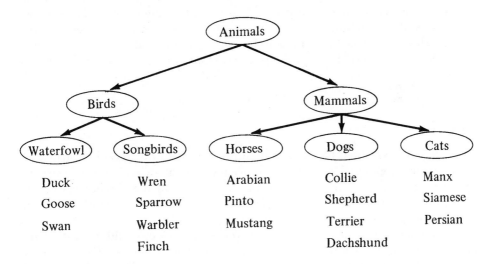

Red, Orange, Yellow, Green, Blue, Indigo, and Violet. As you may have learned in a statistics class, the nominal, ordinal, interval, and ratio scales conveniently spell the French word for *black—noir.*

Students frequently use first-letter mnemonics (Gruneberg, 1978). In one group of medical students, for example, more than half used this technique at least occasionally in preparing for anatomy examinations. The pharmaceutical company Merck, Sharp & Dome (1980) prepared a medical mnemonics handbook for physicians. A typical example is to be used in the treatment of trauma from sports injuries: PRICE (Position, Rest, Ice, Compression, Elevation). However, the effectiveness of the first-letter technique has not been convincingly demonstrated. Morris (1978) reports that the first-letter technique helps recall if the order of the items is important. On the other hand, it is less useful when you need to remember unrelated items. Carlson, Zimmer, and Glover (1981) also found that first-letter techniques did not aid memory, though they admit that they may not have allowed the participants enough study time to benefit fully from the mnemonics. In summary, the first-letter technique is a popular one, and one that many of us *believe* must work; however, it may not really deserve its popularity.

So far, we have seen how organization can enhance memory through the use of chunking, a hierarchy, or a first-letter mnemonic. A fourth organizational method, called the ***narrative technique,*** instructs people to make up stories to link a series of words together. In one study, Bower and Clark (1969) told one group of people to make up narrative stories that incorporated a set of English words. Different people—the control group—spent the same amount of time learning these words, but they were simply told to study and learn each list. In all, each group learned 12 lists. On each of the lists, the narrative group recalled between 80% and 95% of the words. In contrast, the control group recalled between 5% and 30%. In other words, the two groups showed absolutely no overlap in their performance; the narrative technique is clearly an effective strategy for enhancing memory. However, we should stress that techniques such as this are effective only if you can generate the narrative easily and reliably during both learning and recall (Bellezza, 1987). A narrative will not be helpful if it hangs together so loosely that you cannot remember the story!

Practice

So far, we have examined two mnemonic strategies that offer specific instructions on transforming material so that it becomes more memorable. You can construct mental images—perhaps using the keyword method or the method of loci—or you can use one of several organizational techniques. Let us now turn to four more general approaches to memory improvement.

The first of these general memory-improvement strategies sounds almost too obvious to mention: The more you practice, the more you remember. However, even college students forget the rule that "practice makes perfect." Every semester, students in some of my classes will come to my office to discuss how they can improve their performance on examinations. One of my first questions is, "How long did you spend studying for the last test?" An amazing number will say something like, "Well, I read every chapter, and I looked over my notes." Most of us cannot master material with only one exposure to a textbook and a cursory inspection of lecture notes. Instead, the task requires reading the material two or three times; each time, you should also practice retrieving the information (Baddeley, 1993). (For example, what are all the memory techniques we have discussed so far?)

The *total time hypothesis* states that the amount you learn depends on the total time you devote to learning (Baddeley, 1990). Keep in mind, however, that an hour spent actively learning the material—using deep levels of processing—may be more valuable than 2 hours in which your eyes simply drift across the pages.

Also keep in mind a second point called the *spacing effect* or the *distribution of practice effect;* in general, you learn more if you spread your learning trials over time, rather than learning the material all at once. Research consistently supports the spacing effect, and it is one of the most dependable findings in experiments on human memory (Dempster, 1988). Research on real-life material, such as high school math and Spanish vocabulary, confirms the spacing effect (Bahrick, Bahrick, Bahrick, & Bahrick, 1993; Bahrick & Hall, 1991; Bahrick & Phelps, 1987; Payne & Wenger, 1992).

A related technique called expanding retrieval practice is especially helpful if you have a relatively small number of items to remember. Suppose, for example, that you are on a job interview, and you want to remember the names of four important people. Try the *expanding retrieval practice* method; each time you practice retrieving the names, increase the delay period (Bjork, 1988). For instance, you might repeat their names as soon as you have been introduced. Then rehearse them after 2 minutes, then 5 minutes, then 10 minutes. Incidentally, this technique even works well for people with Alzheimer's disease (Camp & McKitrick, 1992; McKitrick et al., 1992).

External Memory Aids

All the other memory strategies discussed in this section involve internal memory techniques. In contrast, an ***external memory aid*** is defined as any device, external to the person, that facilitates memory in some way (Intons-Peterson & Newsome, 1992). Taking notes on a lecture is one obvious external memory aid; research confirms that students typically recall more material if they have taken notes (Intons-Peterson & Newsome, 1992; Kiewra, 1985).

Other external memory aids include a shopping list, a bookmark, asking someone else to remind you to do something, and the ring of an alarm clock, reminding you to make an important phone call (Intons-Peterson & Fournier, 1986; Intons-Peterson, 1993b). Unfortunately, psychologists have not conducted much formal research on external mnemonics (Hertel, 1993). However, one study of everyday memory examined individuals who were learning to become bartenders (Beach, 1993). A common strategy among bartenders who must remember a long list of drinks to be prepared is to place the drink glasses on the counter before beginning. Because most glasses are associated with only a limited number of drinks, the glasses function as an external mnemonic.

Dozens of commercial memory aids are also available (Searleman & Herrmann, 1994). For example, you can buy a case for your credit card that sounds an alarm if you forget to take your credit card back from the clerk (Herrmann & Petro, 1990). In all cases, the external memory aids ease the burden of remembering too much information. However, these aids are helpful only if they can be easily used and if they successfully remind us of what we are supposed to remember. If you switch your ring to another finger to remind you to turn off your stove before leaving the apartment, you may find yourself pondering, "Now what was this reminder supposed to remind me to do?"

The Multimodal Approach

In the past 20 years, psychologists have become increasingly critical of the mnemonics approach to memory improvement. These researchers complain that the traditional approach to memory improvement has been too simplistic; it implies that we can find a single solution to help all people with their memory difficulties (e.g., Herrmann, 1991; Herrmann & Searleman, 1990; Poon, 1980; Wilson, 1984; Zacks & Hasher, 1992).

The most readable summary of the new approaches to memory improvement is a book by Douglas Herrmann (1991) called *Super Memory*. Herrmann's book elaborates on the research of Wilson and of Poon, as well as his own research. It specifically focuses on the **multimodal approach,** which emphasizes that memory problems cannot be solved by a simple, improve-your-memory-overnight strategy. Herrmann stresses that people who seriously want to improve their memory must adopt a complete approach to memory improvement. This complete approach involves attention to physical and mental condition (for example, by getting sufficient sleep and maintaining an optimum level of daily activity).

The multimodal approach also emphasizes the importance of memory attitude. For example, you can keep a memory diary in order to provide an accurate impression of typical memory behavior. The approach also explains how social context influences memory performance. For instance, you can make conversation in order to "buy time" while you gather information to help you remember some critical fact.

Herrmann also makes numerous suggestions about mental manipulations, such as rehearsing an item, focusing attention on details that should be registered, and encouraging deep levels of processing by paying attention to semantic and emotional aspects of the material to be remembered. Finally, Herrmann emphasizes that people who want to improve their memories should develop a repertoire of several memory manipulations. Again, there is no single, perfect mnemonic device. For example, Herrmann gives several pages of recommendations on how to acquire and remember people's names. One of these recommendations for learning a new name involves the following steps:

1. Say the name aloud.
2. Ask the person a question, using his or her name.
3. Say the name at least once in conversation.
4. End the conversation by thinking of a rhyme for the name, deciding whom the person looks like, or—if possible—jotting down the name unobtrusively.

Herrmann and others argue that this more comprehensive multimodal approach to memory improvement is essential because the more traditional methods may have limited usefulness. For example, people who have learned how to use a mnemonic device may indeed show short-term improvement in memory. However, people later fail to apply these methods to new tasks, and they stop using them (Searleman & Herrmann, 1994; Zacks & Hasher, 1992). Memory improvement should involve more comprehensive approaches that attend to the numerous factors affecting memory. In addition, memory improvement must involve the development of a flexible repertoire of techniques to aid each specific kind of memory task.

Metamemory

So far, you have learned that you can improve your memory by using imagery, organization, practice, external memory aids, and the multimodal approach to memory. However, all these techniques are limited in their effectiveness if you fail to use your metamemory. **Metamemory** is your knowledge and awareness about your own memory. We will examine the topic of metamemory much more thoroughly in the chapter on general knowledge (Chapter 7).

To learn most effectively, you need to know what strategies work best for you; a technique that your best friend recommends may fail miserably for you (Bellezza, 1996). You also need to know how long you can study before your attention wanders, the time of day during which you can learn the most, and so forth. In addition to knowing your memory's strengths and weaknesses, you also need to know how to regulate your memory and related processes (Hertzog, 1992; McKeachie et al., 1985; Pressley & El-Dinary, 1992). For example, you need to know how to adapt your memory strategies to new tasks. You need to know how to plan your study activities, how to regulate your attention, and how to monitor whether you understand the material you are reading. You need to know that you should spend more time reviewing a difficult part of the chapter—such as the discussion of explicit versus implicit measures of memory—rather than this more concrete section on memory improvement (Matlin, 1993).

In fact, metamemory is probably the most important component of memory improvement. Consistent with Theme 2 of this book, we humans possess remarkably competent cognitive processes. When we exercise our metamemory appropriately, we can develop study strategies that make the best possible use of these remarkable processes.

SECTION SUMMARY: MEMORY IMPROVEMENT

1. Two specific methods of memory improvement include visual imagery (which, in turn, includes the keyword method and the method of loci) and organization (which includes chunking, hierarchies, the first-letter technique, and the narrative technique).
2. Four more general strategies of memory improvement include practice (including the total time hypothesis, the spacing effect, and the technique of expanding retrieval practice), external memory aids, the multimodal approach (a more comprehensive approach), and metamemory (or knowledge about your own memory).

CHAPTER REVIEW QUESTIONS

1. What is encoding specificity? How is the outshining hypothesis relevant to the research on encoding specificity? How is encoding specificity related to the topic of mood-state dependence, and how strong is the evidence for mood-state dependence?
2. Give several examples of explicit and implicit memory tasks you have performed in the past few days. What is dissociation, and how is it relevant in the research that has been conducted with both amnesia patients and normal adults?
3. According to one saying, "The more you know, the easier it is to learn." What evidence do we have for this statement, based on the material discussed in this chapter? How could educators take advantage of this saying?

4. Define the term *autobiographical memory* and mention several topics that have been studied in this area. How does research in this area differ from more traditional laboratory research? List the advantages and disadvantages of each approach. Point out how Roediger and McDermott's study on false memory for English words highlights the advantages and disadvantages of the laboratory approach.

5. Describe how schemas could lead to a distortion in the recall of a flashbulb memory. How might misleading post-event information also influence this recall? In answering the two parts of this question, use the terms *proactive inhibition* and *retroactive inhibition*.

6. Describe an example of an occasion where you had difficulty on a reality monitoring task. According to Marcia Johnson and her colleagues, how do people decide whether or not an event really happened? The section on memory for action also discussed prospective memory. Describe several prospective memory tasks you currently face. How could external memory aids help you remember to do each of these things?

7. The constructivist approach to memory emphasizes that we actively revise our memories, in the light of new concerns and new information. How is this concept relevant throughout many of the topics in the section on autobiographical memory?

8. Discuss as many of the mnemonic techniques from this chapter as you can remember. In each case, tell how you can use each one to remember some information from this chapter for your next examination in cognitive psychology.

9. Some theorists argue that mnemonic techniques are primarily effective because they encourage more effective processing of the material. Review the techniques and show how most of them emphasize deep processing, rather than shallow processing.

10. Why are some current memory researchers critical of the traditional mnemonics approach to memory improvement? Why do the multimodal approach and the metamemory approach emphasize a more comprehensive and complex view of memory improvement?

NEW TERMS

permastore
encoding specificity
  principle
outshining hypothesis
Pollyanna Principle
mood congruence
mood congruity
mood-state dependence
meta-analysis technique

explicit memory measures
recall
recognition
implicit memory measures
repetition priming task
dissociation
picture superiority effect
expertise

long-term working
  memory
own-race bias
autobiographical memory
everyday memory
flashbulb memory
schema
repisodic memory
reality monitoring

prospective memory	mnemonics	total time hypothesis
retrospective memory	imagery	spacing effect
misinformation effect	keyword method	distribution of practice
proactive inhibition	method of loci	effect
retroactive inhibition	organization	expanding retrieval
constructivist approach	chunking	practice
repressed memory	hierarchy	external memory aid
false memories	first-letter technique	multimodal approach
ecological validity	narrative technique	metamemory

RECOMMENDED READINGS

Cutler, B. L., & Penrod. S. D. (1995). *Mistaken identification: The eyewitness, psychology, and the law.* New York: Cambridge University Press. Here is an ideal overview of the research on eyewitness testimony, emphasizing the factors that affect accuracy; some chapters also examine how eyewitness testimony is used in the courts.

Ericsson, K. A., & Smith, J. (Eds.). (1991b). *Toward a general theory of expertise: Prospects and limits.* New York: Cambridge University Press. This edited volume explores expert knowledge in areas as diverse as chess, music, and sports.

Herrmann, D. J. (1991). *Super memory.* Emmaus, PA: Rodale Press. Herrmann's book describes the multimodal approach to memory improvement. An especially useful part of the book is a list of a wide variety of memory techniques.

Pressley, M., & Grossman, L. R. (Eds.). (1994). Recovery of memories of childhood sexual abuse [Special issue]. *Applied Cognitive Psychology, 8* (4). The journal *Applied Cognitive Psychology* publishes some of the most interesting articles on everyday memory, and this special issue investigates the false memory controversy in some detail.

Rubin, D. C. (1995). *Memory in oral traditions: The cognitive psychology of epic, ballads, and counting-out rhymes.* New York: Oxford University Press. This superb book by one of the leaders in the everyday memory discipline examines how people manage to remember extremely long ballads, poems, and other works in the oral tradition.

Searleman, A., & Herrmann, D. (1994). *Memory from a broader perspective.* New York: McGraw-Hill. This mid-level textbook on memory emphasizes environmental and social factors that influence memory, as well as everyday memory and memory-improvement techniques.

ANSWERS TO DEMONSTRATION 5.1

1. railroad	6. apple	11. street	16. arm
2. cat	7. heart	12. devil	17. skirt
3. sister	8. shoe	13. orange	18. breakfast
4. bed	9. chair	14. bird	19. window
5. head	10. kitchen	15. grandfather	20. moon

CHAPTER

6

IMAGERY

INTRODUCTION

THE CHARACTERISTICS OF MENTAL IMAGES

Imagery and Rotation
Imagery and Size
Imagery and Shape
In Depth: Imagery and Interference
Imagery and Ambiguous Figures
Imagery and Other Vision-Like Processes
Neuropsychological Evidence for the Similarity Between Imagery and Perception
The Imagery Controversy, Revisited

COGNITIVE MAPS

Cognitive Maps and Distance
Cognitive Maps and Shape
Cognitive Maps and Relative Positions
Using Verbal Descriptions to Create Mental Models

====== **Preview** ======

Chapters 3, 4, and 5 have emphasized memory for verbal material. Now we shift our focus to more pictorial material as we investigate mental imagery, specifically, the characteristics of mental images and cognitive maps.

Psychologists have devised some creative research techniques to examine the characteristics of mental images. In many ways, mental images and the perception of real objects are similar; for example, our mental images of elephants are larger than our mental images of rabbits. This section also examines a controversy about how we store mental images in memory—are images stored in a picture-like code or in a more abstract, language-like description?

A cognitive map is an internal representation of your spatial environment. For example, you have developed a cognitive map of the town or city in which your college is located. Our cognitive maps show certain systematic distortions. For example, you may remember that two streets intersect at right angles, even when the angles are far from 90°. As a final topic in this chapter, we will consider how people can use verbal descriptions to create mental models of their environment.

INTRODUCTION

Which is larger, a tennis ball or the rounded portion of a lightbulb? Which has a darker green color, a frozen pea or a pine tree? Which is higher off the ground, the tip of a racehorse's tail or its rear knee? When people try to answer these questions, many report that their "mind's eye" seems to see the tennis ball, the pine tree, or the horse (Kosslyn, 1990). This chapter examines *imagery,* which is the mental representation of stimuli that are not physically present.

We use imagery for a wide variety of different cognitive activities. Imagery is useful when we try to solve a mathematics problem, understand a graph, or construct a mental representation from a technical diagram (Lowe, 1993; Reed, 1993a; Shah & Carpenter, 1995). Some professions require skilled use of mental images; would you want to fly on an airplane with a pilot with weak spatial imagery (Dror et al., 1993)? Imagery also plays an important role in our daily lives when we try to remember where we parked or when we plan the quickest route home from an unfamiliar location (Antonietti & Baldo, 1994; Lutz et al., 1994). We'll also see in Chapter 10 that mental imagery is immensely helpful when we want to solve spatial problems or work on a task that requires creativity (Finke, 1993).

How often do we use imagery? Inspired by the research on everyday cognition in areas such as memory, Stephen Kosslyn and his colleagues (1990) asked students to keep a diary listing the examples of mental imagery that occurred in their daily lives. The students reported that about two-thirds of their images were visual; images involving hearing, touch, taste, and smell were much less common.

Psychologists show a similar lopsidedness in their research preferences. Some psychologists occasionally study topics such as auditory imagery or smell imagery (e.g., Carrasco & Ridout, 1993; Intons-Peterson & McDaniel, 1991; Reisberg, 1992). However, most of the research examines visual imagery.

Imagery—especially visual imagery—has received more than 2,500 years of attention in Western thought (Yuille, 1985). Even the first psychologists considered imagery to be an important part of the discipline (Gardner, 1985). For example, Wundt and his followers carefully analyzed the self-reports provided in the introspections that trained subjects provided about imagery. However, American behaviorists, such as John Watson, were strongly opposed to research on any process as unobservable as mental imagery. As a consequence, research and theories about imagery declined sharply during the 40-year period in which behaviorism was dominant (Kent, 1990; Yuille, 1983). Frederick Bartlett maintained an interest in imagery in Great Britain, and Jean Piaget explored developmental aspects of imagery in continental Europe (Yuille, 1985). Nonetheless, these psychologists were unable to inspire enthusiasm about imagery in the United States. As behaviorism declined in popularity, however, cognitive psychologists rediscovered imagery and have made it one of the most controversial areas in contemporary cognitive psychology.

This chapter explores two aspects of mental images that have especially intrigued contemporary researchers. The first section examines the nature of mental images, with an emphasis on the way these mental images are stored. The second section focuses on cognitive maps, or the representation of geographic information.

THE CHARACTERISTICS OF MENTAL IMAGES

As you might expect, research on mental imagery is difficult to conduct, especially because mental images are not directly observable and because they fade quickly (Finke, 1989). However, during recent decades, psychologists have applied some of the research techniques developed for studying visual perception. As a result, the investigation of imagery has made impressive advances (Finke & Shepard, 1986). Try Demonstration 6.1, which illustrates one important research technique.

One of the major controversies in this field concerns this question: To what extent does mental imagery resemble perceptual processes? We'll introduce that question now and return to discuss it in more detail once we've examined the evidence.

Many theorists—such as Stephen Kosslyn (1990, 1994), Roger Shepard (1981), and Ronald Finke (1989)—argue that information about a mental image is stored in an analog code. An **analog code** (also called a **depictive representation**) is a representation that closely resembles the physical object. (Notice that the word *analog* suggests the word *analogy*, such as the analogy between the real object and the mental picture.) According to the analog-code approach, mental imagery is a close relative of perception (Baird & Hubbard, 1992). When you perceive a picture of a triangle, the physical features of that triangle are registered in the brain in a form

MENTAL ROTATION. SOURCE: SHEPARD & METZLER (1971).

Which of these pairs of objects are the same, and which are different?

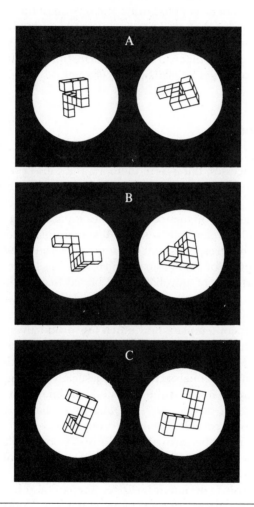

that preserves the physical relationship among the three lines. Those who support analog codes argue that a mental image of a triangle is registered in a similar fashion, preserving the same physical relationship among the lines.

In contrast, other theorists such as Zenon Pylyshyn (1978, 1984, 1989) argue that we store images in terms of a propositional code. A ***propositional code*** (also called a *descriptive representation*) is an abstract, language-like representation; storage is neither visual nor spatial, and it does not resemble the original stimulus. Thus, if you try to create a mental image of a triangle, your brain will register a language-like description of the lines and angles, though the precise nature of the verbal description has not been specified. Those who support propositional codes argue that mental imagery is a close relative of *language,* not perception (Baird & Hubbard, 1992).

The controversy about analog versus propositional coding has not been resolved, although most researchers seem to favor some version of the analog approach. Like most controversies in psychology, both positions are probably at least partially correct. As you read the following pages, you'll find it helpful to decide which studies support each viewpoint, so that you can appreciate our more detailed consideration of the controversy on pages 205–207 of this chapter.

Imagery and Rotation

A major stumbling block to the study of imagery is that researchers typically cannot observe mental processes. Long-term memory, the subject of the preceding chapter, is relatively accessible. We can ask people to write down the words they remember from a list, and their recall provides some hints about memory strategies. Now think how you might study mental images. Compared with verbal memory, this mental process is elusive and inaccessible. It's tempting to suggest that we should simply ask people to introspect about their mental images and use these reports as a basis for a description of mental imagery. However, as Pinker (1985) writes, these introspective reports can be unreliable and biased because we may not have conscious access to the processes involved in imagery. (You'll recall that the consciousness section of Chapter 2 discussed this issue.)

It's interesting to contemplate how much less productive the research on mental imagery might have been if Roger Shepard hadn't had an unusual half-dream on November 16, 1968. He was just emerging from sleep on that morning when he visualized a three-dimensional structure majestically turning in space (Shepard, 1978). This vivid image inspired the first study on imagery that used careful controls and measurement procedures—the first study that made those inaccessible mental images more accessible. It provided objective, quantitative data that could satisfy some of the more permissive behaviorists (Cooper & Shepard, 1984). This study is now considered one of the classics in cognitive psychology, and it helped to earn Roger Shepard the U.S. National Medal of Science in 1995.

You tried this classic experiment by Roger Shepard and his coauthor Jacqueline Metzler(1971) when you worked on Demonstration 6.1. Notice that in the top pair of designs, the left-hand figure can be changed into the right-hand figure by keeping the figure flat on the page and rotating it clockwise. Suddenly, the two figures match up, and you reply "same." The middle pair, however, requires a rotation in a third dimension. You may, for example, take the two-block "arm" that is jutting out toward you and push it over to the left and away from you. Suddenly, again, the figures match up, and you reply "same." In the case of the bottom figure, every attempt to rotate the figure produces a mismatch, and you conclude "different."

Shepard and Metzler asked eight long-suffering people to judge 1,600 pairs of line drawings like these. The participants pulled a lever with their right hand if they judged the figures to be the same, and they pulled another lever with their left hand if they judged the figures to be different. In each case, the experimenters measured the amount of time required for a decision.

Figure 6.1a shows the results for figures that require only a 2-dimensional rotation, similar to rotating a flat picture; Pair a in Demonstration 6.1 required a picture-plane rotation. Figure 6.1b shows the results for figures that require a three-dimensional rotation, or rotating an object in depth; Pair b in Demonstration 6.1 required a depth rotation. As both graphs show, people's decision time was strongly influenced by the amount of rotation required to match a figure up with its mate. For example, rotating a figure 160° requires much more time than rotating it a mere 20°. As you can see, the relationship between rotation and reaction time is strictly linear in both figures. This research supports the analog code, because you would take much longer to rotate an actual physical object 160° than to rotate it a mere 20°.

Does it take longer to rotate pairs in depth than to rotate them in the picture plane? As you can see in Figure 6.1, Shepard and Metzler (1971) found virtually

━━━━━━━━━━━━━━ **FIGURE 6.1** ━━━━━━━━━━━━━━

REACTION TIME FOR DECIDING THAT PAIRS OF FIGURES ARE THE SAME, AS A FUNCTION OF THE ANGLE OF ROTATION AND THE NATURE OF ROTATION. NOTE: THE CENTERS OF THE CIRCLES INDICATE THE MEANS, AND THE BARS ON EITHER SIDE PROVIDE AN INDEX OF THE VARIABILITY OF THOSE MEANS. SOURCE: SHEPARD & METZLER (1971).

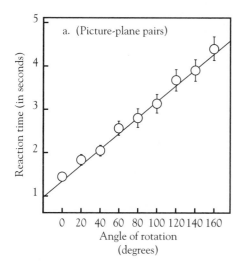
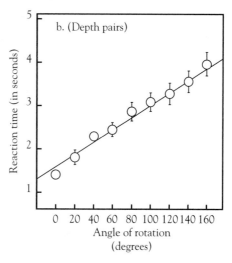

identical reaction times for both tasks. This observation illustrates once more that the operations we *imagine* performing on objects resemble the operations we perform on actual physical objects. If you were holding two figures in your hands, trying to decide whether they were the same, you would find that rotating a figure in depth would take no longer than rotating it while holding it flat. However, a more recent study—using different kinds of stimuli—reported that three-dimensional rotations do take significantly longer than two-dimensional rotations (Kerr, 1993).

The conclusions about 2-D and 3-D rotations may be uncertain. However, the basic findings have been replicated many times. Using other stimuli, such as letters of the alphabet, researchers have found a clear relationship between angle of rotation and reaction time (e.g., Cooper & Shepard, 1973; Jordan & Huntsman, 1990; Just & Carpenter, 1985; Van Selst & Jolicoeur, 1994).

We also know that people rotate familiar figures more quickly than unfamiliar figures, and they rotate clear pictures more rapidly than blurry pictures (Duncan & Bourg, 1983; Jolicoeur et al., 1987). Furthermore, with practice, we can rotate figures more rapidly (Jolicoeur, 1985). You won't be surprised to learn that individual differences in the rate of mental rotation are extremely large (Favreau, 1993; Kail et al., 1979). Finally, elderly people perform more slowly than younger people on a mental-rotation task, though age does not influence other mental imagery abilities, such as constructing or scanning mental images (Dror & Kosslyn, 1994).

In general, then, the research on rotating geometric figures and letters provides some of the strongest support for the analog coding approach. We seem to treat mental images the same way we treat physical objects when we rotate them through space.

Imagery and Size

The first systematic research on imagery demonstrated that people treat mental images the same way they treat physical objects on a mental rotation task. Researchers immediately began to examine other attributes of mental images, such as their size and shape. Try Demonstration 6.2 before you read farther. Then we will discuss Kosslyn's classic research on visual imagery and size, a potential alternative explanation for Kosslyn's results, some research on comparative size, and Intons-Peterson's research on auditory distance.

Kosslyn's Research. Questions like those in Demonstration 6.2 were part of a carefully planned series of experiments conducted by a major researcher in imagery, Stephen Kosslyn. Kosslyn (1975) wanted to discover whether people would make faster judgments about large images than about small images. You can anticipate a major problem with this research area: How can we control the size of someone's mental image? Kosslyn figured that a mental image of an elephant next to a rabbit would force people to imagine a relatively small rabbit. In contrast, a mental image of a fly next to a rabbit would produce a relatively large rabbit.

When you see *real-life* pictures of animals, you can see all the details quite clearly on a large picture. On the other hand, details are squeezed in so close together on a small picture that it is difficult to make judgments about them. If this same rule

DEMONSTRATION 6.2

IMAGERY AND SIZE

A. Imagine an elephant standing next to a rabbit. Now answer this question: *Does a rabbit have a beak?*
B. Imagine a fly standing next to a rabbit. Now answer this question: *Does a rabbit have an eyebrow?*

In which picture was the rabbit the largest, A or B? Which picture seemed to have more detail in the area you were examining for the beak or the eyebrow, A or B?

for real-life pictures also holds true for pictures in our heads, then people should make judgments more quickly with a large mental image (as in a rabbit next to a fly) than with a small mental image (as in a rabbit next to an elephant). In the experiment, people make judgments about objects, for example, whether a rabbit had legs. Kosslyn's results support his prediction; judgments were 0.21 seconds faster with a large mental image than with a small mental image. This difference was very substantial, given the small amount of time required to make these judgments.

In another study, Kosslyn (1975) demonstrated that the rapid judgment of large mental images could not be explained by a potential confounding variable—the relative interest level of rabbits, elephants, and flies. He also showed that people take longer to create a large mental image than a small one, just as it takes longer to fill in all the details on a large painting, compared to a small one.

In other research on the relationship between size and response time, Kosslyn and his colleagues (1978) showed that people required a long time to scan the distance between two widely separated points on a mental map that they had created. In contrast, they scanned the distance between two nearby points quite rapidly.

Experimenter Expectancy. Kosslyn's research had eliminated several alternative explanations that critics might suggest to explain his data. However, Intons-Peterson (1983) has argued that these results could perhaps be produced by experimenter expectancy. In ***experimenter expectancy,*** the experimenters' biases influence the outcomes of the experiment. For example, experimenters who conduct research in mental imagery know that longer distances should require longer search times. Experimenters could somehow transmit these expectations to the participants in the study. These participants might (either consciously or unconsciously) adjust their search speeds according to the expectations.

To answer this criticism, Jolicoeur and Kosslyn (1985a, 1985b) repeated Kosslyn and his coauthors' (1978) mental map experiment. However, the two people who conducted the experiment were not familiar with the research on mental imagery, and they were given elaborate and convincing (but incorrect) explanations about why their results *should* show a U-shaped relationship between distance and scanning time. (The explanation involved Gestalt organizational principles, discussed in Chapter 1.) Participants in the experiment studied a map in order to create a mental image of various locations on the map, such as a large tree and a hut. Then the experimenter named a location on the mental map and instructed the participant to "focus" on this location. The experimenter then named a second location and asked the participant to imagine a small black speck moving in a straight line from the original location toward the second location. The participants were told to press a button when the speck "arrived" at the destination.

Did the results show the typical relationship between distance and time, with longer distances requiring more time, or did they show the U-shaped results that the experimenters had been led to expect the participants to supply? Figure 6.2 illustrates the U-shaped results that the experimenters should have obtained if experimenter expectancy had been operating. It also shows that the results actually obtained in the experiment demonstrated the by-now typical linear relationship, in

═══════════════════ **FIGURE 6.2** ═══════════════════

RELATIONSHIPS BETWEEN DISTANCE AND REACTION TIME, AS PREDICTED BY EXPERIMENTER-EXPECTANCY EXPLANATION AND AS ACTUALLY DEMONSTRATED BY PARTICIPANTS IN THE EXPERIMENT.   BASED ON JOLICOEUR & KOSSLYN (1985a).

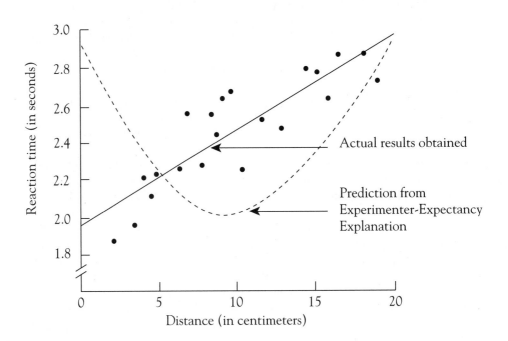

which it takes longer to scan a large mental distance. Experimenter expectancy cannot account for the obtained results.

Moyer's Research. Robert Moyer has provided additional information about how the relative size of mental images corresponds to the relative size of physical objects. Moyer (1973) used a principle from ***psychophysics,*** the area of psychology that measures people's reactions to perceptual stimuli. In psychophysics, we know that when people are asked to judge which of two lines is longer, they take longer to make a decision if the lines are almost equal. If the lines are clearly different from one another, the decision is much faster.

Moyer searched for evidence of an ***internal psychophysics,*** one that operates on images stored inside the head, rather than images on paper. He proposed that people should take longer to decide which was larger, a moth or a flea, than to decide which was larger, a moose or a roach. This prediction, remember, was based on the longer decision times for physical objects when the two choices are similar in size.

Participants in Moyer's (1973) experiment saw many different pairs of names for animals, with the animals ranging in size from a flea to a whale. Moyer measured how long it took people to decide which member of the pair was larger. Then people assigned a number to each animal name, estimating that animal's size. The results showed evidence of an internal psychophysics. There was a ***symbolic distance effect;*** that is, the smaller the difference in size between two animals, the longer the decision time (Moyer & Dumais, 1978). Thus, people took longer to decide whether an ant (whose size was ranked 1) was larger than a bee (size ranking of 2) than it took to compare an ant with an elk (size rankings of 1 and 7). Moyer argued that people convert the animal names into mental images that preserve the sizes of animals. Decisions regarding relative size take a long time if two objects are similar, whether the objects are in our minds or physically in front of us.

Intons-Peterson's Research. So far, we have considered only visual images, asking questions about the sizes of imagined animals and the distances on imagined maps. Margaret Intons-Peterson (one of the creators of the Brown/Peterson & Peterson technique for assessing short-term memory) provides some interesting information about *auditory* distance.

Imagine a cat purring, and create a mental image of its pitch. Now with that auditory image firmly in mind, move the pitch upward to the pitch of a telephone ringing. Intons-Peterson and her colleagues (1992) asked students to perform a similar task in which two imagined sounds were separated by a large distance. She found that people required a long time to "travel" that mental distance. As you can see from Figure 6.3, however, people were able to "travel" a small mental distance much more quickly. For example, a typical participant might require less than 4 seconds to move the pitch upward from "purring cat" to "ticking clock." Just as Kosslyn and his colleagues (1978) showed that long distances require more time on a *visual* mental map, Intons-Peterson showed that long distances require more time on an *auditory* mental map.

=== FIGURE 6.3 ===

AMOUNT OF TIME TAKEN TO "TRAVEL" A MENTAL DISTANCE BETWEEN TWO TONES, AS A FUNCTION OF THE SEPARATION BETWEEN THESE TWO TONES. BASED ON INTONS-PETERSON ET AL. (1992).

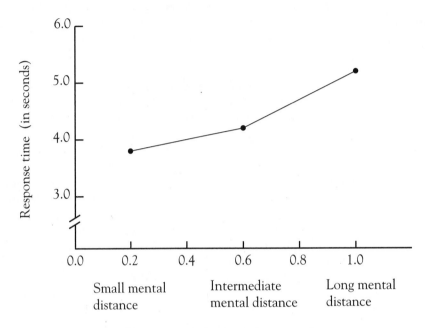

Difference in pitch ratings between the two tones

In addition, Intons-Peterson and her coworkers were able to demonstrate a symbolic distance effect with auditory images. You'll recall from Moyer's research on visual images that people take a long time to decide whether a bee is larger than an ant. In contrast, they could rapidly decide whether an elk is larger than an ant. Basically, then, when two objects are similar in size, it will take a long time to decide which is larger. In a second experiment, Intons-Peterson and her associates (1992) found that people take a long time to decide whether the pitch of a purring cat is lower than the pitch of a ticking clock. However, they could rapidly decide whether the pitch of a purring cat is lower than the pitch of a ringing telephone.

Students in my cognitive psychology classes often have difficulty sorting out the research on size and mental imagery. Remember from Kosslyn's research on mental maps, as well as Intons-Peterson's first study, that people take longer to travel a large mental distance, whether that distance is visual or auditory. In contrast, Moyer's research and Intons-Peterson's second study illustrate the symbolic distance effect; when two stimuli are similar, people take longer to decide which one is bigger (in the case of visual imagery) or which one is lower in pitch (in the case

==
DEMONSTRATION 6.3

IMAGERY AND ANGLES

For each pair below, imagine two standard, nondigital clocks. Each clock should represent one of the specified times. Compare these two mental clocks and decide which clock has the smaller angle between the hour hand and the minute hand. Notice which two tasks seem to take longer.

1. 3:20 and 7:25
2. 4:10 and 9:23
3. 2:45 and 1:05
4. 3:15 and 5:30
==

of auditory imagery). The symbolic distance effect always involves a comparison, making a decision about two visual images or a decision about two auditory images.

Imagery and Shape

Try Demonstration 6.3, which is similar to a study by Allan Paivio, one of the pioneers in research on imagery. In solving each problem in this demonstration, you probably seemed to consult two pictures that you created in your head. The task seemed to require imagery, rather than verbal reasoning.

Paivio (1978a) worked with a very basic kind of shape, the angle formed by the two hands on a mental clock. He decided to work with these particular shapes because these angles could be measured more precisely and consistently than the shape of imagined animals or other objects. Paivio asked people to make decisions, such as the ones described in Demonstration 6.3, and then he measured each decision time.

Paivio's results showed that decision time was related to the size of the difference between the angles. If the hands in the two clocks that were being compared create angles that are almost equal (for example, 3:20 and 7:25), the decision about which angle was smaller required a relatively long time. In contrast, the decision was easy and rapid when the two angles were quite different (for example, 4:10 and 9:23). Figure 6.4 shows a difficult decision and an easy one.

This finding provides more evidence for an "internal psychophysics," like the study by Moyer (1973) that we discussed in the Imagery and Size section. With real objects, people take longer to a make a decision if two objects are similar than if there is a clear-cut difference. In the same way, people should take longer when the mental objects are similar to each other. Paivio therefore tested pairs of times

======= FIGURE 6.4 =======

DECISIONS ABOUT ANGLES

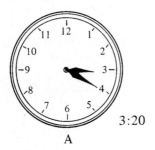

3:20

A

7:25

B

A difficult decision:
Which angle between the hands is smaller, clock A or clock B?

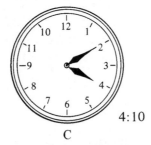

4:10

C

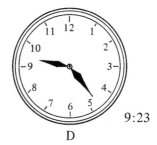

9:23

D

An easy decision:
Which angle between the hands is smaller, clock C or clock D?

corresponding to several angle size differences. For example, some pairs had a difference of 30° between the angles, and some had a difference of 120°.

We mentioned individual differences in connection with mental rotation, and Paivio (1978a) also examined individual differences in connection with judgments about angles on mental clocks. As you can imagine, some people are quite good at mental imagery tasks like this: Just mention the time 9:23 to them, and a mental picture of a clock reading 9:23 pops immediately into their heads. Other people have to struggle to create an image. Slowly they picture the small hand set at the 9, then they try to keep the small hand glued there while they add a large hand pointing to the lower right-hand corner. Paivio gave the participants in his study several standardized tests for mental-imagery ability (e.g., predicting what a colored block would look like if it were subdivided into smaller blocks). Based on these test results, people were categorized as having either high imagery or low imagery.

Let us see how angle difference and imagery ability influenced reaction time, that is, the amount of time required to decide which angle is smaller. As Figure 6.5 shows, the study provided additional evidence for internal psychophysics. Notice how the reaction times are much longer when the two shapes are similar (that is,

━━━━━━━━━━━━━━━━━━━━━━ FIGURE 6.5 ━━━━━━━━━━━━━━━━━━━━━━

THE INFLUENCE OF ANGLE DIFFERENCE ON REACTION TIME, FOR HIGH-IMAGERY AND LOW-IMAGERY PEOPLE.   SOURCE: PAIVIO (1978b).

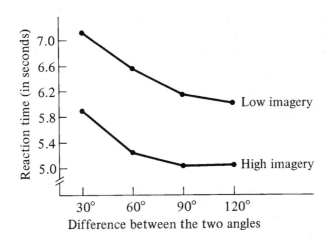

the angle difference is small). Notice, also, that high-imagery people have consistently shorter reaction times than the low-imagery people.

Paivio argues that this study offers strong support for the proposal that people use analog codes—rather than propositional codes—in problems like the mental clock task. First of all, the participants' reaction times were closely related to the angle differences, corresponding to the true, physical differences on "real" clocks. Secondly, the reaction times were related to imagery ability. Additional data showed that reaction times were *not* related to verbal ability; we would expect these two factors to be related if images were stored in a language-like propositional code.

Other research on imagery and shape provides additional support for analog codes. For example, Shepard and Chipman (1970) asked people to construct mental images of the shapes of various states—such as Colorado and West Virginia—and to make judgments about the shape similarity for various pairs of mental images. The participants' judgments were highly similar to the judgments they made when judging actual sketches of the states' shapes. Once again, people's judgments about the shape of mental images are similar to their judgments about the shape of physical stimuli.

Let's review our conclusions about the characteristics of mental images, based on the research we have discussed in the first part of this chapter:

1. When people rotate a mental image, a large rotation takes them longer, just as they take longer when making a large rotation with a physical stimulus.
2. People make size judgments in a similar fashion for mental images and physical stimuli; this conclusion holds true for both visual and auditory images.

3. People make decisions about shape in a similar fashion for mental images and physical stimuli; this conclusion holds true for both simple shapes (angles formed by hands on a clock) and complex shapes (geographic regions, like Colorado or West Virginia).

Now, let's consider some additional research that demonstrates some similarity between mental images and physical stimuli, specifically, the research on interference. As we will see in this in-depth examination, the research shows that the correspondence is strong, but it is less than perfect.

IN DEPTH: Imagery and Interference

Try to get a mental image of a good friend's face, and simultaneously let your eyes wander over this page. You will probably find the task to be difficult, because you are trying to look at the words on the page (a physical stimulus) and to look (with your "mind's eye") at your friend. You experience interference. Research has demonstrated that visual perception can interfere with visual imagery, and visual imagery can also interfere with visual perception.

Visual Tasks Interfering with Visual Imagery. Brooks (1968) demonstrated that visual perception can interfere with a task that requires visual imagery. Participants in this study saw a block letter, such as the **L** in Figure 6.6. Then, the letter was removed. From memory, people were instructed to make a decision about each corner in the figure. Specifically, they were told to answer "yes" if a corner was located

=== FIGURE 6.6 ===

AN EXAMPLE OF A BLOCK DIAGRAM AND AN ANSWER SHEET FOR THE POINTING CONDITION, SIMILAR TO THOSE USED BY BROOKS (1968). (A) A BLOCK LETTER: SUBJECTS CLASSIFIED EACH CORNER AS TO WHETHER IT WAS AT AN EXTREME PART OF THE FIGURE OR NOT. (B) AN ANSWER SHEET FOR THE POINTING CONDITION: SUBJECTS POINTED TO Y OR N TO INDICATE THE ANSWER (CORRECT ANSWERS ARE UNDERLINED).

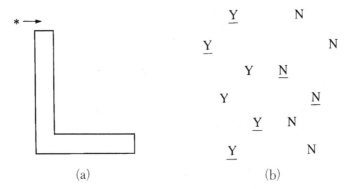

(a) (b)

at an extreme part of the figure (either at the extreme top or the extreme bottom). If a corner was not located at an extreme part (that is, if it was in the middle of the figure), they should answer "no." Starting at the asterisk in Figure 6.6a, for example, and moving clockwise around the figure, notice that the first two responses should be "yes," because these corners are at the extreme top of the figure. The next two responses should be "no," because these corners are neither at the extreme top nor the extreme bottom. The last two responses should both be "yes."

Brooks asked participants to give their answers by responding in one of three different ways. For a vocal response, people simply replied "yes" or "no" when identifying each corner. For a tapping response, people used their left hand to answer "yes" and their right hand to answer "no." For a pointing response, people looked at a complex spatial arrangement of pairs of Y's and N's, such as the one shown in Figure 6.7b; they were instructed to move downward through this answer sheet, marking either "yes" or "no." (You'll note that the correct sequence is Y, Y, N, N, Y, Y.)

Brooks reasoned that the pointing task would require a great deal of visual perception in order to scan the display of Y's and N's. In contrast, visual perception in the vocal or tapping conditions would be minimal. Therefore, if a person's mental image of the letter **L** is visual, then he or she would have trouble providing responses that require visual perception. Brooks's results showed that people spent about twice as long on the pointing task as on the other tasks. That is, visual perception interfered with the visual image. (You'll notice, incidentally, that this study is an excellent demonstration of Baddeley's distinction between the phonological loop and visuo-spatial working memory, which we discussed in Chapter 4.)

You might be suspicious about these results, however. How do we know that the pointing task is not simply a more difficult one, without considering interference? Fortunately, Brooks included another condition, in which people were asked to remember sentences and make judgments about the words in the sentence. This task was largely verbal or vocal, rather than spatial. The participants in this condition responded quickly for tapping and pointing, but they experienced interference when the vocal response was required, and their reaction times were much longer. Thus, visual perception interferes with a visual image, and a verbal task interferes with a verbal image. This experiment thus provides evidence that we store a memory of a picture (such as a picture of the letter **L**) in terms of what it looks like in its arrangement in space rather than in terms of a string of verbal descriptions of its shape.

Visual Imagery Interfering with Visual Tasks. If stimuli we really see can interfere with our visual images, will the reverse also be true? That is, can a visual image interfere when we are trying to see a physical stimulus? The pioneering studies in this area were conducted by Cheves Perky (1910), who reported that the participants in her study had difficulty detecting visual stimuli when they had constructed simultaneous mental images. In her honor, the term ***Perky effect*** is now applied to situations in which visual imagery interferes with performance on visual tasks performed at the same time (Craver-Lemley & Reeves, 1992).

Research on the topic of visual imagery virtually disappeared during the behaviorist era of psychology, and the Perky effect was temporarily forgotten. However, Sydney Segal and Vincent Fusella (1970) revived the phenomenon by asking participants to make a visual image (for example, a volcano or a tree) or an auditory image (for example, the sound of an oboe or a typewriter). As soon as each person had formed the requested image, the experimenters presented either a sound on a harmonica (auditory signal), a small blue arrow (visual signal), or nothing.

Segal and Fusella's results showed that people performed much less accurately in detecting the physical stimulus when the image and the signal were in the same sensory mode. In other words, it was easier for participants to see the arrow when they were imagining the sound of a typewriter than when they were imagining the shape of a tree. On the other hand, they could hear the harmonica better when they were imagining the shape of a tree than when they were imagining the sound of a typewriter. Once again, visual images seem to involve visual activity. In contrast, auditory images seem to involve auditory activity. Additional research by Segal and her coauthor confirmed the Perky effect (Segal, 1971; Segal & Gordon, 1969), but other research by Farah and Smith (1983) failed to demonstrate interference.

Let's examine a series of more recent studies on the Perky effect by Catherine Craver-Lemley and Adam Reeves. In their first study, the basic visual task involved acuity (Craver-Lemley & Reeves, 1987). Specifically, the participants were asked to look at a series of figures with two vertical lines, similar to Part a of Figure 6.7. They were instructed to report, on each trial, whether the bottom line was offset to the left or to the right of the top line. In some conditions, participants simply performed the acuity task. In other conditions, they were shown a sketch of a design (such as those in Parts b and c of Figure 6.7) and were asked to "project" the visual image of this design onto a particular location. While they maintained the visual image in this location, the researcher then presented the acuity task. Sometimes the two lines from the acuity task were in the same location as the visual image, and sometimes the two lines were placed a varying number of degrees off to the side.

═══════════════ **FIGURE 6.7** ═══════════════

FIGURES USED IN CRAVER-LEMLEY AND REEVES'S (1987) RESEARCH. PART a AND SIMILAR FIGURES WERE USED TO TEST ACUITY; PARTICIPANTS WERE ASKED TO CREATE MENTAL IMAGES OF FIGURES SUCH AS IN PART b AND PART c.

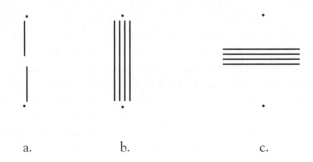

a.   b.   c.

As you can see from Figure 6.8, Craver-Lemley and Reeves found evidence for the Perky effect. Specifically, visual images tended to interfere with visual perception, and the effect was especially strong when the visual image and the visual stimulus were located close together.

In a later paper, Craver-Lemley and Reeves (1992) attempted to identify more precisely just how a visual image interferes with a visual stimulus. Their research eliminated several likely explanations, such as the possibility that people's eyes may wander away from the visual stimulus while maintaining a visual image. They also eliminated another explanation that would be consistent with a strict interpretation of the analog position. Specifically, research in perception shows that an actual visual stimulus does not interfere with another visual stimulus if the two stimuli are slightly separated from each other. Interference occurs only when they actually overlap. In contrast, however, as we saw in Figure 6.8, a visual image still blocks perception, even when the two are separated.

Craver-Lemley and Reeves (1992) prefer a different explanation. They argue that visual images block perception because imagery actually lowers the observer's

═══════════════ **FIGURE 6.8** ═══════════════

THE PERKY EFFECT (REDUCTION IN ACUITY ACCURACY), AS A FUNCTION OF THE SEPARATION BETWEEN THE MENTAL IMAGE AND THE ACUITY-TEST STIMULUS. BASED ON CRAVER-LEMLEY AND REEVES (1987).
NOTE: RESULTS FROM FOUR DIFFERENT MENTAL-IMAGE STIMULI ARE COMBINED.

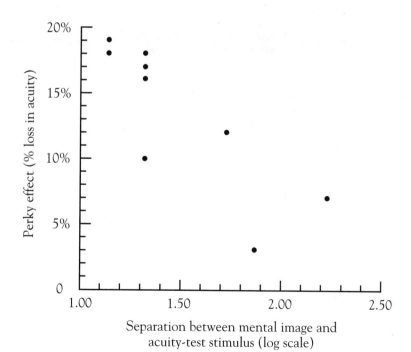

Separation between mental image and
acuity-test stimulus (log scale)

sensitivity. Somewhere along the visual pathway—beyond the retina but before complex visual processing in the cortex—people seem to be less sensitive to a real visual stimulus if they are simultaneously maintaining a mental image. According to the authors, people may need to suppress messages from real physical stimuli in order to create clear mental images.

In later research, Craver-Lemley and her coauthors (1997) provided still further evidence that imagery and perception are not equivalent. Specifically, they found that acuity was reduced when people were instructed to create a visual image in front of the two lines that were being used to test acuity. When the visual image appeared *behind* the two lines, however, acuity remained excellent. In contrast, real lines interfere with accuracy on an acuity test, whether those lines are in front of or behind the acuity-test stimulus.

In short, the research on interference shows that the mystery of visual imagery is complex. Earlier, we mentioned that imagery appears to be related to perception. However, this relationship doesn't seem to involve close kinship. We are probably dealing with two cousins, rather than identical twins!

◀◀

Imagery and Ambiguous Figures

Try Demonstration 6.4 and note whether you were able to reinterpret the figure. Most people have difficulty with tasks like this. Reed (1974) was interested in

---

DEMONSTRATION 6.4

IMAGERY AND AN AMBIGUOUS FIGURE

Look at the figure below, and form a clear mental image of the figure. Then turn to the section labeled "Further Instructions" at the bottom of Demonstration 6.5, on page 202.

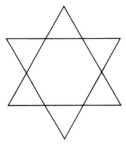

people's ability to decide whether a pattern was a portion of a design they had seen earlier. He therefore presented a series of paired figures: first a pattern like the Star of David in Demonstration 6.4 and then—after a brief delay—a second pattern (for example, a parallelogram). In half of the cases, the second pattern was truly part of the first one; in the other half, it was not (for example, a rectangle).

If people store mental images in their heads that correspond to the physical objects they have seen, then they should be able to produce the mental image of the star and quickly discover the parallelogram shape hidden within the star. However, the participants in Reed's study were correct only 14% of the time on this particular example. Across all stimuli, they were correct only 55% of the time, hardly better than chance.

Reed argued that this lack of accuracy suggests that people could not have stored mental pictures. Instead, Reed proposed that people store pictures as descriptions, in propositional codes. You may have stored the description in Demonstration 6.4 as "two triangles, one pointing up and the other pointing down, placed on top of each other." When asked whether the figure contained a parallelogram, you may have searched through that verbal description and found only triangles, not parallelograms. Notice that Reed's research is not consistent with the analog-code argument.

Similar research has examined whether people are able to provide reinterpretations of ambiguous mental images. For example, you can interpret the ambiguous stimulus in Figure 6.9 in two ways: a rabbit facing to the right or a duck facing to the left. Chambers and Reisberg (1985) showed this figure to participants for 5 seconds, asked them to create a clear mental image of the figure, and then removed it. Participants were then asked to give a second, different interpretation of the figure. None of the 15 people could do so, even though several of them were high-imagery individuals. However, when they were asked to draw the figure from memory and then reinterpret it, all 15 supplied a second interpretation.

FIGURE 6.9

AN EXAMPLE OF AN AMBIGUOUS FIGURE FROM CHAMBERS AND REISBERG'S (1985) STUDY.

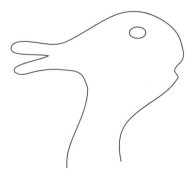

DEMONSTRATION 6.5

REINTERPRETING AMBIGUOUS STIMULI

Imagine the capital letter **H.** Now imagine the capital letter **X** directly on top of the **H,** so that the four corners of each letter match up exactly. From this mental image, what new shapes and objects do you see in your "mind's eye"?

(Further instructions for Demonstration 6.4: Without glancing back at the figure in the previous demonstration, consult your mental image. Does that mental image contain a parallelogram?)

Chambers and Reisberg's (1985) research on ambiguous figures suggests that a language-like propositional code can dominate over an analog code. In this study, people apparently devised a strong interpretation of the figure (Finke, 1989). Therefore, top-down processes—similar to those we explored in Chapter 2—can interfere with alternate interpretations.

Notice the similarity between Chambers and Reisberg's study and Reed's study with parallelograms and other geometric figures. In both cases, participants were asked to manipulate a mental image of an abstract sketch that had been presented and then removed. In contrast, research supporting the analog code typically uses simple figures or asks participants to create their own images of elephants, clocks, or West Virginia. Tasks using abstract shapes may encourage a propositional code requiring verbal labels, rather than an analog code. Similarly, when I work on jigsaw puzzles, I often find myself searching for missing pieces to which I've attached verbal labels such as "angel with outstretched wings." In these cases, storage may be predominantly propositional.

Other authors have pointed out that these studies using ambiguous figures are unusual. For instance, ambiguous figures such as the rabbit-duck are unique. The whole figure must be perceived at once, and when part of the image fades, some of the details are lost (Hyman, 1993; Kaufmann & Helstrup, 1993). In contrast, we can readily revive a fading image of elephants, clocks, and West Virginia.

Further research by Chambers and Reisberg (1992) has clarified that people who construe Figure 6.9 as a rabbit are likely to emphasize the mouth in their mental image, omitting information about the ears. In contrast, those who construe it as a duck are likely to emphasize the beak, omitting information about the back of the head. Notice, then, that the image becomes more schematic as time passes; characteristics that don't match the schema are lost.

In some circumstances, however, people can reinterpret mental images as easily as they reinterpret visual stimuli. For example, they can reinterpret mental images of the classical ambiguous figures when they are given appropriate instructions

(Hyman, 1993) or when they are encouraged to pay attention to specific parts of the image (Peterson et al., 1992).

In other research, Finke and his colleagues (1989) asked people to combine two mental images, as in Demonstration 6.5. The participants in this study were indeed able to come up with new interpretations for these ambiguous stimuli. In addition to a combined **X** and **H** figure, they reported some new geometric shapes (such as a right triangle), some new letters (such as **M**), and some objects (such as a bow tie).

In summary, the research on ambiguous figures shows that mental images can be both descriptive and depictive (Chambers, 1993). That is, we often do use propositional codes to provide verbal labels to describe our mental images. However, when the stimuli and instructions are ideal, we can use an analog code to depict a picture-like representation.

Imagery and Other Vision-Like Processes

So far, we have reviewed a variety of topics, in each case examining two or more studies addressing the similarity between imagery and perception. In this section, we'll look at four other specialized characteristics of visual perception: acuity as a function of retinal location, the oblique effect, stabilized images, and complementary colors. Together, these four topics provide additional evidence that mental imagery resembles visual perception.

One important characteristic of the visual system is that acuity is better for objects that are registered in the center of the retina and worse for objects registered in the periphery. Finke and Kosslyn (1980) presented two dots about a centimeter apart; they asked participants in their study to indicate how far into their peripheral vision the dots could be moved before the acuity was so poor that the dots blurred together. Other participants performed the same task by *imagining* the dots moving out into the periphery. The perception and imagery instructions produced highly similar results, particularly for people with vivid imagery.

Another visual phenomenon discovered by perception researchers is called the ***oblique effect,*** which means that acuity is better for narrow stripes if they are oriented either horizontally or vertically than if they are oriented diagonally. Kosslyn (1983) reproduced the oblique effect using imagery instructions. This study demonstrates once again the similarity between perception and imagery. However, the study has additional significance. Critics have proposed that the experimental results in imagery experiments might be traceable to demand characteristics. Earlier we discussed experimenter expectancy, a process by which the experimenter's expectations might be transmitted to participants in an experiment. ***Demand characteristics*** include all the cues that might convey the experimenter's hypothesis to the participant. Experimenter expectancy is one source of these cues, but there are numerous other demand characteristics, as well. For example, in many cases, participants may be able to guess the results that the experimenter wants. For instance, they may guess that an auditory image is supposed to interfere with an auditory perception. However, the oblique effect is virtually unknown to people without a background in the field of perception. It seems highly unlikely that the participants in Kosslyn's study could have guessed the results.

Other imagery phenomena resembling vision that have been demonstrated with visual imagery include stabilized images. Kosslyn (1983) showed that when people imagine a pattern at a particular location for a long period, they have trouble imagining a new pattern at this same location. This phenomenon is directly parallel to a perceptual phenomenon called the stabilized retinal image, in which an image that is kept on the same part of the retina ultimately stops being perceived.

Finally, another visual phenomenon involves complementary colors as afterimages. After viewing a green stimulus, you will see faint red when you look at a white surface. Finke and Schmidt (1978) demonstrated that color afterimages can be produced by imagery, as well as by physical stimuli. All these four areas of research therefore support the analog-code approach to explaining visual images.

Neuropsychological Evidence for the Similarity Between Imagery and Perception

We have examined many studies that demonstrate how people seem to treat mental images the same way they treat visual stimuli. In general, imagery and perception appear to involve similar psychological processes. But how similar are imagery and perception at the biological level? As Finke (1989) notes, mental imagery does not involve the rods and cones in the retina. Also, the research by Craver-Lemley and Reeves (1992), which we discussed in the In-Depth section, suggests that perceptual stimuli and mental imagery produce interference at different locations in the visual system.

However, physiological structures at more advanced levels of visual processing do seem to be activated when we construct mental images (Simon, 1992b). For example, some relevant research has been gathered by Martha Farah (1988, 1995), who received the Troland Award from the National Academy of Sciences for her research on vision. Farah gathered some compelling evidence that the visual processing areas of the cerebral cortex are implicated in visual mental imagery.

The research summarized in Farah's review uses many of the techniques discussed in the section on neuroscience in Chapter 1. For example, researchers have studied individuals with lesions (damage) in the visual cortex. Many of these people cannot produce mental images, even though their other cognitive abilities are normal. Although exceptions have been reported, most individuals with these lesions show similar impairments in both perception and mental imagery (Farah, 1995; Intons-Peterson, 1993b).

A variety of other studies have used PET scans, fMRIs, and other brain-imaging techniques to assess which areas of the brain show increased blood flow when people work on tasks that require visual imagery. For example, Stephen Kosslyn and his coauthors (1993, 1996) asked people to perform a variety of tasks involving visual imagery. The researchers found that these tasks activated the occipital visual cortex, located at the back of the brain. Furthermore, when people were asked to form small visual images, the most active region of the visual cortex was the same part activated when we look at a small visual stimulus. When people formed large visual images, the most active region was farther forward in the visual cortex—the same part activated when we look at a large visual stimulus.

A third neuroscience technique that is often employed to study mental imagery is the event-related potential technique. Using this method, Farah and Peronnet (1989) tested people who rated themselves as high or low in imagery. When both types of individuals were asked to produce mental images, the high-imagery people showed significantly larger event-related potentials in the occipital visual cortex. Once again, portions of the brain associated with vision are activated when people form mental images.

The neuroscience evidence is particularly compelling because it avoids the problem of demand characteristics that we discussed earlier. As Farah (1988) points out, people are not likely to know which parts of their brain are typically active during vision. Furthermore, they are not likely to be able to voluntarily force more blood into their visual cortex or voluntarily change the electrical activity in their brains. The similarity between perception and imagery is persuasive, because it cannot be explained by social expectations.

The Imagery Controversy, Revisited

As Howard Gardner (1985) writes in his chronicle of the history of cognitive science, "Probably no research in cognitive studies has generated so much controversy as work on imagery" (p. 330). Let's first examine the analog position, and then we will consider the propositional view. The two positions do differ in their emphasis on the similarity between mental images and physical stimuli. However, the two positions are not *completely* different from each other, and they may apply to different kinds of tasks.

The Analog Viewpoint. When we examined the characteristics of mental images, we discovered many ways in which our reactions to mental images resemble our reactions to real objects. (You may wish to review those similarities.) Indeed, the majority of the research supports this position. However, no one argues that vision and mental imagery are *identical*. After all, you can easily differentiate between your mental image of your textbook's cover and your perception of that cover. (However, you may recall from the discussion of reality monitoring in Chapter 5 that we may have trouble remembering whether we actually did something or simply imagined doing it.)

Stephen Kosslyn and others support an analog theory of imagery, which proposes that "similar mechanisms in the visual system are activated when objects or events are imagined as when the same objects or events are actually perceived" (Finke, 1989, p. 41).

Kosslyn has developed his theory of imagery still further by implementing a computer-simulation model (Kosslyn, 1981, 1987, 1994; Kosslyn & Koenig, 1992). This theory is complex, and this textbook will only summarize it briefly. As you'll see, this theory does not *exclude* language-like representations; it differs from the propositional viewpoint because it also includes analog (literal) information.

According to Kosslyn's theory, images have two important components. The first is the ***surface representation,*** which is a quasi-pictorial representation. This representation depicts an object, and it is responsible for the experience we report of having a picture-like mental image. The surface representation is produced in the visual cortex, somewhat similar to the way a visual image is produced when we see a real, physical object. The second component of Kosslyn's theory is the ***deep representation.*** This is the information that is stored in long-term memory and is used to generate the surface representation. Two different kinds of deep representations can generate surface representations: (1) literal information, which consists of encodings of how something looked, and (2) propositional information, which describes an object or a scene in verbal terms.

How does Kosslyn's theory account for the generation of an image? According to Kosslyn, image generation occurs when a surface image is formed on the basis of information stored in long-term memory (that is, the deep representation). This image generation is accomplished by four processing components:

1. The *picture* process converts information encoded in a literal encoding into a surface image. The image can come in different sizes and locations, depending on the "instructions" given to the picture process.
2. The *find* process searches the surface image for a particular part. (For example, suppose someone is describing a person to you and then says, "He has red hair." You must find the neutral-colored hair in your surface image and correct the hair color.)
3. The *put* process performs several functions that are necessary to create a portion of an image at the correct location, for example, by adjusting the size of one part of the image.
4. The *image* process coordinates the other three components and determines other characteristics such as whether the image will be detailed or relatively simple.

Kosslyn proposes additional processes that allow a person to scan to a correct location (for example, to look at the rear end of the mental image of a frog when asked, "Does a frog have a tail?"), to change the size of the mental image, and to rotate the figure.

The Propositional Viewpoint. Pylyshyn (1978, 1984, 1989) has been the strongest opponent of the "pictures-in-the-head" hypothesis. He agrees that people *do* experience mental images; it would be foolish to argue otherwise. However, Pylyshyn says that these images are epiphenomenal, which means that the images are simply "tacked on" later, after an item has been recovered from (propositional) storage. He proposes that information is actually stored in terms of propositions, or abstract concepts that describe relationships between items. People remove a proposition from storage and use that propositional information to construct a mental image. Pylyshyn argues that it would be awkward—and perhaps even unworkable—to store information in terms of mental images, because a huge storage space would be required to store all the images people claim they have.

Pylyshyn also emphasizes the differences between perceptual experiences and mental images. For example, you can reexamine and reinterpret a real photograph. However, Reed's (1974) research showed that people cannot typically reinterpret a mental image in order to locate a hidden part that was not originally noticed. Also, Chambers and Reisberg's (1985) study illustrated that people cannot usually reinterpret an ambiguous stimulus, even though they can easily reinterpret a visual stimulus.

As Pylyshyn also points out, when we perceive real objects, we can perform operations that are impossible for mental images. Pylyshyn (1984) suggests an informal demonstration to illustrate this last point:

> Form a clear, stable image of a favorite familiar scene. Can you now imagine it as a photographic negative, out of focus, in mirror-image inversion, upside down? (pp. 227–228)

Indeed, these transformations will probably be difficult, because mental images do not exactly mimic perceptual experiences.

Some people prefer the propositional viewpoint for reasons of parsimony; why should we introduce a second storage mechanism unless we have a compelling reason to propose analog codes as well as propositional codes (Farah, 1995)? However, others believe that the support for analog codes *is* compelling. Of course, the problem is that imagery is such a hidden process that research is especially difficult. At present, however, the evidence suggests that with most stimuli and most tasks, mental images seem to be stored in an analog code. For some kinds of stimuli and several specific tasks, however, a propositional code may be used. In many respects—though certainly not all—mental images resemble the perceptions of real objects.

SECTION SUMMARY: THE CHARACTERISTICS OF MENTAL IMAGES

1. An important controversy in imagery is whether information is stored in analog or propositional codes; research on the characteristics of mental images addresses this issue.
2. The amount of time it takes to rotate a mental image depends on the extent of the rotation, just as when rotating a real, physical object.
3. People take longer to make judgments about the characteristics of small mental images than of large mental images. Also, people take longer to travel a large mental distance, whether that distance is visual or auditory. Finally, comparisons take longer when two mental images are similar than when they are different.

4. When judging shapes, people take longer to make decisions about two similar angles formed by hands on a clock; when judging the shape of states, people's decisions about mental images resemble people's decisions about physical stimuli.

5. Visual tasks interfere with visual imagery, and verbal tasks interfere with verbal imagery. Furthermore, visual imagery may interfere with visual tasks (The Perky effect), and auditory imagery may interfere with auditory tasks. For example, research by Craver-Lemley and Reeves shows that visual imagery can interfere with performance on an acuity task; however, mental images do not interfere in exactly the same way as do perceptual images.

6. People have difficulty identifying that a part belongs to a whole if they have not included the part in their original verbal description of the whole. Also, some ambiguous figures are difficult to reinterpret in a mental image.

7. Other vision-like properties of mental images include acuity for objects as a function of retinal location, the oblique effect, the stabilized-image phenomenon, and complementary colors as afterimages.

8. Neuropsychological research using case studies, PET scans, and event-related potentials shows that visual imagery involves the visual processing areas of the cerebral cortex.

9. Kosslyn has developed the analog position that includes both surface and deep representations. The propositional viewpoint, as expressed by Pylyshyn, argues that images are simply "tacked on" to the propositional code. At present, most—but not all—research supports the analog position.

COGNITIVE MAPS

You have probably had an experience like this. You have just arrived in a new environment, perhaps for your first year of college. You ask for directions, let's say, to the library. You hear the reply, "OK, it's simple. You go up the hill, staying to the right of the Blake Building. Then you take a left, and Newton will be on your right. The library will be over on your left." You struggle to recall some landmarks from the orientation tour. Was Newton next to the College Union, or was it over near the Administration Building? Valiantly, you try to incorporate this new information into your discouragingly hazy mental map.

So far, this chapter has examined the general characteristics of mental images and how they are stored in memory. Now we consider a related topic, cognitive maps. A *cognitive map* is a mental device that codes and simplifies the way our spatial environment is arranged (Kitchin, 1994; Ormrod et al., 1988). Research on cognitive maps has examined environmental spaces that range widely in size and include classrooms, neighborhoods, cities, countries, and even larger geographic regions (Warren, 1995; Weatherford, 1985). Typically, these studies emphasize real-world settings and ecological validity. The study of cognitive maps is included within the larger topic of *spatial memory*, a broad topic that involves not only cognitive maps, but also the location of words and other objects in a spatial array (Schacter & Nadel, 1991).

In general, researchers have not discussed the way in which cognitive maps are encoded, that is, whether the code is analog or propositional. However, most researchers who have raised this issue conclude that cognitive maps must be both analog and propositional in nature (e.g., Gärling et al., 1985; McNamara et al., 1989; Russell & Ward, 1982). Your mental map for a particular city may therefore include both a picture-like image of the relationship among several streets and buildings, as well as propositions, such as "The Ethiopian restaurant is in northwest Toronto." Information on your mental map may include landmark knowledge and procedural knowledge (for example, "To get to the Ethiopian restaurant, go north from the hotel parking lot and turn left on Bloor").

Your mental map may also include survey knowledge, which is the relationship among locations that can be directly acquired by learning a map or by repeatedly exploring an environment (Schwartz & Kulhavy, 1988; Thorndyke & Goldin, 1983). As you might imagine, your mental map will be much more accurate if you acquire spatial information from a physical map that is oriented in the direction you are facing, so that you do not need to perform a mental rotation (Aretz & Wickens, 1992; Warren, 1994; Warren et al., 1992).

In this section on cognitive maps, we will consider how cognitive maps represent distance, shape, and orientation. Then we'll examine how we can construct mental models of our environment, based on a verbal description.

Theme 2 of this book states that cognitive processes are generally accurate. This generalization also applies to cognitive maps, because our mental representations of the environment usually reflect reality with reasonable accuracy, whether these cognitive maps depict college campuses or larger geographic regions. However, the second part of Theme 2 states that when people do make errors in their cognitive processes, those mistakes can often be traced to a rational strategy. We saw an example of this principle in Chapter 5 on the schematic nature of memory: People tend to believe that certain events occurred in their lives, as long as these events are conceptually similar to the schemas they have already developed. Similarly, the mistakes people make in their cognitive maps "make sense." These mistakes are systematic distortions of reality. They reflect a tendency to base our judgments on variables that are typically relevant, and to judge our environment as being more regular and orderly than it really is. We will see that people tend to show systematic distortions in distance, shape, and orientation.

Cognitive Maps and Distance

How far is it from your college library to the classroom in which your cognitive psychology course is taught? How many miles separate the city in which you were born from the city where your home is currently located? When people make distance estimates like these, their estimates are often distorted by factors such as the number of intervening cities, road-route distance, and semantic categories.

Number of Intervening Cities. In one of the first systematic studies about distance in cognitive maps, Thorndyke (1981) constructed a map of a hypothetical region with cities distributed throughout the map at 100, 200, 300, and 400 miles from each other. Between any two cities on the map, there were 0, 1, 2, or 3 other cities along the route, and Thorndyke was interested in the relationship between the number of intervening cities and distance estimation. Participants in the experiment alternated between study trials and recall trials until they had accurately reconstructed the map on two consecutive trials. Finally, they received a sheet listing the 64 possible city pairs, and they were instructed to estimate the distance between each pair of cities.

The number of intervening cities had a clear-cut influence on their estimates. For example, when the cities were really 300 miles apart on the map, people estimated that they were 280 miles apart when there were no intervening cities, but they were estimated to be 350 miles apart with three intervening cities. Notice that this error is a sensible one, however. In general, if two cities are randomly distributed through a region, any two cities *are* indeed farther apart when there are three other cities between them; two cities with no other intervening cities are likely to be closer together.

Road-Route Distance. Another determinant of distance on our cognitive maps will not surprise you. People consider two cities to be physically closer together "as the crow flies" if the road connecting these cities is a straight line, rather than an indirect route (McNamara et al., 1984). This emphasis on road-route distance is another distortion that makes good sense. In real life, we humans cannot travel along the route that crows fly; instead, we travel along roads. We are therefore perfectly rational to calculate distance in terms of road-route distance, rather than crow-flight distance.

Semantic Categories. The Fine Arts Building on my college campus seems closer to the College Union than it is to Sun Dance Bookstore. This bookstore is actually closer, but my distance estimate is distorted because the Fine Arts Building and the College Union are clustered together in my semantic memory under the category "college buildings." The bookstore does not belong to this cluster, even though no physical boundary divides campus buildings from the stores located off campus.

Research by Stephen Hirtle and his colleagues illustrates how semantic factors influence distance estimates for landmarks located within a town. For example, Hirtle and Mascolo (1986) constructed a hypothetical map of a town that included some landmarks associated with town government (for example, courthouse, police station, town hall) and some landmarks associated with recreation (for example, park, golf course, beach). After participants learned the locations on the map, the map was removed and people estimated the distance between pairs of landmarks. The results showed that people tended to shift each landmark closer to other landmarks that belonged to the same cluster. For example, the courthouse

DEMONSTRATION 6.6

MENTAL MAPS AND CURVES

Look at the portion of the map below, which shows a river and two nearby streets. Study this map for about 5 seconds. Then close the book and try to sketch the map as accurately as possible. The results will be discussed in the next section.

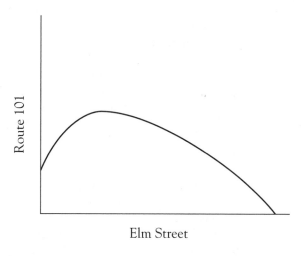

might be remembered as being close to the police station and the town hall. The shifts occurred for members of the same semantic cluster, but not for members of different semantic clusters; the courthouse did not move closer to the park.

The same influence of semantic categories occurred when Hirtle and Jonides (1985) asked University of Michigan students to estimate distances between pairs of landmarks in Ann Arbor. The students showed a clustering bias; members of the same cluster were judged to be closer to each other than members of different clusters—even when the actual distances were the same.

Thus, both laboratory research (Hirtle & Mascolo, 1986) and research using ecologically valid stimuli (Hirtle & Jonides, 1985) confirm an additional distortion in distance estimates: When two places seem semantically close, we believe they are geographically close. Once again, however, this error makes sense; in general, our real-life experience tells us that landmarks with similar functions are likely to be close to each other. Be sure you have tried Demonstration 6.6 at the top of this page before you read further.

Cognitive Maps and Shapes

Our cognitive maps represent not only distances, but shapes. These shapes are evident in map features such as the angles formed by intersecting streets and the curves illustrating the bends in rivers. Once again, the research shows a systematic distortion; people tend to construct cognitive maps in which the shapes are more regular than they are in reality.

Angles. Consider the research by Moar and Bower (1983), who studied people's cognitive maps of Cambridge, England. All the participants in the study had lived in Cambridge for at least 5 years. Moar and Bower wanted to determine people's estimates for the angles formed by the intersection of two streets. They were particularly interested in the angle estimates for sets of three streets that formed large triangles within the city of Cambridge. The participants showed a clear tendency to "regularize" the angles so that they were more like 90-degree angles. For example, three streets formed a triangle that contained real angles of 67°, 63°, and 50°. However, these same angles were estimated to be 84°, 78°, and 88°. In all, seven of the nine angles were significantly biased in the direction of a 90-degree angle. Furthermore, you know that the angles within a triangle should sum to 180°. Notice, however, that the angles in people's cognitive-triangle maps do not necessarily sum to 180°. (In this particular example, for instance, the angles sum to 250°.)

What explains this systematic distortion? Moar and Bower (1983) suggest that we employ a *heuristic,* or simple rule of thumb. In general, as a rule of thumb, when two roads meet, they form a 90-degree angle. It is easier to represent angles in a mental map as being closer to 90° than they really are. Similarly, as you recall from the discussion of schematization of memory, it is easier to store a schematic version of an event, rather than a precise version of the event that accurately represents all the little details.

Curves. The New York State Thruway runs in an east-west direction across the state, though it curves somewhat in certain areas. To me, the upward curve south of Rochester seems symmetrical, equally arched on each side of the city. However, when I checked the map, the curve is much steeper on the eastern side.

Research confirms that people tend to use a *symmetry heuristic;* figures are remembered as being more symmetrical and regular than they truly are. For example, Tversky and Schiano (1989) showed students map-like diagrams in which an irregularly shaped curve was said to be a river, bordered by two streets. These diagrams resembled the figure in Demonstration 6.6. The participants studied each figure for 5 seconds and then drew it from memory.

The results showed that for 7 of the 8 figures, people drew the figure as being more symmetrical than it had been in the original sketch. Now check your own figure from Demonstration 6.6 and see whether the symmetry heuristic also operated in your drawing.

Spatial Arrangement. So far, we have seen how people tend to construct a mental image of a geographic shape that is more regular than it is in reality. We seem to find it easier to store a schematic version of reality, rather than reality itself. Not surprisingly, then, research on mental maps of house layouts shows that people can remember the spatial arrangement of rooms when a house follows a typical layout, with the bedrooms clustered together and the kitchen near the dining room (Arbuckle et al., 1994). In contrast, they have trouble remembering an arrangement in which the bathroom is located near the main entrance and the kitchen lies between two bedrooms—an arrangement that violates our standard architectural schema.

Cognitive Maps and Relative Positions

Which city is farther west, San Diego, California, or Reno, Nevada? If you are like most people—and the participants in a study by Stevens and Coupe (1978)—the question seems ludicrously easy. Of course San Diego is farther west, because California is west of Nevada. However, if you consult a map, you'll discover that Reno is in fact west of San Diego. Which city is farther north, Detroit or its "twin city" across the river, Windsor, in Ontario, Canada? Again, the answer seems obvious; any Canadian city must be north of a U.S. city!

Barbara Tversky (1981) argues that cognitive maps often reveal two additional kinds of heuristics. We use these heuristics when we try to capture the orientation of features on our mental maps. Geographic regions are typically irregular in shape, and landmarks are typically irregularly scattered through space. We tend to represent features as being more regular than they really are—just as we represent the angles of intersecting streets as being close to 90° and we represent curves as being symmetrical. The two heuristics that operate for the relative positions of features are called the rotation heuristic and the alignment heuristic.

The Rotation Heuristic. According to the *rotation heuristic,* figures that are slightly tilted will be remembered as being either more vertical or more horizontal than they really are. For example, Figure 6.10 shows that the coastline of California is slanted at a significant angle. The rotation heuristic makes the orientation more vertical by rotating the coastline. If your cognitive map suffers from the distorting effects of the rotation heuristic, you will conclude (erroneously) that San Diego is west of Reno. Similarly, the rotation heuristic leads you to the wrong decision about Detroit and Windsor; Windsor, in Canada, is actually *south* of Detroit.

Let us look at some research on the rotation heuristic. Tversky (1981) studied people's mental maps for the geographic region of the San Francisco Bay area. This region slants substantially, as Figure 6.10 shows. However, 69% of the students at a Bay area university in this region showed evidence of the rotation heuristic. In their maps, the coastline was rotated in a more north–south direction than is true on a geographically correct map. Keep in mind, though, that some students—in fact,

FIGURE 6.10

ACCORDING TO THE ROTATION HEURISTIC, WE TEND TO ROTATE THE COASTLINE OF CALIFORNIA INTO A MORE NEARLY VERTICAL ORIENTATION AND INCORRECTLY CONCLUDE THAT SAN DIEGO IS FARTHER WEST THAN RENO.

31% of them—were not influenced by this heuristic. Glicksohn (1994) found a similar rotation heuristic in the mental maps of students living in Israel.

The Alignment Heuristic. According to the ***alignment heuristic,*** figures will be remembered as being more lined up than they really are. To test the alignment heuristic, Tversky (1981) presented pairs of cities to students, who were asked to select which member of each pair was north (or, in some cases, east). For example, one of those pairs was Rome–Philadelphia. As Figure 6.11 shows, Rome is actually north of Philadelphia. However, because of the alignment heuristic, people tend to line up the United States and Europe so that they are in the same latitude. Because we know that Rome is in southern Europe and Philadelphia is at the north end of the United States, we conclude—incorrectly—that Philadelphia is north of Rome.

Tversky's results indicated that the students showed a consistent tendency to use the alignment heuristic. For example, 78% judged Philadelphia to be north of Rome, and 12% judged that they were the same latitude. Only 10% correctly answered that Rome is north of Philadelphia. On all eight pairs tested by Tversky, an average of 66% of participants supplied the incorrect answer.

The rotation heuristic and the alignment heuristic may initially sound similar. However, the rotation heuristic involves rotating a single coastline, country, building, or other figure in a clockwise or counterclockwise fashion so that its border is oriented in a nearly vertical or horizontal direction. In contrast, the alignment heuristic involves lining up a number of separate countries, buildings, or other figures in a straight row. Both heuristics are similar, however, because they encourage us to construct cognitive maps that are orderly.

The heuristics we have examined in this chapter makes sense. For example, our cities tend to have right angles, pictures are generally hung on walls in a vertical

======================= **FIGURE 6.11** =======================

ACCORDING TO THE ALIGNMENT HEURISTIC, WE TEND TO LINE UP EUROPE AND THE UNITED STATES AND INCORRECTLY CONCLUDE THAT PHILADELPHIA IS NORTH OF ROME.

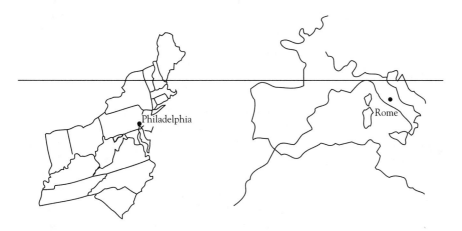

orientation, rather than at a slant, and houses are typically lined up evenly along the streets. However, when we rely too strongly on these heuristics, we miss the important details that make each stimulus unique. When our top-down cognitive processes are too active, we fail to pay sufficient attention to bottom-up information. In fact, the angle at the intersection is really 70°, that coastline does not run exactly north–south, and those continents are not really arranged in a horizontal line.

We have been stressing the similarity among the various heuristics. However, Tversky (1991a) points out some noticeable differences. For example, the symmetry heuristic, which would be used for representing curves, is equally strong in perception and in memory. In contrast, the rotation and alignment heuristics are small in perception; with the actual maps in front of us, we show little distortion. Still, the distortions produced by these two heuristics are much stronger in memory than in perception.

At this point, you may be reasonably skeptical about the validity of Theme 2; perhaps our cognitive processes are *not* impressively accurate. However, Mary Smyth and her coauthors (1994) place these errors in perspective:

> Bias in spatial judgments does not mean that people have a built-in tendency to get things wrong. Rather, the errors people make when they straighten edges, make junctions more like right angles, put things closer to landmarks, and remember average rather than specific positions, are indications of the way in which knowledge of spatial information is dealt with. Like the formation of concepts, the regularizing of spatial information reduces the need to maintain all the features of an environment which

DEMONSTRATION 6.7

CREATING A MENTAL MODEL

Take a piece of paper and cover the portion labeled, "Further Instructions." Read the story. When you have finished reading it, cover up the story and follow the Further Instructions.

The Story

You are at the Jefferson Plaza Hotel, where you have just taken the escalator from the first to the second floor. You will be meeting someone for dinner in a few minutes. You now stand next to the top of the escalator, where you have a view of the first floor as well as the second floor. You first look directly to your left, where you see a shimmering indoor fountain about 10 yards beyond a carpeted walkway. Though you cannot see beyond the low, stone wall that surrounds it, you suppose that its bottom is littered with nickels and pennies that hotel guests have tossed in. The view down onto the first floor allows you to see that directly below you is a darkened, candle-lit tavern. It looks very plush, and every table you see seems to be filled with well-dressed patrons. Looking directly behind you, you see through the window of the hotel's barbershop. You can see an older gentleman, whose chest is covered by a white sheet, being shaved by a much younger man. You next look straight ahead of you, where you see a quaint little giftshop just on the other side of the escalator. You're a sucker for little ceramic statues, and you squint your eyes to try to read the hours of operation posted on the store's entrance. Hanging from the high ceiling directly above you, you see a giant banner welcoming the Elks convention to the hotel. It is made from white lettering sewn onto a blue background, and it looks to you to be about 25 feet long. (Based on Tversky, 1991b, p. 133)

Further Instructions

Now imagine that you have turned to face the barbershop. Cover up the story above and answer the following questions:

1. What is above your head?
2. What is below your feet?
3. What is ahead of you?
4. What is behind you?
5. What is to your right?

might possibly be relevant and allows approximate solutions to problems for which precise location is unnecessary. (p. 326)

Using Verbal Descriptions to Create Mental Models

In everyday life, we often hear or read descriptions of a particular environment. A friend calls to give you directions to her house. You have never traveled there before, yet you find yourself creating a cognitive map to represent the route. Similarly, a neighbor describes the setting in which his car was hit by a truck, or you read a mystery novel explaining where the dead body was found in relation to the broken vase and the butler's fingerprints. Again, you create cognitive maps. These cognitive maps allow us to simulate spatial aspects of our external environment (Rumelhart & Norman, 1988). These representations that depict situations, which we derive from verbal descriptions, are called ***mental models*** (Millis & Cohen, 1994).

One of the themes of this textbook is that cognitive processes are active. When we hear a description, we do not simply store these isolated statements in a passive fashion. Instead, we actively create a mental model that represents the relevant features of a scene. In fact, people who had been asked to draw maps of environments that they had read about were just as accurate in their re-creation as people who learned this same information by studying a map (Taylor & Tversky, 1992).

In this final section, we will examine how people create these mental models, based on verbal description. Let us begin by considering the initial research. Then we will examine the spatial framework model, as well as other information about the characteristics of mental models.

Franklin and Tversky's Research. Before you read further, try Demonstration 6.7, which is based on a story used in a series of studies conducted by Nancy Franklin and Barbara Tversky (1990). Franklin and Tversky presented descriptions of 10 different scenes, depicting a hotel lobby, an opera theater, a barn, and so forth. Each description mentioned five objects located in a plausible position in relation to the observer (either above, below, in front, in back, and to either the left or the right side). Only five objects were mentioned, so that the memory load would not be overwhelming. After reading each description, the participants were instructed to imagine that they were rotating to face a different object. They were then asked to specify which object was located in each of several directions (for example, "above your head"). In all cases, the researchers measured how long the participant took to respond to the question.

Franklin and Tversky were especially interested in discovering whether response time depended upon the location of the object that was being tested. Can we make all those decisions equally quick? In contrast, did your experience with Demonstration 6.7 suggest that some decisions are easier than others?

Franklin and Tversky found that people could rapidly answer which objects were above and below; reaction times were short for these judgments. People required a somewhat longer amount of time to decide which objects were ahead or behind. Furthermore, decisions about which objects were to the right and to the left required the longest amount of time.

Franklin and Tversky (1990) replicated these results in two additional studies; again, the vertical dimension was systematically favored. They also asked participants to describe how they thought they had performed the task. All participants reported that they had constructed images of the environment as they were reading. Most also reported that they had constructed imagery that represented the observer's point of view. Do these reports match your own experience with Demonstration 6.7?

The Spatial Framework Model. To explain their results, Franklin and Tversky propose the spatial framework model (Franklin & Tversky, 1990; Tversky, 1991b). The ***spatial framework model*** emphasizes that certain spatial directions (such as up and down) are especially prominent in our thinking.

Specifically, the spatial framework model states that when we are in a typical upright position, the vertical or above/below dimension is especially prominent. This dimension has special significance for two reasons:

1. The vertical dimension is correlated with gravity, an advantage that neither of the other two dimensions share. Gravity has an important asymmetric effect on the world we perceive; objects fall downward, not upward. Because of its association with gravity, the above/below dimension should be particularly important and thus particularly accessible.
2. The vertical dimension on an upright human's body is physically asymmetric. That is, the top (head) and the bottom (feet) are very easy to tell apart, and so we do not confuse them with each other.

These two factors combine to help make judgments on the above/below dimension very rapid.

The next most prominent dimension is the front/back dimension. This dimension is not correlated with gravity in upright observers. However, we can view and interact with objects in front of us more readily than with objects in back of us, introducing an asymmetry. Also, the human's front half is not symmetric with the back half, again making it easy to distinguish between front and back. These two characteristics lead to judgment times for the front/back dimension that are fast, although not as fast as for the above/below dimension.

The least prominent dimension is right/left. This dimension is not correlated with gravity, and we can perceive objects equally well whether they are on the right or the left. Furthermore, except for the minor preferences most of us have in manipulating objects with our right or left hand, this dimension does not have the degree of asymmetry we find for front versus back. Finally, a human's right half is roughly symmetrical with the left half. You can probably remember occasions when you confused your right and left hands, or when you told someone to turn left when you meant right. Apparently, we need additional processing time to ensure that we do not make this error; therefore, right/left decisions take longer.

In summary, then, Franklin and Tversky's (1990) spatial framework model proposes that the vertical or up/down dimension is most prominent for the upright observer. The front/back dimension is next most prominent, and the right/left dimension is least prominent.

Further Research on Mental Models. So far, all the research we have discussed used scenarios written in the second person. (Notice the number of *you* sentences in Demonstration 6.7, for example.) Perhaps people can construct mental models from verbal descriptions when the text suggests that the reader is observing a scene. However, do people still construct these models when the text involves the third person? If a mystery novel describes what Detective Brown sees upon arriving at the scene of the crime, do we readers jump into the scene and adopt Detective Brown's perspective—or do we remain outside the scene, like a viewer watching a movie? In fact, Bryant, Tversky, and Franklin (1992) found that readers typically prefer to adopt the perspective of an involved person.

Furthermore, Franklin and her colleagues (1992) presented narratives describing objects from the perspective of two different observers in the same environment. Interestingly, participants in these studies did not take the viewpoints of the two observers in turn. Instead, they adopted a neutral perspective that incorporated information from both observers.

We have seen that the mental models we derive from verbal descriptions represent both orientation and point of view. Another important feature of these mental models is landmarks. According to research by Ferguson and Hegarty (1994), we tend to establish important landmarks when we hear or read a story. Then we use those landmarks as reference points for adding other locations to our mental models.

All the research on mental models provides a strong testimony for the active nature of human cognitive processes. We take in information and go beyond the information we have been given, constructing a model to represent our knowledge. As we will see in the next chapter, this tendency to go beyond the given information is an important general characteristic of our cognitive processes.

SECTION SUMMARY: COGNITIVE MAPS

1. Cognitive maps usually reflect reality with reasonable accuracy. However, systematic errors reflect the tendency to base our judgments on variables that are typically relevant and to judge our environment as being more regular than it really is.
2. Estimates of distance on cognitive maps can be distorted by the number of intervening cities, by road-route distance (rather than distance "as the crow flies"), and by the semantic categories representing the landmarks on the cognitive maps.
3. Shapes on cognitive maps can be distorted so that angles of intersecting streets are closer to 90° and curves are more nearly symmetrical; house plans that violate our schemas may be difficult to remember.

4. The relative positions of features on cognitive maps can be distorted so that slightly tilted figures will be remembered as being more vertical or more horizontal than they really are (rotation heuristic). Furthermore, a series of figures will be remembered as being more lined up than it really is (alignment heuristic).

5. We often create mental models of environments on the basis of a verbal description. In these mental models, the vertical dimension has special prominence, followed by the front/back dimension, and then the right/left dimension; these data are explained by the spatial framework model.

CHAPTER REVIEW QUESTIONS

1. Summarize the two theories of the characteristics of mental images: the analog code and the propositional code. Describe the findings about mental rotations, size, shape, reinterpreting ambiguous figures, and any other topics you recall. In each case, note which theory the results support.

2. Almost all of this chapter dealt with *visual* imagery, because little information is available about imagery in the other senses. How might you design a study on taste imagery that would be conceptually similar to one of the studies mentioned in this chapter? See whether you can also design studies to examine smell, hearing, and touch, basing these studies on the research techniques discussed in this chapter.

3. How do the studies on imagery and interference support the viewpoint that visual activity is involved in visual imagery, and auditory activity is involved in auditory imagery?

4. Which areas of research provided the strongest support for the propositional storage of information about objects? I mentioned my own experience with using a propositional code for a jigsaw-puzzle piece; can you think of an occasion where you seemed to use a propositional code for an unfamiliar stimulus?

5. What are experimenter expectancy and demand characteristics? For each of these concepts, describe one study that suggests that the results of imagery experiments are unlikely to be traced to these factors alone.

6. What kind of neuropsychological evidence do we have that suggests visual imagery resembles visual perception? In what respects are the two processes different?

7. Cognitive maps sometimes correspond to reality, but sometimes they show systematic deviations. Discuss the factors that seem to produce systematic distortions when people estimate distances on mental maps.

8. What are the heuristics that cause systematic distortions in geographic shape and in relative position represented on cognitive maps? How are these related to two concepts we discussed in earlier chapters, top-down processing (Chapter 2) and schemas (Chapter 5)?

9. According to Franklin and Tversky, the three dimensions represented in our mental models are not created equal. Which dimension has special prominence? How does the spatial framework model explain these differences?

10. The material we discussed in the first portion of this chapter emphasized that mental imagery resembles perception. However, the material in the second portion emphasizes that cognitive maps may be influenced by our conceptions as well as our perceptions. Discuss these points, including some information about mental models.

NEW TERMS

imagery
analog code
depictive representation
propositional code
descriptive representation
experimenter expectancy
psychophysics
internal psychophysics

symbolic distance effect
Perky effect
oblique effect
demand characteristics
surface representation
deep representation
cognitive map

spatial memory
heuristic
symmetry heuristic
rotation heuristic
alignment heuristic
mental models
spatial framework model

RECOMMENDED READINGS

Craver-Lemley, C., & Reeves, A. (1992). How visual imagery interferes with vision. *Psychological Review, 99*, 633–649. This review article, which focuses on the in-depth topic of Chapter 6, provides a model of how to pursue an explanation for a cognitive phenomenon.

Farah, M. J. (1995). The neural bases of mental imagery. In M. S. Gazzaniga (Ed.), *The cognitive neurosciences* (pp. 963–975). Cambridge, MA: MIT Press. If neuroscience is an area that interests you, this chapter is an ideal overview of the topic.

Intons-Peterson, M. J. (Ed.). (1992). Mental models, pictures, and text: Integration of spatial and verbal information [special issue]. *Memory & Cognition, 20* (5). This special issue includes four articles that examine aspects of mental models, as discussed in the last part of the chapter.

Kosslyn, S. M. (1994). *Image and brain: The resolution of the imagery debate*. Cambridge, MA: MIT Press. Stephen Kosslyn, a leading psychologist in imagery research, reviews both the psychological and neuroscience studies in this comprehensive book.

Reisberg, D. (Ed.). (1992). *Auditory imagery*. Hillsdale, NJ: Erlbaum. This collection of 10 chapters on auditory images offers a helpful supplement to the material in Chapter 6, which primarily emphasizes visual images.

Roskos-Ewoldsen, B., Intons-Peterson, M. J., & Anderson, R. E. (Eds.). (1993). *Imagery, creativity, and discovery: A cognitive perspective*. Amsterdam: North-Holland. This book contains 11 chapters, many focusing on the reinterpretation of ambiguous stimuli; other chapters examine topics such as imagery and creativity, an area we will consider in Chapter 10.

GENERAL KNOWLEDGE

INTRODUCTION

THE STRUCTURE OF SEMANTIC MEMORY

The Feature Comparison Model
Network Models
The Prototype Approach

SCHEMAS

Scripts
Schemas and Memory Selection
Schemas and Memory Abstraction
Schemas and Inferences in Memory
Schemas and Integration in Memory
Conclusions About Schemas

METACOGNITION

The Tip-of-the-Tongue Phenomenon
In Depth: Metamemory

===== **Preview** =====

This chapter covers three major topics: semantic memory, schemas, and metacognition. The first two topics refer to our general knowledge of the outside world, and metacognition examines our knowledge about our own cognitive processes.

Semantic memory refers to our organized knowledge about the world. We will look at three different theories that attempt to explain how all this information could be stored and used in memory.

A schema is a generalized kind of knowledge about situations and events. One kind of schema is called a script; scripts describe an expected sequence of events. For example, most people have a well-defined "restaurant script," which specifies all the events that are likely to occur when you dine in a restaurant. Schemas influence our memories during four processes: selecting the material we want to remember, storing the meaning of a verbal passage, interpreting the material, and forming a single, integrated representation in memory. Schemas can cause inaccuracies during these stages, but we are often more accurate than schema theory proposes.

Metacognition is our knowledge, awareness, and control of our cognitive processes. For example, you often know a characteristic of a word on the tip of your tongue (for instance, the first letter of the target word), even if you cannot recover that word. The In-Depth section on metamemory points out that college students can accurately predict what they will remember from some memory tasks. However, they often spend too much time studying material they already know, and insufficient time on difficult material they have not yet mastered.

INTRODUCTION

Let's briefly review the topics we've considered so far in this textbook. In Chapter 2, on perception, we examined how the senses gather stimuli from the outside world, and how these stimuli are then interpreted by our previous knowledge. In Chapters 3 through 6, we discussed how these stimuli from the outside world are stored in memory. In many cases, we saw that our previous knowledge can influence memory. For example, our knowledge can help us process information deeply (Chapter 3), and it can help us chunk items together to aid short-term memory (Chapter 4). Our knowledge can provide the kind of expertise that enhances long-term memory, and schemas can also influence autobiographical memory (Chapter 5). Our knowledge of general principles such as the rotation heuristic and the alignment heuristic can distort our memories of spatial relationships, making them more regular than they actually are (Chapter 6).

For this first half of the book, then, we've emphasized how these stimuli from the outside world are taken into the cognitive system and are somehow influenced by our general knowledge. Now we need to focus specifically on the nature of this general knowledge. We will examine three components of knowledge.

First, we'll consider semantic memory. If you are a typical adult, you know the meaning of at least 20,000 to 40,000 words (Baddeley, 1990). You also know a tremendous amount of information about each of these words. For example, you know that a cat has fur, that an apple is red, and that a car is a good example of a vehicle . . . but an elevator is a bad example.

Second, we'll consider the nature of schemas, or general knowledge about an object or event. Schemas allow us to know much more than the simple combination of words in a sentence would suggest (Eysenck & Keane, 1990). Consider the following sentence:

> When Lisa was on her way back from the store with the balloon, she fell and the balloon floated away.

Think about all the facts you take for granted and all the reasonable inferences you make. For instance, Lisa is probably a child, not a 40-year-old woman. Also, she bought the balloon in the store; the balloon was attached to a string; the balloon was inflated with a light gas; when she fell, she let go of the string; she may have scraped her knee; it may have bled. A sentence that initially seemed simple is immediately enriched by an astonishing amount of information about objects and events in our world. (Incidentally, Chapter 8 will explore the way we make these inferences during reading.)

Whereas the first and second topics of this chapter focus on our knowledge about the world, the third topic focuses on our knowledge about our own mind, or metacognition. You may know that you know the capital of Utah, but you know that you cannot recall the definition of the alignment heuristic. You may also know that you'll remember a person's name better if you think of some meaningful connection between the person and the name, rather than simply rehearsing the name.

This chapter emphasizes our impressive cognitive abilities; we have an enormous amount of information at our disposal. This chapter also confirms the active nature of our cognitive processes. In the last part of Chapter 6, we saw that people can use the information in a verbal description to actively construct a mental model of an environment. As we'll see in the current chapter, people who are given one bit of information can go beyond the given information to actively retrieve other stored information about word relationships and other likely inferences. Let us explore the nature of general knowledge as we see how people go beyond the given information in semantic memory, schemas, and metacognition.

THE STRUCTURE OF SEMANTIC MEMORY

As we discussed in earlier chapters, *semantic memory* is organized knowledge about the world. We contrasted semantic memory with *episodic memory*, which contains information about time-dated events. As we emphasized, the distinction between semantic and episodic memory is not clear-cut. However, semantic memory involves knowledge without referring to how that information was acquired. An example of semantic memory would be, "The solar system has nine planets." In contrast, episodic memory always implied the phrase "It happened to me," because episodic memory emphasizes when, where, or how this event occurred (Chang, 1986). An example of episodic memory would be, "This morning I was told that the solar system has nine planets."

As you may recall, psychologists use the term *semantic memory* in a broad sense. Semantic memory includes encyclopedic knowledge (for example, "Martin Luther King Jr. was born in Atlanta, Georgia") as well as lexical or language knowledge (for example, "The word *snow* is related to the word *rain*"). As one researcher in the field of semantic memory pointed out,

> Our knowledge of the world will influence most of the cognitive things that we do. Solving a problem, finding our way, or just reading involves our semantic memory. It is clearly one of the building blocks of cognition. (Shoben, 1992, p. 585)

Let us consider several possible models of how semantic memory is organized. These include the feature comparison model, network models, and the prototype approach.

The Feature Comparison Model

One logical way to organize semantic memory would be in terms of lists of features. According to the *feature comparison model*, concepts are stored in memory according to a list of features or attributes (Smith, Shoben, & Rips, 1974). People use a decision process to make judgments about these concepts. Let's first look at the structure that Smith and his colleagues propose for semantic memory, and then we'll consider the research that has been conducted on the feature comparison model. Finally, we'll evaluate this approach to semantic memory.

Structural Components of the Feature Comparison Model. Consider the concept *cat* for a moment. We could make up a list of features that are often relevant to cats:

> has fur
> dislikes water
> has four legs
> meows
> has a tail
> chases mice

The decision process described by Smith and his coauthors becomes relevant when people must answer a question such as "Is a cat an animal?" In the first stage of

========== **FIGURE 7.1** ==========

THE FEATURE COMPARISON MODEL OF SEMANTIC MEMORY, BASED ON SMITH (1978). COURTESY OF LAWRENCE ERLBAUM ASSOCIATES, INC.

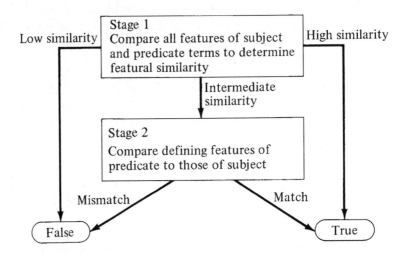

the decision process, people compare all the features of the subject of the sentence, *cat,* and the predicate, *animal.* Figure 7.1 shows an outline of the model.

Three decisions are possible at Stage 1. First of all, the subject term and the predicate term may show low similarity and so the person quickly replies "false" to the question. For example, the question "Is a cat a pencil?" has such little similarity between the two terms that you would immediately answer "false." In a second

========== **DEMONSTRATION 7.1** ==========

THE SENTENCE VERIFICATION TECHNIQUE

For each of the items below, answer *as quickly as possible* either true or false.

1. A poodle is a dog.
2. A squirrel is an animal.
3. A flower is a rock.
4. A carrot is a vegetable.
5. A mango is a fruit.
6. A petunia is a tree.
7. A robin is a bird.
8. A rutabaga is a vegetable.

situation, the subject and the predicate term may show high similarity, leading to a quick "true" answer. "Is a cat an animal?" leads to an immediate "true." However, if the subject and the predicate term shows intermediate similarity, the decision requires a Stage 2 comparison. For example, you might need a Stage 2 comparison for a question such as, "Is a bird a mammal?" As you can imagine, these decisions take longer. Try Demonstration 7.1 now, before you read further.

Smith and his coauthors propose that the features used in the feature comparison model are either defining features or characteristic features. *Defining features* are those features that are necessary to the meaning of the item. For example, the defining features of a robin include that it is living and has feathers and a red breast. *Characteristic features* are those features that are merely descriptive but are not essential. For example, the characteristic features of a robin include that it flies, perches in trees, is not domesticated, and is small in size.

Research on the Feature Comparison Model. The sentence verification technique is one of the major tools used to explore the feature comparison model. In the *sentence verification technique,* people see simple sentences, and they must consult their stored semantic knowledge to determine whether the sentences are true or false (Kounios et al., 1987). Demonstration 7.1 shows the kinds of items presented in the sentence verification technique. In general, people are highly accurate on this task, so researchers do not need to compare the error rate across experimental conditions. Instead, they measure response latencies. Two experimental conditions might produce response latencies that differ by one-tenth of a second. You might initially think this sounds like a trivial difference. However, if this difference is consistently found for most participants, it is worth exploring. A stable difference may reveal something important about the structure of semantic memory.

One common finding in research using the sentence verification technique is the typicality effect. In the *typicality effect,* people reach decisions faster when an item is a typical member of a category, rather than an unusual member. For example, in Demonstration 7.1, you probably decided quickly that a carrot is a vegetable, but you paused before deciding that a rutabaga is a vegetable. In a typical study, Katz (1981) presented high-typicality sentences such as "A globe is round" and low-typicality sentences such as "A barrel is round." Reaction times were about 0.3 seconds faster for typical items than for atypical items.

The feature comparison model can explain these results. For example, a carrot is a typical member of its category, so the features of carrots and vegetables are highly similar. People quickly answer the question "Is a carrot a vegetable?" because they only require Stage 1 processing in the model. However, the rutabaga is an example of an atypical vegetable. People require much longer to answer the question "Is a rutabaga a vegetable?" because the decision requires Stage 2 processing as well as Stage 1 processing.

Unfortunately, the feature comparison model has difficulty explaining other semantic memory findings that have been obtained with the sentence verification technique. For example, a second common finding with this technique (beyond the typicality effect) is the category size effect. According to the ***category size effect,*** people reach decisions faster when an item is a member of a small category, rather than a large category. For example, in Demonstration 7.1, you probably decided quickly that a poodle is a dog, whereas you took longer to decide that a squirrel is an animal. After all, *dog* has fewer category members than *animal* does. However, the feature comparison model would predict the opposite, because small categories have a larger number of defining features (for example, the category *dog* has a greater number of defining features than the category *animal*). Therefore, comparing the features should take *longer* during Stage 2.

Conclusions About the Feature Comparison Model. We have seen that the feature comparison model can account for the typicality effect, but it cannot explain the category size effect. Another major problem with this approach is that nonexperts may not be guided by defining features (Malt, 1990). In many cases, nonexperts may be more influenced by characteristic features. Furthermore, the model does not provide any objective way to distinguish between these defining and characteristic attributes (Eysenck & Keane, 1990). Also, we seem to know that robins are birds without resorting to a formal comparison of features (Cohen, 1983). Finally, the feature comparison model does not explain how the members of categories are related to one another (Barsalou, 1992b). As we'll see, interrelationships are important in network models, which we will discuss next.

Network Models

Think for a moment about the large number of associations you have to the word *apple.* How can we find an effective way to represent the different aspects of meaning for *apple* that are stored in memory? A number of theorists favor network models. Originally, a network was an arrangement of threads in a net-like structure, with many connections among these threads. Similarly, a ***network model*** of semantic memory proposes a net-like organization of concepts in memory, with many interconnections. The meaning of a particular concept, such as *apple,* depends on the concepts to which it is connected.

We will consider the network model developed by Collins and Loftus (1975) and then examine Anderson's (1983a, 1990) ACT* theory. A third network theory, the parallel distributed processing approach, was discussed in Chapter 3. Turn back to Figure 3.6 (page 96) to refresh your memory of a representative network. In brief, the ***parallel distributed processing (PDP) approach*** argues that cognitive processes can be understood in terms of networks that link together neuron-like units (Masson, 1995). The PDP approach does not distinguish between episodic and semantic memory (Johnson & Hasher, 1987), so that episodic facts are intertwined with semantic information.

The Collins and Loftus Network Model. Collins and Loftus (1975) developed a theory in which meaning is represented by hypothetical networks. The ***Collins and Loftus network model*** proposes that semantic memory is organized in terms of

FIGURE 7.2

AN EXAMPLE OF A NETWORK STRUCTURE FOR THE CONCEPT *APPLE*, AS IN THE COLLINS AND LOFTUS NETWORK MODEL.

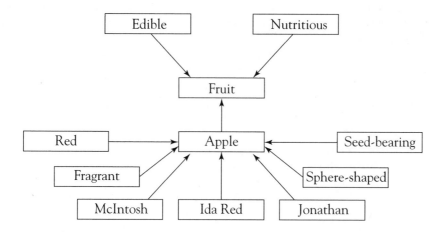

net-like structures, with many interconnections; when we retrieve information, activation spreads to related concepts.

In this model, each concept can be represented as a ***node,*** or location in the network. Links connect a particular node with other concept nodes. Figure 7.2 shows a small portion of the network that might surround the concept *apple.*

How does this network model work? When the name of a concept is mentioned, the node representing that concept is activated. The activation expands or spreads from that node to other nodes with which it is connected, a process called ***spreading activation.*** The activation spreads eventually to the more remote nodes.

Let's consider how the Collins-Loftus model would explain what happens in a sentence verification task. Suppose you hear the sentence, "A McIntosh is a fruit." This model proposes that activation will spread from *McIntosh* and *fruit* to the node *apple.* A search of memory notes the intersection of these two activation patterns. As a consequence, the sentence, "A McIntosh is a fruit" deserves a "yes" answer. However, suppose you hear the sentence, "An apple is a mammal." Activation spreads from *apple* and *mammal,* but no intersection can be found. This sentence deserves a "no" answer.

Collins and Loftus (1975) also propose that frequently used links have greater strengths. As a result, activation travels faster between the nodes. Therefore, the typicality effect is easy to explain; the link between vegetable and carrot is stronger than the link between vegetable and rutabaga.

The concept of spreading activation is an appealing one, and Chapter 3 showed how this concept works in the PDP approach. However, Collins and Loftus's model has been superseded by more complex theories that attempt to explain broader aspects of general knowledge. We already looked at one of these theories, the PDP approach. The other theory that has superseded the Collins and Loftus model is Anderson's ACT* theory.

Anderson's ACT* Theory. One of the most influential theorists in contemporary cognitive psychology is John Anderson of Carnegie Mellon University. Anderson constructed a series of network models (Anderson, 1976, 1983a, 1985, 1990). The most current version is called ***ACT**** (to be read "Act-star"; ACT stands for the Adaptive Control of Thought, and the asterisk indicates that this version is a modification of the original ACT model. ACT* attempts to account for all of cognition, including memory, language, learning, reasoning, decision making, and so forth. Anderson believes that the mind is unitary and that all the higher cognitive processes are different products of the same underlying system. (In contrast, other theorists propose that the language system, for example, is governed by different principles than memory or decision making.) The ACT* model emphasizes the concept of control, which is the feature that provides direction to thought and supervises the transition between thoughts.

Obviously, a theory that attempts to explain all of cognition is extremely complex. We will therefore consider an overview of ACT* as described in Anderson's (1983a) book *The Architecture of Cognition* and then discuss his more specific view of semantic memory. Anderson makes a basic distinction between declarative and procedural knowledge. ***Declarative knowledge*** is knowledge about facts and things (in other words, the essence of this current chapter). In contrast, ***procedural knowledge*** is knowledge about how to perform actions. Another important feature of Anderson's theory is ***working memory,*** which is the active part of the declarative memory system—it is the portion that is currently "working." You'll recall our discussion of the characteristics of working memory from Chapter 4.

Black (1984) presents a simplified example. Suppose you are trying to set the time on a new digital watch, using the instruction booklet. First, you activate the goal of wanting to set the watch; that goal is therefore in working memory. The goal of setting the watch would then activate a procedure such as "If the goal is to set a watch, then look at the instruction booklet." Looking at the instruction booklet activates the procedures of processing the verbal material and the pictures in the booklet. After comprehending the material, the contents of the booklet are stored in the declarative network. The declarative network contains an interconnected set of propositions (for example, "the watch has three buttons"), visual images (for example, the locations of the buttons), and information about the order of events (for example, "set the date first, then hours, then minutes, then the seconds").

Let us now focus on declarative knowledge, which is responsible for semantic memory. According to Anderson (1976, 1983a, 1985), the meaning of a sentence can be represented by a propositional network, or pattern of interconnected propositions. We discussed propositions in Chapter 6. Anderson's definition of a proposition, however, is somewhat more precise: A ***proposition*** is the smallest unit of knowledge that can be judged either true or false. For instance, the phrase *white cat* does not qualify as a proposition because we cannot find out whether it is true

=== **FIGURE 7.3** ===

A PROPOSITIONAL NETWORK REPRESENTING THE SENTENCE "SUSAN GAVE A WHITE CAT TO MARIA, WHO IS THE PRESIDENT OF THE CLUB."

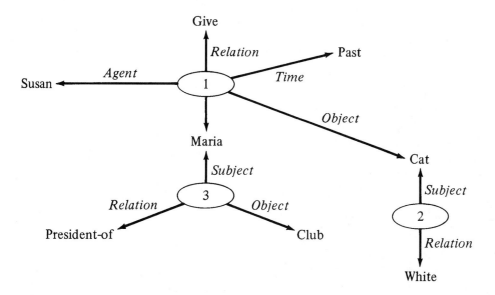

or false unless we know something more about the white cat. However, each of the following three statements is a proposition:

1. Susan gave a cat to Maria.
2. The cat was white.
3. Maria is the president of the club.

These three propositions can appear by themselves, but they can also be combined into a sentence, such as the following:

Susan gave a white cat to Maria, who is the president of the club.

Figure 7.3 shows how this sentence could be represented by a propositional network. As you can see, each of the three propositions in the sentence is represented by a node, and the links are represented by arrows. Notice, too, that the propositional network represents the important relations in the three propositions, but not the exact wording. Propositions are abstract; they do not represent a specific set of words. (Later in the chapter, we will look at research that demonstrates how we tend to remember the gist or general message of language, rather than the specific wording of sentences.)

Furthermore, Anderson suggests that each of the concepts in a proposition can be represented by a network as well. Figure 7.4 illustrates just a small part of the representation of the word *cat* in memory. Try to imagine what the

=== FIGURE 7.4 ===

A PARTIAL REPRESENTATION OF CAT IN MEMORY

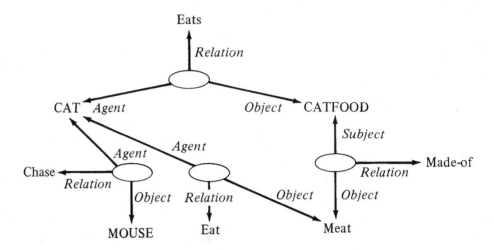

propositional network in Figure 7.3 would look like if each of the concepts in that network were to be replaced by an expanded network representing the richness of meanings you have acquired. Obviously, these networks need to be complicated in order to accurately represent the dozens of associations we have for each item in semantic memory.

Anderson's model of semantic memory makes some additional proposals. For example, similar to the Collins-Loftus model, the links vary in strength, and they become stronger as they are used more often. Also, the model assumes that at any given moment, as many as 10 nodes are represented in working memory. Furthermore, the model proposes that activation can spread. However, Anderson argues that the spread of activation has a limited capacity. Thus, if many links are activated simultaneously, each link receives relatively little activation (Anderson, 1983b).

Anderson's model has been highly praised for its skill in integrating cognitive processes and for its scholarship (e.g., Black, 1984; Lehnert, 1984). However, others have been critical about some of its general attributes. Johnson-Laird and his coauthors (1984), for example, complain that network models only provide connections between words; they do not make connections to the representations of those words in the real world. Future theories of semantic memory will need to be even more comprehensive, and they must also make those final connections to real-world objects.

Conclusions About Network Models. So far, we have considered two categories of semantic memory models: the feature comparison model and three different network models. The feature comparison model suggests that concepts are stored in memory according to a list of attributes. We decide whether a cat is an animal by comparing the features of the concept *cat* with the features of the concept *animal*.

In contrast, the three network models emphasize the interconnections among concepts in memory. These three theories include: (1) an early model by Collins and Loftus (1975), which introduced the concept of spreading activation; (2) the parallel distributed processing approach, discussed in Chapter 3; and (3) Anderson's (1983a) ACT* theory, which describes how sentences—as well as words—can be represented by networks. All three network models emphasize interconnections among concepts, so they focus on how one item in memory leads us to think of related items. Prototype theory, which we will now consider, differs somewhat from the feature comparison model and the network models because it is more concerned with answering questions about category membership. For instance, if we see a strange creature in the zoo, how do we decide whether it is a bird or a mammal?

The Prototype Approach

According to a theory proposed by Eleanor Rosch (1973), we organize categories according to *prototypes*, which are items that are most typical of a category. According to this *prototype approach*, we decide whether an item belongs to a category by comparing that item with a prototype. If the item is similar to the prototype, we include that item in the category. However, if the item is sufficiently different, we place it in another category where it more closely resembles that category's prototype. You'll notice how this approach resembles the prototype view of pattern perception, which we discussed in Chapter 2.

As Rumelhart and Norman (1988) point out, the prototype of category does not really need to exist. For example, if I were to ask you to describe a prototypical animal, you might tell me about a four-legged creature with fur, a tail, and a size somewhere between a large dog and a cow—something exactly like no creature on earth. Thus, a prototype is an idealized example.

Rosch also points out that members of a category differ in their *prototypicality*, or degree to which they are prototypical. A robin and a sparrow are very prototypical birds, whereas ostriches and penguins are nonprototypes. Think of a prototype, or most typical member, for a particular group on your campus, such as a fraternity, sorority, or other club. Also think of a nonprototype ("You mean he's a Theta Kappa? He doesn't seem at all like one!"). Now think of a prototype for a professor, a fruit, and a murder weapon; then think of a nonprototype for each category. For example, a tomato is a nonprototypical fruit, and an icicle is a nonprototypical murder weapon.

The prototype approach represents a very different perspective from the classical view of concepts (Komatsu, 1992; Margolis, 1994; Medin & Ahn, 1992). The *classical view of concepts*, which is compatible with the feature comparison model that we examined in Figure 7.1, proposes that concepts are based on defining features; an item belongs to a category as long as it possesses the necessary and sufficient features. The classical view therefore argues that category membership is very clear-cut. For example, the defining features of *bachelor* are *male* and *unmarried*. But don't you think that your 32-year-old male cousin represents a better example of a bachelor than does your 2-year-old nephew or an elderly Catholic priest? The prototype approach would argue that not all members of the category *bachelor* are created equal. Instead, your cousin is a more prototypical bachelor than your nephew or the priest.

The prototype approach has had an important impact on cognitive psychology, and it has also influenced other disciplines within psychology (Komatsu, 1992; Rosch, 1988). For example, Mayer and Bower (1986) discovered that people use prototypes to organize personality concepts, such as "extrovert." Prototypes are also important when we form attitudes toward social policies (Lord et al., 1994). Clinical psychologists tend to use prototypes for various psychological disorders, such as "aggressive-impulsive child" (Horowitz et al., 1981). Furthermore, emotions such as anger may be organized according to prototypes (Russell, 1990).

Eleanor Rosch and her coauthors, as well as other researchers, have conducted numerous studies on the characteristics of prototypes. They have demonstrated that all members of categories are *not* created equal (Malt & Smith, 1984). Instead, a category tends to have a ***graded structure,*** beginning with the most representative or prototypical members and continuing on through the category's nonprototypical members (Barsalou, 1985, 1987; Neisser, 1987). Let us examine several important characteristics of prototypes. Then we will discuss another important component of Rosch's prototype theory, levels of categorization.

Characteristics of Prototypes. Prototypes differ from the nonprototypical members of categories in several respects. As you will see, prototypes have a special, privileged status (Smith, 1989).

1. *Prototypes are supplied as examples of a category.* Several studies have shown that people judge some items to be "better" examples of a concept than some other items. In one study, for example, Mervis, Catlin, and Rosch (1976) looked at some category norms that had already been collected. The norms had been constructed by asking people to provide examples of eight different categories, such as birds,

---

DEMONSTRATION 7.2

PROTOTYPES AS REFERENCE POINTS

Pairs of items are listed below, together with a sentence containing two blanks. Choose one item to fill the first blank, and place the other item in the second blank. Take your time, try the items both ways, and choose the way in which the "sentence" seems to make the most sense.

1. (10, 11)   _____ is essentially _____.
2. (103, 100)   _____ is sort of _____.
3. (48, 50)   _____ is roughly _____.
4. (1000, 1004) _____ is basically _____.

fruit, sports, and weapons. Other people supplied prototype ratings for each of these examples. A statistical analysis showed that the items that were rated most prototypical were the same items that people supplied most often in the category norms. For instance, for the category *bird,* people would consider *robin* to be very prototypical, and *robin* is very frequently listed as an example of the category *bird.* In contrast, people would rate *penguin* as low on the prototype scale, and *penguin* is only rarely listed as an example of the category *bird.* Thus, if someone asks you to name a member of a category, you will probably name a prototype.

Earlier, we discussed the typicality effect; people reach decisions faster when an item is a typical member of a category. Thus, prototypes are supplied more often as examples, and they are also judged more rapidly. In fact, the prototype approach accounts well for the typicality effect (Komatsu, 1992).

2. *Prototypes serve as reference points.* Before reading further, try Demonstration 7.2, which illustrates how prototypes can serve as reference points. This demonstration is based on a study by Rosch (1975a), in which people saw pairs of numbers, colors, or lines. For the numbers, one member of each pair was a prototype—that is, a multiple of 10 that should be relevant in our decimal number system (for example, 10, 50, or 100). The other member of the pair was a number of about the same size, but not a multiple of 10 (for example, 11, 48, or 103). For the colors, one member of each pair was a prototype color (red, yellow, green, and blue), and the other member was a nonprototype color (for example, purplish red). For the lines, one member was a line in a "standard" position (exactly horizontal, exactly vertical, and 45° diagonal) and the other member was a line in a position rotated 10° from one of the standard positions. In each case, then, Rosch wanted to determine which pair member served as a reference point, that is, the stimulus with which the other member was compared.

Her results showed quite clearly that the prototypes tended to serve as the reference points. For example, people were more likely to say "11 is essentially 10," rather than "10 is essentially 11." Check your answers in Demonstration 7.2. Did the prototypes, which are multiples of 10, occur second in the sentence, as if they were standards to which all other numbers are compared?

3. *Prototypes are judged more quickly after priming.* The **priming effect** means that people respond faster to an item if it was preceded by a similar item. For example, you would make judgments about apples more quickly if you had just seen the word *fruit* than if you had just seen the word *giraffe.*

The research shows that priming helps prototypes more than it helps nonprototypes. Imagine, for example, that you are participating in a study on priming. Your task is to judge pairs of similar colors and to respond whether they are the same or not. On some occasions, the name of the color is shown to you before you must judge the pair of colors; these are the primed trials. On other occasions, no color name is supplied to you as a "warning"; these are the unprimed trials. Rosch (1975b) tried this priming setup for both prototype colors (for example, a good, bright red) and nonprototype colors (for example, a muddy red).

DEMONSTRATION 7.3

SUBSTITUTING PROTOTYPES AND NONPROTOTYPES IN SENTENCES

Examine each of the sentences below and rate them as to how normal or how bizarre each one seems to you. Use this scale:

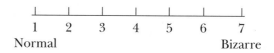

1   2   3   4   5   6   7
Normal   Bizarre

Rating

_____ 1. Twenty birds sat on a telephone wire outside my window.
_____ 2. Twenty sparrows sat on a telephone wire outside my window.
_____ 3. Twenty penguins sat on a telephone wire outside my window.
_____ 4. One of my favorite desserts is fruit pie.
_____ 5. One of my favorite desserts is apple pie.
_____ 6. One of my favorite desserts is olive pie.
_____ 7. How can I go to the fair without a vehicle?
_____ 8. How can I go to the fair without a truck?
_____ 9. How can I go to the fair without an elevator?
_____ 10. The robbers had many weapons.
_____ 11. The robbers had many guns.
_____ 12. The robbers had many bricks.

Rosch's results showed that priming was very helpful when people made judgments about prototypical colors; they responded more quickly after primed trials than after nonprimed trials. However, priming actually inhibited the judgments for nonprototypical colors, even after two weeks of practice. In other words, if you see the word *red,* you expect to see true, fire-engine red colors. If you see, instead, dark, muddy red colors, the priming offers no advantage. Instead, you pause as you work to reconcile your image of a bright, vivid color with the muddy colors you actually see before you.

4. *Prototypes can substitute for a category name in a sentence.* Try Demonstration 7.3, which illustrates a typical study on substituting other words for category names (Rosch, 1977). As you'll probably discover, prototypes can substitute quite well for the category name. However, a sentence is bizarre when a nonprototype is

substituted. Check over your responses from this demonstration. It seems peculiar to have 20 penguins sitting on telephone wires. Sentences 3, 6, 9, and 12 involve nonprototypes and probably seemed more bizarre than those involving prototypes.

5. *Prototypes share common attributes in a family resemblance category.* Before we examine this issue, let's introduce a new term, *family resemblance*. **Family resemblance** means that no single attribute is shared by all examples of a concept; however, each example has at least one attribute in common with some other example of the concept. As the philosopher Wittgenstein (1953) pointed out, some concepts are difficult to describe in terms of specific defining features. For example, consider the concept of *games*. Think about the games you know. What single attribute do they all have in common? How is Monopoly similar to volleyball? You might respond that both involve competition, but then what about the children's game, "Ring around the Rosie"? Some games involve skill, but others depend upon luck. Notice how each game shares some attributes with some other game, yet no one attribute is shared by all games. In fact, the members of the concept *games* have a family resemblance to one another.

Rosch and Mervis (1975) examined the role of prototypes in family resemblance. Specifically, they examined whether the items that people judge to be most prototypical will have the greatest number of attributes in common with other members of the category. First, they asked a group of people to provide prototype ratings for words in several categories. Table 7.1 shows three of these categories. For vehicles, notice that *car* was rated as the most prototypical, whereas *sled* had a low prototype rating. Rosch and Mervis asked a new group of people to list the attributes possessed by each item. For the word *dog*, for instance, participants were told to list attributes like having four legs, barking, having fur, and so on. From this information, the researchers calculated a number that showed what proportion of an item's attributes were also shared by other members of the same category. *Car* received a high score; like most other items on that list, it has wheels, moves horizontally, and uses fuel. In contrast, *sled* received a low score.

Rosch and Mervis demonstrated a significant correlation between the two measures—prototype rating and the "attributes in common" score. In other words, a highly prototypical item—such as *car*—usually has many attributes in common with other category members. In contrast, an item that is not prototypical—such as *sled*—has few attributes in common with other category members. See whether this relationship also holds true for the following concepts: profession, adventure movie, and snack food.

Levels of Categorization. We have just examined five characteristics of prototypes that differentiate them from nonprototypes. The second major portion of Eleanor Rosch's theory looks at the way that our semantic categories are structured in terms of different levels.

Consider these examples. You can call the wooden structure upon which you are sitting by several different names: furniture, chair, or desk chair. You can refer to your pet as a dog, a spaniel, or a cocker spaniel. You can tighten the mirror on your

=== TABLE 7.1 ===

PROTOTYPE RATINGS FOR WORDS IN THREE CATEGORIES. ROSCH AND MERVIS (1975).

<u>Category</u>

Item	Vehicle	Vegetable	Clothing
1	Car	Peas	Pants
2	Truck	Carrots	Shirt
3	Bus	String beans	Dress
4	Motorcycle	Spinach	Skirt
5	Train	Broccoli	Jacket
6	Trolley car	Asparagus	Coat
7	Bicycle	Corn	Sweater
8	Airplane	Cauliflower	Underwear
9	Boat	Brussels sprouts	Socks
10	Tractor	Lettuce	Pajamas
11	Cart	Beets	Bathing suit
12	Wheelchair	Tomato	Shoes
13	Tank	Lima beans	Vest
14	Raft	Eggplant	Tie
15	Sled	Onion	Mittens

car with a tool, a screwdriver, or a Phillips screwdriver. In other words, an object can belong to many different, related categories.

Some category levels are called *superordinate-level categories,* which means higher level or more general. Furniture, animal, and tool are all examples of superordinate category levels. *Basic-level categories* are moderately specific. Chair, cat, and screwdriver are examples of basic-level categories. Finally, *subordinate-level categories* mean lower level or more specific categories. Desk chair, Siamese, and Phillips screwdriver are examples of subordinate categories.

Try reviewing these terms by thinking of some superordinate terms you use often, such as "vehicle," "clothing," and "musical instrument"; can you think of examples of basic-level and subordinate categories for these terms? Keep in mind that *prototype* and *basic-level category* are different terms. A prototype is a best example of a category, whereas a basic-level category refers to a category that is neither too general nor too specific.

Eleanor Rosch and her colleagues (1976) propose that basic-level categories have special status; in general, they are more useful than superordinate-level categories and subordinate-level categories. Apparently, basic-level categories are especially informative and useful for communication within social groups (Corter & Gluck, 1992). Let's examine how these basic-level categories seem to have special privileges, in contrast to the other two category levels.

1. *Basic-level names are used to identify objects.* Try naming some of the objects that you can see from where you are sitting. You are likely to use basic-level names for these objects. You will mention *pen,* for example, rather than the superordinate *writing instrument* or the subordinate *Bic fine-point pen.* Rosch and her colleagues (1976) asked people to look at pictures and identify the objects; they found that people preferred to use basic-level names. Apparently, the basic-level name gives enough information without being overly detailed. Other researchers have demonstrated that this effect is not simply produced by a preference for shorter words (Murphy & Smith, 1982). Furthermore, people use basic-level names to refer to events as well as objects (Morris & Murphy, 1990). In other words, the basic level has special, privileged status.

2. *Members of basic-level categories have attributes in common.* Rosch and her colleagues (1976) found that people listed a large number of attributes shared by members of a basic-level category. For example, for the basic-level category *screwdriver,* someone might list "metal protrusion," "ridged handle," and "about 4–10 inches long." In contrast, people listed very few attributes shared by members of a superordinate-level category, such as *tool.* After all, how many attributes could you supply that would hold true for all the tools you could name? However, people did not supply many more attributes for subordinate-level items than for basic-level items. Again, this makes sense. For the subordinate-level category, *Phillips screwdriver,* we cannot add many attributes to the list we constructed for *screwdriver.*

Tversky and Hemenway (1984) found similar results in their study of category levels. For example, when people were asked to list attributes for various superordinate-level categories, they listed fewer than two attributes for each item. They listed about nine attributes for various basic-level categories—a substantial increase. They listed about 10 attributes for various subordinate-level categories—not much better than for the basic-level categories.

3. *Basic-level names produce the priming effect.* As we saw earlier, members of the same basic-level category share the same general shape. For example, members of the category *chair* look roughly the same. We would expect, therefore, that when people hear the word *chair,* they would form a mental image that would resemble most chairs.

The mental image is relevant because Rosch and her colleagues (1976) wanted to see whether priming with basic-level names would be helpful. In one variation of the priming technique, the experimenter gives the name of the object, and the participants decide whether two pictures that follow are the same or different. For example, you might hear the word *carrot* and see a picture of two identical carrots. Presumably, priming works because the presentation of the word allows you to make a mental image of this word, which helps when you make the later decision.

At any rate, the results showed that priming with basic-level names *was* helpful—it did help to see a basic-level term like *carrot* before judging the carrots. However, priming with superordinate names (such as *vegetable*) was *not* helpful. Apparently, when you hear the word *vegetable,* you do not develop a mental image that is specific enough to prepare you for judging carrots. When you want to warn people that something is happening, warn them with a basic-level term—shout "Fire!" not "Danger!"

4. *Experts use subordinate categories differently.* So far, we have seen that we use basic-level names to identify objects, that members of basic-level categories share attributes in common, and that basic-level names produce the priming effect. Tanaka and Taylor (1991) note that basic-level categories may have special status for those of us who are not experts in an area. However, for an expert, the subordinate-level categories may also have "privileged" status. For example, those of you who are experts on birds may be able to list a large number of attributes for *Baltimore orioles* (subordinate level) that you would not list for *orioles* (basic level).

Tanaka and Taylor located 12 dog experts and 12 bird experts, all with at least 10 years of experience in their field. These experts were asked to list features of either dogs or birds at the superordinate level, the basic level, and the subordinate level. On the average, these experts listed 10 new characteristics for the basic level that were not mentioned at the superordinate level and 10 new characteristics for the subordinate level were not mentioned at the basic level. In contrast, the comparable figures for novices were 11 new characteristics for the basic level and 6 for the subordinate level. In other words, experts show substantially more differentiation at the subordinate level than novices do. Similar findings have been reported for musicians making judgments about musical instruments (Palmer et al., 1989). Apparently, basic-level categories do not have special status for experts. Because of experts' knowledge on the subject, subordinate-level categories are equally privileged.

Conclusions About the Prototype Approach. One advantage of the prototype approach is that it can account for our ability to form concepts for groups that are loosely structured. For example, we can create a concept for stimuli that merely share a family resemblance to one another, such as *games*. As Barsalou (1992b) points out, prototype models work especially well when the members of a category have no single characteristic in common.

Furthermore, the prototype approach explains how we can reduce all the information about a wide variety of stimuli into a single, idealized abstraction. We do not need to retain a vast amount of information about an enormous number of category members. However, in many cases, we do store specific information about these individual examples of a category. An ideal prototype model would therefore need to include a mechanism for storing this specific information, as well as abstract prototypes (Barsalou, 1990, 1992b).

An ideal prototype model must also acknowledge that concepts can be unstable and variable. We saw in the previous section that conceptual structure can change as people acquire expertise; they can fine-tune their subordinate-level categories. Furthermore, our notions about the ideal prototype can shift as the context changes (Barsalou, 1989, 1993). For example, under typical circumstances, Americans regard a robin to be a more prototypical bird than a swan. However, when instructed to take the viewpoint of the average Chinese citizen, Americans believe that a swan is a more prototypical bird.

Another problem with the prototype approach is that most people strongly believe that many categories *do* have clear-cut boundaries, not fuzzy ones (Komatsu, 1992). For example, we feel strongly that a Pomeranian is a dog and should be categorized with German shepherds, rather than with the fluffy Persian cats that they physically resemble.

To account for the complexity of the concepts we store in semantic memory, an ideal theory must explain how concepts are often stable. However, this theory must also explain how concepts can be altered by factors such as expertise and context. Furthermore, this ideal theory must account for our intuitions that categories sometimes seem to be defined by clear-cut boundaries. Unfortunately, however, research on prototype theory has decreased since the 1980s. One neuroscience project using PET scans has shown that subordinate and superordinate terms seem to be processed in different regions of the brain. Specifically, superordinate terms activate the part of the prefrontal cortex that processes associative memory. Subordinate terms activate areas of the brain involved in shifting attention (Kosslyn et al., 1995). Although this research examines how the brain processes information regarding prototypes, the theory of prototypes has not been developed to account for some of the complexities of the categories we use in our daily lives.

SECTION SUMMARY: THE STRUCTURE OF SEMANTIC MEMORY

1. In the previous chapters, we saw how our general knowledge influences our cognitive processes; this chapter illustrates how human cognitive abilities are both impressive and active with respect to general knowledge.

2. The feature comparison model proposes that concepts are stored in terms of a list of features. Some decisions about semantic memory can be made rapidly, whereas others require two stages.

3. Three network models include one proposed by Collins and Loftus (with interconnecting concepts and spreading activation), the PDP approach (whose neuron-like components we discussed in Chapter 3), and Anderson's ACT* approach (in which both sentences and concepts can be represented by a network structure).

4. According to Rosch's prototype theory, people compare new stimuli with an idealized prototype in order to categorize them. Prototypes are frequently supplied when people compile a list of category examples; they serve as reference points; they are judged more quickly after priming; they can substitute for a category name; and they share a large number of attributes with others in a family-resemblance category.

5. Rosch's theory also proposes that basic-level categories are more likely than subordinates or superordinates to be used to identify objects; members of basic-level categories have attributes in common; and basic-level names produce the priming effect. However, experts give as many details for subordinate-level categories as they do for basic-level categories.

SCHEMAS

So far, our discussion of general knowledge has focused on words, concepts, and—occasionally—sentences. However, our cognitive processes also handle knowledge units that are much larger. For example, our knowledge includes information about familiar situations, events, and other "packages" of things we know. These generalized kinds of knowledge about situations and events are called *schemas.* You may recall that we discussed schemas in Chapter 5 in connection with autobiographical memory. In that chapter, we saw how people can develop schemas for certain repeated events in their lives, such as shopping for a gift.

Schema theories propose that people encode this "generic" information in memory and use it to understand and remember new examples of the schema. Specifically, schemas guide our recognition and understanding of new examples by providing expectations about what should occur (Thorndyke, 1984). Schemas therefore exploit top-down processing, a principle of cognitive processes emphasized in Theme 5. Furthermore, schemas allow us to predict what will happen in a new situation (Norman, 1982). In most situations, these predictions will be correct; schemas are *heuristics,* or rules-of-thumb that are generally accurate.

Schemas can sometimes lead us astray, and we make errors. However, these errors usually make sense within the framework of that schema. Consistent with Theme 2, our cognitive processes are generally accurate and our mistakes are typically rational.

Schema theories are useful when psychologists try to explain how people remember complex events (Alba & Hasher, 1983; Shoben, 1988). The term *schema* is now standard in cognitive psychology, and the concept has a long history. For example, Piaget's work in the 1920s investigated schemas in infants, and Bartlett (1932) tested memory for schemas in adults.

DEMONSTRATION 7.4

AN APPLICATION OF A SCRIPT

Read the following paragraph from an article by Abelson (1981, p. 715):

John was feeling very hungry as he entered the restaurant. He settled himself at the table and noticed that the waiter was nearby. Suddenly, however, he realized that he'd forgotten his reading glasses.

Now, explain how Sentence 3 is related to Sentence 2.

```
┌─────────────────────────────────────────────────────────────┐
│              ╭──────────────────────────────╮                │
│              │      DEMONSTRATION 7.5        │                │
│              ╰──────────────────────────────╯                │
```

THE NATURE OF SCRIPTS

Read the following paragraph, which is based on a paragraph from Trafimow and Wyer (1993, p. 368):

After doing this, he found the article. He then walked through the doorway and took a piece of candy out of his pocket. Next, he got some change and saw a person he knew. Subsequently, Joe found a machine. He realized he had developed a slight headache. After he aligned the original, Joe put in the coin and pushed the button. Thus, Joe had copied the piece of paper.

Now, turn to the list of new terms for Chapter 7, on page 267. Look at the first two columns of terms and write out the definition for as many of these terms as you know, taking about 5 minutes on the task. Then look at the additional instructions for the present demonstration, which appear at the bottom of Demonstration 7.6, on page 247.

In this section on schemas, we will first examine one kind of schema called a script. The remainder of the section will explore how schemas operate in memory during the processes of selection, abstraction, interpretation, and integration.

Scripts

A *script* is a simple, well-structured sequence of events associated with a highly familiar activity (Anderson & Conway, 1993). The terms *schema* and *script* are often used interchangeably. However, *script* is actually a narrower term, referring to a sequence of events that happen across a period of time.

Consider the simple story in Demonstration 7.4. This task seems ridiculously easy. Of course John would need his glasses to read the menu that the waiter would bring to him. However, the paragraph did not explicitly mention a menu. Nonetheless, the word *restaurant* immediately activates your expectation of certain predictable events. In fact, this word calls forth something we could call a "restaurant script," involving a standard sequence of events that a customer might expect in a restaurant (Abelson, 1981; Schank & Abelson, 1977). We could also have scripts for visiting a dentist's office, for how a board meeting should be run, and even for events that do not have the outcome we expected (Foti & Lord, 1987; Read & Cesa, 1991). Let's consider some of the research that has been conducted on scripts. Specifically, what is the structure of a script, and can people appreciate the resemblance between two similar scripts?

The Structure of Scripts. This chapter explores scripts and categories, because they are both important components of the structure of knowledge. The two terms differ, however, because a script represents a sequence of events, whereas a category represents clusters of objects.

Barsalou and Sewell (1985) have demonstrated that scripts and categories also differ in the way they are recovered from memory. As part of their experiment, Barsalou and Sewell asked participants to recall items from the script "How to write a letter" and from the category *tools*. On some occasions, they were instructed to recall the items in any order they wished. On other occasions, they were told to recall the items in a specified order, from most typical representative to least typical representative. Barsalou and Sewell measured the number of items recalled in each 5-second period. In the script condition, people recalled roughly a constant number of items for each 5-second period of recall, whereas in the category condition, people started with a burst of examples and rapidly decreased their output toward the end of recall. We saw in the section on natural categories that typical examples are recalled quickly and at the beginning of the list of items. However, the structure of scripts is different. Perhaps because they are often constrained by the sequence of events, the components of a script are recalled at an even, steady pace. Before you read further, be sure you tried Demonstration 7.5 on the previous page.

Other research shows that we can recall the elements in a script much more accurately if the script is clearly identified at the beginning of a description. Trafimow and Wyer (1993) developed four different scripts, each describing a familiar sequence of actions: photocopying a piece of paper, cashing a check, making tea, and taking the subway. Some details irrelevant to the script (such as taking a piece of candy out of a pocket) were also added. In some cases, the schema-identifying event was presented first. In other cases, the schema-identifying event was presented last, as in the sentence about copying the piece of paper in Demonstration 7.5.

After reading all four descriptions, the participants were given a 5-minute filler task, which required recalling the names of U.S. states and their capitals. Then they were asked to recall the events from the four original descriptions. The results for the paragraphs that contained six script-related events (as in Demonstration 7.5) showed that the participants recalled 23% of those events when the schema-identifying event had been presented first. In contrast, they recalled only 10% when the schema-identifying event had been presented last. As you might expect, the events in a sequence are much more memorable if you can appreciate—from the very beginning—that these events are all part of a standard script.

In the section on prototype theory, we noted that experts differ from novices in the richness of their subordinate-level categories. You will not be surprised to learn that experts also differ from novices in their understanding of a script's structure. For example, Pryor and Merluzzi (1985) examined two common social scripts, "getting a date" and "going on a first date." Some of the college students in their study were "experts," because they had been on many dates. These experts were able to place the events in their proper script sequence much more quickly than less socially experienced students.

Appreciating the Similarity of Related Scripts. A script is an abstraction, a proto-type of a sequence of events that share an underlying similarity. Can people appreci-ate an even more advanced level of abstraction? That is, can they see the resemblance between two types of scripts that have similar kinds of motives and outcomes?

Colleen Seifert and her colleagues (1986) examined thematically similar episodes. For example, one episode occurred in an academic setting. It concerned Dr. Popoff, who knew that his graduate student Mike was unhappy with the re-search facilities. When Dr. Popoff discovered that Mike had been accepted at a rival university, he quickly offered Mike abundant research equipment, but by then Mike had already decided to transfer. A second episode occurred in a ro-mance setting. Phil and his secretary were in love, but Phil kept postponing asking her to marry him. Meanwhile, the secretary fell in love with an accountant. When Phil found out, he proposed to her, but by then she and the accountant were al-ready making honeymoon plans. Notice that these two passages show high the-matic similarity.

Seifert and her colleagues used the priming technique described earlier in this book. They wanted to discover whether people would recognize a test sentence more quickly if that sentence were preceded by a priming sentence from the the-matically similar story. Psychologists interpret faster reaction times after a priming stimulus to be an indication that the participant regards the priming stimulus and the test stimulus to be conceptually related.

The results of the study showed that the response time for a test sentence was fa-cilitated by the priming sentence *only* if the participants had been urged to pay at-tention to repeated themes in the stories they were reading. Otherwise, people did not seem to make the connection between the two stories. If you plan to inspire a friend to behave more admirably, and you decide to tell a cautionary tale—based on someone else's experiences—you would be wise to point out that the story might be connected with current behavior! People do not spontaneously detect ab-stract similarities in scripts. In Chapter 10, we will also see that people do not spon-taneously detect abstract similarities between mathematical problems.

Now that we have examined the kind of schema known as a script, let's return to the more general category of schemas and investigate how schemas operate in four phases of memory. According to Alba and Hasher (1983), schemas may operate at four different phases:

1. during the selection of material to be remembered;
2. during abstraction (when you store meaning, but not the specifics of the message);
3. during interpretation (when schemas aid your comprehension); and
4. during integration (when you form a single memory representation).

Schemas and Memory Selection

The research on schemas and memory selection has produced contradictory find-ings. Sometimes people remember material best when it is *consistent* with a schema;

sometimes they remember material best when it is *inconsistent* with the schema. Let's first consider a classic study that favors schema-consistent memory.

Enhanced Memory for Schema-Consistent Material. Try Demonstration 7.6 when you have the opportunity. This demonstration is based on a study by Brewer and Treyens (1981). These authors asked participants in their study to wait, one at a time, in the room pictured in the demonstration. Each time, the experimenter explained that this was his office, and he needed to check the laboratory to see if the previous participant had completed the experiment. After 35 seconds, the experimenter asked the participant to move to a nearby room. Here, each person was given a surprise test: Recall everything in the room in which he or she had waited.

The results showed that people were highly likely to recall objects consistent with the "office schema"—nearly everyone remembered the desk, the chair next to the desk, and the wall. However, few recalled the wine bottle and the coffee pot, and only one remembered the picnic basket. These items were not consistent with the office schema. (In addition, some remembered items that were *not* in the room; nine remembered books, though none had been in sight. This supplying of schema-consistent items represents an interesting reconstruction error.)

As Alba and Hasher (1983) point out, schema theories propose three conditions that determine whether a piece of information will be selected for encoding:

1. A person must have a relevant schema, such as an "office schema."
2. The schema must be activated. For example, the participants in Brewer and Treyen's study must realize that they are in an office.
3. The incoming information must be important with respect to the schema. For example, the chair and the desk are important components of the "office schema."

In the case of Brewer and Treyens's study, people recalled information consistent with the "office schema." Notice, however, that people did not realize that they were going to be asked to remember the items; in other words, the task involved ***incidental learning.*** Incidental learning conditions may encourage us to be more casual about processing the objects we see. As a consequence, we may recall objects more accurately when they match our expectations.

Enhanced Memory for Schema-Inconsistent Material. As you might imagine, we sometimes show better recall for material that *violates* our expectations, especially when that material is especially vivid and interrupts the ongoing schema. In a recent study, Davidson (1994) asked people to read a variety of stories, describing well-known schemas such as going to the movies. The results showed that people were especially likely to recall events that interrupted the normal, expected story. In a "going to the movies" story, for example, they were more likely to remember a schema-inconsistent sentence involving a woman named Sarah—"A child runs through the theater and smashes head on into Sarah"—than they were to remember the schema-consistent sentence, "The usher tears their tickets in half and gives them the stubs" (p. 773).

SCHEMAS AND MEMORY. BASED ON BREWER & TREYENS (1981).

After reading these instructions, cover them and the rest of the text in this demonstration so that only the picture shows. Present the picture to a friend, with the instructions, "Look at this picture of a psychologist's office for a brief time." Half a minute later, close the book and ask your friend to list everything that was in the room.

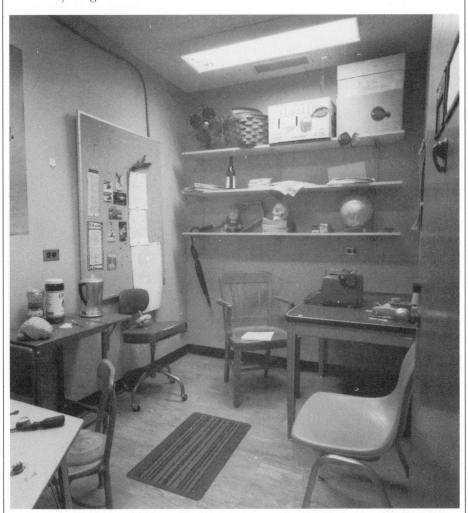

Further instructions for Demonstration 7.5: Now without looking back at Demonstration 7.5, write down the story from that demonstration, being as accurate as possible.

DEMONSTRATION 7.7

CONSTRUCTIVE MEMORY. BASED ON JENKINS (1974).

Part 1

Read each sentence, count to five, answer the question, and go on to the next sentence.

SENTENCE	QUESTION
The girl broke the window on the porch.	Broke what?
The tree in the front yard shaded the man who was smoking his pipe.	Where?
The cat, running from the barking dog, jumped on the table.	From what?
The tree was tall.	Was what?
The cat running from the dog jumped on the table.	Where?
The girl who lives next door broke the window on the porch.	Lives where?
The scared cat was running from the barking dog.	What was?
The girl lives next door.	Who does?
The tree shaded the man who was smoking his pipe.	What did?
The scared cat jumped on the table.	What did?
The girl who lives next door broke the large window.	Broke what?
The man was smoking his pipe.	Who was?
The large window was on the porch.	Where?
The tall tree was in the front yard.	What was?
The cat jumped on the table.	Where?
The tall tree in the front yard shaded the man.	Did what?
The dog was barking.	Was what?
The window was large.	What was?

Part 2

Cover the preceding sentences. Now read each of the following sentences and decide whether it is a sentence from the list in Part 1.

1. The girl who lives next door broke the window.   (old _____, new _____)
2. The tree was in the front yard.   (old _____, new _____)

(*continued on page 249*)

DEMONSTRATION 7.7 (CONTINUED)

3. The scared cat, running from the barking
   dog, jumped on the table. (old _____, new _____)
4. The window was on the porch. (old _____, new _____)
5. The tree in the front yard shaded the man. (old _____, new _____)
6. The cat was running from the dog. (old _____, new _____)
7. The tall tree shaded the man who was
   smoking his pipe. (old _____, new _____)
8. The scared cat was running from
   the dog. (old _____, new _____)
9. The girl who lives next door broke the
   large window on the porch. (old _____, new _____)
10. The tall tree shaded the girl who broke
    the window. (old _____, new _____)
11. The cat was running from the barking dog. (old _____, new _____)
12. The girl broke the large window. (old _____, new _____)
13. The scared cat ran from the barking
    dog that jumped on the table. (old _____, new _____)
14. The girl broke the large window on the
    porch. (old _____, new _____)
15. The scared cat which broke the window on
    the porch climbed the tree. (old _____, new _____)
16. The tall tree in the front yard shaded the
    man who was smoking his pipe. (old _____, new _____)

Rojahn and Pettigrew (1992) conducted a recent meta-analysis of the research on memory and schemas. Most of the studies included in the meta-analysis seemed to involve **intentional learning,** where people realized that they were going to be asked to remember the items. When memory was assessed in terms of recall—as in Davidson's study—people were likely to remember schema-inconsistent material better than schema-consistent material. When memory was assessed in terms of recognition and the results were corrected for guessing, schema-inconsistent material was still favored. However, when memory was assessed in terms of recognition and the results were *not* corrected for guessing, schema-*consistent* material was favored. In other words, if you can't remember whether you've seen a sentence on a recognition test about a movie schema, you're more likely to guess that you saw a sentence about an usher tearing up tickets than a sentence that violates the schema. However, guessing—rather than memory—may be responsible for this difference.

Why should we often remember schema-inconsistent material so accurately? Sherman and Hamilton (1994) suggest an interesting explanation. Perhaps when we encounter some information that violates a schema, we bring back some of the earlier material into our working memory. This new, schema-inconsistent information is then linked with that earlier material; this association may increase the probability of remembering the schema-inconsistent information at a later time. For example, when you read about a child smashing into a moviegoer, you may search the earlier material for an explanation for this bizarre event. In contrast, when you read about an usher tearing up the movie tickets, you don't need to retrieve any earlier material.

The Current Status of Schemas and Memory Selection. Ironically, we cannot establish any clear schema for the research on this important topic! Apparently, we seem to remember schema-consistent material more accurately if the task involves incidental learning or if memory is assessed by recognition—with no correction for guessing. In most cases, however, schema-inconsistent material appears to be more memorable.

Schemas and Memory Abstraction

Abstraction is a memory process that stores the meaning of a message without storing the exact words and grammatical structures. For example, you can recall much of the information about the concept "family resemblance," without recalling a single sentence in its exact original form. In Chapter 5, we saw that people may sometimes have good verbatim recall, or word-for-word recall. For instance, professional actors can recite the exact words from a Shakespeare play. More often, our verbatim memory is far from spectacular a few minutes after a passage has been presented (e.g., Sachs, 1967). However, we tend to recall the gist or general meaning with impressive accuracy. Let's consider two approaches to this issue, the constructive approach and the pragmatic approach.

The Constructive Approach. First, try Demonstration 7.7 on page 248–249, if you have not already done so. This is a simpler version of a study by Bransford and Franks (1971). How many sentences in the second half had you seen before? The answer is at the end of the chapter.

Bransford and Franks asked the participants in their study to listen to sentences that belonged to several different stories. Then they were given a recognition test that included new sentences, many of which were combinations of the earlier sentences. Nonetheless, people were convinced that they had seen them before. They were particularly certain that they had heard complex sentences, such as "The tall tree in the front yard shaded the man who was smoking his pipe." In contrast, they were quite confident that they had not seen simple sentences, such as "The cat was scared." Furthermore, they did not think that they had seen sentences that violated the meaning of the earlier sentences—for example, "The scared cat which broke the window on the porch climbed the tree."

Bransford and Franks proposed a constructive model of memory for prose material. According to the ***constructive model of memory,*** people integrate information from individual sentences in order to construct larger ideas. People therefore think that they have already seen those complex sentences because they have combined the various facts in memory. Once sentences are fused in memory, we cannot untangle them into their original components and recall those components verbatim.

Notice that the constructive view of memory emphasizes the active nature of our cognitive processes, consistent with Theme 1 of this book. Sentences do not passively enter memory, where each is stored separately. Instead, we try to make sense out of sentences that seem to be related to one another. We combine the sentences into a coherent story, fitting the pieces together.

Constructive memory also illustrates Theme 2. Although memory is generally accurate, the errors in cognitive processing can often be traced to generally useful strategies. In real life, a useful heuristic is to fuse sentences together. However, this heuristic can lead us astray if it is applied inappropriately. As it turns out, participants in Bransford and Franks's (1971) study used a constructive memory strategy that is useful in real life but inappropriate in a study that tests verbatim memory.

The Pragmatic Approach. Recently, Murphy and Shapiro (1994) have developed a different view of memory for sentences, which they call the pragmatic view of text memory. The ***pragmatic view of memory*** proposes that people "attend to the level of analysis of text that is most relevant, important, or salient, given their current goals" (p. 87). In other words, people can strategically control their attention. In everyday life, we realize that we should pay attention to the general meaning of a story. As a consequence, we recall the "gist" quite accurately but ignore the specific sentences. However, if we realize that we *should* pay attention to the exact words in a sentence, then word-for-word or ***verbatim memory*** can be accurate. Notice that the pragmatic view of text memory is somewhat similar to some research we discussed in Chapters 3 and 5, in connection with encoding specificity. Specifically, when people focus on the sounds of words during encoding, they can remember acoustical information; when they focus on meaning, they can remember semantic information (Bransford et al., 1979; Moscovitch & Craik, 1976).

In one of their experiments, Murphy and Shapiro (1994) found that people who had been instructed to pay attention to the specific words in a sentence could accurately recognize the correct words on a later test; they were not misled into believing they had seen close synonyms.

In another experiment, Murphy and Shapiro (1994) speculated that people are particularly likely to pay attention to the specific words in a sentence if they are part of a criticism or an insult. After all, from the pragmatic view, the exact words do matter if you are being insulted. In this study, participants read one of two letters, presumably written by a young woman named Samantha. One letter, supposedly written to her cousin Paul, chatted about her new infant in a bland fashion and included a number of neutral sentences such as "It never occurred to me that I would be a mother so young" (p. 91). The other letter was supposedly written by Samantha to her boyfriend Arthur. Ten of the sentences that were neutral in the bland letter to cousin Paul now appeared in a sarcastic context, though the exact words were identical. For example, the sentence "It never occurred to me that I would be a mother so young" now referred to Arthur's infantile behavior.

========== TABLE 7.2 ==========

PERCENTAGE OF "OLD" JUDGMENTS MADE TO TEST ITEMS IN MURPHY AND SHAPIRO'S (1994) STUDY.

		Story condition
	Bland	*Sarcastic*
Irrelevant sentences	4%	5%
Hits (original sentences)	71%	86%
False alarms (paraphrases)	54%	43%
Hits minus false alarms	17%	43%

Memory was later tested on a recognition test that included five of the original sentences, five paraphrased versions of those sentences with a slightly different form (e.g., "I never thought I would be a mother at such a young age"), and four irrelevant sentences. Table 7.2 shows the results. As you can see, people rarely made the mistake of falsely "recognizing" the irrelevant sentences. However, they correctly recognized ("hits") the sarcastic sentences more often than the bland sentences. Furthermore, they made mistakes in thinking they had seen the paraphrases ("false alarms") more often for the bland sentences than for the sarcastic sentences. When we compare the accuracy for the two versions (by subtracting the false alarms from the correct responses), we see that people were much more accurate in their verbatim memory for the sarcastic version than for the bland version. Perhaps we are especially sensitive about emotionally threatening material, so we recall the exact words of the sentences.

The Current Status of Schemas and Memory Abstraction. Some theorists prefer the constructive approach to memory abstraction, whereas others prefer the pragmatic approach. However, the two approaches are actually quite compatible. Specifically, in many cases, we do integrate information from individual sentences so that we can construct large schemas, especially when the situation suggests that the exact words are not crucial. However, in other cases, we know that the specific words *do* matter, and so we allocate extra attention to the precise wording. An actor rehearsing for a play or two people quarreling will need to remember more than just the gist of a verbal message.

Schemas and Inferences in Memory

In many cases, people add their own general knowledge to the material they encounter, and they remember that this information was present in the original material. Thus, recall can contain *inferences* or logical interpretations and conclusions that were never part of the original stimulus material.

Research in this area began with the studies of Frederick Bartlett (1932), a memory researcher who used natural language material. As we've mentioned before, his theories and techniques foreshadowed the approaches of contemporary cognitive psychologists. Whereas Ebbinghaus favored nonsense words, Bartlett believed that the most interesting aspect of memory was the complex interaction between the prior knowledge of the participants in the experiment and the material presented during the experiment. Furthermore, Bartlett argued that, as time passes after hearing the original story, the recalled story borrows more heavily from previous knowledge and less from the information in the original story.

Bransford and his colleagues (1972) provided further evidence about the fusing of previous knowledge and information from the stimulus. These authors studied how people construct mental models, based on verbal descriptions—a topic we considered at the end of Chapter 6. They gave some people a sentence such as:

1. *Three turtles rested beside a floating log, and a fish swam beneath them.*

Other people heard a sentence such as:

2. *Three turtles rested on a floating log, and a fish swam beneath them.*

Notice that the only difference between these two sentences is the word *beside* or *on*.

Later, everyone received a recognition test containing sentences such as:

3. *Three turtles rested (beside/on) a floating log, and a fish swam beneath it.*

Let us discuss this recognition sentence before examining the results. Sentence 3 contains *it* rather than *them* and can be derived from Sentence 2. Our knowledge of spatial relations tells us that if the turtles are on the log and a fish is beneath them, then the fish must also be beneath the log. That recognition sentence is therefore a reasonable inference. Notice, however, that the recognition sentence is not necessarily an inference from Sentence 1; it is ambiguous whether the fish are swimming beneath the log.

The results of the study showed that people who had seen Sentence 2 often reported that they recognized Sentence 3. However, people who had seen Sentence 1 were much less likely to say that they recognized Sentence 3. Bransford and his coauthors (1972) explain that people who saw Sentence 2 construct an idea by fusing that sentence with what they know about the world. As a result, they believe that they have seen a sentence that was never presented, even though it is a reasonable inference.

This study demonstrates that background knowledge can mislead people, causing them to remember inferences that were not actually stated. However, background information is usually helpful in our daily lives. For instance, our background knowledge can help us recall stories. Bower (1976) argues that simple stories have definite, regular structures. People become familiar with the basic structure of stories from their prior experience in their culture. They use this structure in sorting out any new stories they hear. Once again, when background information is consistent with the stimulus materials, this background information is clearly helpful.

This material on schemas and memory interpretations can be applied to advertising. Suppose that an ad says, "Four out of five doctors recommend the ingredients in Gonif's brand medication." You might reasonably infer, therefore, that four out of five doctors would also recommend Gonif's medication itself—even though the ad never said so.

Research by Harris and his colleagues (1989) shows that people who read advertisements may jump to conclusions, remembering inferences that were never actually stated. In their research, college students read stories that contained several advertising slogans. Some slogans made a direct claim (for example, *Tylenol cures colds*), whereas others merely implied the same claim (for example, *Tylenol fights colds*). On a multiple-choice task that followed, people who had seen the implied-claim version often selected the direct-claim version instead. You can see why these results suggest that consumers should be careful. If an advertiser implies that a particular product has outstanding properties, make certain that you do not jump to inappropriate conclusions; you are likely to remember those inferences, rather than the actual stated information.

After reading about the experimental evidence for humans' tendencies to draw inappropriate inferences, you might conclude that people inevitably draw conclusions based on inferences from their daily experience. Alba and Hasher (1983) note, however, that inference-making is not an *obligatory* process. Several researchers have found that inference-making occurs only in limited situations; people often recall material accurately, just as it was originally presented. Further research must address the issue of when memory is schematic and when it is accurate. In many cases, then, schemas can indeed influence inferences in memory. However, consistent with Theme 2, memory can often be highly accurate.

Schemas and Integration in Memory

The final process in memory formation is integration. Schema theories argue that a single, integrated representation is created in memory from the information that was selected in the first phase, abstracted in the second phase, and interpreted (with the aid of background knowledge) in the third phase. In fact, some researchers argue that schemas exert a more powerful effect during the integration and retrieval phases than during the earlier phases of memory (e.g., Bloom, 1988; Kardash et al., 1988).

For example, a number of studies show that background knowledge does not influence recall if that recall is tested immediately after the material is learned. However, after a longer delay, the material has been integrated with existing schemas; recall is now altered. For instance, Harris and his colleagues (1989) asked college students in Kansas to read a story that was consistent with either American or traditional Mexican culture. A representative story about planning a date in the Mexican culture included a sentence about the young man's older sister accompanying the couple as a chaperone; the American version had no chaperone. When story recall was tested 30 minutes after reading the material, the students showed no tendency for the Mexican-schema stories to shift in the direction consistent with American schemas. After a 2-day delay, however, the students had shifted a significant number of story details.

As Harris and his colleagues (1988) point out, schemas about our culture can influence our initial understanding of a story about another culture. However, an important additional source of cultural distortion occurs during delayed recall. We do not remember the details, so we reconstruct information that is consistent with our own cultural schemas.

People often do integrate material in memory. However, Alba and Hasher (1983) cite experimental evidence that fails to demonstrate integration. In many cases, people store within memory several separate, unintegrated units of the original stimulus complex. Memory integration does occur, but it is not inevitable.

Conclusions About Schemas

In summary, schemas can influence memory, from the initial selection of material, during abstraction, during interpretation, and even in the final process of integration. However, we must emphasize the following points:

1. We may be especially likely to select material that is *inconsistent* with our schemas, and we sometimes select material that is not relevant to those schemas.
2. We frequently recall the exact words of a passage as it was originally presented—otherwise, chorus directors would have resigned long ago.
3. We often fail to apply our background knowledge when we need to interpret new material.
4. We may keep the elements in memory isolated from each other, rather than integrated together.

Thus, schemas clearly influence memory. However, the influence is far from complete. After all, our cognitive processes are guided by bottom-up processing, as well as top-down processing. Therefore, we select, recall, interpret, and integrate many unique features of each stimulus, in addition to the schema-consistent features that match our background knowledge.

SECTION SUMMARY: SCHEMAS

1. According to research on scripts, people show different patterns in recalling material from scripts, as opposed to categories; we can also recall the elements in a script more accurately if the script is identified at the outset. Also, experts are better than novices at understanding a script's structure.

2. People may not detect abstract similarities between two scripts unless the similarities are pointed out.

3. Schemas operate in the selection of memories; for example, people recall items consistent with an office schema, but schema-inconsistent information is often favored.

4. According to the constructive model of memory, schemas encourage memory abstraction, so that the general meaning is retained, even if the details of the original message are lost. According to the pragmatic view of memory, people can shift their attention to remember the exact words—when the specific words really matter.

5. Schemas influence the interpretations in memory; people may recall inferences that never appeared in the original material. However, background information is often helpful, for example, in recalling stories. Unfortunately, people often recall incorrect inferences from advertisements.

6. Schemas encourage an integrated representation in memory; research shows that people may misremember material so that it is more consistent with their schemas, including the schemas from their own culture.

METACOGNITION

We have discussed several kinds of knowledge in this chapter, including knowledge about words, concepts, situations, and events. Every topic so far has emphasized our knowledge about the outside world. Our last topic is somewhat different, because it focuses on our knowledge about the inside world—the processes inside our head, or metacognition. *Metacognition* is our knowledge, awareness, and control of our cognitive processes.

Think about the variety of metacognitive knowledge you possess. For example, if I ask you the name of the researcher who is associated with the prototype approach to semantic memory, you can tell me whether or not the researcher's name is on the tip of your tongue. You also know what kind of factors influence your own cognitive processes (for example, time of day, motivation, type of material, and social circumstances). You can also assess whether you are adequately prepared for the next exam you will take. Furthermore, your metacognitive processes allow you to *control* your cognitive activities (Nelson, 1994). For example, your assessment that you are not yet prepared to take a test on semantic memory may encourage you to spend extra time studying that section.

Metacognition is an intriguing topic because we use our cognitive processes to contemplate our cognitive processes. Metacognition is important because our knowledge about our cognitive processes can guide us in arranging circumstances and selecting strategies to improve future cognitive performance.

The previous chapters in this book have discussed topics related to metacognition. For instance, in Chapter 2, we saw that people often have limited consciousness about their higher mental processes. For example, they may not be able to identify which factors helped them solve a problem (Nisbett & Wilson, 1977). In

Chapter 5, we discussed how people may have difficulty on reality monitoring tasks. For instance, they may not be able to recall whether they actually gave a book to a friend—or whether they merely imagined they had done so (Johnson, 1988; Johnson, 1995). Metacognition is also featured prominently in two memory theories discussed in earlier chapters. For instance, Atkinson and Shiffrin's (1968) classic model emphasizes that control processes are strategies that people use flexibly and voluntarily. Baddeley's (1992b) theory of working memory proposes that the central executive integrates information from the other components of working memory and plays a role in planning and controlling behavior.

In the current chapter, we will examine two very important kinds of metacognition: the tip-of-the-tongue phenomenon and metamemory. In Chapter 8, we will look at metacomprehension, which focuses on your knowledge about whether you have understood a passage you have just read. In Chapter 10, we will discuss whether people can accurately judge how close they are to solving a cognitive problem. Finally, Chapter 12 addresses the development of metacognition.

The Tip-of-the-Tongue Phenomenon

Try Demonstration 7.8 to see whether any of the definitions encourage you into a tip-of-the-tongue experience. The *tip-of-the-tongue phenomenon* refers to the sensation we have when we are confident that we know the word for which we are searching, yet we cannot recall it. In our discussion of this topic, let's first consider the classic study by Brown and McNeill (1966). Then we'll examine some of the more recent research, including the related topic of the feeling of knowing.

Brown and McNeill's (1966) Research. Roger Brown and David McNeill conducted the first formal investigation in this area. Their description of a man "seized" by a tip-of-the-tongue state may capture the torment you sometimes feel when you fail to snatch a word from the tip of your tongue:

> The signs of it were unmistakable; he would appear to be in mild torment, something like the brink of a sneeze, and if he found the word his relief was considerable. (p. 326)

The similarity between "the brink of a sneeze" and the irritating tip-of-the-tongue experience is amazing! Don't you wish you had a substance similar to pepper that could coax the missing word out of memory?

In their research, Brown and McNeill produced the tip-of-the-tongue state by giving people the definition for an uncommon English word, such as *cloaca, ambergris,* and *nepotism.* Sometimes people supplied the appropriate word immediately, and other times they were confident that they did not know the word. However, in some cases, the definition produced a tip-of-the-tongue state. In these cases, the experimenter asked people to provide words that resembled the target word in terms of sound, but not meaning. For example, when the target word was *sampan,* people provided these similar-sounding words: *Saipan, Siam, Cheyenne, sarong, sanching,* and *symphoon.*

DEMONSTRATION 7.8

THE TIP-OF-THE-TONGUE PHENOMENON

Look at each of the definitions below. For each definition, supply the appropriate word if you know it. Indicate "Don't know" for those that you are certain you don't know. Mark TOT next to those for which you are reasonably certain you know the word, though you can't recall it now. For these words, supply at least one word that sounds similar to the target word. The answers appear at the end of the chapter. Check to see whether your similar-sounding words actually do resemble the target words.

1. An absolute ruler, a tyrant.
2. A stone having a cavity lined with crystals.
3. A great circle of the earth passing through the geographic poles and any given point on the earth's surface.
4. Worthy of respect or reverence by reason of age and dignity.
5. Shedding leaves each year, as opposed to evergreen.
6. A person appointed to act as a substitute for another.
7. Five offspring born at a single birth.
8. A special quality of leadership that captures the popular imagination and inspires unswerving allegiance.
9. The red coloring matter of the red blood corpuscles.
10. Flying reptiles that were extinct at the end of the Mesozoic Era.
11. A spring from which hot water, steam, or mud gushes out at intervals, found in Yellowstone National Park.
12. The second stomach of a bird, which has thick, muscular walls.

When Brown and McNeill analyzed the results, they found that the similar-sounding words were indeed very similar to the target words. The similar-sounding words matched the target's first letter 49% of the time, and they matched the target's number of syllables 48% of the time.

Brown and McNeill (1966) proposed that our long-term memory for words and definitions is like a dictionary. However, our mental dictionaries are much more flexible than the dictionary you have on your bookshelf. We can recover words from memory by either their meaning or their sound, and we need not examine the entries in alphabetical order.

Think about the reason why the tip-of-the-tongue phenomenon is one kind of metacognition. People know enough about their memory to report, "This word is on the tip of my tongue." Their knowledge is indeed fairly accurate, because they are likely to be able to identify the first letter and the number of syllables in the target word. They are also likely to provide similar-sounding words that really do resemble the target word.

More Recent Research on the Tip-of-the-Tongue Phenomenon. Alan Brown
(1991) has reviewed 25 years of research on the tip-of-the-tongue experience.
He concludes that people report about one of these experiences each week
in their daily lives, although elderly people report it somewhat more often
than younger adults. People successfully retrieve the word they are seeking
about half the time, often within the first two minutes of the tip-of-the-tongue
experience.

In general, the research also shows that people correctly guess the first letter of
the target word between 50% and 70% of the time (Brown, 1991). They are also
highly accurate in identifying the appropriate number of syllables, with accuracy
rates between 47% and 83%. However, these figures are less impressive when you
consider that people could be quite accurate by simply guessing. The higher accuracy rates are usually obtained with proper names, which are usually just one or two
syllables long. Thus, people's guesses could be counted as accurate simply because
they are unlikely to report that the person's name on the tip of their tongue is
longer than two syllables.

One active area within the tip-of-the-tongue research concerns the role of "interlopers." Suppose, for example, that you are searching for the word that refers to
a young goose, and a friend says to you, "It's something like *goblet*." Will the interloper *goblet* block you from achieving your target word, *gosling*? Unfortunately, we
don't yet have clear-cut answers on this question; sometimes the interloper facilitates recall of the target word, sometimes it blocks recall, and sometimes it has no
effect (Meyer & Bock, 1992; Perfect & Hanley, 1992). The answer probably depends
upon such factors as the unusualness of the target word and the similarity between
the interloper and the target word.

Another active area within the tip-of-the-tongue research focuses on the nature
of the ***feeling of knowing,*** or the judgment that some information is on the tip of
your tongue. For example, Koriat (1993, 1994) argues that when we are searching
for a target and trying to retrieve it, we directly assess our feeling of knowing. That
is, we base our feeling of knowing on the accessibility of that partial information.
Also, if we have a strong feeling of knowing about a particular target, we know that
we should keep on searching (Miner & Reder, 1994). For example, several pages
ago, I was writing about the classic research by Brown and McNeill (1966), and I
wanted to add the first names of these two researchers. Ironically, I was seized by a
tip-of-the-tongue state when trying to recall McNeill's first name. However, I had a
very strong feeling of knowing about the target, so I knew that further searching
would be worthwhile. Sure enough, 10 seconds later, the name "David" jumped into
memory. Not surprisingly, strong feelings of knowing are associated with rapid remembering (Smith & Clark, 1993).

Feeling of knowing is a predictive kind of metacognition; it indicates how likely
you will be to recall some information. In contrast, confidence in your memory is
a retrospective kind of metacognition; your confidence reflects your judgment that
some information has been correctly retrieved from memory (Miner & Reder,
1994). In general, we base our confidence in a target memory on the ease with
which that target came to mind (Kelley & Lindsay, 1993).

A final new emphasis within the research on the tip-of-the-tongue phenomenon is to place it within the context of the parallel distributed processing approach, which we discussed on pages 94–99 (McClelland, Rumelhart, & the PDP group, 1986; Rumelhart et al., 1986). Specifically, the tip-of-the-tongue experience is consistent with the concept of graceful degradation. That is, we often remember some partial information, even when we cannot recall the exact target we are seeking in memory.

IN DEPTH: Metamemory

Have you ever been in this situation? You thought that you knew the material for a midterm, and—in fact—you expected to receive a fairly high grade. However, when the midterms were handed back, you received a C. If this sounds familiar, you have experienced a metamemory failure. *Metamemory* refers to people's knowledge, awareness, and control of their memory. Metamemory is relevant when you learn new material and when you try to remember previously learned material (Nelson, 1992a).

In this in-depth section, let's first examine the accuracy of metamemory and next consider how metamemory is related to memory performance. Then we will ask whether students are aware of the factors that can affect memory. Our final topic is whether students are effective in using metamemory to regulate and control their study strategies.

Chapter 5 foreshadowed the importance of metamemory. In the section on memory improvement, we introduced a number of memory strategies. However, these strategies will not greatly improve your memory unless you use your metamemory to decide what you already know and what you need to review in more detail. Metamemory also helps you identify which memory strategies work best for you and which ones are inefficient. This in-depth section therefore suggests some practical tips for improving both your everyday memory and your performance on examinations. As you read this material, try to identify areas in which your metamemory could be improved. Then figure out how you can apply the information you learn in this section to remedy these problems.

The Accuracy of Metamemory. Under ideal conditions, metamemory can be outstandingly accurate. Consider a study by Eugene Lovelace (1984). Lovelace presented pairs of unrelated English words, such as *disease-railroad*. The participants were told that they would be tested for paired-associate learning; that is, they would later see the first word in each pair and be asked to supply the second word. They learned the pairs under four different exposure conditions: S1 people saw each pair for 8 seconds on a single study trial; S2 people saw each pair for 4 seconds on each of two successive study trials; S4 people saw each pair for 2 seconds on each of four successive study trials; and T2 people saw each pair for 4 seconds on each of two successive study trials with a test trial in between. After the final exposure of each pair, the participants rated each pair for the likelihood of their answering the item correctly on a later test. Finally, they were tested for recall.

FIGURE 7.5

PROBABILITY OF RECALLING AN ITEM, AS A FUNCTION OF EXPERIMENTAL CONDI-
TION AND RATED LIKELIHOOD OF ANSWERING THE QUESTION.   LOVELACE (1984).

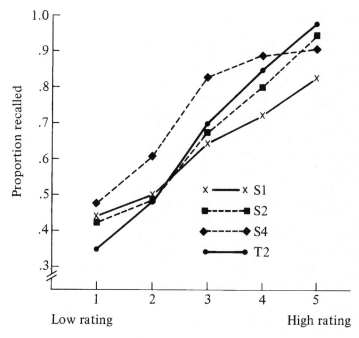

Rated likelihood of answering the question correctly
on a later test

Figure 7.5 shows the results, which were similar for all four conditions. The most
striking finding is that people can accurately predict which items they will recall.
When they give a rating of 5 to an item, they do in fact recall it about 90% of the
time when they are tested later. In contrast, when they give a rating of 1, they recall
it less than half the time. You can apply these findings to your classroom performance. If you know that you'll be tested on a specific list of items—such as Spanish
vocabulary or definitions for specific psychology terms—you are likely to be reasonably accurate in estimating whether you know the material.

Metamemory is less accurate when the task is not so clear-cut. In most college
courses, you seldom know exactly what material will be on the test. Furthermore,
you need to master concepts, not pairs of words. Metamemory judgments about
conceptual material seem to be more difficult.

We have noted that the kind of material influences the accuracy of one's
metamemory. What other factors affect whether your metamemory will accurately
reflect the status of your memory? Remember that, in this case, we are no longer
discussing *memory accuracy,* the central topic in Chapters 4 and 5. Instead, we are

discussing *metamemory accuracy*. For example, the participants in Lovelace's (1984) study had high metamemory accuracy, because they were much more likely to remember those items they predicted they would remember, in contrast to those items they predicted they would not remember. Here are some of the conditions in which metamemory accuracy is likely to be especially *high*:

1. When material has been overlearned, rather than just barely mastered (Nelson & Narens, 1994);
2. When the material is easy, rather than difficult (Schraw & Roedel, 1994);
3. When learning is intentional, rather than incidental (Mazzoni & Nelson, 1995); and
4. When people delay their judgments, rather than making them immediately after learning (Dunlosky & Nelson, 1994; Nelson, 1996; Nelson & Dunlosky, 1991).

Why should these factors affect the accuracy of metamemory? One possibility is that we are realistically optimistic about our memories when we know the material fairly well (because we overlearned it, because it's easy, or because we intentionally learned it). In contrast, we may use "magical thinking" and show inappropriate optimism when we have not mastered the material.

Furthermore, delayed judgments are more likely to provide accurate assessments of our memory performance because they assess long-term memory . . . and the actual memory task involves long-term memory.[1] In contrast, immediate judgments assess working memory, which is less relevant to the memory task. These particular findings suggest an important practical application. When you are studying your notes for an exam—and you are trying to determine which topics need more work—wait a few minutes before assessing your memory (Dunlosky & Nelson, 1994). Your metamemory is more likely to be accurate than when you make an immediate judgment.

The Relationship Between Metamemory and Memory Performance. Are people with excellent metamemory likely to perform better on memory tests? Leal (1987) gave introductory psychology students a questionnaire to test their knowledge about metamemory. Typical questions assessed whether students knew that relearning is easier than learning material for the first time, and that material at the beginning and end of a list is learned better than material in the middle. The results showed that some of the individual metamemory questions were significantly correlated with performance on classroom examinations. For instance, students who reported that they organize material in a meaningful manner and test themselves prior to an exam were likely to do well on classroom exams. However, the total score on the metamemory questionnaire was not correlated with exam performance. Apparently, some components of metamemory are not really related to exam scores. Also, the research in this area shows that metamemory is difficult to measure reliably (Thompson & Mason, 1996).

---

[1]In fact, it could be argued that this measure is actually a long-term memory test, rather than a true assessment of metamemory (Lovelace, 1996).

As you may know from other courses, an ideal study for examining cause-and-effect relationships in psychology should involve an experiment, rather than correlational methods. Unfortunately, I've not been able to locate any experiments showing a *causal* relationship between metamemory and memory performance. Here is an important question, ready to be tested experimentally: If we were to teach metacognitive skills to college students, would they score higher than students in a control group, who had not been instructed in metacognitive techniques?

Awareness of Factors Affecting Memory. Think about someone you know with a high grade point average. Can this person's high grades be traced more to high ability or to hard work? According to Devolder and Pressley (1989), North American students give more credit to innate ability than to hard work. However, students need to be aware that effort and strategic factors can be just as important as ability, or sometimes even more important.

Are students aware that some memory strategies are more effective than others? Here again, students are not sufficiently aware of the importance of strategic factors. Suzuki-Slakter (1988) instructed one group of students to memorize material by simply repeating it—a strategy that you know is relatively ineffective. These students seriously overestimated their performance. Another group was told to make up stories and images about the items—a strategy you know to be effective. These students *underestimated* their performance.

Other students have found that people are not aware that the keyword method (which was illustrated in Figure 5.5) is more effective than mere repetition (Pressley et al., 1984, 1988). However, when people practiced both methods and saw their superior performance with the keyword method, they were much more likely to use this method in the future. This research highlights an important point: Try using various study strategies, then test yourself. Identify which method or methods were most effective. You'll be much more likely to revise your strategies if you can demonstrate that they improve your own performance.

Regulating Study Strategies. You may have developed your metamemory to the point that you know exactly which study strategies work best in which circumstances. However, your exam performance may still be less than ideal if you have not effectively regulated your study strategies. Specifically, you need to control your time allotment so that you spend much more time on the items you have not yet mastered than on those that you know you'll remember.

Thomas Nelson and R. Jacob Leonesio (1988) examined how students distribute their study time when they are allowed to study at their own pace. They found that students did allocate more study time for the items they believed would be difficult to master. The correlations here averaged about +.30 (where .00 would indicate no relationship and +1.00 would be a perfect correlation between study time and judged difficulty).

One of my professors in graduate school made an interesting observation (Martin, 1967). He pointed out that—whenever you see a number—you should ask yourself, "Why is it so high, and why is it so low?" In this case, the correlation of +.30 is high because students do realize that they should study more difficult items more diligently. This general relationship has been replicated in more recent research (Nelson et al., 1994).

Why is this crucial correlation as *low* as +.30? Unfortunately, students are less than ideal in regulating their study strategies. They spend longer than necessary studying items they already know, and not enough time studying the items they have not yet mastered. Let's translate these findings to apply to the way you might study this current chapter for an examination tomorrow—assuming that you are a typical student. You may decide that you know the material on the tip-of-the-tongue phenomenon fairly well, but you are not confident about the theories of semantic memory. You might indeed spend somewhat longer studying semantic memory. However, you would be likely to distribute your study time too evenly across the chapter, reviewing the comfortably familiar topics you already know. Can't you see yourself pausing to reminisce about your experiences with the tip-of-the-tongue effect, but breezing too quickly over the finer points of the network models of semantic memory?

Another reason that this correlation is as low as +.30 is that students may make a strategic decision not to waste time on the most difficult items—the ones that would require an enormous investment of time to master (Mazzoni & Cornoldi, 1993). Instead, they may concentrate on the moderately difficult items, which could be learned with modest effort. Also, we can hardly condemn a student for pausing to think about an intriguing part of a textbook (Phillips, 1995). After all, efficient studying is not the only goal in a student's education!

However, let's assume that you *do* want to figure out how to distribute your study time more strategically across items that vary in difficulty. Some research by Cull and Zechmeister (1994) provides useful information based on something you learned in the section on the accuracy of metamemory. On page 262, you learned that metamemory is more accurate when people delay their judgments, rather than making them immediately after learning (Dunlosky & Nelson, 1994; Nelson & Dunlosky, 1991). Perhaps students would distribute their study time more appropriately if they had the opportunity to assess their metamemory after a delay, rather than immediately after learning.

To test this hypothesis about delayed metamemory assessments, Cull and Zechmeister (1994) asked students to learn pairs of words. In each pair, the first word was an unusual English word, such as *fugue* or *rheum*. The second word in each pair was either easy (e.g., *brown*) or hard (e.g., *siege*). Thus, the task was set up to resemble a situation in which students were learning new English vocabulary words. Students in the immediate-judgment condition were asked to assess whether they knew each pair immediately after seeing it. In contrast, students in the delayed-judgment condition waited until they had seen all 36 pairs before assessing whether they knew each item. Then the researchers recorded the number of times the students studied each pair during the rest of the study session.

Figure 7.6 shows the results. As you would expect, students devoted more study trials to the hard items than to the easy items. However, the more interesting finding is the statistical interaction between item type and testing condition (immediate versus delay). As you can see, people who assessed their metamemory immediately after seeing each pair showed a relatively flat distribution of study time; they didn't spend much longer on the hard items than on the easy items. In contrast, people who assessed their metamemory after a delay used a wiser study strategy, allocating substantially more time to the hard items than to the easy items. (Of course, a truly wise student would show an even stronger preference for studying the hard items.) Incidentally, students in the delayed-judgment condition also *recalled* more items—both easy and hard—than students in the immediate condition.

Here's how you can apply Cull and Zechmeister's findings. Let's say you want to learn the new terms used in the present chapter. Read through the chapter as you normally would. Then turn to the list of new terms at the end of the chapter and assess whether you know each term. This delayed assessment would presumably be a more accurate measure of your knowledge than would an immediate assessment, and you should distribute your subsequent study time more wisely.

═══════════════ **FIGURE 7.6** ═══════════════

NUMBER OF STUDY TRIALS FOR EASY AND HARD PAIRS OF WORDS, AS A FUNCTION OF IMMEDIATE AND DELAYED JUDGMENT.   CULL & ZECHMEISTER (1994).

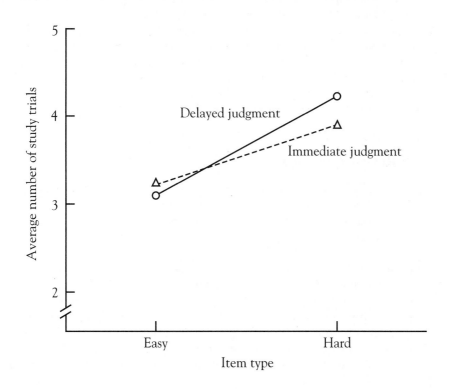

Throughout this section on metamemory, we have discussed how attention to your metamemory can improve performance. Naturally, you need to know memory strategies, such as those described in Chapter 5. However, you also need to know how to use them effectively by selecting the strategies that work well for you and by distributing your study time appropriately.

SECTION SUMMARY: METACOGNITION

1. Whereas other parts of this chapter have focused on our knowledge of the outside world, the part on metacognition focuses on our knowledge of the world inside our heads, specifically the tip-of-the-tongue phenomenon and metamemory.
2. According to research on the tip-of-the-tongue phenomenon, when people cannot remember the word for which they are searching, they often can identify its important attributes.
3. When you have a strong feeling of knowing about a target, you're likely to retrieve the item rapidly; you are also likely to be confident that the information you retrieved from memory is correct if the target came easily to mind.
4. People's metamemories are quite accurate when the task is clear-cut, when material is extremely familiar or easy, when learning has been intentional, and when judgments about an item's memorability are delayed.
5. Some components of metamemory are correlated with memory performance; however, students are not sufficiently aware that effort is related to test scores or that some memory strategies are more effective than others.
6. Students spend somewhat more time studying difficult material, rather than easy material; when judgments about memorability are delayed, students spend even longer on the difficult material.

CHAPTER REVIEW QUESTIONS

1. Suppose that you read the following question on a true-false examination: "A script is a kind of schema." Describe how you would process that question in terms of the feature comparison model and the two network models discussed in this chapter.
2. Think of a prototype for the category *household pet*, and contrast it with a non-prototypical pet. Compare these two animals with respect to: (a) whether they would be supplied as examples of the category; (b) whether they could be used as a reference point in trying to describe another kind of household pet; (c) how quickly they could be judged after priming; and (d) whether they can substitute for a category name in a sentence.
3. Consider the basic-level category *dime*, in contrast to the superordinate *money* and the subordinate *1986 dime*. Discuss how the basic-level name

would be used to identify objects. Also discuss how members of this basic-level category share attributes in common.

4. Describe three scripts with which you are very familiar. How would these scripts be considered heuristics, rather than exact predictors of what will happen the next time you find yourself in one of the situations described in the script?

5. Human cognitive processes seem to prefer prototypes, basic-level categories, and schemas. Discuss this general statement, providing experimental support from the current chapter.

6. You probably have a fairly clear schema of the concept "dentist's office." Focus on the section of the chapter called "Schemas and Memory Selection" and point out the circumstances in which you would be likely to remember (a) schema-consistent material and (b) schema-inconsistent material.

7. Think of a schema or a script with which you are especially familiar. Explain how that schema might influence your memory during four different phases: selection, abstraction, interpretation, and integration.

8. In general, how accurate is our metacognition? Provide examples from the tip-of-the-tongue phenomenon and various metamemory tasks. Also describe several factors that could influence the accuracy of your metamemory. Finally, describe how you could design a new experiment in which college students are taught metacognitive skills, to see whether their test performance improves.

9. An important part of the section on metacognition examined how people regulate and control their memory activities. Discuss this information, pointing out how study strategies are somewhat effective, but they could be better.

10. Think about someone you know who is just beginning college. Imagine that this person is asking you for advice on how to study. What information can you provide from the discussion of metamemory? Give as many hints as possible.

NEW TERMS

semantic memory
episodic memory
feature comparison model
defining features
characteristic features
sentence verification technique
typicality effect
category size effect
network model

parallel distributed processing (PDP) approach
Collins and Loftus network model
node
spreading activation
ACT*
declarative knowledge
procedural knowledge
working memory

proposition
prototypes
prototype approach
prototypicality
classical view of concepts
graded structure
priming effect
family resemblance
superordinate-level categories

basic-level categories
subordinate-level
  categories
schemas
heuristics
script
incidental learning

intentional learning
abstraction
constructive model of
  memory
pragmatic view of memory
verbatim memory

inferences
metacognition
tip-of-the-tongue phenom-
  enon
feeling of knowing
metamemory

RECOMMENDED READINGS

Barsalou, L. W. (1992a). *Cognitive psychology: An overview for cognitive scientists.* Hillsdale, NJ: Erlbaum. Lawrence Barsalou is a prominent researcher in the area of semantic memory. His chapters on categorization and knowledge in memory would be useful for students who want a theoretical, advanced-level treatment of these topics.

Brown, A. S. (1991). A review of the tip-of-the-tongue experience. *Psychological Bulletin, 109,* 204–223. Brown's article provides a solid review of the topic, including questions for which we do not yet have answers.

Metcalfe, J., & Shimamura, A. P. (Eds.). (1994). *Metacognition: Knowing about knowing.* Cambridge, MA: MIT Press. This book contains a number of well-written chapters by the major figures in the area of metacognition, and it includes such topics as memory monitoring, the tip-of-the-tongue phenomenon, feeling of knowing, and metacognitive aspects of eyewitness testimony.

Nelson, T. O. (Ed.). (1992b). *Metacognition: Core readings.* Boston, MA: Allyn & Bacon. A library could provide a superb overview of metacognition by purchasing both this book and the Metcalfe and Shimamura book. Nelson's book contains an excellent collection of theoretical and empirical articles about metacognition.

Rojahn, K., & Pettigrew, T. F. (1992). Memory for schema-relevant information: A meta-analytic resolution. *British Journal of Social Psychology, 31,* 81–109. This article is a clearly written summary of the conflicting research on schema-consistent and schema-inconsistent material.

Vosniadou, S., & Ortony, A. (Eds.). (1989). *Similarity and analogical reasoning.* New York: Cambridge University Press. The first part of the book contains some excellent articles on the structure of concepts.

ANSWER TO DEMONSTRATION 7.7

Every sentence in Part 2 is *new.*

ANSWER TO DEMONSTRATION 7.8

1. despot; 2. geode; 3. meridian; 4. venerable; 5. deciduous; 6. surrogate; 7. quintuplets; 8. charisma; 9. hemoglobin; 10. pterodactyl; 11. geyser; 12. gizzard.

LANGUAGE COMPREHENSION: LISTENING AND READING

INTRODUCTION

THE NATURE OF LANGUAGE

Phrase Structure
Transformational Grammar
Factors Affecting Comprehension
Neurolinguistics

SPEECH PERCEPTION

Characteristics of Speech Perception
Theories of Speech Perception

BASIC READING PROCESSES

Perceptual Processes in Reading
Discovering the Meaning of an Unfamiliar Word
Reading and Working Memory
Theories About the Role of Sound in Word Recognition

UNDERSTANDING DISCOURSE

Forming a Coherent Representation of the Text
In Depth: Inferences in Reading
Artificial Intelligence and Reading
Metacomprehension

============================ **Preview** ============================

In Chapters 8 and 9 we'll examine the pyschological aspects of language. Specifically, Chapter 8 emphasizes language comprehension in the form of listening and reading. In contrast, Chapter 9 will emphasize speaking and writing, as well as bilingualism.

We'll begin Chapter 8 by exploring the nature of language. In particular, we'll look at the structure of language and at the biological underpinnings of language.

A necessary first stage in comprehending spoken language is speech perception, which requires translating sounds into speech units. When we perceive speech, we fill in missing sounds, we use visual cues to help us, and we determine the boundaries between words. In this section, we'll also consider theoretical approaches to speech perception.

Reading requires perceptual processes such as eye movement. Context is important when we need to understand the meaning of an unfamiliar word, and working memory also plays an important role in decoding sentences. This section also examines several theories about the role of sound in word recognition; we'll see that these theories suggest important implications for teaching reading to children.

The last part of Chapter 8 moves beyond small linguistic units to consider how we understand discourse, or language units that are larger than a sentence. Some important components of discourse comprehension include forming a coherent representation of a passage and drawing inferences that were not actually stated in the passage. Research on artificial intelligence emphasizes the impressive competence of humans in comprehending language. However, college students are not exceptionally accurate in their metacomprehension. For example, college students cannot accurately predict how well they will perform on a reading comprehension test. This section on metacomprehension may help you improve your ability to predict which topics you understand well and which require more careful review.

INTRODUCTION

"Two seniors for dead man," muttered the man standing in front of me. Did I suddenly fear that a bizarre new cult was permeating tranquil upstate New York? No. In fact, my understanding of language and my familiarity with the context of this utterance immediately informed me that two individuals over the age of 65 wanted to purchase movie tickets to see the film *Dead Man Walking*. Our general background knowledge is supplemented by the vast storehouse of specific information stored in memory. Almost instantaneously, we can decode puzzling conversations—an impressive testimony to the second theme of this book.

Another equally impressive characteristic of our language skills is our extraordinary ability to master thousands of words. For instance, Wingfield (1993) estimates that the average college-educated North American has a speaking vocabulary in the range of 75,000 to 100,000 words.

Furthermore, as Pinker (1993) points out, "Human language is one of the wonders of the natural world, because it is an infinite system mastered by creatures with finite brains" (pp. 59–60). In fact, there are no limits to the productivity of language. For example, if we only consider the number of 20-word sentences that you could potentially generate, you would need 10,000,000,000,000 years—or 2,000 times the age of the earth—to say them all (Miller, 1967; Pinker, 1993).

In Chapters 8 and 9, we will examine *psycholinguistics,* or the pyschological aspects of language. Psycholinguistics examines how people learn and use language to communicate ideas (Taylor & Taylor, 1990). Language provides the best example of the fourth theme of this textbook, the interrelatedness of the cognitive processes. In fact, virtually every topic discussed so far in this book makes some contribution to language processing. For example, perception allows us to hear speech and read words. Echoic memory and short-term memory help us store the stimuli long enough to process and interpret them. Long-term memory provides contiguity between the material we processed long ago and the material we now encounter (Garman, 1990). Furthermore, language is related to imagery, semantic memory, schemas, and the tip-of-the-tongue phenomenon.

The two chapters on language should also convince you that humans are active information processors (Theme 1). Rather than passively listening to language, we actively consult our previous knowledge, use various strategies, form expectations, and draw conclusions. When we speak, we must determine what our listeners already know and what other facts must be conveyed. Language is not only our most remarkable cognitive achievement, but it is also our most social cognitive process.

The first of our two chapters on language focuses on language comprehension. After an introductory discussion about the nature of language, we will examine speech perception, reading, and the more complex processes involved in understanding discourse. In Chapter 9, we will switch our focus from the understanding of language to the production of language. Three topics we will consider in that chapter are speaking, writing, and bilingualism.

THE NATURE OF LANGUAGE

Psycholinguists have developed a specialized vocabulary for language terms; let's now consider these terms. A *phoneme* (pronounced "*foe*-neem") is the basic unit of spoken language, such as the sounds *a, k,* and *th.* In contrast, a *morpheme* (pronounced "*more*-feem") is the basic unit of meaning. For example, the word *reactivated* actually contains four morphemes, *re-, active-, -ate,* and *-ed* (Gazdar, 1993). Each of those segments conveys meaning, including both those morphemes that can stand on their own (like *active*) and those that must be attached to other morphemes in order to convey their meaning; for example, *re*-indicates a repeated action (Newman, 1994).

Semantics is the area of psycholinguistics that examines the meanings of words and sentences (Carroll, 1994). The related term, *semantic memory,* refers to our organized knowledge about the world. We have discussed semantic memory throughout earlier chapters of this book, but especially in Chapter 7.

Another important component of psycholinguistics is syntax. *Syntax* refers to the grammatical rules that govern how words can be combined into sentences (Maratsos & Matheny, 1994). A final important term is *pragmatics,* which is our knowledge of the social rules that underlie language use (Carroll, 1994). Pragmatics is an especially important topic when we consider the production of speech (Chapter 9), but pragmatic factors also influence comprehension.

As you can see from reviewing the terms in this section, psycholinguistics encompasses a broad range of topics, involving sounds, several levels of meaning, and grammar. Let's now consider some additional background information about psycholinguistics: phrase structure, transformational grammar, factors affecting comprehension, and neurolinguistics.

Phrase Structure

A central concept in understanding language is called phrase structure. *Phrase structure* involves organizing a sentence into phrases or *constituents.* For example, suppose we have the following sentence:

The young woman carried the heavy painting.

We can divide this sentence into two broad constituents, *the young woman* and *carried the heavy painting.* Each of these constituents can be further subdivided, creating a hierarchy of constituents with a tree-like diagram. These diagrams, like the one in Figure 8.1, help us appreciate that a sentence is not simply a chain of words, strung like beads on a necklace. Instead, we appreciate more complicated relationships among the elements of a sentence.

Why should we humans bother with constituents, either in listening to spoken language or in reading written language? Why shouldn't we simply process the words one at a time? As it turns out, we often need information from the entire unit in order to give us cues about the meaning of the words. For example, consider the word *painting* in the sentence we just analyzed. *Painting* could be either a verb or a noun. However, from the context in which *painting* appears in the constituent *the heavy painting,* we know that the noun version is appropriate. Other words are even more ambiguous. The word *block,* for example, has many meanings in isolation; the other words in the constituent help to identify the appropriate meaning. Thus, context within a constituent helps us figure out the meaning of words.

What evidence do we have that people actually use phrase structure when they encounter a sentence? A representative study by Jarvella (1971) demonstrates the psychological reality of constituent structure. Specifically, he demonstrated that people remember words better if the words are from the constituent they are currently processing, rather than an earlier constituent. Jarvella presented two kinds of passages, such as:

FIGURE 8.1

AN EXAMPLE OF CONSTITUENTS

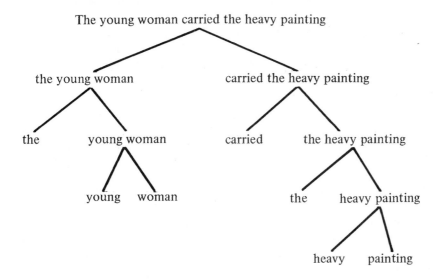

1. The confidence of Kofach was not unfounded.
   To stack the meeting for McDonald,
   the union had even brought in outsiders.

2. Kofach had been persuaded by the international
   to stack the meeting for McDonald.
   The union had even brought in outsiders.

Notice that the actual words in the second and third lines are identical in Passage 1 and Passage 2. However, in Passage 1, *to stack the meeting for McDonald* belongs with the third line. In contrast, in Passage 2, this same phrase belongs with the first line.

Jarvella interrupted people just after they had finished reading the third line and asked them to recall what they had read. As you would expect, recall in both conditions was excellent for the very most recent material, such as the line *the union had even brought in outsiders*. The interesting finding was that recall of the second line, *to stack the meeting for McDonald*, was excellent for people who saw Passage 1. That second line was part of a constituent that they were currently processing. In contrast, recall of the second line was poor for people who saw Passage 2. For them, that line was part of a constituent that they had already completed. Consequently, they did not need to remember it verbatim. In another study, Jarvella demonstrated that people remembered the general meaning of these previous constituents (e.g., the second line of Passage 2), even though their verbatim recall was poor.

Language comprehension clearly depends on memory processes (Pinker, 1994). This theme has been further developed by theorists who propose that part of short-term memory is set aside as a buffer that contains verbatim information about constituents from earlier in the text (Kintsch & van Dijk, 1978; Miller & Kintsch, 1980; Singer, 1990). New information is presented in a new cycle, and it enters short-term memory; this new information is interpreted with the aid of the old information in the buffer. Information is then transferred to long-term memory, and a new cycle begins. Fletcher (1981) tested this hypothesis by presenting material from *Reader's Digest* articles; the memory status of portions of this material had been established by pretesting. Participants were then shown a probe word, which was selected from one of four locations in the cycle, as based on the theories of Kintsch and his colleagues.

1. words from earlier cycles, not held in memory buffer;
2. words from the next-to-last cycle, not held in memory buffer;
3. words from the next-to-last cycle, held in memory buffer; and
4. words from the most recent cycle.

The participants in the study pressed buttons to indicate whether or not each specified probe word had occurred in the passage. Fletcher's results showed that words from Category 2 were recalled no better than the words from Category 1. However, words from Category 3 were recalled much more accurately. In summary, words that are currently held in the memory buffer have a greater likelihood of being recalled.

We have seen that phrase structure can be used to organize a sentence into its constituents. People actually use phrase structure, because research like Jarvella's (1971) and Fletcher's (1981) suggests that they hold the constituent in memory while they process it. In the following section, we'll see how Chomsky developed phrase structure into transformational grammar.

Transformational Grammar

People usually think of a sentence as an orderly sequence of words that are lined up in a row on a piece of paper. Noam Chomsky (1957) caused great excitement among psychologists and linguists by proposing that there is more to a sentence than meets the eye. His work on the psychology of language was mentioned in the Introduction to this textbook as one of the forces that led to the decreased popularity of behaviorism. The behaviorists emphasized the observable aspects of language behavior. In contrast, Chomsky argued that human language abilities could only be explained in terms of a complex system of rules and principles represented in the minds of speakers. He is clearly one of the most influential theorists in modern linguistics (Harris, 1993; Pinker, 1994).

Specifically, Chomsky devised a model of ***transformational grammar*** to convert underlying, deep structure into the surface structure of a sentence. ***Surface structure*** is represented by the words that are actually spoken or written. In contrast, ***deep structure*** is the underlying, more abstract meaning of the sentence. Let us examine these two kinds of structures in more detail.

Chomsky pointed out that two sentences may have very different surface structures, but very similar deep structures. Consider the following two sentences:

Sara threw the ball.
The ball was thrown by Sara.

Notice that the surface structures are different: None of the words occupies the same position in the two sentences, and three of the words in the second sentence do not appear in the first sentence. The phrase-structure diagrams would also represent these two sentences differently. However, "deep down," speakers of English feel that the sentences have identical core meanings.

Chomsky also pointed out that two sentences may have very similar surface structures but very different deep structures, as in these two sentences:

John is easy to please.
John is eager to please.

These sentences differ by only a single word, yet their meanings are quite different.

Two sentences can also have identical surface structures but very different deep structures; these are called **ambiguous sentences.** Here are three ambiguous sentences:

The shooting of the hunters was terrible.
They are cooking apples.
The lamb is too hot to eat.

Notice that each sentence can be represented by two very different phrase-structure diagrams. In fact, try making two diagrams like the one in Figure 8.1 to represent the two underlying meanings for the sentence *They are cooking apples.* We will discuss ambiguity in more detail later in this section.

Chomsky proposed that people understand sentences by transforming the surface structure into a basic, deep structure or **kernel** form. They use **transformational rules** to convert surface structure to deep structure during understanding. They also use transformational rules to convert deep structure to surface structure during speech production or writing.

Chomsky's ideas about transformational grammar inspired dozens of studies during the 1960s and 1970s. For example, Mehler (1963) found that people recalled kernel sentences, such as *The biologist has made the discovery,* much more accurately than sentences that involved several transformations, such as *Hasn't the discovery been made by the biologist?* (a negative-passive-question variant of the kernel).

Not all the evidence for Chomsky's theory was favorable, however. For example, the sentence *The cookies were smelled by John* should theoretically take less time to process than the sentence *The cookies were smelled* because the second sentence requires an additional transformation to drop the *by John.* However, Slobin's

(1966) research demonstrated that the second sentence actually took *less* time to verify.

In general, psychologists support Chomsky's notion about the distinction between surface and deep structure (Bock et al., 1992). However, research such as Slobin's (1966) has made many psychologists less enthusiastic about the notion that the number of transformations closely corresponds to psychological complexity (Carroll, 1994).

Furthermore, Chomsky's more recent theories provide more sophisticated linguistic analyses. For example, the early versions of transformational grammar could generate implausible sentences, as well as plausible ones (Leonard & Loeb, 1988). Chomsky's current approach places constraints on the possible hypotheses that the language-learner can make about the structure of language.

Chomsky's *government-binding theory* argues that grammar consists of seven systems that work independently (Chomsky, 1981; Leonard & Loeb, 1988). For example, one of these systems describes how grammatical units such as pronouns are "bound" or related to other words in a segment of language. For example, consider the following two sentences:

> Tanya gave herself the day off.
> Tanya gave her the day off.

You'll notice that in the first sentence you immediately appreciate that *Tanya* and *herself* are the same individual. In other words, *herself* is bound to *Tanya*. In contrast, in the second sentence, you realize that *Tanya* and *her* refer to different individuals; *her* is not bound to *Tanya*.

Chomsky's new approach also places more emphasis on the information contained in the individual words of a sentence. For example, the word *greet* not only conveys information about the word's meaning, but it also specifies the requirement that *greet* must be followed by a noun, as in the sentence, *Joe greeted his opponent* (Ratner & Gleason, 1993).

Factors Affecting Comprehension

The research on transformational grammar sparked an interest in the factors that can influence our understanding of sentences. As this section will demonstrate, we have more difficulty understanding sentences (1) if they contain negatives, such as *not;* (2) if they are in the passive rather than the active voice; and (3) if they are ambiguous.

Negatives. Several years ago, the first sentence in a newspaper article read,

> ALBANY—The Assembly yesterday overwhelmingly approved a state Equal Rights Amendment free of revisions intended to restrict its influence on a woman's right to an abortion.

This sentence requires several readings to understand exactly what the Assembly decided, because it contains so many implied negatives. If a sentence contains a negative word, such as *no* or *not*, or an implied negative, the sentence almost always requires more processing time than a similar affirmative sentence (Taylor & Taylor, 1990).

In a classic study, Clark and Chase (1972) asked people to verify statements, such as:

Star is above plus.　　＊
　　　　　　　　　　　　＋

The participants responded more quickly if the sentences were affirmative than if they contained the negative form *isn't* (for example, *Plus isn't above star*). They also made fewer errors with affirmative sentences.

As you can imagine, readers' understanding decreases as the number of negative terms increases. For example, Sherman (1976) gave people sentences with several negative terms. If you had been a participant in this study, how would you judge this sentence? "Few people strongly deny that the world is not flat" (p. 145). Sherman found that people understood every one of the affirmative sentences. Their accuracy decreased for sentences with two negatives and three negatives (like the sentence you just read). With four negatives, they understood only 59% of the sentences. In other words, performance in this condition was only slightly better than guessing (which would produce 50% correct responses).

The Passive Voice. As we discussed earlier, Chomsky (1957, 1965) pointed out that the active and passive forms of a sentence may differ in their surface structure but have similar deep structures. However, the active form is more basic; the transformation to the passive form requires additional words. Svartik (1966) provides additional evidence that the active form is more basic; it is used seven times as often as the passive in samples of modern English.

The active form is also easier to understand. In a typical study, adults in their thirties correctly understood 94% of active sentences and 81% of passive sentences (Obler et al., 1991). In other words, you can understand a sentence such as *The woman rescued the dog* more readily than *The dog was rescued by the woman*.

In previous eras, articles in psychology and other scientific disciplines typically overused the passive voice. As a result, scientific writing often sounded extremely pompous. Fortunately, current style manuals now recommend the active voice. For example, the current *Publication Manual of the American Psychological Association* points out that the active-voice sentence *"Gould (1994) designed the experiment"* is much more direct and vigorous than *"The experiment was designed by Gould (1994)"* (American Psychological Association, 1994, p. 32).

Ambiguity. Suppose that you saw the following headline in your local newspaper: "Two Sisters Reunited After 18 Years in Checkout Counter." As you might imagine, ambiguous sentences like this one are difficult to understand—just like sentences containing negatives or the passive voice. We discussed ambiguous sentences in connection with Chomsky's transformational grammar. But what happens when people try to understand these sentences?

In a classic study, Foss (1970) asked people to listen to ambiguous and unambiguous sentences. At the same time, they performed an additional task, which involved pressing a button every time they heard the sound *b* in a sentence. People took longer to press the button if they were listening to an ambiguous sentence. Foss reasoned that ambiguous sentences are more difficult to understand, so listeners have less processing capacity "left over" to use for other tasks.

However, theorists disagree about *how* listeners process ambiguous material (Holmes et al., 1987; Simpson, 1994). For example, theorists who favor a parallel distributed processing approach argue that, when people encounter a potential ambiguity, the activation builds up for all meanings of the ambiguous item. Furthermore, the degree of activation depends on the frequency of the meanings and on the context (Simpson, 1984; Simpson & Burgess, 1985). Consider the sentence, *Pat took the money to the bank.* Here, the "financial institution" interpretation of *bank* would receive the most activation. After all, this is the most common interpretation of *bank,* and the context of *money* suggests this meaning. But, presumably, some minimal activation also builds up for other meanings of *bank* (as in *riverbank* and *blood bank.*)

In contrast, other theorists argue that context constrains the meaning-activation from the very beginning, limiting meaning-access to only a single interpretation that is appropriate to the sentence context (Glucksberg et al., 1986).

One resolution to this controversy is that some individuals may use the approach in which all meanings are activated, whereas others activate only a single interpretation at any given time. In a study by Miyake and his coauthors (1994), people read sentences such as *Since Ken really liked the boxer, he took a bus to the nearest pet store to buy the animal.* Those readers who had large working-memory capacity were able to activate both meanings of the word *boxer* (the fighter and the dog). In contrast, those readers with small working-memory capacity had more difficulty reading the sentence when the ambiguous word involved the less common meaning (as in this sentence). Apparently, these readers initially constructed only a single interpretation for *boxer,* and then they needed to struggle to construct the alternate meaning.

As Rueckl (1995) observes, "Ambiguity is a fact of life. Happily, the human cognitive system is well-equipped to deal with it" (p. 501). Indeed, we can understand ambiguous sentences, just as we can understand negative sentences and sentences using the passive voice. However, we typically respond more quickly and more accurately when the language we encounter is straightforward. Now that you are familiar with the concept of ambiguity, try Demonstration 8.1.

Neurolinguistics

Neurolinguistics is the discipline that examines the relationship between the brain and language. Research in this area has become increasingly active in recent years, and it demonstrates that the neurological basis of language is impressively complex.

DEMONSTRATION 8.1

SEARCHING FOR AMBIGUOUS LANGUAGE

Perhaps the best source of ambiguous phrases is newspaper headlines. After all, these headlines must be very brief, so they often omit the auxiliary words that could resolve the ambiguity. Here are some actual newspaper headlines that I've seen:

1. "Eye drops off shelf"
2. "Squad helps dog bite victims"
3. "British left waffles on Falkland Islands"
4. "Enraged cow injures farmer with ax"
5. "Teacher strikes idle kids"

For the next few weeks, search the headlines of the newspapers you normally read. Keep a list of any that seem to be ambiguous. Try to notice whether your first interpretation of the ambiguous portion involved a correct or incorrect understanding of the phrase. If you find any particularly intriguing ambiguities, please send them to me! My address is: Department of Psychology, SUNY Geneseo, Geneseo, NY 14454.

For example, consider one "fact" that is most likely to be common knowledge about language: Language is localized in the left hemisphere of the brain. Even this straightforward statement is incorrect, however. For about 10% of right-handers and 35% of left-handers, language is either localized in the *right* hemisphere or is processed equally by both hemispheres (Blumstein, 1995; Maratsos & Matheny, 1994). Keeping in mind these individual differences, let's examine two sources of information about neurolinguistics: aphasia during adulthood and brain-imaging techniques.

Adults With Aphasia. Until recently, almost all the information scientists had acquired about neurolinguistics was based on people with ***aphasia,*** or damage to the speech areas of the brain that produces difficulty in speaking, understanding, or writing (Thompson, 1993). Figure 8.2 illustrates two relevant regions of the brain; a stroke or other damage to either region frequently causes aphasia.

Damage to ***Broca's area*** (toward the front of the brain) produces speech that is slow and effortful (Blumstein, 1995). For example, one person with Broca's aphasia produced this sentence:

> Me . . . build-ing . . . chairs, no, no cab-in-nets. One, saw . . . then, cutting wood . . . working . . . . (Jackendoff, 1994, p. 146)

Broca's aphasia is therefore characterized by an expressive-language deficit. However, people with Broca's aphasia also have some trouble understanding several language distinctions. For example, they may be unable to tell the difference

=========== FIGURE 8.2 ===========

TWO REGIONS OF THE BRAIN, BROCA'S AREA AND WERNICKE'S AREA, THAT ARE COMMONLY ASSOCIATED WITH APHASIA.

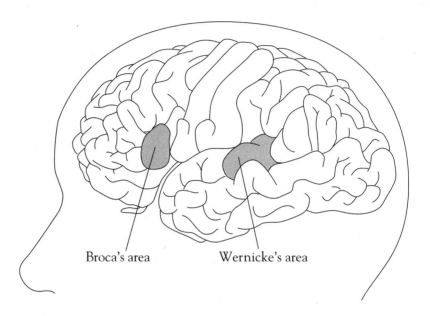

Broca's area   Wernicke's area

between "He showed her baby the pictures" and "He showed her the baby pictures" (Jackendoff, 1994, p. 149).

The other major aphasia is called Wernicke's aphasia (pronounced "*Ver*-nih-kee"). Damage to ***Wernicke's area*** (toward the back of the brain) produces speech that is too abundant and often makes little sense; people with Wernicke's aphasia also have serious difficulties comprehending speech (Blumstein, 1995). For example, one person with Wernicke's aphasia produced these sentences:

> Well, this is . . . mother is away here working out o'here to get her better, but when she's working, the two boys looking in the other part. One their small tile into her time there. She's working another time because she's getting, too. (Jackendoff, 1994, p. 147)

However, Wernicke's aphasia is characterized by an even more severe receptive-language deficit; people with this disorder cannot follow basic instructions such as "point to the telephone" or "show me the picture of the watch."

The basic information about these two kinds of aphasia has been known for about a century. The more recent research—using neuroscience techniques such as brain imaging—provides a more complete picture of the biological basis of language.

Recent Neuroscience Research. During the past decade, researchers have used two techniques to investigate language in the human brain. Let's first examine the results of research using the **PET scan**, or **positron emission tomography**, which measures the blood flow within regions of the brain in order to obtain a picture of brain activity. Then we will consider the research using the **ERP technique**, or **event-related potential**, which records the small fluctuations in the electrical activity of the brain, in response to a stimulus.

The research of Petersen and his colleagues provides an elegant analysis of brain activity by using the PET scan (Petersen et al., 1989; Posner & Raichle, 1994). Their technique used the following logic: (1) present an increasingly complex series of language tasks; and (2) "subtract" the blood flow pattern created by the simpler tasks from the blood flow pattern created by the next most complex task. This technique therefore identifies the brain activity associated with each component of language.

Figure 8.3 shows the typical setup for this kind of PET-scan approach. During the simplest task, at the first level, the participant simply looks at the crosshair (+) on the television monitor. During the second-level, visual task, the participant passively views a word. During the second-level, auditory task, the participant passively hears a word. During the third-level task, the participant must speak the word that was either seen or heard. Finally, during the fourth-level task, the participant must provide a verb that describes the function of the word that was either seen or heard. (For example, a *hammer* can be used to *pound*.)

Now turn to Color Figure 3, inside the back cover of this textbook. Here you can see the PET scans that were generated after subtracting the blood-flow pattern associated with the simpler tasks. For example, the upper-left portion shows the PET scan for passively viewing words, after subtracting the blood-flow patterns associated with simply looking at the crosshair. The red and yellow colors indicate the greatest brain activity in a PET scan.

You can see, therefore, that when people passively view words, the most active region is the occipital cortex—the rear part of the brain that processes visual stimuli. When people passively listen to words, their temporal cortex—near the ear—is most active. The task of speaking words activates the motor regions in the parietal portion of the cortex. Finally, the task of generating meaning (thinking of a related verb) produces activation in the frontal cortex and in the back portion of the temporal cortex. Take a moment to look at Figure 8.3 and Color Figure 3 simultaneously. Imagine that you are participating in each phase of this study, and place your hand on the portion of your head near the brain region activated by each task.

One of the most impressive findings in these PET-scan studies is the variety of brain regions involved in processing language. Although other research groups report somewhat different results (e.g., Menard et al., 1996), the PET-scan research clearly illustrates the multiple processes involved in understanding and producing language (Posner & Rothbart, 1994).

The research using event-related potentials (ERPs) is still in its beginning stages. This technique allows researchers to trace the rapid changes in the brain's electrical activity by focusing on the regions identified by the PET scans. For example, when people process a word and think of a related verb (e.g., *hammer–pound*), the frontal cortex is active after 200 milliseconds, and the temporal cortex is active after 700 milliseconds (Snyder et al., 1995). Other research has shown that the pattern of electrical activity is different when people process content words (nouns and

FIGURE 8.3

THE SETUP FOR POSNER AND RAICHLE'S (1994) SERIES OF TASKS. SEE TEXT FOR EXPLANATION.

First Level

Second Level, Visual

Second Level, Auditory "Hammer"

Third Level "Hammer"

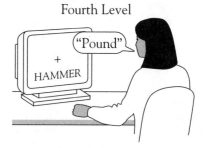

Fourth Level "Pound"

verbs) versus words that simply serve a grammatical function—such as *therefore* (Nobre & McCarthy 1994).

So far in this chapter, we have examined the basic vocabulary of psycholinguistics, as well as phrase structure, transformational grammar, factors affecting comprehension, and basic neurolinguistics. Now that you have acquired this background knowledge, let's turn our attention to the general topics of speech perception, basic reading process, and discourse comprehension.

SECTION SUMMARY: THE NATURE OF LANGUAGE

1. Some of the central concepts in psycholinguistics are the phoneme, the morpheme, semantics, and syntax.
2. People use the information in constituents to determine meaning; part of short-term memory stores the previous constituents in a segment of language.
3. Chomsky's theory of transformational grammar proposed that deep structure is converted to surface structure via transformational rules. Chomsky's more recent government-binding theory emphasizes the role of seven independent language systems, as well as the grammatical implications contained in individual words.
4. Sentences are more difficult to understand if they contain negatives, if they are in the passive voice, and if they are ambiguous.
5. Neurolinguistic research on adults with aphasia points out the importance of Broca's area and Wernicke's area in normal language processing. Research using PET scans and ERPs highlights a variety of brain regions involved in separate language-related activities.

SPEECH PERCEPTION

When we hear spoken language, we must first analyze the sounds of speech. During *speech perception,* the listener's auditory system translates sound vibrations into a string of sounds that the listener perceives to be speech. Speech perception seems perfectly easy and straightforward . . . until you begin to think about some of the components of this process. For example, adult speakers produce about 15 sounds each second (Kuhl, 1994a). In other words, a listener must somehow perceive 900 sounds each minute! In order to perceive a word, an adult listener must distinguish the sound pattern of one word from the tens of thousands of irrelevant words that are stored in memory (Goldinger et al., 1989). And—if these tasks are not challenging enough—the listener must separate the voice of the speaker from a background that typically includes other simultaneous conversations as well as a wide variety of nonspeech sounds (Remez, 1994). In fact, it's astonishing that we ever manage to perceive spoken language!

Speech perception is extremely complex, and more details on the process may be pursued in other books (Coren et al., 1994; Kuhl, 1994a; Matlin & Foley, 1997; Miller & Eimas, 1995a). We'll consider two aspects of speech perception in this section: (1) characteristics of speech perception and (2) theories of speech perception.

Characteristics of Speech Perception

The next time you listen to a radio announcer, pay attention to the sounds you are hearing, rather than the meaning of the words. You hear some vowels for which the vocal tract remains open (for example, the sounds *a* and *e*), stop consonants for which the vocal tract closes completely and then quickly opens up (for example, the sounds *p* and *k*), and other sounds (such as *f* and *r*) in which the vocal tract performs other contortions. You may hear brief quiet periods throughout this string of sounds. However, most of the words are simply run together in a continuous series.

Let's consider several characteristics of speech perception:

1. Phoneme pronunciation varies tremendously.
2. Context allows listeners to fill in missing sounds.
3. Visual cues from the speaker's mouth help us interpret ambiguous sounds.
4. Listeners can impose boundaries between sounds.

All these characteristics provide further evidence for the second theme of this book. Despite a less-than-perfect speech stimulus, we perceive speech with remarkable accuracy and efficiency.

Variability in Phoneme Pronunciation. Perceiving phonemes does not initially seem like a challenging task. After all, don't we simply hear a phoneme and instantly perceive it? Actually, phoneme perception is not that easy. For example, speakers vary tremendously in the pitch of their voices and their rate of producing phonemes. Fortunately, listeners seem to retain information about speakers' phoneme production in their long-term memory (Pisoni, 1993). We use this information to help us perceive a speaker's stream of phonemes (Miller & Eimas, 1995b).

A second source of variability is that speakers often fail to produce phonemes in a precise fashion. For example, Remez (1994) found that speakers were sloppy when they carried on normal conversations; they seldom produced the appropriate features of the phonemes. For instance, they rarely stopped completely when producing a stop consonant such as *p* or *k*.

A third source of variability is called ***coarticulation;*** when you are pronouncing a particular phoneme, you are typically also pronouncing a small portion of the previous phoneme and the following phoneme—at the same time. As a result, the phoneme you produce varies slightly from time to time, depending upon the surrounding phonemes (Kuhl, 1994a; Miller & Eimas, 1995b). For example, the *d* in *idle* is slightly different from the *d* in *don't*.

Despite this remarkable variability in phoneme pronunciation, we still manage to appreciate the speaker's intended phoneme. Factors such as context, visual cues, and word boundaries help us achieve this goal.

Context and Speech Perception. People are active listeners, consistent with Theme 1. Instead of passively receiving speech sounds, they can use context as a cue to help them figure out a sound or a word.

Warren and his colleagues have demonstrated in several experiments that people tend to show ***phonemic restoration:*** They can fill in sounds that are missing, using context as a cue. For example, Warren (1970) played a recording of a sentence: *The state governors met with their respective legi*latures convening in the capital city.* The first *s* in the word *legislatures* was replaced with an ordinary cough lasting 0.12 seconds. Of the 20 people who heard the recording, 19 reported that there were no sounds missing from the recording! (The one remaining person reported the wrong sound as missing.)

We are accustomed to having occasional phonemes masked by extraneous noises, and we are quite good at reconstructing the missing sounds. Think about the number of times extraneous noises have interfered with your professors' lectures. People knock books off desks, cough, turn pages, and whisper. Still, you can figure out the appropriate words.

Warren and Warren (1970) showed that people are skilled at using the meaning of a sentence to select the correct word from several options. They played four sentences for their subjects:

> It was found that the *eel was on the axle.
> It was found that the *eel was on the shoe.
> It was found that the *eel was on the orange.
> It was found that the *eel was on the table.

The four sentences were identical with one exception: A different word was spliced onto the end of each sentence. As before, a cough was inserted in the location shown by the asterisk. The "word" *eel was heard as *wheel* in the first sentence, *heel* in the second sentence, *peel* in the third, and *meal* in the fourth. In this study, then, people could not use surrounding sounds to reconstruct the word, yet they were able to reconstruct the word on the basis of a context cue that occurred four words later!

Notice that phonemic restoration is a kind of illusion (Warren, 1984). People think they hear a phoneme, even though the correct sound vibrations never reached their ears. Phonemic restoration is a well-documented phenomenon, and it has been demonstrated in numerous studies (e.g., Samuel, 1981, 1987; Samuel & Ressler, 1986). Other research has demonstrated that people are highly accurate in reconstructing a word that is missed during speech perception, particularly when that word is highly predictable from context (Cooper et al., 1985; Salasoo & Pisoni, 1985).

DEMONSTRATION 8.2

CONTEXT AND MISPRONUNCIATIONS

Practice reading these sentences until you can read them smoothly. Then read them to a friend. Ask your friend to report which word in each sentence was mispronounced and to identify which sound in the word was incorrect.

1. In all the gunfusion, the mystery man escaped from the mansion.
2. When I was working pizily in the library, the fire alarm rang out.
3. The messemger ran up to the professor and handed her a proclamation.
4. It has been zuggested that students be required to preregister.
5. The president reacted vavorably to all of the committee's suggestions.

Our ability to perceive a word on the basis of context also allows us to handle sloppy pronunciations. Try Demonstration 8.2, which is a modification of a study by Cole (1973). In Cole's study, people often did not notice mispronunications when they occurred in the context of a sentence (for example, the *gunfusion* sentence). However, they accurately distinguished syllables such as *gun* and *con* when the isolated syllables were presented.

Because we are so tolerant of mispronunciations in sentences, we often fail to notice startling mispronunciations that children make. Think back about a song that you sang when you were a child in which you included totally inappropriate words. One of my students recalled singing a Christmas carol in which the shepherds "washed their socks by night," rather than "watched their flocks by night." Another student recalled singing a Christmas carol with the words, "O come all ye hateful: Joy, Phil, and their trumpet." Many songs that children learn are never explained to them, and so they make up versions that make sense. However, these versions sound close enough to the standard that adults will not detect the errors. A classroom may have 25 second-graders, all reciting their own variants of the "Pledge of Allegiance"!

We have seen in this section that context has an important influence on the speech we hear. You may recall a similar discussion about the effects of context in Chapter 2 when we examined the influence of context on visual pattern perception. In the context of a kitchen scene, we see a loaf of bread, rather than a mailbox. In the context of an axle, we hear the word *wheel*, rather than *peel*. One likely explanation for the influence of context on perception is top-down processing, although other explanations have also been offered (e.g., Kintsch, 1988; Miller & Eimas, 1995b). The top-down processing approach argues that we use our knowledge and expectations to facilitate recognition, whether we are looking or listening. Understanding language is not merely a passive process in which words flow into our ears, providing data for bottom-up processing. Instead, we actively use the information we know to create expectations about what we might hear. Consistent with Theme 5 of this textbook, top-down processing influences our cognitive activities.

Visual Cues as an Aid to Speech Perception. Try Demonstration 8.3 when you have the opportunity. As Smyth and her colleagues (1987) point out, this simple exercise illustrates how visual cues contribute to speech perception. Information from the speaker's lips and face helps resolve ambiguities from the speech signal, much as phoneme contextual cues help us choose between *wheel* and *peel* (Dodd & Campbell, 1986). Similarly, you can hear conversation more accurately when people speak to you directly, instead of speaking over the telephone (Massaro, 1989). Even with a superb telephone connection, we miss the lip cues that would inform us whether the speaker was discussing *Harry* or *Mary*.

Adults with normal hearing seldom learn to notice or take full advantage of these visual cues. In fact, we are likely to appreciate visual cues only in unusual circumstances. For example, you may notice a poorly dubbed movie, in which the actors' lips move independently of the sounds presumably coming from those lips (Massaro, 1987). However, researchers have demonstrated that we do integrate visual cues with auditory cues during speech perception—even if we don't

---

DEMONSTRATION 8.3

VISUAL CUES AND SPEECH PERCEPTION. BASED ON SMYTH ET AL. (1987).

The next time you are in a room with both a television and a radio, try this exercise. Switch the TV set to the news or some other program where some-one is talking straight to the camera; keep the volume low. Now turn on your radio and tune it between two stations, so that it produces a hissing noise. Turn the radio's volume up until you have difficulty understanding what the person on television is saying; the radio's "white noise" should nearly mask the speaker's voice. Face the TV screen and close your eyes; try to understand the spoken words. Now open your eyes. Do you find that speech perception is now much easier?

---

recognize the usefulness of these visual cues. These results have been replicated for speakers of English, Spanish, Japanese, and Dutch (Massaro et al., 1995).

Word Boundaries. Have you ever heard a conversation in an unfamiliar language? The words seem to run together in a continuous stream, with no boundaries sepa-rating them. You may think that the boundaries between words seem much more distinct in English—almost as clear-cut as the white spaces that identify the bound-aries of written English. In most cases, however, the actual acoustical stimulus of spoken language shows no clear-cut pauses to mark the boundaries (Kuhl, 1994a; Lively et al., 1994; Miller & Eimas, 1995b). An actual physical event—such as a pause—marks a word boundary less than 40% of the time (Cole & Jakimik, 1980; Flores d'Arcais, 1988).

Consider this visual analog of the auditory word-boundary problem (Jusczyk, 1986) as you read the following line:

THEREDONATEAKETTLEOFTENCHIPS

Without the white spaces (the visual equivalent of pauses in speech), you probably found the task difficult. Did you read the line as, "There, Don ate a kettle of ten chips," "There, donate a kettle of ten chips," or "The red on a teakettle often chips"?

We sometimes make boundary errors in everyday conversation. For example, Safire (1979) comments on a grandmother who made an interesting misinterpre-tation of "the girl with kaleidoscope eyes" from the Beatles' song "Lucy in the Sky with Diamonds." Because of her greater familiarity with illness than with psyche-delic experiences, she thought that the line was "the girl with colitis goes by." We use our knowledge to interpret ambiguous phonemes and to impose boundaries between words. Most of the time, this knowledge leads us to the correct conclusions, but it sometimes leads to humorous misinterpretations.

Theories of Speech Perception

The theories that explain speech perception generally fall into two categories (Kuhl, 1989). Some theorists believe that speech requires a special mechanism to explain our impressive skill in this area. Others admire humans' skill in speech perception, but they argue that the same general mechanism that handles other cognitive processes also handles speech perception.

The Special Mechanism Approach. According to the ***special mechanism approach,*** humans have a specialized device that allows them to decode speech stimuli by connecting the stimuli they hear with the way these sounds are produced by the speaker. In other words, speech perception is closely linked with speech production. The major proponents of this approach, Alvin Liberman and Ignatius Mattingly, argue that this unique ability to perceive speech resembles the special sound localization abilities found in barn owls and bats (Liberman, 1992; Liberman & Mattingly, 1989; Mattingly & Liberman, 1988).

More specifically, Liberman and Mattingly argue that humans possess a ***phonetic module,*** a special-purpose neural mechanism that facilitates speech perception. This phonetic module enables listeners to perceive ambiguous phonemes and to segment the blurred stream of auditory information that reaches their ears, so that they can perceive distinct phonemes and words.

One argument in favor of the phonetic module was thought to be categorical perception. Computers can generate a range of sounds that form a gradual continuum between two speech sounds—for example, between the phonemes *b* and *p.* These stimuli form a smooth continuum. However, people who hear this series of sounds typically show categorical perception, hearing either a clear-cut *b* or a clear-cut *p.* Intriguingly, people do *not* report hearing a sound partway between a *b* and a *p.* When it was originally proposed, supporters of the special mechanism approach argued that people processed speech sounds very differently than nonspeech sounds. Specifically, they believed that people show categorical perception for speech sounds, but nonspeech sounds are heard as a smooth continuum.

Notice that the special mechanism approach suggests that the brain is organized in a special way. Specifically, the module that handles speech perception does not rely on the general cognitive functions we have discussed in earlier chapters—functions such as iconic memory, working memory, and pattern recognition (Carroll, 1994). More information on speech as a modular system can be found in other resources (e.g., Gunnar & Maratsos, 1992; Pinker, 1994). The modular approach is not consistent with Theme 4 of this textbook, which argues that the cognitive processes are interrelated and dependent upon one another.

The General Mechanism Approaches. In contrast, a variety of ***general mechanism approaches*** argue that we can explain speech perception without any special phonetic module. People who favor these approaches believe that humans use the same neural mechanisms to process both speech sounds and nonspeech sounds. Speech perception is therefore a learned ability—indeed, a very impressive learned ability. Speech perception is not an innate ability, highly developed in the newborn.

Current research seems to favor the general mechanism approach, with the strongest evidence from the following studies:

1. The same categorical perception found in humans has also been demonstrated with an impressive variety of nonhuman animals, including chinchillas, Japanese quail, and macaque monkeys (Kuhl, 1989; Miller, 1990; Moody et al., 1990). Because these nonhuman species do not have human language abilities, they should not have a special phonetic module.
2. Humans exhibit categorical perception for complex *nonspeech* sounds (Pastore et al., 1990). In other words, these first two points demonstrate that categorical perception is a general characteristic, not limited to humans and not limited to speech (Jusczyk, 1986).
3. People's judgments about phonemes are influenced by visual cues, as we saw in an earlier section. For example, suppose that people hear the auditory stimulus *ba* and see lip movements appropriate to a sound somewhere between *ba* and *da*. According to Massaro, they are extremely unlikely to report hearing the clear-cut sound *ba*—even though that was the sound reaching their ears (Massaro, 1987; Massaro & Cohen, 1990, 1995). Thus, speech perception is more flexible than the special mechanism approach suggests; phoneme perception is influenced by nonspeech information.

Several different general-mechanism theories of speech perception have been developed (e.g., Marslen-Wilson, 1987; Marslen-Wilson et al., 1994; Massaro, 1989; Massaro & Oden, 1995; Yeni-Komshian, 1993), and you may wish to pursue further details on these approaches. These theories tend to argue that speech perception proceeds in stages and that it depends upon familiar cognitive processes such as feature recognition and decision making.

In summary, our ability to perceive speech sounds is impressive. However, this ability can probably be explained by our general perceptual skill, combined with our other cognitive abilities—rather than any special, inborn speech mechanism. We learn to distinguish speech sounds, the same as we learn to master other cognitive skills.

SECTION SUMMARY: SPEECH PERCEPTION

1. Speech perception is an extremely complex process that demonstrates humans' impressive cognitive skills.
2. The pronunciation of a specific phoneme varies greatly, depending upon the speaker, imprecise pronunciation, and variability caused by coarticulation.

3. When a sound is missing from speech, listeners demonstrate phonemic restoration, using context to help them perceive the missing sound.
4. People also use visual cues to facilitate speech perception.
5. Even when the acoustical stimulus contains no clear-cut pauses, people are able to determine the boundaries between words with impressive accuracy.
6. According to the special mechanism approach, humans have a special brain device (or module) that allows them to perceive phonemes.
7. At present, the evidence supports a general mechanism approach to speech perception; research suggests that humans do not perceive speech sounds differently than nonspeech sounds, and phoneme perception can be influenced by other cognitive processes.

BASIC READING PROCESSES

In just a few decades, the topic of reading has gained an important status within psychology. As recently as the 1960s, psychologists knew embarrassingly little about the reading process. In fact, one of the major books on reading during that earlier era was a reprint of a book originally published in 1908 (Huey, 1968). The introduction to the 1968 edition pointed out that no new information had been gathered on many aspects of reading during the previous 60 years! As we approach the 21st century, reading is one of the most important topics in cognitive psychology. When I revised the material on reading for this fourth edition of your textbook, for example, I had assembled 19 new books and 82 new articles published within the previous 5 years. Students who want more information about this complex topic might be especially interested in the books by Crowder and Wagner (1992), Lorch and O'Brien (1995), Rayner (1992), and Willows and her coauthors (1993).

Our discussion of reading is not confined just to Chapter 8, because we have already discussed several components of reading, such as letter recognition (Chapter 2), memory for written material (Chapters 4, 5, and 7), and the construction of mental models from written text (Chapter 6). In Chapter 10 we will examine how reading is related to problem solving, and in Chapter 12 we'll mention children's knowledge about the reading process. As emphasized throughout this book, the cognitive processes are interrelated. Reading is an important cognitive activity that uses virtually every process discussed in this textbook, demonstrating how the cognitive processes are interrelated (Theme 4).

This section begins with a discussion of the more perceptual aspects of reading and then considers how we manage to read isolated words. We'll also see how working memory plays a role in reading, and then we will consider some theories about word recognition. The final section in this chapter, on discourse processing, examines how we understand larger units of language—such as sentences and stories—in both written and spoken language.

Perceptual Processes in Reading

As we change our focus from spoken language to written language, consider how these two cognitive activities differ in important ways (Ferreira & Anes, 1994; Lively et al., 1994; Perfetti, 1994):

1. Writing is spread out across space, whereas speech is spread out across time.
2. Readers can control the rate of input, whereas listeners usually cannot.
3. Readers can re-scan the written input, whereas listeners must rely much more heavily on their working memory.
4. Writing shows discrete boundaries between words, whereas speech does not.
5. Writing is confined to the words on a page, whereas speech is supplemented by additional auditory cues—such as stressed words and variations in pace—that enrich the linguistic message.

An important perceptual process that is central to reading involves eye movement. For a moment, become aware of the way your eyes are moving as you read this paragraph. Notice that your eyes make a series of little jumps as they move across the page. These very rapid movements of the eyes from one spot to the next are known as ***saccadic movement*** (pronounced suh-*ka*-dik). Your eyes must make these movements in order to bring the center of the retina—where vision is sharpest—into position over the words you want to read. ***Fixations*** occur during the period between these saccadic movements; during each fixation, the visual system acquires the information that is useful for reading (Rayner, 1993). Researchers have estimated that people make between 150,000 and 200,000 saccadic movements every day (Abrams, 1992; Cooper & Hochberg, 1994).

Researchers have developed a number of methods for assessing perceptual processes during reading (Müller et al., 1993; Rayner & Sereno, 1994). One very useful method is called the ***moving window technique,*** which involves tracking a reader's eye movements as he or she reads material displayed on a cathode-ray tube; the text display is changed as the reader progresses through a passage (Pollatsek, 1993). With this technique, researchers can selectively replace letters in certain regions of the display. However, a window of text—which includes the reader's fixation point—remains unaltered. For example, researchers can replace all letters more than 10 letters to the right of the letter that the reader is viewing; a string of irrelevant letters and spaces can be substituted (e.g., rmot lfe . . .). The researchers note whether this text alteration changes any measures of reading. If the measures do change, then the researchers conclude that the letters in the altered region would normally be included within the ***perceptual span***—the region seen during the pause between saccadic movements (Underwood & McConkie, 1985).

The moving window technique has been used to demonstrate that the perceptual span normally includes letters lying about four positions to the left of the letter you are directly looking at, and the letters about 15 positions to the right of that central letter. Thus, the perceptual span is definitely lopsided, probably because we are looking for reading cues in the text that lies to the right. The letters in the extreme right side of the perceptual span are useful for providing information about word length; we usually cannot identify a word that lies more than eight spaces to the right of the fixation point (Rayner, 1995).

Other research has demonstrated that saccadic eye movements show several predictable patterns. For example, when the eye jumps forward in a saccadic movement, it rarely moves to a blank space between sentences or between words (McConkie & Zóla, 1984). The eye usually jumps past short words, function words such as *the,* and words that are highly predictable in a sentence (Pollatsek, 1993; Rayner & Sereno, 1994). However, the size of the saccadic movement is small if the next word in a sentence is misspelled or if it is unusual (Inhoff & Topolski, 1994; Rayner, 1993). All these strategies make sense, because a large saccadic movement would be unwise if the material is puzzling or challenging.

Our saccadic movements are also sensitive to thematic aspects of the material we are reading. For example, if we read a story with a surprise ending, we make a larger number of saccadic movements as we reread the puzzling passage (Blanchard & Iran-Nejad, 1987).

Good readers differ from poor readers with respect to their saccadic eye movements. Figure 8.4 shows how two readers might differ in their eye movements. The good reader makes larger jumps and is also less likely to make **regressions,** by moving backward to earlier material in the sentence (Crowder & Wagner, 1992; Rayner, 1995). Furthermore—although this cannot be seen in Figure 8.4—the good reader pauses for a shorter time before making the next saccadic movement. A typical good reader might pause for $\frac{1}{5}$ second each time, whereas a poor reader might pause for $\frac{1}{2}$ second. Thus, good and poor readers differ with respect to the size of the saccadic movement, the number of regressions, and the duration of the fixation pause.

You may wish to review the section in Chapter 2 on pattern recognition, which provides information on how we recognize letters when we read. That section considers theories of pattern recognition and discusses how context aids the visual recognition of letters and other patterns.

Discovering the Meaning of an Unfamiliar Word

Chapter 2 examined how context aids the visual recognition of letters, and an earlier portion of this chapter examined how context aids the auditory recognition of

FIGURE 8.4

EYE MOVEMENT PATTERNS AND FIXATIONS FOR A GOOD READER (TOP NUMBERS) AND A POOR READER (BOTTOM NUMBERS).

1   2   3   4   5   6

The handsome frog kissed the princess and turned her into an eggplant.

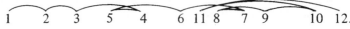

1   2   3   5   4   6 11 8   7   9   10   12.

DEMONSTRATION 8.4

FIGURING OUT THE MEANING OF A WORD FROM CONTEXT. BASED ON STERNBERG & POWELL (1983).

Read the paragraph below. Then define, as precisely as possible, the two words that are italicized.

Two ill-dressed people—the one a tired woman of middle years and the other a tense young man—sat around a fire where the common meal was almost ready. The mother, Tanith, peered at her son through the *oam* of the bubbling stew. It had been a long time since his last *ceilidh* and Tobar had changed greatly; where once he had seemed all legs and clumsy joints, he now was well-formed and in control of his hard, young body. As they ate, Tobar told of his past year, re-creating for Tanith how he had wandered long and far in his quest to gain the skills he would need to be permitted to re-join the company. Then all too soon, their brief *ceilidh* over, Tobar walked over to touch his mother's arm and quickly left.

---

phonemes. You won't be surprised to learn that context also helps you recognize words. Specifically, you perceive words more accurately when they are embedded within the context of a sentence (Chawarski & Sternberg, 1993; Potter et al., 1993).

Context is also vitally important when people want to discover the meanings of unfamiliar words. Try Demonstration 8.4, which is an example of the passages used by Sternberg and Powell (1983) in their work on verbal comprehension.

Sternberg and Powell point out that when we read, we often come upon a word whose meaning is unfamiliar. We then typically attempt to use the context in which the word occurs to figure out its meaning. Sternberg and Powell propose that context can provide several kinds of information cues about meaning, including the following:

1. Temporal cues indicate how often X (the unknown word) occurs or how long it lasts.
2. Spatial cues identify X's location.
3. Value cues suggest the emotion that X arouses.
4. Functional descriptive cues describe the possible actions X can perform.
5. Stative descriptive cues concern the physical properties of X (that is, its physical state).

For example, consider the following sentence:

At dawn, the *blen* arose on the horizon and shone brightly.

This sentence contains several contextual cues that make it easy to infer the meaning of *blen*. The phrase *at dawn* provides a temporal cue, about the time at which the arising of the *blen* occurred. *Arose* is a functional descriptive cue, describing an action that a *blen* could perform. (Notice how this cue limits the possible candidates for *blen* to those things that move or appear to move.) *On the horizon* provides a spatial cue. *Shone* is an additional functional descriptive cue, further limiting the possible candidates for *blen*. Finally, *brightly* provides a stative descriptive cue, describing a property of the shining of the *blen,* that is, its brightness. With all these different cues, an experienced reader can easily understand that the nonsense word *blen* is a synonym for the familiar word *sun.*

Naturally, we do not always use contextual cues in decoding a word's meaning, and when we do use them, they do not always work. For example, we are more likely to use contextual cues if an unknown word appears in a variety of different contexts. A variety of contexts increases the likelihood that a wide range of cues will be supplied about the word. In this case, the reader is more likely to obtain a full picture of the scope of the word's meaning. In contrast, merely repeating an unknown word in the same context is *not* particularly helpful.

To test their theory about the importance of contextual cues, Sternberg and Powell (1983) asked high-school students to read passages like the one in Demonstration 8.4. Then the students provided a definition for each of the italicized words in the passage (for example, *oam* and *ceilidh* in Demonstration 8.4). Three trained raters judged the quality of these definitions, and then they calculated a "definition goodness" score for each of the words. Powell herself then examined each of the passages and counted the number of occurrences of each kind of contextual cue. The results showed a strong correlation between the two measures: Words that appeared in a rich context of different cues were more likely to be accurately defined.

As you might expect, the students in Sternberg and Powell's study showed large individual differences in their ability to use contextual cues and to provide accurate definitions for the unfamiliar words. The students who were particularly good at this task were also found to have higher scores on tests of vocabulary, reading comprehension, and general intelligence. (Incidentally, in the passage in Demonstration 8.4, *oam* means steam and a *ceilidh* is a visit.)

Reading and Working Memory

Working memory plays an important role during reading. For example, researchers have demonstrated that people who have large working-memory spans are especially skilled in guessing the meaning of unusual words on the basis of sentence context (Daneman & Green, 1986). Apparently, the large memory span allows them to read efficiently, so that they have more attention "left over" to remember the important contextual cues.

Working memory also plays a role in decoding sentences. As we discussed earlier in the chapter, readers who have a large working-memory span can process ambiguous sentences efficiently (Miyake et al., 1994). They can maintain both potential interpretations of a phrase until they have read several words farther in the sentence. In contrast, readers who have smaller working-memory spans keep only the most obvious interpretation in their working memory. Later, when they read the ending of the sentence, they may have to struggle to retrieve the less obvious interpretation (MacDonald et al., 1992).

Working memory also helps us to understand complicated sentences (Carpenter et al., 1994; Engle et al., 1992; Just & Carpenter, 1992). People who can maintain many items in memory while they unravel a sentence are more accurate and more rapid in understanding complex sentences such as *The reporter that the senator attacked admitted the error.*

All this research on reading and working memory is an excellent illustration of Theme 4. The cognitive processes do not operate in isolation. Instead, reading skill depends heavily on other cognitive abilities, such as working memory.

Theories About the Role of Sound in Word Recognition

So far, our examination of basic reading processes has emphasized the sacccadic eye movements our eyes make as they scan a line of text, the way we discover the meaning of an unfamiliar word, and the role that working memory plays in reading. Now we'll address a difficult and controversial question about reading: How do we look at a pattern of letters and actually recognize that word? For example, how do you manage to look at the eight letters in the first word of this section's title and realize that it says *theories?*

Three different hypotheses have been developed to explain how readers recognize printed words when they read to themselves. One hypothesis, which we will call the ***direct-access hypothesis,*** states that readers can recognize a word directly from the printed letters. That is, you look at the word *theories,* and the visual pattern is sufficient to let you locate information about the meaning of the word in semantic memory (Seidenberg, 1995).

Another hypothesis, which we will call the ***phonologically mediated hypothesis*** or the ***indirect-access hypothesis,*** states that we must translate the ink marks on the page into some form of sound before we can locate information about a word's meaning (Besner et al., 1981; Perfetti, 1996). Notice that this process is indirect because—according to this hypothesis—we *must* go through the intermediate step of converting the visual stimulus into a phonological (sound) stimulus.

Think about whether you seem to use this intermediate step when you read. As you read this sentence, for example, do you have a speech-like representation of the words? You probably don't actually move your lips when you read, and you certainly don't say the words out loud. But do you seem to have an auditory image of what you are reading?

The third hypothesis, called the ***dual-route hypothesis,*** states that semantic memory can be reached either directly—through the visual route—or indirectly—through the sound route (Coltheart et al., 1993; Coltheart & Rastle, 1994). In other words, our reading processes can be flexible. Let's examine the evidence for the three hypotheses, and then we'll consider their implications for teaching reading to children.

The Direct-Access Hypothesis. One kind of evidence for the hypothesis that words can be recognized directly—without a translation into sound—comes from an analysis of homonyms. As you may recall, homonyms are words that are spelled differently but sound the same. When you see the two homonyms *their* and *there*, you know that they have different meanings. If each of those visual stimuli were translated into sound, as the indirect-access hypothesis claims, then we would be left with two identical sounds. It would be difficult to explain how those two identical sounds could then lead to the two different meanings.

More support for the direct-access hypothesis comes from a study by Bradshaw and Nettleton (1974). They presented pairs of words that were similar in spelling but not in sound, such as *mown–down, horse–worse,* and *quart–part.* When subjects pronounced the first member of the pair out loud, it took them somewhat longer to pronounce the second member—interference arose because the two words were not pronounced similarly. However, this effect did not occur in silent reading. When people read the first word silently, there was no delay in pronouncing the second word. This finding suggests that silent reading does not lead to a silent pronunciation of the word, because there was no evidence for any interference.

Perhaps the strongest evidence for the direct-access hypothesis comes from clinical observations of ***deep dyslexia,*** a severe reading disorder in which people are unable to translate printed words into sounds. For example, these people are unable to pronounce simple nonsense words, such as *dap, ish,* and *lar.* They also are unable to judge which visually presented words rhyme with each other. Clearly, these people cannot use the intermediate step of translating words into sound. Nevertheless, they are able to look at a printed word and identify its meaning (Besner et al., 1981; Coltheart, et al., 1980). Thus, it is possible to read without an obligatory translation into a speech code.

The Phonologically Mediated Hypothesis. Many studies indicate that visual stimuli are translated into sound during reading. Hardyck and Petrinovitch (1970), for example, noted that people often sound out words when the material is difficult. (Incidentally, did you sound out the name *Petrinovitch* when you read it?) When people were prevented from making any lip movements, they had trouble reading difficult material. These results indicate that people are translating the visual stimulus into sound.

Word sounds may be especially important when children begin to read. Numerous studies demonstrate that children with high phonological awareness have superior reading skills. That is, the children who are able to identify sound patterns in a word also receive higher scores on reading achievement tests (Seidenberg, 1995; Vellutino, 1991; Wagner & Torgesen, 1987). Furthermore, Byrne and Fielding-Barnsley (1991) trained some preschool children in phoneme skills, and they trained other preschool children in semantic skills. The phoneme-training children performed better on a word-identification test.

A study by Doctor and Coltheart (1980) also supports the phonologically mediated hypothesis. Children saw sentences such as, "He ran threw the street," and they were asked to decide whether the sentences were meaningful. Doctor and

Coltheart found that the children were likely to judge sentences as meaningful if they *sounded* meaningful. For example, "He ran threw the street" would be pronounced just the same as the meaningful sentence, "He ran through the street." Therefore, the children judged that sentence to be meaningful. In contrast, they did not judge sentences as meaningful if they remained meaningless when they were pronounced. For example, children judged that "He ran sew the street" was not meaningful.

Perhaps you're thinking that *children* may need to translate the printed word into sound—after all, children even move their lips when they read—but adults do not. Try Demonstration 8.5 and see whether you change your mind. Adults read "tongue twisters" very slowly, which indicates that they are indeed translating the printed words into sounds (Perfetti, 1996).

Other evidence for the phonologically mediated hypothesis comes from Van Orden (1987), who found that readers made frequent errors when they were instructed to categorize homonyms. In a typical task, readers were instructed to decide whether a particular stimulus (for example, *rose*) belonged to a previously specified category (for example, *flower*). The interesting question is how readers would respond to homonyms (for example, *rows*, rather than *rose*). Van Orden found that the participants in his study often agreed that a *rows* is in fact, a *flower*, suggesting that the printed word was indeed translated into a sound representation.

The Dual-Route Hypothesis. Some results favor a direct access to word recognition, whereas others favor an intermediate step involving a word's sound. The dual-route hypothesis is currently very popular (Crowder & Wagner, 1992; Van Orden et al., 1990). The flexibility of this hypothesis is certainly one of its strengths. It

---

DEMONSTRATION 8.5

READING TONGUE TWISTERS

Read each of the following tongue twisters silently to yourself:

1. The seasick sailor staggered as he zigzagged sideways.
2. Peter Piper picked a peck of pickled peppers. A peck of pickled peppers Peter Piper picked.
3. She sells seashells down by the seaside.
4. Congressional Caucus questions controversial CIA-Contra-Crack connection.
5. Sheila and Celia slyly shave the cedar shingle splinter.

Now be honest. Could you "hear" yourself pronouncing these words as you were reading? Did you have to read them more slowly than other sentences in this book?

argues that the characteristics of the reader and the characteristics of the reading material determine whether access is direct or phonologically mediated.

For example, Baron and Strawson (1976) identified both direct-access and phonologically mediated readers in their study. One set of readers read words more quickly if the words conformed to the standard spelling-sound rules (for example, *sweet*) than if they violated these rules (for example, *sword*). Furthermore, in a different test, these people relied heavily on spelling-sound correspondence rules. These are the people who prefer the phonologically mediated route; they encode the visual stimulus into sound before recognition. The other set of readers did not show much difference in reading speed between regular and irregular words. Also, they did not rely heavily on the spelling-sound correspondence rules. These are the direct-access readers.

In addition, Mason (1978) found that "mature readers"—for example, college students—are more likely to use the direct-access method. This makes sense. When children first learn to read, they rely on sound; as they mature, they can skip that intermediate step.

Other factors may also determine whether people select the direct-access or the phonologically mediated route. For example, you will recall that Hardyck and Petrinovitch (1970) found that people sounded out words when the words were difficult. Also, as you might expect, very common words can be recognized with little or no input from the phonologically mediated route (Seidenberg, 1995). Try to notice whether you are more likely to sound out unfamiliar words than ones you know well.

Furthermore, we sometimes choose the phonologically mediated method when we are under stress. When you are reading the questions on an essay examination, you might find yourself *subvocalizing,* sounding out the words silently. However, if you are by yourself in a quiet room, you probably will not subvocalize when you are reading the Sunday comics. Word sounds may be important if the text is difficult and if it requires elaborate processing of grammatical structure. In these cases, comprehension may involve storing the phonological information in working memory for several seconds (Besner et al., 1981).

At present, the dual-route hypothesis seems like a wise compromise. However, several researchers are currently arguing for the phonologically mediated hypothesis. Based on research like the studies we considered earlier, they are convinced that virtually all reading requires a translation into sound (e.g., Perfetti, 1996; Perfetti & Bell, 1991; Van Orden et al., 1990).

Implications for Teaching Reading to Children. The debate about theories of word recognition has some important implications about the way we should teach reading. Those who favor the direct-access hypothesis would suggest that educators should use the whole-word approach. The ***whole-word approach*** argues that readers can directly connect the written word—as an entire pattern—with the meaning that the word represents (Chialant & Caramazza, 1995; Crowder & Wagner, 1992). The whole-word approach emphasizes that the correspondence between the written and spoken codes in English is notoriously complex

(Seidenberg & McClelland, 1989). They therefore argue against emphasizing the way a word *sounds*.

In contrast, people who favor the phonologically mediated hypothesis would tend to favor the phonics approach. The ***phonics approach*** states that readers recognize words by sounding out the individual letters in the word. If your second-grade teacher told you to "sound it out" when you stumbled on a new word, they championed the phonics approach. The phonics approach stresses that speech-sound is a necessary intermediate step in reading. The phonics approach emphasizes developing young children's awareness of phonemes (Griffith & Olson, 1992; Yopp, 1992). As you might imagine, children who have received phonics training are better spellers than those with no training (Castle et al., 1994).

The argument between the whole-word supporters and the phonics supporters is just as feverish among educators as is the argument between direct-access supporters and phonologically mediated supporters within psychology. This argument among educators is further complicated by a prominent movement within education called *whole language*. The ***whole-language approach*** suggests that children should read storybooks, experiment with writing before they are expert spellers, try to guess the meaning of a word from the sentence's context, and use reading throughout the classroom (Adams & Bruck, 1995; Liberman & Liberman, 1992; Murray, 1995). Those who favor this approach also support the whole-word approach, rather than the phonics approach. Notice, however, that a strong supporter of the phonics approach might admire many components of the *whole-language* approach, while rejecting the specific emphasis on the *whole-word* approach.

SECTION SUMMARY: BASIC READING PROCESSES

1. The topic of reading is currently one of the most important research areas in cognitive psychology.
2. The eyes make saccadic movements during reading; using the moving window technique, researchers have determined that the perceptual span during the fixation pause extends about four letters to the left of center and 8 to 15 spaces to the right.
3. Saccadic movement patterns are influenced by such factors as the predictability of the text and individual differences among readers (e.g., the number of regressions during reading).
4. Readers use a variety of contextual cues to determine the meaning of an unfamiliar word.
5. Working memory aids reading when readers encounter unfamiliar words, when they decode ambiguous sentences, and when they unravel the meaning of a complex sentence.
6. Three theories of word recognition include the direct-access hypothesis, the phonologically mediated hypothesis, and the dual-route hypothesis; research shows that phonological information is often accessed during reading.

7. Educators who use the whole-word approach agree with the direct-access hypothesis; educators who use the phonics approach agree with the phonologically mediated hypothesis.

UNDERSTANDING DISCOURSE

We began this chapter with an overview of the nature of language—considering both linguistic theory and the biological basis of language. Then we explored speech perception and basic reading processes. You'll notice that these three topics all focused on the way we process small units of language, such as a phoneme, a letter, a word, or an isolated sentence. In your daily life, however, you are continually processing connected **discourse,** or language units that are larger than a sentence (Carroll, 1994). You listen to the news on the radio, you hear a friend telling a story, you follow the instructions for assembling a bookcase . . . and you read your cognitive psychology textbook.

Frederick Bartlett (1932) was concerned about these larger linguistic units when he conducted research on memory for stories more than half a century ago. However, for the next few decades, psychologists and linguists concentrated primarily on words and isolated sentences. The topic of discourse processing was not revived until the mid-1970s (Kintsch, 1994).

During the 1990s, research on discourse processing has branched out into new areas. Some representative new topics include research on the reader's point of view in a story (Albrecht et al., 1995), the reader's problem-solving strategies in suspenseful stories (Gerrig & Bernardo, 1994), and the reader's emotional responses to a narrative (Gernsbacher, 1995; Gerrig, 1993). Our exploration of discourse comprehension focuses on the following selected topics: forming a coherent representation of the text, drawing inferences during reading, artificial intelligence and reading, and metacomprehension.

Throughout the previous sections, we emphasized how context can help us understand sounds, letters, and words. In this section, we will see that context is also important when we consider larger linguistic units. As Chapter 7 explained, general background knowledge and expertise help to facilitate conceptual understanding. Research on discourse comprehension also emphasizes the importance of expertise, scripts, and schemas (e.g., Moravcsik & Kintsch, 1993; Smith & Swinney, 1992; Spilich et al., 1979). At all levels of language comprehension, we find an interaction between the processing of the physical stimuli (bottom-up processing) and the context provided by our expectations and previous knowledge (top-down processing), as Theme 5 suggests. This interaction is especially prominent when we form a coherent representation of the text and when we draw inferences during reading.

Forming a Coherent Representation of the Text

Reading comprehension is enormously more complicated than simply fitting words and phrases together. In addition, readers must gather information together, making the message both cohesive and stable. Readers assume that writers intend their messages to "hang together." As a result, readers interpret confusing sections as clearly as they can, and they seek relevance and connections even when the material is not well structured (Foss & Speer, 1991). We should note that listeners—as well as readers—form coherent representations and draw inferences when they hear spoken language (e.g., Marslen-Wilson et al., 1993). However, virtually all the research examines discourse processing during reading.

In order to form a coherent representation, we often construct mental models of the material we are reading. In Chapter 6, we saw that people construct mental models based on a written description of an environment. Similarly, readers construct internal representations that include descriptions of the cast of characters in a story. This descriptive information may include the characters' occupations, relationships, personal traits, goals, plans, and actions (Bower, 1989; Bower & Morrow, 1990; Trabasso et al., 1995).

Walter Kintsch, one of the pioneers in the research on discourse processing, describes the processing cycles we use when we understand a passage (Kintsch, 1993, 1994). According to the concept of *processing cycles,* we understand each new sentence within the context of the previous text. Because we cannot retain the entire previous text, we keep only the most important portions. Specifically, we retain the portions that are likely to help us maintain the general coherence of the material we are reading.

When people try to form a coherent representation of the text they are reading, they often make inferences that go beyond the information supplied by the writer. Let's consider this topic in more detail.

IN DEPTH: Inferences in Reading

Shortly before I began revising this chapter on language, I read a novel called *Ladder of Years* by Anne Tyler, one of my favorite contemporary authors. I zealously followed the heroine, Delia, as she explored new opportunities. And, based on my growing familiarity with Delia's character, I made inferences about how the book should turn out. However, the book didn't end that way. After discovering that my husband and several friends shared the same reaction, I even wrote to the author. Her reply clarified that she had made a different set of inferences about Delia and her family members. This interchange emphasized to me the importance of the mental processes we activate during reading, when we go beyond the information presented on the printed page. You've undoubtedly had a similar experience when a book's ending didn't match your expectations.

When we make an *inference* during reading, we activate information that is not explicitly stated in a written passage (van den Broek, 1994). We discussed inferences in Chapter 7 in connection with the influence of schemas on memory. People combine their information about the world with the information presented in a passage, and they draw a reasonable conclusion based on that combination. Consistent with Theme 1, people are active information processors.

Let's explore several issues that have been raised in connection with inferences during reading. First, we'll consider two contrasting views of these inferences. Then we'll discuss factors that encourage inferences. Our final topic in this in-depth section is higher level inferences.

The Constructionist versus Minimalist Views of Inferences. According to the widely accepted ***constructionist view*** of inference, readers usually draw inferences about the causes of events and the relationships between events. When you read a novel, for instance, you construct inferences about a character's motivations, characteristics, and emotions. You develop expectations about new plot developments, about the writer's point of view, and so forth (Graesser & Kreuz, 1993; Huitema et al., 1993).

In 1992, Gail McKoon and Roger Ratcliff presented a startling alternative, which they called the minimalist hypothesis. The ***minimalist hypothesis*** argues that readers do *not* consistently construct inferences when they read. According to these theorists, the only inferences that readers automatically create are (1) based on information that is readily available or (2) necessary to make sense of sentences that are next to each other. This proposal immediately stimulated numerous replies from both theorists and researchers (e.g., Dopkins et al., 1993; Perfetti, 1993; Singer et al., 1994).

Let's consider some research by John Huitema and his coauthors (1993), who argued that McKoon and Ratcliff had not tested the constructionist view adequately; the stories they had used were not especially compelling and didn't seem to require inferences. Before you read further, try Demonstration 8.6, which shows one

---

DEMONSTRATION 8.6

READING A PASSAGE OF TEXT. BASED ON HUITEMA ET AL. (1993), p. 1054.

Read the following passage, and notice whether it seems to flow smoothly and logically.

1. Dick had a week's vacation due
2. and he wanted to go to a place
3. where he could swim and sunbathe.
4. He bought a book on travel.
5. Then he looked at the ads
6. in the travel section of the Sunday newspaper.
7. He went to his local travel agent
8. and asked for a plane ticket to Alaska.
9. He paid for it with his charge card.

version of a story that Huitema and his colleagues used—a story that these authors judged to be more compelling.

You'll notice that in Demonstration 8.6, the introductory material leads you to believe that Dick will soon be lounging on a sunny beach. You drew this inference on line 3, and this inference is contradicted five lines later, not in the very next sentence. McKoon and Ratcliff (1992) would argue that you would not work hard to resolve this puzzling inconsistency. Because the sentences are far apart, you would not draw an inference.

Huitema and his colleagues tested four conditions. You saw the far/inconsistent version of the story, in which several lines separated the sentence stating the goal from the inconsistent statement. In the near/inconsistent version, the goal and the inconsistent statement were in adjacent sentences. In the far/consistent version, the goal and a consistent statement (in which Dick asked for a plane ticket to Florida—a place consistent with swimming) were separated by several lines. In the near/consistent version, the goal and the consistent statement were in adjacent sentences.

The dependent measure in this experiment was the amount of time that participants needed to read the crucial line about Dick's travel destination (line 8). This variable could be easily measured, because participants pressed a key after reading each line in order to advance the text to the next line.

As you can see from Figure 8.5, in the near condition, participants read the inconsistent version significantly more slowly than the consistent version. Both McKoon and Ratcliff (1992) and Huitema and his coworkers (1993) would predict this result. However, you'll notice that participants also read the inconsistent version significantly more slowly than the consistent version in the *far* condition, when the relevant portions of the task were separated by four intervening lines. McKoon and Ratcliff would argue that people wouldn't be bothered by this inconsistency because the separation was too great. However, the data support the constructionist view. Readers clearly try to connect material within a text passage, and they consult information stored in long-term memory. During discourse processing, we try to construct a representation of the text that is internally consistent.

Other support for the constructionist view comes from research by Soyoung Suh and Tom Trabasso. These researchers instructed participants to talk out loud as they were reading text passages, in order to explain their interpretations of the stories (Suh & Trabasso, 1993; Trabasso & Suh, 1993). In these stories, the main character had an initial goal that was blocked. When the goal was fulfilled on the last line of the story, about 90% of the participants specifically mentioned the original goal when they were commenting on the last line. Suh and Trabasso argue that readers create causal inferences in order to integrate discourse and construct an organized structure.

Factors That Encourage Inferences. Naturally, we do not always draw inferences when we read a passage. As you might expect, people are more likely to draw inferences during reading when they have been instructed to read a passage carefully (Van Oostendorp, 1991). When reading slowly and cautiously, we have the time to search for connections that we might otherwise miss.

===== **FIGURE 8.5** =====

AMOUNT OF TIME TAKEN TO READ THE CRUCIAL LINE IN THE STUDY BY HUITEMA AND HIS COLLEAGUES (1993), AS A FUNCTION OF THE AMOUNT OF SEPARATION BETWEEN THE GOAL AND THE CRUCIAL LINE AND THE COMPATIBILITY BETWEEN THE GOAL AND THE CRUCIAL LINE (CONSISTENT VERSUS INCONSISTENT).

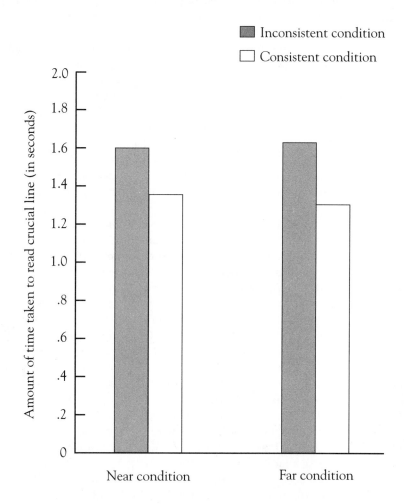

Another factor that determines whether we draw inferences is the kind of inference required by the passage. For instance, we are especially likely to make inferences about events, specifically about a character's goals, plans, and actions (Seifert, 1990; Seifert et al., 1985). We don't have the processing capacity to make every possible inference when we are reading, so we may fail to make inferences about issues that do not advance the plot. For example, we may not make inferences about the physical locations of objects unless this information is critical to the story.

Other research shows that people may fail to construct inferences when they are reading scientific texts. For example, Noordman and his colleagues (1992) presented sentences such as "Chlorine compounds make good propellants, because they react with almost no other substances" (p. 573); this sentence appeared in a paragraph on spray cans. Now if you analyze this sentence carefully, you can make the inference that a manufacturer would not want the propellants to react with the material in the spray can. Under normal conditions, readers did not draw this inference, consistent with McKoon and Ratcliff's (1992) minimalist hypothesis. However, readers do make inferences when the task is structured appropriately. For instance, when participants were instructed to answer questions such as, "How do spray cans work?" they did construct the relevant inferences. Other research shows that people reading scientific texts do draw inferences that are necessary to make the text appear coherent, but they do not draw inferences about what they expect to happen next in the passage (Millis & Graesser, 1994).

This section has focused on factors that affect inferences, and we have seen that some inferences are more probable than others. In discussing these factors, however, let's recall an important point from Chapter 7. We are sometimes just as likely to remember our inferences as to remember statements that actually occurred in the text. Our inferences blend with the text, forming a cohesive story. We often retain the gist or general meaning of a passage, forgetting that we actually constructed some of the elements of that story.

Higher Level Inferences. Researchers are beginning to explore higher levels of inferences, including very abstract themes. Colleen Seifert (1990), for example, presents a passage describing a man who was being considered for a Supreme Court appointment some years ago.

> Ginsberg has been accused of using marijuana during his teaching years, threatening his appointment to the Supreme Court. A lawyer who is said to have been a close friend of Ginsberg during his days at Harvard refused to comment. (p. 115)

In order to make sense of this passage, we need to make inferences based on a wide variety of "facts" from our general knowledge storehouse.

Another higher level inference involves our own preference for the way we want a story to turn out. Perhaps you've turned the pages of a fast-paced spy novel and mentally shouted to our favorite character, "Watch out!" In fact, Allbritton and Gerrig (1991) found that readers did generate what they called *participatory responses* when they became involved in a story. These mental preferences for the story's outcome can be so strong that they can actually interfere with readers' ability to judge how the story actually turned out, making us pause as we try to decide whether that unhappy ending really did occur. In fact, you may find yourself so hopeful about a happy ending you've constructed that you read the final sentences over several times, trying to convince yourself that the hero or heroine didn't die!

In summary, we often draw inferences when we read. We are especially likely to draw inferences when we read carefully and when the inferences are necessary to advance the plot or answer questions. In addition, we draw higher level, more abstract inferences about people's intentions, as well as inferences based on our own plot preferences.

Artificial Intelligence and Reading

As discussed earlier in this textbook, *artificial intelligence (AI)* is the area of computer science that attempts to construct computers that can execute human-like cognitive processes. As Judith Greene (1986) writes, the goal of AI is to develop computer programs that will make a computer behave "as if" it were intelligent. When developing AI models of language, the basic rationale of the approach we will discuss is that computers are dumb. They start off with no knowledge whatsoever about *natural language,* that is, ordinary human language with all its sloppiness, ambiguities, and complexities. The researcher has to write into the program all the information that is necessary to make the computer behave as if it comprehends sentences typed on its keyboard. The program must be in the form of detailed instructions, and the computer must be given specific programming operations for analyzing all input.

Researchers in artificial intelligence claim three benefits from developing computer programs capable of language comprehension:

1. The operations have to be stated very precisely in the form of objective instructions that a computer program can carry out. This requirement forces researchers to be very specific about the components of their theory of language comprehension.

2. The process of deciding what information should be provided to the computer database may reveal insights about what processes must be involved in human language comprehension.

3. Researchers' theories of language can be tested by running the program to see whether it responds correctly to the typed sentences (J. Greene, 1986).

How can researchers tell whether a computer really "understands" a fragment of language? Perhaps the sentences it generates may simply reflect the information that the programmer put into the program. Typically, researchers demand that the output must be in a different format from the input. For example, if the input is a story, the output must be a summary that captures the important points. The output cannot simply match the input.

Chapter 1 pointed out the distinction between artificial intelligence (specifically "pure AI") and computer simulation. *Pure AI* seeks to accomplish a task as efficiently as possible, whereas *computer simulation* tries to take human limitations into account. Thus, a computer simulation model of sentence comprehension should reflect the difficulty humans have in understanding ambiguous sentences, and it should also have problems interpreting long, complex sentences (Singer, 1990).

Researchers have been intrigued with computer simulation of language comprehension since the discipline of artificial intelligence began about 40 years ago. In the 1950s, for example, some researchers tried to program a computer to translate English into Russian. This may seem like a fairly easy task until you consider the problems presented by ambiguities and idioms. Legend has it that an early researcher programmed his computer to translate "the spirit is willing but the flesh is weak," initially into Russian and then back into English. The retranslated English read: "The vodka is good but the meat is rotten" (Tartter, 1986). Clearly, any accurate translation would involve extensive familiarity with both language and world knowledge, more comparable to an encyclopedia than a dictionary.

Let us consider one example of a program designed to perform reading tasks. One specific script-based program has been given the unattractive name of **FRUMP,** standing for Fast Reading Understanding and Memory Program (De Jong, 1982). The goal of FRUMP is to summarize newspaper stories, written in ordinary language. When it was developed, FRUMP could interpret about 10% of news wires issued by United Press International (Kintsch, 1984). It works by applying world knowledge, based on 48 different scripts. The program is designed to make a guess about which scripts are relevant to a story, and then to search the text to see if the guess is confirmed. FRUMP summarizes only the main points of the script; everything else is disregarded.

FRUMP uses a bottom-up approach at only one point—when it is searching the words to decide which script to use. The rest of the process is top-down, because it is based on script information.

Consider, for example, the "vehicle accident" script, which is activated when the text contains information about some kind of vehicle striking some physical object in some location. The script contains information involving the number of people killed, number of people injured, and the cause of the accident. On the basis of the "vehicle accident" script, FRUMP reported on a news article, "A vehicle accident occurred in Colorado. A plane hit the ground. 1 person died." FRUMP did manage to capture the facts of the story. However, it missed the major reason that the item was newsworthy: Yes, one person was killed, but 21 survived!

Furthermore, FRUMP sometimes misinterprets figures of speech. For example, it interpreted the newspaper headline "Pope's Death Shakes the Western Hemisphere" as, "There was an earthquake in the Western Hemisphere. The Pope died." As it happened, FRUMP had been programmed to interpret the word *shake* as belonging to the "earthquake" script!

We can be impressed that FRUMP manages to process a reasonable number of newspaper stories, but its errors tend to highlight the extensive capabilities of human readers. Other research with computer simulation has demonstrated the difficulty of designing machines that can understand speech, decode a handwritten address scrawled on an envelope, or pronounce words (Brennan, 1991; Kosslyn & Koenig, 1992; Kuhl, 1994a; Seidenberg, 1995). Humans' impressive linguistic capacities emphasize the importance of Theme 2 of this textbook.

Still, cognitive scientists are continuing to develop programs designed to understand discourse. For example, a program called MIDAS has been developed to represent standard metaphors and apply this knowledge in order to learn new metaphors (Martin, 1992). NEXUS is another program, which searches semantic memory in order to understand sentences and connect a new event to a previous event (Alterman & Bookman, 1992). Furthermore, researchers are now expanding the parallel distributed processing approach so that it can understand and recall stories (Golden & Rumelhart, 1993). Once again, the artificial intelligence approach to reading illustrates humans' tremendous cognitive flexibility, as well as the breadth of semantic memory and world knowledge.

Metacomprehension

Did you understand the material on artificial intelligence and reading? How much longer can you read today before you feel that you can't absorb any more? Are you aware that you've started a new section under the topic of reading? As you think about these issues, you are engaging in metacomprehension. *Metacomprehension* refers to our thoughts about reading comprehension; it is one kind of metacognition. Incidentally, if your metacomprehension is excellent, you now realize that this topic is going to be related to the material in Chapter 7, on the tip-of-the-tongue phenomenon and metamemory.

Let's consider two topics in connection with metacomprehension. First, how accurate is the typical college student's metacomprehension? Second, how can we improve a person's metacomprehension skills?

Metacomprehension Accuracy. In general, college students are not very accurate in their metacomprehension skills. For example, they may *think* that they understood something they read because they are familiar with its general topic. However, they often fail to retain specific information (Glenberg et al., 1987).

Let us consider a representative study on metacomprehension. Pressley and Ghatala (1988) tested introductory psychology students to assess their metacomprehension as well as their performance on two other metacognitive tasks. Metacomprehension was tested using the reading comprehension tests from the Scholastic Aptitude Test (SAT). If you took the SAT, you'll recall that items on this portion of the SAT typically contain between one and three paragraphs, in essay form, followed by several multiple-choice questions. After the students in Pressley and Ghatala's study had answered the multiple-choice questions, they then rated how certain they were that they had answered the questions correctly. If they were absolutely certain that their answer had been correct, they were told to answer 100%. If they were just guessing, they were told to report 20% (representing guessing at the chance level among five possible answers on the test). This certainty rating served as the measure of metacomprehension.

Figure 8.6 shows the students' average certainty ratings for the items they had actually answered correctly and for those answered incorrectly. When they had actually answered the reading comprehension questions correctly, they supplied an average certainty rating of 73%. In other words, they were fairly confident about these items, which is appropriate. However, notice the average certainty rating for the items that they answered *incorrectly*. Here, they supplied an average certainty rating of about 64%. Unfortunately, this is about the same level of confidence they showed for the items they answered correctly! Furthermore, these data suggest that students are highly overconfident in many cases; they believe they know what they have just finished reading, even when they answer the questions incorrectly.

=========== **FIGURE 8.6** ===========

AVERAGE CERTAINTY OF CORRECTNESS RATINGS FOR ITEMS ANSWERED CORRECTLY AND ITEMS ANSWERED INCORRECTLY. BASED ON PRESSLEY & GHATALA (1988).

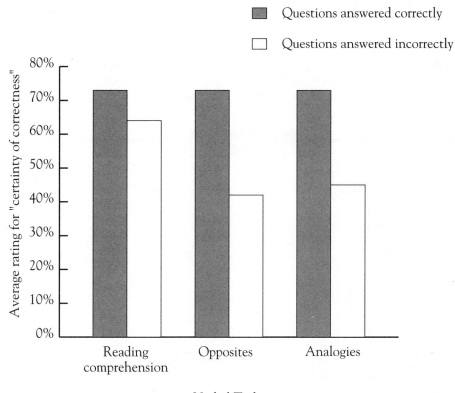

For comparison's sake, let's see how those same students performed on two other metacognition tests, based on other verbal portions of the SAT. If you took the SAT, you may remember that one verbal task asks you to select a word that is the opposite of a listed word. (For example, "Which word is the opposite of *irreparable? amiable, mendable, grateful, confusing,* or *divisible.*") Notice that the students were much more confident about the items they had answered correctly (73%) than the items they had answered incorrectly (42%). The third verbal task involved the analogies test (for example, "*intruder* is to *privacy* as *animal* is to *forest, ripple* is to *calm . . .*"). Once more the contrast is clear; they were much more certain about items they had answered correctly (72%) than about items they had answered incorrectly (46%). In short, students are reasonably accurate in assessing their performance on two vocabulary tests, but they are not very accurate in assessing their reading comprehension.

As you might expect, people with excellent metacomprehension tend to receive higher scores on tests of reading comprehension (Maki & Berry, 1984; Maki et al., 1994; Schraw, 1994). For example, Maki and her coauthors (1994) reported that readers who were good at assessing which sections of a text they had understood were also likely to receive higher scores on a reading comprehension test. In fact, metacomprehension accuracy and reading comprehension scores were significantly correlated ($r = +.43$). Furthermore, students become somewhat more accurate in assessing their performance as they gain experience in reading the text and as they receive feedback (Maki & Berry, 1984; Maki & Serra, 1992). However, the improvement is not dramatic. College students clearly need some hints on how to increase their metacomprehension abilities and how to take advantage of their reading experiences.

DEMONSTRATION 8.7

ASSESSING YOUR METACOMPREHENSION SKILLS

Answer each of the following questions about your own metacomprehension. If you answer "no" to any question, devise a plan for improving metacomprehension that you can apply as you read the next assigned chapter in this textbook.

1. Before beginning to read an assignment, do you try to assess how carefully you should read the material?
2. In general, are you accurate in predicting your performance on exam questions related to reading?
3. After reading a chapter in this textbook, do you test yourself on the list of new terms and on the review questions?
4. After you read a short section (roughly a page in length), do you make yourself summarize what you have just read—using your own words?
5. Do you reread a portion when it doesn't make sense or when you realize that you haven't been paying attention?
6. Do you try to draw connections between the ideas in the textbook?
7. When you read a term you do not know, do you try to determine its meaning by looking it up in a dictionary or in the index of this textbook?
8. When you review material prior to a test, do you spend more time reviewing the reading that you consider difficult than the reading you consider easy?
9. When reading through a variety of resources to see whether they might be relevant for a paper, do you try to assess—without reading every word—the general scope or findings of the article?

Improving Metacomprehension. Ideally, students should be accurate in assessing whether they understand what they have read; their subjective assessments should match their performance on an objective test. One effective way to improve metacomprehension is to take a pretest, which can supply feedback about comprehension before taking the actual examination (Glenberg et al., 1987).

As we have seen, metacomprehension involves accurately assessing whether or not you understand a written passage. However, metacomprehension also involves regulating your reading, so that you know how to read more effectively. For example, Kaufman and her colleagues (1985) found that good and poor readers differed in their awareness that certain reading strategies are useful. Good readers were more likely to report that they found it helpful to try to make connections among the ideas they had read; they also tried to create visual images, based on descriptions in the text.

Psychologists and editors have also discovered that good readers can categorize different kinds of reading situations. They know that they must adopt a different reading approach when reading a chemistry chapter in preparation for an exam than when reading a Shakespeare play before writing an essay (Lorch et al., 1995; Pressley & Afflerbach, 1995). Good readers also try to determine whether the reading is relevant to their goals. For example, they assess whether a particular article contains information and whether the content seems trustworthy. Demonstration 8.7 will help you consider your own metacomprehension skills and think about some strategies for self-management.

SECTION SUMMARY: UNDERSTANDING DISCOURSE

1. The research on discourse processing now examines a variety of components of understanding language units that are larger than a sentence.
2. Readers try to form coherent representations of discourse, and they often do so by constructing mental models.
3. Research on inferences in reading emphasizes how people use their world knowledge.
4. The research on theories of inferences generally supports the constructionist view; people actively draw inferences that connect parts of the text. Inferences are especially likely when people read carefully and when inferences concern a character's goals, plans, and actions. The minimalist hypothesis is often supported when people read scientific texts. Finally, people also draw higher level inferences.
5. Computer simulation programs, such as one called FRUMP—which is designed to understand newspaper stories—point out human competence in a wide variety of reading tasks.
6. Research on metacomprehension shows that college students are not highly accurate in predicting whether they have understood a written passage.

CHAPTER REVIEW QUESTIONS

1. Why is language one of the most impressive human accomplishments, and why does it illustrate the interrelatedness of the cognitive processes?

2. Construct a simple sentence and divide it into constituents. Explain how these constituents are important in language comprehension. Next, construct a different sentence, one that has the same deep structure as your original sentence, but different surface structure. Finally, think of a pun that has a single surface structure but two different deep structures.

3. What does the information on aphasia and brain-imaging techniques tell us about the regions of the brain that are involved in language?

4. What evidence do we have that speech stimuli are less than ideal? Describe several sources of variability, and explain why these factors present a problem when psychologists try to explain speech perception.

5. Context is an important concept throughout this chapter. Explain how context is important in (a) speech perception; (b) processing ambiguous words; (c) discovering the meaning of an unfamiliar word; and (d) background knowledge in reading.

6. What kinds of arguments support the general mechanism approach to speech perception? Contrast this approach with the special mechanism approach, and describe why the general mechanism approach is more consistent with the view that cognitive processes are interrelated.

7. Describe the processes you are using right now as you move your eyes while reading this sentence. Also, review the three theories of word recognition; describe the situations in which the direct-access hypothesis is most likely to apply and those in which the phonologically mediated hypothesis is most likely. If you can recall how you were taught to read, comment on whether that method was effective.

8. Describe the two theories of inference discussed in the in-depth section of this chapter. Think about several kinds of reading tasks you have performed in the last two days, and speculate about which kind of task used which pattern of inferences.

9. What kind of metacomprehension tasks are relevant when you are reading this textbook? List as many tasks as possible. Why do you suppose that metacomprehension for reading passages of text would be less accurate than metamemory for vocabulary words (discussed in Chapter 7)?

10. This chapter discussed both listening and reading. Compare the two kinds of language tasks. Which processes are similar, and which are different?

NEW TERMS

psycholinguistics	morpheme	semantic memory
phoneme	semantics	syntax

pragmatics
phrase structure
constituents
transformational grammar
surface structure
deep structure
ambiguous sentence
kernel
transformational rules
government-binding theory
neurolinguistics
aphasia
Broca's area
Wernicke's area
PET scan (positron emission tomography)
ERP technique (event-related potential)

speech perception
coarticulation
phonemic restoration
special mechanism approach
phonetic module
general mechanism approaches
saccadic movement
fixations
moving window technique
perceptual span
regressions
direct-access hypothesis
phonologically mediated hypothesis
indirect-access hypothesis
dual-route hypothesis

deep dyslexia
subvocalizing
whole-word approach
phonics approach
whole-language approach
discourse
processing cycles
inference
constructionist view
minimalist hypothesis
artificial intelligence (AI)
natural language
pure AI
computer simulation
FRUMP
metacomprehension

RECOMMENDED READINGS

Carroll, D. W. (1994). *Psychology of language* (2nd ed.). Pacific Grove, CA: Brooks/Cole. I strongly recommend this textbook to any student who wants a clear and accessible overview of psycholinguistics.

Crowder, R. G., & Wagner, R. K. (1992). *The psychology of reading: An introduction* (2nd ed.). New York: Oxford University Press. This is an excellent summary of the psychological components of reading; in addition to the topics covered in Chapter 8, this book also examines reading development, spelling, and dyslexia.

Gernsbacher, M. A. (Ed.). (1994). *Handbook of psycholinguistics*. San Diego: Academic Press. This comprehensive handbook contains 34 chapters on all aspects of the psychology of language, from saccadic eye movements to understanding discourse.

Kuhl, P. K. (1994a). Speech perception. In F. D. Minifie (Ed.), *Introduction to communication sciences and disorders* (pp. 77–148). San Diego: Singular Publishing Group. Patricia Kuhl is one of the leading experts in the field of speech perception; her summary is both clear and current.

Lorch, R. F., Jr., & O'Brien, E. J. (Eds.). (1995). *Sources of coherence in reading*. Hillsdale, NJ: Erlbaum. Here is an ideal book for more discussion of discourse comprehension. It includes chapters on eye movements and discourse processing, readers' standards for coherence, and inference generation.

Miller, J. L., & Eimas, P. D. (Eds.). (1995a). *Speech, language, and communication*. San Diego: Academic Press. This advanced-level book includes chapters on such topics as speech perception, visual word recognition, and the neurobiology of language.

LANGUAGE PRODUCTION: SPEAKING, WRITING, AND BILINGUALISM

INTRODUCTION

SPEAKING

> The Production Process
> Selecting the Active or the Passive Voice
> Speech Errors
> Producing Discourse
> The Social Context of Speech

WRITING

> Planning
> Sentence Generation
> Revision

BILINGUALISM

> Advantages of Bilingualism
> In Depth: Maintenance of the First Language Among Immigrants
> Second-Language Proficiency as a Function of Age of Acquisition

=========================== **Preview** ===========================

Whereas Chapter 8 examined language comprehension (listening and reading), Chapter 9 focuses on language production. The specific topics to be covered include speaking, writing, and bilingualism.

Speaking requires impressive planning. For example, we need to plan how to arrange the words in an orderly sequence. Although most of our spoken language is accurate, we sometimes make speech errors such as slips of the tongue. When we tell a story, the narrative typically follows a specific structure. The social context of speech is crucial; for example, your conversational partner must share the same background information.

Although writing occupies a large portion of college students' course work, psychologists have only recently begun to study the writing process. Writing consists of three tasks that often overlap in time: planning, sentence generation, and revision.

Bilingual people seem to have a number of advantages over those who are monolingual. For example, they are more aware of language structure, and they perform better on tests of cognitive flexibility and nonverbal intelligence. Bilinguals may become as proficient as monolinguals in their new language, without losing their skill in their first language. Finally, children may learn to speak a new language with a less pronounced accent than an adult. However, adults and children are similar in vocabulary acquisition. They are also similar in their mastery of grammar, at least when the first and second language are reasonably similar.

INTRODUCTION

Every sentence that is comprehended by one person must have been produced by someone else. If psychologists distributed their research equitably, we would know just as much about language production as we know about language comprehension. Furthermore, Chapter 9 would be just as long as Chapter 8.

However, psychologists have ignored language production from the very beginning of the discipline's history, and only about 5% of published papers in psycholinguistics focus on language production (Dell, 1985; Levelt, 1994). One reason that researchers ignore language production is that they cannot control what a person wishes to say or write. In contrast, they can easily control what a person hears or reads (Fromkin, 1993; Stemberger, 1991). Fortunately, psychologists have recently begun to investigate several components of language production (Foss, 1988).

Let us begin by examining spoken language, and then we'll consider written language. Our final topic, bilingualism, involves all the impressive skills of both language comprehension and language production, so it will serve as the final section of these two chapters on language.

SPEAKING

Every day, we spend hours telling stories, chatting, talking on the telephone, quarreling, and speaking to ourselves. Indeed, speaking is one of our most complex cognitive and motor skills (Levelt, 1989, 1994). In this section of the chapter, we will first examine the production process. Then we'll consider how people select the active or passive voice when they produce a sentence, as well as the kinds of speech errors they produce. Finally, we'll move beyond the sentence as we examine the production of discourse and the social context of speech.

The Production Process

Every time you produce a sentence, you must overcome the limits of your memory and attention in order to plan and deliver that sentence (Bock, 1995; Jou & Harris, 1992). Speech production requires a series of stages. We begin by working out the gist or the overall meaning of the message we intend to generate. Then we devise the general structure of the sentence, without selecting the exact words. During the third stage, we choose both the words and their forms (for example, not just the word *eat,* but the form *am eating).* In the fourth and final stage, we convert these intentions into speech by articulating the phonemes (Garrett, 1984; Levelt, 1994). As you might expect, these stages of speech production typically overlap in time. We often pronounce several phonemes in a sentence before we have completely worked out the structure for the last part of the sentence.

Typically, we pause as we plan what we intend to say, with the pauses being longer for lengthy utterances (Bock, 1995). We often plan ahead for more than one sentence when we are speaking (Holmes, 1984). When we are talking for an extended period (for example, telling a friend about summer plans), we alternate between hesitant phases and fluent phases. We therefore speak haltingly as we plan what we will say. Then, during the fluent phase, we are rewarded for our earlier planning, and the words flow more easily (Beattie, 1983; Levelt, 1989).

We sometimes tackle an important problem when we are planning a sentence. We may have a general thought that we want to express, or we may have a mental image that needs to be conveyed verbally. These rather shapeless ideas need to be translated into a statement that has a disciplined, linear shape, with words following one another in time. This problem of arranging words in an ordered, linear sequence is called *the linearization problem* (Bock, 1987; Levelt, 1994). Try noticing how linearization usually occurs quite effortlessly. Consistent with Theme 2, we accomplish this challenging task quite readily. However, you may occasionally find yourself struggling, trying to describe everything at the very beginning.

The speech production process is more complex than you might initially imagine. For example, we must also plan the *prosody* of an utterance, or the "melody" of its intonation and stress (Carroll, 1994; Ferreira, 1993). When you actually speak a sentence, more than 100 different muscles must coordinate their interactions

(Levelt, 1994). Let's consider, in somewhat more detail, the portion of the production process that involves choosing the active or the passive voice.

Selecting the Active or the Passive Voice

In Chapter 8, we noted that people can understand the active voice much better than the passive voice. For example, the sentence *She saw the car* is easier to understand than *The car was seen by her*. Other research shows that people also produce the active voice more frequently. For example, in Taylor and Taylor's (1990) tabulation of spoken language samples, the active form was used about six times as often as the passive form.

Our selection of the active versus the passive voice can be influenced by a number of factors. For instance, you are more likely to use the passive voice if you heard a passive sentence immediately beforehand. Participants in a study by Bock (1986) heard isolated sentences, with the instructions that they would be asked to recognize them later. In fact, the true purpose of each sentence was to act as a prime for a picture-description task that followed immediately after. For example, a participant might read either the active priming sentence *A brick struck the car's windshield* or the passive priming sentence *The car's windshield was struck by a brick*. Then the participant saw a target picture, which might show a bolt of lightning striking a church. Bock asked the participant to describe the picture, and she noted whether the sentence produced was active or passive.

When human agents were responsible for the picture's activity, people almost always used the active voice. It is far more natural to say, "The boy punched the man" than to say, "The man was punched by the boy." The priming condition (active vs. passive) had no influence on people's choices, as shown in Figure 9.1. However, when there was a nonhuman agent (as in the example of lightning striking the church), people were more likely to use the active voice in the sentence they produced if the prime had been active. If the prime had been passive, people used the passive voice relatively often. People therefore tend to mimic the form of a preceding sentence, in the case of a nonhuman agent.

Certain kinds of verbs and nouns are especially likely to encourage us to use the passive voice. For example, Ferreira (1994) found that people use the passive voice about one-third of the time when the subject of the sentence is experiencing an emotional reaction to something, as in the sentences, *Bill was disgusted by the movie* or *Sarah was pleased by her grade*. Notice, then, that psycholinguists can study language production by manipulating the linguistic context in which a sentence appears or the nature of the words in the sentence. Ironically, however, researchers are more likely to study language production by examining speech errors.

Speech Errors

The speech that most people produce is generally very well formed (Bock, 1995; Deese, 1984), consistent with Theme 2. In spontaneous language samples, people

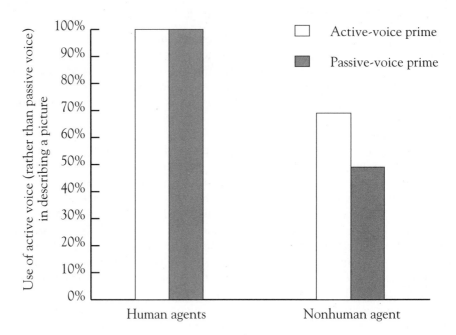

FIGURE 9.1

THE INFLUENCE OF THE PRIME IN WORD CHOICE IN DESCRIBING A PICTURE. BASED ON BOCK (1986).

make an error only about once every 200 sentences. However, we may pause in the middle of a sentence or start a new sentence before finishing the previous one. We sometimes use extra words, such as *oh, well,* and *um.* Naturally, the circumstances of the conversation can influence the number of speech errors. For example, people calling to make airplane reservations made errors that they later corrected at the rate of one error every 10 to 20 utterances (Nakatani & Hirschberg, 1994).

Even high-status speakers do not always produce flawless English. For instance, when former U.S. President George Bush was asked by reporters about his accomplishments, he replied:

> I see no media mention of it, but we entered in—you asked what time it is and I'm telling you how to build a watch here—but we had Boris Yeltsin here the other day. And I think of my times campaigning in Iowa, years ago, and how there was a—Iowa has kind of, I single out Iowa, it's kind of an international state in a sense and has a greater interest in all these things—and we had Yeltsin standing here in the Rose Garden, and we entered into a deal to eliminate the biggest and most threatening ballistic missiles . . . and it was almost, "Ho-hum, what have you done for me recently?" ("Overheard," 1992)

Researchers have been particularly interested in the kind of speech errors called slips-of-the-tongue. *Slips-of-the-tongue* are errors in which sounds or entire words are rearranged between two or more different words. Dell (1986) proposes three kinds of errors:

1. Sound errors occur when sounds in nearby words are exchanged, for example, *Snow flurries → flow snurries.*
2. Morpheme errors occur when morphemes (or smallest meaningful units in language, such as *-ly* or *in-*) are exchanged in nearby words, for example, *Self-destruct instruction → self-instruct destruction.*
3. Word errors occur when words are exchanged, for example, *Writing a letter to my mother → writing a mother to my letter.*

Each of these three kinds of errors can take several forms, in addition to the exchange errors in the previous examples. For example, people make anticipation errors *(Reading list → leading list)*, perseveration errors *(Waking rabbits → waking wabbits)*, and deletions *(Same state → same sate)*.

In almost all cases, the errors occur across items from the same category. For instance, in sound errors, initial consonants interact with initial consonants (as in the *flow snurries* example). In morpheme errors, prefixes substitute for prefixes (as in the *self-instruct* example). In word errors, people interchange members of the same grammatical category (as in the *mother to my letter* example).

Dell (1986) has proposed an elaborate and comprehensive theory for speech errors that is similar to the parallel distributed processing approach and includes the concept of spreading activation. Let us consider a brief overview of what might happen to encourage a sound error. Dell proposes that when a speaker is constructing a sentence, he or she constructs a representation at the word level. This representation must be fairly well constructed before representation can be constructed at the sound level. When a person wants to speak, the words required for a sentence will activate the sound elements to which they are linked. For example, Figure 9.2

FIGURE 9.2

AN EXAMPLE OF DELL'S MODEL OF SOUND PROCESSING IN SENTENCE PRODUCTION (SIMPLIFIED).

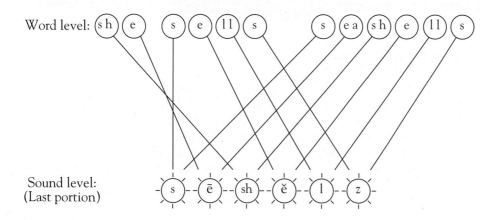

shows how the activation might work for the sounds in the last word of the tongue-twister *She sells seashells.*

Usually, we utter the sounds that are most highly activated, and usually these highly activated sounds are the appropriate ones. However, each sound can be activated by several different words. Notice, for example, that the *sh* sound in the sound level representation of seashells (that is, *seshelz*) is highly "charged" because it receives activation from the first word in the sentence, *she,* as well as the *sh* in *seashells.* As Dell says, errors are a natural result from the theory's assumptions. Incorrect items can sometimes have activation levels that are just as high as (or higher than) the correct items. In Figure 9.2, the activation level for *sh* is just as high as the activation level for *s.* By mistake, an incorrect item may be selected. A speaker is highly likely to say, *She sells sheashells,* particularly because the rhythm of the sentence encourages a further resemblance between the *she* and the *sea* in *seashells.*

More recent research has examined factors that influence speech errors. For example, people are not likely to make sound errors for very common words that perform a grammatical function in a sentence (Dell, 1990). People are also not likely to substitute an inappropriate word for the verb in a sentence. In contrast, noun, adjective, and adverb substitutions are much more common (Bock & Levelt, 1994).

Try Demonstration 9.1 to determine the form and function of the slips-of-the-tongue that you typically make or hear. Incidentally, Ferber (1991) suggests that listeners often fail to detect slips-of-the-tongue, thereby committing what we could call "slips-of-the-ear." As you know from the material on context and phonemic restoration in Chapter 8, we often fail to notice speech errors because context effects and top-down processing (Theme 5) are often so strong that we fail to notice speech errors.

Producing Discourse

When we speak, we typically produce *discourse,* or language units that are larger than a sentence (Carroll, 1994). Psycholinguists have conducted several studies on

---

DEMONSTRATION 9.1

SLIPS-OF-THE-TONGUE

Keep a record of all the slips-of-the-tongue that you either hear or make yourself in the next week. Classify each slip as a sound error, morpheme error, or word error. Furthermore, decide whether the error is an exchange error, an anticipation error, or some other problem. Also note whether the error occurs across items from the same category. Finally, see if you can determine why the error occurred, using an analysis similar to Dell's.

discourse production. For example, research has shown that people who are describing the layout of their apartment tend to give a guided tour of their home (Linde & Labov, 1975). Research shows that when people have been asked to make a list, they describe items that are the same in some ways, but different in other ways. Their descriptions are very focused on the goal of producing the list, and the portions of the list tend to have a similar grammatical structure (Schiffrin, 1994).

However, psycholinguists have paid the most attention to ***narratives,*** the type of discourse in which someone describes a series of events (H. H. Clark, 1994). Some narratives describe actual events, and some are fictional. The research shows that narratives differ from lists because events are described in a time-related sequence, and they are more emotionally involving than lists (Schiffrin, 1994). In a narrative, the storyteller has a specific goal that must be conveyed, but the organization is not fully preplanned at the beginning of the story (H. H. Clark, 1994).

The format of a narrative is unusual, because it allows the speaker to "hold the floor" for an extended period. During that time, six parts of the narrative are usually conveyed: the brief overview of the story, a summary of the characters and setting of the story, an action that made the situation complicated, the point of the narrative, the resolution of the story, and the final signal that the narrative is complete (e.g., . . . *and so that's how I ended up traveling to Colorado with a complete stranger.*). These features tend to make the narrative cohesive and well organized (H. H. Clark, 1994; Labov, 1972). Now that you know something about the function and structure of narratives, try Demonstration 9.2.

Another characteristic of the narrative is that the storyteller typically keeps track of what the listeners know, and how they are making sense of the story (Clark & Bly, 1995). To explore these interpersonal factors in more detail, let's now consider the social context of speech.

DEMONSTRATION 9.2

THE STRUCTURE OF NARRATIVES

During the next few weeks, try to notice, in your daily conversations, what happens when someone you know begins to tell a story. First, how does the storyteller announce that she or he is about to begin the narrative? Does the structure of the narrative match the six-part sequence we discussed? Does the storyteller attempt to check to see whether the listeners have the appropriate background knowledge? What other characteristics do you notice that distinguish this kind of discourse from a normal conversation that involves standard turn-taking?

The Social Context of Speech

When we speak, we need to plan the content of our language. We also need to produce relatively error-free speech, and we need to plan the format of our discourse. However, in addition to these challenging assignments, we also need to be attuned to the social context of speech. As we saw in the discussion of narratives, we must ascertain that our listeners can grasp the information we are trying to convey.

As Herbert Clark (1985, 1994) argues, language is really a social instrument. We direct our words to other people, and our goal is not merely to express our thoughts aloud, but also to affect the people with whom we are talking. Clark proposes that conversation is like a complicated dance. Speakers cannot simply utter words aloud and expect to be understood. Instead, speakers must consider their conversation partners, make numerous assumptions about those partners, and design their utterances appropriately.

This complicated dance requires precise coordination. Two people going simultaneously through a doorway need to coordinate their motor actions. Similarly, two speakers need to coordinate turn-taking, they need to coordinate their understanding of ambiguous terms, and they need to understand each other's intentions. When Helen tells Sam, *The Bakers are on their way,* both participants in the conversation need to understand that this is an indirect invitation for Sam to start dinner, rather than to call the police for protection (Clark, 1985). Conversation involves an implicit contract in which the speaker must ensure that the listener has the proper contextual background for the message (Harris et al., 1980).

The knowledge of these social rules that underlie language use is called ***pragmatics*** (Carroll, 1994). Included in the topic of pragmatics are common ground, knowledge about conversational format, and an understanding of directives.

Common Ground. Suppose that a young man named Andy asks Lisa, "How was your weekend?" and Lisa answers, "It was like being in Conshohocken again." Andy will understand this reply only if they share a similar understanding about the characteristics or events that took place in Conshohocken. In fact, we would expect Lisa to make this remark only if she is certain that she and Andy shared the appropriate common ground (Gerrig & Littman, 1990).

Common ground means that the conversationalists share the similar background knowledge, schemas, and experiences that are necessary for mutual understanding (Clark, 1992). To guarantee conversational coherence, the speakers must collaborate to make certain that they share common ground. For instance, the listener must provide positive evidence of understanding, such as the comment *uh-huh* or perhaps a nod of the head (Clark & Brennan, 1991). Speakers also monitor their conversational partners to make certain that they are paying attention, and they must clarify any misunderstandings if their listeners look puzzled.

Recently, our plumber called me from the hardware store, where he was trying to locate some handles for our washbowl faucet. As he described the various models over the telephone, I instantly realized that we were replicating a study by Clark and Wilkes-Gibbs (1986) on the collaboration process involved in establishing

DEMONSTRATION 9.3

COLLABORATING TO ESTABLISH COMMON GROUND

For this demonstration, you need to make two photocopies of the figures below. Then locate two volunteers and a watch that can measure time in seconds. Cut the figures apart, keeping each sheet's figures in a separate pile and making certain the dot is at the top of each figure. Appoint one person to be the "director"; this person should arrange the figures in random order in two rows of six figures each. This person's task is to describe the first figure in enough detail so that the "matcher" is able to identify that figure and place it in position 1 in front of him or her. (Neither person should be able to see the other's figures.) The goal is for the matcher to place all 12 figures in the same order as the director's figures. They may use any kind of verbal descriptions they choose, but no gestures or imitation of body position. Record how long it takes them to reach their goal, and then make sure that the figures do match. Ask them to try the game two more times, with the same person serving as director. Record the times again, and note whether the time decreases on the second and third trials; are they increasingly efficient in establishing common ground? Do they tend to develop a standard vocabulary (for example, "the ice skater") to refer to a given figure?

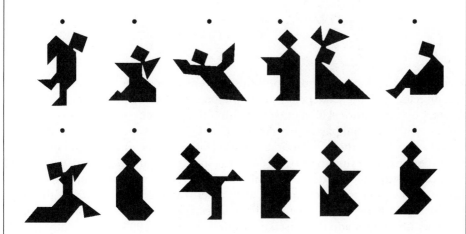

common ground. Demonstration 9.3 is a modification of their study, which involves people working together to arrange complex figures.

The participants in Clark and Wilkes-Gibbs's study played this game for six trials. (Each trial consisted of arranging all 12 figures in order.) On the first trial, the director required an average of nearly four turns to describe a figure and make

FIGURE 9.3

AVERAGE NUMBER OF TURNS THAT DIRECTORS REQUIRED FOR EACH FIGURE, AS A FUNCTION OF TRIAL NUMBER. CLARK AND WILKES-GIBBS (1986).

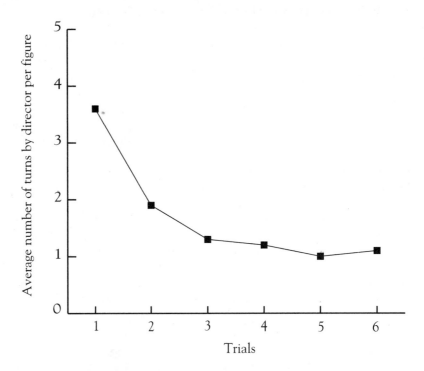

certain that the matcher understood the reference. However, as Figure 9.3 shows, the director and the matcher soon developed a mutual shorthand. Just as two dancers become more skilled at coordinating their movements as they practice together, conversational partners become more skilled in communicating efficiently.

Naturally, not all these collaborative conversations succeed. You've no doubt had the experience of trying to work together to establish common ground, yet you and your conversational partner never really seemed to achieve mutual understanding. Interestingly, when college students were asked to judge conversations that contained a pragmatic error, they rated the *listeners* even more negatively than the speakers who had made the mistake (Kreuz & Roberts, 1993). Apparently, people feel that conversation must be a collaborative effort, and the listener must be responsible for signaling any breakdown in pragmatic communication.

Conversational Format. Just as we have social rules for establishing common ground, we also have social rules about the format of our conversations. For example, one rule is that the speakers should alternate (H. H. Clark, 1994; McLaughlin, 1984). Speakers do not talk at the same time, and they should take turns. In fact, if

=== DEMONSTRATION 9.4 ===

THE IMPORTANCE OF SHORT CONVERSATIONAL PAUSES. NOTE: THIS DEMONSTRATION WAS SUGGESTED BY W. D. PHILLIPS (1995).

To demonstrate the importance of short pauses, find some time when you can have a short conversation with a friend. Be sure to select a topic that is not consequential, and be prepared to debrief your friend after you are done with this demonstration.

   During the conversation, force yourself to pause for several seconds after the person completes his or her statement, and before you begin your own response. Notice, first of all, your own difficulty in sustaining the silence! Also notice what your friend does, perhaps continuing to "hold the floor" by saying "um" or "er." Alternately, does your friend adjust his or her pauses—after several unnatural-sounding interchanges—by matching the length of your pauses? How many sentences can you utter before conversation becomes unbearable?

you have tried Demonstration 9.2, you may have noticed that a person who wants to relate a narrative must first negotiate with the listeners (H. H. Clark, 1994). After all, the listener must relinquish their right to speak in order to make way for the storyteller. This negotiation is necessary because other conversations routinely require turn-taking.

   Furthermore, when people take turns in a conversation, they are supposed to allow only very short pauses between speakers. In fact, analyses of conversations between two individuals reveal that the silence between speakers is typically less than one second (Ervin-Tripp, 1993). Try Demonstration 9.4 to illustrate the importance of keeping these conversational pauses very short.

   Proper etiquette specifies that the closing of conversations must also be highly structured (Ervin-Tripp, 1993). Pay attention to this structure the next time you overhear a telephone conversation. The speakers may require numerous alternations to "wind down" a conversation. Certainly, a polite adult cannot end a conversation by flinging a simple "good-bye" into a random pause in the interchange. After all, the two speakers must make pre-closing statements so that they can negotiate being ready to leave the conversation at the same time (H. H. Clark, 1994). To soften the leave-taking, people often comment about plans for speaking again in the future (Clark, 1985).

Directives. Susan Ervin-Tripp (1976, 1993) has studied the social aspects of a particular kind of statement called a directive. A ***directive*** is a sentence that requests someone to do something. Ervin-Tripp gathered large samples of speech in natural settings and found six different kinds of directives used in American English. Each kind of directive seemed to be used in certain, well-defined circumstances. For example, one kind of directive was used to express need. It was used either by a higher-ranking person in a work setting, as when a physician says to a nurse, "I'll need an ear curette in room 3," or in families, as when a child says to a parent, "I need a drink, Daddy." Another kind of directive is very abbreviated, because the necessary action is obvious. Thus, a customer in a restaurant may say to a server, "Tea, with lemon."

In general, the most polite directives require more words (Brown & Levinson, 1987). For example, "Could you possibly by any chance lend me your car for just a few minutes?" would be considered more polite than, "Could you lend me your car?"

Sometimes, directives are asked in the form of indirect questions. However, the speaker really needs a service, rather than information (Clark & Bly, 1995). For example, a teacher might ask a class, "What are you laughing at?" The teacher is not really concerned about the source of the laughter. Instead, he or she is requesting silence. Also, some directives take the form of hints. You probably know someone who asks questions like, "I wonder if there is any butter in the refrigerator?" instead of the more *direct* directive, "Would you get me some butter, please?" Finally, some people may issue directives in the form of complaints, but they do not really intend that any action should be taken (Kowalski, 1996). Obviously, directives offer numerous opportunities for misunderstandings!

Notice that many requests are in the form of questions that provide listeners with options. The options allow listeners either to comply with the request or to give some good reason why they cannot comply. These questions whose syntax does not match their intended purpose are called **indirect speech acts** (Green, 1989). Gibbs (1986) investigated the hypothesis that speakers will state their requests in a format that anticipates potential obstacles to compliance. Participants in this study read scenarios of everyday situations, such as going to a restaurant and ordering something that might no longer be available. They are asked to imagine themselves in this scenario and write down one sentence that they might say.

The results showed that people were most likely to frame their requests in terms of a possible obstacle that might create a problem. In the restaurant scenario, for example, 68% of the sentences began, "Do you have . . ."; requests such as "I'd like . . . " were much less common. Try noticing how you word your own requests. Do you tend to address a potential obstacle? For example, I recall an occasion when I wanted to call a professor at a large university. Aware that I would speak to one of many secretaries, who might not know about this professor's habits, I asked almost automatically, "Do you know what Dr. New's schedule will be for the day?"

Also, consider how we may occasionally phrase a request in an extremely indirect fashion. Valian (1985) provides an example of how we communicate more than we say. On seeing her neighbor in the elevator, she asked, "Has your designer made any progress on the soundproofing?" After a blank moment, the neighbor smiled and answered, "Oh, has our music been bothering you again?" The question about the designer let the neighbor know that the noise had still been bothersome and reminded him of an earlier promise. Notice, also, that if the neighbor had been somewhat less pragmatically skilled, these conversational partners would have failed to achieve common ground!

SECTION SUMMARY: Speaking

1. Research on language production is much less common than studies on language comprehension, but some components of production are now being examined.
2. Four stages in speech production include working out the gist, formulating the general structure of the sentence, making the word choice, and articulating the phoneme.
3. People typically select the active voice; however, they may prefer the passive voice when the preceding sentence is passive and when using certain kinds of nouns and verbs.
4. According to Dell, slips-of-the-tongue occur because a speech sound other than the intended one is highly activated.
5. A narrative is a kind of discourse that typically includes certain specified story components.
6. The pragmatic rules of speech regulate components of speech production such as common ground, appropriate conversational format, and the skillful use of directives.

WRITING

Writing is a cognitive task that integrates virtually every cognitive activity described in this textbook. Think about the last writing project you completed, and consider how that project required attention, memory, imagery, background knowledge, metacognition, problem solving, creativity, reasoning, and decision making (Kellogg, 1994).

Writing is also an important component of many people's occupations. For example, technical and professional people report that in a typical working day they spend an average of about 30% of their time writing (Faigley & Miller, 1982; Kellogg, 1989). However, writing is one of the least understood linguistic tasks; research in this area is relatively limited (Hayes, 1989a; Levy & Ransdell, 1995). We noted earlier in this chapter that research on *understanding* speech is more common than research on speech production. The contrast is even more dramatic when we compare written language. Reading inspires hundreds of books and research articles each year, whereas writing inspires only a handful.

Writing and speaking share many similar cognitive components. However, writing is more likely to be performed in isolation, with more complex syntax and more extensive revisions (Ellis & Beattie, 1986). In contrast, when you speak, you are more involved with your audience, and you are also more likely to refer to yourself (Chafe & Danielewicz, 1987).

The cognitive tasks that comprise writing include planning, sentence generating, and revising. However—like the similar stages we discussed in both understanding and producing spoken language—these tasks often overlap (Hayes, 1989a; Hayes & Flower, 1986; Kellogg, 1987, 1994). For example, you may be planning your overall writing strategy while generating parts of several sentences. All components of the task are complex, and they strain the limits of attention (Kellogg, 1994). As Flower and Hayes (1980) describe the process,

> Writing is the act of dealing with an excessive number of simultaneous demands or constraints. Viewed this way, a writer in the act is a thinker on a full-time cognitive overload. (p. 33)

Still, consistent with Theme 2, we generally manage to coordinate these tasks quite skillfully as we produce written language. Let's examine the three phases of writing.

Planning

A writing plan includes at least three kinds of elements: (1) goals to express content knowledge about the topic; (2) goals unrelated to content, such as the form of the essay or persuasive techniques; and (3) goals to use certain words and phrases that sound appropriate. Research has shown that the amount of planning and the quality of planning are both highly correlated with the quality of the written text (Hayes, 1989a).

Perhaps you had a high school teacher who insisted that you outline a paper before you began to write. Research by Kellogg (1988, 1990, 1994) strongly supports this strategy. College students who were instructed to prepare a written outline later wrote significantly better essays than students in a control group. Kellogg suggests that an outline may help to alleviate attention overload. In addition, an outline may help students resolve the linearization problem, which occurs in writing as well as in speaking. You've probably had the experience of beginning to write a paper, only to find that each of several interrelated ideas needs to be placed first! An outline helps sort these ideas into an orderly, linear sequence.

Some researchers have begun to explore the influence of computer use on the planning process. Hayes (1989a) cites research by Haas showing that writers were less likely to preplan writing when they used a computer than when they used pen and paper. They also planned less at a conceptual level when they used a computer. In his book on writing, Kellogg (1994) concludes that overall writing quality and writing fluency are similar when people compose with a computer, rather than with a pen and paper.

Sentence Generation

Before you read farther, try Demonstration 9.5, which requires you to generate some sentences. During sentence generation, the writer must translate the general

DEMONSTRATION 9.5

GENERATING SENTENCES

For this exercise, you should be alone in a room, with no one else present to inhibit your spontaneity. Take a piece of paper on which you will write two sentences. For this writing task, however, say out loud the thoughts you are considering while you write each sentence. The results will be discussed later in this section.

1. Write one sentence to answer the question, "What are the most important characteristics that a good student should have?"
2. Write one sentence to answer the question, "What do you consider to be your strongest personality characteristics—the ones that you most admire in yourself?"

ideas developed during planning, thus creating the actual sentences of the text. Even the most detailed outline must be greatly expanded during this process.

One important characteristic of sentence generation is that the final essay is typically at least eight times longer than even the most elaborate outline. Another important characteristic is that hesitant phases tend to alternate with fluent phases, just as we discussed for spoken language. Think back on your own pattern when you were writing the sentences in Demonstration 9.5. Did you show a similar pattern of pauses alternating with fluent writing?

Revision

In order to revise what you have written, you need to reconsider the goals of the text, to predict how well the text accomplishes these goals, and to propose improved ways to accomplish those goals (Hayes, 1989a). College students in one study reported that they had spent 30% of their writing time on revising their papers, but observation of their actual writing behavior showed that they never spent more than 10% of their time on revisions (Levy & Ransdell, 1995). We have seen that students' metacognitions about reading comprehension are not very accurate (Chapter 7); their metacognitions about writing are also inaccurate.

Furthermore, college students show tremendous individual differences in their revision strategies. Hayes (1989a) studied college students who were writing research papers for a class. Some students revised their original papers dramatically, often completely abandoning earlier drafts to begin a new version. Others showed little or no global revision, making changes only at the word or the sentence level.

In another study, Hayes and his colleagues (1987) compared the revision strategies of seven expert writers and seven first-year college students. Everyone was given the same poorly written two-page letter and was asked to revise it for an audience of young college students. The first-year students were likely to approach the text one sentence at a time, fixing relatively minor problems with spelling and grammar, but ignoring problems of organization, focus, and transition between ideas. The students were also more likely to judge some defective sentences as being appropriate. For example, several students found no fault with the sentence, "In sports like fencing for a long time many of our varsity team members had no previous experience anyway." Finally, the students were less likely than the expert writers to diagnose the source of a problem in a sentence. For example, a student might say, "This sentence just doesn't sound right," whereas an expert might say, "The subject and the verb don't agree here."

In other situations, however, expertise can be a drawback. Specifically, if you know too much, you may not recognize that the text could be unclear to readers with little background knowledge. Hayes (1989a) found that students who had acquired background knowledge on a topic were *less* likely to identify problem passages in an unclear essay on that topic. Ideally, writers should be sensitive to grammatical and organizational problems when they are revising a writing sample. However, they must also be able to adopt the viewpoint of a naive reader, who may not have enough background knowledge to understand a difficult technical paper.

One final caution about the revision process focuses on the proofreading stage. Daneman and Stainton (1993) confirmed what many of us already suspected: You can proofread someone else's writing more accurately than your own. Our extreme familiarity with what we have written helps us overlook the errors in the text; top-down processing triumphs again! Many of my students also seem to assume that the spell-check feature on their word processor will locate every mistake, but it only identifies the nonwords. It doesn't protest when you've entered the word *line*, rather than the word *like*. Furthermore, you've probably discovered that you cannot proofread your papers for spelling when you are focusing on the paper's content.

As you can see, research on the psychology of writing is still in its beginning phase. Ironically, most psychologists spend hours each week on various writing tasks. Nevertheless, very few have conducted empirical research on this extremely complex cognitive task.

SECTION SUMMARY: WRITING

1. Writing is a task that involves numerous other cognitive activities, but it has received little research attention.
2. Writing is typically performed in isolation, with more complex syntax and more extensive revisions, whereas speaking involves both the audience and the speaker.
3. The quality of writing is related to the amount and the quality of planning; outlining also improves one's writing.

4. When people generate sentences during writing, the final essay is much longer than the outline; writers' fluent phases alternate with hesitant phases.

5. Expert writers are more likely than beginning college students to revise a paper thoroughly; they are also more likely to diagnose defective sentences; however, people who have background knowledge in an area may not be sensitive to text difficulty. Finally, people proofread others' writing more accurately than their own.

BILINGUALISM

In these two chapters on language, we have considered four astonishingly complicated cognitive tasks: speech comprehension, reading, speaking, and writing. These tasks require the simultaneous coordination of cognitive skills and social knowledge. We can marvel that human beings can manage all these tasks in one language. But then we must remind ourselves that many people master two or more languages.

Most of the people in the world are at least somewhat bilingual. Some people live in bilingual countries, such as Canada, Belgium, and Switzerland. Others become bilingual because their home language is not the language used for school and business; for example, Zulu speakers in South Africa must learn English. Immigrants frequently need to master the language of their new country. Figure 9.4 shows a message sent to Boston residents, reminding us that people who learn

===== FIGURE 9.4 =====

A NOTICE SENT TO BOSTON RESIDENTS BY A TELEPHONE COMPANY. THE LANGUAGES ON THE NOTICE INCLUDE ENGLISH, PORTUGUESE, SPANISH, VIETNAMESE, FRENCH, CHINESE, AND CAMBODIAN.

What You Should Know About Automatic Dialing Services.

This is an important notice. Please have it translated.
Este é um aviso importante. Queira mandá-lo traduzir.
Este es un aviso importante. Sírvase mandarlo traducir.
ĐÂY LÀ MỘT BẢN THÔNG CÁO QUAN TRỌNG
XIN VUI LÒNG CHO DỊCH LẠI THÔNG CÁO ẤY
Ceci est important. Veuillez faire traduire.

本通知很重要。请将之译成中文。
នេះគឺជាដំណឹងល្អ សូមមេត្តាបកប្រែជូនផង

a second language often need to learn new written characters, as well as words and syntax. People also become bilingual because colonization has imposed another language upon them, because they have studied language in school, or because they grew up in homes where two languages were used routinely.

For many years, North Americans were accustomed to considering themselves monolinguals. However, 10% of couples in Canada are mixed-language couples— for example, one person originally spoke English and the other spoke French (Turcotte, 1993). Canada's bilingual status encourages many Canadians to master a second language. In the United States, about 32 million people speak a language other than English at home (Bialystok & Hakuta, 1994). This number includes about 17 million speakers of Spanish, nearly 2 million speakers of French, and more than 1 million speakers of each of three other languages: German, Italian, and Chinese. Bilingualism therefore figures prominently in the lives of many North Americans.

A *bilingual* speaker is a person who uses two languages that differ in speech sounds, vocabulary, and syntax. Technically, we should use the term *multilingual* to refer to someone who uses more than two languages, but psycholinguists often use the term *bilingual* to include *multilinguals* as well (Taylor & Taylor, 1990). The bilingual's native language is referred to as the *first language* or *L1,* and the non-native language is the *second language* or *L2.*

A pioneer in research on bilingualism, Wallace Lambert, introduced an important distinction between additive and subtractive bilingualism. In *additive bilingualism,* an individual acquires proficiency in a second language with no loss in his or her first language; both languages are associated with respect and prestige. For example, English speakers in Quebec usually learn French if they run a business. In *subtractive bilingualism,* the new language replaces the first language. Unfortunately, linguistic minorities in many areas of the United States and Canada are pressured to develop high-level skills in English at the expense of their first language, producing subtractive bilingualism (Lambert, 1990).

The North American educational system values additive bilingualism; we want European-American middle-class children to acquire French or German. However, this same educational system seldom appreciates the value of keeping a child fluent in a first language such as Korean, Arabic, or Spanish; subtractive bilingualism often predominates for immigrant children.

As you can imagine, the topic of bilingualism has important political and social psychological implications, especially when educators and politicians make statements about various ethnic groups. These same social psychological forces are important when an individual wants to become bilingual. One of the most important predictors in acquiring a second language is a person's attitude toward the people who speak that language. In fact, researchers have tried to predict how well English-Canadian high school students will learn French. The students' *attitude* toward French Canadians was just as important as their cognitive, language-learning *aptitude* (Gardner & Lambert, 1959; Lambert, 1992). Not surprisingly, the relationship between attitudes and language proficiency also works in the reverse direction. Specifically, elementary school English Canadians who learn French develop more positive attitudes toward French Canadians than do children in a monolingual control group.

The topic of bilingualism is so interesting and complicated that some colleges offer an entire course in the subject. Several recent books also explore bilingualism and second-language learning (Bialystok & Hakuta, 1994; Selinker & Gass, 1994; Tarone et al., 1994). We will limit our discussion here to three cognitive issues: (1) the advantages of bilingualism, (2) an in-depth examination of how immigrants maintain their first-language skills, and (3) the relationship between age of acquisition and proficiency in the second language.

Advantages of Bilingualism

The early theorists suggested that bilingualism is harmful. For example, Jespersen (1922) said, "The brain effort required to master the two languages instead of one certainly diminishes the child's power of learning other things which might and ought to be learnt" (p. 148). According to that view, an individual's cognitive capacity is limited, and thought is less efficient because the brain stores two linguistic systems (Lambert, 1990). The early research on bilingualism seemed to support that conclusion. However, this research was seriously flawed; lower-class bilinguals were compared with middle-class monolinguals, with all the achievement and IQ testing conducted in the monolingual child's language (Reynolds, 1991).

You can imagine, then, the impact caused by the first well-controlled study comparing monolinguals with bilinguals: Bilinguals were found to be more advanced in school, they scored better on tests of first-language skills, and they showed greater mental flexibility (Peal & Lambert, 1962). The original research was conducted in Montreal, and the results have been confirmed by carefully conducted research in Singapore, Switzerland, South Africa, Israel, and New York (Lambert, 1990).

In addition to gaining fluency in a second language, bilinguals seem to have a number of advantages over monolinguals.

1. Bilinguals actually acquire more expertise in their native (first) language. For example, English-speaking Canadian children whose classes are taught in French gain greater understanding of English language structure (Diaz, 1985; Lambert et al., 1991).
2. Bilinguals excel at paying selective attention to relatively subtle aspects of a language task, ignoring more obvious linguistic characteristics (Bialystok, 1992).
3. Bilinguals are more aware that the names assigned to concepts are arbitrary (Bialystok, 1987, 1988; Hakuta, 1986). For example, monolingual children cannot imagine that a cow could just as easily have been assigned the name, *dog.* A number of studies have examined *metalinguistics,* or knowledge about the form and structure of language. On many measures of metalinguistic skill—but not all of them—bilinguals outperform monolinguals (Bialystok, 1988, 1992; Campbell & Sais, 1995; Galambos & Goldin-Meadow, 1990; Galambos & Hakuta, 1988).
4. Bilingual children are more sensitive to some pragmatic aspects of language. For example, English-speaking children whose classes are taught in French are more aware than monolinguals that when you speak to a blindfolded child, you need to supply additional information (Genesee et al., 1975).

5. Bilingual children are better at following complicated instructions (Hamers & Blanc, 1989; Powers & López, 1985).

6. Bilingual children perform better than monolinguals on tests of creativity, such as thinking of a wide variety of different uses for a paper clip (Hamers & Blanc, 1989; Ricciardelli, 1992; Scott, 1973).

7. Bilinguals perform better on concept formation tasks and on tests of non-verbal intelligence that require reorganization of visual patterns (Peal & Lambert, 1962).

The *disadvantages* of being bilingual are trivial. People who use two languages extensively may subtly alter their pronunciation of some speech sounds in both languages (Caramazza et al., 1973). Bilinguals are also slightly slower in making some kinds of decisions about language, though these are unlikely to hamper communication. For example, an English-French bilingual may be momentarily uncertain whether a passage is written in English or in French (Taylor & Taylor, 1990). Bilinguals may also take somewhat longer to decide whether a string of letters (either a nonsense word or an English word) is actually an English word (Ransdell & Fischler, 1987). As Insup Taylor—a multilingual who speaks Korean, Japanese, and English—concludes in her psycholinguistics textbook,

> Bilinguals may experience a slight disadvantage in language-processing speed over monolinguals, but this disadvantage is far outweighed by the advantages of being able to function in two languages. (Taylor & Taylor, 1990, p. 340)

IN DEPTH: Maintenance of the First Language Among Immigrants

Earlier, we noted that many immigrants are discouraged from retaining fluency in their first language, once they come to North America. However, some immigrants move to communities in the United States or Canada where their first language is widely spoken. How do these individuals manage linguistically? Do they master English? If so, does their original language deteriorate?

These questions have been addressed in an extensive study by Harry Bahrick and his coauthors (1994). You may recall Bahrick's work on everyday memory, which we examined in Chapter 5. In this study, Bahrick and his coauthors moved beyond people's memory for material learned long ago in school in order to examine some important questions about bilingual memory.

Bahrick and his colleagues tested a total of 801 Spanish-speaking immigrants from Cuba and Mexico, the majority of whom lived in either Miami, Florida, or El Paso, Texas. These individuals had immigrated to the United States when they were between 10 and 26 years of age, and they had been living there between 0 and 50 years since immigration. The researchers administered many tests in both English and Spanish, as well as questionnaires about language experiences.

How well did the immigrants learn English? Bahrick and his colleagues compared the scores of these bilingual immigrants with the scores of English monolinguals, who were similar in age and education. The results showed that the bilinguals and monolinguals performed similarly on a number of measures, such as recognizing English vocabulary and generating examples of English categories (e.g., kinds of clothing). However, the immigrants did receive somewhat lower scores on a test of English oral comprehension.

FIGURE 9.5

PERFORMANCE ON FOUR TESTS OF SPANISH LANGUAGE SKILL, FOR SPANISH MONOLINGUALS AND SPANISH-ENGLISH BILINGUALS. BAHRICK ET AL. (1994).

-------- Spanish monolinguals
———— Spanish-English bilinguals

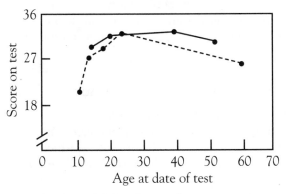

a. Spanish Test Comprehension

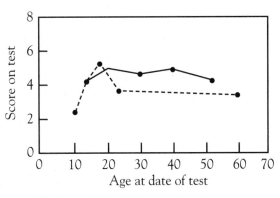

b. Spanish Oral Comprehension

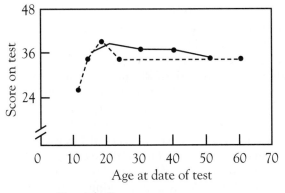

c. Spanish Grammar

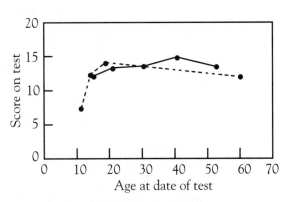

d. Spanish Vocabulary Recognition

How well did the immigrants remember their Spanish? Bahrick and his colleagues compared the scores of the bilinguals with the scores of Spanish monolinguals, who were similar in age and education and who had recently arrived in the United States. As you can see from Figure 9.5, the bilinguals performed slightly *better* on tests of Spanish text comprehension, Spanish oral comprehension, and Spanish grammar, but similarly on Spanish vocabulary recognition. Notice that these results contrast sharply with the findings on North American students who have learned Spanish in school. As we saw in Chapter 5, these students had forgotten more than half the Spanish vocabulary they had learned in high school (Bahrick, 1984).

You may wonder whether the bilinguals' Spanish usage was somehow impaired by their learning English; perhaps English vocabulary or sentence structure may corrupt their proper usage of Spanish. To answer this question, Bahrick and his coauthors (1994) devised a set of items to test Anglicisms. The bilinguals were just as accurate as the monolinguals in identifying which expressions were Anglicisms (e.g., *defrostiar,* a contrived translation for the verb *to defrost*), rather than genuine Spanish terms.

As you might imagine, the researchers discovered substantial individual differences on most language measures. However, the results suggest an optimistic outlook for bilinguals: They can achieve English language skills without compromising their ability to speak Spanish.

Second-Language Proficiency as a Function of Age of Acquisition

One of the most controversial topics in the study of bilingualism is whether young children have an advantage over older adults in learning a second language. The answers to this controversy seem to depend upon a number of factors, such as which aspect of language is being measured and the similarity between the two languages.

You probably will not be surprised to learn that age of acquisition influences the mastery of *phonology,* or speech sounds. Specifically, people who acquire a second language during early childhood are more likely to pronounce words like a native speaker of that language; those who acquire a second language during adulthood will be more likely to have a foreign accent when they speak their new language (Bialystok & Hakuta, 1994; Kilborn, 1994; Snow, 1993; Tahta et al., 1981).

When our measure of language proficiency is vocabulary, age of acquisition does not seem to be related to language skills (Bialystok & Hakuta, 1994). That is, adults and children are equally skilled in learning words in their new language.

The controversy about age of acquisition is strongest when we consider mastery of grammar. For example, Johnson and Newport (1989) studied Chinese and Korean speakers who had learned English as a second language. These researchers found that people who had arrived in the United States when they were younger than 7 received scores identical to scores received by native speakers of English. Specifically, the two groups performed similarly in their mastery of the past tense, pronouns, prepositions, and word order. In contrast, scores on this test were significantly lower for those who had learned English as teenagers or adults. These results led Johnson and Newport to conclude, "Human beings appear to have a special capacity for acquiring language in childhood, regardless of whether the language is their first or second" (p. 95).

However, young children may not have this advantage when their first language is more similar to English. For example, in the study by Bahrick and his colleagues (1994)—which we just discussed—Spanish speakers who were older when they immigrated showed greater mastery of English than those who were younger. Similar findings were reported by Snow and Hoefnagel-Hohle (1978) for speakers of Dutch, another language that is fairly similar to English.

We will need to wait until additional research has been performed on a wider variety of language combinations—hopefully with some second languages other than English. However, at present, the conclusions of Bialystok and Hakuta (1994) seem appropriate: "Thus, learners of a second language, even adult learners, continue to have 'access' to the ability to learn abstract linguistic structures" (p. 75).

As a final exercise in helping you understand bilingualism, try Demonstration 9.6 at your next opportunity. Quite clearly, bilinguals and multilinguals provide the best illustration of how Theme 2 applies to language, because they manage to master accurate and rapid communication in at least two languages.

DEMONSTRATION 9.6

EXPLORING BILINGUALISM

If you are fortunate enough to be bilingual or multilingual, you can answer these questions yourself. If you are not, locate someone you know well enough to ask the following questions:

1. How old were you when you were first exposed to your second language?
2. Under what circumstances did you acquire this second language? For example, did you have formal lessons in this language?
3. When you began to learn this second language, did you find yourself becoming any less fluent in your native language? If so, can you provide any examples?
4. Do you think you have any special insights about the nature of language that a monolingual may not have?
5. Does the North American culture (including peer groups) discourage bilinguals from using their first language?

SECTION SUMMARY: BILINGUALISM

1. In additive bilingualism, both languages are associated with prestige; in subtractive bilingualism, the first language is considered less prestigious. Attitudes are an important determinant of bilingual skills.

2. Well-controlled research shows that bilinguals have an advantage over monolinguals in their understanding of first-language structure, their ability to pay attention to subtle aspects of language, their awareness of the arbitrary nature of concept names, their sensitivity to pragmatics, their ability to follow instructions, their creativity, and their capacity for concept formation. However, bilinguals may pronounce some speech sounds differently, and they may take longer to make some language-processing decisions.

3. According to Bahrick and his colleagues, Spanish-speaking immigrants may learn English as well as English monolinguals, while retaining their Spanish as well as Spanish monolinguals.

4. People who acquire a second language during early childhood are less likely than adult learners to speak their new language with an accent, but adults and children are equally skilled in acquiring vocabulary. When the new language resembles English, adults are even more skilled than children in mastering English grammar.

CHAPTER REVIEW QUESTIONS

1. Describe some of the important cognitive tasks that are involved in language production (Chapter 9)—tasks that are not required in language comprehension (Chapter 8).

2. Think of someone you know whom you might be likely to see very soon, and construct a brief imaginary conversation with that person. What elements of the production process, discussed in this chapter, are illustrated in this conversation?

3. What is the linearization problem? Why is it more relevant in language production (either speaking or writing) than it would be when you create a mental image (Chapter 6)?

4. Think of a speech error that you recently made or heard in a conversation. What kind of error is this, according to Dell's classification, and how would Dell's theory explain this particular error?

5. How would you describe the structure of a typical narrative? How does a narrative differ from other kinds of discourse?

6. Analyze the next conversation you overhear from the viewpoint of the social context of speech. Pay particular attention to (a) the establishment of common ground, (b) the format of the conversation, and (c) directives.

7. How does writing differ from speaking? What cognitive tasks do these two activities share?

8. Based on the material in the section on writing, what hints could you adopt to produce a better paper the next time you are given a formal writing assignment?

9. What are additive and subtractive bilingualism? Describe several tasks in which bilinguals are likely to perform better than monolinguals. Which tasks would monolinguals probably perform better than bilinguals?

10. Several decades ago, theorists believed that bilinguals had a linguistic disadvantage; because of the second language, the first language would suffer. How would the research of Bahrick and his colleagues address this concern? Why might the results of this study be limited by the nature of the population they studied?

NEW TERMS

the linearization problem
prosody
slips-of-the-tongue
discourse
narratives
pragmatics

common ground
directive
indirect speech acts
bilingual
multilingual
first language (L1)

second language (L2)
additive bilingualism
subtractive bilingualism
metalinguistics
phonology

RECOMMENDED READINGS

Bialystok, E., & Hakuta, K. (1994). *In other words: The science and psychology of second-language acquisition.* New York: Basic Books. Ellen Bialystok and Kenji Hakuta are well-known researchers in the area of bilingualism, and they have written an interesting and accessible summary of the research on this topic.

Gernsbacher, M. A. (Ed.). (1994). *Handbook of psycholinguistics.* San Diego: Academic Press. This excellent handbook includes chapters on the grammatical aspects of language production, discourse production, and second-language learning.

Gleason, J. B., & Ratner, N. B. (Eds.). (1993a). *Psycholinguistics.* Fort Worth, TX: Harcourt Brace Jovanovich. Two well-written chapters in this book—one on conversational discourse and one on bilingualism—are especially strong, current discussions of the research.

Kellogg, R. T. (1994). *The psychology of writing.* New York: Oxford University Press. Ronald Kellogg is one of the pioneers of research on writing, and his book should help give the topic the attention it deserves.

Miller, J. L., & Eimas, P. D. (Eds.). (1995a). *Speech, language, and communication.* San Diego: Academic Press. This advanced-level book includes useful chapters on sentence production and on the pragmatics of discourse.

PROBLEM SOLVING AND CREATIVITY

INTRODUCTION

UNDERSTANDING THE PROBLEM

The Requirements for Problem Understanding
Paying Attention to Important Information
Methods of Representing the Problem

PROBLEM-SOLVING APPROACHES

The Means-Ends Heuristic
In Depth: The Analogy Approach

FACTORS THAT INFLUENCE PROBLEM SOLVING

Expertise
Mental Set
Functional Fixedness
Insight and Noninsight Problems

CREATIVITY

Definitions
Approaches to Creativity
Factors Influencing Creativity

──────────── **Preview** ════════════

$\mathbf{W}$e use problem solving when we want to reach a particular goal, but we can't immediately figure out the appropriate pathway to that goal. This chapter considers four aspects of problem solving: (1) understanding the problem, (2) problem-solving approaches, (3) factors that influence problem solving, and (4) creativity.

When you understand a problem, you need to pay attention to the relevant parts of the problem. Then you can use many alternate methods to represent the problem, such as lists, graphs, and visual images.

Some problem-solving approaches use algorithms, which are methods that will always produce a solution. Heuristics, in contrast, do not always produce a solution, though they require less time. One heuristic is the means-ends heuristic, which breaks a problem into subproblems and then solves these individual subproblems. A second heuristic is the analogy approach; unfortunately, people often select an inappropriate previous problem to develop the analogy for the current problem.

The section on factors that influence problem solving emphasizes how top-down and bottom-up processing are both important in effective problem solving. Experts make good use of their well-developed top-down processing. In contrast, the sections on mental set, functional fixedness, and insight versus noninsight problems demonstrates that top-down processing can sometimes interfere with effective problem solving.

Creativity can be defined as finding a solution that is both unusual and useful. After discussing several approaches to creativity, we'll examine how creativity can be influenced by taking a break (incubation) and by social factors, such as having your work evaluated.

INTRODUCTION

Every day, you solve dozens of problems. Think about all the problems you solved yesterday, for example. Perhaps you wanted to leave a note for a professor, but you had no pen or pencil. An essay may have asked you to compare two theories that seemed entirely unrelated. Perhaps you had planned to make an interesting main course for dinner but arrived home to find bare cupboards. Although you spent most of the day solving problems, you may have decided to relax late at night . . . by solving even more problems. Maybe you played a card game or read a mystery novel or solved a crossword puzzle.

Problem solving is inescapable in everyday life. In fact, most jobs require some kind of problem solving; auto mechanics, computer programmers, physicians, teachers, and counselors all use problem solving (Lesgold, 1988; M. U. Smith, 1991).

You use ***problem solving*** when you want to reach a certain goal, but the path toward that goal is not immediately obvious (Squire, 1992). You face a problem whenever you encounter a gap between where you are now and where you want to be—and you do not know how to cross that gap (Hayes, 1989b; Mayer, 1985; M. U. Smith, 1991).

Every problem contains three features: (1) the initial state, (2) the goal state, and (3) the obstacles. For example, suppose you want to go shopping in a nearby town. The *initial state* describes the situation at the beginning of the problem. In this case, your initial state might be, "I am in my room, five miles from that town, with no car and no public transportation." The *goal state* is reached when the problem is solved. Here, it would be, "I'm shopping in a town five miles away." The *obstacles* describes the restrictions that make it difficult to proceed from the initial state to the goal state (Davidson et al., 1994). The obstacles in this hypothetical problem might include the following: "I can't borrow a car from a stranger" and "I can't drive a stick-shift car." Take a moment to recall a problem you have recently solved. Determine the initial state, the goal state, and the obstacles, so that you are familiar with these three terms.

One aspect of problem solving that has received relatively little attention is problem *finding* (Brown & Walter, 1990; Hennessey, 1994). However, problem finding—like problem solving—is a crucial component of many occupations (Runco, 1994). For example, agencies that are trying to do social intervention work in a community must first try to identify the most important problems that need to be solved (Suarez-Balcazar et al., 1992).

Another example of problem finding was reported by leaders of a British company, who discovered that they were requesting unnecessary paperwork from their employees. The company leaders had previously been unaware that any problem existed. One year after finding this problem, 26 million cards and sheets of paper were eliminated—and the employees presumably felt less overwhelmed (Bransford et al., 1987). However, the solution would never have occurred if the problem hadn't first been discovered.

Children seem to seek out problems spontaneously, although adults typically do not (Thomas, 1989). Some educators argue that our formal education discourages us from learning to find problems and ask questions (Brown & Walter, 1990). For instance, one writer observed:

> Recently a teacher was overheard to announce: "When I want your questions, I'll give them to you." Much of school practice consists of giving definite, almost concrete answers. Perhaps boredom sets in as answers are given to questions that were never asked. (Gowin, 1981, p. 127)

Because we have so little information on problem finding, this chapter will emphasize problem solving. Throughout this chapter, we will note the active nature of cognitive processes in problem solving, consistent with Theme 1. When people solve problems, they seldom take a random, trial-and-error approach, blindly trying different options until they find a solution. Instead, they typically show extraordinary flexibility (Hinrichs, 1992). They plan their attacks, often breaking a problem into its component parts and devising a plan for solving each part. In addition to plans, problem solvers also use strategies. We will emphasize that people frequently use certain kinds of strategies that are likely to produce a solution relatively quickly. As this textbook stresses, humans are not passive beings that absorb information from the environment. Instead, we plan our approach to problems, choosing strategies that are likely to provide useful solutions.

Our first topic in this chapter is understanding the problem. Then we will consider a variety of problem-solving approaches, as well as several factors that influence problem solving. Our final topic is a particularly puzzling area of problem solving: creativity.

UNDERSTANDING THE PROBLEM

Some years ago, the companies located in a New York City skyscraper faced a major problem. The people in the building were continually complaining that the elevators moved too slowly. Numerous consultants were brought in, but the complaints only increased. When people threatened to move out, plans were drawn up to add an extremely expensive new set of elevators. Before reconstruction began, however, someone decided to add mirrors in the lobbies next to the elevators. The complaints stopped. Apparently, the original problem solvers had not properly understood the problem. In fact, the real problem wasn't the speed of the elevators, but the boredom of waiting for them to arrive (Thomas, 1989).

The Requirements for Problem Understanding

What do we mean when we say that we understand a problem? According to Greeno (1977, 1991), *understanding* involves constructing an internal representation. For example, if you understand a sentence, you create some internal representation or pattern in your head so that concepts are related to each other in the same way that they are related to each other in the original sentence. To create this pattern in your head, you must use background knowledge, such as the meaning of the various words in the sentence.

Greeno believes that understanding has three requirements: coherence, correspondence, and relationship to background knowledge. Let us look at each of these components in more detail.

A coherent representation is a pattern that is connected, so that all parts make sense. For example, consider Greeno's sentence, "Tree trunks are straws for thirsty leaves and branches" (p. 44). That sentence remains at the level of complete nonsense unless you see that it is based on the similarity of tree trunks and straws in moving liquid. Once you see the analogy, the fragments of the sentence become united. Similarly, look back at Demonstration 7.5. When you originally read that paragraph, it had no coherent representation in your head because many fragments were unrelated. However, once you had been told that the paragraph was about photocopying, everything made sense. You had a coherent representation.

Greeno also proposes that understanding require a close correspondence between the internal representation and the material that is being understood. Sometimes the internal representation is incomplete, and sometimes it is inaccurate. Important relations among the parts may be left out or mismatched. Think about an occasion when you noticed that an internal representation and the material to be understood did not correspond. I recall my mother giving her friend a recipe for homemade yogurt, which included the sentence, "Then you put the yogurt in a warm blanket." The friend looked quite pained and asked, "But isn't it awfully messy to wash the blanket out?" Unfortunately, the friend's internal representation had omitted the fact that the yogurt was in a container.

Greeno's third criterion for good understanding is that the material to be understood must be related to the understander's background knowledge. In many everyday situations, people underutilize their background knowledge when they try to solve problems (Perkins et al., 1991). In other words, they fail to make sufficient use of top-down processing.

DEMONSTRATION 10.1

THE FIVE-HANDED-MONSTER PROBLEM. SIMON & HAYES, 1976 (P. 168).

Read over this problem and underline the parts of the sentences you consider most important.

1. Three five-handed extraterrestrial monsters were holding three crystal globes.
2. Because of the quantum-mechanical peculiarities of their neighborhood, both monsters and globes come in exactly three sizes with no others permitted: small, medium, and large.
3. The medium-sized monster was holding the small globe; the small monster was holding the large globe; and the large monster was holding the medium-sized globe.
4. Since this situation offended their keenly developed sense of symmetry, they proceeded to transfer globes from one monster to another so that each monster would have a globe proportionate to his own size.
5. Monster etiquette complicated the solution of the problem since it requires: that only one globe may be transferred at a time; that if a monster is holding two globes, only the larger of the two may be transferred; and that a globe may not be transferred to a monster who is holding a larger globe.
6. By what sequence of transfers could the monsters have solved this problem?

This third criterion has probably occurred to you if you've found yourself enrolled in an advanced-level course without the proper prerequisite courses or if you have ever looked at a professional article in a subject that is unfamiliar. Vocabulary and concepts must be familiar for material to be understood. Greeno (1977) summarizes his previous research on this topic, which involved people solving probability problems. Those who had been told the meanings of basic concepts in probability were better at solving word problems than those who had been taught only the formulas.

We've considered three criteria for problem understanding. Now let's examine two important steps during this stage of problem solving. The first step is to pay attention to the relevant information, ignoring irrelevant material. The second step is to decide how to represent the problem.

Paying Attention to Important Information

To understand a problem, you must decide which information is most relevant to the problem's solution and then attend to it. Notice, then, that one cognitive task—problem solving—relies on other cognitive activities—decision making and attention. This is another example of the inter-relatedness of our cognitive processes (Theme 4). Read over the problem in Demonstration 10.1 and decide which parts are most important.

Simon and Hayes (1976) asked people to solve this problem, thinking aloud as they worked. The authors recorded what the participants said, as well as the number of times each sentence was reread. The sentences that were most frequently reread were Sentence 3, which describes the initial situation, Sentence 4, which describes the goal state, and Sentence 5, which describes the obstacles—the rules that must be followed to reach the goal. The other three sentences were rarely read a second time. Notice, then, that people pay attention to the information that is relevant to the task. They also pay attention to information that is difficult to store in memory. After all, problem solving depends heavily on working memory (Logie et al., 1994).

DEMONSTRATION 10.2

USING SYMBOLS IN PROBLEM SOLVING

Solve the following problem: Mary is ten years younger than twice Susan's age. Five years from now, Mary will be eight years older than Susan's age at that time. How old are Mary and Susan? (The answer is found in the discussion in the text.)

Were your judgments about the importance of the sentences of Demonstration 10.1 similar to the rereading patterns that Simon and Hayes found? For example, did you realize that you could safely ignore the jargon phrase, "Because of the quantum-mechanical peculiarities . . ."?

Attention is also important in problem understanding because competing thoughts can produce divided attention. Bransford and Stein (1984) presented algebra word problems to a group of college students. You remember these problems—a typical one might ask about a train traveling in one direction and a bird flying in another direction. The students were asked to note their thoughts and feelings as they inspected the problem. For a substantial number of students, their initial reactions to the problem included thoughts such as "Oh no, this is a mathematical word problem—I hate those things" and "Boy, am I going to look stupid!" These negative thoughts occurred frequently throughout the 5 minutes allotted to the task. Clearly, they drained attention from the central task of problem solving. Real-world problem solving frequently requires divided attention. Hunt and Lansman (1986) point out, for example, that the task of driving a car through an unfamiliar city in rush-hour traffic is a divided-attention issue. You must solve the problem of reaching your goal while watching other cars, pedestrians, and traffic lights.

Consider, too, the number of problems we face in everyday life in which the major challenge is discovering what information is important and what is irrelevant. Your statistics professor, for example, may include a problem on a test that has many details about the experimental design that are really not important for the solution of the problem. There may even be extra statistical information that you will not need in finding the answer. The challenge in the problem may really be to decide what information merits attention. Also, consider how this idea of discovering essential information can be applied to some riddles. Halpern (1996) poses this one:

> Suppose you are a bus driver. On the first stop you pick up 6 men and 2 women. At the second stop 2 men leave and 1 woman boards the bus. At the third stop 1 man leaves and 2 women enter the bus. At the fourth stop 3 men get on and 3 women get off. At the fifth stop, 2 men get off, 3 men get on, 1 woman gets off and 2 women get on. What is the bus driver's name? (p. 356)

A major problem in understanding a problem is focusing on the appropriate part of the problem (Mayer, 1989). If you paid attention to the bus driver problem, you could solve it without rereading it. However, if you didn't pay attention, you can locate the answer in the first sentence.

Methods of Representing the Problem

As soon as the problem solver has decided which information is essential and which can be disregarded, the next step is to find a good way to represent the problem.

Simon and Hayes (1976) argue that people regard problems like the one in Demonstration 10.1 as a "cover story" for the real problem. Therefore, they must discover the abstract puzzle underneath all the details, and then they must find a good way to represent this abstract puzzle. Think about your own reaction to Demonstration 10.1, for example. Did you really think it was a problem about five-handed monsters? Instead, you probably saw it as a puzzle in which certain objects were to be exchanged according to certain rules.

If people regard problems as being abstract, then a difficulty arises. After all, an abstract problem is difficult to keep in memory while you perform operations. Therefore, people typically invent some method of representing the abstract problem in a concrete way—a particular concrete way that shows only the essential information. Some of the most effective methods of representing problems include symbols, lists, matrices, hierarchical tree diagrams, graphs, and visual images. These methods help reduce the demands on working memory and help problem solvers to organize the information effectively (Davidson et al., 1994).

Symbols. Sometimes the most effective way to represent an abstract problem is by using symbols, as students learn to do in high-school algebra. Consider Demonstration 10.2, on page 345. The usual way of solving this problem is to let a symbol such as m represent Mary's age and a symbol such as s represent Susan's age. We can then "translate" each sentence into a formula. The first sentence becomes:

$$m = 2s - 10$$

The second sentence becomes:

$$m + 5 = s + 5 + 8$$

Now we can substitute for m in the second equation:

$$2s - 10 + 5 = s + 5 + 8$$

Therefore we find that:

$$s = 18$$

Substituting for s in the first equation, we find that:

$$m = 26$$

Finally, we have to translate the symbols back into words: Susan is 18 and Mary is 26.

Of course, a major problem is learning to translate words into symbols. This translation must meet Greeno's (1977) three requirements for problem understanding: coherence, correspondence, and relationship to background knowledge. The problem solver may make mistakes here. For example, Schoenfeld (1982) describes how calculus students were asked to rephrase simple algebra problem statements so that they were more understandable. About 10% of the rephrasings included information that directly contradicted the input, and 20% contained information that was so confused that it was unintelligible. If you misunderstand a problem you will not translate it accurately into symbols. (And, incidentally, a proper understanding of a problem does not guarantee an appropriate translation into symbols!)

Many errors occur in translating words into symbols, either because people have difficulty with the linguistic interpretation of the words or because they fail to remember all the critical material. In previous chapters, we have seen that people often remember material that is consistent with their prior schemas. This same schema-consistent processing also occurs when people try to solve problems (Mayer, 1989).

One common problem in translating sentences into symbols is that the problem solver often simplifies the sentence, thereby misrepresenting the information. Mayer (1982, 1985) asked college students to read a series of eight algebra story problems, and then recall them later. The problems contained some relational propositions such as "the rate in still water is 12 miles per hour more than the rate of the current" and simpler propositions such as "the cost of the candy is $1.70 per pound." The participants recalled only 71% of the relational propositions correctly, in contrast to 91% of the simpler propositions. Further analysis showed that the errors on the relational propositions frequently involved changing those statements into simpler forms, such as "the rate in still water is 12 miles per hour."

A further problem arises in the translation process because people bring their previous misconceptions with them when they begin to solve a problem. For example, several researchers have asked students without any background in physics to solve physics problems (Donley & Ashcraft, 1992; Green et al., 1985). Many of them hold misconceptions about the way objects move. Unfortunately, these misconceptions interfere with the proper translation of words into symbols.

Lists. In many problems, however, we will not go far by translating words into symbols. For example, the monster problem in Demonstration 10.1 cannot be handled by the symbols used in an algebra problem. We could approach the problem by making a list, as in Table 10.1. However, notice how quickly the list becomes bulky. We cannot keep track of which monster has which globe, so in this instance a list is not very helpful.

Matrices. Simon and Hayes (1976) found that more than 50% of their participants spontaneously constructed some kind of matrix to represent the monster problem. A *matrix* is a chart that shows all possible combinations of items. In the case of the monster problem, the matrix shows which monster holds which globe at different times, as in Table 10.2. A matrix is an excellent way to keep track of items, particularly when the problem is complex and the relevant information is

=== **TABLE 10.1** ===

REPRESENTING THE MONSTER PROBLEM IN A LIST

	Monster size	*Globe size*
Step 1	Small	Medium
	Medium	Large
	Large	Small
Step 2	Small	Medium
	Medium	—
	Large	Large, Small
Step 3	Small	—
	Medium	Medium
	Large	Large, Small

categorical (Halpern, 1996). For example, you might use a matrix if you have 20 people who need to be conveyed to an event in five cars. The matrix lets you assess all the possible combinations, taking into account personal preferences ("Kim and Sid won't want to be together in a car for two hours!").

Hierarchical Tree Diagrams. Suppose that you are playing a coin game with two children, Chris and Pat. You toss each of three coins. If it's heads, the coin goes to Chris; if it's tails, it goes to Pat. What is the probability that one child will get to keep all three coins? Solving this problem with a list format typically leads to an incorrect response (Keren, 1984).

A more satisfactory alternative for representing this problem is a ***hierarchical tree diagram,*** a figure that uses a treelike structure to specify every possible

=== **TABLE 10.2** ===

REPRESENTING THE MONSTER PROBLEM IN A MATRIX

			Monster size
	Small	*Medium*	*Large*
Step 1	Medium	Large	Small
Step 2	Medium	—	Large, Small
Step 3	—	Medium	Large, Small

A HIERARCHICAL TREE DIAGRAM USED TO SOLVE A PROBABILITY PROBLEM.

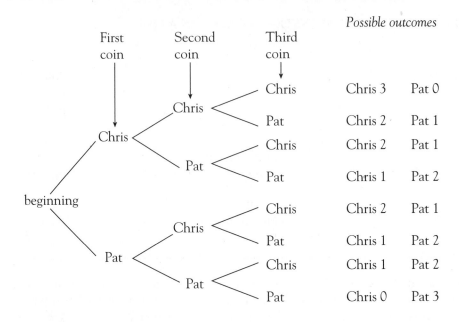

Possible outcomes

Probability of one outcome: One child 3 coins/other child 0 = 25%

DEMONSTRATION 10.3

THE BUDDHIST MONK PROBLEM

Exactly at sunrise one morning, a Buddhist monk set out to climb a tall mountain. The narrow path was not more than a foot or two wide, and it wound around the mountain to a beautiful, glittering temple at the mountain peak.

The monk climbed the path at varying rates of speed. He stopped many times along the way to rest and to eat the fruit he carried with him. He reached the temple just before sunset. At the temple, he fasted and meditated for several days. Then he began his journey back along the same path, starting at sunrise and walking, as before, at variable speeds with many stops along the way. However, his average speed going down the hill was greater than his average climbing speed.

Prove that there must be a spot along the path that the monk will pass on both trips at exactly the same time of day. (The answer is found in Figure 10.2.)

outcome and is especially effective in assessing the mathematical probability of various outcomes (Halpern, 1996). Notice that in Figure 10.1 the hierarchical tree diagram shows that the 3 coins/0 coin distribution can occur in two ways, out of the eight possible outcomes. Students who used this kind of diagram in solving probability problems were twice as successful at solving the problem as were those who used the simple list (Keren, 1984). Try Demonstration 10.3 before reading further.

Graphs. For some problems, however, symbols, lists, matrices, and hierarchical tree diagrams are not useful. Consider, for example, the Buddhist monk problem in Demonstration 10.3. A graph is an effective way to approach this problem. As Figure 10.2 shows, we can use one line to show the monk going up the mountain on the first day. We use a second line to show the monk coming down the mountain several days later. The point at which the lines cross tells us the spot that the monk will pass at the same time on each of the two days. I have drawn the lines so that they cross at a point 1,200 feet up the mountain at 1:00 P.M. However, the two paths must always cross at *some* point, even if you vary the monk's rate of ascent and descent.

Visual Images. Other people prefer to solve problems like the one about the Buddhist monk by using visual imagery. One young woman who chose a visual approach to this problem reported the following:

> I tried this and that, until I got fed up with the whole thing, but the image of that monk in his saffron robe walking up the hill kept persisting in my mind. Then a moment came when, superimposed on this image, I saw another, more transparent one, of the monk walking *down* the hill, and I realized in a flash that the two figures *must* meet at some point some time—regardless at what speed they walk and how often each of them stops. Then I reasoned out what I already knew: whether the monk descends two days or three days later comes to the same; so I was quite justified in letting him descend on the same day, in duplicate so to speak. (Koestler, 1964, p. 184)

As Koestler points out, a visual image has an advantage—it can be *irrational.* After all, how could the monk meet himself coming down the mountain? Thus, the visual image can let us escape from the boundaries of traditional representations. At the same time, however, the visual image is somewhat concrete; it serves as a symbol for a theory that has not yet been thoroughly developed. This may partially explain why visual representations are particularly useful in solving novel problems (Kaufmann, 1985). Good visual-imagery skills also provide an advantage on problems that require construction of a figure (Adeyemo, 1994).

We need to point out that problem solvers use neither exclusively verbal means nor exclusively visual imagery to solve a puzzle. For example, the image of the monk must be associated with some words (Gellatly, 1986). Also, some imagery representations may be more effective than others. For example, Adeyemo (1990) asked college students to construct a novel coat rack, given only specified equipment. Students who created a visual image of an imaginary structure were much more successful in solving the problem than were students who created an image of a familiar coat rack.

===== FIGURE 10.2 =====

A GRAPHIC REPRESENTATION OF THE BUDDHIST MONK PROBLEM

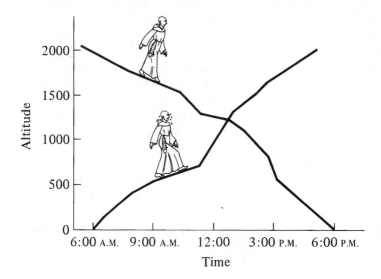

DEMONSTRATION 10.4

REPRESENTATIONS OF PROBLEMS

Read the following information and answer the question at the bottom of the demonstration. (The answer is at the end of the chapter.)

Five people are in a hospital. Each person has only one disease, and each has a different disease. Each one occupies a separate room; room numbers are 101–105.

1. The person with asthma is in Room 101.
2. Ms. Jones has heart disease.
3. Ms. Green is in Room 105.
4. Ms. Smith has tuberculosis.
5. The woman with mononucleosis is in Room 104.
6. Ms. Thomas is in Room 101.
7. Ms. Smith is in Room 102.
8. One of the patients, other than Ms. Anderson, has gall bladder disease.

What disease does Ms. Anderson have and in what room is she?

Which Method Is Best? We have seen that problems can be represented by symbols, lists, matrices, hierarchical tree diagrams, graphs, and visual images. Naturally, few problems can be represented by all methods. For example, the Buddhist monk problem will not fit into a matrix. Furthermore, some problems will quickly outgrow the boundaries of a list or a matrix.

Of course, some methods work better than others for a particular problem. Try Demonstration 10.4, and see which of the six methods works best for this kind of problem. Schwartz (1971) gave people problems that involved matching individuals with situations, as in the hospital-room problem. The participants were encouraged to show all their work, so that Schwartz could observe how they represented the problem.

Schwartz found that the success on this problem was related to the method people had used to represent the situation. When people used a matrix, 74% reached the correct solution. Other representations produced a solution between 40% and 55% of the time. Furthermore, people who did not use any particular representation method were successful only 25% of the time. For this kind of problem (though clearly not for all problems), the matrix representation was by far the most effective.

We should point out, however, that Schwartz's study shows only that the representation method is *related to* the frequency of solution. We may be tempted to conclude that this method *caused* a higher frequency of solution, so that problem solvers could improve their accuracy by shifting to matrix representation. However, another interpretation for these correlational data is that people who choose matrix representations are already good problem solvers, and people who choose other representations happen to be poor problem solvers. Teaching these other people about matrix representation may not aid them substantially. At present, though, we can conclude that people who spontaneously use matrix representations tend to be effective in solving this kind of problem.

SECTION SUMMARY: UNDERSTANDING THE PROBLEM

1. Problem finding is a crucial part of problem solving; formal education does not emphasize this part of the task.
2. Understanding the problem requires constructing an internal representation of the problem, which should have coherence, correspondence between the internal representation and the material to be understood, and an appropriate relationship to the problem solver's background knowledge.
3. People pay the most attention to the parts of the problem that seem relevant to the task and that are difficult to remember.
4. Methods for representing problems include symbols, lists, matrices, hierarchical tree diagrams, graphs, and visual images. For certain problems, problem solvers who spontaneously use some techniques are more successful than problem solvers who use other techniques.

PROBLEM-SOLVING APPROACHES

Once you have represented the problem, you can use many different strategies to attack it. Some strategies are very time consuming. For instance, an ***algorithm*** is a method that will always produce a solution to the problem, sooner or later. One example of an algorithm is a method called ***exhaustive search,*** in which you try out all possible answers using a specified system. For instance, a high-school student faced with the algebra problem in Demonstration 10.2 could begin with $m = 0$ and $s = 0$ and try all possible values for m and s until the solution is reached. With such an inefficient algorithm, however, the exam would probably be over before this one problem is solved.

In general, the time you take to search for an answer to a problem is roughly proportional to the total size of the problem space. The ***problem space*** is all the possible solutions to the problem that have occurred to the problem solver. The problem may have other solutions. However, if the problem solver is not aware of these solutions, they are not included in the problem space. Notice how the problem space can vary. When you try to solve the anagram YBO, the problem space is very small. In contrast, the problem space for the anagram LSSTNEUIAMYOUL is enormous.

Algorithms are often inefficient and unsophisticated. Other, more sophisticated methods cut down the part of the space that must be explored to find a solution. The problem solver thus begins with a large space at first. However, she or he applies relevant information about the problem in order to reduce the size of the problem space, leaving a relatively small space to examine. For example, to solve that lengthy anagram, you might pick out initial combinations of letters that are pronounceable, thereby narrowing the problem space (Greeno & Simon, 1988). Perhaps you would reject combinations such as LS, LT, and LN, but consider LE, LU, and hopefully SI. This strategy would probably lead you to a solution much faster than a systematic random search of all the more than 87 billion possible arrangements of the 14 letters in SIMULTANEOUSLY.

The strategy of looking only for pronounceable letter combinations is an example of a heuristic. As you know from other chapters, a heuristic is a rule of thumb. In problem solving, a **heuristic** is a rule of thumb involving a selective search, looking at only the portions of the problem space that are most likely to produce a solution.

We noted that algorithms such as an exhaustive search will always produce a solution, although you may age a few years in the process. Heuristics, in contrast, do not guarantee a solution. For instance, suppose you were given the anagram IPMHYLOD, and you use the heuristic of rejecting unlikely initial combinations of letters. If you reject words beginning with LY, you would fail to find the correct solution, LYMPHOID. When making a decision, you'll need to weigh the benefits of an algorithm's speed against the costs of possibly missing the correct solution (Anderson, 1991; Du Boulay, 1989).

Psychologists have conducted more research on problem solvers' heuristics than on their algorithms. One reason is that most everyday problems cannot be solved by algorithms. For example, no algorithm can be applied to the problem of getting to a nearby town when you don't own a car. Furthermore, people are more likely to use heuristics. Two of the most widely used heuristics are means-ends analysis and the analogy. (Try Demonstration 10.5 before you read further.)

The Means-Ends Heuristic

The **means-ends heuristic** has two important components: (1) first you divide the problem into a number of **subproblems,** or smaller problems, and (2) then you try to reduce the difference between the initial state and the goal state for each of the

---

DEMONSTRATION 10.5

THE HOBBITS-AND-ORCS PROBLEM

Try solving this problem. (The answer is at the end of the chapter.)

   Three Hobbits and three Orcs arrive at a river bank, and they all wish to cross to the other side. Fortunately, there is a boat, but unfortunately, the boat can hold only two creatures at one time. There is another problem. Orcs are vicious creatures, and whenever there are more Orcs than Hobbits on one side of the river, the Orcs will immediately attack the Hobbits and eat them up. Consequently, you should be certain that you never leave more Orcs than Hobbits on any river bank. How should the problem be solved? (It must be added that the Orcs, though vicious, can be trusted to bring the boat back!)

subproblems. The name *means-ends analysis* is appropriate because it involves figuring out the "ends" you want and then figuring out the "means" you will use to reach those ends. Means-ends analysis concentrates the problem solver's attention on the difference between the initial problem state and the goal state, and this method is one of the most useful characteristics of human problem solvers (Stillings et al., 1995; Sweller & Levine, 1982).

Every day we all solve problems by using means-ends analysis. For example, several years ago, a student I knew well came running into my office saying, "Can I use your stapler, Dr. Matlin?" When I handed her the stapler, she immediately inserted the bottom edge of her skirt into the stapler and deftly tacked up the hem. As she explained at a more leisurely pace later that day, she had been faced with a problem: At 11:50, she realized that the hem of her skirt had come loose, and she was scheduled to deliver a class presentation in 10 minutes. Using means-ends analysis, she divided the problem into two subproblems: (1) identifying some object that could fix the hem, and (2) locating that object.

When you use means-ends analysis to solve a problem, you can proceed in either the forward direction, from the initial state to the goal state, or backward from the goal state to the initial state. Thus, you may solve the second subproblem prior to the first subproblem. Try noticing the kinds of problems you might solve using means-ends analysis, perhaps writing a term paper for a history course, solving a problem in a statistics class, or figuring out the solution to numerous everyday dilemmas. Let us now examine some of the research showing how people use means-ends analysis in solving problems, as well as computer simulation investigations of this heuristic.

Research on the Means-Ends Heuristic. Research demonstrates that people do organize problems in terms of subproblems. Greeno (1974) used the Hobbits-and-Orcs problem in Demonstration 10.5. His study showed that people pause at points in the problem and plan their strategy for the next few moves. They do not move ahead at a steady pace through a long series of individual moves. Specifically, people took a long time before the first move and before two other critical moves. At each of these points, they were tackling a subproblem and needed to organize a group of moves.

In some cases, means-ends analysis might not be the best approach. Sometimes the solution to a problem depends on temporarily *increasing* the difference between the initial state and the goal state. For example, how did you solve the Hobbits-and-Orcs problem in Demonstration 10.5? Maybe you concentrated on reducing the difference between the initial state (all creatures on the right side) and the goal state (all creatures on the left side), and you therefore only moved them from right to left. If you did, you would have ignored some steps that were crucial for solving the problem: moving creatures *backward* across the river to the river bank on the right.

Research by Thomas (1974) confirmed that people are reluctant to move away from the goal state—even if the correct solution ultimately depends on this temporary detour. In one of the conditions, participants began by solving the last part of the Hobbits-and-Orcs problem, starting at one of the points that required moving away from the goal. People in this group were somewhat more willing to move away from the goal state; the detour probably did not seem to be so annoying. Later, they were asked to solve the problem again, starting at the very beginning. Now, they strongly resisted moving away from the goal state. In fact, their performance did not differ from the performance of people in the control group, who had no previous experience with the problem. We humans strongly resist going backwards in order to go forward (Gilhooly, 1982).

In real life, as in the Hobbits-and-Orcs problem, the most effective way to move forward is sometimes to move backward temporarily. Think about an occasion when you were working on one of the later subproblems within a problem, and you discovered that a solution to an earlier subproblem was inadequate. For example, when you are writing a paper based on library research, you might discover that the resources you gathered during an earlier stage were not appropriate. Now you need to move backward to that earlier subproblem and revisit the library. My students tell me that this situation is particularly frustrating, especially because it seems to increase the difference between the initial state and the goal state. In short, when we try to solve a problem with means-ends analysis, we must sometimes violate a strict difference-reduction strategy.

Computer Simulation. One of the most widely discussed examples of computer simulation was devised to account for the way humans use means-ends analysis (Baron, 1994; Stillings et al., 1995). Specifically, Allen Newell and Herbert Simon developed a theory that featured subgoals and reducing the difference between the initial state and the goal state (Newell & Simon, 1972; Simon, 1995). Let's first consider some general characteristics of computer simulation, when applied to problem solving. Then we'll briefly discuss Newell and Simon's approach, as well as more recent developments in computer simulation.

As discussed earlier in the book, when researchers use ***computer simulation,*** they write a computer program that will perform a task the same way that a human would. For example, a researcher might try to write a computer program for the Hobbits-and-Orcs problem. The program should make some false starts, just as the human would. The program should be no better at solving the problem than a human would be, and it also should be no worse. The researcher tests the program by having it solve a problem and noting whether the steps it takes match the steps that humans would take in solving the problem. In studying problem solving, computer simulation offers the same advantage mentioned in connection with computer simulation of language processes: It forces the theorist to be clear and unambiguous about the components of the theory (Gilhooly, 1982; Greeno & Simon, 1988).

Sometimes the computer program's performance does not match the performance of human problem solvers. This failure indicates to the researchers that their theory needs to be revised. If the researchers have created a program that does mimic human behavior, however, this success does *not* automatically imply that humans actually solve problems in this fashion. It is possible, for example, that another task could be devised for which the computer program and the human problem solver would perform differently. In psychology, we cannot "prove" that a theory is correct; we can only demonstrate that it is compatible or consistent with behavior. Thus, if a program does predict how humans will solve a problem, a theory can be tentatively accepted. If it does not predict problem solutions, a theory can be rejected.

What is the advantage of computer simulation? Why is it preferable to a theory stated in standard English? Many cognitive psychologists favor computer simulation because it allows them to express their theories in precise computer language. In contrast, standard English is much less explicit.

In 1972, Newell and Simon developed a now-classic computer simulation, called General Problem Solver. **General Problem Solver,** or **GPS,** is a program whose basic strategy is means-ends analysis. The goal of the GPS is not simply to solve problems in the most efficient way. Instead, it mimics the processes that normal humans use when they tackle these problems (Gardner, 1985; Stillings et al., 1995). GPS has several different methods of operating. For example, the "reduce method" involves searching for an operator that would help reduce the difference between the initial state and the goal state. Then the operator is applied to the initial state to produce a new state.

The General Problem Solver was the first program to simulate a variety of human symbolic behaviors (Gardner, 1985). GPS therefore has had an important impact on the history of cognitive psychology. It was used to simulate human performance on transport problems like that of the Hobbits and Orcs, as well as to study a number of other problems.

In addition, researchers used the GPS to simulate human performance on a wide variety of tasks, such as the grammatical analysis of sentences, proofs in logic, and trigonometry problems. The GPS was eventually discarded by Newell and Simon because its generality was not as great as they had wished (Gardner, 1985). However, GPS remains important because it helped us understand how humans solve problems using means-ends analysis (Greeno & Simon, 1988).

One of the most active projects involving computer simulation of problem solving has been directed by John Anderson and his colleagues at Carnegie Mellon University (1995). This project is an outgrowth of Anderson's ACT* theory, which was summarized in Chapter 7. Anderson and his coworkers have now developed programs for solving problems in algebra, geometry, and computer science. These programs were developed originally in order to learn more about how students acquire skills in problem solving. More recently, the programs have been developed into "cognitive tutors" that can be used in education. For example, the tutor can assist students who can work at their own rate outside the classroom. In some high school classes, students alternate between classroom activities and work in a computer laboratory (Anderson et al., 1995). Thus, a project that was initially designed to examine theoretical questions can be applied to real-life situations.

IN DEPTH: The Analogy Approach

Every day you use analogies to solve problems. When confronted with a problem in a mathematics course, you refer to previous examples in your textbook. To pronounce an unfamiliar English word, you think about other words with similar spellings. Analogies also figure prominently in creative breakthroughs in art and science (Keane, 1988; Lawson & Lawson, 1993). For example, some of Einstein's theories developed out of analogies.

When we use the **analogy approach** in problem solving, we use a solution to an earlier problem to help solve a new one. Analogies pervade human thinking. Whenever we try to solve a new problem by referring to a known, familiar problem, we are using an analogy (Halpern et al., 1990).

Educators are clearly aware of the power of analogies. For example, in a survey conducted by Halpern (1987), virtually every college-level course in critical thinking or creative thinking emphasized course instruction on using analogies. More generally, any instruction that is designed to improve thinking should focus on analogies (Halpern, 1993). After all, students must learn to see the similarities between the problems they master in the classroom and the problems they encounter in real life. Moreover, an important new concept in education is called **situated learning;** learning depends upon the situation in which the learning occurs, rather than representing knowledge that a person can bring to every environment (Greeno et al., 1993). As a result, educators try to determine how to maximize the transfer to new situations.

Let's consider the general structure of the analogy approach, and then we'll discuss a representative study in some detail. Later, we'll look at some of the factors that can encourage problem solvers to use the analogy approach most effectively.

The Structure of the Analogy Approach. The challenge for people who use the analogy strategy is to determine the *real* problem, that is, the abstract puzzle underneath all the details. In the section on understanding problems, we emphasized that the problem solver must peel away the unimportant layers in order to reach the core of the problem. For example, when you attacked Demonstration 10.5, you did not really need to know anything about Hobbits and Orcs—except for any characteristics that were relevant for getting them across the stream. The story could just as well have concerned residents of different countries. These sets of problems with the same underlying structures and solutions—but with different specific details—are called **problem isomorphs.**

Let's introduce some other standard terminology for analogical problem solving. Imagine that you are currently trying to solve a problem; this current problem is called the **target problem.** To solve the target problem, you should look for a similar problem you solved in the past, called a **source problem.**

Researchers have determined that college students can classify algebra problems fairly accurately into general categories, such as work-rate problems and river-current problems (Hinsley et al., 1977). They are also fairly accurate in matching complex target problems with complex source problems, while matching simple target problems with simple source problems (Reed et al., 1994).

The major barrier to using the analogy approach, however, is that people tend to focus more on the superficial content of the problem than on the abstract, underlying meaning of the problem (Reeves & Weisberg, 1993, 1994; VanderStoep & Seifert, 1994). In other words, they pay more attention to the salient **surface**

DEMONSTRATION 10.6

A TYPICAL PROBLEM FROM NOVICK'S (1988) RESEARCH. BASED ON NOVICK (1988), p. 513.

Mr. and Mrs. Renshaw were planning how to arrange vegetable plants in their new garden. They agreed on the total number of plants to buy, but not on how many of each kind to get. Mr. Renshaw wanted to have a few kinds of vegetables and ten of each kind. Mrs. Renshaw wanted more kinds of vegetables, so she suggested having only four of each kind. Mr. Renshaw didn't like that because if some of the plants died, there wouldn't be very many of each kind. So they agreed to have five of each vegetable. But then their daughter pointed out that there was room in the garden for two more plants, although then there wouldn't be the same number of each kind of vegetable. To remedy this, she suggested buying six of each vegetable. Everyone was satisfied with this plan. Given this information, what is the fewest number of vegetable plants the Renshaws could have in their garden? (The answer to this problem appears at the end of the chapter.)

features, which are the specific objects and terms used in the question. Unfortunately, these problem solvers may fail to emphasize the *structural features,* the underlying core that must be understood in order to solve the problem correctly. Several studies have demonstrated that people often fail to see the analogy between a problem they have solved and a new problem isomorph that is structurally similar (e.g., Holyoak & Koh, 1987; Reed, 1977, 1993b). Let's look at a representative study by Novick (1988) in more detail.

Novick's Research. Laura Novick wanted to see how the ability of the problem solvers influenced the way they selected a source problem when they were tackling algebra word problems. In particular, she proposed that low-ability problem solvers would select a source problem that resembled the surface features of the target problem. In contrast, high-ability problem solvers should be more likely to select a source problem that resembled the structural features of the target problem.

Novick tested college undergraduates and categorized them into ability categories (high, medium, and low) on the basis of their scores on the mathematics section of the Scholastic Aptitude Test (SAT). She argued that the SAT is a valid way to categorize students in her research because the problems on that test are similar to the problems she presented to the students. Try Demonstration 10.6, which shows a typical problem from Novick's research.

Imagine that you are participating in Novick's study. In the beginning, you are given three problems to solve, including the one in Demonstration 10.6; these serve as the source problems. Each problem is also accompanied by an explanation of the solution. For example, you might see the explanation for Demonstration 10.6 that

====== FIGURE 10.3 ======

KIND OF SOURCE PROBLEM SELECTED FOR SOLVING THE TARGET PROBLEM, AS A FUNCTION OF LEVEL OF EXPERTISE OF PROBLEM SOLVER. BASED ON NOVICK (1988).

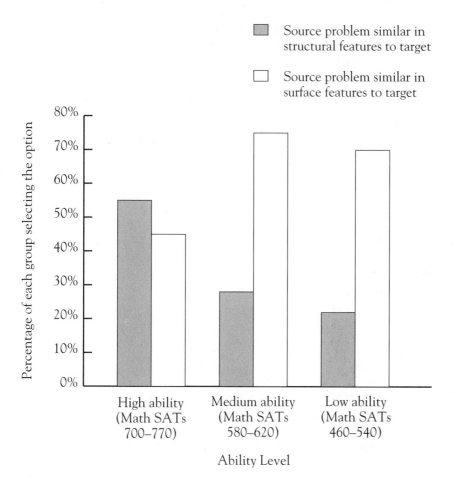

Source problem similar in structural features to target

Source problem similar in surface features to target

is shown at the end of this chapter, on pages 381–382. After these three problems, Novick hands you the target problem, and you are instructed to solve it. This target problem resembles the *surface* features of the first source problem. However, it also resembles the *structural* features of the second problem, because both problems required you to figure out the lowest common multiple (for example, 10 × 4 × 5 in Demonstration 10.6). The only similarity between the target problem and the third source problem is that both require some arithmetic calculations.

Novick examined the students' calculations for the target problem in this study to determine whether their solution relied on the earlier problem that had been similar in surface features or the one that had been similar in structural features. As you can see in Figure 10.3, the high-ability students were slightly more likely to emphasize structural similarity, rather than surface similarity. In contrast, medium- and low-ability students were much more likely to emphasize surface similarity.

Thus, Novick's research shows us that people skilled in mathematics are often able to peel away the layers of math problems and notice that, at the core, two problems share structural similarities. In contrast, people with less mathematical skill often miss the appropriate analogy, relying instead on similarities that are unimportant. As you may recall from Chapter 7, people sometimes fail to notice that a new story uses the same underlying script as an old story. In summary, people may fail to make apropriate use of top-down processing.

Factors Encouraging Appropriate Use of Analogies. How can we help people use the analogy method more effectively, so that they consult a source problem based on structural similarity, rather than surface similarity? Researchers have found that people are more likely to use analogies effectively under the following circumstances:

1. When people are required to compare two or more problems that have different surface structure (Cummins, 1992, 1994; VanderStoep & Seifert, 1994);
2. When people are exposed to many structurally similar problems before they tackle the target problem (VanderStoep & Seifert, 1994); and
3. When people actually try to solve the source problem, rather than simply studying that problem (Needham & Begg, 1991).

The research on using analogies to solve problems suggests that this technique is extremely useful—when it is used appropriately. Unfortunately, however, people are often distracted by superficially similar problems, especially if their problem-solving ability is low. Still, we noted three techniques that can be used to encourage active processing of the source problem; these techniques help people solve new problems more effectively.

SECTION SUMMARY: PROBLEM-SOLVING APPROACHES

1. With algorithms, such as exhaustive search, the problem solver eventually reaches a solution, but this method is very time consuming; in contrast, heuristics are faster and they examine only part of the problem space, but they do not guarantee a solution.
2. One heuristic is the means-ends heuristic, which requires dividing a problem into subproblems and trying to reduce the difference between the initial state and the goal state for each of the subproblems. The General Problem Solver (GPS) is a computer program designed to use means-ends analysis.
3. Another heuristic is the analogy approach, in which people solve a new problem by referring to an earlier problem. However, they may be distracted by superficial similarity and ignore structural similarity. People with strong

mathematical abilities and people who have been actively involved with the source problems are more likely to draw analogies with structurally similar source problems.

FACTORS THAT INFLUENCE PROBLEM SOLVING

How will you approach the next problem you face, and how successfully will you solve it? To answer that question, we need to know some information about you—the problem solver—and about the problem you are about to attack. For example, we would want to know about your level of expertise, a factor that demonstrates how top-down processing helps you solve problems. We would also want to know about any mental set or functional fixedness that might interfere with solving the problem; both of these factors show that top-down processing can sometimes block effective problem solving. Finally, we would want to know whether the problem requires insight. In order to solve an insight problem, you must also overcome overactive top-down processing. Thus, effective problem solving requires an appropriate mixture of both top-down and bottom-up processing (Theme 5).

Expertise

An individual with *expertise* demonstrates consistently exceptional performance on representative tasks for a particular area (Ericsson & Lehmann, 1996). Most cognitive psychologists specify that it takes at least 10 years of intense practice to achieve expertise (Anderson, 1993; Ericsson & Charness, 1994; Reynolds, 1992). The most effective practice requires appropriately difficult tasks, useful feedback, and the opportunity to correct errors (Ericsson, 1996a). Expertise does not come easily. For example, Ericsson and his colleagues (1993) discovered that a group of 20-year-old expert violinists had each devoted more than 10,000 hours to deliberate practice!

We know that experts aren't simply "smarter" than other people. For instance, Ceci and Liker (1986, 1988) found that people who were experts at betting on horse races did not have higher IQs than nonexperts. Furthermore, experts excel primarily in their own domains of expertise (Glaser & Chi, 1988). You wouldn't expect a racetrack expert to excel at the problem of creating a Northern Italian meal from unfamiliar ingredients!

Let's trace how experts differ from novices during many phases of problem solving. We'll begin with some of the basic, early advantages, then explore differences in problem-solving approaches, and finally consider more general issues, such as metacognition.

Knowledge Base. Novices and experts differ substantially in their knowledge base, or schemas (Hunt, 1989; Reed, 1993b). For example, Chi (1981) found in her study of physics problem solving that the novices simply lacked important knowledge about the principles of physics. As we discussed in previous chapters, you need the appropriate schemas in order to understand a topic properly.

Memory. Experts differ from novices with respect to their memory for information related to their area of expertise (Chi et al., 1982; Glaser & Chi, 1988). In Chapter 5, for example, we saw that memory experts can use retrieval cues from their "regular," short-term working memory in order to access a large, stable body of information in long-term working memory (Ericsson & Kintsch, 1995).

The memory skills of experts seem to be very specific. For example, expert chess players have much better memory than novices for various chess positions. De Groot (1966) briefly showed chess positions to novices and experts and then requested recall. The experts were far superior in recalling the chess positions. However, other researchers have discovered that experts are no better at remembering *random* arrangements of the chess pieces (Simon & Chase, 1973; Vicente & de Groot, 1990). In other words, experts' memory is better only if the chess arrangement fits into a particular schema. Similarly, people who are experts at the game Othello are also superior at recalling meaningful game patterns, but not random positions (Wolff et al., 1984). Ericsson and Hastie (1994) reviewed a large number of studies that contrast experts' memory for meaningful versus random patterns. Experts have an advantage over novices only on meaningful patterns— whether their area of expertise is chess, bridge, electronics, computer programming, or figure skating. Experts have a clear advantage over novices in game performance because memory for relevant information is such an important part of problem solving (Anderson, 1987).

Representation. Furthermore, novices and experts represent the problems differently. Larkin (1983, 1985) asked people to solve a variety of physics problems. She found that the novices in her study were likely to use naive problem representations, depicting objects in the real world such as blocks, pulleys, and toboggans. In contrast, the experts were able to construct physical representations about abstract ideas such as force and momentum. Other researchers have found similar results (e.g., De Jong & Ferguson-Hessler, 1986; Ferguson-Hessler & De Jong, 1987). In other words, novices tend to emphasize surface characteristics in their representations, whereas experts emphasize structural features (Novick, 1992).

Experts and novices also differ in the form they use for problem representation. Specifically, experts are more likely to use appropriate mental images or diagrams, which are likely to facilitate problem solving (Clement, 1991; Larkin & Simon, 1987).

Problem-Solving Approaches. When experts encounter a novel problem in their area of expertise, they are more likely than novices to use the means-ends heuristic. That is, they divide a problem into several subproblems, which they solve in a specified order (Schraagen, 1993). Experts are also more competent than novices at devising a grand plan for solving the problem, prior to beginning work (Priest & Lindsay, 1992).

Experts and novices also differ in the way they use the analogy approach. When solving physics problems, experts are more likely than novices to appreciate the structural similarity between problems. In contrast, novices are more likely to be distracted by surface similarities, and they therefore often choose an inappropriate source problem (Glaser & Chi, 1988; Hardiman et al., 1989). You'll notice that these findings resemble Novick's (1988) results for algebra problem solvers. She found that high-ability students were more likely to select a source problem on the basis of structural similarity. (Now try Demonstration 10.7 before you read further.)

Elaborating on Initial States. Experts are more thorough than novices in thinking about the initial states of a problem. For example, Voss and his colleagues

---

DEMONSTRATION 10.7

MENTAL SET

Try these two examples to see the effects of mental set.

a. Luchin's (1942) Water-Jar Problem
Imagine that you have three jars, A, B, and C. In each of seven problems, the capacity of the three jars is listed. You must use these jars in order to obtain the amount of liquid specified in the Goal column. You may obtain the goal amount by adding or subtracting the quantities listed in A, B, and C. (The answers can be found in the discussion of the experiment.)

Problem	A	B	C	Goal
1	24	130	3	100
2	9	44	7	21
3	21	58	4	29
4	12	160	25	98
5	19	75	5	46
6	23	49	3	20
7	18	48	4	22

b. A Number Puzzle
You are no doubt familiar with the kind of number puzzles in which you try to figure out the pattern for the order of numbers. Why are these numbers arranged in this order?

$$8, \quad 5, \quad 4, \quad 9, \quad 1, \quad 7, \quad 6, \quad 3, \quad 2, \quad 0$$

The answer appears at the end of the chapter.

(1991) asked experts and novices in the field of international relations to solve a problem involving the Soviet response to German reunification. The experts began by discussing the historical background of the problem, as well as a description of the Soviet goals. Novices did not provide any background framework; instead, they immediately began generating alternative responses.

Of course, the experts' extensive knowledge base allows them to elaborate in detail on the initial states. For example, medical experts who are trying to diagnose a patient will retrieve many types of information from memory. Any inconsistencies in this information will direct their search for new information (Patel et al., 1996).

Speed and Accuracy. As you might expect, experts are much faster than novices, and they solve problems very accurately (Bédard & Chi, 1992). Their operations become more automatic, and a particular stimulus situation also quickly triggers a response (Glaser & Chi, 1988). Experts also seem to have a more efficient and coherent plan for problem solving (Hershey et al., 1990).

On some tasks, experts may solve problems faster because they use parallel processing, rather than serial processing. As the discussion on attention in Chapter 2 noted, parallel processing handles two or more items at the same time. In contrast, serial processing handles only one item at a time. Novick and Coté (1992) examined experts, who reported that they could solve anagrams quickly, and novices, who said their anagram-solving skills were "awful." The experts solved the anagrams so quickly that they must have been considering several alternate solutions at the same time. To experts, the solution to anagrams such as DNSUO, RCWDO, and IASYD seemed to "pop out" in less than 2 seconds. In contrast, the novices were probably using serial processing. (Incidentally, are you a novice or an expert anagram solver?)

Metacognitive Skills. Experts are better at monitoring their problem solving; you may recall that Chapter 7 discusssed how self-monitoring is a component of metacognition. Experts seem to be better at judging the difficulty of a problem. They are also more aware when they are making an error, and they are more skilled at allocating their time appropriately when solving problems (Glaser & Chi, 1988). In short, experts are more skilled at numerous phases of problem solving and are even more skilled at knowing how well they are doing in solving the problem at hand.

Mental Set

Before you read farther, be sure to try the two parts of Demonstration 10.7, which illustrate mental set. When problem solvers have a ***mental set,*** they keep trying the same solution they have used in previous problems, even though the problem could be approached via other, easier ways. Mental sets involve a kind of mental rut or mindless rigidity that blocks effective problem solving (Langer, 1989; Smith, 1995a).

We noted earlier that problem solving demands both top-down and bottom-up processing (Theme 5). Expertise makes appropriate use of top-down processing, because experts can employ their previous knowledge to solve problems both quickly and accurately. In contrast, both mental set and functional fixedness—which we'll discuss in the next section—represent *overactive* top-down processing. In these two cases, problem solvers are so strongly guided by their previous experience that they fail to see some obvious solutions to their problems.

The classic experiment on mental set is the Luchins (1942) water-jar problem, illustrated in the first part of Demonstration 10.7. The best way to solve Problem 1 is to fill up jar B and remove one jarful with jar A and two jarsful with jar C. Because Problems 1–5 can all be solved in this fashion, they create a set for the problem solver. Most people will keep using this method when they reach Problems 6 and 7. However, this past learning will actually produce a disadvantage, because these later problems can be solved by easier, more direct methods. For example, Problem 6 can be solved by subtracting C from A, and Problem 7 can be solved by adding C to A.

Luchins found that almost all participants to whom he gave such complex problems as 1–5 persisted in the same complex kind of solution on later problems. On the other hand, control-group participants—who began right away with problems such as 6 and 7—almost always solved the problem in the easier fashion. These

---

DEMONSTRATION 10.8

TWO INSIGHT PROBLEMS

a. The Nine-Dot Problem
Connect these nine dots with four connected straight lines. Do not lift your pencil from the paper when you draw the four lines.

b. The Triangle Problem
With six matches, construct four equilateral triangles. One complete match must make up one side of each triangle.

The answers to these two problems appear at the end of the chapter.

same findings have been replicated in a series of three experiments by McKelvie (1990).

A mental set can interfere with the quality of the problem solution, as well as the speed of problem solving. For example, in one study, college students were asked to create ideas for toys and extraterrestrial creatures (Smith, 1995b; S. M. Smith et al., 1993). Half the students briefly saw three examples of toys or creatures before they began to create the objects; the other half served as the control group, and they saw no examples. The students who had seen the examples were much more likely to borrow one of the characteristics from the examples when they designed their own items. For example, those who had seen a toy example that featured a ball were three times as likely to show a ball in their "original" design, compared to those in the control group.

A mental set often works against us in our everyday experiences. Consider, for example, the problem of getting to a particular location in a nearby city. Perhaps you devised a long, elaborate route involving many turns—a route that you have used for years. At some point, you may learn that a friend has discovered a much simpler, more direct route on the first try!

Functional Fixedness

Like a mental set, functional fixedness occurs when our top-down processing is overactive. However, mental set refers to our problem-solving strategies, whereas functional fixedness refers to the way we think about objects. Specifically, *functional fixedness* means that the functions or uses we assign to objects tend to remain fixed or stable.

To overcome functional fixedness, we need to think flexibly about other ways that objects can be used. My sister, for example, described a creative solution to a problem she had faced on a business trip. She had purchased a take-out dinner from a wonderful Indian restaurant. Back in her hotel, she discovered that the bag contained no plastic spoons or forks, and the hotel dining room had closed several hours earlier. What to do? She searched the hotel room, discovered an attractive new shoehorn in the "complimentary packet," washed it thoroughly, and enjoyed her chicken biriyani. She conquered functional fixedness by realizing that an object designed for one particular function (putting on shoes) can also serve another function (conveying food to the mouth).

The classic study in functional fixedness is called Duncker's candle problem (Duncker, 1945). Imagine that you have been led to a room that contains a table. On the table are three objects, a candle, a box of matches, and a box of thumbtacks. Your task is to find a way to attach a candle to the wall of the room so that it burns properly, using no other objects than those on the table. Most people approach this problem by trying to tack the candle to the wall or by using melted wax to try to glue it up; both tactics fail miserably! The solution requires overcoming functional fixedness by tacking the empty matchbox to the wall to serve as a candle holder.

In the situations most of us encounter in everyday life, we have access to a variety of tools and objects, so functional fixedness is not a major issue. However, consider the quandry of Dr. Angus Wallace and Dr. Tom Wong. These physicians had just taken off for Hong Kong when they learned that another passenger was experiencing a collapsed lung. The only surgical equipment they had brought on board was a segment of rubber tubing and a scalpel. They operated on the woman and saved her life, using only this modest equipment and objects that normally have fixed functions—a coathanger, a knife, a fork, and a bottle of Evian water (Adler & Hall, 1995).

Functional fixedness and mental sets are two more examples of a part of Theme 2, which states that mistakes in cognitive processing can often be traced to a strategy that is basically very rational. In general, objects in our world have fixed functions. For example, we use a hammer to pound a nail, and we use a wrench to tighten a bolt. The strategy of using one tool for one task and another tool for another task is generally appropriate; after all, each was specifically designed for its own task. Functional fixedness occurs, however, when we apply that strategy too rigidly and fail to realize, for instance, that if all other tools are missing, a wrench could be used to pound the nail. Similarly, it is generally a wise strategy to use the knowledge you learned in solving earlier problems to solve the present dilemma. If an old idea works well, keep using it! However, in the case of mental sets, we apply the strategy gained from past experience too rigidly and fail to notice more efficient solutions.

Insight and Noninsight Problems

Demonstration 10.8, on page 367, illustrates two typical insight problems. When we solve an *insight problem*, the solution to a problem suddenly enters our minds, and we immediately realize that the solution is correct (Baron, 1994). In contrast, when we work on a *noninsight problem*, we solve the problem gradually, using reasoning skills and a routine set of procedures (J. E. Davidson, 1995; Schooler et al., 1995). For example, Demonstration 10.2 was a noninsight problem, because you pursued the answer in a logical, step-by-step fashion, gradually solving the algebra problem.

Let's examine the nature of insight in somewhat more detail. Then we'll compare insight and noninsight problems on two dimensions: metacognition about problem solving and the role of language in problem solving.

The Nature of Insight. The concept of insight was very important to Gestalt psychologists. As Chapter 1 described, Gestalt psychologists emphasized organizational tendencies. They argued that the parts of a problem may initially seem unrelated to one another, but a sudden flash of insight could make the parts instantly fit together into a solution. If you solved the problems successfully in Demonstration 10.8, you experienced this feeling of sudden success.

Behaviorist psychologists rejected the concept of insight because insight's emphasis on sudden cognitive reorganization was not compatible with their emphasis on observable behavior. However, with the rise of the cognitive approach, psychologists once again use the term freely.

Cognitive psychologists argue that people working on an insight problem usually hold some unwarranted assumptions when they begin to solve the problem. For example, when you began to solve part b of Demonstration 10.8, you probably assumed that the six matches needed to be arranged on a flat surface. In other words, you were searching the wrong problem space (Schooler & Melcher, 1994; Schooler et al., 1995). Therefore, top-down processing inappropriately dominated your thinking. In addition, the more you persevere in your top-down thinking, the more you spin your wheels, and the rut becomes even deeper (Smith, 1995a). To solve the problem correctly, you may need to take a break so that the misleading information no longer dominates your thinking (Schooler et al., 1995; Smith, 1995a).

Notice, in contrast, that noninsight problems typically benefit from top-down processing. The strategies you learned in high-school math classes offer guidance as you work, step by step, toward the proper conclusion of an algebra problem.

Metacognition During Problem Solving. When we are working on a problem, how confident are we that we are on the right track? Janet Metcalfe (1986) argues that the pattern of our metacognitions differs for noninsight and insight problems. Specifically, our confidence builds gradually for problems that do not require insight, such as standard high-school algebra problems. In contrast, when we work on insight problems, we experience a sudden leap in confidence when we are close to a correct solution. In fact, the sudden rise in confidence can be used to distinguish insight from noninsight problems (Metcalfe & Wiebe, 1987).

Let us examine Metcalfe's (1986) paper on metacognitions about insight problems. Metcalfe asked students problems like this one:

> A stranger approached a museum curator and offered him an ancient bronze coin. The coin had an authentic appearance and was marked with the date 544 B.C. The curator had happily made acquisitions from suspicious sources before, but this time he promptly called the police and had the stranger arrested. Why? (p. 624)

As students worked on this problem, they supplied ratings every 10 seconds on a "feeling-of-warmth" scale. A rating of 0 indicated that they were completely "cold" about the problem, with no glimmer of a solution. A score of 10 meant that they were certain they had a solution.

As you can see from Figure 10.4, the warmth ratings showed only gradual increases until they soared dramatically with the discovery of the correct solution. If you figured out the answer to the coin question, did you experience this same sudden burst of certainty? (Incidentally, the answer to this problem is that someone who had actually lived in 544 B.C. could not possibly have used the designation B.C. to indicate the birth of Christ half a millennium later.) Metcalfe's results have recently been replicated (J. E. Davidson, 1995), demonstrating that insight problems are characterized by a dramatic increase in the metacognition that the problem solver has located the solution.

=== **FIGURE 10.4** ===

"WARMTH RATINGS" FOR ANSWERS THAT WERE CORRECT AS A FUNCTION OF TIME OF RATING PRIOR TO ANSWERING.   BASED ON METCALFE (1986).

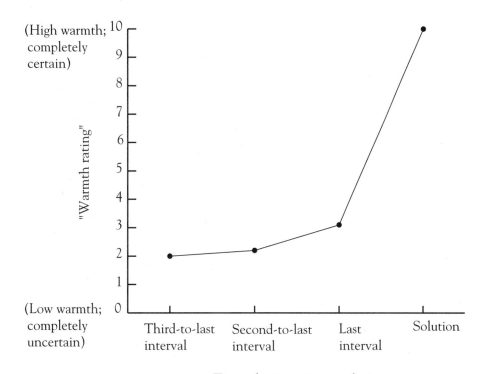

The Role of Language in Problem Solving. Insight and noninsight problems also differ with respect to the role that language can play during problem solving. In particular, talking about the problem may be helpful for a noninsight problem, but it may interfere with the solution of an insight problem.

For example, Berardi-Coletta and her colleagues (1995) asked some students to explain what they were doing as they worked on noninsight problems. They tended to discuss their strategies, their errors, and their expectations about the effectiveness of future steps in the problem-solving process. These students were significantly more effective in solving future problems, compared to students in control groups. Apparently, the use of language had forced them to focus on their metacognitions, and their greater awareness of problem-solving strategies transferred to the later problems. Similar research by Chi and her colleagues (1989) showed that these self-generated explanations led to improved performance for high-ability problem solvers, but no improvement for low-ability problem solvers.

Schooler and his colleagues asked students to talk out loud while solving both noninsight and insight problems (Schooler & Melcher, 1994; Schooler et al., 1993). They found that talking out loud had no influence on performance for noninsight problems. Looking at the results of all these studies, language sometimes helps people solve noninsight problems—but not always.

However, Schooler and his colleagues asked other students to solve insight problems. Those who had been instructed to verbalize their strategies solved substantially *fewer* problems than students in a control group (Schooler et al., 1993). Apparently, when we talk out loud while solving an insight problem, we somehow disrupt the kind of thinking we need to produce sudden insights. As Metcalfe (1986) showed, people don't know they are about to solve an insight problem until the solution leaps out; thus, they should not be able to report gradual progress toward a solution. When problem solvers are instructed to verbalize their strategies, these verbalizations may overshadow the less analytical, less conscious processes that would encourage effective solutions for insight problems.

SECTION SUMMARY: FACTORS THAT INFLUENCE PROBLEM SOLVING

1. Experts differ from novices with respect to their knowledge base, memory for task-related material, method of problem representation, problem-solving approaches, the extent of elaboration on initial states, speed and accuracy, and metacognitive skills.
2. Problem solving is also influenced by an individual's mental set (in which people keep trying the same solution strategy, when another strategy would be more effective) and functional fixedness (in which people assign a fixed use to an object). In both cases, top-down processing is overactive, but these strategies are basically rational.
3. Insight problems are solved when the answer appears suddenly; noninsight problems are solved gradually, using reasoning skills. Top-down processing is overactive in the case of insight problems and appropriately helpful in the case of noninsight problems.
4. Research on metacognition shows that confidence builds gradually for noninsight problems; for insight problems, confidence suddenly increases when the problem is solved. Also, for noninsight problems, performance is either enhanced or unaffected by explaining one's strategies; for insight problems, performance is disrupted.

CREATIVITY

Perhaps you breathed a sigh of relief as you finished the sections on problem solving and prepared to read a section on creativity. Problem solving sounds so routine—people who solve problems work out their means-ends analyses. In contrast, creativity sounds inspired—people who think creatively experience moments of genius, and light bulbs flash above their heads.

Truthfully, however, creativity is an area of problem solving. Creativity, like the areas of problem solving we have already considered, requires moving from an initial state to a goal state. However, creativity is more controversial because we have no standardized definition of creativity, and the theoretical approaches to creativity are so diverse.

One characteristic of creativity is *not* controversial: As we approach the 21st century, creativity has become an extremely popular topic, both within and beyond psychology. Numerous general books on creativity have been published in the last few years (e.g., Boden, 1994; Feldman et al., 1994; Finke et al., 1992; Goleman et al., 1992; Roskos-Ewoldsen et al., 1993; Russ, 1993; Sternberg & Lubart, 1995; Weisberg, 1993). Other books explore creativity in specific domains, such as architecture (Gero & Maher, 1993), storytelling (Turner, 1994), inventions (Weber, 1992; Weber & Perkins, 1992), and the visual arts (Freeman, 1993; Wakefield, 1992).

Let's begin our exploration of creativity by discussing definitions, as well as several approaches to creativity. Then we'll consider several factors that may influence creativity.

Definitions

An entire chapter could be written on the variety of ways creativity can be defined. However, most theorists agree that novelty is a necessary component of creativity (e.g., Baron, 1994; Eysenck, 1990; Feldman et al., 1994; Weisberg, 1993). But novelty is not enough. The answer we seek must also allow us to reach our goal; it must be practical and useful. Suppose I asked you to creatively answer the question, "How can you roast a pig?" The 19th-century essayist Charles Lamb observed that one way to roast a pig would be to put it into a house and then burn down the house. The answer certainly meets the criterion of novelty, though it does not fulfill the usefulness requirement. To most theorists, then, *creativity* involves finding a solution that is both novel and useful.

Although many theorists agree on the basic definition of creativity, their views diverge on other characteristics. For instance, Weisberg (1993) argues that creativity is based on ordinary thinking, something related to everyday problem solving. In contrast, Feldman and his colleagues (1994) argue that an ordinary person will not be likely to produce a creative product. Instead, certain people are creative within limited domains; a person who is creative in writing may be very *uncreative* in music or science.

Approaches to Creativity

If theorists disagree about the definition of creativity, how can they possibly agree about how to study it? Let's consider three methods that have been

DEMONSTRATION 10.9

DIVERGENT PRODUCTION TESTS

Try the following items, which are similar to Guilford's (1967) Divergent Production Tests.

1. Many words begin with an L and end with an N. In one minute, list as many words as possible that have the form L _____ N. (The words can have any number of letters between the L and the N.)
2. Suppose that people reached their final height at the age of 2, and so normal adult height is less than 3 feet. In one minute, list as many consequences as possible that would result from this change.
3. Here is a list of names. They can be classified in many ways. For example, one classification would be in terms of the number of syllables; SALLY, MAYA, and HAROLD have two syllables, whereas BETH, GAIL, and JOHN have one syllable. Classify them in as many ways as possible in one minute.

   BETH   HAROLD   GAIL   JOHN   MAYA   SALLY

4. Here are four shapes. In one minute, combine them to make each of the following objects: a face, a lamp, a piece of playground equipment, a tree. Each shape may be used once, many times, or not at all in forming each object, and it may be expanded or shrunk to any size.

proposed for measuring creativity, as well as one theoretical approach that is currently popular.

Divergent Production. Guilford (1967) proposed that creativity should be measured in terms of ***divergent production,*** or the number of varied responses made to each test item. Demonstration 10.9 shows some of the ways in which Guilford measured divergent production. These test items allow the test taker to explore in many different directions from the initial problem state, and some items may require test takers to overcome functional fixedness (Finke et al., 1992).

Research on tests of divergent production have found modest correlations between people's test scores and other judgments of their creativity (Guilford, 1967).

==
DEMONSTRATION 10.10
==

REMOTE ASSOCIATES

For each set of three words, try to think of a fourth word that is related to all three words. For example, the words ROUGH, COLD, and BEER suggest the word DRAFT, because of the phrases ROUGH DRAFT, COLD DRAFT, and DRAFT BEER. (The answers are at the end of the chapter.)

1. CHARMING	FROG	VALIANT
2. FOOD	CATCHER	HOT
3. HEARTED	FEET	BITTER
4. DARK	SHOT	SUN
5. CANADIAN	GOLF	SANDWICH
6. TUG	GRAVY	SHOW
7. ATTORNEY	SELF	SPENDING
8. MAGIC	PITCH	POWER
9. ARM	COAL	PEACH
10. TYPE	GHOST	STORY

However, even Guilford admitted that the support for his test was not spectacular. Others have pointed out that different measures of divergent production are not as highly correlated with one another as they should be (Brown, 1989). Finally, the *number* of different ideas may not be the best measure of creativity (Nickerson et al., 1985). After all, this measure does not assess whether the solutions meet the two criteria for creativity—that solutions should be both novel and useful.

Remote Associates Test. The ***Remote Associates Test (RAT)*** is a test of creativity; the items consist of three words that must be linked together with a single word. Try Demonstration 10.10, which contains some items like those on the RAT. The RAT was devised by Mednick and Mednick (1967) to measure their concept of creativity. According to Mednick and Mednick, creativity requires the ability to see relationships among ideas that are remote from one another. Creative people can take far-flung ideas and combine them into new associations that meet certain criteria.

Notice that the RAT items also require you to reach down into your hierarchy of associations to each word (Finke et al., 1992). For example, when you saw the word ROUGH, your first associations were probably words such as TOUGH and SOFT. The word DRAFT was probably a fairly remote association in your hierarchy!

Scores on the RAT seem to be moderately correlated with creativity as measured by school performance. However, many studies conducted outside of school settings show much weaker correlations (Baron, 1994; Brown, 1989; Nickerson et al., 1985). For example, Andrews (1975) studied scientists who had directed research projects. RAT scores were correlated with scientific output only for those scientists who worked in environments where they felt professionally secure and could work independently. Of course, Andrews' observation may tell us something important about creativity. Specifically, even the most creative individuals may not produce creative work unless their environment nurtures their productivity.

Consensual Assessment Technique. Teresa Amabile has developed a third alternative to measuring creativity. She points out that we can look at creativity as a property of *products,* rather than of *people.* According to her **consensual assessment technique,** a product should be considered creative if observers who are familiar with the field agree that the product is indeed creative (Amabile, 1983, 1990, 1994). Her research indicates that judges who are familiar with an area tend to agree with one another in their creativity assessments. In one study, for example, trained artists rated young girls' artwork, and they agreed with one another in their judgments about which artwork was creative and which was not (Amabile, 1982). Their ratings also tended to agree with the ratings of art teachers and the ratings of novices.

Amabile's technique has some clear advantages. For example, it'a hard to argue with the logic of a definition of creativity that can be paraphrased, "If experts think this work is creative, then it is." In addition, this straightforward measurement technique facilitates research on the factors that can influence creativity. We will look at some of this research in the final section.

Investment Theory of Creativity. Financial experts tell us that the route to wise investment is to buy low and sell high. Similarly, Sternberg and Lubart (1995) propose that creative people, who deal in the world of ideas, also buy low and sell high. That is, they produce a creative idea when no one else is interested in the "investment." At a later time, when the idea has become popular, they move on to a new creative project.

What are the characteristics of these people who are wise creative investors? According to Sternberg and Lubart's **investment theory of creativity,** the essential attributes are intelligence, knowledge, motivation, an encouraging environment, and appropriate thinking style and personality. In order to work creatively, you'll need all six of these attributes. In other words, a person may qualify in five of the characteristics, but he or she may lack motivation; this person will probably not produce anything creative. You'll notice that this approach to creativity is consistent with Andrews' (1975) research on scientists. People who have creative personal attributes—but lack a supportive work environment—will not work creatively.

The investment theory of creativity is inherently appealing, especially because it emphasizes the complex prerequisites for creativity. We'll look forward to seeing whether the research confirms that multiple factors must be combined in order to produce creative performance.

Factors Influencing Creativity

Psychologists may disagree about definitions and theoretical approaches to creativity. However, they would agree that we should search for factors that might influence creativity, so that we can determine how to enhance creative performance. In this section, we'll explore two potentially influential factors—incubation and social factors.

Incubation and Creativity. Have you ever worked on a creative project and come to an impasse—then found that the solution leapt into your mind after you took a break? Many artists, scientists, and other creative people testify that incubation helps them solve problems creatively. *Incubation* is defined as a situation in which you are initially unsuccessful in solving a problem, but you are more likely to solve the problem after taking a break, rather than continuing to work on the problem without interruption (Smith, 1995b).

Incubation sounds plausible, and some research shows that incubation improves creative problem solving (e.g., Houtz & Frankel, 1992). However, in well-controlled research, incubation is not consistently demonstrated (Baron, 1994; Gilhooly, 1988). Perhaps more ecologically valid research should be conducted with creative individuals solving real-life artistic, scientific, and conceptual problems. You may want to try your own informal research to see whether incubation facilitates your creative problem solving. If your efforts seem to be blocked, set the problem aside and work on something completely different. Does a solution occur to you shortly after you return to the problem?

In those cases in which incubation *does* work, what would be a likely mechanism? Some theorists propose that unconscious processes are at work during that incubation period. Another possibility, currently favored by cognitive psychologists, is that top-down factors such as mental set and functional fixedness may temporarily block you from going beyond the problem space. If you keep working on the problem in those circumstances, you'll keep retrieving the same useless ideas. However, if you wait a while or change the location in which you are working, you are likely to represent the problem differently. With a different problem representation, you may now solve the problem creatively (Finke et al., 1992; Smith, 1995b).

Social Factors Influencing Creativity. In the research by Andrews (1975) and in Sternberg and Lubart's (1995) investment theory of creativity, we found that social factors in people's environment can influence their creativity. Theresa Amabile (1983, 1990, 1994) has examined these social factors in more detail.

For example, Amabile (1983, 1990) has shown that people are less creative when they know that others will be evaluating their work. In a representative experiment, college students were told to compose a poem. Half were told that the experimenter was simply interested in their handwriting, not the content of the poem, and therefore they did not expect to be evaluated on their poems. The other half were told that the experimenter was interested in the poem's content, and they would receive a copy of the judges' evaluations of their poems. Therefore, these

=== FIGURE 10.5 ===

THE INFLUENCE OF EVALUATION EXPECTATION AND WORKING CONDITION ON CREATIVITY. BASED ON AMABILE (1983).

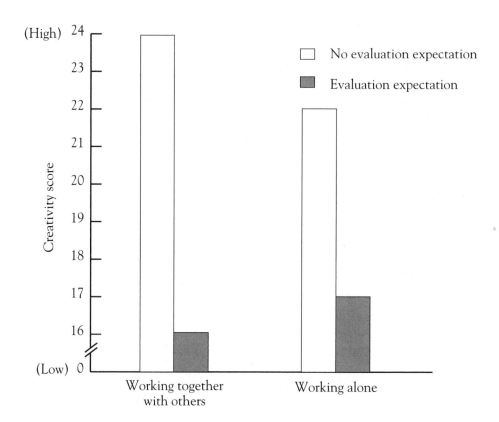

people expected to be evaluated. Half the people in each group worked alone, and half worked with others who were also composing poems.

Each poem was judged according to the consensual assessment technique, using judges who were poets. Figure 10.5 shows the results. As you can see, people produced poems that were much less creative when they expected to be evaluated. Creativity was inhibited by evaluation expectation, whether people worked in isolation or with others. However, people were equally creative in the "working together" and "working alone" conditions.

Amabile (1983) presents other convincing evidence that evaluation expectation can undermine creativity. For instance, the effect holds true for both adults and children, and for both artistic creativity and verbal creativity (Amabile, 1983, 1990; Hennessey & Amabile, 1984, 1988). When you expect your work to be evaluated, the product may not be less appealing or less technically appropriate, but it may be less creative.

Additional research has documented how other social factors can also influence creativity. For example, creativity may be reduced when someone is watching you while you are working, when you must compete for prizes, and when someone restricts your choices about how you can express your creativity (Amabile, 1990, 1994). In some cases—but not all—creativity may be reduced when you are offered a reward for being creative (Amabile, 1990; Eisenberger & Selbst, 1994).

Undergraduate students in psychology often think that all the interesting research questions have already been answered. In the area of creativity, we certainly have not answered all the questions. Furthermore, if we seriously accept the challenge of problem finding that was raised at the beginning of the chapter, we probably have not yet discovered many of the interesting questions!

SECTION SUMMARY: CREATIVITY

1. Numerous definitions have been proposed for creativity; one common definition is that creativity involves finding a solution that is both unusual and useful.
2. Creativity can be measured by Guilford's Divergent Production Test and Mednick and Mednick's Remote Associates Test; results on the validity of these two tests are mixed. A newer method is Amabile's consensual assessment technique, in which a product is considered to be creative if experts in that area agree that it is creative.
3. A new approach to creativity, called investment theory, proposes that creativity requires intelligence, knowledge, motivation, an encouraging environment, and appropriate thinking style and personality.
4. Well-controlled research sometimes fails to support the idea that incubation encourages creative problem solving.
5. The social conditions that can influence creativity include the anticipation of evaluation, being watched while working, competition, restricted choice, and being offered a reward.

CHAPTER REVIEW QUESTIONS

1. Try to recall a problem that you found difficult to understand, either from an academic area or from other aspects of your life. Which of Greeno's three requirements for understanding (coherence, correspondence, and relationship to background knowledge) were not met in this problem?
2. This chapter examined six different methods of representing a problem. Return to the description of these methods and point out how each method could be used to solve a problem you have faced either in college classes or in your personal life during recent weeks.
3. In problem solving, how do algorithms differ from heuristics? When you solve problems, what situations encourage which of these two approaches?

Describe a situation in which the means-ends heuristic was more useful than an algorithm.

4. What barriers prevent our successful use of the analogy approach to problem solving? Think of an area in which you are an expert (an academic subject, a hobby, or work-related knowledge) and point out whether you are skilled in recognizing the structural similarities shared by problem isomorphs.

5. Think of a different area of expertise that you have, and point out the seven cognitive areas in which you are likely to have an advantage over a novice.

6. How are mental set and functional fixedness related to each other, and how do they limit problem solving? Why would incubation—when it works—help in overcoming these two barriers to effective problem solving?

7. Metacognition was mentioned twice in this chapter. Discuss these two applications, and point out how metacognitive measures can help us determine which problems require insight and which do not.

8. Think of a kind of problem that you seem to solve more effectively by talking aloud as you work on the problem. Similarly, what kind of problem seems to be solved less effectively by talking aloud? Does this match the conclusions in the section on the effects of language on problem solving?

9. The influence of the environment on problem solving was discussed in several places—in connection with the analogical approach, an approach to creativity, and factors influencing creativity. Using this information, point out why environmental factors are important in problem solving.

10. Imagine that you are a supervisor of 10 employees in a small company. Describe how you might use the material in this chapter to encourage more effective problem solving and greater creativity.

NEW TERMS

problem solving
initial state
goal state
obstacles
understanding
matrix
hierarchical tree diagram
algorithm
exhaustive search
problem space
heuristic
means-ends heuristic
subproblems

computer simulation
General Problem Solver
  (GPS)
analogy approach
situated learning
problem isomorphs
target problem
source problem
surface features
structural features
expertise
mental set

functional fixedness
insight problem
noninsight problem
creativity
divergent production
Remote Associates Test
  (RAT)
consensual assessment
  technique
investment theory of
  creativity
incubation

RECOMMENDED READINGS

Ericsson, K. A. (Ed.). (1996b). *The road to excellence: The acquisition of expert performance in the arts and sciences, sports, and games.* Mahwah, NJ: Erlbaum. One of the most widely published experts in expertise is K. Anders Ericsson; chapters in his edited book examine expertise in problem solving, but also expertise in areas such as music and sports.

Finke, R. A., Ward, T. B., & Smith, S. M. (1992). *Creative cognition: Theory, research, and applications.* Cambridge, MA: MIT Press. This book on creative problem solving includes chapters on visual imagery, inventions, and imagination—as well as topics we have explored in the current chapter.

Halpern, D. F. (1996). *Thought and knowledge: An introduction to critical thinking* (3rd ed.). Mahwah, NJ: Erlbaum. Diane Halpern writes clearly and engagingly about critical thinking and higher mental processes; her book helps you understand the relationship between problem solving and critical thinking.

Sternberg, R. J., & Davidson, J. E. (Eds.). (1995). *The nature of insight.* Cambridge, MA: MIT Press. This book contains 17 chapters on the role of insight in problem solving; the final chapter by Jonathan Schooler and his colleagues provides a particularly useful summary of the book.

Weisberg, R. W. (1993). *Creativity: Beyond the myth of genius.* New York: Freeman. Weisberg argues that creativity is simply an extension of ordinary thinking and problem solving. Although his view may not currently be most dominant, he offers one of the most comprehensive and readable summaries of the research on problem solving.

ANSWERS TO DEMONSTRATIONS

Demonstration 10.4   In the hospital room problem, Ms. Anderson has mononucleosis, and she is in Room 104.

Demonstration 10.5   In the Hobbits-and-Orcs problem (with R representing the right bank and L representing the left bank), here are the steps in the solution:

1. Move 2 Orcs, R to L.
2. Move 1 Orc, L to R.
3. Move 2 Orcs, R to L.
4. Move 1 Orc, L to R.
5. Move 2 Hobbits, R to L.
6. Move 1 Orc, 1 Hobbit, L to R.
7. Move 2 Hobbits, R to L.
8. Move 1 Orc, L to R.
9. Move 2 Orcs, R to L.
10. Move 1 Orc, L to R.
11. Move 2 Orcs, R to L.

Demonstration 10.6   In the beginning, Mr. and Mrs. Renshaw both agree upon the number of plants to buy. Therefore, we know that 10, 4, and 5 must all go evenly into that number—whatever it is. Thus, the first thing to do is to find the smallest number that is evenly divisible by 10, 4, and 5; that number is 20. So we know that the original number of vegetable plants the Renshaws were thinking of buying could be any multiple of 20 (that is, 20, 40, 60, 80, and so on). But then they decide to buy 2 additional plants they had not originally planned to buy. Thus, the total number of plants they actually end up buying must be 2 more than the multiples of 20 listed earlier (that is, 22, 42, 62, 82, and so on). This means that 10, 4, and 5 will no longer go evenly into the total number of plants. However, the problem states that they eventually agree to buy 6 of each vegetable, so the total number of plants must be evenly divisible by 6. The smallest total number of plants that is evenly divisible by 6 is 42, so the answer is 42 (based on Novick, 1988, p. 513).

Demonstration 10.7 The numbers are in alphabetical order; your mental set probably suggested that the numbers were in some mathematical sequence, not a language-based sequence.

Demonstration 10.8 (a)

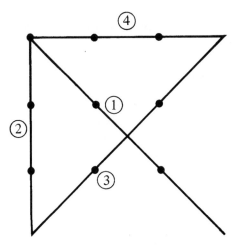

Incidentally, Adams (1979) lists a number of other, nontraditional solutions, such as cutting the puzzle apart into thirds, taping the dots together in a row, and drawing a single line through all nine dots.

Demonstration 10.8 (b)

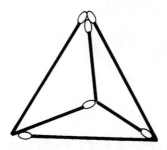

Demonstration 10.10   Answers to the remote associates items:

1. PRINCE
2. DOG
3. COLD
4. GLASSES
5. CLUB
6. BOAT
7. DEFENSE
8. BLACK
9. PIT
10. WRITER

DEDUCTIVE REASONING AND DECISION MAKING

INTRODUCTION

DEDUCTIVE REASONING

An Overview of Conditional Reasoning
Difficulties with Negative Information
Difficulties with Abstract Reasoning Problems
The Belief-Bias Effect
Constructing Only One Model of the Premises
Making an Illicit Conversion
Trying to Confirm a Hypothesis, Rather Than Trying to Disprove It
Failing to Transfer Knowledge to a New Task

DECISION MAKING

The Representativeness Heuristic
The Availability Heuristic
The Anchoring and Adjustment Heuristic
In Depth: The Framing Effect
Overconfidence in Decisions
New Developments in Decision Making: The Optimists versus the Pessimists

========================= **Preview** =========================

This chapter considers how people perform two complex cognitive tasks, deductive reasoning and decision making. The topics of problem solving (Chapter 10), deductive reasoning, and decision making are all included within the topic of thinking.

In deductive reasoning tasks, you must infer the logical consequences of the given information; in this chapter, we will focus on conditional reasoning, which describes "if . . . then . . ." relationships. People make several systematic errors on conditional reasoning tasks; for example, they may be influenced by their prior beliefs, and they may fail to appreciate all possible interpretations of the premises.

Decision making means assessing and choosing among several alternatives; we often use heuristics or "rules of thumb" to make decisions. Heuristics *usually* lead to the correct decision, but we sometimes apply them inappropriately. One heuristic is representativeness, in which we judge a sample to be likely because it looks similar to the population from which it was selected. For example, if you toss a coin six times, the outcome H T H H T T looks very likely. We pay so much attention to representativeness that we sometimes ignore important information such as sample size and base rates. A second heuristic, the availability heuristic, is used when we estimate frequency in terms of how easily we can think of examples of something. For example, you estimate the number of students from Illinois at your college to be large if you can easily think of examples. Unfortunately, availability is often influenced by two irrelevant factors—recency and familiarity—and so we often make decision errors when we use this heuristic. The third heuristic, the anchoring and adjustment heuristic, is used when we begin by guessing a first approximation (an anchor) and then make an adjustment, based on other information. This strategy is reasonable, except that our adjustments are typically too small. Other topics we'll discuss in this chapter include (1) how context and wording influence decisions, (2) why people are often overconfident, and (3) some new, more optimistic interpretations of human decision making.

INTRODUCTION

You use deductive reasoning every day, although you might not spontaneously choose that formal-sounding label. For example, a friend tells you, "If I find that newspaper ad for the apartment, I'll give you a call." The afternoon passes without a phone call, and you draw the logical conclusion, "My friend did not find the ad." Every day, you also make dozens of decisions. Should you ask Professor Adams for the letter of recommendation, or should you try Professor Sanchez?

Problem solving (which we discussed in the previous chapter), deductive reasoning, and decision making are all interrelated, and we will note several similarities among these tasks throughout this chapter. All three topics are included in the general category called *thinking*. ***Thinking*** is defined as going beyond the information given (Galotti, 1989). That is, you begin with several pieces of information, and you must manipulate that information to solve a problem, to draw a conclusion on a deductive reasoning task, or to make a decision.

Our topics for this chapter—deductive reasoning and decision making—are clearly related. ***Deductive reasoning*** requires people to infer the logical consequences of information that they are given or to evaluate whether a logical argument is valid (Evans, 1993). In reasoning, the premises are either true or false, and the rules for drawing conclusions are clearly specified. Our second topic, ***decision making,*** refers to assessing and choosing among several alternatives. In contrast to deductive reasoning, decision making is much more ambiguous. Much of the information may be missing. In addition, no clear-cut rules tell us how to proceed from the information to the conclusions. Furthermore, the consequences of that decision won't be immediately apparent (Evans, Over, & Manketelow, 1993). (In fact, you may never know whether you would have been wiser to choose Professor Adams or Professor Sanchez.) As you might imagine, people who make wise decisions are likely to be successful both in school and in the workplace.

In real life, the uncertainty of decision making is more common than the certainty of deductive reasoning. However, we humans find both deductive reasoning and decision making to be difficult tasks. As this chapter also demonstrates, we do not always reach the appropriate conclusions.

DEDUCTIVE REASONING

One of the most common kinds of deductive reasoning tasks is called conditional reasoning. ***Conditional reasoning*** or ***propositional reasoning*** problems tells us about the relationship between conditions. Here's a typical conditional reasoning task:

> If the moon is shining, I can see without a flashlight.
> I cannot see without a flashlight.
> Therefore, the moon is not shining.

Notice that this problem tells us about the relationship between conditions, such as the relationship between the moon shining and the need for a flashlight. The kind of conditional reasoning we consider in this section explores "if . . . then . . ." relationships, and people are instructed to judge whether the conclusion is valid or invalid. In this example, the conclusion "Therefore, the moon is not shining" is indeed valid.

Another common kind of deductive reasoning task is called a syllogism. A ***syllogism*** consists of two statements that we must assume to be true, plus a conclusion. Syllogisms involve quantities, so they use the words *all, none, some,* and other similar terms. Here's a typical syllogism:

> Some bankers are college graduates.
> Some college graduates are friendly.
> Therefore, some bankers are friendly.

People are instructed to judge whether the conclusion is true, false, or indeterminate. (In this case, the answer is indeterminate, especially because those bankers who are not college graduates may not be friendly.)

You could take a philosophy course in logic that would spend an entire semester teaching you about the structure and solution of deductive reasoning problems like these. However, this section focuses on the *cognitive* factors that influence deductive reasoning. Accordingly, we will limit ourselves to conditional reasoning—the more straightforward kind of deductive reasoning task. However, syllogisms are influenced by virtually the same set of cognitive factors (Matlin, 1994). Let's first explore the nature of conditional reasoning. Then we'll see how reasoning is influenced by two factors: whether the statements include negative information and whether the problem is concrete or abstract. Then we'll discuss five different cognitive strategies that people typically use when they solve these problems.

An Overview of Conditional Reasoning

Conditional reasoning situations occur frequently in daily life, yet these problems are surprisingly difficult to solve correctly. Let's examine the formal principles that have been devised for solving these problems. First, however, try the conditional reasoning problems that are shown in Demonstration 11.1.

This demonstration illustrates **the propositional calculus,**[1] which is a system for categorizing the kinds of reasoning used in analyzing propositions or statements. Let's first introduce some basic terminology. The word **antecedent** means the proposition or statement that comes first; the antecedent is contained in the "if . . ." part of the sentence. The word **consequent** refers to the proposition that follows; it is the consequence. The consequent is contained in the "then . . ." part of the sentence. Sometimes we affirm part of the sentence, saying that it is true; sometimes we deny part of the sentence, saying that it is false.

By combining the two parts of the sentence with the two actions, we have four conditional reasoning situations:

1. **Affirming the antecedent** means that you say the "if . . ." part of the sentence is true. This kind of reasoning leads to a valid, or correct, conclusion.
2. **Affirming the consequent** means that you say the "then . . ." part of the sentence is true. This kind of reasoning leads to an incorrect conclusion. Notice in the second item that the conclusion, "Therefore, Nereyda is a psychology major" is incorrect because she could be an engineering major, a Spanish major, or any major in addition to psychology.

---

[1] By tradition, the word *the* is inserted here, forming the phrase *the propositional calculus,* rather than simply *propositional calculus.*

DEMONSTRATION 11.1

THE PROPOSITIONAL CALCULUS

Decide which of the following conclusions are valid and which are invalid. The answers are at the end of the chapter.

1. Affirming the antecedent.

   If today is Tuesday, then I have my bowling class.
   Today is Tuesday.
   Therefore, I have my bowling class.

2. Affirming the consequent.

   If Nereyda is a psychology major, then she is a student.
   Nereyda is a student.
   Therefore, Nereyda is a psychology major.

3. Denying the antecedent.

   If I am a first-year student, then I must register for next semester's classes today.
   I am not a first-year student.
   Therefore, I must not register for next semester's classes today.

4. Denying the consequent.

   If the judge is fair, then Susan is the winner.
   Susan is not the winner.
   Therefore, the judge is not fair.

We can easily see why people are tempted to affirm the consequent: In real life, we are often correct when we make this kind of reasoning error (Bell & Staines, 1981; Nickerson et al., 1985). For example, consider the propositions, "If a person is a talented singer, then he or she has musical abilities" and "Paula has musical abilities." It is a good bet that we can conclude Paula is indeed a talented singer; however, in logical reasoning we cannot rely on statements such as "It's a good bet that . . . ." (Furthermore, I remember a student whose musical skills as a violinist were exceptional, yet she sang off-key. The conclusion about her singing would have been incorrect.) As Theme 2 emphasizes, many cognitive errors can be traced to a strategy that usually works well. In this case, however, "it's a good bet that" is not the same as "always."

3. **Denying the antecedent** means that you say the "if . . ." part of the sentence is false. Denying the antecedent also leads to an incorrect conclusion. The conclusion of Item 3 in Demonstration 11.1—"I must not register for next semester's classes today"—is false, because it is possible that the members of your own class, as well as first-year students, must register today.

4. **Denying the consequent** means that you say the "then . . ." part of the sentence is false. This kind of reasoning leads to a correct conclusion.[2]

The four kinds of reasoning are presented in a matrix in Table 11.1. Make certain that you understand these and can make up your own examples for each kind.

Try noticing how often you use the two correct kinds of reasoning. For example, a traffic sign might read, "Left turns permitted on weekends." This sign could be translated into the "if . . . then . . ." form: "*If* it is a weekend, *then* left turns are permitted." You know that it is Saturday, a weekend day. By the method of affirming the antecedent, you conclude that left turns are permitted. Similarly, a judge says, "If I find Tom Smith guilty, he is going to jail." You learn that Tom Smith did not go to jail, so you conclude by the method of denying the consequent that Tom was judged not guilty.

═══════════════════ **TABLE 11.1.** ═══════════════════

THE PROPOSITIONAL CALCULUS: THE FOUR KINDS OF REASONING WITH EXAMPLES FOR THE STATEMENT, *"IF THIS IS AN APPLE, THEN THIS IS A FRUIT."*

		Portion of the statement
Action taken	*Antecedent*	*Consequent*
Affirm	Affirming the Antecedent (valid) *This is an apple; therefore this is a fruit.*	Affirming the Consequent (invalid) *This is a fruit; therefore this is an apple.*
Deny	Denying the Antecedent (invalid) *This is not an apple; therefore this is not a fruit.*	Denying the Consequent (valid) *This is not a fruit; therefore this is not an apple.*

───────

[2]If you have taken courses in research methods or statistics, you will recognize that scientific reasoning is based on the strategy of denying the consequent, that is, ruling out the null hypothesis.

Also, watch out for logical errors that you might be making. Think how the method of affirming the consequent might produce the wrong conclusion in the sentence, "If Mary likes me, then she will smile at me." Similarly, the method of denying the antecedent produces the wrong conclusion for the sentence, "If I get a D on this test, then I'll get a D in the course."

As you might guess, the four kinds of conditional reasoning tasks vary in their difficulty. Affirming the antecedent is easiest. In fact, people's performance in this condition is typically close to perfect (E. E. Smith et al., 1993). Taplin's (1971) research demonstrated that people were indeed most accurate in affirming the antecedent, next best in denying the consequent, and worst in denying the antecedent and in affirming the consequent. (Performance was equally poor for these last two kinds of reasoning.) Notice, then, that people are best at the correct kinds of reasoning. They are worst at the incorrect kinds of reasoning, which they mistakenly believe to be correct.

According to Theme 4, the cognitive processes are interrelated. Our ability on conditional reasoning tasks certainly illustrates this theme. Obviously, this kind of task requires language skills. Furthermore, research has confirmed that conditional reasoning relies upon working memory—primarily the central executive component of working memory that we discussed in Chapter 4 (Toms et al., 1993). We would expect the burden on working memory to be especially heavy when some of the propositions contain negative terms (rather than just positive ones) and when people are trying to solve abstract reasoning problems (rather than concrete ones). Let's examine these two topics before we consider several cognitive tendencies that are revealed on conditional reasoning tasks.

Difficulties With Negative Information

Theme 3 of this book states that people can handle positive information better than negative information. This principle is certainly true for conditional reasoning tasks. For example, try the following reasoning problem:

> If today is not Friday, then the office staff cannot wear casual clothes today.
> The office staff cannot wear casual clothes today.
> Therefore, today is not Friday.

This problem is much more challenging than a similar problem that begins "If today is Friday . . . ."

Research shows that people take longer to evaluate problems that contain negative information, and they are also more likely to make errors on these problems (Galotti, 1989; Garnham & Oakhill, 1994; Johnson-Laird et al., 1992; Ormerod et al., 1993). Working memory is especially likely to be strained when the problem involves denying the antecedent or denying the consequent. Most of us squirm when we see a reasoning problem that includes a statement like, "It is not true that today is not Friday." We are likely to make an error in translating either the initial statement or the conclusion into more accessible, positive forms.

Difficulties With Abstract Reasoning Problems

In general, people are more accurate when they solve reasoning problems that use concrete examples, rather than abstract ones. For example, you probably worked through the examples in Table 11.1 quite easily. In contrast, even short reasoning problems are difficult if they are abstract (Wason & Johnson-Laird, 1972). Try this abstract problem, for example:

> If an object is red, then it is rectangular.
> This object is not rectangular.
> Therefore, it is not red. (True or false?)

Other related research demonstrates that performance is better if the propositions are high in imagery (Clement & Falmagne, 1986). Furthermore, accuracy increases when people use diagrams to make the problem more concrete (Bauer & Johnson-Laird, 1993; Halpern, 1996). However, reasoning can sometimes be more difficult when the problems are concrete if our everyday knowledge interferes with logical principles. Let's see how this principle operates in the next section, on the belief-bias effect.

The Belief-Bias Effect

In our lives outside the psychology laboratory, our background knowledge helps us function well. Inside the psychology laboratory—and in a course on logic—this background information is counterproductive. For example, try the following problem (Cummins et al., 1991, p. 276):

> If my finger is cut, then it bleeds.
> My finger is bleeding.
> Therefore, my finger is cut.

In everyday life, that conclusion is almost certainly correct; why else would your finger be bleeding unless it was cut? (Of course, you might suggest that the finger was *punctured.*) However, in the world of logic, this cut-finger problem commits the error of affirming the consequent, so it cannot be correct. As Cummins and her colleagues (1991) found, people often accepted the logic as being correct when the conclusion matched people's "common sense" and when few alternative explanations were available. In contrast, they usually caught the flaw in the logic when many alternative explanations were available, as in this problem:

> If I eat candy often, then I have cavities.
> I have cavities.
> Therefore, I eat candy often. (p. 276)

The *belief-bias effect* occurs in reasoning when people make judgments based on prior beliefs, rather than on the rules of logic. The research on the belief-bias effect frequently examines its influence on syllogisms—those reasoning problems involving words such as *all, none,* and *some*—which we mentioned at the beginning of the chapter. In general, people are likely to make errors when the logic of the problem conflicts with their background knowledge (Evans, Newstead, & Byrne, 1993; Hilton et al., 1990; Newstead et al., 1992).

In a typical study, Markovitz and Nantel (1989) gave French-Canadian college students a series of syllogisms. The English translation for one of them is:

> All eastern countries are communist.[3]
> Canada is not an eastern country.
> Therefore, Canada is not communist.

Many of the students responded that the logic in this syllogism was correct, even though it used the invalid strategy of denying the antecedent. One explanation for results like these may be that people solve logical problems by trying to construct a mental model of the situation. If they can create a model that is consistent with the believable conclusions (e.g., that Canada is not communist), they announce that the reasoning is correct. As a consequence, they fail to construct other models to represent other possibilities—for example, one in which some non-eastern countries could be communist (Newstead et al., 1992).

The belief-bias effect is one more example of top-down processing (Theme 5). Our prior expectations help us organize our experiences and understand the world. When we see new information, in the form of a reasoning problem, we fit this information into our familiar framework. Thus, we do not pay enough attention to the specific information contained in the problem (Cohen, 1993a). We fail to question an invalid conclusion. Fortunately, however, when people receive appropriate instructions, the belief-bias effect is substantially reduced (Evans et al., 1994).

Constructing Only One Model of the Premises

According to Johnson-Laird and Byrne (1991), people often create only one model of a conditional reasoning problem—even in situations where the belief-bias effect is not relevant. This proposal is consistent with something you learned in Chapter 10: People may not search the problem space as thoroughly as they should.

For instance, consider this reasoning problem:

> If she meets her friend, then she will go to a play.
> She did not meet her friend.

---

[3]In deductive reasoning problems, you must accept that the premises are valid, even when they violate your background knowledge. Thus, the validity of a conclusion depends on the structure of an argument, rather than its validity in the real world.

Byrne (1989) found that 46% of her college-student participants erroneously concluded, "She will not go to a play." Apparently, students constructed a single mental model in which the only way she could go to the play was by meeting her friend. In another condition, Byrne added an extra premise, "If she meets her brother, then she will go to a play." Now only 4% drew the wrong conclusion, "She will not go to a play." Apparently, this extra hint encouraged them to construct an additional mental model involving the brother. They now saw that she might go to the play, even without the friend.

Inspecting a wide variety of reasoning problems, Johnson-Laird (1995) points out how reasoners tend to be prematurely satisfied with their answers on these problems: "If they reach a congenial conclusion they tend not to search for alternative models" (p. 1003). This premature focusing prevents us from exploring other ways of representing the reasoning problem (Legrenzi et al., 1993).

Making an Illicit Conversion

Another interpretive error that people often make in conditional reasoning problems is called an illicit conversion. An *illicit conversion* means that you inappropriately change part of the problem into another form. Wason and Johnson-Laird (1972) point out how this works when people use the method of denying the antecedent—an invalid method. The general form of this method is:

> If p, then q.
> p is not true.
> Therefore, q is not true.

The problem is that people use illicit conversion when they see the first statement. They convert it—inappropriately—into:

> If q, then p.

Then they attack that converted statement, using the method of denying the consequent, which is a valid method when used appropriately. They conclude, therefore, that q is not true.

In everyday reasoning situations, we can often use an illicit conversion and still reach a correct conclusion. For example, suppose that your dormitory consistently serves a different breakfast menu for each day of the week. Suppose that a friend is trying to guess what the dorm will serve for breakfast on a particular day, and she says, "If it's Tuesday, then we are having pancakes." You can reasonably conclude that the two parts of the statement can be converted to yield the statement, "If we are having pancakes, then it is Tuesday." However, in a formal reasoning task—unlike in real life—we must consider that pancakes may be served more often than once a week.

DEMONSTRATION 11.2

THE CONFIRMATION BIAS. BASED ON WASON (1968).

Imagine that each square below represents a card. Imagine that you are participating in a study in which the experimenter has told you that every card has a letter on one side and a number on the other side.

You are then given this rule about these four cards: "If a card has a vowel on one side, then it has an even number on the other side."

Your task is to decide which card or cards you would need to turn over in order to find out whether this rule is true or false. What is your answer? The correct answer is discussed in the text.

Trying to Confirm a Hypothesis, Rather Than Trying to Disprove It

Try Demonstration 11.2 now, before reading farther. Wason's (1968) selection task has inspired more research than any other deductive reasoning problem—and it has also raised many questions about whether humans are basically rational (Oaksford & Chater, 1994; Platt & Griggs, 1993a).

This task illustrates the ***confirmation bias;*** people would rather try to confirm a hypothesis than try to disprove it. Most people working on this classical selection task choose to turn over the *E* card. One review of the literature showed than an average of 89% of research participants selected this appropriate strategy (Oaksford & Chater, 1994). This strategy allowed them to confirm the hypothesis by the valid method of affirming the antecedent, because this card has a vowel on it. If this card has an even number on the other side, the rule is correct. If the number is odd, the rule is incorrect.

The other valid method in deductive reasoning is to deny the consequent. To accomplish this goal, you must choose to turn over the *7* card. The information about the other side of the *7* is very valuable— just as valuable as the information about the *E*. Remember that the rule is:

If a card has a vowel on its letter side, then it has an even number on its number side.

To deny the consequent, we need to check out a number side that is *not* an even number (in this case, the 7). People are eager to affirm the antecedent, but they are reluctant to deny the consequent by searching for counterexamples. This would be a wise attempt to reject a hypothesis, but people avoid this strategy. In a review of the literature, only 25% of research participants selected this appropriate strategy (Oaksford & Chater, 1994).

You may wonder why we did not need to check on the *J* and the *6*. If you reread the rule, you will notice that the rule did not say anything about consonants, such as *J*. The other side of the *J* could show an odd number, an even number, or even a Renoir painting, and we wouldn't care. The rule also doesn't specify what must appear on the other side of the even numbers, such as *6*. However, many people select the *6* to turn over because they perform an illicit conversion on the rule, so that it reads, "If a card has an even number on its number side, then it has a vowel on its letter side." Thus, they make an error by choosing the *6*.

Perhaps you notice that this preference for confirming a hypothesis—rather than disproving it—corresponds to Theme 3 of this book. On the selection task, we see that people who are given a choice would rather seek out positive information than negative information. We would rather know what something *is* than what it *is not*. This preference is so strong that even people with PhD degrees are no more likely than people with bachelor's degrees to answer the problem correctly (Jackson & Griggs, 1988).

In recent years, researchers have tested numerous versions of the classic selection task. Even a subtle change in the wording of the problem can change the results dramatically (Jackson & Griggs, 1990; Markovitz & Savary, 1992). Careful instructions about strategy can also have an impact (Griggs, 1995; Griggs & Jackson, 1990; Platt & Griggs, 1993a, 1995). As you may have guessed, performance is much better when the task is concrete and familiar (e.g., Cheng & Holyoak, 1985; Oakhill & Johnson-Laird, 1985; Pollard & Evans, 1987).

Let's consider a representative study that demonstrates how well people can do on a concrete version of this task, rather than the standard, abstract version you saw in Demonstration 11.2. Griggs and Cox (1982) tested college students in Florida using a variation of the selection task. This task focused on the drinking age, which was then 19. The problem was much more concrete and relevant to most college students. The participants in this study saw the following problem:

> On this task imagine that you are a police officer on duty. It is your job to ensure that people conform to certain rules. The cards in front of you have information about four people sitting at a table. On one side of a card is a person's age and on the other side of the card is what the person is drinking. Here is a rule: IF A PERSON IS DRINKING BEER, THEN THE PERSON MUST BE OVER 19 YEARS OF AGE. Select the card or cards that you definitely need to turn over to determine whether or not the people are violating the rule. (p. 415)

Four cards were presented, labeled DRINKING A BEER, DRINKING A COKE, 16 YEARS OF AGE, and 22 YEARS OF AGE, respectively.

Griggs and Cox found that 73% of the students who tried the drinking age problem made the correct selection, in contrast to 0% who tried the standard, abstract form of the selection task. The difference in performance between concrete and abstract tasks is especially dramatic when the wording of the selection task implies some kind of social contract designed to prevent people from cheating (Cosmides,

1989; Gigerenzer & Hug, 1992; Platt & Griggs, 1993b). Cosmides argues that evolution may have encouraged people to develop specialized skills in understanding important, adaptive problems. In particular, we humans may be especially competent in understanding the kinds of rules that are necessary for cooperative interactions in a society. In contrast, we may be less skilled in understanding rules that have no implications for social interactions—for example, abstract problems about cards, letters, and numbers.

How can we translate the confirmation bias into everyday experiences? One example is that consumers may keep using their favorite, familiar brand, rather than seek evidence that it doesn't work. Police investigators and juries in legal cases may also be eager to confirm a suspect's guilt, rather than seek ways to disprove the guilt (Davidsson & Wahlund, 1992; Kuhn et al., 1994). In any case, try noticing your own behavior when you are searching for evidence. Do you consistently look for information that will confirm that you are *right*, or do you valiantly pursue ways in which your conclusion can be *wrong*?

Failing to Transfer Knowledge to a New Task

So far, we have seen that people struggle with conditional reasoning problems that include negative or abstract information. Their accuracy is also reduced because of the belief-bias effect. In addition—because they construct only one model of the premises—they make illicit conversions, and they only try to confirm their hypotheses. Perhaps you could have predicted the final source of errors, based on the information in the chapter on problem solving. In that chapter, we saw that people have trouble appreciating the similarity between a math problem that they are currently working on and one they solved earlier. Similarly, people have trouble appreciating the similarity between two versions of the selection task illustrated in Demonstration 11.2 (Klaczynski et al., 1989). Other research has shown that students who study formal logic in philosophy classes also have difficulty applying their knowledge in new situations (Salmon, 1991).

This overview of conditional reasoning does not provide much evidence for Theme 2 of this book. At least in the psychology laboratory, people are not especially accurate when they try to solve "if . . . then . . ." kinds of problems. However, the circumstances are usually more favorable in our daily lives, where problems are concrete and situations are consistent with our belief biases. Deductive reasoning is such a difficult task that we are not as efficient and accurate as we are in perception and memory—two areas in which humans truly excel.

SECTION SUMMARY: DEDUCTIVE REASONING

1. Conditional reasoning involves "if . . . then . . ." relationships; performance is most accurate for the two valid categories, for affirmative (rather than negative) statements, and for concrete problems.

2. The belief-bias effect interferes with conditional reasoning; top-down processing encourages people to trust their prior expectations, rather than the principles of logic.

3. Another factor that interferes with conditional reasoning is that people often create only one representation of a conditional reasoning problem, so they do not search for alternative answers to the problem.

4. Additional errors are created by illicit conversions, in which people convert the premise "If q, then p" into "If p, then q."

5. Furthermore, people typically try to confirm a hypothesis, rather than trying to reject it. A variety of factors influence performance on the selection task (which assesses this confirmation bias); for example, accuracy is enhanced when the task is concrete.

6. Finally, people often fail to transfer their knowledge to a new task.

7. Although people do not perform well on these reasoning tasks in the laboratory, their accuracy may be greater in real-life situations.

DECISION MAKING

As you have just seen, reasoning uses established rules to draw clear-cut conclusions. In contrast, when we make decisions, we have no established rules, and we also do not know the consequences of those decisions (Tversky & Fox, 1995). You may be missing some critical information, and you may not trust other information. Should you apply to graduate school or get a job after college? Should you take social psychology in the morning or in the afternoon? Given all the sources of potential uncertainty, no list of rules—such as the propositional calculus—can help you assess the relative merits of each option.

Psychologists have approached the study of decision making in several different ways. These different approaches are described in recent books about decision making (e.g., Klein et al., 1993; Mellers & Baron, 1993; Payne et al., 1993; Piatelli-Palmarini, 1994; Poulton, 1994; Plous, 1993). For example, several approaches weigh the various costs and benefits of various outcomes, and then researchers determine whether humans actually choose the outcome with the highest expected value (Frisch & Clemen, 1994; Smyth et al., 1994).

In this section, however, we will emphasize the approach that focuses on decision-making heuristics. As you'll recall from previous chapters, *heuristics* are rules of thumb or strategies that are likely to produce a correct solution. As a consequence, we humans do not always make wise decisions because we fail to appreciate the limitations of these heuristics. As one theorist wrote, humans are "sometimes systematically irrational" (Baron, 1991, p. 487).

Throughout this section, you will often see the names of two researchers, Daniel Kahneman and Amos Tversky. These two individuals proposed that a small number of heuristics guide human decision making. As they emphasize, the strategies that normally guide us toward the correct decision may sometimes lead us astray—consistent with Theme 2 of this book.

Throughout this part of the chapter, we will discuss many studies that illustrate errors in decision making. However, these errors should not lead us to conclude that humans are limited, foolish creatures (Crandall, 1984). Instead, keep in mind a caution expressed by Nisbett and Ross (1980). They argue that people's decision-making strategies are well adapted to handle a wide range of problems. However, these same strategies become a liability when they are applied beyond that range. Cognitive psychologists interested in decision making often emphasize the errors that people make (Robins & Craik, 1993). This emphasis on what can go wrong is parallel to perception researchers' interest in visual illusions:

> Perception researchers have shown that in spite of, and largely because of, people's exquisite perceptual capacities, they are subject to certain perceptual illusions. No serious scientist, however, is led by such demonstrations to conclude that the perceptual system under study is inherently faulty. Similarly, we conclude from our own research that we are observing not an inherently faulty cognitive apparatus but rather, one that manifests certain explicable flaws. Indeed, in human inference as in perception, we suspect that many of people's failings will prove to be closely related to, or even an unavoidable cost of, their greatest strengths. (Nisbett & Ross, p. 14)

In decision making—as in other cognitive areas—a heuristic that usually leads to correct conclusions can produce errors if it is used inappropriately. Let us explore three classic decision-making heuristics: representativeness, availability, and anchoring and adjustment. Then we will consider two general issues in decision making: (1) how wording and context influence decisions and (2) overconfidence in decision making. In the final section, we will examine some of the new approaches to decision making. (Try Demonstrations 11.3 and 11.4 before reading further.)

The Representativeness Heuristic

Here's a remarkable coincidence: President's Kennedy's secretary was named Lincoln, and President Lincoln's secretary was named Kennedy. Many people who learn about this symmetry consider it proof of a mysterious harmony in the universe (Paulos, 1989). Somehow that coincidence does not look random enough to be explained away by chance.

Now consider this example. Suppose that you have a regular penny with one head (H) and one tail (T), and you toss it six times. Which outcome seems most likely, T H H T H T or H H H T T T?

If you are like most people, you would guess that T H H T H T would be the most likely outcome of those two possibilities. After all, you know that coin tossing should produce heads and tails in random order, and the order T H H T H T looks much more random than H H H T T T.

A sample looks *representative* if it is similar in important characteristics to the population from which it was selected. For example, if a sample was selected by a random process, then that sample must look random in order for people to say it looks representative. Thus, T H H T H T is a sample that would be judged representative because it has an equal number of heads and tails (which would be

DEMONSTRATION 11.3

SAMPLE SIZE AND REPRESENTATIVENESS

A nearby town is served by two hospitals. About 45 babies are born each day in the larger hospital. About 15 babies are born each day in the smaller hospital. Approximately 50% of all babies are boys, as you know. However, the exact percentage of babies who are boys will vary from day to day. Some days it may be higher than 50%, some days it may be lower. For a period of one year, both the larger hospital and the smaller hospital recorded the number of days on which more than 60% of the babies born were boys. Which hospital do you think recorded more such days?

_____ The larger hospital
_____ The smaller hospital
_____ About the same (say, within 5% of each other)

DEMONSTRATION 11.4

BASE RATES AND REPRESENTATIVENESS. KAHNEMAN AND TVERSKY (1973), p. 241.

Imagine that some psychologists have administered personality tests to 30 engineers and 70 lawyers, all people who are successful in their fields. Brief descriptions were written for each of the 30 engineers and the 70 lawyers. A sample description follows. Judge that description by indicating the probability that the person described is an engineer. Use a scale from 0 to 100.

> Jack is a 45-year-old man. He is married and has four children. He is generally conservative, careful, and ambitious. He shows no interest in political and social issues and spends most of his free time on his many hobbies which include home carpentry, sailing, and mathematical puzzles.

The probability that the man is one of the 30 engineers in the sample of 100 is _____ %.

the case in random coin-tosses). Furthermore, T H H T H T would be judged representative because the order of the T's and H's looks random rather than orderly.

According to Kahneman and Tversky (1972), we often use the ***representativeness heuristic***, judging a sample to be likely on the basis of similarity to the population from which a sample was selected, as well as on the basis of random-looking appearance. Here is another way of viewing representativeness, related to a topic we discussed in Chapter 7. A sample looks representative if it resembles a prototype (Pitz & Sachs, 1984). The sample T H H T H T looks like a prototypical sample of coin tosses, whereas the sample H H H T T T does not.

According to the representativeness heuristic, we believe that random-looking outcomes are more likely than orderly looking outcomes—as long as the outcome has been produced by a random process. In reality, however, a random process occasionally produces an outcome that looks too orderly. Has a cashier ever added up your bill, and the sum looked *too* orderly, say, $22.22? You might even be tempted to check the arithmetic, because addition is a process that should yield a random-looking outcome. You would be less likely to check the bill if it were $21.97, because that very random-looking outcome is a more representative kind of answer. But chance alone often produces an orderly sum like $22.22, just as chance alone often produces orderly pairings like Kennedy-Lincoln and Lincoln-Kennedy.

Kahneman and Tversky (1972) conducted several experiments that emphasize the importance of representativeness. In one study, for example, they asked people to make judgments about families with six children. People judged the sequence G B B G B G to be more likely than the sequence B B B G G G. People base their decisions on representativeness, rather than on actual probability. Be sure you tried Demonstration 11.3 on page 399 before you read further.

Sample Size and Representativeness. When we make a decision, representativeness is such a compelling heuristic that we often ignore other important information, such as sample size. How did you respond to Demonstration 11.3? When Kahneman and Tversky (1972) asked college students this question, 56% responded, "About the same." In other words, the majority of students thought that a large hospital and a small hospital were equally likely to report having at least 60% baby boys born on a given day. Thus, they ignored sample size.

In reality, however, sample size is an important characteristic that should be considered whenever you make decisions. A large sample is statistically more likely than a small sample to reflect the true proportions in a population. For example, if approximately 50% of all babies are boys in a population, then a large sample is likely to have close to 50% boy babies. For instance, it is unlikely that 40 of the 45 babies in the large hospital—about 90%—would be boys. It is much more likely for about 90% of the babies in the small hospital to be boys; 13 boys out of 15 babies would not be an unusual outcome. However, people are often unaware that deviations from a population proportion are more likely in these small samples. Instead, representativeness often guides their decisions: Deviations from representativeness— such as more than 60% boy babies—seem equally likely, whether the sample is large or small.

Tversky and Kahneman (1971) point out that we should believe in the **law of large numbers,** which states that large samples will be representative of the population from which they are selected. The law of large numbers is a correct law. However, we often commit the **small-sample fallacy** by assuming that small samples will be representative of the population from which they are selected (Poulton, 1994). The small-sample fallacy leads us to incorrect decisions.

We often commit the small-sample fallacy in social situations, as well as in relatively abstract statistics problems. For example, we may draw unwarranted conclusions about a group of people on the basis of a small number of group members (Hamilton & Sherman, 1994; Rothbart & John, 1985). We often form stereotypes when we fall victim to the small-sample fallacy. One effective way of combating inappropriate stereotypes is to become acquainted with a large number of people from the target group, for example, through exchange programs with groups of people from other countries.

In some cases, however, people appropriately favor the law of large numbers, and they do not commit the small-sample fallacy (Poulton, 1994). For example, research by Well and his colleagues (1990) showed that college students know that the statistical mean (average) for a large sample is likely to be close to the mean for the entire population. They also know that the mean for a small sample can be very different from the population mean. However, students fail to understand the implications of this information. Specifically, they do not realize that if the mean for a small sample shows more variability, you are more likely to find a deviant mean (for example, more than 60% boys in a sample of babies).

Other research has shown that there are tremendous individual differences in answering sample-size problems (Pollard & Evans, 1983). Some people find the task difficult, whereas others realize that large sample sizes are less likely to contain deviant distributions.

Furthermore, people with expertise in a given area are less likely to commit the small-sample fallacy. For example, people with experience in team sports appropriately use the law of large numbers for a prediction about the probable outcome of a football game (Kunda & Nisbett, 1986). Also, Fong and his colleagues (1986) found that people could be trained to appreciate the law of large numbers by being taught about the concept and seeing some typical examples of the small-sample fallacy.

In summary, representativeness is such a strong heuristic that people often ignore other characteristics of the sample that should be important, such as sample size. However, people will often pay appropriate attention to the law of large numbers when they judge the mean, when they have had experience in a problem area, and when they have received formal training.

Base Rate and Representativeness. Representativeness is such a compelling heuristic that people also ignore the **base rate,** or how often the item occurs in the population. Be sure you tried Demonstration 11.4 before we proceed. Using problems like the one in this demonstration, Kahneman and Tversky (1973) showed that people rely on representativeness when they are asked to judge category membership. They focus almost exclusively on whether a description is representative of members of each category. By emphasizing representativeness, they commit the ***base-rate fallacy,*** underemphasizing important information about base rate (Hinsz & Tindale, 1992).

In one study, people were presented with a personality sketch of an imaginary person named Steve. Steve was described in the following words:

> Steve is very shy and withdrawn, invariably helpful, but with little interest in people, or in the world of reality. A meek and tidy soul, he has a need for order and structure, and a passion for detail. (Tversky & Kahneman, 1974, p. 1124)

After reading the passage, people were asked to judge Steve's occupation. A list of possibilities—such as farmer, salesperson, airline pilot, librarian, and physician—was supplied. If people pay attention to base rates, they should select a profession that has a high base rate in the population, such as a salesperson. However, people used the representativeness heuristic, and they tended to guess that Steve was a librarian. The description of Steve was highly similar to (that is, representative of) the stereotype of a librarian.

You might argue, however, that the experiment with Steve was unfair. After all, Tversky and Kahneman did not make the base rates of the various professions at all prominent in the problem. People may not have considered the fact that salespeople are more common than librarians. Well, the base rate was made very clear in Demonstration 11.4; you were told that the base rate was 30 engineers and 70 lawyers in the population. Did you make use of this base rate and guess that Jack was highly likely to be a lawyer? Most people ignored this base-rate information and judged on the basis of representativeness. In fact, this description is highly representative of our stereotype for engineers, and so people guess a high percentage for the answer to the question (Kahneman & Tversky, 1973).

Kahneman and Tversky (1973) point out how their studies are related to Bayes' theorem. ***Bayes' theorem*** states that judgments should be influenced by two factors, base rate and the likelihood ratio. The ***likelihood ratio*** is the ratio of the probability that the description came from population A, divided by the probability that the description came from population B. For example, in the engineer-versus-lawyer decision, let us say that engineers represent population A and lawyers represent population B. Now the description in Demonstration 11.4 is probably much more representative of a typical engineer than of a typical lawyer. Thus, the likelihood ratio is very high, because the probability that the passage describes an engineer (from population A) is much greater than the probability that the passage describes a lawyer (from population B). We seem to base our decision on this likelihood ratio; meanwhile, we ignore base rates. Because people often ignore base rates, they are not obeying Bayes' theorem, and they can make unwise decisions.

We should emphasize, however, that people vary widely in the way they tackle problems. Furthermore, some problems—and some alternative wordings of problems—produce more accurate decisions (Gigerenzer & Hoffrage, 1995; Pollard &

DEMONSTRATION 11.5

THE CONJUNCTION FALLACY

Read the following paragraph:

> Linda is 31 years old, single, outspoken, and very bright. She majored in philosophy. As a student, she was deeply concerned with issues of discrimination and social justice, and also participated in antinuclear demonstrations.

Now rank the following options in terms of their likelihood in describing Linda. Give a ranking of 1 to the most likely option and a ranking of 8 to the least likely option:

_____ Linda is a teacher at an elementary school.

_____ Linda works in a bookstore and takes Yoga classes.

_____ Linda is active in the feminist movement.

_____ Linda is a psychiatric social worker.

_____ Linda is a member of the League of Women Voters.

_____ Linda is a bank teller.

_____ Linda is an insurance salesperson.

_____ Linda is a bank teller and is active in the feminist movement.

Evans, 1983; Poulton, 1994). Training sessions also encourage students to use base-rate information appropriately (Gebotys & Claxton-Oldfield, 1989; Ginossar & Trope, 1987).

Unfortunately, however, decision makers often fail to evaluate the credibility of the source for information (Carlson, 1995). For example, Hinsz and Tindale (1992) found that college students did not carefully consider the trustworthiness of their source for the likelihood ratio. Specifically, they trusted this source more when it was provided by a human source (an eyewitness report) than when it was provided by a technical source (a report from a laboratory). As you know from Chapter 5, eyewitness reports can often be inaccurate. Think about some well-known court trials; can you recall any where jurors tended to discount information from lab reports?

You should also be alert for other everyday examples of the base-rate fallacy. For instance, one study of pedestrians killed at intersections showed that 10% were killed when crossing at a signal that said "walk." In contrast, only 6% were killed when crossing at a signal that said "stop" (Poulton, 1994). Does that mean that—for your own safety—you should only cross the street when the signal says "stop"? I'd prefer to urge you to reconsider the base rates; many more people cross the street when the signal says "walk." (Try Demonstration 11.5 now.)

======================= FIGURE 11.1 =======================

THE INFLUENCE OF TYPE OF STATEMENT AND LEVEL OF STATISTICAL SOPHISTICATION ON LIKELIHOOD RATINGS. (NOTE: LOW NUMBERS ON THE RANKING INDICATE THAT PEOPLE THINK THE EVENT IS MORE LIKELY.)

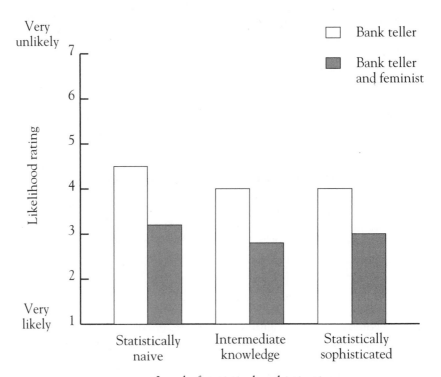

Level of statistical sophistication

The Conjunction Fallacy and Representativeness. Try Demonstration 11.5 before you read farther. Now inspect your answers. Which did you rank more likely, that Linda is a bank teller, or that Linda is a bank teller and is active in the feminist movement? Demonstration 11.5 is one of the questions that Tversky and Kahneman (1983) tested in their study on the conjunction fallacy. Let us examine their experiment and then discuss the nature of the conjunction fallacy.

Tversky and Kahneman presented the "Linda" problem and another similar problem to three groups of people. One was a statistically naive group of undergraduates. The second group consisted of first-year graduate students who had taken one or more courses in statistics; this group had intermediate knowledge about the principles of probability. The third group consisted of doctoral students in a decision science program of a business school who had taken several advanced courses in probability and statistics; they were labeled the sophisticated group. In each case, the participants were asked to rank all eight statements according to their probability, with the rank of 1 assigned to the most likely statement.

Figure 11.1 shows the average rank for each of the three groups for the two critical statements: (1) "Linda is a bank teller" and (2) "Linda is a bank teller and is active in the feminist movement." Notice that the people in all three groups thought that the second statement would be more likely than the first.

Think for a moment why this conclusion is statistically impossible. The **conjunction rule** states that the probability of a conjunction of two events cannot be larger than the probability of its constituent events. In the Linda problem, the conjunction of the two events—bank teller and feminist—cannot occur more often than either event by itself, for example, being a bank teller, (Contemplate some other examples of the conjunction rule; for example, the number of psychology majors who were born in the state of Iowa cannot be greater than the number of psychology majors.)

Tversky and Kahneman (1983) discovered, however, that most people commit the **conjunction fallacy:** They judge the probability of the conjunction to be greater than the probability of a constituent event. Tversky and Kahneman trace the conjunction fallacy to the representativeness heuristic. They argue that people judge the conjunction of "bank teller" and "feminist" to be more likely than the simple event "bank teller," because "feminist" is a characteristic that is very representative of (that is, similar to) someone who is single, outspoken, bright, a philosophy major, concerned about social justice, and an antinuclear activist. A person with these characteristics doesn't seem very likely to become a bank teller. However, she seems highly likely to be a feminist. By adding the extra detail of "feminist" to "bank teller," we have made the description seem more representative and plausible— even though that description is statistically less likely.

Psychologists have been very intrigued with the conjunction fallacy, especially because it demonstrates that people can ignore one of the most basic principles of probability theory. The results on the conjunction fallacy have been replicated many times, with generally consistent findings (Birnbaum et al., 1990; D. Davidson, 1995; Shafir et al., 1990; Wolford et al., 1990).

Some skeptics have wondered whether the conjunction fallacy can be traced to a simple verbal misunderstanding. For example, perhaps people interpret the statement, "Linda is a bank teller" to mean that Linda is a bank teller who is *not* active in the feminist movement. However, we do not have much evidence for this explanation (Agnoli & Krantz, 1989). Other theorists have proposed explanations for the results of the "Linda problem" that do not involve the representativeness heuristic (e.g., Epstein et al., 1995; Massaro, 1994). For example, people may consider this problem to be a pattern-recognition test, not a test requiring statistical expertise (Massaro, 1994).

Before we discuss a second decision-making heuristic, let's briefly review the representativeness heuristic. We use the representativeness heuristic when we make decisions based on whether a sample looks similar in important characteristics to the population from which it is selected. The representativeness heuristic is so appealing that we tend to ignore other important characteristics that *should* be considered, such as sample size and base rate. We also fail to acknowledge that the probability of two events occurring together (for example, bank teller and feminist) needs to be smaller than the probability of just one of those events (for example, bank teller). In summary, the representativeness heuristic is basically helpful in our daily lives, but we sometimes use it inappropriately.

The Availability Heuristic

A second important heuristic that people use in making decisions is availability. You use the *availability heuristic* whenever you estimate frequency or probability in terms of how easy it is to think of examples of something (Tversky & Kahneman, 1973). In other words, people judge frequency by assessing whether relevant examples can be easily retrieved from memory or whether this memory retrieval requires great effort.

The availability heuristic is generally helpful in everyday life. For example, suppose that someone asked you whether your college had more students from Illinois or more from Idaho. You have probably not memorized the geography statistics, so you would be likely to answer the question in terms of the relative availability of examples of Illinois students and Idaho students. Perhaps your memory has stored the names of dozens of Illinois students, and so you can easily retrieve their names ("Cynthia, Akiko, Bob . . ."). Perhaps your memory has stored only one name of an

---

DEMONSTRATION 11.6

AVAILABILITY AND LETTER ESTIMATES

Some linguistics researchers studied the frequency of various letters in the English language. They selected a typical passage in English and recorded the relative frequency with which various letters of the alphabet appeared in the first and the third positions in words. For example, in the word *language*, *l* appears in the first position and *n* appears in the third position. In this study, words with fewer than three letters were not examined.

Consider the letter *k*. Do you think that the letter *k* is more likely to appear in the first position or in the third position? Now estimate the ratio for the number of times it appears in the first position, in comparison to the number of times it appears in the third position. For example, if you guess 2:1, this means that it appears in the first position twice as often as in the third position. If you guess 1:2, this means that it appears in the third position twice as often as in the first position.

Idaho student, so it's difficult to think of examples of this category. Because examples of Illinois students were relatively easy to retrieve, you conclude that your college has more Illinois students. In general, then, this availability heuristic is a relatively effective method for making decisions about frequency. Now try Demonstration 11.6 before you read further.

As you'll recall, a heuristic is a rule of thumb that is generally accurate. The availability heuristic is accurate as long as availability is correlated with true, objective frequency—and it usually is. However, the availability heuristic can lead to errors. As we will see in this section, several factors that can influence memory retrieval are *not* correlated with true, objective frequency. These factors distort availability and therefore decrease the accuracy of our decisions. We will see that recency and familiarity—both factors that influence memory—can potentially influence availability. Figure 11.2 clarifies this relationship.

We mentioned at the beginning of the chapter that deductive reasoning and decision making are interrelated. One example of this principle is the belief-bias effect in reasoning, in which people base their conclusions on their prior beliefs that come readily to mind. People seem to treat the reasoning task as a decision-making problem, and the *logically* correct answer is so unbelievable that it does not come readily to mind (Rips, 1994). As a result, people give the incorrect answer.

Let's make certain that you understand how availability differs from representativeness. When we use the representativeness heuristic, we are given a specific example (such as T H H T H T or Linda the bank teller). We then make judgments about whether the specific example is similar to the general category it is supposed to represent (such as coin tosses or philosophy majors concerned about social justice). In contrast, when we use the availability heuristic, we are given a general

━━━━ FIGURE 11.2 ━━━━

THE RELATIONSHIP BETWEEN TRUE FREQUENCY AND ESTIMATED FREQUENCY, WITH RECENCY AND FAMILIARITY AS "CONTAMINATING" FACTORS.

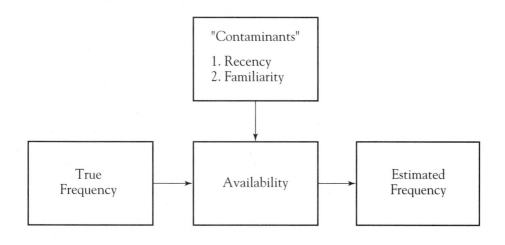

category, and we must supply the specific examples (such as examples of Illinois students). Then we make decisions based on whether the specific examples come easily to mind. So here is a way to remember the two heuristics.

1. If the problem begins with a specific example of a person or a possible outcome, you are dealing with the representativeness heuristic.
2. If the problem begins with a general category, you are dealing with the availability heuristic.

A classic study on the availability heuristic asked people to consider two general categories, words with *k* in the first position and words with *k* in the third position; this task was illustrated in Demonstration 11.6. Tversky and Kahneman (1973) found that most people guess that about twice as many words have *k* in the first position, compared to words that have *k* in the third position. However, in reality, about twice as many *k*'s appear in the third position as in the first position.

Can you see why people overestimate the frequency of first-position *k*'s? Well, consider how you approached the question in Demonstration 11.6. You probably found it easy to think of examples of words beginning with *k* (kitty, king, koala, karate, and so forth). In contrast, it is difficult to search for words in terms of their third letter. If we make judgments on the basis of how easily examples come to mind, the first-position task wins by a wide margin. Consequently, we erroneously judge first-letter *k*'s to be more common.

We'll begin our exploration of availability by considering two factors that influence availability—recency and familiarity. Then we will examine a consequence of availability, called illusory correlations. Finally, we will see how availability operates when people try to imagine an event in the future.

Recency and Availability. As you know, memory for items generally declines with the passage of time. Thus, you recall the more recent items more accurately. As a result, more recent items are more available, and we judge them to be more likely than they really are. For example, suppose you had been asked in May of 1995— following the bombing at the federal building in Oklahoma City—to estimate the frequency of terrorist bombings. Your estimate would probably have been high. Recency also influences judgments about the probability of natural hazards. People rush to purchase earthquake insurance immediately after an earthquake. However, they are much less likely to purchase insurance after several months have passed, and the earthquake fades into history (Slovic et al., 1982).

An article in the *New England Journal of Medicine* points out how physicians' decisions can be influenced by the recency effect. The article describes a physician who was reluctant to recommend a particular medical procedure because a serious neurological disorder had developed in a patient of his who had recently undergone this procedure. As the authors of this article pointed out, "Recalling a patient who suffered a complication is an example of the availability heuristic" (Pauker & Kopelman, 1992, p. 42). Researchers in decision making should be delighted that their findings have been discussed in a prestigious medical journal. This kind of information can help physicians become more unbiased decision makers. Research confirms the importance of the availability heuristic in medical decision making. Specifically, physicians were more likely to select a particular diagnosis if they had recently diagnosed a similar case (Weber et al., 1993).

Other research suggests implications for clinical psychology. MacLeod and Campbell (1992) found that when people were encouraged to recall pleasant events from their past, they judged pleasant events to be more likely in their future. In contrast, those who were encouraged to recall unpleasant events judged unpleasant events to be more likely in their future. Psychotherapists might be able to encourage depressed clients to envision a more hopeful future by recalling and focusing on previous pleasant events. In short, the availability heuristic suggests many practical applications.

Familiarity and Availability. The familiarity of the examples—as well as their recency—can also produce a distortion in frequency estimation. For instance, people who know many divorced individuals often provide higher estimates of national divorce rates than do people who have rarely encountered divorce (Kozielecki, 1981).

Familiarity also contaminates medical judgments. For example, genetic counselors often overestimate the probability of genetic risks—not surprising, given their experience with counseling people about birth defects (Shiloh, 1994). Also, physicians often have distorted ideas about the dangers of various diseases that are discussed frequently in medical journals. Specifically, the number of journal articles about a disease is highly correlated with physicians' estimates about whether that disease is likely to be fatal (Christensen-Szalanski et al., 1983). This correlation holds true, regardless of what the article actually said about the disease. If journal coverage leads a doctor to believe that a disease is more dangerous than it really is, he or she may order screening tests that are not actually necessary (Schwartz & Griffin, 1986).

Journalists and news reporters overexpose us to some events and underexpose us to others (Breyer, 1993; Slovic, 1992; Slovic et al., 1982). For example, they tell us about violent events such as fires and murders much more often than less dramatic (and more common) causes of death. One hundred times as many people die from diseases as are murdered, yet the newspapers carry three times as many articles about murders.

Did you know that the media can even influence your estimates of a country's population? Brown and Siegler (1992) found that students estimated the population of El Salvador as 12 million, though its actual population was only 5 million. In contrast, their estimate for Indonesia was 19.5 million, though its actual population was 180 million. At the time the study was conducted, El Salvador was frequently in the news because of U.S. intervention in Latin America. Because students were not familiar with news about Indonesia, they severely underestimated its population. Try asking a friend to estimate the population of Israel (population = 5,143,000) and Paraguay (population = 5,358,000). Are your friend's estimates distorted by the frequency of media coverage?

The media can also influence viewers' ideas about the prevalence of different points of view. As Nisbett and Ross (1980) remark about news coverage during the Vietnam era, the media would often devote only slightly more time to the 100,000 antiwar protesters than to several dozen counterprotestors. Viewers might therefore reach inaccurate conclusions about the size of the two groups. Notice whether you can spot the same tendency in current news broadcasts. Do the media still create our cognitive realities?

Try Demonstration 11.7, a modification of a study by Tversky and Kahneman (1973). See whether your friends respond according to the familiarity of the examples, rather than true frequency. Tversky and Kahneman presented people with lists of 39 names. A typical list might contain the names of 19 famous women and 20 less famous men. After hearing the list, participants were asked to judge whether the list contained more men's names or more women's names. About 80% of the participants erroneously guessed that the group with the most famous (familiar) names was the more frequent, even though it was objectively less frequent. Similar results were obtained in a replication by Manis and his coauthors (1993).

DEMONSTRATION 11.7

FAMILIARITY AND AVAILABILITY

Read this list of names to several friends. After you have finished the entire list, ask your friends to estimate whether there were more men or women listed. Do not allow them to answer "about the same." (In reality, 14 women's names and 15 men's names are listed.)

Louisa May Alcott	Maxine Hong Kingston
John Dickson Carr	Virginia Woolf
Alice Walker	Robert Lovett
Thomas Hughes	Judy Blume
Laura Ingalls Wilder	George Nathan
Jack Lindsay	Allan Nevins
Edward George Lytton	Jane Austen
Margaret Mitchell	Henry Crabb Robinson
Michael Drayton	Joseph Lincoln
Edith Wharton	Emily Brontë
Henry Vaughan	Arthur Hutchinson
Judith Krantz	James Hunt
Agatha Christie	Anne Tyler
Richard Watson Gilder	Brian Hooker
	Harriet Beecher Stowe

Illusory Correlation and Availability. So far, we have seen that availability—or the ease with which examples come to mind— is typically a useful heuristic. However, this heuristic can become "contaminated" by factors such as recency and frequency, leading to inappropriate decisions about an event's frequency. Now we turn to a third topic, to see how the availability heuristic can contribute to a cognitive error called an illusory correlation.

As you know, a correlation is a statistical relationship between two variables, and *illusory* means deceptive or unreal. Therefore, an **illusory correlation** occurs when people believe that two variables are statistically related, when there is no real evidence for this relationship. In particular, numerous studies show that we often believe that a certain group of people tends to have certain kinds of characteristics, even though an accurate tabulation would show that the relationship is not statistically significant (Crocker, 1981; Hamilton et al., 1993; Trolier & Hamilton, 1986).

Think of some examples of stereotypes that arise from illusory correlations. These illusory correlations may either have no basis in fact or much less basis than is commonly believed. For example, consider the following illusory correlations: females are unskilled at math, blondes are not very bright, gay males and lesbians have psychological problems, and so forth. According to an important current approach, our stereotypes are mediated by cognitive processes such as availability (Hamilton et al., 1993).

An early investigation of illusory correlation was performed by Chapman and Chapman (1967, 1969), who approached the problem from a clinical psychology viewpoint. In particular, these researchers investigated a projective test called the Draw-a-Person test. This test assumes that people project their emotions and motivations onto the figure they draw. For example, paranoid or suspicious individuals are supposed to exaggerate the eyes, whereas dependent individuals are supposed to exaggerate the mouth (because they like to be cared for and fed). However, Chapman and Chapman proposed that clinicians' trust in this test is based on an illusory correlation.

Chapman and Chapman (1967) asked psychiatric patients in a state hospital to take the Draw-a-Person test. These drawings were then paired *completely at random* with six symptoms, such as suspiciousness and dependence. College students then examined these drawings, labeled with the symptoms of the people who had presumably drawn them. Afterward, they were asked to report what features of the drawings were most often paired with each symptom. Remember, now, that the stimuli had been arranged so that the drawings were not systematically related to the symptoms. Nonetheless, the college students reported the same kinds of associations that clinical psychologists had reported. For example, they reported that paranoid people had frequently drawn exaggerated eyes, whereas dependent people had frequently drawn exaggerated mouths. Chapman and Chapman (1969) also extended their findings to reports of homosexuality on the Rorschach test.

Theorists have proposed a variety of alternate explanations for illusory correlations, including unevenly distributed attention and characteristics of the memory trace (e.g., Slovic et al., 1974; E.R. Smith, 1991). However, let's explore the availability explanation in more detail.

When we try to determine whether two variables are related to each other, we really ought to consider four kinds of information. For example, suppose that we want to determine whether people who are lesbians or gay males are more likely than heterosexuals to have psychological problems. Incidentally, some people seem to believe in this illusory correlation, even though the research shows no consistent relationship between sexual orientation and psychological problems (e.g., Gonsiorek, 1996; Kurdek, 1987; Mannion, 1981). To do the research properly, we need to pay attention to the frequency of four possible combinations: gay people who have psychological problems, gay people who do not have psychological problems, straight people who have psychological problems, and straight people who do not have psychological problems. Imagine, for example, that researchers gathered the data in Table 11.2. Their decision should be based on a comparison of two ratios:

$$\frac{\text{gay people with psychological problems}}{\text{total number of gay people}} \quad \text{versus} \quad \frac{\text{straight people with psychological problems}}{\text{total number of straight people}}$$

Using the data from Table 11.2, for example, we would find that 6 out of 60 gay people (or 10%) have psychological problems, and 8 out of 80 straight people (also 10%) have psychological problems. We should therefore conclude that sexual orientation is not related to psychological problems.

Unfortunately, however, people often pay attention to only one cell in the matrix, especially if the two characteristics are statistically less frequent (Hamilton et al., 1993). In this example, many people are likely to notice only gay people who have psychological problems, ignoring the important information in the other three cells. People with a bias against gay people might be especially likely to pay attention to this cell, and they continue to look for information that confirms their hypothesis that gay people have problems. You'll recall from the section on

---

TABLE 11.2

A MATRIX SHOWING HYPOTHETICAL INFORMATION ABOUT SEXUAL ORIENTATION AND PSYCHOLOGICAL PROBLEMS.

	Number in each category	
	Gay people	*Straight people*
People With Psychological Problems	6	8
People Without Psychological Problems	54	72
Totals	60	80

conditional reasoning that people would rather try to confirm a hypothesis than try to disprove it, consistent with Theme 3 of this book.

Recent research has focused on the conditions that influence the formation of illusory correlations. For example, illusory correlations are more likely when the descriptions of the target people are extreme, rather than moderate (Sanbonmatsu et al., 1994). Furthermore, people are more likely to form illusory correlations when their mood is neutral, rather than positive or negative (Hamilton et al., 1993). Apparently, positive and negative moods seem to decrease people's ability to process distinctive information about groups.

Try applying the information about illusory correlations to some stereotype that you hold. Notice whether you have tended to focus on only one cell in the matrix, ignoring the other three. Have you specifically tried to *disconfirm* the stereotypes? Also, notice how politicians often base their arguments on illusory correlations. For example, they may focus on the number of welfare recipients with fraudulent claims. This number is meaningless unless we also know the number of welfare recipients *without* fraudulent claims, or else the number of people who do not receive welfare who have other kinds of fraudulent claims.

The Simulation Heuristic and Availability. So far, we have discussed decisions you can make by thinking of examples and judging the relative frequency of those examples. The correct answer to these decisions could be obtained by counting an unbiased list of the examples. For instance, you could answer the question about first-letter versus third-letter *k*'s by counting letters in a passage of text.

In real life, however, we often judge probabilities in situations that cannot be evaluated by simply counting the list of examples. For instance, what is the probability that Bill and Jane will get divorced? What is the probability that you will become a clinical psychologist? Each marriage and each career are unique, so we cannot provide an answer by counting examples of other people's marriages or careers.

Kahneman and Tversky (1982) propose that the simulation heuristic is a special example of the availability heuristic. However, the availability heuristic refers to the ease with which we can *recall* examples, whereas the **simulation heuristic** refers to the ease with which we can *imagine* examples or scenarios (Poulton, 1994).

For example, suppose that you want to judge the likelihood of your becoming a clinical psychologist. You might construct a scenario in which you do extremely well in your coursework, receive superb scores on the Graduate Record Exam, receive strong letters of recommendation from your professors, get accepted into the graduate school of your choice, receive your PhD in good time, complete your internship, and set up your practice. If you have no difficulty imagining each event in this scenario, then you may judge the entire scenario as being likely. On the other hand, constructing a scenario for your becoming the president of the United States may be more difficult, and so you would judge the scenario as being unlikely.

Let's consider a study by Gregory and his colleagues (1982) that shows how the simulation heuristic operates. These researchers examined how imagining a scenario about using a cable television service actually influenced later attitudes and subscriptions to the service. A door-to-door canvasser provided one group of residents with concrete information about cable television. They encouraged a second group of residents to develop their own scenarios, imagining how much more convenient and inexpensive the cable service would be. The results showed that people were much more positive about cable television if they had constructed their own scenarios. Furthermore, the cable television service reported—three months later—that 20% of the people in the information condition had subscribed to the service, in contrast to 47% in the imagination condition! Clearly, the simulation heuristic has implications for consumer behavior.

The simulation heuristic also has implications for personality psychology. For example, Cervone (1989) examined whether the power of imagination could extend to people's self-efficacy, which is the feeling individuals have that they are competent and effective. Students who had been instructed to think about factors that could enhance their performance on a spatial problem rated themselves as being much higher in self-efficacy than students who had been instructed to think about factors that could inhibit their performance. Furthermore, those who envisioned positive scenarios also persisted much longer on the problems. The implications are clear: If you want to boost your confidence and persistence on a task, think about your strengths, rather than your weaknesses.

The simulation heuristic also explains why we are especially frustrated when we just miss reaching a goal. Kahneman and Tversky (1982) asked students to judge which of two individuals should be more upset, someone who missed his plane by 5 minutes or someone who missed it by 30 minutes. You won't be surprised to learn that 96% of the respondents answered that the more upsetting experience would be to miss the flight by 5 minutes. Kahneman and Tversky propose that we can envision this individual constructing a simulation in which he *didn't* stop to buy a newspaper or some other trivial event—thereby arriving on time. In contrast, we have trouble seeing how a person could construct a scenario that would save 30 minutes.

Let us review what we've discussed about the availability heuristic, in which we estimate frequency or probability in terms of how easily we can think of examples of something. This heuristic is generally accurate in our daily lives, but availability can be contaminated by two factors that are not related to objective frequency—recency and familiarity. Furthermore, availability helps create illusory correlations, another error in decision making. Finally, we often judge likelihood in terms of the simulation heuristic, in which we imagine possible events, rather than recalling examples of them. We apparently use the simulation heuristic when we buy products, make judgments about our performance, and make decisions about whether an event might have turned out differently.

The Anchoring and Adjustment Heuristic

Has this ever happened to you? You're shopping for a coat, and you describe to the salesperson what you are looking for. He shows you a coat that is clearly the top of the line—and very expensive. After gulping and asking to see some other styles, you find that you walk out of the store with a coat that was fairly expensive. The clever clerk may have encouraged you to fall for the anchoring and adjustment heuristic (Poulton, 1994).

According to the *anchoring and adjustment heuristic,* we begin with a first approximation—an *anchor*—and then we make adjustments to that number on the basis of additional information (Poulton, 1994; Slovic et al., 1974; Tversky & Kahneman, 1982). This heuristic often leads to a reasonable answer, just as the representativeness and availability heuristics often lead to reasonable answers. However, people typically rely too heavily on the anchor, and their adjustments are too small. Notice, incidentally, that the anchoring and adjustment heuristic depends upon the availability heuristic, because highly available information is likely to serve as an anchor.

The anchoring and adjustment heuristic illustrates once more that we humans tend to endorse our current hypotheses or beliefs (Baron, 1994). We've seen several other examples of this tendency in the present chapter: (1) We prefer to confirm a current hypothesis, rather than to reject it; (2) we rely too heavily on prior beliefs; and (3) we rely too strongly on one cell in a data matrix, failing to seek information about the other three cells. All these tendencies are further examples of Theme 5, which emphasizes top-down processing.

Let's begin by considering some research on the anchoring and adjustment heuristic. Then we will see how this heuristic can be applied to estimating confidence intervals. Finally, we'll examine several applications to areas beyond cognitive psychology.

DEMONSTRATION 11.8

THE ANCHORING AND ADJUSTMENT HEURISTIC

Copy the two multiplication problems listed below on separate pieces of paper. Show each problem to at least five friends. In each case, ask the friend to estimate the answer within 5 seconds.

a. $8 \times 7 \times 6 \times 5 \times 4 \times 3 \times 2 \times 1$

b. $1 \times 2 \times 3 \times 4 \times 5 \times 6 \times 7 \times 8$

Now tally the answers separately for the two problems, listing the answers from smallest to largest. Calculate the median for each problem. (If you have an odd number of participants, the median is the answer in the middle of the distribution—with half larger and half smaller. If you have an even number of participants, the median is the average of the two answers in the middle of the distribution.)

Research on the Anchoring and Adjustment Heuristic. In a classic study, Tversky and Kahneman (1974) asked people to estimate various quantities. For example, a typical question might ask participants to estimate the percentage of United Nations delegates who were from African countries. Before requesting the reply, the experimenters spun a wheel while the participants looked on. Completely at random, the wheel selected a number between 0 and 100. The participants were asked to indicate whether their answer to the question was higher or lower than the selected number. They replied by moving upward or downward from that selected number.

Tversky and Kahneman (1974) found that the arbitrarily selected number acted as an anchor for the estimates. For example, if the wheel had stopped on 10, people estimated that 25% of U.N. delegates were from Africa. If the wheel stopped on 65, people estimated 45%. In other words, a number that had no real relationship to the question acted as an anchor for the response. People then made adjustments from this number, based on their knowledge of information related to the question. However, these adjustments were usually far too conservative.

Try Demonstration 11.8 for another example of the anchoring and adjustment heuristic. When high-school students were asked to estimate the answers—and were allowed only 5 seconds to do so—they provided widely different answers for the two problems. When starting with a large number—8—the median estimate was 2,250 (that is, half the students estimated higher than 2,250, and half estimated lower). In contrast, when starting with a small number—1—the median estimate was only 512 (Tverksy & Kahneman, 1982). Interestingly, both groups seem to have anchored too heavily on the single-digit numbers in the question, because both estimates are far too low: The correct answer is 40,320. Notice whether the people you tested were influenced by the anchoring and adjustment heuristic.

Estimating Confidence Intervals. We use anchoring and adjustment when we estimate a single number. We also use this heuristic when we estimate ***confidence intervals,*** or ranges within which we expect a number to fall a certain percentage of the time. (For example, you might guess that the 98% confidence interval for the population of a particular town is 2,000–7,000. This guess would mean that you think there is a 98% chance that the population is between 2,000 and 7,000.)

Try Demonstration 11.9 to test the accuracy of your estimates for various kinds of almanac information. The answers can be found at the end of this chapter. Check to see how many of your confidence interval estimates included the correct answer. If a large number of people were to answer a large number of questions, we would expect their confidence intervals to include the correct answer about 98% of the time—if their estimation techniques are correct. However, studies have shown that the confidence intervals actually include the correct answer only about 60% of the time (Fischhoff, 1982; Slovic et al., 1974; Tversky & Kahneman, 1974). In other words, the confidence intervals that we estimate are too narrow.

Tversky and Kahneman (1974) point out how the anchoring and adjustment heuristic is relevant when we make confidence-interval estimates. We first provide

=== DEMONSTRATION 11.9 ===

ESTIMATING CONFIDENCE INTERVALS

For each of the following questions, answer in terms of a range, rather than a single number. Specifically you should supply a 98% confidence interval, which is the range within which you expect the correct answer to fall. For example, if you answer a question by supplying a 98% confidence interval that is 2,000 to 7,000, this means that you think there is only a 2% chance that the real answer is either less than 2,000 or more than 7,000. All questions are based on information in the *World Almanac* and the *Canadian Global Almanac.* (The correct answers can be found at the end of the chapter.)

1. What percentage of the Canadian population identifies themselves as having a French ethnic background?
2. What percent of mothers with children between the ages of 6 and 17 are in the U.S. labor force?
3. What was the population of Georgia in 1992?
4. What is the size of Brazil, in square miles?
5. How many universities are there in Canada?
6. How many languages are represented in the books, documents, and other items in the Library of Congress in Washington, DC?
7. In what year did the philosopher Plato die?
8. What is the literacy rate in Cuba?
9. What percent of the voting-age population in the United States did not vote in the 1992 presidential election?
10. What is the average annual snowfall in Toronto?

a best estimate and use this figure as an anchor. Then we make adjustments upward and downward from this anchor to construct the confidence interval estimate. However, our adjustments are too small. For example, perhaps you initially guessed that the percentage of U.S. nonvoters was 25%. You might then say that your confidence interval was between 15% and 35%. This range is too narrow, especially given the potential for large error in your original estimate. Again, we establish our anchor and we do not wander far from it in the adjustment process.

Think about applications of the anchoring and adjustment heuristic. Suppose that you are trying to guess how much you will make in tips in your summer job. You will probably make a first guess and then base your range on this figure. However, your final answer will depend too heavily on that first guess, which may not have been carefully chosen. Your adjustments will not adequately reflect all the

---

DEMONSTRATION 11.10

THE FRAMING EFFECT AND BACKGROUND INFORMATION. BASED ON TVERSKY & KAHNEMAN (1981).

Try the following two problems:

Problem 1
Imagine that you decided to see a play and you paid $20 for the admission price of one ticket. As you enter the theater, you discover that you have lost the ticket. The theater keeps no record of ticket purchasers, so the ticket cannot be recovered. Would you pay $20 for another ticket for the play?

Problem 2
Imagine that you have decided to see a play where the admission price of one ticket is $20. As you enter the theater, you discover that you have lost a $20 bill. Would you still pay $20 for a ticket for the play?

---

additional factors that you should consider after you made your first guess. When we shut our eyes to new evidence, we demonstrate a pattern we saw in Chapter 10: We fail to conduct an adequate search of the problem space.

Applications of the Anchoring and Adjustment Heuristic. Researchers and theorists have suggested numerous applications of the anchoring and adjustment heuristic, including many outside of psychology. For example, risk assessors might try to calculate the probability of a disaster on an oil rig in the North Sea, based on data derived from the Gulf of Mexico as an anchor. They may depend too heavily on that anchor and fail to make sufficient adjustments for factors such as climate and construction differences (Holtgrave et al., 1994). Another application concerns genetic counseling. According to the research in this area, people who seek counseling about the risk of a genetic disorder in the family will tend to base their final risk estimates very heavily on their own, original risk estimates. In contrast, they give much less weight to the information provided by the genetic counselor (Shiloh, 1994).

Most of the applications of the anchoring and adjustment heuristic have been developed in connection with financial issues. For example, Smith and Kida (1991) examined whether the anchoring and adjustment heuristic operates among auditors, who are accountants responsible for checking a company's financial records. In general, well-trained professionals were not heavily influenced by this heuristic. Reassuringly, experts in this field are reasonably accurate in adjusting their original results to reflect new information.

People also use the anchoring and adjustment heuristic when they make real-estate decisions. Northcraft and Neale (1987) asked real-estate agents to estimate

DEMONSTRATION 11.11

THE FRAMING EFFECT AND THE WORDING OF A QUESTION. BASED ON TVERSKY & KAHNEMAN (1981).

Try the following two problems:

Problem 1
Imagine that the United States is preparing for the outbreak of an unusual Asian disease, which is expected to kill 600 people. Two alternative programs to combat the disease have been proposed. Assume that the exact scientific estimate of the consequences of the programs are as follows:

If Program A is adopted, 200 people will be saved.
If Program B is adopted, there is a one-third probability that 600 people will be saved, and two-thirds probability that no people will be saved.

Which program would you favor?

Problem 2
Now imagine the same situation, with these two alternatives:

If Program C is adopted, 400 people will die.
If Program D is adopted, there is a one-third probability that nobody will die, and two-thirds probability that 600 people will die.

Which program would you favor?

the value of a particular house. Everyone was given a 10-page packet of information about the house. However, some were given a listing price of about $66,000, whereas others were given a listing price of $84,000. Those who had been supplied with the lower anchor suggested that the lowest acceptable offer should be $65,000, whereas the comparable figure for those who had been supplied with the higher anchor was $73,000.

We should note, however, that people may not be strongly influenced by an extremely implausible anchor (Chapman & Johnson, 1994; Kahneman, 1992). For example, an anchor of $300,000 would probably have little effect on the agents' estimates. (Be sure to try Demonstrations 11.10 and 11.11 before you turn the page.)

Let's review the last of the three major decision-making heuristics. When we use the anchoring and adjustment heuristic, we begin by guessing a first approximation or anchor. Then we make adjustments to that anchor. This heuristic is generally useful, but we typically fail to make large enough adjustments. The anchoring and adjustment heuristic also accounts for our errors when we estimate confidence intervals; we usually supply ranges that are far too narrow, given the degree of uncertainty they should reflect. Finally, the anchoring and adjustment heuristic can be applied to a variety of areas, such as risk assessment, genetic counseling, accounting, and real estate.

▶▶ IN DEPTH: The Framing Effect

Recently I received a phone call from a group called, "The Committee to Defeat Jesse Helms," and I pledged a fairly generous donation. Later, I wondered whether I had been influenced by the framing effect. Would my donation have been as large if the group had been called "The Committee to Elect Harvey Gantt"? Are Senate campaign committees perhaps hiring psychologists?

The *framing effect* demonstrates that the outcome of a decision can be influenced by (1) the background context of the choice and (2) the way in which a question is worded (framed). In this in-depth section, let's first consider the research on background context. Then we will turn to research on the wording of the question. Finally, we will consider some possible reasons for the framing effect. However, before you read further, be sure you tried Demonstration 11.10 on page 418.

Background Information and the Framing Effect. Reread Demonstration 11.10 and notice that the amount of money involved is $20 in both cases. However, the decision frame differs for the two situations; they seem "psychologically different." As Kahneman and Tversky (1984) point out, we organize our mental expense accounts according to topics. Specifically, we view going to the theater as a transaction in which the cost of the ticket is exchanged for the experience of seeing a play. If you buy another ticket, the cost of seeing that play has increased to a level that many people find unacceptable. When Kahneman and Tversky asked people what they would do, only 46% said that they would pay for another ticket (Problem 1). In contrast, in Problem 2, we don't tally the lost bill in the same account; the loss is viewed as being generally irrelevant to the ticket. In Kahneman and Tversky's study, 88% of the participants said that they would purchase the ticket. As you can see, the background information provides different frames for the two problems, and the frame strongly influences the decision.

The Wording of a Question and the Framing Effect. Before you read further, try Demonstration 11.11. The concept of a question's wording arose as part of Kahneman and Tversky's (1979) theories about the way people construct internal representations of a decision problem. You'll recall that in Chapter 10 we discussed the internal representation of a problem as an important first step in problem solving. We also saw in that chapter that people often fail to realize that two problems share a deep-structure similarity. That is, people are distracted by the surface-structure differences. We will see that these same statements apply when people make decisions between various options.

Tversky and Kahneman (1981) presented Problem 1 to students in both Canada and the United States. They found that 72% chose Program A; only 28% chose Program B. Notice that the participants in this study were "risk averse"; that is, they preferred the certainty of saving 200 lives, rather than the risky prospect of a one-in-three possibility of saving 600 lives. Notice, however, that the benefits of the two programs in Problem 1 are statistically equal.

Now inspect your answer to Problem 2. When Tversky and Kahneman (1981) presented this problem to a different group of students, only 22% favored Program C, but 78% favored Program D. Here the participants were "risk taking"; they preferred the two-in-three chance that 600 would die, rather than the guaranteed death of 400 people. Again, however, the benefits of the two programs are statistically equal. Furthermore, notice that Problem 1 and Problem 2 have identical deep structure. The only difference is that the outcomes are described in Problem 1 in terms of the lives saved, but in Problem 2 in terms of the lives lost.

The way that the question is framed—lives saved or lives lost—has an important effect on people's decisions. This framing changes people from focusing on the possible gains (lives saved) to focusing on the possible losses (lives lost). The change in focus is important because people tend to be risk-avoiding when dealing with possible gains, but risk-seeking when dealing with possible losses. In the case of Problem 1, we tend to prefer having 200 lives saved for sure; we avoid the option where it's possible that no lives will be saved. In the case of Problem 2, we tend to prefer the risk that nobody will die (even though there is a good chance that 600 will die) rather than choose the option where 400 face certain death.

Kahneman and Tversky (1984) note that the influence of framing on decision making is both pervasive and robust. That is, the framing effect is as common among statistically sophisticated people as among naive people, and the magnitude of the effect is large. Furthermore, the framing effect is not eliminated when the experimenters point out to participants that their answers are contradictory. Even after participants reread the problems, they still are risk averse in the "lives saved" version and risk seeking in the "lives lost" version.

Numerous studies have replicated the framing effect (Levin et al., 1988; Mayer, 1992). For example, similar results were obtained when the "unusual Asian disease" problem was tested in two separate studies in Sweden (Bohm & Lind, 1992; Svenson & Benson, 1993).

The framing effect also has an important impact on consumer behavior. For instance, Johnson (1987) confirmed that people are much more positive about ground beef that is labeled "80% lean," rather than "20% fat." The framing effect has also been demonstrated for people buying refrigerators (Neale & Northcraft, 1986) and for people making real-estate decisions (Northcraft & Neale, 1987).

Several studies have also examined how framing can influence medical decisions. The framing effect holds true for decisions about receiving vaccinations (Slovic et al., 1982), treating lung cancer (McNeil et al., 1982), and genetic counseling (McNeil et al., 1988). Physicians—as well as patients—may be influenced by this effect. The framing effect has also been demonstrated in situations as diverse as paying for public services (Green et al., 1994), using automobile seat belts (Slovic et al., 1988), and making gambling choices (Elliott & Archibald, 1989).

Let us consider two of these framing studies in more detail. Huber and her colleagues (1987) examined the effects of framing on personnel selection decisions. Imagine that you are an executive who needs to hire three new employees for a job. Should you approach the task by rejecting the applicants who are less qualified, or by accepting the applicants who are more qualified? The participants in the study by Huber and her coauthors were students in courses on organizational behavior, and they were asked to read the resumes from 20 applicants for a position as a computer technician's assistant. They were informed that it would cost the company $300 to interview each job applicant. When people were instructed to accept the applicants who were high on the selection criteria, they chose to interview an average of 6 applicants. In contrast, when they were instructed to reject the applicants who were low on the selection criteria, they chose to interview an average of 10 applicants.

As you can see, this study demonstrates once more that the wording of a question determines whether people show risk-averse or risk-seeking behavior. *Accepting* the candidates for interviews implies gains, so people demonstrate risk aversion; that is, they do not choose to interview risky candidates. *Rejecting* the candidates for interviews implies losses, so people demonstrate risk seeking; that is, they decide that they do want to interview those borderline candidates.

Incidentally, the way to remember this general effect—which may initially seem backwards—is that when people think the situation is good, they want to maintain the status quo, so they avoid risks. However, when they think the situation is bad, they want things to change, so they seek risks. In summary, a positive frame makes people avoid risks; a negative frame makes them seek risks (Schooler, 1992).

Let's consider one final example of how a question's wording influences decisions. Levin and his colleagues (1988) asked college students to estimate the incidence of cheating at their university. Before making these estimates, half the students were informed about a national survey reporting that 65% of students had cheated during their college career; the other half read a version reporting that 35% of students had never cheated. Those who saw the "cheated" version rated their university's incidence of cheating as being significantly higher than did those who saw the "never cheated" version.

As Huber and her colleagues (1987) concluded in connection with the general framing effect, decision making often depends on whether the choice is presented as, "Is the pitcher half *empty?*" or, "Is the pitcher half *full?*" This area of research confirms Theme 4 of this textbook; the cognitive processes are indeed interrelated. In this case, language has a profound effect on decision making.

Reasons for the Framing Effect. Perhaps as you read the previous pages, you had an uneasy feeling that the various kinds of problems seemed quite diverse. For example, the problem about the unusual Asian disease presents two versions that yield identical results; in each version, 200 people live and 400 people die. But the lost

DEMONSTRATION 11.12

OTHER EXAMPLES OF THE FRAMING EFFECT. BASED ON FRISCH (1993).

Try the following problems.

Problem 1

Version a: You are lying on the beach on a hot day. All you have to drink is ice water. For the last hour you have been thinking about how much you would enjoy a nice cold bottle of your favorite cola drink. A friend offers to bring back a drink from the only nearby place where beverages are sold, a fancy hotel. He says that the cola may be expensive, though. How much would you be willing to pay? _____

Version b: Imagine the same scenario, except that your friend will be going to a small, run-down grocery store. How much would you be willing to pay? _____ (If your answer is different for the two versions, explain why.)

Problem 2

Version a: Imagine that you go to purchase a calculator for $15. The calculator salesman informs you that the calculator you wish to buy is on sale for $10 at the other branch of the store, which is 10 minutes away. Would you drive to the other store? _____

Version b: Imagine that you go to purchase a jacket for $125. The jacket salesman informs you that the jacket you wish to buy is on sale for $120 at the other branch of the store, which is 10 minutes away. Would you drive to the other store? _____ (If your answer is different for the two versions, explain why.)

ticket situation "feels" subjectively different from the lost money situation. Although the objective cost is the same, you feel as if you are paying $40 for the new ticket in the first problem, but only $20 in the second problem.

Deborah Frisch (1993) decided to determine whether people really did consider the two versions of several framing problems to be similar—and whether they responded the same to all problems. Before you read further, though, try Demonstration 11.12.

Frisch asked students to try each of nine problems, including the "unusual Asian disease" problem and the two you worked on in Demonstration 11.12. Two independent judges then classified the students' responses into four categories: (1) student agrees the two versions are the same; (2) student believes there is an *objective*

====== **TABLE 11.3** ======

PERCENTAGE OF EACH TYPE OF JUSTIFICATION, AS PROVIDED BY THE STUDENTS WHO TREATED THE TWO VERSIONS OF THE PROBLEM DIFFERENTLY. BASED ON FRISCH (1993).

Problem	Same	Objective difference	Subjective difference	No justification given
Asian disease	69	0	10	21
Drink on beach	32	27	23	18
Calculator/jacket	24	0	56	19

difference between the two versions, even though it was not explicitly stated; (3) student believes there is a *subjective* difference between the two versions, involving psychological factors such as fairness or wastefulness; (4) student gave no justification response.

Table 11.3 shows the categories for three problems you have tried. As you can see, most of the students believed that the two versions of the Asian disease problem really were the same, though many did not provide any answer. In the "drink-on-the-beach" problem (which was actually beer in the original version), the responses were fairly evenly split. However, a large number of students argued for an objective difference—maybe the bottle had been sitting around the wretched grocery store for several years. In contrast to these two problems, notice that most of the students in the "calculator/jacket" problem argued for a subjective difference—it wouldn't seem worthwhile to save $5 on a $125 jacket; in contrast, $5 is a large percentage of the $15 calculator price.

In other words, framing effects are not homogeneous. In problems like the Asian disease scenario, most people agree that the two situations are identical. So we can call this a true bias; people are not acting rationally. In the drink-on-the-beach problem, people bring their world knowledge to the problem and make an inference that the two situations are objectively different. Given those premises, people *are* acting rationally. But are people acting rationally in the calculator/jacket problem? An economist would probably say "no," in a purely dollars-and-cents fashion. However, most psychologists would probably argue that these subjective, psychological factors may indeed play an important role, and we do not need to classify this behavior as irrational decision making.

Let's review how the framing effect operates. Background information can influence decisions; we do not make choices in a vacuum, devoid of knowledge about the world (Payne et al., 1992). In addition, the wording of the question can influence decisions, so that people avoid risks when the wording implies gains, and they seek risks when the wording implies losses. Furthermore, these framing effects have been replicated in a variety of situations. Finally, the work of Deborah Frisch clarifies that people have different reasons for being influenced by framing effects.

Sometimes, they acknowledge that the two versions of a problem are identical, but sometimes they argue that the two versions are either objectively or subjectively different.

◀◀

Overconfidence in Decisions

So far, we have seen that decisions can be influenced by three decision-making heuristics. Furthermore, the framing effect demonstrates that background information and wording can influence decision making inappropriately. Given these sources of error, people should not be very confident about their decision-making skills. Unfortunately, however, the research shows that they are overconfident. ***Overconfidence*** means that people's confidence judgments are higher than they should be, based on the relative frequencies of the correct answers (Gigerenzer et al., 1991).

We have already seen two examples of overconfidence in decision making in this chapter. In the section on illusory correlations, we emphasized that people are confident that two variables are related, when in fact the relationship is either weak or nonexistent. In the discussion of anchoring and adjustment, we saw that people are so confident in their estimation abilities that they supply very narrow confidence intervals for their estimates.

Overconfidence is a characteristic of other cognitive tasks, in addition to decision making. For example, you may recall from Chapter 8 that people are overconfident about how well they understood material they had read, even though they had answered many questions incorrectly.

A wide variety of studies show that humans are overconfident in numerous decision-making situations. For example, they are overconfident about how long people with a fatal disease will live, which firms will go bankrupt, which psychiatric inpatients have serious disorders, whether the defendant is guilty in a court trial, and which students will do well in graduate school (Kahneman & Tversky, 1995). People consistently have more confidence in their own decisions than in predictions that are based on statistically objective measurements.

Other studies on the topic of overconfidence demonstrate that amateur bridge players are overconfident, though expert players are not (Keren, 1987). Furthermore, physicians are overconfident in judging that patients with coughs have pneumonia (Schwartz & Griffin, 1986). Are you surprised to learn that students are overly optimistic about how long it will take them to complete a project (Buehler et al., 1994)?

Overconfidence also plays a role in international policy. For example, politicians may be overly confident that an emerging political situation is similar to a situation they have already encountered (Peterson, 1985). In international conflict, each side tends to overestimate its chances of success (Kahneman & Tversky, 1995).

In many situations, overconfidence has real consequences for people's lives. For example, in 1988, Captain Will Rogers was aboard the USS *Vincennes* in the Persian Gulf. The ship's radar had just detected an unknown aircraft, and Rogers had to decide whether the aircraft was simply a civilian airplane or whether it was actually attacking his ship. He decided to launch two missiles at the aircraft. As both Rogers and the rest of the world soon learned, the plane was only a civilian airline, and all 290 passengers aboard the plane died when it was shot down. A panel of decision-making theorists pointed out that the captain had been overconfident about his original judgment and failed to verify critical characteristics of the situation (Bales, 1988).

Let us begin by examining some of the reasons for people's overconfidence. Then we will consider a specific kind of overconfidence, called the hindsight bias.

Reasons for Overconfidence. Our overconfidence in the correctness of our decisions arises from errors during many different stages in the decision-making process:

1. People are often unaware that their knowledge is based on very tenuous and uncertain assumptions and on information from unreliable or inappropriate sources (Carlson, 1995; Greenberg et al., 1995; Griffin & Tversky, 1992; Slovic et al., 1982).

2. Examples confirming our hypotheses are readily available, whereas we resist searching for counterexamples (Baron, 1994; Cohen, 1993a; Dawes, 1988). You'll recall from the discussion of deductive reasoning that people persist in confirming their current hypothesis, rather than looking for negative evidence.

3. People have difficulty *recalling* the other possible hypotheses, and decision making depends on memory (Theme 4). If you cannot recall the competing hypotheses, you will be overly confident about the hypothesis you have endorsed.

4. A self-fulfilling effect operates (Einhorn & Hogarth, 1978, 1981). For example, admissions officers who judge that a candidate is particularly well qualified for admission to a program may feel that their judgment is supported when their candidate does well. However, the candidate's success may be due primarily to the positive effects of the program itself. Even the people who had been rejected might have been successful if they had been allowed to participate in the program.

5. When people are informed that most people are overconfident about the accuracy of their decisions, they fail to take this information into account when providing confidence judgments (Gigerenzer et al., 1991). In other words, they remain overconfident. Keep these findings in mind, and try to reduce your own overconfidence when you make important decisions.

The Hindsight Bias. We have been discussing how people are overconfident about predictions for events that will happen in the future. In contrast, ***hindsight*** refers to our overconfidence about events that have already happened (Poulton, 1994). Specifically, the ***hindsight bias*** is our tendency to falsely report that we would have accurately predicted an outcome—even if we had not been told about that outcome in advance (Cannon & Quinsey, 1995). Not only do people say that

THE HINDSIGHT BIAS

Find two friends who can spare a few minutes for an experiment. They should be tested separately, one friend hearing version A and one friend hearing version B. In each case, announce that you will read a paragraph and then ask a question.

Version A (foresight)

A goose egg was placed in a soundproof, heated box from time of laying to time of cracking. Approximately two days before it cracked, the experimenter began intermittently to play sounds of ducks quacking into the box. On the day after birth, the gosling was placed on a smooth floor equidistant from a duck and a goose, each of which was in a wire cage. The gosling was observed for two minutes. The possible outcomes were (a) the gosling approached the caged duck or (b) the gosling approached the caged goose (Slovic & Fischhoff, 1977, p. 546). If the gosling does approach the caged duck, what is the probability that in a replication of this experiment with ten additional goslings,

    a. all will approach the duck? _____%
    b. some will approach the duck _____%
    c. none will approach the duck _____%

Note that these must sum to 100%.

Version B (hindsight)

Read the same story as in version A up to the Slovic and Fischhoff reference. Then read this ending:
    The initial gosling that was tested in this experiment approached the caged duck. Suppose that a replication of the experiment was performed with ten additional goslings. What is the probability that in this replication,

    a. all will approach the duck? _____%
    b. some will approach the duck? _____%
    c. none will approach the duck? _____%

Note that these must sum to 100%.

After you have tested your two subjects (or better still, five on each version), compare the percentages. Were people in the hindsight condition more likely to guess that all the goslings would approach the duck?

they "knew it all along," but they also insist that the information about the outcome had no influence on their judgment (Hawkins & Hastie, 1990).

Fischhoff (1975) provides a good example of a hindsight bias. In 1974, a prisoner named Cletus Bowles—who had been previously convicted of murder and bank robbery—was allowed to leave the penitentiary on a 4-hour social pass. He promptly fled and later allegedly murdered two people. The public then demanded the resignation of the prison warden who had issued the pass. However, the prison warden may well have made a good decision, given the information he had at the time. Bowles had in fact been a model prisoner before he left the penitentiary. Unfortunately, however, good decisions can have bad outcomes. Notice why a hindsight bias is operating here. As you were reading about Cletus Bowles, weren't you tempted to conclude that the prison warden had been a fool? In fact, you probably overestimated the extent to which he should have been able to predict that Bowles would harm someone.

Demonstration 11.13 is based on a classic study by Slovic and Fischhoff (1977). Perhaps you've had the experience these researchers examined. You are reading about a study in a textbook, and then you read about the study's results. You think to yourself, "Well, of course! Who needed to do a study to demonstrate that?" In reality, the hindsight bias may have led you to overestimate your confidence.

Slovic and Fischhoff (1977) asked people to make judgments about either a foresight version (such as Version A) or a hindsight version (such as Version B). The people in the foresight version were not told which outcome occurred, whereas the people in the hindsight condition were told the results. Slovic and Fischhoff found that people assigned much higher probabilities to the stated outcome if they had been in the hindsight condition. Specifically, the average estimated probability was .55 for those who had read the hindsight version and .38 for those who had read the foresight version. (Now, be honest. Did you "know it all along" that hindsight is better than foresight?)

The hindsight bias has been demonstrated in a number of different situations, though the effect is not always strong (e.g., Agans & Shaffer, 1994; Cannon & Quinsey, 1995; Christensen-Szalanski & Willham, 1991; Creyer & Ross, 1993; Hawkins & Hastie, 1990). For example, doctors showed the hindsight bias when guessing a medical diagnosis (Arkes et al., 1981), and students showed the hindsight bias when judging that Clarence Thomas would be confirmed as a Supreme Court Justice (Dietrich & Olson, 1993).

In a review of the literature, Christensen-Szalanski and Willham (1991) located 122 studies on the hindsight bias. They then conducted a meta-analysis on these studies. As discussed earlier in the book, the *meta-analysis technique* provides a statistical method for synthesizing numerous studies on a single topic. The meta-analysis on the hindsight studies showed that the overall magnitude of the effect was small. However, it was especially likely to operate when people made judgments about almanac-type information and when people were working on an unfamiliar task.

Hawkins and Hastie (1990) discuss a variety of possible explanations for the hindsight bias. For example, people may reconstruct their prior judgment by rejudging the outcome. In other words, people may use cognitive strategies to make their judgments consistent with reality. Another cognitive explanation is that people might use anchoring and adjustment. They have been told that a particular outcome actually happened—that it was 100% certain. Therefore, they use this 100% value as an anchor, and they do not adjust their certainty downward as much as they should. An additional explanation is motivational, rather than cognitive. Perhaps people simply want to look good in the eyes of the experimenter or other people who may be evaluating them. Did Hawkins and Hastie's explanation surprise me? Of course not; I knew it all along!

In discussing the topic of overconfidence, we have seen several examples in which people are overly confident about their decisions, and we've also seen several explanations for this overconfidence. We've also noted that people are often influenced by the hindsight bias; they overestimate the likelihood that they would have been able to predict an outcome.

New Developments in Decision Making: The Optimists versus the Pessimists

So far, the material on decision making has provided little evidence for Theme 2. Especially compared to some of our astonishing perceptual, memory, and linguistic capabilities, we humans do not seem to be especially wise decision makers. We rely too heavily on three decision-making heuristics, and we are plagued by both framing effects and overconfidence. This is the admittedly pessimistic view presented by researchers such as Tversky and Kahneman. However, they would argue that the three heuristics usually serve us well in our everyday life.

In recent years, however, a group of optimistic decision theorists has emerged. One of the most prominent of these optimists is Gerd Gigerenzer (e.g., Gigerenzer, 1993, 1994; Gigerenzer & Hoffrage, 1995). These theorists argue that people may not be perfectly rational decision makers, but the research hasn't tested them fairly and hasn't used naturalistic settings (Cohen, 1993b; McClelland & Bolger, 1994; Orasanu & Connolly, 1993). Specifically, they argue that people would perform better if psychologists eliminated trick questions that encourage decision makers to ignore important information like base rate. They also argue that people perform better when the question is asked in terms of frequencies, rather than probabilities (e.g., Gigerenzer, 1993).

The optimists also note that research participants may interpret the decision-making task differently than the experimenters had intended. For example, participants might consider that the experimenters are lying—for example, about the relative frequency of engineers and lawyers in Demonstration 11.4 (Cohen, 1993a). As you saw in Frisch's (1993) study, participants bring their world knowledge into the experiment, and they apply this information to the decision. It's "illegal" to rely on world knowledge in deductive reasoning, but this strategy seems quite rational in decision making!

As in most controversies, both positions are probably at least partially correct. The optimists may have a point; the methods used by Kahneman and Tversky—

and others who study decision-making heuristics—may underestimate our potential. However, the pessimists also have a point; they have always argued that the heuristics usually serve us well, and we can become more effective decision makers by realizing the limitations of these rules of thumb.

SECTION SUMMARY: DECISION MAKING

1. Decision-making heuristics are typically useful in our daily lives; many errors in decision making occur because we use heuristics beyond the range for which they are intended.

2. According to the representativeness heuristic, we judge that a sample is likely if it resembles the population from which it was selected.

3. We are so impressed by representativeness that we tend to ignore sample size and base rates; the representativeness heuristic also produces the conjunction fallacy.

4. According to the availability heuristic, we estimate frequency or probability in terms of how easily we can remember examples of something.

5. The availability heuristic produces errors when recency and familiarity influence availability. When we use the simulation heuristic (which is related to availability), we judge likelihood in terms of how easily we can imagine possible events.

6. According to the anchoring and adjustment heuristic, we establish an anchor and then make adjustments based on other information; the problem is that these adjustments are usually too small.

7. We also use the anchoring and adjustment heuristic when we estimate confidence intervals. We arrive at a single best estimate, and then we make very narrow adjustments upwards and downwards to establish a confidence interval.

8. The way in which a question is framed or worded can influence our decisions; background information can influence our decisions inappropriately. Also, when the wording implies gains, we tend to avoid risks; when the wording implies losses, we tend to seek out risks.

9. People are frequently overconfident about their decisions; this overconfidence also produces a hindsight bias.

10. A group of decision-making theorists argues that humans are reasonably skilled at making decisions, and they argue that researchers who emphasize heuristics have not tested people fairly.

CHAPTER REVIEW QUESTIONS

1. Describe the basic differences between deductive reasoning and decision making. Provide at least one example from your daily life that illustrates each cognitive process. Why do they both qualify as thinking?

2. To make certain that you understand conditional reasoning, begin with the sentence, "If a student is a psychology major, then he or she takes a course in statistics before graduating." Apply the four conditional reasoning situations (the propositional calculus) to this sentence, and point out which are valid and which are invalid. Finally, note which of these four tasks are easier and which are most difficult to solve.

3. What factors (other than the conditional reasoning situation) influence people's accuracy on deductive reasoning tasks? Give an example of each of these factors.

4. Many of the errors that people make in reasoning can be traced to overreliance on previous knowledge or overactive top-down processes. Discuss this point, and relate it to the anchoring and adjustment heuristic.

5. Chapter 10 emphasized the importance of understanding problems. Explain how some of the errors in reasoning can be traced to difficulty in understanding. How is this related to the information on the framing effect in decision making?

6. Throughout this chapter, you have seen many examples of a cognitive tendency related to top-down processing: We tend to accept the status quo, without sufficiently exploring other options. How does this statement apply to both deductive reasoning and decision making?

7. Decide which heuristic each of the following everyday errors represents: (a) you decide that you will be more likely to live in Massachusetts than in New Mexico, because you can more easily envision a sequence of events that brings you to Massachusetts; (b) someone asks you whether cardinals or robins are more common, and you decide on the basis of the number of birds of each kind that you have seen this winter; (c) one of your classes has 30 students, including two people named Scott and three named Michele, which seems too coincidental to be due to chance alone; and (d) you estimate the number of bottles of soda you will need for the Fourth of July picnic based on the Christmas party consumption, taking into account the fact that the weather will be warmer in July.

8. In the case of the representativeness heuristic, people fail to take into account two important factors that should be emphasized. In the case of the availability heuristic, people take into account two important factors that should be ignored. Discuss these statements, with reference to the information in this chapter. Give examples of each of these four kinds of errors.

9. Describe the variety of ways in which people tend to be overconfident in their decision making. Think of relevant examples from your own experience. Be sure to include the hindsight bias in your list.

10. Imagine that you have been hired by your local high-school district to create a course in critical thinking. Review the chapter and make 15 to 20 suggestions (each only a sentence long) about precautions that should be included in such a program.

NEW TERMS

thinking
deductive reasoning
decision making
conditional reasoning
propositional reasoning
syllogism
the propositional calculus
antecedent
consequent
affirming the antecedent
affirming the consequent
denying the antecedent
denying the consequent
belief-bias effect

illicit conversion
confirmation bias
heuristics
representative
representativeness
 heuristic
law of large numbers
small-sample fallacy
base rate
base-rate fallacy
Bayes' theorem
likelihood ratio
conjunction rule
conjunction fallacy

availability heuristic
illusory correlation
simulation heuristic
anchoring and adjustment
 heuristic
anchor
confidence intervals
framing effect
overconfidence
hindsight
hindsight bias
meta-analysis technique

RECOMMENDED READINGS

Evans, J. St. B. T., Newstead, S. E., & Byrne, R. M. J. (1993). *Human reasoning: The psychology of deduction.* Hove, England: Erlbaum. This book includes three chapters on conditional reasoning, as well as coverage on syllogisms and inferences involving a series of items.

Hawkins, S. A., & Hastie, R. (1990). Hindsight: Biased judgments of past events after the outcomes are known. *Psychological Bulletin, 107,* 311–327. This article provides a superb review of the topic, giving examples of both laboratory research and real-life decision making.

Klein, G. A., Orasanu, J., Calderwood, R., & Zsambok, C. E. (Eds.). (1993). *Decision making in action: Models and methods.* Norwood, NJ: Ablex. Here's a book that presents a good overview of the "optimist" position on decision making; the two chapters by Martin Cohen are especially relevant to the chapter you have just read.

Nisbett, R. E. (Ed.). (1993). *Rules for reasoning.* Hillsdale, NJ: Erlbaum. Useful chapters in this book cover topics such as heuristics, statistical training, and how to teach reasoning.

Piattelli-Palmarini, M. (1994). *Inevitable illusions: How mistakes of reason rule our minds.* New York: Wiley. As you might guess from the grim title, this book presents the "pessimist" view of decision making; it is written for the intelligent general reader, and it includes many interesting anecdotes.

Poulton, E. C. (1994). *Behavioral decision theory: A new approach.* Cambridge, England: Cambridge University Press. Although the level of writing in this book is fairly sophisticated, students will appreciate the broad range of topics, including overconfidence, hindsight, the small-sample fallacy, the conjunction fallacy, base-rate neglect, and the major heuristics.

ANSWERS TO DEMONSTRATIONS

Demonstration 11.1
1. valid
2. invalid
3. invalid
4. valid

Demonstration 11.9
1. 27% French
2. 76% of the mothers
3. 6,751,404 people
4. 3,286,470 square miles
5. 57 universities
6. 470 languages
7. 347 B.C.
8. 99% literacy rate
9. 44% nonvoters
10. 139 cm (55 inches)

COGNITIVE DEVELOPMENT

INTRODUCTION

THE DEVELOPMENT OF MEMORY

Memory in Infants
In Depth: Memory in Children
Memory in Elderly People

THE DEVELOPMENT OF METACOGNITION

Metacognition in Children
Metacognition in Elderly People

THE DEVELOPMENT OF LANGUAGE

Language in Infants
Language in Children

==================== **Preview** ====================

$\mathbf{T}$his chapter examines how cognitive processes develop in three areas: memory, metacognition, and language. Some skills improve as children mature to adulthood, and some decline as adults reach old age. However, other skills show less change than might be expected.

According to recent research, even young infants can remember people, objects, and events. For example, 6-month-olds can remember how to repeat an action that they learned 2 weeks earlier. Children's recognition memory is surprisingly accurate, but their working memory and long-term recall memory is considerably less accurate than in adults. Young children also fail to use memory strategies spontaneously when they want to remember something. Elderly adults are somewhat similar to young adults in sensory memory and on some working memory and long-term memory tasks. However, other kinds of memory (for example, memory for people's names) may decline.

Studies on metacognition reveal that children change in their metamemory as they grow older. For example, older children are more accurate than young children in estimating their own memory span. Older children are also more skilled in measures of metacomprehension. However, young adults and elderly adults are generally comparable in their metamemory.

With respect to language development, young infants are remarkably competent in perceiving speech. As children mature, their skills increase dramatically in areas such as word meaning, grammatical relationships, and the social aspects of language.

INRODUCTION

The following conversation between two 4-year-old children was overheard in a playroom:

GIRL: (*on toy telephone*) David!
BOY: (*not picking up second phone*) I'm not home.
GIRL: When you'll be back?
BOY: I'm not here already.
GIRL: *But when you'll be back?*
BOY: Don't you know if I'm gone already, I went *before* so I can't talk to you!
(Miller, 1981)

This dialogue captures the considerable language skills of young children, while illustrating some ways in which they differ from adults. As another 4-year-old boy remarked to his mother one morning, "You know, I thought I'd be a grown-up by now .

. . . It sure is taking a long time!" (Rogoff, 1990, p. 3). As we will see in this chapter, the boy is absolutely correct. Four-year-olds have mastered some aspects of memory and language, but they still need to develop their skills in memory performance, memory strategies, metacognition, syntax, and pragmatics.

This chapter will examine not only the cognitive development of young children, but also the cognitive skills of elderly people. The chapter will emphasize that some cognitive skills decline during the aging process, but many other capabilities remain stable.

When we study the cognitive abilities of the very young and the very old, the research problems are even more complex than when we study young adults. How can young infants convey what they know, given their limited language and motor skills? As Jean Mandler (1990) remarked, researchers "have tended to confuse infants' motor incompetence with conceptual incompetence" (p. 240). Research with the elderly presents a different set of methodological problems. Many studies have compared the performance of young, healthy college students with the performance of elderly people whose health, self-confidence, and education are relatively poor. Furthermore, college students have had extensive recent experience with memorizing material and taking tests, whereas elderly people have not. Of course, confounding variables like these cannot account for all age-related cognitive differences; however, they do explain a substantial portion of the differences (Birren & Schaie, 1996; Kausler, 1990; Salthouse, 1991).

This chapter focuses on cognitive development in three areas: memory, metacognition, and language.[1] The final chapter therefore allows you to review the important concepts in three important areas within cognitive psychology. In addition, you will learn not only that infants and young children possess cognitive skills you might not have suspected, but also that elderly people are quite cognitively competent.

THE DEVELOPMENT OF MEMORY

Many parts of this textbook have examined memory. Chapters 3, 4, and 5 focused specifically on memory, and the remaining chapters discussed the contribution of memory to other cognitive processes. Now we will examine how memory develops from infancy and childhood through old age.

Memory in Infants

Think about an infant you know, a baby under one year of age. Would you expect that this baby would recognize his or her mother, remember the location of hidden

---

[1]This chapter does not cover theoretical approaches to cognitive development, such as the approach of Jean Piaget. This controversial topic would require a lengthy discussion, and many students who read this book are likely to have learned about these theories in previous courses.

objects, or imitate simple actions? Naturally, we cannot expect sophisticated memory feats from a young infant. After all, the synaptic connections in the portions of the cortex most relevant to long-term memory will not be fully developed for several more years, perhaps as late as 7 years of age (Bauer, 1996; Siegler, 1989). Furthermore, we will underestimate infants' memory capacities unless we can create a task that depends upon a response the infant has already mastered (Kail, 1990; Rovee-Collier & Boller, 1995).

Fortunately, developmental psychologists have recently devised several methods to test infants' ability to remember people and objects. The research shows that infants have greater memory capabilities than you might expect. Indeed Theme 2—which emphasizes cognitive competence—can even be applied to infants.

Recognizing Mother. In our North American culture, infants generally spend more time with their mother than with any other person. Research on visual recognition shows that even 2-day-olds seem to be able to distinguish their mother from a stranger (Bushnell & Sai, 1987). In a representative study, Walton and her coauthors (1992) found that infants younger than 3 days of age made significantly more sucking responses in order to produce a video of their mother's face, rather than a video of a visually similar stranger's face.

Infants' ability to recognize their mother's voice is equally remarkable. DeCasper and Fifer (1980) found that 3-day-old babies sucked on pacifiers at different rates to produce either the voice of their mother or the voice of a female stranger. Impressively, these tiny babies produced their mother's voice more often than the stranger's. They probably become accustomed to mother's voice while still in the uterus. DeCasper and Spence (1986) demonstrated that newborns prefer a particular Dr. Seuss passage that their mother read aloud each day during the last three months of pregnancy, rather than a similar passage that had never been read.

Infants can even smell the difference between their mother and a stranger. In typical research on smell recognition, infants demonstrate their memory by turning their heads to a breastpad worn by their mother, rather than a breastpad worn by a stranger. Researchers have not established exactly when infants acquire smell recognition. However, estimates vary between 6 days and 6 weeks of age (Cernoch & Porter, 1985; Macfarlane, 1977; Russell, 1976).

The Conjugate Reinforcement Technique. The most extensive program of research on infant memory has been conducted by Carolyn Rovee-Collier and her colleagues, using the conjugate reinforcement technique. In the ***conjugate reinforcement technique,*** a mobile is placed above an infant's crib; a ribbon connects the infant's ankle and the mobile, so that the infant's kicks produce motion in the mobile. (See Figure 12.1.) According to Rovee-Collier and Boller (1995), 2- to 6-month-old infants seem to like this game. After several minutes, they begin to kick rapidly and pump up the mobile; then they lie quietly and watch parts of the mobile move. As the movement dies down, they typically shriek and then kick vigorously, thereby pumping it up again. In operant conditioning terms, the *response* is a foot kick, and the *reinforcement* is the movement of the mobile.

===================== **FIGURE 12.1** =====================

THE CONJUGATE REINFORCEMENT SETUP IN ROVEE-COLLIER'S RESEARCH.

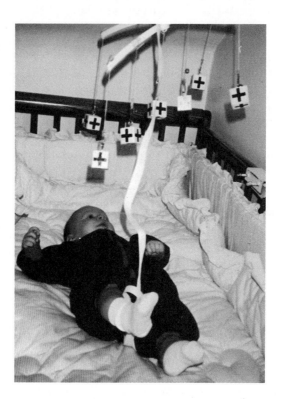

Let's see how the conjugate reinforcement technique can be used to assess infant memory. All the training and testing take place in the infant's crib at home, so that measurements are not distorted by the infant's reactions to the new surroundings. For a 3-minute period at the beginning of the first session, the experimenter takes a baseline measure. During this time, the ribbon is attached to an "empty" mobile stand, rather than to the mobile. Thus, the experimenters can measure the amount of spontaneous kicking that occurs in the presence of the mobile, prior to learning (Rovee-Collier, 1987; Rovee-Collier & Boller, 1995).

Next, the experimenter moves one end of the ribbon from the empty mobile stand to the stand from which the mobile is hung. The babies are allowed 9 minutes to discover that their kicks can activate the mobile and to enjoy playing with it; this is the acquisition phase. The infants typically receive two training sessions like this, spaced 24 hours apart. At the end of the second session, the ribbon is unhooked and returned to the empty stand for 3 minutes in order to measure what they remember; this is the immediate retention test.

Long-term memory is then measured after 1 to 42 days have elapsed. The mobile is once again hung over the infant's crib, with the ribbon hooked to the empty stand. If the infant recognizes the mobile and recalls how kicking had produced movement, then he or she will produce the foot-kick response. Notice, then, that Rovee-Collier has devised a clever way to "ask" infants if they remember how to activate the mobile. She has also devised an objective method for measuring memory, because she can compare the number of kicks produced following the delay to the number of kicks produced in the immediate retention test.

Rovee-Collier and Boller (1995) recently devised a similar task that would be more appealing to infants between the ages of 6 and 12 months. In this task, infants learn to press a lever in order to make a miniature train move along a circular track. Figure 12.2 shows how much time can pass before infants no longer show significant recall for the task. For example, 6-month-olds can recall how to move the

FIGURE 12.2

THE MAXIMUM DURATION FOR WHICH INDEPENDENT GROUPS OF INFANTS EXHIBITED SIGNIFICANT RETENTION; INFANTS BETWEEN 2 AND 6 MONTHS OF AGE KICKED TO ACTIVATE A MOBILE, AND INFANTS BETWEEN 6 AND 12 MONTHS PRESSED A LEVER TO ACTIVATE A TRAIN.   ROVEE-COLLIER & BOLLER (1995).

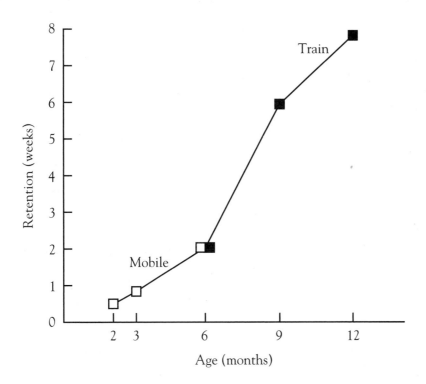

mobile and also how to move the train, even after a 2-week delay. As you can see, retention shows a steady improvement during the first months of life.

We saw in Chapter 5 that context sometimes influences adult memory; contextual effects are even stronger for infants. For example, Rovee-Collier and her colleagues (1985) used the conjugate reinforcement technique to test 3-month-old infants whose cribs were lined with a fabric that had a distinctive, colorful pattern. The infants' recall was excellent when they were tested after a 7-day delay. However, another group of infants was tested with the same mobile and the same delay—but with a different crib liner. This second group of infants showed no retention whatsoever! Without the proper environmental context, infants' memories decline sharply.

You'll also recall from Chapter 5 that young adults' eyewitness testimony for details of an accident was modified if they learned new information—about a stop sign, rather than a yield sign—after witnessing the events. (See pages 163–164.) Similarly, Rovee-Collier and her coauthors (1993) measured "eyewitness testimony" in 3-month-olds. Immediately after the infants had learned how to produce movement in one particular mobile, they were shown a novel mobile for just 3 minutes. When long-term memory was later tested, they showed significantly less recall for the original mobile than did babies in a control group, who had seen no second mobile. Infants—like adults—recall an event less accurately if they have been exposed to post-event information.

In subsequent research, Rovee-Collier and her associates have discovered yet another similarity between infant and adult memory. You may recall the *spacing effect* from Chapter 5; students learn most effectively if their practice is distributed over time, rather than if they learn the material all at once (page 176). A number of studies have now demonstrated that infants also remember better if their practice is distributed (Rovee-Collier, 1995; Rovee-Collier et al., 1995).

To explain this spacing phenomenon, Rovee-Collier proposed a concept called a time window. A *time window* is a limited period—between the first exposure and a second exposure—during which the infant can integrate the new information with the old. Babies remember most effectively if several days pass before the second exposure. However, if you wait too long, the time window has closed, and the baby can no longer integrate the two events. (I'm hopeful that your own time window has remained open long enough for you to recall similar information that you saw seven chapters ago!)

Remembering the Location of Objects. Infants can also remember the location of a hidden object. Baillargeon and Graber (1988) presented 7- and 8-month-old infants with a distinctive-looking object, a white Styrofoam cup decorated with stars and dots, located on one of two placemats. After 3 seconds of viewing, identical screens were placed in front of the two placemats so that the object was no longer visible. Then a human hand emerged, wearing a long silver glove and a jingle-bell bracelet. The hand "tiptoed" back and forth for 15 seconds, then reached behind one of the two screens, and came out holding the white cup. Half of the time the cup came from behind the screen where it was supposed to be located, thereby representing a possible event. In the remaining instances, the cup came from behind the other screen, representing an impossible event.

Baillargeon and Graber found that 8-month-old infants looked significantly longer at the cup in the impossible-event condition, indicating that they were puzzled by its unexpected location. However, the 7-month-olds looked at the cup for an equal amount of time in both conditions, thus indicating they do not seem to remember the original location of an object after it has been hidden for a 15-second period. Thus, memory for location seems to emerge between 7 and 8 months of age.

Imitation. Most parents can remember examples of their infant imitating an action he or she had previously seen. But how can we encourage imitation so that it can be studied objectively? Mandler and McDonough (1995) showed 11-month-old infants a two-step sequence of actions. For example, the experimenter pushed a button through a slot in a transparent box and then shook the box, saying "Shake, shake, shake." Three months later, the infants returned to the laboratory, and 50% of them spontaneously imitated the previous action. In contrast, this action was performed by only 25% of infants in a control group, who had not had previous experience on the task.

Other infants in this study learned a two-step sequence of actions that was *not* causally related. For example, the experimenter placed a hat on a toy bunny and fed it a carrot. Infants in this condition did not perform significantly better on this arbitrary-sequence task than did the infants in a control group who had no previous experience on the task. You'll recall that we discussed scripts and schemas in Chapter 7. Apparently, 11-month-old infants already appreciate the structure of a two-event script!

In summary, infants demonstrate memory on a number of tasks. Newborns can recognize the sight, sound, and smell of their mothers, and babies a few months older can remember how to activate a mobile after a 2-week delay. Eight-month-olds can recall the location of hidden objects, and 11-month-olds can remember how to imitate actions after a 3-month delay.

IN DEPTH: Memory in Children

We have seen that researchers need to be extremely inventive when they study infant memory. By using the conjugate reinforcement technique, imitation tasks, and other creative methods, they have concluded that infants' memory is reasonably impressive.

Assessing children's memory is much easier, because children can respond verbally. However, the task is still far from simple, because children may have trouble understanding task instructions, and they may not be able to identify certain stimuli (for example, letters of the alphabet). This in-depth section considers three components of children's memory: (1) sensory and working memory, (2) long-term memory, and (3) memory strategies.

Sensory and Working Memory. In general, studies of sensory memory show that children and adults have similar kinds of sensory memory (Engle et al., 1981; Hoving et al., 1978). Reviews of the literature in cognitive development conclude that the capacity is similar for adults and for 5-year-old children with respect to both iconic (visual) and echoic (auditory) memory. The decay rates are also thought to be similar (Kail & Siegel, 1977; Rosser, 1994).

Working memory is often measured in terms of memory span. Tests of memory span usually measure the number of items that can be correctly recalled in order immediately after presentation. As you might expect, memory span improves dramatically during childhood; a 2-year-old can recall an average of two numbers in a row, whereas a 9-year-old can recall six (Kail, 1992). In other words, older children's working memory capacity is close to the adult level. Now let's turn our attention to a general consideration of long-term memory in children, followed by a discussion of some of the important issues in children's autobiographical memory.

Long-Term Memory: General. Children typically have excellent recognition memory but poor recall memory (e.g., Brown & Scott, 1971; Peters, 1987; Small, 1990). In a classic study, Myers and Perlmutter (1978) performed experiments similar to those in Demonstration 12.1, using 2- and 4-year-old children. To test recognition, the researchers showed children 18 objects. Then they presented 36 items, including the 18 previous objects and 18 new objects. The 4-year-olds recognized about 90% of the items, and even the 2-year-olds recognized about 80% of the items. When different groups of children were tested for their ability to *recall* nine objects, the 4-year-olds recalled about 40% of the items, and the 2-year-olds recalled about 20% of the items.

You may recall that Chapter 5 discussed ***reality monitoring,*** which is the process of trying to decide which memories are real and which are simply imagined. In general, children have more difficulty than adults in distinguishing between reality and fantasy (Foley & Ratner, 1996; Ratner & Foley, 1994). For example, I know an extremely bright child who had participated in an imaginary trip to the moon one day at school. Later that day, she claimed that she really *had* visited the moon.

Research has demonstrated age-related changes in reality monitoring. For example, in research by Foley and her colleagues (1987) and by Harris and Foley (1992), children and adults either drew objects or imagined themselves drawing objects. Young children had more difficulty than older children in remembering which activities they had actually done and which they had imagined doing; older children also had more difficulty than adults. Similarly, in another study, 4-year-olds worked together with adults in making collages (Foley et al., 1993). The 4-year-olds made many errors in deciding which pieces they had placed on the collage and which had been placed there by adults. The children frequently claimed, "I did it," when the adult had actually contributed the pieces.

DEMONSTRATION 12.1

AGE DIFFERENCES IN RECALL AND RECOGNITION

In this experiment you will need to test a college-age person and a preschool child. You should reassure the child's parents that you are simply testing memory as part of a class project.

You will be examining both recall and recognition in this demonstration. First, assemble 20 common objects, such as a pen, pencil, piece of paper, leaf, stick, rock, book, key, apple, and so on. Place the objects in a box or cover them with a cloth.

You will use the same testing procedure for both people, although the preschool child will require more extensive explanation. Remove 10 objects in all, 1 at a time. Show each object for about 5 seconds and then conceal it again. After all 10 objects have been shown, ask each person to recall as many of the objects as possible. Do not provide feedback about the correctness of the responses. After recall is complete, test for recognition. Remove one object at a time, randomly presenting the old objects mixed in sequence with new objects. In each case, ask whether the object is old or new.

Count the number of correct recalls and the number of correct recognitions for each person. You should find that they both show a similar high level of performance on the *recognition* measures. However, the older person will *recall* far more than the younger person.

Other research has demonstrated that children use scripts in their memories (Small, 1990). For example, children as young as 3 years of age can supply script-like answers to general questions such as "Can you tell me what happens when you have lunch at the day-care center?" (Nelson, 1986). Children respond by listing the critical actions in the appropriate time sequence; they rely on generic information, rather than on specific episodes. In fact, children are more attentive to the typical, script-type aspects of events than to the distinctive aspects that make each event unique (Farrar & Goodman, 1990; Fivush & Hamond, 1990).

Children also use schemas in their memory. For example, children in a study by Davidson and her colleagues (1995) were asked to recall information about a person who had been described as elderly. Their recall showed some systematic distortions, so that recall was more consistent with children's schemas about the elderly. For example, when they had been told that an elderly person was healthy, they tended to recall that the elderly person was sick.

Long-Term Memory: Autobiographical Memory. The research on children's autobiographical memory is the most controversial topic in this chapter. This controversy has theoretical implications for the nature of young children's memory, as well as practical implications for children's eyewitness testimony.

One area of interest is often called *infantile amnesia,* a term that refers to adults' general inability to remember events that occurred in their lives prior to the age of about 3 (Howe & Courage, 1993). Some argue that children can remember important events—such as the birth of a sibling—if they occurred even earlier, at age 2 (Usher & Neisser, 1993). However, others point out that this "recall" is not based on true memories, but on educated guesses or stories heard from other family members (Loftus, 1993b).

As you might imagine—based on what you know about infant memory—young children often reveal impressive memory skills when they are appropriately tested. For example, McDonough and Mandler (1994) found that 23-month-old children recalled feeding a teddy bear with a plastic cylinder—an action they had performed 12 months earlier! In fact, very young children can recall suprisingly well when the circumstances are ideal: (1) when recall is tested nonverbally rather than verbally; (2) when they experience an event several times; and (3) when they are provided with reminders (Bauer, 1995). However, true autobiographical memory for life events may require more sophisticated cognitive abilities, such as a well-developed sense of self (Howe & Courage, 1993).

A second important topic within the area of children's autobiographical memory concerns the accuracy of their eyewitness testimony. Let's first consider a court case in which a child's testimony played an important role, and then we'll discuss research on suggestibility in children's testimonies. We'll conclude by briefly examining some other factors that need to be considered in evaluating the accuracy of children's eyewitness reports.

In 1984, Frederico Martinez Macias was accused of the armed robbery and murder of an elderly couple (Ceci & Bruck, 1995; Leichtman & Ceci, 1995). Another man, who had been found with stolen property belonging to the couple, accused Macias of the actual murder. Two witnesses said that Macias was elsewhere on the night of the murder, and the only witness testifying against Macias was not compelling. So the police began to search for another person who had seen Macias. (Incidentally, if you've just read Chapter 11, you might notice the confirmation bias. The police were trying to gather evidence for their hypothesis that Macias might be guilty, rather than a hypothesis that he might be innocent.) An investigator happened to have a conversation with a 9-year-old girl named Jennifer F., who mentioned that she had seen Macias with blood spattered on his shirt and hands, on about the date of the murder. The trial did not emphasize that Jennifer's mother had frequently told her that Macias was a bad man, or that Macias worked in a salsa factory.

Four years later—and two weeks before Macias was scheduled to be executed by a lethal injection—Jennifer made a statement. In retrospect, she hadn't been certain whether the red stain was blood or salsa. Many people had asked her questions, and they encouraged her to be more certain than she felt. Ultimately, she had supplied answers because she had wanted to help the adults. (Fortunately, a stay of execution was issued, and Macias was eventually set free.)

The Macias case inspired an experiment by Michelle Leichtman and Stephen Ceci (1995) that examined the influence of stereotypes and suggestions on children's eyewitness testimony. They tested 176 preschoolers, assigning each child to one of four conditions. In the *control condition,* a stranger named Sam Stone visited the classroom, strolling around, and making several bland comments for a period of about 2 minutes. In the *stereotype condition,* a research assistant presented one story each week to the children for three weeks prior to Sam Stone's visit; each story emphasized that Sam Stone was nice but very clumsy and bumbling. In the *suggestion condition,* children had no knowledge of Sam Stone prior to his visit. However, during interviews after his visit, the interviewer provided two incorrect suggestions—that Sam Stone had ripped a book and spilled chocolate on a white teddy bear. In the *stereotype-plus-suggestion* condition, children were exposed to both the stereotype before Sam Stone's visit and the suggestions afterwards.

Ten weeks after Sam Stone's classroom visit, a new interviewer, whom no child had previously met, asked what Sam Stone had done during his visit. As part of the interview, the children were asked whether they had actually seen him tear up the book and pour chocolate on the teddy bear. Figure 12.3 shows the results for the percentage of children who said they had witnessed at least one of these events.

Notice, first of all, that children in the control group were highly accurate; only 5% of the younger children and *none* of the older children claimed to have witnessed something that Sam Stone had not actually done. However, a worrisome number of children claimed they had witnessed these actions if a previous stereotype had been established. (Notice that this condition mimicked the stereotype that Jennifer F.'s mother had established about Frederico Macias.) Even more of the younger children claimed they had witnessed the actions when suggestions had been made prior to the final interview. Most alarming is that nearly half the younger children claimed to have witnessed the actions when they had received both the stereotype and the suggestions.

But shouldn't a trained observer be able to detect these inaccurate reports? The researchers showed videotaped interviews to more than one thousand clinicians and researchers who worked with children. Despite their expertise, these professionals thought that a child who made up a detailed description of Sam Stone's "offenses" was more believable than a child who firmly—and correctly—denied seeing either offense (Ceci, 1994; Leichtman & Ceci, 1995).

Several other factors also decrease the accuracy of children's eyewitness testimonies. We've already discussed how children have trouble deciding which memories are real and which are simply imagined (Ratner & Foley, 1994). Children also confuse details that occurred during similar events. For example, Howe and his colleagues (1995) questioned preschoolers six months after the children had been treated for trauma in an emergency room. About half the 3-year-olds inserted details from a different traumatic event. Finally, children are extremely reluctant to say "I don't know" when an adult questions them about what they know (Ceci & Bruck, 1993).

The topic of children's eyewitness testimony is far too complicated to construct any simple guidelines for when to trust children and when to suspect their reports

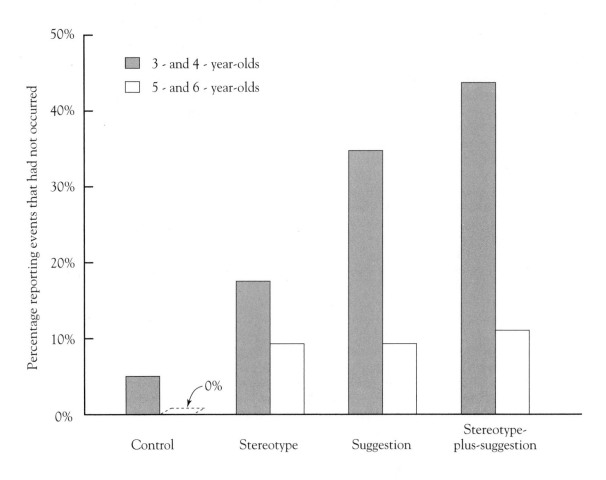

FIGURE 12.3

THE EFFECTS OF STEREOTYPES AND SUGGESTIONS ON YOUNG CHILDREN'S EYEWIT-
NESS TESTIMONY: THE PERCENTAGE WHO REPORTED ACTUALLY SEEING EVENTS
THAT HAD NOT OCCURRED. BASED ON LEICHTMAN & CECI (1995).

(e.g., Ceci & Bruck, 1995; Dent & Flin, 1992; Goodman & Bottoms, 1993). Under
ideal circumstances, most older children are reasonably trustworthy. However, children's reports may be questionable when they are young, when they have been supplied with stereotypes and suggestive comments, when reality may be confused with
fantasy or with other real-life events, and when adults pressure them to make a
clear-cut response.

Memory Strategies. So far, our exploration of children's memory has demonstrated that children are most similar to adults in their sensory memory and their

recognition memory. In contrast, they differ most from adults in their recall memory. When adults want to remember something that must be recalled at a later time, they are likely to use memory strategies. A possible explanation for children's relatively poor performance in recall is that they are not able to use memory strategies effectively.

Strategies are deliberate, goal-oriented behaviors we use to improve our memories (Kail, 1990). Young children may not realize that strategies can be helpful. Furthermore, their strategies may be faulty, and the children may not use the strategies effectively (Flavell, Miller, & Miller, 1993; Wellman, 1988). In contrast, older children typically realize that strategies are helpful. In addition, they choose their strategies more carefully and use them more consistently (e.g., Cairns & Valsiner, 1984; Kail, 1990; Small, 1990). Let's survey three major kinds of memory strategies: rehearsal, organization, and imagery.

1. *Rehearsal,* or merely repeating items over and over, is not a particularly effective strategy, but it may be useful for maintaining items in working memory. Research suggests that 4- and 5-year-olds do not rehearse (Flavell et al., 1966; Gathercole et al., 1994). However, 7-year-olds do use rehearsal strategies, often rehearsing several words together (Flavell et al., 1966; Kail, 1990). As children grow older, they also begin to rehearse at a faster rate (Hulme & Tordoff, 1989). As we saw in Chapter 4, working memory capacity is related to the number of items that can be rehearsed in a short period of time. Part of the reason that adults have larger working memory capacities may be that they can rehearse more quickly than children.

Another important point is that younger children benefit from rehearsal strategies, but they may not use these strategies spontaneously (e.g., Baker-Ward et al., 1984; Flavell, 1985; Liben, 1982). As we will see in the section on metacognition, young children often fail to realize that they could improve their memory performance by using strategies.

2. *Organizational strategies,* such as categorizing and grouping, are frequently used by adults, as we saw in Chapter 5. However, young children do not spontaneously group similar items together to aid memorization. Try Demontration 12.2 and see whether children are reluctant to adopt organizational strategies.

This demonstration is based on a study by Moely and her colleagues (1969), in which children studied pictures from four categories: animals, clothing, furniture, and vehicles. During the 2-minute study period, they were told that they could rearrange the pictures in any order they wished. Younger children rarely moved the pictures next to other similar pictures, but older children frequently organized the pictures into categories. Other groups of children were specifically urged to organize the pictures. This training procedure encouraged even the younger children to adopt an organizational strategy, and this strategy increased their recall. Thus, children often have the ability to organize, though they are not aware that organization will enhance recall. Other research has shown that grade-school children can use spatial organization to remember the names of the other students in their classroom (Bjorklund & Zeman, 1982).

ORGANIZATIONAL STRATEGIES IN CHILDREN

Make a photocopy of the pictures on this page and use scissors to cut them apart (or, alternatively, cut four different categories of pictures out of magazines). In this experiment you will test a child between the ages of 4 and 8; ideally, it would be interesting to test children of several different ages. Arrange these pictures in random order in a circle facing the child. Instruct him or her to study the pictures so that they can be remembered later. Mention that the pictures can be rearranged in any order. After a two-minute study period, remove the pictures and ask the child to list as many items as possible. Notice two things in this demonstration: (1) Does the child rearrange the items at all during the study period? (2) Does the child show clustering during recall, with similar items appearing together?

3. *Imagery,* a topic discussed in Chapters 5 and 6, is an extremely useful device for improving memory in adults. Research has demonstrated that children as young as 6 can also effectively use visual imagery on memory tasks (Foley et al., 1993; Kosslyn, 1976). Furthermore, Yuille and Catchpole (1977) found that first-graders' memories improved after they had been trained to form interactive images. Specifically, these authors displayed pairs of objects, one at a time, and asked children to imagine the two objects playing together. Compared to children in a control group, these children recalled significantly more material, both in immediate recall and after a 1-week delay. Thus, just 5 minutes of training can lead to a long-lasting improvement in learning. Grade-school teachers should offer more instruction on how to learn. In particular, young children can benefit from training that is designed to improve their memory (Fry & Lupart, 1986).

In short, preschool children are unlikely to use memory strategies in a careful, consistent fashion. In fact, as we have suggested here—and will further discuss in the section on metamemory—children are not likely to appreciate that they need to use memory strategies. However, as children develop, they learn how to use memory strategies such as rehearsal, organization, and imagery. Furthermore, they become aware that if they want to remember something, they would be wise to use these memory strategies, rather than merely trusting that they will remember important material.

Memory in Elderly People

Irene Hulicka (1982) provides an illustration of the way people judge cognitive errors made by elderly people. A 78-year-old woman served a meal to her guests, and the meal was excellent except that she had used Clorox instead of vinegar in the salad dressing. Her concerned relatives attributed the error to impaired memory and general intellectual decline, and they discussed placing her in a nursing home. As it turned out, someone else had placed the Clorox in the cupboard where the vinegar was kept. Understandably, the woman had reached for the wrong bottle, which was similar in size, shape, and color to the vinegar bottle.

Some time later, the same people were guests in another home. A young woman in search of hair spray reached into a bathroom cabinet and found a can of the right size and shape. She proceeded to drench her hair with Lysol. In this case, however, no one suggested that the younger woman be institutionalized; they merely teased her about her absentmindedness. Apparently, people are so convinced that elderly people have cognitive deficits that an incident considered humorous in a younger person provides proof of incompetence in an older person.

During the last decade, research on memory in the elderly has increased dramatically, and a wide variety of review articles and books have been published (e.g., Birren & Schaie, 1996; Cerella et al., 1993; Craik & Salthouse, 1992; Light, 1991; Lovelace, 1990a). The picture that emerges suggests large individual differences and complex developmental trends in various components of memory (Lachman, 1991; Whitbourne & Powers, 1996). Let us consider the research on sensory memory, working memory, and long-term memory; then we will examine some potential explanations for the memory changes during aging.

Sensory Memory. In general, researchers have not discovered major developmental changes in sensory memory, that fragile storage system that retains information for less than two seconds (Kausler, 1994). Some studies, however, have reported moderate decline in iconic (or visual sensory) memory when using the Sperling technique, described in Chapter 4 (Walsh & Thompson, 1978). One explanation for the age-related difference may be that elderly people tend to concentrate their attention on the top row of letters (Kausler, 1994; Rebok, 1987). In contrast, younger people distribute their attention more evenly throughout the visual display, thereby increasing their scores on Sperling-type tests. When other tests are used, iconic memory is fairly similar for younger and older adults (Gilmore et al., 1986; Kausler, 1994).

Echoic memory, or auditory sensory memory, may be difficult to assess because hearing declines somewhat in many elderly people (Kausler, 1994). Many tests of echoic memory also use divided-attention tasks, which may be difficult for older adults (Erber, 1982). In general, however, both researchers and theorists have concluded that the echoic memory of younger people and of elderly adults does not differ substantially (Craik, 1977; Crowder, 1980; Kausler, 1994). In summary, if we want to discover major ways in which the memory of 80-year-olds differs from the memory of 20-year-olds, we will have to look beyond sensory memory. Let us turn our attention to working memory and then long-term memory.

Working Memory. How well do elderly people perform on tasks requiring working memory, when material must be retained in memory for less than a minute? If you have taken several previous psychology courses, you'll probably agree that your professors and your textbooks frequently use the phrase, "It all depends on . . . ." In the case of working memory, factors such as the nature of the task determine whether we find age similarities or age differences. In general, we find age similarities when the task is relatively straightforward; we find age differences when the task is complicated and requires manipulation of information (Craik, 1992; Smith, 1996).

For example, Craik (1990) reports that younger and older adults performed similarly on a standard digit-span test, where people were instructed to recall a list of numbers in order. However, age differences were substantial for a task in which people were given short lists of unrelated words, with the instructions to report the words in correct alphabetical order. For example, the average young participant reported 3.2 correct items on the alphabetical-order task, whereas the average elderly participant reported only 1.7 correct items.

Another example of the complex nature of working memory comes from Stine and her coauthors (1989), who tested people's recall for spoken English. When the sentences had normal syntax and were spoken at the normal rate, the younger and older participants performed similarly. However, when the words were in random order and the speech rate was much faster than normal, the younger participants recalled about twice as many items. We should keep in mind, then, that elderly people perform well on the task they are most likely to encounter in everyday life.

Researchers have found that elderly people encounter some difficulties on working-memory tasks in which they must keep some information in memory while processing or manipulating material. For instance, older people are more likely than younger people to make errors on mental arithmetic problems (Salthouse & Babcock, 1991). Once again, age differences are likely to emerge when the task is complicated and requires manipulation of information.

Long-Term Memory. Do elderly people differ from younger adults in their long-term memory? Once again, the answer is, "It all depends on . . . ." In general, the age differences are smallest on tasks that involve recognition memory and on tasks that can be performed relatively automatically. However, age differences emerge on more challenging tasks.

A number of research papers and reviews of the literature argue that long-term *recognition* memory declines either slowly or not at all as people grow older (Craik et al., 1987; Craik & McDowd, 1987; Lavigne & Finley, 1990). However, elderly people may have a significantly higher false-alarm rate; they may say that an item is old, when in fact they have never seen it before (Trahan et al., 1986).

Chapter 5 discussed the difference between explicit and implicit memory measures. As you may recall, an ***explicit memory measure*** requires the participant to remember information in an active fashion (for example, recall or recognition). In contrast, an ***implicit memory measure*** requires the participant to perform a perceptual or cognitive task. For instance, Light and her colleagues (1995) measured implicit memory in terms of the time required to say a letter sequence that was formed by combining two familiar one-syllable words (e.g., *fishdust*). Implicit memory would be demonstrated when people performed more quickly on the letter sequences that they had seen on previous trials, compared to letter sequences formed by recombining words from the previous trials (e.g., when they had seen *artmale* and *pointinch,* then seeing the recombined item, *artinch*). In other words, people demonstrate memory by showing that they read a familiar sequence faster than an unfamiliar sequence. On this task, adults between the ages of 64 and 78 remembered as well as adults between the ages of 18 and 24.

Other research on implicit memory shows either similar performance by older and younger adults, or else just a slight deficit for older adults (e.g., La Voie & Light, 1994; Light & Albertson, 1989; Light & La Voie, 1993; Lovelace & Coon, 1991; Russo & Parkin, 1993). Thus, age differences are minimal when the memory task involves fairly automatic processing.

Let us now turn to performance on long-term *recall* tasks, where age differences are more substantial. For example, older people make more errors in recalling names and in recalling details of historical events (Cohen, 1993; Cohen et al., 1994). Also, consider the research on recall for lengthy passages of standard English. Zelinski and Gilewski (1988) conducted a meta-analysis on this extensive research. As you may recall, the ***meta-analytic technique*** is a statistical method for synthesizing numerous studies on a single topic. This meta-analysis of 36 studies showed that—overall—younger adults recalled significantly more material than older adults. However, age differences were much more prominent when the verbal material told a story; age differences were minimal on essays. Furthermore, age differences were more prominent in people who were low in verbal ability; age differences were minimal for people who were high in verbal ability.

Notice how the research on long-term memory obeys the "It all depends on . . ." principle. Elderly people are fairly similar to younger people in recognition memory and in implicit-memory performance. Even when we examine an area in which age differences are more prominent—such as prose recall—we cannot draw a simple conclusion, because essays are less likely to cause problems, and highly verbal elderly people are less likely to show deficits. In other words, memory deficits are far from universal among elderly people.

Explanations for Age Differences in Memory. As you probably suspected, a complex pattern of results requires a complex explanation. Also, we must emphasize that we are seeking explanations for memory changes that accompany the normal aging process; disease-related memory deficits involve different mechanisms (e.g., Elias et al., 1991). To account for normal memory changes, we probably need to rely on several mechanisms, because no single explanation is sufficient. Let's consider some possible explanations, using the framework proposed by Leah Light (1991).

1. Elderly people could have impaired memory because they use memory strategies and metamemory less effectively. Some research suggests that elderly individuals are less likely to use organizational strategies and imagery (e.g., Smith, 1980; Weinstein et al., 1979). However, numerous studies conclude that elderly and young adults report using similar memory strategies (Light, 1991; Salthouse, 1991). Furthermore—as we will see later in this chapter—age differences in metamemory do not seem to be consistent enough to explain differences in memory performance.

2. Elderly people have problems in deliberate recollection. As we saw earlier, elderly people experience the greatest problems with memory tasks that require the most effortful, deliberate processing. Recall suffers the most as we grow older; recognition and implicit memory suffer less. Light (1991) agrees that the data show a reasonably consistent pattern. However, we cannot yet identify any mechanisms to explain why some performance is spared and some is impaired.

3. The hypothesis that has been most extensively researched in the past decade is that elderly people have reduced processing resources. For example, young adults may be able to use selective attention more effectively, so that inhibitory processes eliminate competing stimuli. In contrast, older adults may have a more limited attention capacity; their working memory may be flooded by irrelevant information (e.g., Hartman & Hasher, 1991; Hasher & Zacks, 1988). However, the evidence for attention capacity is mixed (Light, 1991). A second "reduced processing resources" explanation is that

the capacity of working memory may be reduced in elderly people. Light concludes that this explanation can account for some of the age-related differences in memory, but not all. A third "reduced processing resources" explanation is that elderly people often experience cognitive slowing, or a slower rate of responding on cognitive tasks (e.g., Hale et al., 1991; Hunt, 1993; Lima et al., 1991; Salthouse, 1991; Smith, 1996). However, Light (1991) argues that the cognitive slowing hypothesis does not predict how elderly people perform on tasks requiring large memory loads.

At present, none of these mechanisms adequately accounts for the pattern of age-related differences in memory (Craik & Jennings, 1992; Light, 1991). Perhaps a more refined version of one of these hypotheses may be developed, or additional hypotheses may be proposed. However, we currently have a complex set of findings about memory in the elderly, but no satisfying explanation for these results.

SECTION SUMMARY: THE DEVELOPMENT OF MEMORY

1. Psychologists interested in the development of cognition encounter methodological problems in their research, particularly with studies on infants and elderly people.
2. Research demonstrates that newborns can recognize their mothers, 6-month-olds can recall how to move a mobile following a 2-week delay, 8-month-olds can recall the location of hidden objects, and 14-month-olds can remember how to imitate actions after a 3-month delay.
3. Compared to adults, children have similar sensory memory but reduced working memory; children have reasonably strong recognition memory, but poor recall memory. In addition, children have poor reality monitoring; however—like adults—their memory is based on scripts and schemas.
4. One controversy about children's long-term memory concerns infantile amnesia; some argue that children forget life events that occurred prior to age 3, but others are more optimistic.
5. Children's eyewitness testimony is also controversial; under ideal circumstances, their reports can be trustworthy, but such reports may be unreliable when children are young, when they have been supplied with stereotypes and suggestive questions, when they are confused about reality, and when they receive pressure from adults.
6. As they grow older, children increasingly use memory strategies such as rehearsal, organization, and imagery.
7. As adults grow older, sensory memory does not decline substantially; working memory remains intact for some tasks, but it is limited when the task is complicated and requires manipulation of information.
8. With respect to long-term memory, age differences are smallest for recognition memory tasks and for implicit memory tasks; age differences in long-term recall are more substantial, especially for story recall and for people with low verbal ability.

9. Potential explanations for age-related memory changes include (a) memory strategies and metamemory, (b) the deliberate-recollection hypothesis, and (c) the hypothesis about reduced processing resources. Unfortunately, none of the current forms of these hypotheses is strongly supported by the data.

THE DEVELOPMENT OF METACOGNITION

As we discussed in Chapter 7, *metacognition* is knowledge, awareness, and control of cognitive processes—or our thoughts about thinking. Two important kinds of metacognition are metamemory (for example, realizing that you need to use a strategy to remember someone's name) and metacomprehension (for example, trying to decide whether you understood that definition of *metacognition*). In this section of the chapter, we will look at metacognition in children and in elderly adults.

Metacognition in Children

Research on metacognition in children has been thriving for nearly three decades. In fact, the first major research in metacognition focused on children rather than on college students (Flavell, 1971). Flavell argued that young children have extremely limited metacognition; they seldom monitor their memory, language, problem solving, or decision making (Flavell, 1979). More recent research on children's metacognition has focused on children's theories about the mind— children's ideas on how their minds work, on their understanding of the stream of consciousness, and on their beliefs about other people's thoughts (e.g., Astington, 1993; Bartsch & Wellman, 1995; Flavell, Green, & Flavell, 1993; Wellman & Gelman, 1992). Our discussion of children's metacognition will focus on several components of children's metamemory, as well as the topic of metacomprehension.

Metamemory: How Memory Works. An important component of metamemory is your knowledge about how memory works. Demonstration 12.3 includes some questions about this aspect of metamemory. Even young children, 3 and 4 years of age, know that a small set of pictures can be remembered better than a large set (Flavell et al., 1993; Yussen & Bird, 1979). These young children also know that personal variables, such as mood and fatigue, can affect how easily you learn new material (D.S. Hayes et al., 1987). Children as young as 6 years of age also know that familiar items are easier to remember than unfamiliar ones (Kreutzer et al., 1975).

However, children often have unsophisticated ideas about how their memories work. For example, 5-year-olds are not yet aware that words are easier to remember when they are part of a narrative, rather than a list. They also do not realize that the gist of a passage is easier to remember than the exact words (Brown, 1975; Kreutzer et al., 1975).

DEMONSTRATION 12.3

METAMEMORY IN ADULTS AND CHILDREN

Ask a child the following questions. (Ideally, try to question several children of different ages.) Compare the accuracy and/or the completeness of the answers with your own responses. Note that some questions should be reworded to a level appropriate for the individuals you are testing.

1. A child will be going to a party tomorrow, and she wants to remember to bring her skates. What kinds of things can she do to help her remember them?
2. Suppose that I were to read you a list of words. How many words do you think you could recall in the correct order? (Then read the following list and count the number of words correctly recalled. Use only part of the list for the child.)

   cat   rug   chair   leaf   sky   book   apple   pencil   house   teacher

3. Two children want to learn the names of some rocks. One child learned the names last month but forgot them. The other child never learned the names. Who will have an easier time in learning the names?
4. Suppose that you memorize somebody's address. Will you remember it better after 2 minutes have passed or after 2 days have passed?
5. Suppose that you are memorizing two kinds of words. One kind of word is abstract (refers to things you cannot see or touch, such as *idea* or *religion*) and the other kind is concrete (refers to things that you can see and touch, such as *notebook* or *zebra*). Which kind of word will you learn better?
6. Two children want to remember some lists of words. One child has a list of 10 words, and the other has a list of 5 words. Which child will be more likely to remember all the words on the list correctly?
7. Two children are reading the same paragraph. The teacher tells one child to remember all the sentences in the paragraph and repeat them word for word. The teacher tells the other child to remember the main ideas of the paragraph. Which child will have an easier job?

Metamemory: Realizing the Necessity of Effort. Another important component of metamemory is the awareness that if you really want to remember something, you must make an effort (Flavell & Wellman, 1977; Kail, 1992). However, young children do not appreciate this principle. When preschoolers and kindergartners are given a list of items to learn—with instructions to notify the experimenter when the list has been memorized—they spend most of the study time in unproductive activities. They are also even more likely than adults to keep studying information that they already know (Kail, 1992). Finally, they do not understand when something has been committed to memory. They typically report to the experimenter that they have satisfactorily memorized a list, yet they recall little on a test (Gross, 1985).

Even older children have naive ideas about the effort required in memorization. I recall a visit from a sixth-grade neighbor, who had been memorizing some information about the U.S. Constitution. My husband asked her how she was doing and whether she would like him to quiz her on the material. She replied that she knew the material well, but he could quiz her if he wanted. Her recall turned out to be minimal for both factual and conceptual information. She had assumed that by allowing her eyes to wander over the text several times, the material had magically worked its way into memory. Of course, magical thinking is not limited to children. If your high-school courses were relatively easy for you, perhaps you reached college before you realized that you needed effortful processing in order to retain difficult material.

Metamemory: Accuracy of Predictions. In general, older children and adults are reasonably accurate in predicting their memory performance. In contrast, younger children are unrealistically optimistic (Bjorklund & Green, 1992).

In a classic study, Yussen and Levy (1975) studied preschool children (mean age of 4.6 years), third-graders (mean age of 8.9), and college students (mean age of 20.2). Each person was first asked to estimate the number of picture names that he or she would be able to recall in correct order. Notice that this question measures metamemory because it asks people to think about their memory abilities. Next, Yussen and Levy measured everyone's true memory span on this task.

Figure 12.4 shows both memory estimates and actual memory spans for the three age groups. Notice that the preschoolers are wildly optimistic when estimating their memory. Unfortunately, this optimism may lull them into a false sense of security; they may not believe that they need to spend any effort or use any strategies to memorize material (Kail, 1990). However, as people grow older, their estimates become more modest while their actual memory spans increase. Consequently, college students are fairly realistic in their memory-span estimates.

Metamemory: The Relationship Between Metamemory and Memory Performance. Let us summarize several observations related to memory in young children: (1) their metamemory is faulty—they do not realize that they need to put effort into memorizing, and they do not realize how little they can remember; (2) they do not spontaneously use helpful memory strategies; and (3) relative to older children, their memory performance is poor.

Does a causal relationship link these three observations? Perhaps the three are related in this fashion:

Metamemory → Strategy use → Memory Performance

In other words, a faulty metamemory means that children are not aware that they must use strategies to commit material to memory. If they do not use strategies, then memory performance will suffer.

We have some evidence that metamemory is related to strategy use. For example, children with more sophisticated metacognitive abilities are more likely to report using strategies (Alexander & Schwanenflugel, 1994). Also, children who are given metacognitive instruction are more likely to use organizational strategies (Lange & Pierce, 1992). We also have extensive evidence to support the second link in the chain. As we saw on pages 447 to 449, children's strategy use is related to memory performance.

So, metamemory is linked to strategy use and strategy use is linked to memory performance. Are the two ends in that chain—that is, metamemory and memory performance—related to each other? Analysis of the research shows that metamemory and memory performance are moderately correlated (Andreassen & Waters, 1989; Schneider & Pressley, 1989; Wellman, 1985). In a typical study, Weed and her colleagues (1990) asked children whether they believed that they could control

---

FIGURE 12.4

ESTIMATED VERSUS ACTUAL MEMORY SPAN, AS A FUNCTION OF AGE.

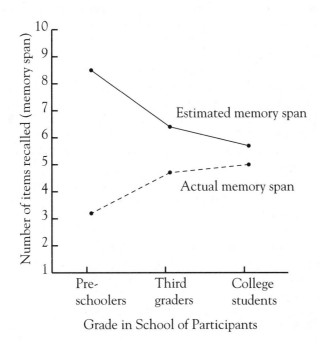

their academic success. For example, could they do things to raise their grades in school? Children who scored high on this measure (which is a component of metamemory) also tended to perform better on a memory test.

Further analysis of the relationship between metamemory and memory performance shows an interesting pattern. Specifically, the correlations are much stronger when metamemory is assessed in terms of children's monitoring their own knowledge. In contrast, correlations between metamemory and performance are lower when metamemory is assessed in terms of children's knowledge about memory strategies (Schneider, 1984).

Schneider's conclusions make sense, especially because metamemory has many separate components; some components are more closely linked to memory performance. Nine-year-old Suzy may *know* that organization helps memory. However, if she doesn't *use* that strategy, that knowledge will not help her. In contrast, if she is very skilled in knowing when she is ready to be tested, she will probably perform well on a memory test.

In summary, we can probably conclude that metamemory—particularly memory monitoring—is related fairly strongly to memory performance. Consequently, the proposed causal sequence (Metamemory → Strategy Use → Memory Performance) probably accounts for a substantial portion of the improvement in memory performance as children grow older.

Metacomprehension. ***Metacomprehension*** involves assessing whether you understand what you are reading or what is being said to you; it also involves your knowledge and thoughts about comprehension. An important component of metacomprehension is your awareness of whether or not you understand what you are reading. You have probably had the sensation of reading a passage in a book, and suddenly becoming aware that you have not understood what you have been reading. You search back through the passage, trying to locate the point where the material first became unclear. As we grow older, we become increasingly skilled in identifying problems with comprehension.

Even young children can reveal that they do not understand a spoken message— though they may not be able to verbalize this confusion. For example, Flavell and his colleagues (1981) found that young children sometimes failed to identify a garbled message as being flawed. However, they revealed their difficulty in understanding by giving nonverbal messages: They looked puzzled, made funny expressions with their faces, and produced other body language that indicated, "I don't understand this message." This study is particularly interesting because it reveals that children know more about metacomprehension than they reveal verbally.

In the discussion of metamemory, we noted that metamemory measures are somewhat correlated with memory performance. Is metacomprehension correlated with comprehension scores? Research by Cross and Paris (1988) revealed that the two factors were not closely related in their sample of third-graders, but these factors were related in their sample of fifth-graders. Apparently, by fifth grade, children can use their understanding about reading strategies to enhance their reading performance.

Metacognition in Elderly People

Research on metacognition in the elderly is limited almost exclusively to the topic of metamemory (Salthouse, 1991). Any of you who are concerned that all the interesting or worthwhile topics in psychology have already been examined should consider the possible research areas that are still unexplored. For example, we know little about elderly people's thoughts about their comprehension, problem solving, and other cognitive processes. Our discussion of metacognition in the elderly is therefore limited to the area of metamemory.

Actually, we have already given away the "punch line" about age comparisons in metamemory. Earlier in the chapter, we discussed possible explanations for age differences in some areas of memory. One explanation we rejected stated that young and elderly adults might differ substantially in their metamemory. The evidence does not seem to support major age differences in metamemory. Let us consider the evidence in more detail:

1. Older and younger adults share similar beliefs about the properties of memory tasks (Light, 1991; Salthouse, 1991). Both groups have the same fundamental knowledge about how memory works, which strategies are most effective, and what kinds of material can be remembered most readily.

2. Older and younger adults have similar ability to monitor their memory performance (Bieman-Copland & Charness, 1994; Hertzog & Dixon, 1994; Lovelace, 1990b). For example, the two groups are similar in their ability to predict, on an item-by-item basis, which items they can recall at a later time (Lovelace & Marsh, 1985). The similarity in accuracy rates holds true for three different memory tasks—free recall, paired-associate learning, and sentence memory (Rabinowitz et al., 1982).

3. The research on people's estimates of their memory performance is not consistent (Hertzog & Dixon, 1994). Some research shows that older adults are more likely than younger adults to underestimate the difficulty of a memory task (e.g., Bruce et al., 1982; Herrmann, 1990; Lovelace & Marsh, 1985; Salthouse, 1991). However, other studies are not consistent with that conclusion (e.g., Hertzog et al., 1990; Salthouse, 1991). The results probably depend on the sample of elderly people who are being tested, as well as the methods of measuring memory estimates.

4. Elderly people are likely to report problems with their everyday memory (Pollina et al., 1993). They are also likely to say that their memory failures have increased over the years. Lovelace and Twohig (1990) asked people whose average age was 68 to report whether they had noticed a change in their memory for certain items. The results showed that 42% reported that they were now more likely to have problems recalling the word they wanted during a conversation. In addition, 40% said that they were more likely to forget what they had intended to do (for example, why they went into a

particular room). They also reported an increased incidence of forgetting the point of a conversation they had begun and an increased problem with remembering whether they had done a routine task. However, Lovelace and Twohig also found that in this sample of healthy, articulate adults, not a single person reported that memory failures seriously hampered his or her daily activities. Although their memory difficulties had increased in some areas, these adults were still managing quite well.

In summary, our examination of metamemory in the elderly has revealed many age similarities in memory knowledge, memory monitoring, memory self-confidence, and reported memory problems. As Salthouse (1991) concludes in his review of metamemory in the elderly, "Results from the available studies do not appear to provide much support for the hypothesis of age differences in metacognitive functioning" (p. 211). Thus, young children's metamemory may be inferior compared to young adults' metamemory; however, elderly adults experience no overwhelming metamemory impairment.

SECTION SUMMARY: The Development of Metacognition

1. Young children have some awareness of the way memory works, and their knowledge increases as they mature.
2. Young children are not aware that they must make an effort and use strategies to learn a list of items.
3. Older children and adults are much more accurate than younger children in predicting their memory performance; young children are far too overconfident.
4. When metamemory is measured in terms of children's monitoring of their own knowledge, metamemory is correlated with memory performance. As children grow older, their metamemory improves, leading to increased strategy use, in turn producing better memory performance.
5. Young children may reveal that they do not understand a message by giving nonverbal signals.
6. Older and younger adults have similar knowledge about their memory and similar ability to monitor their memory; age is not consistently related to overconfidence in predicting one's memory performance.
7. The elderly report an increase in the frequency of some memory problems, but they do not believe that these memory problems greatly impair their daily functioning.

THE DEVELOPMENT OF LANGUAGE

"Mama!" (8 months old)

"Wash hair." (1 year, 4 months old)

"Don't tickle my tummy, Mommy!" (1 year, 11 months old)

"My Grandma gave me this dolly, Cara. My Grandma is my Mommy's Mommy. I have another Grandma, too. She's my Daddy's Mommy. And Aunt Elli is my Daddy's sister." (2 years, 9 months old)

These selections from the early language of my daugher Sally are typical of the remarkable accomplishment involved in language acquisition. Individual children differ in the rate at which they master language (e.g., Bates et al., 1988). Still, within a period of two to three years, all normal children progress from one-word utterances to complex descriptions.

Language acquisition is often said to be the most spectacular of human accomplishments, and children's linguistic skills clearly exemplify Theme 2. For instance, the average 6-year-old has some mastery of about 14,000 words. To acquire a vocabulary this large, children must learn about nine new words each day from the time they start speaking until their sixth birthday (Clark, 1991). If you are not impressed by a 14,000-word vocabulary, consider how much effort high-school students must exert to acquire 1,000 words in a foreign language—and those 6-year-old language learners are only waist high! Furthermore, children combine these words into phrases that they have never heard before, such as "My dolly dreamed about toys" (2 years, 2 months).

Researchers have typically ignored language skills in the elderly, although some new research is beginning to emerge (e.g., Kemper, 1992; Light, 1992; Stine et al., 1995). Our discussion of language development will therefore be limited to infancy and childhood.

Language in Infants

Let us begin by considering infants' early perception of speech sounds. Then we will look at their language production, including both verbal language and nonverbal gestures, as well as the characteristics of the language that parents use with infants.

Speech Perception in Infancy. To acquire language, infants must distinguish between *phonemes,* or the smallest sound units in a language. However, the ability to make distinctions is only half the struggle; infants must also be able to group together the sounds that are phonetically equivalent. Thus, language acquisition requires the ability to recognize that the sounds *b* and *p* are different from each other, whereas the sound *b* spoken by the deepest bass voice, in the middle of a word, is the same as the sound *b* spoken by the highest soprano voice, at the end of a word.

If you have recently seen a baby who is less than 6 months old, you might have been tempted to conclude that the baby's mastery of language was roughly equivalent to that of a tennis shoe. Until the early 1970s, psychologists were not much more optimistic. However, research has demonstrated that infants' speech perception is surprisingly advanced. They can perceive almost all the speech contrasts used in language, either at birth or within the first few weeks of life (Bates, Thal, & Janowsky, 1992). Infants can also recognize similarities, an important early stage in the understanding of language. Infants' abilities are highly conducive to language learning (Kuhl, 1987; Miller & Eimas, 1983).

Peter Eimas and his coauthors (1971) were among the first to discover infants' capacity for speech perception. They used a method called **nonnutritive sucking,** in which babies suck on nipples to produce a particular sound. No liquid is delivered through the nipple, but the infant is required to suck at least two times each second to maintain the sound. Typically, babies begin each session by sucking frequently to maintain the sound. However, they then show habituation. As you may know, **habituation** occurs when a stimulus is presented frequently, and the response rate decreases. Presumably, the sound is now too boring, and it is not worth the hard work of frequent sucking.

How can the nonnutritive sucking technique be used to provide insight into speech perception? Eimas and his colleagues shifted the speech sound after the 1- to 4-month-old infants had habituated to the first sound. For example, an infant who had shown habituation to *bah* was suddenly presented with a highly similar sound, *pah*. These infants show dishabituation. That is, when *pah* was presented, they suddenly started sucking vigorously once more. In contrast, infants showed no dishabituation when they continued to hear the *bah* sound; their response rate continued to decrease. Thus, the nonnutritive sucking technique revealed that infants respond at different rates to different sounds, and so they can perceive the difference between them.

Other research has demonstrated that 2-month-old infants can distinguish between the syllables *bad* and *bag*. Furthermore, 6-month-old infants can distinguish between the similar nonsense words *kokodu* and *kokoba* (Eimas & Tartter, 1979; Goodsitt et al., 1984).

In some cases, young infants are even better than older infants and adults in making phonemic distinctions. For example, infants raised in English-speaking homes can make distinctions between phonemic contrasts that are important in Hindi, a language spoken in India. In Hindi, the *t* sound is sometimes made by placing the tongue against the back of the teeth and sometimes by placing the tongue farther back along the roof of the mouth. In contrast, English does not distinguish between these two *t* sounds. However, Werker and Tees (1984) demonstrated that English-speaking infants can distinguish between these phonemes with about 95% accuracy when they are 6 to 8 months old. Accuracy drops to about 70% at 8 to 10 months of age, and to about 20% at 10 to 12 months of age. As Werker (1994) explains, the development of speech perception encourages infants to reorganize their perceptual categories.

Patricia Kuhl and her coworkers (1992) have tested infants in the United States and Sweden to determine when linguistic experience alters the perception of phonemes. They tested 6-month-old infants in both countries for their perception of two speech sounds. One vowel, the *ee* sound in American English, is a prototype vowel in American English, but it is not found in Swedish. A second vowel that is somewhat similar to *ee* but pronounced with a rounded mouth (we'll call it *y*) is a prototype in Swedish, but it is not found in American English.

As you can imagine, the methodology in this study was crucially important. Borrowing from operant conditioning methods, Kuhl and her colleagues trained the infants to turn their heads whenever they heard the vowel change from the prototype vowel to a computerized version that was slightly different from the prototype. The infants' head-turning responses were rewarded by activating a toy bear that pounded a miniature drum. This drumming bear was so enchanting that infants paid close attention to the prototype vowel, trying to detect any change in the sound.

The researchers analyzed the data to see if they could detect a phenomenon called the magnet effect. Adult speakers of a given language often demonstrate the ***magnet effect;*** they perceive nonprototypic sounds to be similar to their nearest prototype. Thus, a prototype acts like a magnet, drawing other speech sounds closer to it, much like a magnet attracts iron filings. If infants demonstrate the magnet effect, they will *not* turn their heads when the speech sound changes from the prototype to a variant. By not turning their head, infants are indicating that they regard the new, nonprototypic speech sound to be similar to the prototype.

FIGURE 12.5

INFANTS' RESPONSES TO SOUNDS THAT WERE SIMILAR TO PROTOTYPES IN AMERICAN ENGLISH AND IN SWEDISH.   BASED ON KUHL ET AL. (1992).

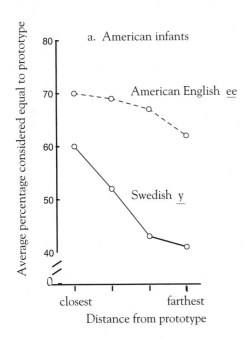
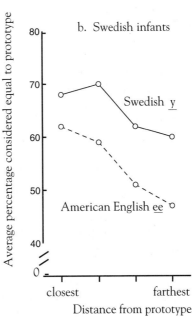

Figure 12.5 shows the results. Let's first look at the results for the American infants. Part a of Figure 12.5 shows that the infants considered between 60% and 70% of those nonprototypic speech sounds to be similar to the American English prototype *ee;* the magnet effect operated to draw even the more distant sounds in closer to the *ee* sound. However, their pattern was different for the Swedish sound *y.* They were able to detect the difference between the prototype for the *y* sound and other sounds that were different—especially those that were far-removed from the *y* sound. Notice that only 40% of those distant sounds were considered equal to the prototype *y.* In other words, infants turned their heads more often when the Swedish sound changed; they showed the magnet effect for the Swedish sound much less often than for the American English sound.

As you can see, the pattern is neatly reversed for the Swedish infants. As part b of Figure 12.5 shows, the Swedish infants demonstrated the magnet effect toward the prototypical *y* sound. Furthermore, they were more likely to notice when the sound changed from the American English sound *ee* to its variants.

We need to emphasize the significance of this study. Basically, it illustrates that infants are well prepared to perceive speech (Kuhl, 1993a, 1993b). This research illustrates that infants can learn about sounds merely by being exposed to language. These tiny infants are only 6 months old, and they have not yet uttered a single meaningful word in their native language. However, they already identify the prototypical sounds in their language, and they have already learned not to notice slight variations from those prototypes.

We have examined in some detail infants' appreciation of the auditory components of language. In addition, infants have a remarkable understanding of some social aspects of language. For example, Walker-Andrews (1986) played recordings of either a happy voice or an angry voice to 7-month-old infants. Meanwhile, the infants saw a pair of films—of one happy speaker and one angry speaker— projected side-by-side. The mouth region of the faces was covered so that the infants could not rely on lip movements to match the voice with the film. The results showed that infants who heard a happy voice tended to watch the happy face, whereas infants who heard an angry voice tended to watch the angry face. Thus even young infants appreciate that facial expression must correspond with vocal intonation.

The word *infant* originally meant "not speaking." Infant's speech *production* is certainly limited. However, their speech *perception* is impressively sophisticated, even when they are only a few months old.

Language Production in Infancy. The early vocalizations of infants pass through a series of stages. By about 2 months of age, infants begin to make **cooing** noises, sounds that involve vowels such as *oo.* By about 6 to 8 months they have developed **babbling,** a vocalization that uses both consonants and vowels, often repeating sounds in a series such as *dadada* (Locke, 1994; Menyuk et al., 1995). Interestingly, deaf infants who have been exposed to sign language also begin at about this time to "babble" with their hands, producing systematic but meaningless actions that are not found in hearing children (Petitto & Marentette, 1991).

Researchers do not know what function babbling serves. Perhaps it is a form of language (Carroll, 1994). We do know that it is not purely communicative, because it often occurs when no other people are present.

The first attempts at intentional communication occur at about 9 months of age. *Intentional communication* involves the expectation that another person will help in reaching a desired goal (Bates, 1979). For example, an 8-month-old who wants a ball will reach out toward the ball and fuss. However, a 9-month-old who uses intentional communication will alternate eye contact between the ball and the parent, while fussing. The young infant apparently sees some relationship among the goal, the adult, and the communication signal.

These advances in intentional communication may be linked to biological developments in the brain. Bates and her colleagues (1992) report that brain-imaging research has detected increased metabolic activity in the frontal lobe of the cortex in 8- to 10-month-old infants. We know that the frontal lobe is associated with many "executive functions" that monitor behavior in adults. Links between other regions of the brain and the frontal lobe may be necessary before infants can master relatively sophisticated tasks such as intentional communication, imitation, and retrieving hidden objects.

Infants typically begin to point to objects at about 10 months of age (Sachs, 1993). Psychologists believe that pointing is particularly important because it calls another person's attention to an object or an event. Preverbal infants may point simply to attract the parent's attention, but an older infant often points and names simultaneously.

Another important social component of early language is turn-taking. Parents treat their babies as active conversational partners, each alternating politely and waiting for a response from the other (Carroll, 1994; Owens, 1996). Turn-taking increases dramatically between the ages of 8 and 12 months (Menyuk et al., 1995). Here is a sample conversation between a mother and her 12-month-old daughter, Rachael, who is sitting with a tissue on her head:

Mom: Can we put it on my head?

Rachael: (Removes tissue.)

Mom: Put it on mommy's head.

Rachael: (Touches mom's head with tissue.) (Menyuk et al., 1995, p. 145)

Parents' Language to Infants. Infant's language acquisition is facilitated by their impressive auditory skills, their memory capacity, and their receptivity to language. However, they also receive superb assistance from their parents and other adults. Adults who raise children tend to make language acquisition somewhat simpler by adjusting their language when speaking with the children. The term *motherese* is used to refer to the language spoken to children; motherese language uses simple vocabulary and syntax, clear pronunciation, slow speech, varying intonation, a focus on the here and now, and exaggerated facial expressions (Kuhl, 1994b; Garton, 1992; Menyuk et al., 1995). Demonstration 12.4 illustrates motherese (DeHart, 1989).

You probably caught the gender-bias in the term *motherese*. Many fathers probably speak "motherese" to their infants and children. However, fathers who are secondary caregivers seem to be less "tuned in" to their offspring's communication needs, and their speech to infants tends to be more like their speech to adults. Also, when fathers do not understand something spoken by their children, they usually respond with a nonspecific question, such as "What?" In contrast, mothers make more specific requests for clarification, such as "Where should I put the Raggedy Andy?" (Sroufe et al., 1992; Tomasello et al., 1990). Obviously, it would be interesting to study the language patterns of fathers who are primary caregivers, as well as mothers who are secondary caregivers. When confounding variables are eliminated, gender differences are typically minimal (Matlin, 1996).

Research in a variety of language communities throughout the world shows major similarities in the language adults use with infants and children (Fernald, 1985). The rhythm of the speech helps young language learners break the stream of conversation into its major syntactic units (e.g., Gleason & Ratner, 1993b; Hirsh-Pasek et al., 1987). As Gleason and Ratner write:

> Parents say things like "See the birdie? Look at the birdie! What a pretty birdie!" These features probably make it easier for the infant to decode the language than if they heard, "Has it come to your attention that one of our better looking feathered friends is perched upon the windowsill?" (p. 311)

Language in Children

Sometime around their first birthday, most infants speak their first word. Let's look at the characteristics of these initial words, as well as the words spoken by older

---

DEMONSTRATION 12.4

SPEAKING MOTHERESE

Locate a doll that resembles an infant as closely as possible in features and size. Select a friend who has had experience with infants, and ask him or her to imagine that the doll is a niece or nephew who just arrived with parents for a first visit. Encourage your friend to interact with the baby as he or she normally would. Observe your friend's language for qualities such as pitch, variation in pitch, vocabulary, sentence length, repetition, and intonation. Also observe nonverbal communication. What qualities are different from the language used with adults?

children. Then we will consider children's grammar, specifically morphology and syntax. Finally, we will examine how children master pragmatics, or the social rules of language.

Words. A child's first words usually refer to people, objects, and their own activities (Clark, 1993; de Villiers & de Villiers, 1992). In a large-scale study involving samples from three cities, parents estimated that their children produced an average of 12 words at 12 months of age, 179 words at 20 months, and 380 words at 28 months. However, we need to emphasize the tremendous range in vocabulary size for normal children. For example, the production vocabulary for 12-month-olds in this study ranged between 0 and 52 words (Fenson et al., 1991). The sudden increase in vocabulary size between 12 and 28 months may be linked to rapid increases in synaptic connections in the cortex, which occur during this period (Bates et al., 1992).

One factor that facilitates children's acquisition of new words is that they have already mastered some impressively sophisticated concepts before their first birthday. For example, even 3-month-olds can perceptually differentiate dogs and cats (Quinn et al., 1993). By the age of 9 months, infants can distinguish between toy birds and toy airplanes that are visually very similar (Mandler, 1996; Mandler & McDonough, 1993).

Another factor that helps children learn new words is called ***fast mapping,*** or using context to make a reasonable guess about a word's meaning after just one or two exposures (de Villiers & de Villiers, 1992). Chapter 8 emphasized that adults are guided by word context, and fast mapping demonstrates that context is also critically important for young children. In a relevant study, Heibeck and Markman (1987) showed preschoolers pairs of objects and asked the children to select one of them. The request specifically used one familiar term and one unfamiliar term, such as "Bring me the chartreuse one. Not the blue one, the chartreuse one." Other requests used familiar and unfamiliar terms for shape and texture, as well as color. The children understood the requests, bringing the appropriate object with the unfamiliar label. When tested several minutes later, even 2-year-olds remembered the unfamiliar terms.

Furthermore, children make a ***taxonomic assumption;*** they assume that a label can apply to other objects of the same category. For example, Markman (1990) showed children a puppet, who spoke to them and made certain requests. For instance, the puppet might say, "I'm going to show you a *dax,* then I want you to think carefully and find another one." The children were shown a picture of a cow, and they were encouraged to select one of two pictures, either a pig or a pail of milk. The children selected the pig 65% of the time. They made the taxonomic assumption that *dax* referred to all members of the taxonomic category *animal* or *farm animal*—rather than focusing on the specific properties of cows (for example, milk-givers).

Naturally, young children may apply a newly learned label to a category that is either too broad or too narrow. An ***overextension*** is the use of a word to refer to other objects in addition to objects that adults would consider appropriate (Clark, 1993). For example, my daughter Beth used the word *baish* to refer initially to her blanket. Then she later applied the term to a diaper, a diaper pin, and a vitamin pill. Often an object's shape or function is important in determining overextensions, but sometimes (as in the case of the vitamin pill) overextensions defy adult explanation. Incidentally, they frequently occur for properly pronounced English words, as well as for children's own invented words. You've probably heard of children who call every adult male—including the mailman—"Daddy."

Research by Thomson and Chapman (1977) demonstrated that children around the age of 2 often show overextension for words such as *dog* and *ball*. For example, one child produced the name *dog* for nine species of dog and one toy dog—all correct answers. However, he also used the word *dog* for two bears, a wolf, a fox, a doe, a rhinoceros, a hippopotamus, and a fish—all overextensions.

Children may also supply an **underextension,** using a word in a narrower sense than adults do (Clark, 1993). For example, they may apply the name *doggie* only to the family pet. Older children may refuse to believe that the word *animal* could apply to a praying mantis (Anglin, 1977).

Try Demonstration 12.5 to illustrate another important aspect of children's word usage. Specifically, the characteristics of children's word meaning change as they

---

DEMONSTRATION 12.5

THE RELATIVE IMPORTANCE OF CHARACTERISTIC AND DEFINING FEATURES. KEIL & BATTERMAN (1984), p. 227.

Locate two or more children between the ages of 5 and 10. Read these four stories to each of them individually. Try to decide whether the child bases word meaning more on characteristic features or defining features.

1. These two girls look alike, dress alike, do well in the same subjects in school, like the same vegetables, and live in the same house. One of them, however, is 2 years older than the other one. Could these be twin sisters?
2. There are two girls who were born at the same time on the same day in the same room from the same mommy, but one of them lives in California and the other one lives in New York. Could these be twin sisters?
3. There is this place that sticks out of the land like a finger. Coconut trees and palm trees grow there, and the girls sometimes wear flowers in their hair because it's so warm all the time. There is water on all sides except one. Could that be an island?
4. On this piece of land, there are apartment buildings, snow, and no green things growing. This piece of land is surrounded by water on all sides. Could that be an island?

mature, particularly with respect to defining and characteristic features (Keil, 1989). As discussed in Chapter 7, *defining features* are the features that are essential to the meaning of the item, whereas *characteristic features* are those that are merely descriptive, but not essential. As you can see from Demonstration 12.5, for example, the defining features of twins are that they were born on the same day and have the same mother. The characteristic features are that they look alike, act alike, and live together.

Keil and Batterman (1984) read brief stories like those in Demonstration 12.5 to children who ranged in age from preschool to fourth grade. Each child was then asked if the thing or person described could be an *x* (twin, island, and so on). For each concept they investigated, one story had the correct defining features but lacked important characteristic features; the other story had important characteristic features but lacked the correct defining features. Children's responses changed very significantly as they grew older. Preschoolers and kindergartners relied heavily on characteristic features, as revealed in the following dialog with the experimenter about whether your mother's brother, who was 2 years old, could be your uncle:

EXPERIMENTER: Could he be an uncle?

CHILD: No . . . because he's little and 2 years old.

EXPERIMENTER: How old does an uncle have to be?

CHILD: About 24 or 25.

EXPERIMENTER: If he's 2 years old can he be an uncle?

CHILD: No . . . he can be a cousin. (p. 229)

Children in the second grade seemed to be in transition. For instance, they tended to know that sisters of different ages could not be twins. However, they usually insisted that people needed to live in the same house to be twins. By fourth grade, defining features predominated. These older children realized that characteristic features were nice to have, but not essential. As Nelson (1985) stresses, language development is basically a problem in the acquisition of culture. In American culture, uncles must meet kinship criteria, rather than age criteria.

Morphology. Children initially use the simple form of a word in every context, for example, "girl run," rather than "girl runs." However, they soon begin to master how to add on ***morphemes*** (basic units of meaning, which include endings such as *-s* and *-ed,* as well as simple words such as *run). **Morphology*** is the study of these basic units of meaning.

English-speaking children acquire morphemes in a fairly regular order between the ages of 1 ½ and 3 ½. For example, the first morpheme to develop is *-ing* (for example, *running);* plurals develop next, using the morpheme *-s* (for example, *girls);*

and the regular past tense develops still later (for example, *kicked*) (Brown, 1973; Kuczaj, 1977).

After children begin learning the regular plurals and past tenses—like *girls* and *kicked*—they start to create their own regular forms, such as *mouses* and *runned*. This tendency to add the most customary morphemes to create new forms of irregular words is called **overregularization.** (Keep in mind, then, that *overgeneralization* refers to the tendency to broaden a word's meaning inappropriately, whereas *over-regularization* refers to the tendency to add regular morphemes inappropriately.)

Theorists have developed two different explanations of children's overregularizations. One approach is based on parallel distributed processing, which we discussed in previous chapters. According to the **parallel distributed processing** framework, cognitive processes can be understood in terms of networks that link groups of neuron-like units. Rumelhart and McClelland (1986, 1987) propose that the language system keeps a tally of the morpheme patterns for forming past tenses. The system notes that *-ed* is the statistically most likely pattern, and so this ending is extended to new verbs. The child therefore forms inappropriate past tenses, such as *runned, growed, goed,* and *eated.* Rumelhart and McClelland believe that a child does not need to consult an internal set of rules to make these over-regularizations. Instead, patterns of excitation within neural networks can account for the phenomenon.

Steven Pinker has proposed an alternative explanation for overregularization (Pinker, 1990; Pinker & Prince, 1988). According to Pinker's **blocking-plus-retrieval-failure theory,** children have developed a general rule for past-tense verbs—add *-ed;* however, they block this rule if their mental dictionary holds an irregular form. If they fail to retrieve the irregular form, they fall back on the familiar rule of adding *-ed.* Pinker's (1990) data show that children who have learned the "add *-ed*" rule typically make mistakes on fewer than 5% of the irregular verbs. Furthermore, they may produce one correct past tense (e.g., *went*) and one incorrect past tense (e.g., *sanged*) in the same utterance. As you might expect, they master the most common past tenses before the rare ones.

Syntax. At about 18 to 24 months of age, the average child begins to combine two words—usually after acquiring between 50 and 100 words (Bates, 1991; de Villiers & de Villiers, 1992). An important issue that arises at this point is *syntax,* or the organizational rules for determining word order, sentence organization, and the relationship between words (Owens, 1996). As children struggle with syntax, their rate of combining words is initially slow. However, it increases rapidly after the age of 2 (Anisfeld, 1984). Another factor that probably contributes to this rapid increase in word combinations is the growing capacity of working memory (Bates et al., 1988).

Children's two-word utterances express many different kinds of relationships, such as possessor-possession ("Mama dress"), action-object ("Eat cookie"), and agent-action ("Teddy fall"). Furthermore, a two-word phrase can have different meanings in different contexts. "Daddy sock" may signify that the father is putting the girl's sock on her foot, or that a particular sock belongs to the father (de Villiers & de Villiers, 1992).

Children learning all languages—not just English—use telegraphic speech (de Villiers & de Villiers, 1992; Slobin, 1979). *Telegraphic speech* is speech that includes content words, such as nouns and verbs, but omits the extra words that serve only a grammatical function, such as prepositions and articles. The name *telegraphic speech* is appropriate because when adults need to conserve words (for example, when sending a telegram or placing an advertisement in a newspaper), they also omit the extra words. Similarly, a child who wants to convey, "The puppy is sitting on my blanket," will say, "Puppy blanket."

After children have reached the two-word stage, they begin to fill in the missing words and word endings, and they also improve their word order. "Baby cry" becomes "The baby is crying," for example.

We need to emphasize that language learning is an active process, consistent with Theme 1 of this book. As Rogers (1985) emphasizes, children learn language by actively constructing their own speech. Their speech includes phrases that adults would never say, such as "Allgone sticky," "Bye-bye hot," and "More page." Children's speech is far richer than a simple imitation of adult language.

Another example of the active nature of children's language is **crib speech,** or monologs that children produce when they are alone in their cribs. Kuczaj (1983) studied crib speech in 1- and 2-year-old children and found that they often practiced their linguistic skills when they were alone. One frequent pattern in their practice involved building longer phrases, as in the sequence, "Block. Yellow block. Look at all the yellow blocks." Substitutions were common, too: "What color blanket? What color map? What color glass?"

As children grow increasingly skilled in producing sophisticated language, they also grow increasingly skilled in understanding it. Consider, for example, how a child comes to understand the sentence, "Pat hit Chris." How does the child know who is the actor in that sentence and who is the recipient of the action? In English, the word order of the sentence is the most important cue, so we may be tempted to assume that word-order is similarly helpful in all languages. However, as Weist (1985) notes, young children learning Turkish or Polish use the endings of words, rather than word-order information, to decode the meaning of sentences. Children seem to be clever strategists, who can use whatever syntax cues are available in their language.

Pragmatics. As we discussed in Chapter 9, the term *pragmatics* refers to the social rules of language. Children must learn what should be said (and what should *not* be said) in certain circumstances. They must learn how two speakers coordinate conversation, and they must learn how to behave as listeners, as well as speakers.

Every family has its stories about children's wildly inappropriate remarks to elderly relatives, friendly neighbors, and complete strangers. A 2-year-old I knew once told a woman that her husband looked like a monkey. The child's description was stunningly accurate, yet both the child's mother and the woman reacted more strongly to the fact that the child had broken a pragmatic rule than to the fact that she had produced a grammatically perfect and factually accurate sentence.

As Garvey (1984) notes, conversations could not operate without a system to reduce friction and minimize potential conflicts and embarrassments. An important component of children's developing language involves mastering the markers of courtesy such as *please, excuse me,* and *may I.* Garvey's observation of nursery-school children showed that 3- and 4-year-olds frequently requested permission using socially appropriate phrases such as "Can I _____" and "May I _____." Teachers, parents, and other caregivers encourage this kind of courtesy. For example, they may tell a child, "Ask Judy nicely if you can play with the bear" (Garvey, 1984; Snow et al., 1990). Furthermore, children learn to ask a question a second time—perhaps in a different way—if the first attempt was unsuccessful (Ervin-Tripp et al., 1990).

Children must also learn how to coordinate conversations. We discussed earlier that mothers and infants develop turn-taking in their social interactions. Sophisticated turn-taking requires each speaker to anticipate when the conversational partner will complete his or her remark—clearly a requirement that demands an impressive knowledge of the language structure (McTear, 1985). Young children have longer gaps in turn-taking than adults do, perhaps because they are not as skilled in anticipating the completion of a remark. Two-year-olds have conversational gaps that average about 1.5 seconds, in contrast to gaps of about 0.8 seconds in adults (McTear, 1985).

Children also learn how to adapt their language to the listener. Psychologists used to believe that children's language ignored the level of understanding of the listener, but we now acknowledge that they make appropriate adjustments. For example, Shatz and Gelman (1973) found that 4-year-olds modified their speech substantially when the listener was a 2-year-old rather than a peer or an adult. Specifically, the 4-year-olds described a toy to their 2-year-old listeners using short, simple utterances. However, when describing the toy to another 4-year-old or an adult, their utterances were much longer and more complex. Thus children understand some of the social aspects of language, such as the need to modify speech for younger listeners.

The next time you observe two adults conversing, notice how the listener responds to the speaker by smiling, gazing, and other gestures of interest. In one study, researchers recorded these kinds of listener responses in young children who were discussing with an adult such topics as toys, a popular film, and siblings (Miller et al., 1985). All these listener responses were more abundant in the older children. For example, 8% of 3-year-olds said "uh-hum" at some point while the adult was speaking, in contrast to 50% of 5-year-olds. Furthermore, head nods increased from 67% to 100%. Thus, children learn how to be pragmatically skilled listeners, as well as speakers.

Infants and children seem to be specially prepared to notice and interact socially (Wellman & Gelman, 1992). As Marilyn Shatz commented in an interview several years ago:

> Children are very impatient to be members of the family, genuine members. They learn very early that speech is the way to realize and maintain contact with other family members and, at the same time, to be taken seriously. A 2-year-old already has the

goal of being a person in the family instead of a baby, of being someone to interact linguistically with instead of an object of discussion. (Roşu & Natanson, 1987, p. 5)

This enthusiasm about learning language encourages children to master the words, morphemes, syntax, and pragmatics of speech.

Throughout this chapter, we have seen examples of the early competence of infants and children. For instance, young infants are remarkably skilled at remembering faces and distinguishing speech sounds. These early skills foreshadow the impressive cognitive skills that adults exhibit (Theme 2). Furthermore, children's active, inquiring interactions with the people, objects, and concepts in their world (Theme 1) help them develop memory, metamemory, and language. Finally, the research on the cognitive skills of elderly people reveals some deficits. However, their cognitive abilities usually remain both accurate and active throughout the lifespan.

SECTION SUMMARY: THE DEVELOPMENT OF LANGUAGE

1. Studies with infants reveal remarkable speech perception abilities; they can perceive differences between similar phonemes, show the magnet effect for prototypical phonemes in their language environment, and appreciate that a person's voice tone must correspond to the facial expression.
2. Language production in infancy includes cooing and babbling; other early skills are intentional communication, pointing, and turn-taking. The language that parents use with infants encourages their verbal development.
3. Young children rapidly acquire new words from context, but their word usage shows both overextensions and underextensions. As they mature, they begin to emphasize the defining features of words, rather than the characteristic features.
4. During language acquisition, children show overregularization, adding regular morphemes to words that have irregular plurals and past tenses; this phenomenon has been explained in terms of parallel distributed processing and in terms of Pinker's blocking-plus-retrieval-failure theory.
5. Children's early word combinations are telegraphic; children also make active efforts to master language.
6. Although young children frequently break pragmatic rules, they realize the importance of courtesy terms at an early age. As children mature, they develop turn-taking, and they adapt their language to the listener. They also learn how listeners are supposed to respond to speakers.

CHAPTER REVIEW QUESTIONS

1. Until the early 1970s, psychologists were pessimistic about the cognitive skills of infants and young children. In 1979, Gelman said, "The time has come for us to turn our attention to what young children can do as well

as what they cannot do" (p. 904). If you wanted to impress someone with infants' and children's cognitive abilities, what would you describe about their memory, metacognition, and language abilities?

2. Part of the difficulty with infant research is designing experiments that reveal the infant's true abilities. Describe how experimental procedures have been developed to uncover infants' skills in memory and language.

3. Compare children, young adults, and elderly people with respect to sensory memory, working memory, implicit memory, long-term recognition memory, and long-term recall memory. Be sure to list factors that might influence your conclusions.

4. Describe the proposed explanation for children's memory performance, which involves memory strategies and metamemory. Discuss the evidence for this explanation, including information on the correlation between metamemory and memory performance.

5. Imagine that a court case in your community involves the testimony of a young child. What kind of factors would you want to know about before you could decide whether to trust the child's report?

6. In general, what kinds of memory tasks are especially difficult for elderly people? What explanations have been proposed for memory deficits in the elderly? Can metamemory account for these problems?

7. Given what you know about children's metamemory and strategy use, what could a third-grade teacher do to encourage students' memory skills?

8. Branthwaite and Rogers (1985) note that being a child is like being a spy, trying to break a code to discover the way in which the world works. Apply this idea to the development of word meaning, morphology, word order, and pragmatic rules.

9. Describe some of the pragmatic rules of language that are important in our culture. Note how the mastery of these rules changes with development.

10. Considering the information in this chapter, are infants as different from young adults as you had originally thought? Do the findings on elderly people surprise you, or do they match your original impressions?

New Terms

conjugate reinforcement technique
spacing effect
time window
reality monitoring
infantile amnesia
strategies
explicit memory measure
implicit memory measure
meta-analytic technique

metacognition
metacomprehension
phonemes
nonnutritive sucking
habituation
magnet effect
cooing
babbling
intentional communication
motherese

fast mapping
taxonomic assumption
overextension
underextension
defining features
characteristic features
morphemes
morphology
overregularization
parallel distributed processing

blocking-plus-retrieval-
   failure theory

syntax
telegraphic speech

crib speech
pragmatics

RECOMMENDED READINGS

Ceci, S. J., & Bruck, M. (1995). *Jeopardy in the courtroom: A scientific analysis of children's testimony.* Washington, DC: American Psychological Association. Here is an ideal book for students who want to know more about this controversial topic; the book is an excellent blend of empirical research and descriptions from court cases.

Craik, F. I. M., & Salthouse, T. A. (Eds.). (1992). *The handbook of aging and cognition.* Hillsdale, NJ: Erlbaum. The chapters in this handbook are superbly written, covering topics related to cognitive aging, such as attention, memory, spatial abilities, language, and neurophysiology.

de Villiers, P. A., & de Villiers, J. G. (1992). Language development. In M. H. Bornstein & M. E. Lamb (Eds.), *Developmental psychology: An advanced textbook* (3rd ed., pp. 337–418). Hillsdale, NJ: Erlbaum. This chapter succinctly reviews such topics as lexical development, word meaning, syntax, and cross-linguistic variation.

Kail, R. V., Jr. (1990). *The development of memory in children* (3rd ed.). New York: Freeman. This interesting book emphasizes the development of memory, memory strategies, and metamemory in children; it also includes a chapter on infants' memory.

Light, L. L. (1991). Memory and aging: Four hypotheses in search of data. *Annual Review of Psychology, 42,* 333–376. Light's comprehensive review article is clearly written and honest, not bending the empirical research to fit any favored explanation.

Owens, R. E., Jr. (1996). *Language development: An introduction* (4th ed.). Boston: Allyn & Bacon. Owens' textbook offers a very readable, comprehensive overview of language development; it covers topics such as neurolinguistics, pragmatics, adult language development, bilingualism, and language disorders.

ONE LAST TASK

To review this book as comprehensively as possible, try this final task. On separate sheets of paper, list each of the five themes of this book. Then skim through each chapter, noting on the appropriate sheet each time a theme is mentioned. You can check the completeness of your lists by consulting the entries "Themes 1, 2, 3, 4, and 5" in the subject index. After completing your lists, try to synthesize the material within each of the five themes.

REFERENCES

Abelson, R. P. (1981). Psychological status of the script concept. *American Psychologist, 36,* 715–729.

Abrams, R. A. (1992). Planning and producing saccadic eye movements. In K. Rayner (Ed.), *Eye movements and visual cognition* (pp. 66–88). New York: Springer-Verlag.

Adams, J. L. (1979). *Conceptual blockbusting* (2nd ed.). New York: Norton.

Adams, M. J., & Bruck, M. (1995, Summer). Resolving the great debate. *American Educator,* pp. 7, 10–20.

Adelson, E. H. (1978). Iconic storage: The role of rods. *Science, 201,* 544–546.

Adeyemo, S. A. (1990). Thinking imagery and problem solving. *Psychological Studies, 35,* 179–190.

Adeyemo, S. A. (1994). Individual differences in thinking and problem solving. *Personality and Individual Differences,* 17, 117–124.

Adler, J., & Hall, C. (1995, June 5). Surgery at 33,000 feet. *Newsweek,* 36.

Adler, T. (1991, July). Memory researcher wins Troland award. *APA Monitor,* pp. 12–13.

Agans, R. P., & Shaffer, L. S. (1994). The hindsight bias: The role of the availability heuristic and perceived risk. *Basic and Applied Social Psychology, 15,* 439–449.

Agnoli, F., & Krantz, D. H. (1989). Suppressing natural heuristics by formal instruction: The case of the conjunction fallacy. *Cognitive Psychology, 21,* 515–550.

Alba, J. W., & Hasher, L. (1983). Is memory schematic? *Psychological Bulletin, 93,* 203–231.

Albrecht, J. E., O'Brien, E. J., Mason, R. A., & Myers, J. L. (1995). The role of perspective in the accessibility of goals during reading. *Journal of Experimental Psychology: Learning, Memory, and Cognition, 21,* 364–372.

Alexander, J. M., & Schwanenflugel, P. J. (1994). Strategy regulation: The role of intelligence, metacognitive attributions, and knowledge base. *Developmental Psychology, 30,* 709–723.

Allbritton, D. W., & Gerrig, R. J. (1991). Participatory responses in text understanding. *Journal of Memory and Language, 30,* 603–626.

Allport, A. (1989). Visual attention. In M. Posner (Ed.), *Foundations of cognitive science* (pp. 631–682). Cambridge, MA: MIT Press.

Alterman, R., & Bookman, L. A. (1992). Reasoning about a semantic memory encoding of the connectivity of events. *Cognitive Science, 16,* 205–232.

Amabile, T. M. (1982). Social psychology of creativity: A consensual assessment technique. *Journal of Personality and Social Psychology, 43,* 997–1013.

Amabile, T. M. (1983). *The social psychology of creativity.* New York: Springer-Verlag.

Amabile, T. M. (1990). Within you, without you: The social psychology of creativity, and beyond. In M. A. Runco & R. S. Albert (Eds.), *Theories of creativity* (pp. 61–91). Newbury Park, NY: Sage.

Amabile, T. M. (1994). The "atmosphere of pure work": Creativity in research and development. In W. R. Shadish & S. Fuller (Eds.), *The social psychology of science* (pp. 316–328). New York: Guilford.

American Psychological Association. (1994). *Publication manual of the American Psychological Association* (4th ed.). Washington, DC: Author.

Anderson, J. R. (1976). *Language, memory, and thought.* Hillsdale, NJ: Erlbaum.

Anderson, J. R. (1983a). *The architecture of cognition.* Cambridge, MA: Harvard University Press.

Anderson, J. R. (1983b). Retrieval of information from long-term memory. *Science, 220,* 25–30.

Anderson, J. R. (1985). *Cognitive psychology and its implications* (2nd ed.). New York: W. H. Freeman.

Anderson, J. R. (1987). Skill acquisition: Compilation of weak-method problem solutions. *Psychological Review, 94,* 192–210.

Anderson, J. R. (1990). *The adaptive character of thought.* Hillsdale, NJ: Erlbaum.

Anderson, J. R. (1991). Is human cognition adaptive? *Behavioral and Brain Sciences, 14,* 471–517.

Anderson, J. R. (1993). Problem solving and learning. *American Psychologist, 48,* 35–44.

Anderson, J. R., Corbett, A. T., Koedinger, K. R., & Pelletier, R. (1995). Cognitive tutors: Lessons learned. *The Journal of the Learning Sciences, 4,* 167–207.

Anderson, J. R., & Reder, L. (1979). An elaborative processing explanation of depth of processing. In L. S. Cermak & F. I. M. Craik (Eds.), *Levels of processing in human memory.* Hillsdale, NJ: Erlbaum.

Anderson, R. E. (1984). Did I do it or did I only imagine doing it? *Journal of Experimental Psychology: General, 113,* 594–613.

Anderson, S. J., & Conway, M. A. (1993). Investigating the structure of autobiographical memories. *Journal of Experimental Psychology: Learning, Memory, and Cognition, 19,* 1178–1196.

Andreassen, C., & Waters, H. S. (1989). Organization during study: Relationships between metamemory, strategy use, and performance. *Journal of Educational Psychology, 81,* 190–195.

Andrews, F. M. (1975). Social and psychological factors which influence the creative process. In I. A. Taylor & J. W. Getzels (Eds.), *Perspectives in creativity.* Chicago: Aldine.

Anglin, J. M. (1977). *Word, object, and conceptual development.* New York: Norton.

Anisfeld, M. (1984). *Language development from birth to three.* Hillsdale, NJ: Erlbaum.

Anthony, T., Cooper, C., & Mullen, B. (1992). Cross-racial facial identification: A social cognitive integration. *Personality and Social Psychology Bulletin, 18,* 296–301.

Antonietti, A., & Baldo, S. (1994). Undergraduates' conceptions of cognitive functions of mental imagery. *Perceptual and Motor Skills, 78,* 160–162.

Arbuckle, T. Y., Cooney, R., Milne, J., & Melchior, A. (1994). Memory for spatial layout in relation to age and schema typicality. *Psychological Aging, 9,* 467–480.

Aretz, A. J., & Wickens, C. D. (1992). The mental rotation of map displays. *Human Performance, 5,* 303–328.

Arkes, H. R., Wortmann, R. L., Saville, P. D., & Harkness, A. R. (1981). Hindsight bias among physicians weighing the likelihood of diagnoses. *Journal of Applied Psychology, 66,* 252–254.

Astington, J. W. (1993). *The child's discovery of the mind.* Cambridge, MA: Harvard University Press.

Atkinson, R. C., & Shiffrin, R. M. (1968). Human memory: A proposed system and its control processes. In K. W. Spence & J. T. Spence (Eds.), *The psychology of learning and motivation: Advances in research and theory* (Vol. 2). New York: Academic Press.

Baars, B. J. (1992). A plea for simplicity. *American Journal of Psychology, 105,* 591–597.

Baddeley, A. D. (1984). The fractionation of human memory. *Psychological Medicine, 14,* 259–264.

Baddeley, A. D. (1986). *Working memory.* Oxford, England: Clarendon Press.

Baddeley, A. D. (1988). Cognitive psychology and human memory. *Trends in Neurosciences, 11,* 176–181.

Baddeley, A. D. (1989). The uses of working memory. In P. R. Solomon, G. R. Goethals, C. M. Kelley, & B. R. Stephens (Eds.), *Memory: Interdisciplinary approaches* (pp. 107–123). New York: Springer-Verlag.

Baddeley, A. D. (1990). *Human memory: Theory and practice.* Boston: Allyn & Bacon.

Baddeley, A. D. (1992a). Working memory: Humans. In L. R. Squire (Ed.), *Encyclopedia of learning and memory* (pp. 638–642). New York: Macmillan.

Baddeley, A. D. (1992b). Working memory. *Science, 255,* 556–559.

Baddeley, A. D. (1993). *Your memory: A user's guide.* London: Prion.

Baddeley, A. D. (1994). The magical number seven: Still magic after all these years? *Psychological Review, 101,* 353–356.

Baddeley, A. D., & Hitch, G. J. (1974). Working memory. In G. Bower (Ed.), *Recent advances in learning and memory* (Vol. 8, pp. 47–90). New York: Academic Press.

Baddeley, A. D., Thomson, N., & Buchanan, M. (1975). Word length and the structure of short-term memory. *Journal of Verbal Learning and Verbal Behavior, 14,* 575–589.

Bahrick, H. P. (1984). Semantic memory content in permastore: Fifty years of memory for Spanish learned in school. *Journal of Experimental Psychology: General, 113,* 1–35.

Bahrick, H. P., Bahrick, L. E., Bahrick, A. S., & Bahrick, P. E. (1993). Maintenance of foreign language vocabulary and the spacing effect. *Psychological Science, 4,* 316–321.

Bahrick, H. P., & Hall, L. K. (1991). Lifetime maintenance of high school mathematics content. *Journal of Experimental Psychology: General, 120,* 20–33.

Bahrick, H. P., Hall, L. K., & Dunlosky, J. (1993). Reconstructive processing of memory content for high versus low test scores and grades. *Applied Cognitive Psychology, 7,* 1–10.

Bahrick, H. P., Hall, L. K., Goggin, J. P., Bahrick, L. E., & Berger, S. A. (1994). Fifty years of language maintenance and language dominance in bilingual Hispanic immigrants. *Journal of Experimental Psychology: General, 123,* 264–283.

Bahrick, H. P., & Phelps, E. (1987). Retention of Spanish vocabulary over 8 years. *Journal of Experimental Psychology: Learning, Memory, and Cognition, 13*, 344–349.

Baillargeon, R., & Graber, M. (1988). Evidence of location memory in 8-month-old infants in a nonsearch AB task. *Developmental Psychology, 24*, 502–511.

Baird, J. C., & Hubbard, T. L. (1992). Psychophysics of visual imagery. In D. Algom (Ed.), *Psychophysical approaches to cognition* (pp. 389–440). Amsterdam: Elsevier.

Baker, L. (1989). Metacognition, comprehension monitoring, and the adult reader. *Educational Psychology Review, 1*, 3–38.

Baker-Ward, L., Ornstein, P. A., & Holden, D. J. (1984). The expression of memorization in early childhood. *Journal of Experimental Child Psychology, 37*, 555–575.

Bales, J. (1988, December). Vincennes: Findings could have helped avert tragedy, scientists tell Hill panel. *APA Monitor,* pp. 10–11.

Banaji, M. R., & Crowder, R. G. (1989). The bankruptcy of everyday memory. *American Psychologist, 44*, 1185–1193.

Banks, W. P., & Barber, G. (1977). Color information in iconic memory. *Psychological Review, 84*, 536–546.

Banks, W. P., & Krajicek, D. (1991). Perception. *Annual Review of Psychology, 42*, 305–331.

Barber, P. (1988). *Applied cognitive psychology.* London: Methuen.

Barclay, C. R. (1986). Schematization of autobiographical memory. In D. C. Rubin (Ed.), *Autobiographical memory* (pp. 82–99). New York: Cambridge University Press.

Barclay, C. R., & Wellman, H. M. (1986). Accuracies and inaccuracies in autobiographical memories. *Journal of Memory and Language, 25*, 93–103.

Baron, J. (1991). Some thinking is irrational. *Behavioral and Brain Sciences, 14*, 486–487.

Baron, J. (1994). *Thinking and deciding* (2nd ed.). New York: Cambridge University Press.

Baron, J., & Strawson, C. (1976). Use of orthographic and word-specific knowledge in reading words aloud. *Journal of Experimental Psychology: Human Perception and Performance, 2*, 386–393.

Barsalou, L. W. (1985). Ideals, central tendency, and frequency of instantiation as determinants of graded structure in categories. *Journal of Experimental Psychology: Learning, Memory, and Cognition, 11*, 629–654.

Barsalou, L. W. (1987). The instability of graded structure: Implications for the nature of concepts. In U. Neisser (Ed.), *Concepts and conceptual development: Ecological and intellectual factors in categorization.* New York: Cambridge University Press.

Barsalou, L. W. (1989). Intra-concept similarity and its implications for inter-concept similarity. In S. Vosniadou & A. Ortony (Eds.), *Similarity and analogical reasoning* (pp. 76–121). New York: Cambridge University Press.

Barsalou, L. W. (1990). On the indistinguishability of exemplar memory and abstraction in category representation. In T. K. Srull & R. S. Wyer (Eds.), *Advances in social cognition* (Vol. 3, pp. 61–88). Hillsdale, NJ: Erlbaum.

Barsalou, L. W. (1992a). *Cognitive psychology: An overview for cognitive scientists.* Hillsdale, NJ: Erlbaum.

Barsalou, L. W. (1992b). Frames, concepts, and conceptual fields. In A. Lehrer & E. F. Kittay (Eds.), *Frames, fields, and contrasts* (pp. 21–74). Hillsdale, NJ: Erlbaum.

Barsalou, L. W. (1993). Flexibility, structure, and linguistic vagary in concepts: Manifestations of a compositional system of perceptual symbols. In A. F. Collins, S. E. Gathercole, M. A. Conway, & P. E. Morris (Eds.), *Theories of memory* (pp. 29–101). Hove, England: Erlbaum.

Barsalou, L. W., & Sewell, D. R. (1985). Contrasting the representation of scripts and categories. *Journal of Memory and Language, 24*, 646–665.

Bartlett, F. C. (1932). *Remembering: An experimental and social study.* Cambridge, England: Cambridge University Press.

Bartsch, K., & Wellman, H. M. (1995). *Children talk about the mind.* New York: Oxford University Press.

Bates, E. (1979). *The emergence of symbols: Cognition and communication in infancy.* New York: Academic Press.

Bates, E. (1991). *Normal and abnormal language development.* Paper presented at the Venice Conference on Developmental Neuropsychology, San Servolo, Italy.

Bates, E., Bretherton, I., & Snyder, L. (1988). *From first words to grammar: Individual differences and dissociable mechanisms.* New York: Cambridge University Press.

Bates, E., & Elman, J. (1993). Connectionism and the study of change. In M. Johnson (Ed.), *Brain development and cognition: A reader.* Oxford, England: Blackwell.

Bates, E., Thal, D., & Janowsky, J. S. (1992). Early language development and its neural correlates. In I. Rapin & S. Segalowitz (Eds.), *Handbook of neuro-psychology* (Vol. 6). Amsterdam: Elsevier.

Bauer, M. I., & Johnson-Laird, P. N. (1993). How diagrams can improve reasoning. *Psychological Science, 4,* 372–378.

Bauer, P. J. (1995). Recalling past events: From infancy to early childhood. *Annals of Child Development, 11,* 25–71.

Bauer, P. J. (1996). What do infants recall of their lives? Memory for specific events by one- to two-year-olds. *American Psychologist, 51,* 29–41.

Beach, K. (1993). Becoming a bartender: The role of external memory cues in a work-directed educational activity. *Applied Cognitive Psychology, 7,* 191–204.

Beattie, G. (1983). *Talk: An analysis of speech and nonverbal behaviour in conversation.* Milton Keynes, England: Open University Press.

Bechtel, W., & Abrahamsen, A. (1991). *Connectionism and the mind: An introduction to parallel processing in networks.* Cambridge, MA: Basil Blackwell.

Bédard, J., & Chi, M. T. H. (1992). Expertise. *Current Directions in Psychological Science, 1,* 135–137.

Begg, I. (1982). Imagery, organization, and discriminative processes. *Canadian Journal of Psychology, 36,* 273–290.

Begg, I., & White, P. (1985). Encoding specificity in interpersonal communication. *Canadian Journal of Psychology, 39,* 70–87.

Bell, P. B., & Staines, P. J. (1981). *Reasoning and argument in psychology.* London: Routledge and Kegan Paul.

Bellezza, F. S. (1984). The self as a mnemonic device: The role of internal cues. *Journal of Personality and Social Psychology, 47,* 506–516.

Bellezza, F. S. (1986). Mental cues and verbal reports in learning. In G. H. Bower (Ed.), *The psychology of learning and motivation* (Vol. 20, pp. 237–273). New York: Academic Press.

Bellezza, F. S. (1987). Mnemonic devices and memory schemes. In M. McDaniel & M. Pressley (Eds.), *Imagery and related mnemonic processes* (pp. 34–55). New York: Springer-Verlag.

Bellezza, F. S. (1992a). Recall of congruent information in the self-reference task. *Bulletin of the Psychonomic Society, 30,* 275–278.

Bellezza, F. S. (1992b). The mind's eye in expert memorizers' descriptions of remembering. *Metaphor and Symbolic Activity, 7,* 119–133.

Bellezza, F. S. (1992c). Mnemonic devices. In L. R. Squire (Ed.), *Encyclopedia of learning and memory* (pp. 418–424). New York: Macmillan.

Bellezza, F. S. (1994). Chunking. In V. S. Ramachandran (Ed.), *Encyclopedia of Human Behavior* (Vol. 1, pp. 579–589). Orlando, FL: Academic Press.

Bellezza, F. S. (1996). Mnemonic method to enhance storage and retrieval. In E. Bjork & R. Bjork (Eds.), *Handbook of perception and cognition* (Vol. 10) San Diego, CA: Academic Press.

Bellezza, F. S., & Buck, D. K. (1988). Expert knowledge as mnemonic cues. *Applied Cognitive Psychology, 2,* 147–162.

Bellezza, F. S., & Hoyt, S. K. (1992). The self-reference effect and mental cueing. *Social Cognition, 10,* 51–78.

Berardi-Coletta, B., Buyer, L. S., Dominowski, R. L., & Rellinger, E. R. (1995). Metacognition and problem solving: A process-oriented approach. *Journal of Experimental Psychology: Learning, Memory, and Cognition, 21,* 205–223.

Bereiter, C., & Bird, M. (1985). Use of thinking aloud in identification and teaching of reading comprehension strategies. *Cognition and Instruction, 2,* 131–156.

Berz, W. L. (1995). Working memory in music: A theoretical model. *Music Perception, 12,* 353–364.

Besner, D., Davies, J., & Daniels, S. (1981). Reading for meaning: The effects of concurrent articulation. *Quarterly Journal of Experimental Psychology, 33A,* 415–437.

Besner, D., Twilley, L., McCann, R. S., & Seergobin, K. (1990). On the association between connectionism and data: Are a few words necessary? *Psychological Review, 97,* 432–446.

Bialystok, E. (1987). Words as things. Development of word concept by bilingual children. *Studies in Second Language Acquisition, 9,* 133–140.

Bialystok, E. (1988). Levels of bilingualism and levels of linguistic awareness. *Developmental Psychology, 24,* 560–567.

Bialystok, E. (1992). Selective attention in cognitive processing: The bilingual edge. In R. J. Harris (Ed.), *Language processing in bilingual children* (pp. 501–513). Amsterdam: Elsevier.

Bialystok, E. The effects of bilingualism and biliteracy on children's emerging concepts of print. *Developmental Psychology,* in press.

Bialystok, E., & Hakuta, K. (1994). *In other words: The science and psychology of second-language acquisition.* New York: Basic Books.

Biederman, I. (1987). Recognition-by-components: A theory of human image understanding. *Psychological Review, 94,* 115–147.

Biederman, I. (1990). Higher-level vision. In E. N. Osherson, S. M. Kosslyn, & J. M. Hollerbach (Eds.), *An invitation to cognitive science* (Vol. 2, pp. 41–72). Cambridge, MA: MIT Press.

Bieman-Copland, S., & Charness, N. (1994). Memory knowledge and memory monitoring in adulthood. *Psychology and Aging, 9,* 287–302.

Birnbaum, M. H., Anderson, C. J., & Hynan, L. G. (1990). Theories of bias in probability judgment. In J. P. Caverni, J. M. Fabre, & M. Gonzalez (Eds.), *Cognitive biases* (pp. 477–498). Amsterdam: Elsevier.

Birren, J. E., & Schaie, K. W. (Eds.). (1996). *Handbook of the psychology of aging* (4th ed.). San Diego, CA: Academic Press.

Bjork, E. L., & Bjork, R. A. (1988). On the adaptive aspects of retrieval failure in autobiographical memory. In M. M. Gruneberg, P. E. Morris, & R. N. Sykes (Eds.), *Practical aspects of memory* (Vol. 2). London: Academic Press.

Bjork, R. A. (1988). Retrieval practice and the maintenance of knowledge. In M. M. Gruneberg, P. Morris, & R. Sykes (Eds.), *Practical aspects of memory* (Vol. 2, pp. 396–401). London: Academic Press.

Bjork, R. A., & Richardson-Klavehn, A. (1987). On the puzzling relationship between environmental context and human memory. In C. Izawa (Ed.), *Current issues in cognitive processes* (pp. 313–344). Hillsdale, NJ: Erlbaum.

Bjorklund, D. F., & Green, B. L. (1992). The adaptive nature of cognitive immaturity. *American Psychologist, 47,* 46–54.

Bjorklund, D. F., & Zeman, B. R. (1982). Children's organization and metamemory awareness in the recall of familiar information. *Child Development, 53,* 799–810.

Black, J. B. (1984). The architecture of the mind [Review of *The architecture of cognition*]. *Contemporary Psychology, 29,* 853–854.

Blanchard, H. E., & Iran-Nejad, A. (1987). Comprehension processes and eye movement patterns in the reading of surprise-ending stories. *Discourse Processes, 10,* 127–138.

Blaney, P. H. (1986). Affect and memory: A review. *Psychological Bulletin, 99,* 229–246.

Bloom, C. P. (1988). The roles of schemata in memory for text. *Discourse Processes, 11,* 305–318.

Bloom, L. C., & Mudd, S. A. (1991). Depth of processing approach to face recognition: A test of two theories. *Journal of Experimental Psychology: Learning, Memory, and Cognition, 17,* 556–565.

Blumstein, S. E. (1995). The neurobiology of language. In J. L. Miller & P. D. Eimas (Eds.), *Speech, language, and communication* (pp. 339–370). San Diego, CA: Academic Press.

Bock, J. K. (1986). Syntactic persistence in language production. *Cognitive Psychology, 18,* 355–387.

Bock, J. K. (1987). Co-ordinating words and syntax in speech plans. In A. W. Ellis (Ed.), *Progress in the psychology of language* (Vol. 3, pp. 337–390). London: Erlbaum.

Bock, K. (1995). Sentence production: From mind to mouth. In J. L. Miller & P. D. Eimas (Eds.), *Speech, language, and communication* (pp. 181–216). San Diego, CA: Academic Press.

Bock, K., & Levelt, W. (1994). Language production: Grammatical encodings. In M. A. Gernsbacher (Ed.), *Handbook of psycholinguistics* (pp. 945–984). San Diego, CA: Academic Press.

Bock, K., Loebell, H., & Morey, R. (1992). From conceptual roles to structural relations: Bridging the syntactic cleft. *Psychological Review, 99,* 150–171.

Boden, M. A. (Ed.). (1994). *Dimensions of creativity.* Cambridge, MA: MIT Press.

Bohm, P., & Lind, H. (1992). A note on the robustness of a classical framing result. *Journal of Economic Psychology, 13,* 355–361.

Bothwell, R. K., Brigham, J. C., & Malpass, R. S. (1989). Cross-racial identification. *Personality and Social Psychology Bulletin, 15,* 19–25.

Bower, G. H. (1970). Analysis of a mnemonic device. *American Scientist, 58,* 496–510.

Bower, G. H. (1976). Experiments on story understanding and recall. *Quarterly Journal of Experimental Psychology, 28,* 511–534.

Bower, G. H. (1987). Commentary on mood and memory. *Behavior Research Therapy, 25,* 443–455.

Bower, G. H. (1989). Mental models in text understanding. In A. F. Bennett & K. M. McConkey (Eds.), *Cognition in individual and social contexts* (pp. 129–144). Amsterdam: Elsevier Science.

Bower, G. H. (1992). How might emotions affect learning? In S. A. Christianson (Ed.), *Handbook of emotion and memory* (pp. 3–31). Hillsdale, NJ: Erlbaum.

Bower, G. H., & Clark, M. C. (1969). Narrative stories as mediators for serial learning. *Psychonomic Science, 14,* 181–182.

Bower, G. H., Clark, M. C., Lesgold, A. M., & Winzenz, D. (1969). Hierarchical retrieval schemes in recall of categorized word lists. *Journal of Verbal Learning and Verbal Behavior, 8,* 323–343.

Bower, G. H., & Gilligan, S. G. (1979). Remembering information related to one's self. *Journal of Research in Personality, 13,* 420–432.

Bower, G. H., & Mayer, J. D. (1985). Failure to replicate mood-dependent retrieval. *Bulletin of the Psychonomic Society, 23,* 39–42.

Bower, G. H., & Mayer, J. D. (1989). In search of mood-dependent retrieval. *Journal of Social Behavior and Personality, 4,* 121–156.

Bower, G. H., & Morrow, D. G. (1990). Mental models in narrative comprehension. *Science, 247,* 44–48.

Bower, G. H., & Springston, F. (1970). Pauses as recoding points in letter series. *Journal of Experimental Psychology, 83,* 421–430.

Bower, G. H., & Winzenz, D. (1970). Comparison of associative learning strategies. *Psychonomic Science, 20,* 119–120.

Bowers, K. S. (1984). On being unconsciously influenced and informed. In K. S. Bowers & D. Meichenbaum (Eds.), *The unconscious reconsidered* (pp. 227–272). New York: Wiley.

Bradshaw, J. L., & Nettleton, N. C. (1974). Articulatory inference and the MOWN-DOWN heterophone effect. *Journal of Experimental Psychology, 102,* 88–94.

Brandimonte, M. A., Hitch, G. J., & Bishop, D. V. M. (1992). Influence of short-term memory codes on visual image processing: Evidence from image transformation tasks. *Journal of Experimental Psychology: Learning, Memory, and Cognition, 18,* 157–165.

Bransford, J. D., Barclay, J. R., & Franks, J. J. (1972). Sentence memory: A constructive versus interpretive approach. *Cognitive Psychology, 3,* 193–209.

Bransford, J. D., & Franks, J. J. (1971). Abstraction of linguistic ideas. *Cognitive Psychology, 2,* 331–350.

Bransford, J. D., Franks, J. J., Morris, C. D., & Stein, B. S. (1979). Some general constraints on learning and memory research. In L. S. Cermak & F. I. M. Craik (Eds.), *Levels of processing in human memory* (pp. 331–354). Hillsdale, NJ: Erlbaum.

Bransford, J. D., & Johnson, M. K. (1972). Contextual prerequisites for understanding: Some investigations of comprehension and recall. *Journal of Verbal Learning and Verbal Behavior, 11,* 717–726.

Bransford, J. D., Sherwood, R. D., & Sturdevant, T. (1987). Teaching thinking and problem solving. In J. B. Baron & R. J. Sternberg (Eds.), *Teaching thinking skills* (pp. 162–181). New York: Freeman.

Bransford, J. D., & Stein, B. S. (1984). *The IDEAL problem solver.* New York: Freeman.

Branthwaite, A., & Rogers, D. (1985). Introduction. In A. Branthwaite & D. Rogers (Eds.), *Children growing up* (pp. 1–2). Milton Keynes, England: Open University Press.

Brennan, S. E. (1991). Conversation with and through computers. *User Modeling and User-Adapted Interaction, 1,* 67–86.

Brewer, W. F. (1992). The theoretical and empirical status of the flashbulb memory hypothesis. In E. Winograd & U. Neisser (Eds.), *Affect and accuracy in recall: Studies of "flashbulb" memories* (pp. 274–305). New York: Cambridge University Press.

Brewer, W. F., & Treyens, J. C. (1981). Role of schemata in memory for places. *Cognitive Psychology, 13,* 207–230.

Breyer, S. (1993). *Breaking the vicious circle: Toward effective risk regulation.* Cambridge, MA: Harvard University Press.

Briere, J., & Conte, J. (1993). Self-reported amnesia for abuse in adults molested as children. *Journal of Traumatic Stress, 6,* 21–31.

Brigham, T. C., & Malpass, R. S. (1985). The role of experience and context in the recognition of faces of own- and other-race. *Journal of Social Issues, 41,* 139–155.

Broadbent, D. E. (1958). *Perception and communication.* New York: Pergamon.

Brooks, L. R. (1968). Spatial and verbal components of the act of recall. *Canadian Journal of Psychology, 22,* 349–368.

Brown, A. L. (1975). The development of memory: Knowing, knowing about knowing, and knowing how to know. In H. W. Reese (Ed.), *Advances in child development and behavior* (Vol. 10). New York: Academic Press.

Brown, A. L., & Scott, M. S. (1971). Recognition memory for pictures in preschool children. *Journal of Experimental Child Psychology, 11,* 401–412.

Brown, A. S. (1991). A review of the tip-of-the-tongue experience. *Psychological Bulletin, 109,* 204–233.

Brown, J. A. (1958). Some tests of the decay theory of immediate memory. *Quarterly Journal of Experimental Psychology, 10,* 12–21.

Brown, N. R. (1990). Organization of public events in long-term memory. *Journal of Experimental Psychology: General, 119,* 297–314.

Brown, N. R., & Siegler, R. S. (1992). The role of availability in the estimation of national populations. *Memory & Cognition, 20,* 406–412.

Brown, P., Keenan, J. M., & Potte, G. R. (1986). The self-reference effect with imagery encoding. *Journal of Personality and Social Psychology, 51,* 897–906.

Brown, P., & Levinson, S. C. (1987). *Politeness: Some universals of language usage.* Cambridge, England: Cambridge University Press.

Brown, R. (1973). *A first language: The early stages.* Cambridge, MA: Harvard University Press.

Brown, R. (1990). Foreword. In M. G. Johnson & T. B. Henley (Eds.), *Reflections on the Principles of Psychology: William James after a century* (pp. xv–xvii). Hillsdale, NJ: Erlbaum.

Brown, R., & Kulik, J. (1977). Flashbulb memories. *Cognition, 5,* 73–99.

Brown, R., & McNeill, D. (1966). The "tip of the tongue" phenomenon. *Journal of Verbal Learning and Verbal Behavior, 5,* 325–377.

Brown, R. T. (1989). Creativity: What are we to measure? In J. A. Glover, R. R. Ronning, & C. R. Reynolds (Eds.), *Handbook of creativity* (pp. 3–32). New York: Plenum.

Brown, S. I., & Walter, M. I. (1990). *The art of problem posing* (2nd ed.). Hillsdale, NJ: Erlbaum.

Bruce, P. R., Coyne, A. C., & Botwinick, J. (1982). Adult age differences in metamemory. *Journal of Gerontology, 37,* 354–357.

Bruce, V. (1988). Perceiving. In G. Claxton (Ed.), *Growth points in cognition* (pp. 32–65). New York: Routledge.

Bruce, V. (1994). Stability from variation: The case of face recognition. *Quarterly Journal of Experimental Psychology, 47A,* 5–28.

Bruce, V., Burton, A. M., Hanna, E., Healey, P., Mason, O., Coombes, A., Fright, R., & Linney, A. (1993). Sex discrimination: How do we tell the difference between male and female faces. *Perception, 22,* 131–152.

Bruce, V., Cowey, A., Ellis, A. W., & Perrett, D. I. (1992). *Processing the facial image.* Oxford, Great Britain: Clarendon Press.

Bruck, M., Cavanagh, P., & Ceci, S. J. (1991). Fortysomething: Recognizing faces at one's 25th reunion. *Memory & Cognition, 19,* 221–228.

Bryant, D. J., Tversky, B., & Franklin, N. (1992). Internal and external spatial frameworks for representing described scenes. *Journal of Memory and Language, 31,* 74–98.

Buehler, R., Griffin, D., & Ross, M. (1994). Exploring the "planning fallacy." Why people underestimate their task completion times. *Journal of Personality and Social Psychology, 67,* 366–381.

Buehler, R., & Ross, M. (1993). How do individuals remember their past statements? *Journal of Personality and Social Psychology, 64,* 538–551.

Burgess, N., & Hitch, G. J. (1992). Toward a network model of the articulatory loop. *Journal of Memory and Language, 31,* 429–460.

Busey, T. A., & Loftus, G. R. (1994). Sensory and cognitive components of visual information acquisition. *Psychological Review, 101,* 446–469.

Bushnell, I. W. R., & Sai, F. (1987). *Neonatal recognition of the mother's face.* University of Glasgow Report, 87/1.

Butters, N., Heindel, W. C., & Salmon, D. P. (1990). Dissociation of implicit memory in dementia: Neurological implications. *Bulletin of the Psychonomic Society, 28,* 359–366.

Byrne, B., & Fielding-Barnsley, R. (1991). Evaluation of a program to teach phonemic awareness to young children. *Journal of Educational Psychology, 83,* 451–455.

Byrne, R. M. J. (1989). Suppressing valid inferences with conditionals. *Cognition, 31,* 61–83.

Cairns, R. B., & Valsiner, J. (1984). Child psychology. *Annual Review of Psychology, 35,* 553–577.

Calkins, M. W. (1894). Association: I. *Psychological Review, 1,* 476–483.

Camp, C. J., & McKitrick, L. A. (1992). Memory interventions in Alzheimer's type dementil populations: Methodological and theoretical issues. In R. I. West & J. D. Sinott (Eds.), *Everyday memory and aging: Current research and methodology* (pp. 155–172). New York: Springer.

Campbell, R., & Sais, E. (1995). Accelerated meta-linguistic (phonological) awareness in bilingual children. *British Journal of Developmental Psychology, 13,* 61–68.

Cannon, C. K., & Quinsey, V. L. (1995). The likelihood of violent behaviour: Predictions, postdictions, and hindsight bias. *Canadian Journal of Behavioural Science, 27,* 92–106.

Caramazza, A., Yenni-Komshian, G., Zurif, E., & Carbone, E. (1973). The acquisition of a new phonological contrast: The case of stop consonants in French-English bilinguals. *Journal of the Acoustical Society of America, 54,* 421–428.

Carlson, E. R. (1995). Evaluating the credibility of sources: A missing link in the teaching of critical thinking. *Teaching of Psychology, 22,* 39–41.

Carlson, L., Zimmer, J. W., & Glover, J. A. (1981). First-letter mnemonics: DAM (Don't Aid Memory). *Journal of General Psychology, 104,* 287–292.

Carlson, R. A., Sullivan, M. A., & Schneider, W. (1989). Practice and working memory effects in building procedural skill. *Journal of Experimental Psychology: Learning, Memory, and Cognition, 15,* 517–526.

Carpenter, P. A., Miyake, A., & Just, M. A. (1994). Working memory constraints in comprehension. In M. A. Gernsbacher (Ed.), *Handbook of psycholingusitics* (pp. 1075–1122). San Diego, CA: Academic Press.

Carrasco, M., & Ridout, J. B. (1993). Olfactory perception and olfactory imagery: A multidimensional analysis. *Journal of Experimental Psychology: Human Perception and Performance, 19,* 287–301.

Carroll, D. W. (1994). *Psychology of language* (2nd ed.). Pacific Grove, CA: Brooks/Cole.

Castle, J. M., Riach, J., & Nicholson, T. (1994). Getting off to a better start in reading and spelling: The effects of phonemic awareness instruction within a whole language program. *Journal of Educational Psychology, 86,* 350–359.

Cattell, J. M. (1886). The time it takes to see and name objects. *Mind, 11,* 63–65.

Cave, C. B., & Kosslyn, S. M. (1993). The role of parts and spatial relations in object identification. *Perception, 22,* 229–248.

Ceci, S. J. (1994). Cognitive and social factors in children's testimony. In B. D. Sales & G. R. Vanden-Bos (Eds.), *Psychology in litigation and legislation* (pp. 13–54). Washington, DC: American Psychological Association.

Ceci, S. J., & Bronfenbrenner, U. (1991). On the demise of everyday memory: "The rumors of my death are much exaggerated" (Mark Twain). *American Psychologist, 46,* 27–31.

Ceci, S. J., & Bruck, M. (1993). Suggestibility of the child witness: A historical review and synthesis. *Psychological Bulletin, 113,* 403–439.

Ceci, S. J., & Bruck, M. (1995). *Jeopardy in the courtroom: A scientific analysis of children's testimony.* Washington, DC: American Psychological Association.

Ceci, S. J., & Liker, J. K. (1986). A day at the races: A study of IQ, expertise, and cognitive complexity. *Journal of Experimental Psychology: General, 115,* 255–266.

Ceci, S. J., & Liker, J. K. (1988). Stalking the IQ-Expertise relation: When the critics go fishing. *Journal of Experimental Psychology: General, 117,* 96–100.

Ceci, S. J., & Loftus, E. F. (1994). "Memory work": A royal road to false memories? *Applied Cognitive Psychology, 8,* 351–364.

Cerella, J., Rybash, J., Hoyer, W., & Commons, M. L. (1993). *Adult information processing: Limits on loss.* San Diego, CA: Academic Press.

Cernoch, J. M., & Porter, R. H. (1985). Recognition of maternal axillary odors by infants. *Child Development, 56,* 1593–1598.

Cervone, D. (1989). Effects of envisioning future activities on self-efficacy judgments and motivation: An availability heuristic interpretation. *Cognitive Therapy and Research, 13,* 247–261.

Chafe, W., & Danielewicz, J. (1987). Properties of spoken and written language. In R. Horowitz & S. J. Samuels (Eds.), *Comprehending oral and written language* (pp. 83–113). San Diego, CA: Academic Press.

Chambers, D. (1993). Images are both depictive and descriptive. In B. Roskos-Ewoldson, M. J. Intons-Peterson, & R. E. Anderson (Eds.), *Imagery, creativity, and discovery: A cognitive perspective* (pp. 77–97). Amsterdam: Elsevier.

Chambers, D., & Reisberg, D. (1985). Can mental images be ambiguous? *Journal of Experimental Psychology: Human Perception and Performance, 11,* 317–328.

Chambers, D., & Reisberg, D. (1992). What an image depicts depends on what an image means. *Cognitive Psychology, 24,* 145–174.

Chang, T. M. (1986). Semantic memory: Facts and models. *Psychological Bulletin, 99,* 199–220.

Chapman, G. B., & Johnson, E. J. (1994). The limits of anchoring. *Journal of Behavioral Decision Making, 7,* 223–242.

Chapman, L. J., & Chapman, J. P. (1967). Genesis of popular but erroneous psychodiagnostic observations. *Journal of Abnormal Psychology, 72,* 193–204.

Chapman, L. J., & Chapman, J. P. (1969). Illusory correlations as an obstacle to the use of valid psychodiagnostic signs. *Journal of Abnormal Psychology, 74,* 271–280.

Chastain, G. (1981). Phonological and orthographic factors in the word-superiority effect. *Memory & Cognition, 9,* 389–397.

Chastain, G. (1986). Word-to-letter inhibition: Word-inferiority and other interference effects. *Memory & Cognition, 14,* 361–368.

Chawarski, M. C., & Sternberg, R. J. (1993). Negative priming in word recognition: A context effect. *Journal of Experimental Psychology: General, 122,* 195–206.

Cheng, P. W. (1985). Restructuring versus automaticity: Alternative accounts of skill acquisition. *Psychological Review, 92,* 414–423.

Cheng, P. W., & Holyoak, K. J. (1985). Pragmatic reasoning schemas. *Cognitive Psychology, 17,* 391–416.

Cherry, C. (1953). Some experiments on the recognition of speech with one and with two ears, *Journal of the Acoustical Society of America, 25,* 975–979.

Chi, M. T. H. (1981). Knowledge development and memory performance. In M. Friedman, J. P. Das, & N. O'Connor (Eds.), *Intelligence and learning* (pp. 221–230). New York: Plenum.

Chi, M. T. H., Bassok, M., Lewis, M. W., Reimann, P., & Glaser, R. (1989). Self-explanations: How students study and use examples in learning to solve problems. *Cognitive Science, 13,* 145–182.

Chi, M. T. H., Glaser, R., & Rees, E. (1982). Expertise in problem solving. In R. Sternberg (Ed.), *Advances in the psychology of human intelligence* (Vol. 1, pp. 7–75). Hillsdale, NJ: Erlbaum.

Chialant, D., & Caramazza, A. (1995). Where is morphology and how is it processed? The case of written word recognition. In L. B. Feldman (Ed.), *Morphological aspects of language processing* (pp. 55–76). Hillsdale, NJ: Erlbaum.

Chomsky, N. (1957). *Syntactic structures.* The Hague: Mouton Publishers.

Chomsky, N. (1965). *Aspects of the theory of syntax.* Cambridge, MA: M.I.T. Press.

Chomsky, N. (1981). *Lectures on government and binding.* Dordrecht, Netherlands: Foris.

Christensen-Szalanski, J. J. J., Beck, D. E., Christensen-Szalanski, C. M., & Koepsell, T. D. (1983). The effect of journal coverage on physicians' perception of risk. *Journal of Applied Psychology, 68,* 278–284.

Christensen-Szalanski, J. J. J., & Willham, C. F. (1991). The hindsight bias: A meta-analysis. *Organizational Behavior and Human Decision Processes, 48,* 147–168.

Church, B. A., & Schacter, D. L. (1994). Perceptual specificity of auditory priming: Implicit memory for voice intonation and fundamental frequency. *Journal of Experimental Psychology: Learning, Memory, and Cognition, 20,* 521–533.

Churchland, P. M., & Churchland, P. S. (1990, January). Could a machine think? *Scientific American,* 32–37.

Clark, D. M., Winton, E., & Thynn, L. (1993). A further experimental investigation of thought suppression. *Behavioral Research and Therapy, 31,* 207–210.

Clark, E. V. (1993). *The lexicon in acquisition.* Cambridge, England: Cambridge University Press.

Clark, H. H. (1985). Language use and language users. In G. Lindzey & E. Aronson (Eds.), *Handbook of social psychology* (2nd ed., Vol. 2, pp. 179–231). New York: Random House.

Clark, H. H. (1991). Words, the world, and their possibilities. In G. R. Lockhead & J. R. Pomerantz (Eds.), *The perception of structure* (pp. 263–277). Washington, DC: American Psychological Association.

Clark, H. H. (1992). *Arenas of language use.* Chicago: University of Chicago Press.

Clark, H. H. (1994). Discourse in production. In M. A. Gernsbacher (Ed.), *Handbook of psycholinguistics* (pp. 985–1021). San Diego, CA: Academic Press.

Clark, H. H., & Bly, B. (1995). Pragmatics and discourse. In J. L. Miller & P. D. Eimas (Eds.), *Speech, language, and communication* (pp. 371–410). San Diego, CA: Academic Press.

Clark, H. H., & Brennan, S. E. (1991). Grounding in communication. In L. B. Resnick, J. M. Levine, & S. D. Teasley (Eds.), *Perspectives on socially shared cognition* (pp. 127–149). Washington, DC: American Psychological Association.

Clark, H. H., & Chase, W. G. (1972). On the process of comparing sentences against pictures. *Cognitive Psychology, 3,* 472–517.

Clark, H. H., & Wilkes-Gibbs, D. (1986). Referring as a collaborative process. *Cognition, 22,* 1–39.

Clark, L. F. (1994). Social cognition and health psychology. In R. S. Wyer, Jr. & T. K. Srull (Eds.), *Handbook of social cognition* (2nd ed., Vol. 2, pp. 239–288). Hillsdale, NJ: Erlbaum.

Clement, C. A., & Falmagne, R. J. (1986). Logical reasoning, world knowledge, and mental imagery: Interconnections in cognitive processes. *Memory & Cognition, 14,* 299–307.

Clement, J. (1991). Nonformal reasoning in experts and in science students: The use of analogies, extreme cases, and physical intuition. In J. Voss, D. Perkins, & J. Siegel (Eds.), *Informal reasoning and education.* Hillsdale, NJ: Erlbaum.

Cohen, G. (1983). *The psychology of cognition* (2nd ed.). London: Academic Press.

Cohen, G. (1989). *Memory in the real world.* London: Erlbaum.

Cohen, G. (1993). Memory and ageing. In G. M. Davies & R. H. Logie (Eds.), *Memory in everyday life* (pp. 419–446). Amsterdam: North-Holland.

Cohen, G., Conway, M. A., & Maylor, E. A. (1994). Flashbulb memories in older adults. *Psychology and Aging, 9,* 454–463.

Cohen, G., Eysenck, M. W., & LeVoi, M. E. (1986). *Memory: A cognitive approach.* Milton Keynes, England: Open University Press.

Cohen, J. D., Dunbar, K., & McClelland, J. L. (1990). On the control of automatic processes: A parallel distributed processing account of the Stroop effect. *Psychological Review, 97,* 332–361.

Cohen, J. D., & Servan-Schreiber, D. (1992). Context, cortex, and dopamine: A connectionist approach to behavior and biology in schizophrenia. *Psychological Review, 99,* 45–77.

Cohen, M. S. (1993a). The naturalistic basis of decision biases. In G. A. Klein, J. Orasanu, R. Calderwood, & C. E. Zsambok (Eds.), *Decision making in action: Models and methods* (pp. 51–99). Norwood, NJ: Ablex.

Cohen, M. S. (1993b). Three paradigms for viewing decision biases. In G. A. Klein, J. Orasanu, R. Calderwood, & C. E. Zsambok (Eds.), *Decision making in action: Models and methods* (pp. 36–50). Norwood, NJ: Ablex.

Cole, R. A. (1973). Listening for mispronunciations: A measure of what we hear during speech. *Perception & Psychophysics, 14,* 153–156.

Cole, R. A., & Jakimik, J. (1980). A model of speech perception. In R. A. Cole (Ed.), *Perception and production of fluent speech* (pp. 133–163). Hillsdale, NJ: Erlbaum.

Collins, A. M., & Loftus, E. F. (1975). A spreading-activation theory of semantic memory. *Psychological Review, 82,* 407–428.

Coltheart, M. (1980). Iconic memory and visual persistence. *Perception & Psychophysics, 27,* 183–228.

Coltheart, M., Curtis, B., Atkins, P., & Haller, M. (1993). Models of reading aloud: Dual-route and parallel-distributed-processing approaches. *Psychological Review, 100,* 589–608.

Coltheart, M., Patterson, K. E., & Marshall, J. C. (1980). *Deep dyslexia.* London: Routledge and Kegan Paul.

Coltheart, M., & Rastle, K. (1994). Serial processing in reading aloud: Evidence for dual-route models of reading. *Journal of Experimental Psychology: Human Perception and Performance, 20,* 1197–1211.

Conway, A. R. A., & Engle, R. W. (1994). Working memory and retrieval: A resource-dependent inhibition model. *Journal of Experimental Psychology: General, 12,* 354–373.

Conway, M. A. (1991). In defense of everyday memory. *American Psychologist, 46,* 19–26.

Conway, M. A. (1995). *Flashbulb memories.* Hove, England: Erlbaum.

Conway, M. A., Anderson, S. J., Larsen, S. F., Donnelly, C. M., McDaniel, M. A., McClelland, A. G. R., Rawles, R. E., & Logie, R. H. (1994). The formation of flashbulb memories. *Memory & Cognition, 22,* 326–343.

Conway, M. A., Cohen, G., & Stanhope, N. (1991). On the very long-term retention of knowledge acquired through formal education: Twelve years of cognitive psychology. *Journal of Experimental Psychology: General, 120,* 395–409.

Conway, M. A., Cohen, G., & Stanhope, N. (1992). Very long-term memory for knowledge acquired at school and university. *Applied Cognitive Psychology, 6,* 467–482.

Conway, M. A., & Rubin, D. C. (1993). The structure of autobiographical memory. In A. F. Collins, S. E. Gathercole, M. A. Conway, & P. E. Morris

(Eds.), *Theories of memory* (pp. 103–137). Hove, England: Erlbaum.

Cooper, L. A., & Hochberg, J. (1994). Objects of the mind: Mental representations in visual perception and cognition. In S. Ballesteros (Ed.), *Cognitive approaches to human perception* (pp. 223–239). Hillsdale, NJ: Erlbaum.

Cooper, L. A., & Schacter, D. L. (1992). Dissociations between structural and episodic representations of visual objects. *Current Directions in Psychological Science, 1,* 141–146.

Cooper, L. A., & Shepard, R. N. (1973). Chronometric studies of the rotation of mental images. In W. G. Chase (Ed.), *Visual information processing.* New York: Academic Press.

Cooper, L. A., & Shepard, R. N. (1984). Turning something over in the mind. *Scientific American, 251*(6), 106–114.

Cooper, W. E., Tye-Murray, N., & Eady, S. J. (1985). Acoustical cues to the reconstruction of missing words in speech perception. *Perception & Psychophysics, 38,* 30–40.

Corballis, M. C. (1986). Memory scanning: Can subjects scan two sets at once? *Psychological Review, 93,* 113–114.

Corbetta, M., Meizin, F. M., Shulman, G. L., & Petersen, S. E. (1991). Shifting attention in space, direction versus visual hemifield: Psychophysics and PET. *Journal of Blood Flow and Metabolism, 11,* 909.

Coren, S., Ward, L. M., & Enns, J. T. (1994). *Sensation and perception* (4th ed.). Fort Worth, TX: Harcourt Brace.

Corteen, R. S., & Wood, B. (1972). Autonomic responses to shock-associated words in an unattended channel. *Journal of Experimental Psychology, 94,* 308–313.

Corter, J. E., & Gluck, M. A. (1992). Explaining basic categories: Feature predictability and information. *Psychological Bulletin, 111,* 291–303.

Cosmides, L. (1989). The logic of social exchange: Has natural selection shaped how humans reason? Studies with the Wason selection task. *Cognition, 31,* 187–276.

Cowan, N. (1984). On short and long auditory stores. *Psychological Bulletin, 96,* 341–370.

Cowan, N. (1988). Evolving conceptions of memory storage, selective attention, and their mutual constraints within the human information-processing system. *Psychological Bulletin, 104,* 163–191.

Cowan, N. (1994). Mechanisms of verbal short-term memory. *Current Directions in Psychological Science, 3,* 185–189.

Cowan, N. (1995). *Attention and memory: An integrated framework.* New York: Oxford University Press.

Craik, F. I. M. (1977). Age differences in human memory. In J. E. Birren & K. W. Schaie (Eds.), *Handbook of the psychology of aging.* New York: Van Nostrand Reinhold.

Craik, F. I. M. (1979). Levels of processing: Overview and closing comments. In L. S. Cermak & F. I. M. Craik (Eds.), *Levels of processing in human memory* (pp. 447–461). Hillsdale, NJ: Erlbaum.

Craik, F. I. M. (1990). Changes in memory with normal aging: A functional view. In R. J. Wurtman (Ed.), *Advances in neurology: Vol. 51. Alzheimer's disease* (pp. 201–205). New York: Raven Press.

Craik, F. I. M. (1991). Will cognitivism bury experimental psychology? *Canadian Psychology/Psychologie canadienne, 32,* 440–444.

Craik, F. I. M. (1992). Aging and memory in humans. In L. R. Squire (Ed.), *Encyclopedia of learning and memory* (pp. 12–16). New York: Macmillan.

Craik, F. I. M., Byrd, M., & Swanson, J. M. (1987). Patterns of memory loss in three elderly samples. *Psychology and Aging, 2,* 79–86.

Craik, F. I. M., & Jennings, J. M. (1992). Human memory. In F. I. M. Craik & T. A. Salthouse (Eds.), *The handbook of aging and cognition* (pp. 51–110). Hillsdale, NJ: Erlbaum.

Craik, F. I. M., & Lockhart, R. S. (1972). Levels of processing: A framework for memory research. *Journal of Verbal Learning and Verbal Behavior, 11,* 671–684.

Craik, F. I. M., & Lockhart, R. S. (1986). CHARM is not enough: Comments on Eich's model of cued recall. *Psychological Review, 93,* 360–364.

Craik, F. I. M., & McDowd, J. M. (1987). Age differences in recall and recognition. *Journal of Experimental Psychology: Learning, Memory, and Cognition, 13,* 474–479.

Craik, F. I. M., & Salthouse, T. A. (Eds.). (1992). *The handbook of aging and cognition.* Hillsdale, NJ: Erlbaum.

Craik, F. I. M., & Tulving, E. (1975). Depth of processing and the retention of words in episodic memory. *Journal of Experimental Psychology: General, 104,* 268–294.

Cranberg, L. D., & Albert, M. L. (1988). The chess mind. In L. K. Obler & D. Fein (Eds.), *The exceptional brain: Neuropsychology of talent and special abilities* (pp. 156–190). New York: Guilford Press.

Crandall, C. S. (1984). The overcitation of examples of poor performance: Fad, fashion, or fun? *American Psychologist, 39,* 1499.

Craver-Lemley, C., Arterberry, M. E., & Reeves, A. (1997). The effects of imagery on vernier acuity under conditions of induced depth. *Journal of Experimental Psychology: Human Perception and Performance, 23.*

Craver-Lemley, C., & Reeves, A. (1987). Visual imagery selectively reduces vernier acuity. *Perception, 16,* 599–614.

Craver-Lemley, C., & Reeves, A. (1992). How visual imagery interferes with vision. *Psychological Review, 99,* 633–649.

Crevier, D. (1993). *AI: The tumultuous history of the search for artificial intelligence.* New York: Basic Books.

Creyer, E., & Ross, Jr., W. T. (1993). Hindsight bias and inferences in choice: The mediating effect of cognitive effort. *Organizational Behavior and Human Decision Processes, 55,* 61–77.

Crick, F. (1994). *The astonishing hypothesis: The scientific search for the soul.* New York: Scribner's.

Crocker, J. (1981). Judgment of covariation by social perceivers. *Psychological Bulletin, 90,* 272–292.

Cross, D. R., & Paris, S. G. (1988). Developmental and instructional analyses of children's metacognition and reading comprehension. *Journal of Educational Psychology, 80,* 131–142.

Crovitz, H. F. (1990). Association, cognition, and neural networks. In M. G. Johnson & T. B. Henley (Eds.), *Reflections on the Principles of Psychology: William James after a century* (pp. 167–182). Hillsdale, NJ: Erlbaum.

Crowder, R. G. (1980). Echoic memory and the study of aging memory systems. In L. W. Poon, J. L. Fozard, L. S. Cermak, D. Arenberg, & L. W. Thompson (Eds.), *New directions in memory and aging: Proceedings of the George A. Talland Memorial Conference* (pp. 181–204). Hillsdale, NJ: Erlbaum.

Crowder, R. G. (1982a). Decay of auditory memory in vowel discrimination. *Journal of Experimental Psychology: Learning, Memory, and Cognition, 8,* 153–162.

Crowder, R. G. (1982b). The demise of short-term memory. *Acta Psychologica, 50,* 291–323.

Crowder, R. G. (1993). Short-term memory: Where do we stand? *Memory & Cognition, 21,* 142–155.

Crowder, R. G., & Wagner, R. K. (1992). *The psychology of reading: An introduction* (2nd ed.). New York: Oxford University Press.

Cull, W. L., & Zechmeister, E. B. (1994). The learning ability paradox in adult metamemory research: Where are the metamemory differences between good and poor learners? *Memory & Cognition, 22,* 249–257.

Cummins, D. D. (1992). Role of analogical reasoning in the induction of problem categories. *Journal of Experimental Psychology: Learning, Memory, and Cognition, 18,* 1103–1124.

Cummins, D. D. (1994). Analogical reasoning. In V. S. Ramachandran (Ed.), *Encyclopedia of human behavior* (Vol. 1, pp. 125–130). San Diego, CA: Academic Press.

Cummins, D. D., Lubart, T., Alksnis, O., & Rist, R. (1991). Conditional reasoning and causation. *Memory & Cognition, 19,* 274–282.

Cunningham, T. F., Healy, A. F., Till, R. E., Fendrich, D. W., & Dimitry, C. Z. (1993). Is there really very rapid forgetting from primary memory? The role of expectancy and item importance in short-term recall. *Memory & Cognition, 21,* 671–688.

Cutler, B. L., & Penrod, S. D. (1995). *Mistaken identification: The eyewitness, psychology, and the law.* New York: Cambridge University Press.

Cutler, B. L., Penrod, S. D., & Martens, T. K. (1987). The reliability of eyewitness identification: The role of system and estimator variables. *Law and Human Behavior, 11,* 233–258.

Daneman, M., & Green, I. (1986). Individual differences in comprehending and producing words in context. *Journal of Memory and Language, 25,* 1–18.

Daneman, M., & Stainton, M. (1993). The generation effect in reading and proofreading. *Reading and Writing: An Interdisciplinary Journal, 5,* 297–313.

Darke, S. (1988). Anxiety and working memory capacity. *Cognition and Emotion, 2,* 145–154.

Darwin, C. J., Turvey, M. T., & Crowder, R. G. (1972). An auditory analogue of the Sperling partial report procedure: Evidence for brief auditory storage. *Cognitive Psychology, 3,* 255–267.

Davidson, D. (1994). Recognition and recall of irrelevant and interruptive atypical actions in script-based stories. *Journal of Memory and Language, 33,* 757–775.

Davidson, D. (1995). The representativeness heuristic and the conjunction fallacy effect in children's decision making. *Merrill-Palmer Quarterly, 41,* 328–346.

Davidson, D., Cameron, P., & Jergovic, D. (1995). The effects of children's stereotypes on their memory for elderly individuals. *Merrill-Palmer Quarterly, 41,* 70–90.

Davidson, J. E. (1995). The suddenness of insight. In R. J. Sternberg & J. E. Davidson (Eds.), *The nature of insight* (pp. 125–155). Cambridge, MA: MIT Press.

Davidson, J. E., Deuser, R., & Sternberg, R. J. (1994). The role of metacognition in problem solving. In J. Metcalfe & A. P. Shimamura (Eds.), *Metacognition: Knowing about knowing* (pp. 207–226). Cambridge, MA: MIT Press.

Davidsson, P., & Wahlund, R. (1992). A note on the failure to use negative information. *Journal of Economic Psychology, 13,* 343–353.

Davies, G. M. (1988). Faces and places: Laboratory research on context and face recognition. In G. M. Davies & D. M. Thomson (Eds.), *Memory in context: Context in memory* (pp. 35–53). Chichester, England: Wiley.

Davies, G. M., & Jenkins, F. (1985). Witnesses can be misled by police composite pictures: How and when. In F. L. Denmark (Ed.), *Social/ecological psychology and the psychology of women* (pp. 103–115). Amsterdam: Elsevier Science Publishers.

Dawes, R. M. (1988). *Rational choice in an uncertain world.* San Diego, CA: Harcourt Brace Jovanovich.

DeCasper, A. J., & Fifer, W. P. (1980). Of human bonding: Newborns prefer their mothers' voices. *Science, 208,* 1174–1176.

DeCasper, A. J., & Spence, M. J. (1986). Prenatal maternal speech influences newborns' perception of speech sounds. *Infant Behavior and Development, 9,* 133–150.

Deese, J. (1984). *Thought into speech: The psychology of language.* Englewood Cliffs, NJ: Prentice-Hall.

de Groot, A. (1966). Perception and memory versus thought: Some old ideas and recent findings. In B. Kleinmuntz (Ed.), *Problem solving.* New York: Wiley.

DeHart, G. (1989). *Personal communication.*

De Jong, G. (1982). Skimming stories in real time: An experiment in integrated understanding. In W. Lehnert & M. H. Ringle (Eds.), *Natural language processing.* Hillsdale, NJ: Erlbaum.

De Jong, R. (1993). Multiple bottlenecks in overlapping task performance. *Journal of Experimental Psychology: Human Perception and Performance, 19,* 965–980.

De Jong, T., & Ferguson-Hessler, M. G. M. (1986). Cognitive structures of good and poor novice problem solvers in physics. *Journal of Educational Psychology, 78,* 279–288.

Dell, G. S. (1985). Putting production back in psycholinguistics [Review of *Language production, Vol. 2: Development, writing, and other language processes*]. *Contemporary Psychology, 30,* 129–130.

Dell, G. S. (1986). A spreading-activation theory of retrieval in sentence production. *Psychological Review, 93,* 283–321.

Dell, G. S. (1990). Effects of frequency and vocabulary type on phonological speech errors. *Language and Cognitive Processes, 5,* 313–349.

Dember, W. N. (1990). William James on sensation and perception. *Psychological Science, 1,* 163–166.

Dempster, F. N. (1985). Proactive interference in sentence recall: Topic-similarity effects and individual differences. *Memory & Cognition, 13,* 81–89.

Dempster, F. N. (1988). The spacing effect: A case study in the failure to apply the results. *American Psychologist, 43,* 627–634.

Dennett, D. C. (1991). *Consciousness explained.* Boston: Little, Brown and Company.

Dent, H., & Flin, R. (Eds.). (1992). *Children as witnesses.* Chichester, England: John Wiley & Sons.

Desimone, R., Albright, T. D., Gross, C. G., & Bruce, C. J. (1984). Stimulus-selective responses of inferior temporal neurons in the macaque. *Journal of Neuroscience, 4,* 2051–2062.

Desrochers, A., & Begg, I. (1987). A theoretical account of encoding and retrieval processes in the use of imagery-based mnemonic techniques: The special case of the keyword method. In M. A. McDaniel & M. Pressley (Eds.), *Imagery and related mnemonic processes* (pp. 56–77). New York: Springer-Verlag.

Deutsch, J. A., & Deutsch, D. (1963). Attention: Some theoretical considerations. *Psychological Review, 70,* 80–90.

de Villiers, P. A., & de Villiers, J. G. (1992). Language development. In M. H. Bornstein & M. E. Lamb (Eds.), *Developmental psychology: An advanced textbook* (3rd ed., pp. 337–418). Hillsdale, NJ: Erlbaum.

Devolder, P. A., & Pressley, M. (1989). Metamemory across the adult lifespan. *Canadian Psychology, 30,* 578–587.

Diaz, R. M. (1985). Bilingual cognitive development: Addressing three gaps in current research. *Child Development, 56,* 1376–1388.

Dietrich, D., & Olson, M. (1993). A demonstration of hindsight bias using the Thomas confirmation vote. *Psychological Reports, 72,* 377–378.

Di Lollo, V. (1977). Temporal characteristics of iconic memory. *Nature, 267,* 241–243.

Di Lollo, V. (1980). Temporal integration in visual memory. *Journal of Experimental Psychology: General, 109,* 75–97.

Di Lollo, V. (1992). *Personal communication.*

Di Lollo, V., & Dixon, P. (1988). Two forms of persistence in visual information processing. *Journal of Experimental Psychology: Human Perception and Performance, 14,* 671–681.

Di Lollo, V., & Hogben, J. H. (1987). Suppression of visible persistence as a function of spatial separation between inducing stimuli. *Perception & Psychophysics, 41,* 345–354.

Doctor, E. A., & Coltheart, M. (1980). Children's use of phonological encoding when reading for meaning. *Memory & Cognition, 8,* 195–209.

Dodd, B., & Campbell, R. (1986). *Hearing by eye: The psychology of lip reading.* London: Erlbaum.

Donley, R. D., & Ashcraft, M. H. (1992). The methodology of testing naive beliefs in the physics classroom. *Memory & Cognition,* 381–391.

Dopkins, S., Klin, C., & Myers, J. L. (1993). Accessibility of information about goals during the processing of narrative texts. *Journal of Experimental Psychology: Learning, Memory, and Cognition, 19,* 70–80.

Dror, I. E., & Kosslyn, S. M. (1994). Mental imagery and aging. *Psychology and Aging, 9,* 90–102.

Dror, I. E., Kosslyn, S. M., & Waag, W. L. (1993). Visual-spatial abilities of pilots. *Journal of Applied Psychology, 78,* 763–773.

Du Boulay, B. (1989). Nonadversary problem solving by machine. In K. J. Gilhooly (Ed.), *Human and machine problem solving* (pp. 13–37). New York: Plenum.

Duncan, E. M., & Bourg, T. (1983). An examination of the effects of encoding and decision processes on the rate of mental rotation. *Journal of Mental Imagery, 7,* 33–56.

Duncan, J. (1993). Coordination of what and where in visual attention. *Perception, 22,* 1261–1270.

Duncker, K. (1945). On problem solving. *Psychological Monographs, 58* (Whole No. 270).

Dunlosky, J., & Nelson, T. O. (1994). Does the sensitivity of judgments of learning (JOLs) to the effects of various study activities depend on when the JOLs occur? *Journal of Memory and Language, 33,* 545–565.

D'Ydewalle, G., Delhaye, P., & Goessens, L. (1985). Structural, semantic, and self-reference processing of pictorial advertisements. *Human Learning, 4,* 29–38.

Ebbinghaus (1885/1913). *Memory: A contribution to experimental psychology.* New York: Columbia Teacher's College.

Egeth, H. (1994). Emotion and the eyewitness. In P. M. Niedenthal & S. Kitayama (Eds.), *The heart's eye: Emotional influences in perception and attention* (pp. 245–267). San Diego, CA: Academic Press.

Eimas, P. D., Siqueland, E. R., Jusczyk, P., & Vigorito, J. (1971). Speech perception in infants. *Science, 171,* 303–306.

Eimas, P. D., & Tartter, V. C. (1979). On the development of speech perception: Mechanisms and analogies. In H. W. Reese & L. P. Lipsitt (Eds.), *Advances in child development and behavior* (pp. 155–194). New York: Academic Press.

Einhorn, H. J., & Hogarth, R. M. (1978). Confidence in judgment: Persistence of the illusion of validity. *Psychological Review, 85,* 395–416.

Einhorn, H. J., & Hogarth, R. M. (1981). Behavioral decision theory: Processes of judgment and choice. *Annual Review of Psychology, 32,* 53–88.

Einstein, G. O., & McDaniel, M. A. (1987). Distinctiveness and the mnemonic benefits of bizarre imagery. In M. A. McDaniel & M. Pressley (Eds.), *Imagery and related mnemonic processes* (pp. 78–102). New York: Springer-Verlag.

Einstein, G. O., McDaniel, M. A., & Lackey, S. (1989). *Journal of Experimental Psychology: Learning, Memory, and Cognition, 15,* 137–146.

Eisenberger, R., & Selbst, M. (1994). Does reward increase or decrease creativity? *Journal of Personality and Social Psychology, 66,* 1116–1127.

Eiser, J. R. (1994). *Attitudes, chaos, and the connectionist mind.* Oxford, England: Blackwell.

Elias, J. W., Elias, M. F., & Elias, P. K. (1991). Normal aging and disease as contributors to the study of cognitive processing in aging. In J. D. Sinnott &

J. C. Cavanaugh (Eds.), *Bridging paradigms: Positive development in adulthood and cognitive aging* (pp. 27–41). New York: Praeger.

Elliott, C. S., & Archibald, R. B. (1989). Subjective framing and attitudes toward risk. *Journal of Economic Psychology, 10,* 321–328.

Ellis, A., & Beattie, G. (1986). *The psychology of language and communication.* New York: Guilford.

Ellis, H. D. (1984). Practical aspects of face memory. In G. L. Wells & E. F. Loftus (Eds.), *Eyewitness testimony: Psychological perspectives* (pp. 12–37). Cambridge: Cambridge University Press.

Engle, R. W., Cantor, J., & Carullo, J. J. (1992). Individual differences in working memory and comprehension: A test of four hypotheses. *Journal of Experimental Psychology: Learning, Memory, and Cognition, 18,* 972–992.

Engle, R. W., Fidler, D. S., & Reynolds, L. H. (1981). Does echoic memory develop? *Journal of Experimental Child Psychology, 32,* 459–473.

Epstein, S., Denes-Raj, V., & Pacini, R. (1995). The Linda problem revisited from the perspective of cognitive-experiential self-theory. *Personality and Social Psychology Bulletin, 21,* 1124–1138.

Erber, J. T. (1982). Memory and age. In T. M. Field, A. Huston, H. C. Quay, L. Troll, & G. E. Finley (Eds.), *Review of human development* (pp. 569–585). New York: Wiley.

Erdelyi, M. H. (1992). Psychodynamics and the unconscious. *American Psychologist, 47,* 784–787.

Ericsson, K. A. (1985). Memory skill. *Canadian Journal of Psychology, 39,* 188–231.

Ericsson, K. A. (1988). Analysis of memory performance in terms of memory skill. In R. J. Sternberg (Ed.), *Advances in the psychology of human intelligence* (Vol. 4, pp. 137–179). Hillsdale, NJ: Erlbaum.

Ericsson, K. A. (1996a). The acquisition of expert performance: An introduction to some of the issues. In K. A. Ericsson (Ed.), *The road to excellence: The acquisition of expert performance in the arts and sciences, sports and games.* Mahwah, NJ: Erlbaum.

Ericsson, K. A. (Ed.). (1996b). *The road to excellence: The acquisition of expert performance in the arts and sciences, sports and games.* Mahwah, NJ: Erlbaum.

Ericsson, K. A., & Charness, N. (1994). Expert performance: Its structure and acquisition. *American Psychologist, 49,* 725–747.

Ericsson, K. A., & Hastie, R. (1994). Contemporary approaches to the study of thinking and problem solving. In R. J. Sternberg (Ed.), *Thinking and problem solving* (pp. 37–79). San Diego, CA: Academic Press.

Ericsson, K. A., & Kintsch, W. (1995). Long-term working memory. *Psychological Review, 102,* 211–245.

Ericsson, K. A., Krampe, R. T., & Tesch-Römer, C. (1993). The role of deliberate practice in the acquisition of expert performance. *Psychological Review, 100,* 363–406.

Ericsson, K. A., & Lehmann, A. C. (1996). Expert and exceptional performance: Evidence of maximal adaptation to task constraints. *Annual Review of Psychology, 47,* 273–305.

Ericsson, K. A., & Pennington, N. (1993). The structure of memory performance in experts: Implications for memory in everyday life. In G. M. Davies & R. H. Logie (Eds.), *Memory in everyday life* (pp. 241–272). Amsterdam: Elsevier.

Ericsson, K. A., & Simon, H. A. (1993). *Protocol analysis: Verbal reports as data* (rev. ed.). Cambridge, MA: MIT Press.

Ericsson, K. A., & Smith, J. (1991a). Prospects and limits of the empirical study of expertise: An introduction. In K. A. Ericsson & J. Smith (Eds.), *Toward a general theory of expertise: Prospects and limits* (pp. 1–38). New York: Cambridge University Press.

Ericsson, K. A., & Smith, J. (Eds.). (1991b). *Toward a general theory of expertise: Prospects and limits.* New York: Cambridge University Press.

Ervin-Tripp, S. (1976). Is Sybil there? The structure of some American English directives. *Language in Society, 5,* 25–66.

Ervin-Tripp, S. (1993). Conversational discourse. In J. B. Berko-Gleason & N. B. Ratner (Eds.), *Psycholinguistics* (pp. 237–270). Fort Worth, TX: Harcourt Brace Jovanovich.

Ervin-Tripp, S., Guo, J., & Lampert, M. (1990). Politeness and persuasion in children's control acts. *Journal of Pragmatics, 14,* 307–331.

Estes, W. K. (1988). Human learning and memory. In R. C. Atkinson, R. J. Herrnstein, G. Lindzey, & R. D. Luce (Eds.), *Stevens' handbook of experimental psychology* (Vol. 2, pp. 351–415). New York: Wiley.

Estes, W. K. (1991). Cognitive architectures from the standpoint of an experimental psychologist. *Annual Review of Psychology, 42,* 1–28.

Evans, J. St. B. T. (1983). Introduction. In J. St. B. T. Evans (Ed.), *Thinking and reasoning: Psychological approaches* (pp. 1–15). London: Routledge & Kegan Paul.

Evans, J. St. B. T. (1993). The cognitive psychology of reasoning: An introduction. *The Quarterly Journal of Experimental Psychology, 46A,* 561–567.

Evans, J. St. B. T., Newstead, S. E., Allen, J. L., & Pollard, P. (1994). Debiasing by instruction: The case of belief bias. *European Journal of Cognitive Psychology, 6,* 263–285.

Evans, J. St. B. T., Newstead, S. E., & Byrne, R. M. J. (1993). *Human reasoning: The psychology of deduction.* Hove, England: Erlbaum.

Evans, J. St. B. T., Over, D. E., & Manketelow, K. I. (1993). Reasoning, decision making and rationality. *Cognition, 49,* 165–187.

Evans, R. B. (1990). William James and his *Principles.* In M. G. Johnson & T. B. Henley (Eds.), *Reflections on The Principles of Psychology: William James after a century* (pp. 11–31). Hillsdale, NJ: Erlbaum.

Eysenck, M. W. (1982). *Attention and arousal.* Berlin: Springer-Verlag.

Eysenck, M. W. (1984). *A handbook of cognitive psychology.* London: Erlbaum.

Eysenck, M. W. (1990a). Introduction. In M. W. Eysenck (Ed.), *Cognitive psychology: An international review* (pp. 1–7). Chichester, Great Britain: John Wiley & Sons.

Eysenck, M. W. (1990b). Creativity. In M. W. Eysenck (Ed.), *The Blackwell dictionary of cognitive psychology* (pp. 86–87). Oxford, England: Basil Blackwell.

Eysenck, M. W. (1993). *Principles of cognitive psychology.* Hove, England: Erlbaum.

Eysenck, M. W., & Keane, M. T. (1990). *Cognitive psychology: A student's handbook.* London: Erlbaum.

Faigley, L., & Miller, T. P. (1982). What we learn from writing on the job. *College English, 44,* 557–559.

Farah, M. J. (1988). Is visual imagery really visual? Overlooked evidence from neuropsychology. *Psychological Review, 95,* 307–317.

Farah, M. J. (1990). *Visual agnosia: Disorders of object recognition and what they tell us about normal vision.* Cambridge, MA: MIT Press.

Farah, M. J. (1992). Is an object an object an object? Cognitive and neuropsychological investigations of domain specificity in visual object recognition. *Current Directions in Psychological Science, 1,* 164–169.

Farah, M. J. (1995). The neural bases of mental imagery. In M. S. Gazzaniga (Ed.), *The cognitive neurosciences* (pp. 963–975). Cambridge, MA: MIT Press.

Farah, M. J., & Peronnet, F. (1989). Event-related potentials in the study of mental imagery. *Journal of Psychophysiology, 3,* 99–109.

Farah, M. J., & Smith, A. F. (1983). Perceptual interference and facilitation with auditory imagery. *Perception & Psychophysics, 33,* 475–478.

Farrar, M. J., & Goodman, G. S. (1990). Developmental differences in the relation between scripts and episodic memory: Do they exist? In R. Fivush & J. A. Hudson (Eds.), *Knowing and remembering in young children* (pp. 30–64). New York: Cambridge University Press.

Farthing, G. W. (1992). *The psychology of consciousness.* Englewood Cliffs, NJ: Prentice-Hall.

Favreau, O. E. (1993). Do the Ns justify the means? Null hypothesis testing applied to sex and other differences. *Canadian Psychology/Psychologie Canadienne, 34,* 64–78.

Feldman, D. H., Csikszentmihalyi, M., & Gardner, H. (1994). *Changing the world: A framework for the study of creativity.* Westport, CT: Praeger.

Fenson, L., Dale, P., Reznick, S., Thal, D., Bates, E., Hartung, J., Pethick, S., & Reilly, J. (1991). *The MacArthur Communicative Development Inventories: Technical Manual.* San Diego, CA: San Diego State University.

Ferber, R. (1991). Slip of the tongue or slip of the ear? On the perception and transcription of naturalistic slips of the tongue. *Journal of Psycholinguistic Research, 20,* 105–122.

Ferguson, E. L., & Hegarty, M. (1994). Properties of cognitive maps constructed from texts. *Memory & Cognition, 22,* 455–473.

Ferguson-Hessler, M. G. M., & De Jong, T. (1987). On the quality of knowledge in the field of electricity and magnetism. *American Journal of Physics, 55,* 492–497.

Fernald, A. (1985). Four-month-old infants prefer to listen to motherese. *Infant Behavior and Development, 8,* 181–195.

Ferreira, F. (1993). Creation of prosody during sentence production. *Psychological Review, 100,* 233–253.

Ferreira, F. (1994). Choice of passive voice is affected by verb type and animacy. *Journal of Memory and Language, 33,* 715–736.

Ferreira, F., & Anes, M. (1994). Why study spoken language? In M. A. Gernsbacher (Ed.), *Handbook of psycholinguistics* (pp. 33–56). San Diego, CA: Academic Press.

Finke, R. A. (1989). *Principles of mental imagery.* Cambridge, MA: MIT Press.

Finke, R. A. (1993). Mental imagery and creative discovery. In B. Roskos-Ewoldson, M. J. Intons-Peterson, & R. E. Anderson (Eds.), *Imagery, creativity, and discovery: A cognitive perspective* (pp. 255–285). Amsterdam: Elsevier.

Finke, R. A., & Kosslyn, S. M. (1980). Mental imagery acuity in the peripheral visual field. *Journal of Experimental Psychology: Human Perception and Performance, 6,* 126–139.

Finke, R. A., Pinker, S., & Farah, M. J. (1989). Reinterpreting visual patterns in mental imagery. *Cognitive Science, 13,* 51–78.

Finke, R. A., & Schmidt, M. J. (1978). The quantitative measure of pattern representation in images using orientation-specific color after-effects. *Perception & Psychophysics, 23,* 515–520.

Finke, R. A., & Shepard, R. N. (1986). Visual functions of mental imagery. In K. R. Boff, L. Kaufman, & J. Thomas (Eds.), *Handbook of perception and human performance* (Vol. 2, pp. 37-1–37-55). New York: Wiley.

Finke, R. A., Ward, T. B., & Smith, S. M. (1992). *Creative cognition: Theory, research, and applications.* Cambridge, MA: MIT Press.

Fischhoff, B. (1975). The silly certainty of hindsight. *Psychology Today, 8,* 71–72, 76.

Fischhoff, B. (1982). Debiasing. In D. Kahneman, P. Slovic, & A. Tversky (Eds.), *Judgment under uncertainty: Heuristics and biases* (pp. 422–444). New York: Cambridge University Press.

Fischler, I. (1992). *Personal communication.*

Fisher, D. L. (1984). Central capacity limits in consistent mapping, visual search tasks: Four channels or more? *Cognitive Psychology, 16,* 449–484.

Fiske, S. T., & Taylor, S. E. (1991). *Social cognition* (2nd ed.). New York: McGraw-Hill.

Fivush, R., & Hamond, N. R. (1990). Autobiographical memory across the preschool years: Toward reconceptualizing childhood amnesia. In R. Fivush & J. A. Hudson (Eds.), *Knowing and remembering in young children* (pp. 223–248). New York: Cambridge University Press.

Flavell, J. H. (1971). First discussant's comments. What is memory development the development of? *Human Development, 14,* 272–278.

Flavell, J. H. (1979). Metacognition and cognitive monitoring. *American Psychologist, 34,* 906–911.

Flavell, J. H. (1985). *Cognitive development* (2nd ed.). Englewood Cliffs, NJ: Prentice-Hall.

Flavell, J. H., Beach, D. R., & Chinsky, J. M. (1966). Spontaneous verbal rehearsal in a memory task as a function of age. *Child Development, 37,* 283–299.

Flavell, J. H., Green, F. L., & Flavell, E. R. (1993). Children's understanding of the stream of consciousness. *Child Development, 64,* 387–398.

Flavell, J. H., Miller, P. H., & Miller, S. A. (1993). *Cognitive development* (3rd ed.). Englewood Cliffs, NJ: Prentice-Hall.

Flavell, J. H., Speers, J. R., Green, F. L., & August, D. L. (1981). The development of comprehension monitoring and knowledge about communication. *Monographs of the Society for Research in Child Development, 46* (5, Serial No. 192).

Flavell, J. H., & Wellman, H. M. (1977). Metamemory. In R. V. Kail, Jr. & J. W. Hagen (Eds.), *Perspectives on the development of memory and cognition* (pp. 3–34). Hillsdale, NJ: Erlbaum.

Fletcher, C. R. (1981). Short-term memory processes in text comprehension. *Journal of Verbal Learning and Verbal Behavior, 20,* 564–574.

Flores d'Arcais, G. B. (1988). Language perception. In F. J. Newmeyer (Ed.), *Linguistics: The Cambridge survey* (Vol. 3, pp. 97–123). Cambridge, England: Cambridge University Press.

Flower, L. S., & Hayes, J. R. (1980). The dynamics of composing: Making plans and juggling constraints. In L. W. Gregg & E. R. Steinberg (Eds.), *Cognitive processes in writing* (pp. 31–50). Hillsdale, NJ: Erlbaum.

Fodor, J. A., & Pylyshyn, Z. W. (1988). Connectionism and cognitive architecture: A critical analysis. *Cognition, 28,* 3–71.

Foley, M. A., Aman, C., & Gutch, D. (1987). Discriminating between action memories: Children's use of kinesthetic cues and visible consequences. *Journal of Experimental Child Psychology, 44,* 335–347.

Foley, M.A., & Ratner, H. H. (1996). Biases in children's memory for collaborative exchanges. In D. Herrmann, M. K. Johnson, C. McEvoy, C. Hertzog, & P. Hertel (Eds.), *Basic and applied memory: Research on practical aspects of memory.* Mahwah, NJ: Erlbaum.

Foley, M. A., Wilder, A., McCall, R., & Van Vorst, R. (1993). The consequences for recall of children's ability to generate interactive imagery in the absence of external supports. *Journal of Experimental Child Psychology, 56,* 173–200.

Fong, G. T., Krantz, D. H., & Nisbett, R. E. (1986). The effects of statistical training on thinking about everyday problems. *Cognitive Psychology, 18,* 253–292.

Forster, K. (1981). Priming and the effects of sentence and lexical contexts on naming time: Evidence for autonomous lexical processing. *Quarterly Journal of Experimental Psychology, 33A,* 465–495.

Forward, S., & Buck, C. (1988). *Betrayal of innocence: Incest and its devastation.* New York: Penguin Books.

Foss, D. J. (1970). Some effects of ambiguity upon sentence comprehension. *Journal of Verbal Learning and Verbal Behavior, 9,* 699–706.

Foss, D. J. (1988). Experimental psycholinguistics. *Annual Review of Psychology, 39,* 301–348.

Foss, D. J., & Speer, S. R. (1991). Global and local context effects in sentence processing. In R. R. Hoffman & D. S. Palermo (Eds.), *Cognition and the symbolic processes: Applied and ecological perspectives* (pp. 115–139). Hillsdale, NJ: Erlbaum.

Foti, R. J., & Lord, R. G. (1987). Prototypes and scripts: The effects of alternative methods of processing information on rating accuracy. *Organizational Behavior and Human Decision Processes, 39,* 318–340.

Franklin, N., & Tversky, B. (1990). Searching imagined environments. *Journal of Experimental Psychology: General, 119,* 63–76.

Franklin, N., Tversky, B., & Coon, V. (1992). Switching points of view in spatial mental models. *Memory & Cognition, 20,* 507–518.

Franks, J. J., & Bransford, J. D. (1971). Abstraction of visual patterns. *Journal of Experimental Psychology, 90,* 65–74.

Freeman, M. (1993). *Finding the muse: A sociopsychological inquiry into the conditions of artistic creativity.* New York: Cambridge University Press.

Frensch, P. A., & Miner, C. S. (1994). Effects of presentation rate and individual differences in short-term memory capacity on an indirect measure of serial learning. *Memory & Cognition, 22,* 95–110.

Frick, R. W. (1988). Issues of representation and limited capacity in the auditory short-term store. *British Journal of Psychology, 79,* 213–240.

Frick, R. W. (1990). The visual suffix effect in tests of the visual short-term store. *Bulletin of the Psychonomic Society, 28,* 101–104.

Friedman, W. J. (1993). Memory for the time of past events. *Psychological Bulletin, 113,* 44–66.

Frisch, D. (1993). Reasons for framing effects. *Organizational Behavior and Human Decision Processes, 54,* 399–429.

Frisch, D., & Clemen, R. T. (1994). Beyond expected utility: Rethinking behavioral decision research. *Psychological Bulletin, 116,* 46–54.

Fromkin, V. A. (1993). Speech production. In J. B. Berko-Gleason & N. B. Ratner (Eds.), *Psycholinguistics* (pp. 271–300). Fort Worth, TX: Harcourt Brace Jovanovich.

Fruzzetti, A. E., Toland, K., Teller, S. A., & Loftus, E. F. (1992). Memory and eyewitness testimony. In M. Gruneberg & P. Morris (Eds.), *Aspects of memory* (2nd ed., Vol. 1, pp. 18–50). New York: Routledge.

Fry, P. S., & Lupart, J. L. (1986). *Cognitive processes in children's learning.* Springfield, IL: Charles C. Thomas.

Galambos, S. J., & Goldin-Meadow, S. (1990). The effects of learning two languages on levels of metalinguistic awareness. *Cognition, 34,* 1–56.

Galambos, S. J., & Hakuta, K. (1988). Subject-specific and task-specific characteristics of metalinguistic awareness in bilingual children. *Applied Psycholinguistics, 9,* 141–162.

Galotti, K. M. (1989). Approaches to studying formal and everyday reasoning. *Psychological Bulletin, 105,* 331–351.

Ganellen, R. J., & Carver, C. S. (1985). Why does self-reference promote incidental encoding? *Journal of Experimental Social Psychology, 21,* 284–300.

Gara, M. A., Woolfolk, R. L., Cohen, B. D., Goldston, R. B., Allen, L. A., & Novalany, J. (1993). Perception of self and other in major depression. *Journal of Abnormal Psychology, 102,* 93–100.

Gardner, H. (1985). *The mind's new science: A history of the cognitive revolution.* New York: Basic Books.

Gardner, H. (1988, August). *Scientific psychology: Should we bury it or praise it?* Paper presented at the annual meeting of the American Psychological Association, Atlanta, GA.

Gardner, R. C., & Lambert, W. E. (1959). Motivational variables in second-language acquisition. *Canadian Journal of Psychology, 13,* 266–272.

Gärling, T., Böök, A., & Lindberg, E. (1985). Adults' memory representations of the spatial properties of their everyday physical environment. In R. Cohen (Ed.), *The development of spatial cognition* (pp. 141–184). Hillsdale, NJ: Erlbaum.

Garman, M. (1990). *Psycholinguistics.* Cambridge, England: Cambridge University Press.

Garner, W. R. (1979). Letter discrimination and identification. In A. D. Pick (Ed.), *Perception and its development: A tribute to Eleanor J. Gibson* (pp. 111–144). Hillsdale, NJ: Erlbaum.

Garner, R. (1987). *Metacognition and reading comprehension.* Norwood, NJ: Ablex.

Garnham, A., & Oakhill, J. (1994). *Thinking and reasoning.* Oxford, England: Blackwell.

Garrett, M. F. (1984). The organization of processing structures for language production: Applications to aphasic speech. In D. Caplan, A. R. Lecours, & A. Smith (Eds.), *Biological perspectives on language.* Cambridge, MA: MIT Press.

Garry, M., & Loftus, E. F. (1994). Pseudomemories without hypnosis. *International Journal of Clinical and Experimental Hypnosis, 42,* 363–378.

Garton, A. F. (1992). *Social interaction and the development of language and cognition.* Hove, England: Erlbaum.

Garvey, C. (1984). *Children's talk.* Cambridge, MA: Harvard University Press.

Gathercole, S. E. (1992). The nature and uses of working memory. In P. Morris & M. Gruneberg (Eds.), *Theoretical aspects of memory* (2nd ed., pp. 50–78). New York: Routledge.

Gathercole, S. E., Adams, A., & Hitch, G. J. (1994). Do young children rehearse? An individual-differences analysis. *Memory & Cognition, 22,* 201–207.

Gathercole, S. E., & Baddeley, A. D. (1993). *Working memory and language.* Hove, Great Britain: Erlbaum.

Gazdar, G. (1993). The handling of natural language. In D. Broadbent (Ed.), *The simulation of human intelligence* (pp. 151–177). Oxford, United Kingdom: Blackwell.

Gazzaniga, M. S. (Ed.). (1995). *The cognitive neurosciences.* Cambridge, MA: MIT Press.

Gebotys, R. J., & Claxton-Oldfield, S. P. (1989). Errors in the quantification of uncertainty: A product of heuristics or minimal probability knowledge base? *Applied Cognitive Psychology, 3,* 237–250.

Gegenfurtner, K. R., & Sperling, G. (1993). Information transfer in iconic memory experiments. *Journal of Experimental Psychology: Human Perception and Performance, 19,* 845–866.

Geiselman, R. E., & Glenny, J. (1977). Effects of imagining speakers' voices on the retention of words presented visually. *Memory & Cognition, 5,* 499–504.

Gellatly, A. (1986). Solving problems. In A. Gellatly (Ed.), *The skillful mind: An introduction to cognitive psychology* (pp. 171–182). Milton Keynes, England: Open University Press.

Gelman, R. (1979). Preschool thought. *American Psychologist, 34,* 900–905.

Genesee, F., Tucker, R., & Lambert, W. E. (1975). Communication skills of bilingual children. *Child Development, 46,* 1010–1014.

Gernsbacher, M. A. (Ed.). (1994). *Handbook of psycholinguistics.* San Diego, CA: Academic Press.

Gernsbacher, M. A. (1995). Activating knowledge of fictional characters' emotional states. In C. A. Weaver, III, S. Mannes, & C. R. Fletcher (Eds.), *Discourse comprehension: Essays in honor of Walter Kintsch* (pp. 141–155). Hillsdale, NJ: Erlbaum.

Gero, J. S., & Maher, M. L. (Eds.). (1993). *Modeling creativity and knowledge-based creative design.* Hillsdale, NJ: Lawrence Erlbaum Associates.

Gerrig, R. J. (1993). *Experiencing narrative worlds: On the psychological activities of reading.* New Haven, CT: Yale.

Gerrig, R. J., & Bernardo, A. B. I. (1994). Readers as problem-solvers in the experience of suspense. *Poetics, 22,* 459–472.

Gerrig, R. J., & Littman, M. L. (1990). Disambiguation by community membership. *Memory & Cognition, 18,* 331–338.

Gibbs, R. W. (1986). What makes some indirect speech acts conventional? *Journal of Memory and Language, 25,* 181–196.

Gibson, E. J. (1969). *Principles of perceptual learning and development.* New York: Prentice-Hall.

Gigerenzer, G. (1993). The bounded rationality of probabilistic mental models. In K. I. Manktelow & D. E. Over (Eds.), *Rationality: Psychological and philosophical perspectives* (pp. 284–313). London: Routledge.

Gigerenzer, G. (1994). Why the distinction between single-event probabilities and frequencies is important for psychology (and vice versa). In G. Wright & P. Ayton (Eds.), *Subjective probability* (pp. 129–161). Chichester, England: John Wiley & Sons.

Gigerenzer, G., & Hoffrage, U. (1995). How to improve Bayesian reasoning without instruction: Frequency formats. *Psychological Review, 102,* 684–704.

Gigerenzer, G., Hoffrage, U., & Kleinbölting, H. (1991). Probabilistic mental models: A Brunswikian theory of confidence. *Psychological Review, 98,* 506–528.

Gigerenzer, G., & Hug, K. (1992). Domain-specific reasoning: Social contracts, cheating, and perspective change. *Cognition, 43,* 127–171.

Gilhooly, K. J. (1982). *Thinking: Directed, undirected, and creative.* London: Academic Press.

Gilhooly, K. J. (1988). *Thinking: Directed, undirected, and creative* (2nd ed.). London: Academic Press.

Gilmore, G. C., Allan, T. M., & Royer, F. L. (1986). Iconic memory and aging. *Journal of Gerontology, 41,* 183–190.

Ginossar, Z., & Trope, Y. (1987). Problem solving in judgment under uncertainty. *Journal of Personality and Social Psychology, 52,* 464–474.

Glaser, R., & Chi, M. T. H. (1988). Overview. In M. T. H. Chi, R. Glaser, & M. J. Farr (Eds.), *The nature of expertise* (pp. xv–xxxvi). Hillsdale, NJ: Erlbaum.

Gleason, J. B., & Ratner, N. B. (Eds.). (1993a). *Psycholinguistics.* Fort Worth, TX: Harcourt Brace Jovanovich.

Gleason, J. B., & Ratner, N. B. (1993b). Language development in children. In J. Berko Gleason & N. B. Ratner (Eds.), *Psycholinguistics* (pp. 301–350). Fort Worth, TX: Harcourt Brace Jovanovich.

Glenberg, A. M., Sanocki, T., Epstein, W., & Morris, C. (1987). Enhancing calibration of comprehension. *Journal of Experimental Psychology: General, 116,* 119–136.

Glicksohn, J. (1994). Rotation, orientation, and cognitive mapping. *American Journal of Psychology, 107,* 39–51.

Glucksberg, S., Kreuz, R. J., & Rho, S. H. (1986). Context can constrain lexical access: Implications for models of language comprehension. *Journal of Experimental Psychology: Learning, Memory, and Cognition, 12,* 323–335.

Golden, R. M., & Rumelhart, D. E. (1993). A parallel distributed processing model of story comprehension and recall. *Discourse Processes, 16,* 203–237.

Goldinger, S. D., Luce, P. A., & Pisoni, D. B. (1989). Priming lexical neighbors of spoken words: Effects of competition and inhibition. *Journal of Memory and Language, 28,* 501–518.

Goldman, W. P., & Seamon, J. G. (1992). Very long-term memory for odors: Retention of odor-name associations. *American Journal of Psychology, 105,* 549–563.

Goldstein, A. G., Chance, J. E., & Schneller, G. R. (1989). Frequency of eyewitness identification in criminal cases: A survey of prosecutors. *Bulletin of the Psychonomic Society, 27,* 71–74.

Goldstein, E. B. (1996). *Sensation and perception* (4th ed.). Pacific Grove, CA: Brooks/Cole.

Goleman, D., Kaufman, P., & Ray, M. (1992). *The creative spirit.* New York: Dutton.

Golombok, S., & Fivush, R. (1994). *Gender development.* New York: Cambridge University Press.

Gonsiorek, J. C. (1996). Mental health and sexual orientation. In R. C. Savin-Williams & K. M. Cohen (Eds.), *The lives of lesbians, gays, and bisexuals: Children to adults* (pp. 462–478). Fort Worth, TX: Harcourt Brace.

Goodglass, H., & Butters, N. (1988). Psychobiology of cognitive processes. In R. C. Atkinson, R. J. Herrnstein, G. Lindzey, & R. D. Luce (Eds.), *Stevens' handbook of experimental psychology* (Vol. 2, pp. 863–952). New York: Wiley.

Goodman, G. S., & Bottoms, B. L. (Eds.). (1993). *Child victims, child witnesses: Understanding and improving testimony.* New York: Guilford.

Goodsitt, J. V., Morse, P. A., VerHoeve, J. N., & Cowan, N. (1984). Infant speech recognition in multisyllabic contexts. *Child Development, 55,* 903–910.

Gotlib, I. H. (1992). Interpersonal and cognitive aspects of depression. *Current Directions in Psychological Science, 1,* 149–154.

Gowin, D. B. (1981). *Educating.* Ithaca, NY: Cornell University Press.

Graesser, A. C., & Kreuz, R. J. (1993). A theory of inference generation during text comprehension. *Discourse Processes, 16,* 145–160.

Graf, P., & Schacter, D. (1985). Implicit and explicit memory for new associations in normal and amnesic subjects. *Journal of Experimental Psychology: Learning, Memory, and Cognition, 11,* 501–518.

Green, B. F., McCloskey, M., & Caramazza, A. (1985). The relation of knowledge to problem solving, with examples from kinematics. In S. F.

Chipman, J. W. Segal, & R. Glaser (Eds.), *Thinking and learning skills* (Vol. 2, pp. 127–139). Hillsdale, NJ: Erlbaum.

Green, D. P., Kahneman, D., & Kunreuther, H. (1994). How the scope and method of public funding affect willingness to pay for public goods. *Public Opinion Quarterly, 58,* 49–67.

Green, G. M. (1989). *Pragmatics and natural language understanding.* Hillsdale, NJ: Erlbaum.

Greenberg, J., Pyszczynski, T., Warner, S., & Bralow, D. (1995). *European Journal of Social Psychology, 24,* 593–610.

Greene, J. (1986). *Language understanding: A cognitive approach.* Milton Keynes, England: Open University Press.

Greene, R. L. (1992). *Human memory: Paradigms and paradoxes.* Hillsdale, NJ: Erlbaum.

Greeno, J. G. (1974). Hobbits and Orcs: Acquisition of a sequential concept. *Cognitive Psychology, 6,* 270–292.

Greeno, J. G. (1977). Process of understanding in problem solving. In N. J. Castellan, Jr., D. B. Pisoni, & G. R. Potts (Eds.), *Cognitive theory* (Vol. 2, pp. 43–84). Hillsdale, NJ: Erlbaum.

Greeno, J. G. (1991). A view of mathematical problem solving in school. In M. U. Smith (Ed.), *Toward a unified theory of problem solving* (pp. 69–98). Hillsdale, NJ: Erlbaum.

Greeno, J. G., & Simon, H. A. (1988). Problem solving and reasoning. In R. C. Atkinson, R. J. Herrnstein, G. Lindzey, & R. D. Luce (Eds.), *Stevens' handbook of experimental psychology* (2nd ed., Vol. 2, pp. 589–672). New York: Wiley.

Greeno, J. G., Smith, D. R., & Moore, J. L. (1993). Transfer of situated learning. In D. K. Detterman & R. J. Sternberg (Eds.), *Transfer on trial: Intelligence, cognition, and instruction* (pp. 99–167). Norwood, NJ: Ablex.

Greenwald, A. G. (1992). New Look 3: Unconscious cognition reclaimed. *American Psychologist, 47,* 766–779.

Greenwald, A. G., & Banaji, M. R. (1989). The self as a memory system: Powerful, but ordinary. *Journal of Personality and Social Psychology, 57,* 41–54.

Gregory, W. L., Cialdini, R. B., & Carpenter, K. M. (1982). Self-relevant scenarios as mediators of likelihood estimates and compliance: Does imagining make it so? *Journal of Personality and Social Psychology, 43,* 89–99.

Griffin, D., & Tversky, A. (1992). The weighing of evidence and the determinants of confidence. *Cognitive Psychology, 24,* 411–435.

Griffith, P. L., & Olson, M. W. (1992). Phonemic awareness helps beginning readers break the code. *The Reading Teacher, 45,* 516–523.

Griggs, R. A. (1995). The effects of rule clarification, decision justification, and selection instruction on Wason's abstract selection task. In S. E. Newstead & J. St. B. T. Evans (Eds.), *Perspectives on thinking and reasoning: Essays in honour of Peter Wason.* Hove, England: Erlbaum.

Griggs, R. A., & Cox, J. R. (1982). The elusive thematic-materials effect in Wason's selection task. *British Journal of Psychology, 73,* 407–420.

Griggs, R. A., & Jackson, S. L. (1990). Instructional effects on responses in Wason's selection task. *British Journal of Psychology, 81,* 197–204.

Groninger, L. D. (1971). Mnemonic imagery and forgetting. *Psychonomic Science, 23,* 161–163.

Gross, C. G. (1992). Representation of visual stimuli in inferior temporal cortex. In V. Bruce, A. Cowey, A. W. Ellis, & D. I. Perrett (Eds.), *Processing the facial image* (pp. 3–10). Oxford, Great Britain: Clarendon Press.

Gross, T. F. (1985). *Cognitive development.* Monterey, CA: Brooks/Cole.

Gruneberg, M. M. (1978). The feeling of knowing, memory blocks and memory aids. In M. M. Gruneberg & P. Morris (Eds.), *Aspects of memory* (pp. 186–214). London: Methuen.

Guilford, J. P. (1967). *The nature of human intelligence.* New York: McGraw-Hill.

Gunnar, M. R., & Maratsos, M. (Eds.). (1992). *Modularity and constraints in language and cognition.* Hillsdale, NJ: Erlbaum.

Haaga, D. A. F., Dyck, M. J., & Ernst, D. (1991). Empirical status of cognitive theory of depression. *Psychological Bulletin, 110,* 215–236.

Haber, R. N. (1983a). The impending demise of the icon: A critique of the concept of iconic storage in visual information processing. *The Behavioral and Brain Sciences, 6,* 1–11.

Haber, R. N. (1983b). The icon is really dead. *Behavioral and Brain Sciences, 6,* 43–55.

Haber, R. N. (1985). An icon can have no worth in the real world: Comments on Loftus, Johnson, and Shimamura's "How much is an icon worth?"

Journal of Experimental Psychology: Human Perception and Performance, 11, 374–378.

Hakuta, K. (1986). *Mirror of language: The debate on bilingualism.* New York: Basic Books.

Hale, S., Lima, S. D., & Myerson, J. (1991). General cognitive slowing in the nonlexical domain: An experimental validation. *Psychology and Aging, 6,* 512–521.

Halpern, D. F. (1987). Analogies as a critical thinking skill. In D. E. Berger, K. Pezdek, & W. P. Banks (Eds.), *Applications of cognitive psychology: Problem solving, education, and computing* (pp. 75–86). Hillsdale, NJ: Erlbaum.

Halpern, D. F. (1993). Assessing the effectiveness of critical-thinking instruction. *The Journal of General Education, 42,* 239–254.

Halpern, D. F. (1996). *Thought and knowledge: An introduction to critical thinking* (3rd ed.). Mahwah, NJ: Erlbaum.

Halpern, D. F., Hansen, C., & Riefer, D. (1990). Analogies as an aid to understanding and memory. *Journal of Educational Psychology, 82,* 298–305.

Halpin, J. A., Puff, C. R., Mason, H. F., & Marston, S. P. (1984). Self-reference and incidental recall by children. *Bulletin of the Psychonomic Society, 22,* 87–89.

Hamers, J. F., & Blanc, M. H. A. (1989). *Bilinguality and bilingualism.* Cambridge, England: Cambridge University Press.

Hamilton, D. L., & Sherman, J. W. (1994). Stereotypes. In R. S. Wyer, Jr. & T. K. Srull (Eds.), *Handbook of social cognition* (2nd ed., Vol. 2, pp. 1–68). Hillsdale, NJ: Erlbaum.

Hamilton, D. L., Stroessner, S. J., & Mackie, D. M. (1993). The influence of affect on stereotyping: The case of illusory correlations. In D. M. Mackie & D. L. Hamilton (Eds.), *Affect, cognition, and stereotyping: Interactive processes in group perception* (pp. 39–61). San Diego, CA: Academic Press.

Harder, P., & Togeby, O. (1993). Pragmatics, cognitive science and connectionism. *Journal of Pragmatics, 20,* 467–492.

Hardiman, P. T., Dufresne, R., & Mestre, J. P. (1989). The relation between problem categorization and problem solving among experts and novices. *Memory & Cognition, 17,* 627–638.

Hardyck, C. D., & Petrinovitch, L. R. (1970). Subvocal speech and comprehension level as a function of the difficulty level of reading material. *Journal of Verbal Learning and Verbal Behavior, 9,* 647–652.

Harris, G., Begg, I., & Upfold, D. (1980). On the role of the speaker's expectations in interpersonal communication. *Journal of Verbal Learning and Verbal Behavior, 19,* 597–607.

Harris, J. F., & Foley, M. A. (1992). *Developmental comparisons of memories for real and imagined events.* Unpublished manuscript.

Harris, R. A. (1993). *The linguistic wars.* New York: Oxford University Press.

Harris, R. J., Lee, D. J., Hensley, D. L., & Schoen, L. M. (1988). The effect of cultural script knowledge on memory for stories over time. *Discourse Processes, 11,* 413–431.

Harris, R. J., Sardarpoor-Bascom, F., & Meyer, T. (1989). The role of cultural knowledge in distorting recall for stories. *Bulletin of the Psychonomic Society, 27,* 9–10.

Hartley, A. A. (1993). Evidence for the selective preservation of spatial selective attention in old age. *Psychology and Aging, 8,* 371–379.

Hartman, M., & Hasher, L. (1991). Aging and suppression: Memory for previously relevant information. *Psychology and Aging, 6,* 587–594.

Hasher, L., & Zacks, R. T. (1988). Working memory, comprehension, and aging: A review and a new view. *The Psychology of Learning and Motivation, 22,* 193–225.

Hawkins, H., & Presson, J. (1986). Auditory information processing. In K. R. Boff, L. Kaufman, & J. P. Thomas (Ed.), *Handbook of perception and human performance* (Vol. 2, pp. 26-1–26-64). New York: Wiley.

Hawkins, S. A., & Hastie, R. (1990). Hindsight: Biased judgments of past events after the outcomes are known. *Psychological Bulletin, 107,* 311–327.

Hayes, D. S., Scott, L. C., Chemelski, B. E., & Johnson, J. (1987). Physical and emotional states as memory-relevant factors: Cognitive monitoring by young children. *Merrill-Palmer Quarterly, 33,* 473–487.

Hayes, J. R. (1989a). Writing research: The analysis of a very complex task. In D. Klahr & K. Kotovsky (Eds.), *Complex information processing: The impact of Herbert A. Simon* (pp. 209–234). Hillsdale, NJ: Erlbaum.

Hayes, J. R. (1989b). *The complete problem solver* (2nd ed.). Hillsdale, NJ: Erlbaum.

Hayes, J. R., & Flower, L. S. (1986). Writing research and the writer. *American Psychologist, 41,* 1106–1113.

Hayes, J. R., Flower, L. S., Schriver, K. A., Stratman, J., & Carey, L. (1987). Cognitive processes in revision. In S. Rosenberg (Ed.), *Advances in psycholinguistics, Vol. 2: Reading, writing, and languages processing.* Cambridge, England: Cambridge University Press.

Hayman, C. A. G., Macdonald, C. A., & Tulving, E. (1993). The role of repetition and associative interference in new semantic learning in amnesia: A case experiment. *Journal of Cognitive Neuroscience, 5,* 375–389.

Hearnshaw, L. S. (1987). *The shaping of modern psychology.* London: Routledge & Kegan Paul.

Hearst, E. (1979). One hundred years: Themes and perspectives. In E. Hearst (Ed.), *The first century of experimental psychology* (pp. 1–38). Hillsdale, NJ: Erlbaum.

Hearst, E. (1991). Psychology and nothing. *American Scientist, 79,* 432–443.

Heibeck, T. H., & Markman, E. M. (1987). Word learning in children: An examination of fast mapping. *Child Development, 58,* 1021–1034.

Hennessey, B. A. (1994). Finding (and solving?) the problem [Review of *Problem finding, problem solving and creativity*]. *Contemporary Psychology, 40,* 971–972.

Hennessey, B. A., & Amabile, T. M. (1984, April). *The effect of reward and task label on children's verbal creativity.* Paper presented at the annual meeting of the Eastern Psychological Association, Baltimore, MD.

Hennessey, B. A., & Amabile, T. M. (1988). The conditions of creativity. In R. J. Sternberg (Ed.), *The nature of creativity: Contemporary psychological perspectives* (pp. 11–38). New York: Cambridge University Press.

Herrmann, D. J. (1990). Self-perceptions of memory performance. In W. K. Schaie, J. Rodin, & C. Schooler (Eds.), *Self-directedness and efficacy: Causes and effects throughout the life course* (pp. 199–211). Hillsdale, NJ: Erlbaum.

Herrmann, D. J. (1991). *Super Memory.* Emmaus, PA: Rodale Press.

Herrmann, D. J., & Gruneberg, M. (1993). The need to expand the horizons of the practical aspects of memory movement. *Applied Cognitive Psychology, 7,* 553–565.

Herrmann, D. J., & Petro, S. J. (1990). Commercial memory aids. *Applied Cognitive Psychology, 4,* 439–450.

Herrmann, D. J., & Searleman, A. (1990). The new multimodal approach to memory improvement. *The Psychology of Learning and Motivation, 26,* 175–205.

Hershey, D. A., Walsh, D. A., Read, S. J., & Chulef, A. S. (1990). The effects of expertise on financial problem solving: Evidence for goal-directed, problem-solving scripts. *Organizational Behavior and Human Decision Processes, 46,* 77–101.

Hertel, P. T. (1993). Implications of external memory for investigations of mind. *Applied Cognitive Psychology, 7,* 665–674.

Hertzog, C. (1992). Improving memory: The possible roles of metamemory. In D. J. Herrmann, H. Weingartner, A. Searleman, & C. McEvoy (Eds.), *Memory improvement: Implications for memory theory* (pp. 61–78). New York: Springer-Verlag.

Hertzog, C., & Dixon, R. A. (1994). Metacognitive development in adulthood and old age. In J. Metcalfe and A. P. Shimamura (Eds.), *Metacognition: Knowing about knowing* (pp. 227–251). Cambridge, MA: MIT Press.

Hertzog, C., Dixon, R. A., & Hultsch, D. F. (1990). Relationships between metamemory, memory predictions, and memory task performance in adults. *Psychology and Aging, 5,* 215–227.

Higbee, K. L. (1994). More motivational aspects of an imagery mnemonic. *Applied Cognitive Psychology, 8,* 1–12.

Hill, J. W., & Bliss, J. C. (1968). Modeling a tactile sensory register. *Perception & Psychophysics, 4,* 91–101.

Hill, R. D., Evankovich, K. D., Sheikh, J. I., & Yesavage, J. A. (1987). Imagery mnemonic training in a patient with primary degenerative dementia. *Psychology and Aging, 2,* 204–205.

Hilton, D. J., Jaspars, J. M. F., & Clarke, D. D. (1990). Pragmatic conditional reasoning: Context and content effects on the interpretation of causal assertions. *Journal of Pragmatics, 14,* 791–812.

Hineline, P. N. (1992). Behaviorism. In L. R. Squire (Ed.), *Encyclopedia of learning and memory* (pp. 79–82). New York: Macmillan.

Hinrichs, T. R. (1992). *Problem solving in open worlds: A case study in design.* Hillsdale, NJ: Erlbaum.

Hinsley, D., Hayes, J. R., & Simon, H. A. (1977). From words to equations: Meaning and representation in algebra word-problems. In P. Carpenter & M. Just (Eds.), *Cognitive processes in comprehension* (pp. 89–108). Hillsdale, NJ: Erlbaum.

Hinsz, V. B., & Tindale, R. S. (1992). Ambiguity and human versus technological sources of information in judgments involving base rate and individuating information. *Journal of Applied Social Psychology, 22,* 973–997.

Hintzman, D. L. (1978). *The psychology of learning and memory.* San Francisco: Freeman.

Hintzman, D. L. (1993). Twenty-five years of learning and memory: Was the cognitive revolution a mistake? In D. E. Meyer & S. Kornblum (Ed.), *Attention and performance XIV* (pp. 359–391). Cambridge, MA: MIT Press.

Hirsh-Pasek, K., Kemler Nelson, D., Jusczyk, P., Cassidy, K., Druss, B., & Kennedy, L. (1987). Clauses are perceptual units for young infants. *Cognition, 26,* 269–286.

Hirst, W. (1984). Factual memory? *The Behavioral and Brain Sciences, 7,* 241–242.

Hirst, W. (1986). The psychology of attention. In J. E. LeDoux & W. Hirst (Eds.), *Mind and brain* (pp. 105–141). Cambridge, England: Cambridge University Press.

Hirst, W. (1988). Improving memory. In M. S. Gazzaniga (Ed.), *Perspectives in memory research* (pp. 219–244). Cambridge, MA: Bradford.

Hirst, W. (1989). On consciousness, recall, recognition, and the architecture of memory. In S. Lewandowsky, J. C. Dunn, & K. Kirsner (Eds.), *Implicit memory: Theoretical issues* (pp. 33–46). Hillsdale, NJ: Erlbaum.

Hirst, W. (1995). Cognitive aspects of consciousness. In M. S. Gazzaniga (Ed.), *The cognitive neurosciences* (pp. 1307–1319). Cambridge, MA: MIT Press.

Hirst, W., Spelke, E., Reaves, C. C., Caharack, G., & Neisser, U. (1980). Dividing attention without alternation or automaticity. *Journal of Experimental Psychology: General, 109,* 98–117.

Hirtle, S. C., & Jonides, J. (1985). Evidence of hierarchies in cognitive maps. *Memory & Cognition, 13,* 208–217.

Hirtle, S. C., & Mascolo, M. F. (1986). Effect of semantic clustering on the memory of spatial locations. *Journal of Experimental Psychology: Learning, Memory, and Cognition, 12,* 182–189.

Hoffman, J. E. (1986). The psychology of perception. In J. E. LeDoux & W. Hirst (Eds.), *Mind and brain: Dialogues in cognitive neuroscience* (pp. 7–32). New York: Cambridge University Press.

Hollingworth, H. (1910). The oblivescence of the disagreeable. *Journal of Philosophy, Psychology and Scientific Methods, 7,* 709–714.

Holmes, V. M. (1984). Parsing strategies and discourse context. *Journal of Psycholinguistic Research, 13,* 237–257.

Holmes, V. M., Kennedy, A., & Murray, W. S. (1987). Syntactic structure and the garden path. *Quarterly Journal of Experimental Psychology, 39A,* 277–293.

Holtgrave, D. R., Tinsley, B. J., & Kay, L. S. (1994). Heuristics, biases, and environmental health risk analysis. In L. Heath, R. S. Tindale, J. Edwards, E. J. Posavac, F. B. Bryant, E. Henderson-King, Y. Suarez-Balcazar, & J. Myers (Eds.), *Applications of heuristics and biases to social issues* (pp. 259–285). New York: Plenum.

Holyoak, K. J., & Koh, K. (1987). Surface and structural similarity in analogical transfer. *Memory & Cognition, 15,* 332–340.

Holyoak, K. J., & Spellman, B. A. (1993). Thinking. *Annual Review of Psychology, 44,* 265–315.

Horowitz, L. M., Wright, J. C., Lowenstein, E., & Parad, H. W. (1981). The prototype as a construct in abnormal psychology: 1. A method for deriving prototypes. *Journal of Abnormal Psychology, 90,* 568–574.

Houtz, J. C., & Frankel, A. D. (1992). Effects of incubation and imagery training on creativity. *Creativity Research Journal, 5,* 183–189.

Hoving, K. L., Spencer, T., Robb, K., & Schulte, D. (1978). Developmental changes in visual information processing. In P. A. Ornstein (Ed.), *Memory development in children* (pp. 21–68). Hillsdale, NJ: Erlbaum.

Howard, R. W. (1995). *Learning and memory: Major ideas, principles, issues and applications.* Westport, CT: Praeger.

Howe, M. L., & Courage, M. L. (1993). On resolving the enigma of infantile amnesia. *Psychological Bulletin, 113,* 305–326.

Howe, M. L., Courage, M. L., & Peterson, C. (1995). Intrusions in preschoolers' recall of traumatic childhood events. *Psychonomic Bulletin & Review, 2,* 130–134.

Howes, J. L., & Katz, A. N. (1992). Remote memory: recalling autobiographical and public events from across the lifespan. *Canadian Journal of Psychology, 46,* 92–116.

Hubel, D. H. (1982). Explorations of the primary visual cortex, 1955–1978. *Nature, 299,* 515–524.

Hubel, D. H., & Wiesel, T. N. (1965). Receptive fields of single neurons in two nonstriate visual areas (18 and 19) of the cat. *Journal of Neurophysiology, 28,* 229–289.

Hubel, D. H., & Wiesel, T. N. (1979). Brain mechanisms and vision. *Scientific American, 241* (3), 150–162.

Huber, V. L., Neale, M. A., & Northcraft, G. B. (1987). Decision bias and personnel selection strategies. *Organizational Behavior and Human Decision Processes, 40,* 136–147.

Huey, E. B. (1968). *The psychology and pedagogy of reading.* Cambridge, MA: MIT Press. (Original work published 1908).

Huitema, J. S., Dopkins, S., Klin, C. M., & Myers, J. L. (1993). Connecting goals and actions during reading. *Journal of Experimental Psychology: Learning, Memory, and Cognition, 19,* 1053–1060.

Hulicka, I. M. (1982). Memory functioning in late adulthood. In F. I. M. Craik & S. Trehub (Eds.), *Advances in the study of communication and affect* (Vol. 8, pp. 331–351). New York: Plenum.

Hulme, C., & Tordoff, V. (1989). Working memory development: The effects of speech rate, word length, and acoustic similarity on serial recall. *Journal of Experimental Child Psychology, 47,* 72–87.

Humphreys, M. S., Bain, J. D., & Pike, R. (1989). Different ways to cue a coherent memory system: A theory for episodic, semantic, and procedural tasks. *Psychological Review, 96,* 208–233.

Hunt, E. (1989). Cognitive science: Definition, status, and questions. *Annual Review of Psychology, 40,* 603–629.

Hunt, E. (1993). What do we need to know about aging? In J. Cerella, J. Rybash, W. Hoywer, & M. L. Commons (Eds.), *Adult information processing: Limits on loss* (pp. 587–598). San Diego, CA: Academic Press.

Hunt, E., & Lansman, M. (1986). Unified model of attention and problem solving. *Psychological Review, 93,* 446–461.

Hunt, R. R., & Elliott, J. M. (1980). The role of non-semantic information in memory: Orthographic distinctiveness effects on retention. *Journal of Experimental Psychology: General, 109,* 49–74.

Hyman, I. E., Jr. (1993). Imagery, reconstructive memory, and discovery. In B. Roskos-Ewoldson, M. J. Intons-Peterson, & R. E. Anderson (Eds.), *Imagery, creativity, and discovery: A cognitive perspective* (pp. 99–121). Amsterdam: Elsevier.

Inhoff, A. W., & Topolski, R. (1994). Use of phonological codes during eye fixations in reading and in on-line and delayed naming tasks. *Journal of Memory and Language, 33,* 689–713.

Intons-Peterson, M. J. (1983). Imagery paradigms: How vulnerable are they to experimenters' expectations? *Journal of Experimental Psychology: Learning, Memory, and Cognition, 10,* 699–715.

Intons-Peterson, M. J. (Ed.). (1992). Mental models, pictures, and text: Integration of spatial and verbal information [special issue]. *Memory & Cognition, 20* (5).

Intons-Peterson, M. J. (1993a). External memory aids and their relation to memory. In C. Izawa (Ed.), *Cognitive psychology applied.* Hillsdale, NJ: Erlbaum.

Intons-Peterson, M. J. (1993b). Imagery and classification. In A. F. Collins, S. E. Gathercole, M. A. Conway, & P. E. Morris (Eds.), *Theories of memory* (pp. 211–240). Hove, England: Erlbaum.

Intons-Peterson, M. J., & Fournier, J. (1986). External and internal memory aids: When and how often do we use them? *Journal of Experimental Psychology: General, 115,* 267–280.

Intons-Peterson, M. J., & McDaniel, M. A. (1991). Symmetries and asymmetries between imagery and perception. In C. Cornoldi & M. A. McDaniel (Eds.), *Imagery and cognition* (pp. 47–76). New York: Springer-Verlag.

Intons-Peterson, M. J., & Newsome, G. L., III (1992). External memory aids: Effects and effectiveness. In D. Herrmann, H. Weingartner, A. Searleman, & C. McEvoy (Eds.), *Memory improvement: Implications for memory theory* (pp. 101–121). New York: Springer-Verlag.

Intons-Peterson, M. J., Russell, W., & Dressel, S. (1992). The role of pitch in auditory imagery. *Journal of Experimental Psychology: Human Perception and Performance, 18,* 233–240.

Intons-Peterson, M. J., & Smyth, M. M. (1987). The anatomy of repertory memory. *Journal of*

Experimental Psychology: Learning, Memory, and Cognition, 13, 490–500.

Irwin, D. E., & Yeomans, J. M. (1986). Sensory registration and informational persistence. *Journal of Experimental Psychology: Learning, Memory, and Cognition, 10,* 699–715.

Irwin, D. E., Zacks, J. L., & Brown, J. S. (1990). Visual memory and the perception of a stable visual environment. *Perception & Psychophysics, 47,* 35–46.

Jackendoff, R. (1994). *Patterns in the mind.* New York: Basic Books.

Jackson, S. L., & Griggs, R. A. (1988). Education and the selection task. *Bulletin of the Psychonomic Society, 26,* 327–330.

Jackson, S. L., & Griggs, R. A. (1990). The elusive pragmatic reasoning schemas effect. *The Quarterly Journal of Experimental Psychology, 42A,* 353–373.

Jacoby, L. L. (1983). Remembering the data: Analyzing interactive processes in reading. *Journal of Verbal Learning and Verbal Behavior, 22,* 485–508.

Jacquette, D. (1993). Who's afraid of the Turing test? *Behavior and Philosophy, 20,* 63–74.

James, W. (1890). *The principles of psychology.* New York: Henry Holt.

Jarvella, R. J. (1971). Syntactic processing of connected speech. *Journal of Verbal Learning and Verbal Behavior, 10,* 409–416.

Jenkins, F., & Davies, G. (1985). Contamination of facial memory through exposure to misleading composite pictures. *Journal of Applied Psychology, 70,* 164–176.

Jenkins, J. J. (1974). Remember that old theory of memory? Well, forget it. *American Psychologist, 29,* 785–795.

Jespersen, O. (1922). *Language.* London: George Allen and Unwin.

Johnson, J. S., & Newport, E. L. (1989). Critical effects in second language learning: The influence of maturational state on the acquisition of English as a second language. *Cognitive Psychology, 21,* 60–99.

Johnson, M. K. (1988). Reality monitoring: An experimental phenomenological approach. *Journal of Experimental Psychology: General, 117,* 390–394.

Johnson, M. K. (1995). *The relation between memory and reality.* Paper presented at the annual convention of the American Psychological Association, New York.

Johnson, M. K., & Hasher, L. (1987). Human learning and memory. *Annual Review of Psychology, 38,* 631–668.

Johnson, M. K., Hashtroudi, S., & Lindsay, D. S. (1993). Source monitoring. *Psychological Bulletin, 114,* 3–28.

Johnson, M. K., Kounios, J., & Reeder, J. A. (1994). Time-course studies of reality monitoring and recognition. *Journal of Experimental Psychology: Learning, Memory, and Cognition, 20,* 1409–1419.

Johnson, M. K., & Raye, C. L. (1981). Reality monitoring. *Psychological Review, 88,* 67–85.

Johnson, M. K., & Sherman, S. J. (1990). Constructing and reconstructing the past and the future in the present. In E. T. Higgins & R. M. Sorrentino (Eds.), *Handbook of motivation and cognition* (Vol. 2, pp. 482–526). New York: Guilford.

Johnson, R. D. (1987). Making judgments when information is missing: Inferences, biases, and framing effects. *Acta Psychologica, 66,* 69–72.

Johnson-Laird, P. N. (1988). *The computer and the mind: An introduction to cognitive science.* Cambridge, MA: Harvard University Press.

Johnson-Laird, P. N. (1995). Mental models, deductive reasoning, and the brain. In M. S. Gazzaniga (Ed.), *The cognitive neurosciences* (pp. 999–1008). Cambridge, MA: MIT Press.

Johnson-Laird, P. N., & Byrne, R. M. J. (1991). *Deduction.* Hove, Great Britain: Erlbaum.

Johnson-Laird, P. N., Byrne, R. M. J., & Schaeken, W. (1992). Propositional reasoning by model. *Psychological Review, 99,* 418–439.

Johnson-Laird, P. N., Herrmann, D. J., & Chaffin, R. (1984). Only connections: A critique of semantic networks. *Psychological Bulletin, 96,* 292–315.

Johnston, W. A., & Dark, V. J. (1986). Selective attention. *Annual Review of Psychology, 37,* 43–75.

Jolicoeur, P. (1985). The time to name disoriented natural objects. *Memory & Cognition, 13,* 289–303.

Jolicoeur, P., & Kosslyn, S. M. (1985a). Demand characteristics in image scanning experiments. *Journal of Mental Imagery, 9,* 41–50.

Jolicoeur, P., & Kosslyn, S. M. (1985b). Is time to scan visual images due to demand characteristics? *Memory & Cognition, 13,* 320–332.

Jolicoeur, P., & Landau, M. J. (1984). Effects of orientation on the identification of simple visual patterns. *Canadian Journal of Psychology, 38,* 80–93.

Jolicoeur, P., Snow, D., & Murray, J. (1987). The time to identify disoriented letters: Effects of practice and font. *Canadian Journal of Psychology, 41*, 303–316.

Jonides, J., Naveh-Benjamin, M., & Palmer, J. (1985). Assessing automaticity. *Acta Psychologica, 60*, 157–171.

Jordan, K., & Huntsman, L. A. (1990). Image rotation of misoriented letter strings: Effects of orientation cuing and repetition. *Perception & Psychophysics, 48*, 363–374.

Jordan, T. R., & Bevan, K. M. (1994). Word superiority over isolated letters: The neglected case of forward masking. *Memory & Cognition, 22*, 133–144.

Jou, J., & Harris, R. J. (1992). The effect of divided attention on speech production. *Bulletin of the Psychonomic Society, 30*, 301–304.

Jurden, F. H. (1995). Individual differences in working memory and complex cognition. *Journal of Educational Psychology, 87*, 93–102.

Jusczyk, P. W. (1986). Speech perception. In K. R. Boff, L. Kaufman, & J. P. Thomas (Eds.), *Handbook of perception and human performance* (pp. 27.1–27.57). Hillsdale, NJ: Erlbaum.

Just, M. A., & Carpenter, P. A. (1985). Cognitive coordinate systems: Accounts of mental rotation and individual differences in spatial ability. *Psychological Review, 92*, 137–172.

Just, M. A., & Carpenter, P. A. (1992). A capacity theory of comprehension: Individual differences in working memory. *Psychological Review, 99*, 122–149.

Kahneman, D. (1992). Reference points, anchors, norms, and mixed feelings. *Organizational Behavior and Human Decision Processes, 51*, 296–312.

Kahneman, D., & Tversky, A. (1972). Subjective probability: A judgment of representativeness. *Cognitive Psychology, 3*, 430–454.

Kahneman, D., & Tversky, A. (1973). On the psychology of prediction. *Psychological Review, 80*, 237–251.

Kahneman, D., & Tversky, A. (1979). Prospect theory: An analysis of decision under risk. *Econometrica, 47*, 263–291.

Kahneman, D., & Tversky, A. (1982). The simulation heuristic. In D. Kahneman, P. Slovic, & A. Tversky (Eds.), *Judgment under uncertainty: Heuristics and biases* (pp. 201–208). New York: Cambridge University Press.

Kahneman, D., & Tversky, A. (1984). Choices, values, and frames. *American Psychologist, 39*, 341–350.

Kahneman, D., & Tversky, A. (1995). Conflict resolution: A cognitive perspective. In K. Arrow, R. H. Mnookin, L. Ross, A. Tversky, & R. Wilson (Eds.), *Barriers to conflict resolution* (pp. 44–60). New York: Norton.

Kail, R. V., Jr. (1990). *The development of memory in children* (3rd ed.). New York: Freeman.

Kail, R. V., Jr. (1992). Development of memory in children. In L. R. Squire (Ed.), *Encyclopedia of learning and memory* (pp. 99–102). New York: Macmillan.

Kail, R. V., Jr., Carter, P., & Pellegrino, J. (1979). The locus of sex differences in spatial ability. *Perception & Psychophysics, 26*, 182–186.

Kail, R. V., Jr., & Siegel, A. W. (1977). The development of mnemonic encoding in children. From perception to abstraction. In R. V. Kail, Jr. & J. W. Hagen (Eds.), *Perspectives on the development of memory and cognition* (pp. 61–88). Hillsdale, NJ: Erlbaum.

Kardash, C. A. M., Royer, J. M., & Greene, B. A. (1988). Effects of schemata on both encoding and retrieval of information from prose. *Journal of Educational Psychology, 80*, 324–329.

Kasper, L. F., & Glass, A. L. (1988). An extension of the keyword method facilitates the acquisition of simple Spanish sentences. *Applied Cognitive Psychology, 2*, 137–146.

Katz, A. N. (1981). Knowing about the sensory properties of objects. *Quarterly Journal of Experimental Psychology, 33A*, 39–49.

Katz, A. N. (1987). Self-reference in the encoding of creative-relevant traits. *Journal of Personality, 55*, 97–120.

Kaufmann, G. (1985). A theory of symbolic representation in problem solving. *Journal of Mental Imagery, 9*, 51–70.

Kaufmann, G., & Helstrup, T. (1993). Mental imagery: Fixed or multiple meanings? Nature and function of imagery in creative thinking. In R. Roskos-Ewaldson, M. J. Intons-Peterson, & R. E. Anderson (Eds.), *Imagery, creativity, and discovery: A cognitive perspective* (pp. 123–150). Amsterdam: Elsevier.

Kaufman, N. J., Randlett, A. L., & Price, J. (1985). Awareness of the use of comprehension strategies in good and poor college readers. *Reading Psychology, 6*, 1–11.

Kausler, D. H. (1990). *Experimental psychology, cognition, and human aging* (2nd ed.). New York: Springer-Verlag.

Kausler, D. H. (1994). *Learning and memory in normal aging.* San Diego, CA: Academic Press.

Keane, M. T. (1988). *Analogical problem solving.* Chichester, Great Britain: Ellis Horwood.

Keil, F. C. (1989). *Concepts, kinds, and cognitive development.* Cambridge, MA: The MIT Press.

Keil, F. C. (1991). On being more than the sum of the parts: The conceptual coherence of cognitive science. *Psychological Science, 2,* 283, 287–293.

Keil, F. C., & Batterman, N. (1984). A characteristic-to-defining shift in the development of word meaning. *Journal of Verbal Learning and Verbal Behavior, 23,* 221–236.

Keller, T. A., Cowan, N., & Saults, J. S. (1995). Can auditory memory for tone pitch be rehearsed? *Journal of Experimental Psychology: Learning, Memory, and Cognition, 21,* 635–645.

Kelley, C. M., & Lindsay, D. S. (1993). Remembering mistaken for knowing: Ease of retrieval as a basis for confidence in answers to general knowledge questions. *Journal of Memory and Language, 32,* 1–24.

Kellogg, R. T. (1987). Effects of topic knowledge on the allocation of processing time and cognitive effort to writing processes. *Memory & Cognition, 15,* 256–266.

Kellogg, R. T. (1988). Attentional overload and writing performance: Effects of rough draft and outline strategies. *Journal of Experimental Psychology: Learning, Memory, and Cognition, 14,* 355–365.

Kellogg, R. T. (1989). Idea processors: Computer aids for planning and composing text. In B. K. Britton & S. M. Glynn (Eds.), *Computer writing environments: Theory, research, and design* (pp. 57–92). Hillsdale, NJ: Erlbaum.

Kellogg, R. T. (1990). Effectiveness of prewriting strategies as a function of task demands. *American Journal of Psychology, 103,* 327–342.

Kellogg, R. T. (1994). *The psychology of writing.* New York: Oxford University Press.

Kelly, A. E., & Kahn, J. H. (1994). Effects of suppression of personal intrusive thoughts. *Journal of Personality and Social Psychology, 66,* 998–1006.

Kemper, S. (1992). Language and aging. In F. I. M. Craik & T. A. Salthouse (Eds.), *The Handbook of aging and cognition* (pp. 213–270). Hillsdale, NJ: Erlbaum.

Kendler, H. H. (1987). *Historical foundations of modern psychology.* Pacific Grove, CA: Brooks/Cole.

Kent, D. (1990, January). A conversation with Lynn Cooper. *APS Observer, 3,* 11–13.

Keren, G. (1984). On the importance of identifying the correct "problem space." *Cognition, 16,* 121–128.

Keren, G. (1987). Facing uncertainty in the game of bridge: A calibration study. *Organizational Behavior and Human Decision Processes, 39,* 98–114.

Kerr, N. H. (1993). Rate of imagery processing in two versus three dimensions. *Memory & Cognition, 21,* 467–476.

Kiewra, K. A. (1985). Investigation notetaking and review: A depth of processing alternative. *Educational Psychologist, 20,* 23–32.

Kihlstrom, J. F. (1987). The cognitive unconscious. *Science, 237,* 1445–1452.

Kihlstrom, J. F. (1994). *The social construction of memory.* Paper presented at the annual convention of the American Psychological Society.

Kihlstrom, J. F., & Barnhardt, T. M. (1993). The self-regulation of memory: For better and for worse, with and without hypnosis. In D. M. Wegner & J. W. Pennebaker (Eds.), *Handbook of mental control* (pp. 88–125). Englewood Cliffs, NJ: Prentice-Hall.

Kihlstrom, J. F., Barnhardt, T. M., & Tataryn, D. J. (1992). The psychological unconscious: Found, lost, and regained. *American Psychologist, 47,* 788–791.

Kihlstrom, J. F., Schacter, D. L., Cork, R. C., Hurt, C. A., & Behr, S. E. (1990). Implicit and explicit memory following surgical anesthesia. *Psychological Science, 1,* 303–306.

Kilborn, K. (1994). Learning a language late: Second language acquisition in adults. In M. A. Gernsbacher (Ed.), *Handbook of psycholinguistics* (pp. 917–944). San Diego, CA: Academic Press.

Kintsch, W. (1984). Approaches to the study of the psychology of language. In T. G. Bever, J. M. Carroll, & L. A. Miller (Eds.), *Talking minds: The study of language in cognitive science* (pp. 111–145). Cambridge, MA: MIT Press.

Kintsch, W. (1988). The role of knowledge in discourse comprehension: A construction-integration model. *Psychological Review, 95,* 163–182.

Kintsch, W. (1993). Discourse processing. In G. d'Ydewalle, P. Eelen, & P. Bertelson (Eds.), *International perspectives on psychological science. Volume*

2: The state of the art (pp. 135–155). Hove, England: Erlbaum.

Kintsch, W. (1994). The psychology of discourse processing. In M. A. Gernsbacher (Ed.), *Handbook of psycholinguistics* (pp. 721–739). San Diego, CA: Academic Press.

Kintsch, W., & Buschke, H. (1969). Homophones and synonyms in short-term memory. *Journal of Experimental Psychology, 80*, 403–407.

Kintsch, W., & van Dijk, T. A. (1978). Toward a model of text comprehension and production. *Psychological Review, 85*, 363–394.

Kitchin, R. M. (1994). Cognitive maps: What are they and why study them? *Journal of Environmental Psychology, 14*, 1–19.

Klaczynski, P. A., Gelfand, H., & Reese, H. W. (1989). Transfer of conditional reasoning: Effects of explanations and initial problem types. *Memory & Cognition, 17*, 208–220.

Klein, G. A., Orasanu, J., Calderwood, R., & Zsambok, C. E. (Eds.). (1993). *Decision making in action: Models and methods.* Norwood, NJ: Ablex.

Klein, S. B., & Kihlstrom, J. F. (1986). Elaboration, organization, and the self-reference effect in memory. *Journal of Experimental Psychology: General, 115*, 26–38.

Koestler, A. (1964). *The act of creation.* London: Hutchinson.

Komatsu, L. K. (1992). Recent views of conceptual structure. *Psychological Bulletin, 112*, 500–526.

Koriat, A. (1993). How do we know that we know? The accessibility model of the feeling of knowing. *Psychological Review, 100*, 609–639.

Koriat, A. (1994). Memory's knowledge of its own knowledge: The accessibility account of the feeling of knowing. In J. Metcalfe & A. P. Shimamura (Eds.), *Metacognition: Knowing about knowing* (pp. 115–135). Cambridge, MA: MIT Press.

Koriat, A., Ben-Zur, H., & Nussbaum, A. (1990). Encoding information for future action: Memory for to-be-performed tasks versus memory for to-be-recalled tasks. *Memory & Cognition, 18*, 568–578.

Koriat, A., & Melkman, R. (1987). Depth of processing and memory organization. *Psychological Research, 49*, 183–188.

Kosslyn, S. M. (1975). Information representation in visual images. *Cognitive Psychology, 7*, 341–370.

Kosslyn, S. M. (1976). Using imagery to retrieve semantic information: A developmental study. *Child Development, 47*, 433–444.

Kosslyn, S. M. (1981). The medium and the message in mental imagery: A theory. *Psychological Review, 88*, 46–65.

Kosslyn, S. M. (1983). *Ghosts in the mind's machine: Creating and using images in the brain.* New York: Norton.

Kosslyn, S. M. (1987). Seeing and imagining in the cerebral hemispheres: A computational approach. *Psychological Review, 94*, 148–175.

Kosslyn, S. M. (1990). Mental imagery. In D. N. Osherson, S. M. Kosslyn, & J. M. Hollerback (Eds.), *Visual cognition and action: An invitation to cognitive science* (Vol. 2, pp. 73–97). Cambridge, MA: MIT Press.

Kosslyn, S. M. (1994). *Image and brain: The resolution of the imagery debate.* Cambridge, MA: MIT Press.

Kosslyn, S. M., Alpert, N. M., & Thompson, W. L. (1995). Identifying objects at different levels of hierarchy: A positron emission tomography study. *Human Brain Mapping, 3*, 1–26.

Kosslyn, S. M., Alpert, N. M., Thompson, W. L., Maljkovic, V., Weise, S. B., Chabris, C. F., Hamilton, S. E., Rauch, S. L., & Buonanno, F. S. (1993). Visual mental imagery activates topographically organized visual cortex: PET investigations. *Journal of Cognitive Neuroscience, 5*, 263–287.

Kosslyn, S. M., Ball, T. M., & Reiser, B. J. (1978). Visual images preserve metric spatial information: Evidence from studies of image scanning. *Journal of Experimental Psychology: Human Perception & Performance, 4*, 47–60.

Kosslyn, S. M., & Koenig, O. (1992). *Wet mind: The new cognitive neuroscience.* New York: Free Press.

Kosslyn, S. M., Seger, C., Pani, J. R., & Hillger, L. A. (1990). When is imagery used in everyday life? A diary study. *Journal of Mental Imagery, 14*, 131–152.

Kosslyn, S. M., Thompson, W. L., Kim, I. J., & Alpert, N. M. (1995). Topographical representations of mental images in primary visual cortex. *Nature,* 496–498.

Kounios, J., Osman, A. M., & Meyer, D. E. (1987). Structure and process in semantic memory: New evidence based on speed-accuracy decomposition. *Journal of Experimental Psychology: General, 116*, 3–25.

Kowalski, R. M. (1996). Complaints and complaining: Functions, antecedents, and consequences. *Psychological Review, 119,* 179–196.

Kozielecki, J. (1981). *Psychological decision theory.* Warsaw, Poland: Polish Scientific Publishers.

Kreutzer, M. A., Leonard, C., & Flavell, J. H. (1975). An interview study of children's knowledge about memory. *Monographs of the Society for Research in Child Development, 40* (1, Serial No. 159).

Kreuz, R. J., & Roberts, R. M. (1993). When collaboration fails: Consequences of pragmatic errors in conversation. *Journal of Pragmatics, 19,* 239–252.

Krueger, L. E. (1992). The word-superiority effect and phonological recoding. *Memory & Cognition, 20,* 685–694.

Kuczaj, S. A. (1977). The acquisition of regular and irregular past tense forms. *Journal of Verbal Learning and Verbal Behavior, 16,* 589–600.

Kuczaj, S. A. (1983). *Crib speech and language play.* New York: Springer-Verlag.

Kuhl, P. K. (1987). Perception of speech and sound in early infancy. In P. Salapatek & L. Cohen (Eds.), *Handbook of infant perception* (Vol. 2, pp. 275–382). Orlando, FL: Academic Press.

Kuhl, P. K. (1989). On babies, birds, modules, and mechanisms: A comparative approach to the acquisition of vocal communication. In R. J. Dooling & S. H. Hulse (Eds.), *The comparative psychology of audition: Perceiving complex sounds* (pp. 379–419). Hillsdale, NJ: Erlbaum.

Kuhl, P. K. (1993a). Early linguistic experience and phonetic perception: Implications for theories of developmental speech perception. *Journal of Phonetics, 21,* 125–139.

Kuhl, P. K. (1993b). Developmental speech perception: Implications for models of language impairment. *Annals of the New York Academy of Sciences, 682,* 248–263.

Kuhl, P. K. (1994a). Speech perception. In F. D. Minifie (Ed.), *Introduction to communication sciences and disorders* (pp. 77–148). San Diego, CA: Singular Publishing Group.

Kuhl, P. K. (1994b). Learning and representation in speech and language. *Current Opinion in Neurobiology, 4,* 812–822.

Kuhl, P. K., Williams, K. A., Lacerda, F., Stevens, K. N., & Lindblom, B. (1992). Linguistic experience alters phonetic perception in infants by 6 months of age. *Science, 255,* 606–608.

Kuhn, D., Weinstock, M., & Flaton, R. (1994). How well do jurors reason? Competence dimensions of individual variation in a juror reasoning task. *Psychological Science, 5,* 289–296.

Kunda, Z., & Nisbett, R. E. (1986). The psychometrics of everyday life. *Cognitive Psychology, 18,* 195–224.

Kunda, Z., & Thagard, P. (1996). Forming impressions from stereotypes, traits, and behaviors: A parallel constraint satisfaction theory. *Psychological Review, 103,* 284–308.

Kurdek, L. A. (1987). Sex role self schema and psychological adjustment in coupled homosexual and heterosexual men and women. *Sex Roles, 17,* 549–562.

LaBerge, D. L. (1990). Attention. *Psychological Science, 1,* 156–162.

Labov, W. (1972). The transformation of experience in narrative syntax. In W. Labov (Ed.), *Language in the inner city.* Philadelphia: University of Pennsylvania Press.

Lachman, M. E. (1991). Perceived control over memory aging: Developmental and intervention perspectives. *Journal of Social Issues, 47,* 159–175.

Lambert, W. E. (1990). Persistent issues in bilingualism. In B. Harley, P. Allen, J. Cummins, & M. Swain (Eds.), *The development of second language proficiency* (pp. 201–218). Cambridge, England: Cambridge University Press.

Lambert, W. E. (1992). Challenging established views on social issues. *American Psychologist, 47,* 533–542.

Lambert, W. E., Genesee, F., Holobow, N., & Chartrand, L. (1991). *Bilingual education for majority English-speaking children.* Montreal, Quebec, Canada: McGill University, Psychology Department.

Laming, D. (1992). Analysis of short-term retention: Models for Brown-Peterson experiments. *Journal of Experimental Psychology: Learning, Memory, and Cognition, 18,* 1342–1365.

Lange, G., & Pierce, S. H. (1992). Memory-strategy learning and maintenance in preschool children. *Developmental Psychology, 28,* 453–462.

Langer, E. J. (1989). *Mindlessness/mindfulness.* Reading, MA: Addison-Wesley.

Larkin, J. H. (1983). The role of problem representation in physics. In D. Gentner & A. L. Stevens

(Eds.), *Mental models* (pp. 75–98). Hillsdale, NJ: Erlbaum.

Larkin, J. H. (1985). Understanding, problem representations, and skill in physics. In S. F. Chipman, J. W. Segal, & R. Glaser (Eds.), *Thinking and learning skills* (Vol. 2, pp. 141–159). Hillsdale, NJ: Erlbaum.

Larkin, J. H., & Simon, H. A. (1987). Why a diagram is (sometimes) worth ten thousand words. *Cognitive Science, 11,* 65–99.

Lave, J. (1988). *Cognition in practice.* New York: Cambridge University Press.

Lavigne, V. D., & Finley, G. E. (1990). Memory in middle-aged adults. *Educational Gerontology, 16,* 447–461.

La Voie, D., & Light, L. L. (1994). Adult age differences in repetition priming: A meta-analysis. *Psychology and aging, 9,* 539–553.

Lawson, D. I., & Lawson, A. E. (1993). Neural principles of memory and a neural theory of analogical insight. *Journal of Research in Science Teaching, 30,* 1327–1348.

Leal, L. (1987). Investigation of the relation between metamemory and university students' examination performance. *Journal of Educational Psychology, 79,* 35–40.

Legrenzi, P., Girotti, V., & Johnson-Laird, P. N. (1993). Focussing in reasoning and decision making. *Cognition, 49,* 37–66.

Lehnert, W. G. (1984). The architecture of the mind [Review of *The architecture of cognition*]. *Contemporary Psychology, 29,* 854–856.

Leichtman, M. D., & Ceci, S. J. (1995). The effects of stereotypes and suggestions on preschoolers' reports. *Developmental Psychology, 31,* 568–578.

Leonard, L. B., & Loeb, D. F. (1988). Government-binding theory and some of its applications: A tutorial. *Journal of Speech and Hearing Research, 31,* 515–524.

Lesgold, A. (1988). Problem solving. In R. J. Sternberg & E. E. Smith (Eds.), *The psychology of human thought* (pp. 188–213). Cambridge, England: Cambridge University Press.

Levelt, W. J. M. (1989). *Speaking: From intention to articulation.* Cambridge, MA: MIT Press.

Levelt, W. J. M. (1994). The skill of speaking. In P. Bertelson, P. Eelen, & G. d'Ydewalle (Eds.), *International perspectives on psychological science* (Vol. 1, pp. 89–103). Hove, England: Erlbaum.

Levin, I. P., Schnittjer, S. K., & Thee, S. L. (1988). Information framing effects in social and personal decisions. *Journal of Experimental Social Psychology, 24,* 520–529.

Levy, C. M., & Ransdell, S. (1995). Is writing as difficult as it seems? *Memory & Cognition, 23,* 767–779.

Lewandowsky, S. (1993). The rewards and hazards of computer simulations. *Psychological Science, 4,* 236–243.

Lewandowsky, S., & Li, S. C. (1995). Catastrophic interference in neural networks: Causes, solutions, and data. In F. N. Dempster & C. J. Brainerd (Eds.), *Interference and inhibition in cognition* (pp. 329–361). San Diego, CA: Academic Press.

Lewandowsky, S., & Murdock, B. B. (1989). Memory for serial order. *Psychological Review, 96,* 25–57.

Liben, L. S. (1982). The developmental study of children's memory. In T. M. Field, A. Huston, H. C. Quay, L. Troll, & G. E. Finley (Eds.), *Review of human development* (pp. 269–289). New York: Wiley.

Liberman, A. M. (1992). The relation of speech to reading and writing. In R. Frost & L. Katz (Eds.), *Orthography, phonology, morphology, and meaning.* Amsterdam: Elsevier.

Liberman, A. M., & Mattingly, I. G. (1989). A specialization for speech perception. *Science, 243,* 489–494.

Liberman, I. Y., & Liberman, A. M. (1992). Whole language versus code emphasis: Underlying assumptions and their implications for reading instruction. In P. B. Gough, L. C. Ehri, & R. Treiman (Eds.), *Reading acquisition* (pp. 343–366). Hillsdale, NJ: Erlbaum.

Light, L. L. (1991). Memory and aging: Four hypotheses in search of data. *Annual Review of Psychology, 42,* 333–376.

Light, L. L. (1992). The organization of memory in old age. In F. I. M. Craik & T. A. Salthouse (Eds.), *The handbook of aging and cognition* (pp. 111–165). Hillsdale, NJ: Erlbaum.

Light, L. L., & Albertson, S. A. (1989). Direct and indirect tests of memory for category exemplars in young and older adults. *Psychology and Aging, 4,* 487–492.

Light, L. L., & La Voie, D. (1993). Direct and indirect measures of memory in old age. In P. Graf & M. E. J. Masson (Eds.), *Implicit memory: New directions in cognition, development, and neuropsychology* (pp. 207–230). Hillsdale, NJ: Erlbaum.

Light, L. L., La Voie, D., & Kennison, R. (1995). Repetition priming of nonwords in young and older adults. *Journal of Experimental Psychology: Learning, Memory, and Cognition, 21,* 327–346.

Lima, S. D., Hale, S., & Myerson, J. (1991). How general is general slowing? Evidence from the lexical domain. *Psychology and Aging, 6,* 416–425.

Linde, C., & Labov, W. (1975). Spatial networks as a site for the study of language and thought. *Language, 51,* 924–939.

Lindsay, D. S. (1990). Misleading suggestions can impair eyewitnesses' ability to remember event details. *Journal of Experimental Psychology: Learning, Memory, and Cognition, 16,* 1077–1083.

Lindsay, D. S., & Read, J. D. (1994). Psychotherapy and memories of childhood sexual abuse: A cognitive perspective. *Applied Cognitive Psychology, 8,* 281–338.

List, J. A. (1986). Age and schematic differences in the reliability of eyewitness testimony. *Developmental Psychology, 22,* 50–57.

Lively, S. E., Pisoni, D. B., & Goldinger, S. D. (1994). Spoken word recognition: Research and theory. In M. A. Gernsbacher (Ed.), *Handbook of psycholinguistics* (pp. 265–301). San Diego, CA: Academic Press.

Locke, J. L. (1994). Phases in the child's development of language. *American Scientist, 82,* 436–445.

Lockhart, R. S. (1989). The role of theory in understanding implicit memory. In S. Lewandowsky, J. C. Dunn, & K. Kirsner (Eds.), *Implicit memory: Theoretical issues* (pp. 3–13). Hillsdale, NJ: Erlbaum.

Lockhart, R. S., & Craik, F. I. M. (1990). Levels of Processing: A retrospective commentary on a framework for memory research. *Canadian Journal of Psychology, 44,* 87–112.

Loftus, E. F. (1992). When a lie becomes memory's truth: Memory distortion after exposure to misinformation. *Current Directions in Psychological Science, 1,* 121–123.

Loftus, E. F. (1993a). The reality of repressed memories. *American Psychologist, 48,* 518–537.

Loftus, E. F. (1993b). Desperately seeking memories of the first few years of childhood: The reality of early memories. *Journal of Experimental Psychology: General, 122,* 274–277.

Loftus, E. F., Donders, K., Hoffman, H. G., & Schooler, J. W. (1989). Creating new memories that are quickly accessed and confidently held. *Memory & Cognition, 17,* 607–616.

Loftus, E. F., & Hoffman, H. G. (1989). Misinformation and memory: The creation of new memories. *Journal of Experimental Psychology: General, 118,* 100–104.

Loftus, E. F., & Ketcham, K. (1991). *Witness for the defense.* New York: St. Martin's Press.

Loftus, E. F., & Ketcham, K. (1994). *The myth of repressed memory.* New York: St. Martin's Press.

Loftus, E. F., & Klinger, M. R. (1992). Is the unconscious smart or dumb? *American Psychologist, 47,* 761–765.

Loftus, E. F., Miller, D. G., & Burns, H. J. (1978). Semantic integration of verbal information into visual memory. *Journal of Experimental Psychology: Human Learning and Memory, 4,* 19–31.

Loftus, G. R. (1985). On worthwhile icons: Reply to DiLollo and Haber. *Journal of Experimental Psychology: Human Perception and Performance, 11,* 384–388.

Loftus, G. R., Duncan, J., & Gehrig, P. (1992). On the time course of perceptual information that results from a brief visual presentation. *Journal of Experimental Psychology: Human Perception and Performance, 18,* 530–549.

Logie, R. H. (1995). *Visuo-spatial working memory.* Hove, Great Britain: Erlbaum.

Logie, R. H., Gilhooly, K. J., & Wynn, V. (1994). Counting on working memory in arithmetic problem solving. *Memory & Cognition, 22,* 395–410.

Long, G. M. (1980). Iconic memory: A review and critique of the study of short-term visual storage. *Psychological Bulletin, 88,* 785–820.

Long, G. M., & Beaton, R. J. (1982). The case for peripheral persistence: Effects of target and background luminance on a partial-report task. *Journal of Experimental Psychology: Human Perception and Performance, 8,* 383–391.

Lorch, R. F., Jr., Klusewitz, M. A., & Lorch, E. P. (1995). Distinctions among reading situations. In R. F. Lorch, Jr. & E. J. O'Brien (Eds.), *Sources of coherence in reading* (pp. 375–398). Hillsdale, NJ: Erlbaum.

Lorch, R. F., Jr., & O'Brien, E. J. (Eds.). (1995). *Sources of coherence in reading.* Hillsdale, NJ: Erlbaum.

Lord, C. G., Desforges, D. M., Fein, S., Pugh, M. A., & Lepper, M. R. (1994). Typicality effects in attitudes toward social policies: A concept-mapping approach. *Journal of Personality and Social Psychology, 66,* 658–673.

Lovelace, E. A. (1984). Metamemory: Monitoring future recallability during study. *Journal of*

Experimental Psychology: Learning, Memory, and Cognition, 10, 756–766.

Lovelace, E. A. (Ed.). (1990a). *Aging and cognition: Mental processes, self-awareness and interventions.* Amsterdam: North-Holland.

Lovelace, E. A. (1990b). Aging and metacognitions concerning memory function. In E. A. Lovelace (Ed.), *Aging and cognition: Mental processes, self-awareness and interventions* (pp. 157–188). Amsterdam: Elsevier.

Lovelace, E. A. (1996). *Personal communication.*

Lovelace, E. A., & Coon, V. E. (1991). Aging and word finding: Reverse vocabulary and Cloze tests. *Bulletin of the Psychonomic Society, 29,* 33–35.

Lovelace, E. A., & Marsh, G. R. (1985). Prediction and evaluation of memory performance by young and old adults. *Journal of Gerontology, 40,* 192–197.

Lovelace, E. A., & Twohig, P. T. (1990). Healthy older adults' perceptions of their memory functioning and use of mnemonics. *Bulletin of the Psychonomic Society, 28,* 115–118.

Lowe, R. K. (1993). Constructing a mental representation from an abstract technical diagram. *Learning and Instruction, 3,* 157–179.

Lu, A. L., Williamson, S. J., & Kaufman, L. (1992). Behavioral lifetime of human auditory sensory memory predicted by physiological measures. *Science, 258,* 1668–1670.

Luchins, A. S. (1942). Mechanization in problem solving. *Psychological Monographs, 54* (Whole No. 248).

Luger, G. F. (1994). *Cognitive science: The science of intelligent systems.* San Diego, CA: Academic Press.

Lupker, S. J. (1990). Information processing: A reminder of past glories [Review of *Experimental psychology: An information processing approach*]. *Contemporary Psychology, 35,* 1140–1142.

Lutz, J., Means, L. W., & Long, T. E. (1994). Where did I park? A naturalistic study of spatial memory. *Applied Cognitive Psychology, 8,* 439–451.

MacDonald, M. C., Just, M. A., & Carpenter, C. M. (1992). Working memory constraints on the processing of syntactic ambiguity. *Cognitive Psychology, 24,* 56–98.

Macfarlane, A. (1977). *The psychology of childbirth.* Cambridge, MA: Harvard University Press.

MacLeod, C., & Campbell, L. (1992). Memory accessibility and probability judgments: An experimental evaluation of the availability heuristic. *Journal of Personality and Social Psychology, 63,* 890–902.

MacLeod, C., & Donnellan, A. M. (1993). Individual differences in anxiety and the restriction of working memory capacity. *Personality and Individual Differences, 15,* 163–173.

MacLeod, C. M. (1991). Half a century of research on the Stroop effect: An integrative review. *Psychological Bulletin, 109,* 163–203.

MacLeod, C. M., & Bassili, J. N. (1989). Are implicit and explicit tests differentially sensitive to item-specific vs. relational information? In S. Lewandowsky, J. C. Dunn, & K. Kirsner (Eds.), *Implicit memory: Theoretical issues* (pp. 159–172). Hillsdale, NJ: Erlbaum.

Madigan, S., & O'Hara, R. (1992). Short-term memory at the turn of the century: Mary Whiton Calkins's memory research. *American Psychologist, 47,* 170–174.

Maier, N. R. F. (1931). Reasoning in humans: II. The solution of a problem and its appearance in consciousness. *Journal of Comparative Psychology, 12,* 181–194.

Maki, R. H., & Berry, S. L. (1984). Metacomprehension of text material. *Journal of Experimental Psychology: Learning, Memory, and Cognition, 10,* 663–679.

Maki, R. H., Jonas, D., & Kallod, M. (1994). The relationship between comprehension and metacomprehension ability. *Psychonomic Bulletin & Review, 1,* 126–129.

Maki, R. H., & Serra, M. (1992). The basis of test prediction for text material. *Journal of Experimental Psychology: Learning, Memory, and Cognition, 18,* 116–126.

Malt, B. C. (1990). Features and beliefs in the mental representation of categories. *Journal of Memory and Language, 29,* 289–315.

Malt, B. C., & Smith, E. E. (1984). Correlated properties in natural categories. *Journal of Verbal Learning and Verbal Behavior, 23,* 250–269.

Mandler, G. (1985). *Cognitive psychology: An essay in cognitive science.* Hillsdale, NJ: Erlbaum.

Mandler, J. M. (1990). A new perspective on cognitive development in infancy. *American Scientist, 78,* 236–243.

Mandler, J. M. (1996). Development of categorization: Perceptual and conceptual categories. In G.

Bremner, A. Slater, & G. Butterworth (Eds.), *Infant development: Recent advances,* in press.

Mandler, J. M., & McDonough, L. (1993). Concept formation in infancy. *Cognitive Development, 8,* 291–318.

Mandler, J. M., & McDonough, L. (1995). Long-term recall of event sequences in infancy. *Journal of Experimental Child Psychology, 59,* 457–474.

Manis, M., Shedler, J., Jonides, J., & Nelson, T. E. (1993). Availability heuristic in judgments of set size and frequency of occurrence. *Journal of Personality and Social Psychology, 65,* 448–457.

Mannion, K. (1981). Psychology and the lesbian: A critical review of the research. In S. Cox (Ed.), *Female psychology* (pp. 256–274). New York: St. Martin's Press.

Mäntysalo, S., & Näätänen, R. (1987). The duration of a neuronal trace of an auditory stimulus as indicated by event-related potentials. *Biological Psychology, 24,* 183–195.

Maratsos, M., & Matheny, L. (1994). Language specificity and elasticity: Brain and clinical syndrome studies. *Annual Review of Psychology, 45,* 487–516.

Margolis, E. (1994). A reassessment of the shift from the classical theory of concepts to prototype theory. *Cognition, 51,* 73–89.

Markman, E. M. (1990). Constraints children place on word meanings. *Cognitive Science, 14,* 57–77.

Markovits, H., & Nantel, G. (1989). The belief-bias effect in the production and evaluation of logical conclusions. *Memory & Cognition, 17,* 11–17.

Markovits, H., & Savary, F. (1992). Pragmatic schemas and the selection task: To reason or not to reason. *The Quarterly Journal of Experimental Psychology, 45A,* 133–148.

Marr, D. (1982). *Vision.* San Francisco: Freeman.

Marshall, J. C. (1977). Minds, machines and metaphors. *Social Studies of Science, 7,* 475–488.

Marslen-Wilson, W. D. (1987). Functional parallelism in spoken word recognition. *Cognition, 25,* 71–102.

Marslen-Wilson, W. D., Tyler, L. K., & Koster, C. (1993). Integrative processes in utterance resolution. *Journal of Memory and Language, 32,* 647–666.

Marslen-Wilson, W. D., Tyler, L. K., Waksler, R., & Older, L. (1994). Morphology and meaning in the English mental lexicon. *Psychological Review, 101,* 3–33.

Martin, E. (1967). *Personal communication.*

Martin, J. H. (1992). Computer understanding of contentional metaphoric language. *Cognitive Science, 16,* 233–170.

Martin, R. C. (1993). Short-term memory and sentence processing: Evidence from neuropsychology. *Memory & Cognition, 21,* 176–183.

Martindale, C. (1991). *Cognitive psychology: A neural-network approach.* Pacific Grove, CA: Brooks/Cole.

Mason, M. (1978). From print to sound in mature readers as a function of reader ability and two forms of orthographic regularity. *Memory & Cognition, 6,* 568–581.

Massaro, D. W. (1987). *Speech perception by ear and eye: A paradigm for psychological inquiry.* Hillsdale, NJ: Erlbaum.

Massaro, D. W. (1989). Testing between the TRACE model and the fuzzy logical model of speech perception. *Cognitive Psychology, 21,* 398–421.

Massaro, D. W. (1994). A pattern recognition account of decision making. *Memory & Cognition, 22,* 616–627.

Massaro, D. W., & Cohen, M. M. (1990). Perception of synthesized audible and visible speech. *Psychological Science, 1,* 55–63.

Massaro, D. W., & Cohen, M. M. (1995). Perceiving talking faces. *Current Directions in Psychological Science, 4,* 104–109.

Massaro, D. W., Cohen, M. M., & Smeele, P. M. T. (1995). Cross-linguistic comparisons in the integration of visual and auditory speech. *Memory & Cognition, 23,* 113–131.

Massaro, D. W., & Cowan, N. (1993). Information processing models: Microscopes of the mind. *Annual Review of Psychology, 44,* 383–425.

Massaro, D. W., & Oden, G. C. (1995). Independence of lexical context and phonological information in speech perception. *Journal of Experimental Psychology: Learning, Memory, and Cognition, 21,* 1053–1064.

Masson, M. E. J. (1995). A distributed memory model of semantic priming. *Journal of Experimental Psychology: Learning, Memory, and Cognition, 21,* 3–23.

Matlin, M. (1993). *"But I thought I was going to ace that test!": Metacognition and the college student.* Paper presented at the meeting of the Southeastern Psychological Association, Atlanta, GA.

Matlin, M. W. (1994). *Cognition* (3rd ed.). Fort Worth, TX: Harcourt Brace.

Matlin, M. W. (1996). *The psychology of women* (3rd ed.). Fort Worth, TX: Harcourt Brace.

Matlin, M. W., & Foley, H. J. (1997). *Sensation and perception* (4th ed.). Boston: Allyn & Bacon.

Matlin, M. W., & Stang, D. J. (1978). *The Pollyanna Principle: Selectivity in language, memory, and thought.* Cambridge, MA: Schenkman.

Matlin, M. W., Stang, D. J., Gawron, V. J., Freedman, A., & Derby, P. L. (1979). Evaluative meaning as a determinant of spew position. *Journal of General Psychology, 100,* 3–11.

Mattingly, I. G., & Liberman, A. M. (1988). Specialized perceiving systems for speech and other biologically significant sounds. In G. M. Edelman, W. E. Gall, & W. M. Cowan (Eds.), *Auditory function* (pp. 775–793). New York: Wiley.

Mayer, J. D. (1986). How mood influences cognition. In N. E. Sharkey (Ed.), *Advances in cognitive science* (pp. 290–314). Chichester, West Sussex: Ellis Horwood Limited.

Mayer, J. D., & Bower, G. H. (1986). Learning and memory for personality prototypes. *Journal of Personality and Social Psychology, 51,* 473–492.

Mayer, R. (1992). To win and lose: Linguistic aspects of prospect theory. *Language and Cognitive Processes, 7,* 23–66.

Mayer, R. E. (1982). The psychology of mathematical problem solving. In F. K. Lester & J. Garofalo (Eds.), *Mathematical problem solving: Issues in research* (pp. 1–13). Philadelphia, PA: The Franklin Institute.

Mayer, R. E. (1983). *Thinking, problem solving, cognition.* New York: Freeman.

Mayer, R. E. (1985). Implications of cognitive psychology for instruction in mathematical problem solving. In E. A. Silver (Ed.), *Teaching and learning mathematical problem solving* (pp. 123–138). Hillsdale, NJ: Erlbaum.

Mayer, R. E. (1989). Human nonadversary problem solving. In K. J. Gilhooly (Ed.), *Human and machine problem solving* (pp. 39–81). New York: Plenum.

Mazzoni, G., & Cornoldi, C. (1993). Strategies in study time allocation: Why is study time sometimes not effective? *Journal of Experimental Psychology: General, 122,* 47–60.

Mazzoni, G., & Nelson, T. O. (1995). Judgments of learning are affected by the kind of encoding in ways that cannot be attributed to the level of recall. *Journal of Experimental Psychology: Learning, Memory, and Cognition, 21,* 1–12.

McClelland, A. G. R., & Bolger, F. (1994). The calibration of subjective probabilities: Theories and models 1980–94. In G. Wright & P. Ayton (Eds.), *Subjective probability* (pp. 453–482). Chichester, England: John Wiley & Sons.

McClelland, J. L. (1981). Retrieving general and specific knowledge from stored knowledge of specifics. *Proceedings of the Third Annual Conference of the Cognitive Science Society, 170–172.*

McClelland, J. L. (1988). Connectionist models and psychological evidence. *Journal of Memory and Language, 27,* 107–123.

McClelland, J. L., & Rumelhart, D. E. (1981). An interactive activation model of context effects in letter perception: Part 1: An account of basic findings. *Psychological Review, 88,* 375–407.

McClelland, J. L., Rumelhart, D. E., & Hinton, G. E. (1986). The appeal of parallel distributed processing. In D. E. Rumelhart, J. L. McClelland, and the PDP Research Group (Eds.), *Parallel distributed processing* (Vol. 1, pp. 3–44). Cambridge, MA: MIT Press.

McClelland, J. L., Rumelhart, D. E., & the PDP Research Group. (1986). *Parallel distributed processing (Vol. 2).* Cambridge, MA: MIT Press.

McCloskey, M. (1992). Special versus ordinary memory mechanisms in the genesis of flashbulb memories. In E. Winograd & U. Neisser (Eds.), *Affect and accuracy in recall: Studies of "flashbulb" memories* (pp. 227–235). New York: Cambridge University Press.

McCloskey, M., & Cohen, N. J. (1989). Catastrophic interference in connectionist networks: The sequential learning problem. *The Psychology of Learning and Motivation, 24,* 109–165.

McCloskey, M., Wible, C. G., & Cohen, N. J. (1988). Is there a special flashbulb-memory mechanism? *Journal of Experimental Psychology: General, 11,* 171–181.

McConkie, G. W., & Zóla, D. (1984). Eye movement control during reading: The effect of word units. In W. Prinz & A. F. Sanders (Eds.), *Cognition and motor processes* (pp. 63–74). Berlin: Springer-Verlag.

McDaniel, M. A., Einstein, G. O., DeLosh, E. L., May, C. P., & Brady, P. (1995). The bizarreness effect: It's not surprising, it's complex. *Journal of Experimental Psychology: Learning, Memory, and Cognition, 21,* 422–435.

McDaniel, M. A., & Pressley, M. (Eds.) (1987). *Imagery and related mnemonic processes.* New York: Springer-Verlag.

McDaniel, M. A., Pressley, M., & Dunay, P. K. (1987). Long-term retention of vocabulary after keyword and context learning. *Journal of Educational Psychology, 79,* 87–89.

McDonough, L., & Mandler, J. M. (1994). Very long-term recall in infants: Infantile amnesia reconsidered. *Memory, 2,* 339–352.

McKeachie, W. J., Pintrich, P. R., & Lin, Y. (1985). Teaching learning strategies. *Educational Psychology, 20,* 153–160.

McKelvie, S. J. (1990). Einstellung: Luchins' effect lives on. *Journal of Social Behavior and Personality, 5,* 105–121.

McKelvie, S. J., Sano, E. K., & Stout, D. (1994). Effects of colored separate and interactive pictures on cued recall. *Journal of General Psychology, 12,* 241–251.

McKitrick, L. A., Camp, C. J., & Black, F. W. (1992). Prospective memory intervention in Alzheimer's disease. *Journal of Gerontology: Psychological Sciences, 47,* P337–P343.

McKoon, G., & Ratcliff, R. (1986). Automatic activation of episodic information in a semantic memory task. *Journal of Experimental Psychology: Learning, Memory, and Cognition, 12,* 108–115.

McKoon, G., & Ratcliff, R. (1992). Inference during reading. *Psychological Review, 99,* 440–466.

McKoon, G., Ratcliff, R., & Dell, G. S. (1986). A critical evaluation of the semantic-episodic distinction. *Journal of Experimental Psychology: Learning, Memory, and Cognition, 12,* 295–306.

McLaughlin, M. L. (1984). *How talk is organized.* Beverly Hills, CA: Sage.

McNamara, T. P., Hardy, J. K., & Hirtle, S. C. (1989). Subjective hierarchies in spatial memory. *Journal of Experimental Psychology: Learning, Memory, and Cognition, 15,* 211–217.

McNamara, T. P., Ratcliff, R., & McKoon, G. (1984). The mental representation of knowledge acquired from maps. *Journal of Experimental Psychology: Learning, Memory, and Cognition, 10,* 723–732.

McNeil, B. J., Pauker, S. G., & Tversky, A. (1988). On the framing of medical decisions. In D. E. Bell, H. Raiffa, & A. Tversky (Eds.), *Decision making: Descriptive, normative, and prescriptive interactions* (pp. 562–568). New York: Cambridge University Press.

McNeil, B. J., Pauker, S. G., Sox, H. C., & Tversky, A. (1982). On the elicitation of preferences for alternative therapies. *New England Journal of Medicine, 306,* 1259–1262.

McTear, M. F. (1985). *Children's conversations.* Oxford, England: Basil Blackwell.

McTear, M. F. (1988). *Understanding cognitive science.* Chichester, England: Ellis Horwood.

Meacham, J. A. (1982). A note on remembering to execute planned actions. *Journal of Applied Developmental Psychology, 3,* 121–133.

Meacham, J. A., & Singer, J. (1977). Incentive in prospective remembering. *Journal of Psychology, 97,* 191–197.

Medin, D. L., & Ahn, W.-K. (1992). Concepts and categories. In L. R. Squire (Ed.), *Encyclopedia of learning and memory* (pp. 116–119). New York: Macmillan.

Mednick, S. A., & Mednick, M. T. (1967). *Examiner's manual, Remote Associates Test.* Boston: Houghton Mifflin.

Mehler, J. (1963). Some effects of grammatical transformation on the recall of English sentences. *Journal of Verbal Learning and Verbal Behavior, 2,* 346–351.

Mellers, B. A., & Baron, J. (Eds.). (1993). *Psychological perspectives on justice: Theory and applications.* New York: Cambridge University Press.

Melton, A. W. (1963). Implications of short-term memory for a general theory of memory. *Journal of Verbal Learning and Verbal Behavior, 2,* 1–21.

Menard, M. T., Kosslyn, S. M., Thompson, W. L., Alpert, N. M., & Rauch, S. L. (1996). Encoding words and pictures: A positron emission tomography study. *Neuropsychologia, 34,* 185–194.

Menyuk, P., Liebergott, J. W., & Schultz, M. C. (1995). *Early language development in full-term and premature infants.* Hillsdale, NJ: Erlbaum.

Merck, Sharp, & Dome. (1980). *Medical mnemonics handbook.* West Point, PA: Merck, Sharp, & Dome.

Mervis, C. B., Catlin, J., & Rosch, E. (1976). Relationships among goodness-of-example, category norms, and word frequency. *Bulletin of the Psychonomic Society, 7,* 283–284.

Metcalfe, J. (1986). Premonitions of insight predict impending error. *Journal of Experimental Psychology: Learning, Memory, and Cognition, 12,* 623–634.

Metcalfe, J., & Shimamura, A. P. (Eds.). (1994). *Metacognition: Knowing about knowing.* Cambridge, MA: MIT Press.

Metcalfe, J., & Wiebe, D. (1987). Intuition in insight and noninsight problem solving. *Memory & Cognition, 15,* 238–246.

Meyer, A. S., & Bock, K. (1992). The tip-of-the-tongue phenomenon: Blocking or partial activation? *Memory & Cognition, 20,* 715–726.

Miller, G. A. (1956). The magical number seven, plus or minus two: Some limits on our capacity for processing information. *Psychological Review, 63,* 81–97.

Miller, G. A. (1962). *Psychology: The science of mental life.* New York: Harper & Row.

Miller, G. A. (1967). The psycholinguists. In G. A. Miller (Ed.), *The psychology of communication* (pp. 70–92). London: Penguin Books.

Miller, G. A. (1979). *A very personal history.* Address to Cognitive Science Workshop. Massachusetts Institute of Technology, Cambridge, MA.

Miller, G. A. (1981). *Language and speech.* San Francisco: Freeman.

Miller, J. L. (1990). Speech perception. In D. N. Osherson & H. Lasnik (Eds.), *Language: An invitation to cognitive science* (pp. 69–93). Cambridge, MA: MIT Press.

Miller, J. L., & Eimas, P. D. (1983). Studies on the categorization of speech by infants. *Cognition, 13,* 135–166.

Miller, J. L., & Eimas, P. D. (Eds.). (1995a). *Speech, language, and communication.* San Diego, CA: Academic Press.

Miller, J. L., & Eimas, P. D. (1995b). Speech perception: From signal to word. *Annual Review of Psychology, 46,* 467–492.

Miller, J. R., & Kintsch, W. (1980). Readability and recall of short prose passages. A theoretical analysis. *Journal of Experimental Psychology: Human Learning and Memory, 6,* 335–354.

Miller, L. C., Lechner, R. E., & Rugs, D. (1985). Development of conversational responsiveness: Preschoolers' use of responsive listener cues and relevant comments. *Developmental Psychology, 21,* 473–480.

Millis, K. K., & Cohen, R. (1994). Spatial representations and updating situation models. *Reading Research Quarterly, 29,* 369–380.

Millis, K. K., & Graesser, A. C. (1994). The time-course of constructing knowledge-based inferences for scientific texts. *Journal of Memory and Language, 33,* 583–599.

Mills, C. J. (1983). Sex-typing and self-schemata effects on memory and response latency. *Journal of Personality and Social Psychology, 45,* 163–172.

Milner, B. (1966). Amnesia following operation on the temporal lobes. In C. W. M. Whitty & O. L. Zangwill (Eds.), *Amnesia following operation on the temporal lobes* (pp. 109–133). London: Butterworth.

Mineka, S., & Sutton, S. K. (1992). Cognitive biases and the emotional disorders. *Psychological Science, 3,* 65–69.

Miner, A. C., & Reder, L. M. (1994). A new look at feeling of knowing: Its metacognitive role in regulating question answering. In J. Metcalfe & A. P. Shimamura (Eds.), *Metacognition: Knowing about knowing* (pp. 47–70). Cambridge, MA: MIT Press.

Mitchell, D. B. (1991). Implicit memory, explicit theories [Review of *Implicit memory: Theoretical issues*]. *Contemporary Psychology, 36,* 1060–1061.

Miyake, A., Just, M. A., & Carpenter, P. A. (1994). Working memory constraints on the resolution of lexical ambiguity: Maintaining multiple interpretations in neutral contexts. *Journal of Memory and Language, 33,* 175–202.

Moar, I., & Bower, G. H. (1983). Inconsistency in spatial knowledge. *Memory & Cognition, 11,* 107–113.

Moely, B. E., Olson, F. A., Halwes, T. G., & Flavell, J. H. (1969). Production deficiency in young children's clustered recall. *Developmental Psychology, 1,* 26–34.

Moody, D. B., Stebbins, W. C., & May, B. J. (1990). Auditory perception of communication signals by Japanese monkeys. In W. C. Stebbins & M. A. Berkley (Eds.), *Comparative perception: Complex signals* (pp. 311–343). New York: Wiley.

Moravcsik, J. E., & Kintsch, W. (1993). Writing quality, reading skills, and domain knowledge as factors in text comprehension. *Canadian Journal of Experimental Psychology, 47,* 360–374.

Moray, N. (1959). Attention in dichotic listening: Affective cues and the influence of instructions. *Quarterly Journal of Experimental Psychology, 11,* 56–60.

Moray, N. (1993). Designing for attention. In A. Baddeley & L. Weiskrantz (Eds.), *Attention: Selection, awareness, and control* (pp. 111–134). Oxford, Great Britain: Clarendon Press.

Morris, M. W., & Murphy, G. L. (1990). Converging operations on a basic level in event taxonomies. *Memory & Cognition, 18,* 407–418.

Morris, N., & Jones, D. M. (1990). Memory updating in working memory: The role of the central executive. *British Journal of Psychology, 81,* 111–121.

Morris, P. E. (1978). Sense and nonsense in traditional mnemonics. In M. M. Gruneberg, P. E. Morris, & R. N. Sykes (Eds.), *Practical aspects of memory* (pp. 155–163). London: Academic Press.

Morris, P. E. (1988). Memory research: Past mistakes and future prospects. In G. Claxton (Ed.), *Growth points in cognition* (pp. 91–110). London: Routledge.

Morris, P. E. (1992). Prospective memory: Remembering to do things. In M. Gruneberg & P. Morris (Eds.), *Aspects of memory* (2nd ed., Vol. 1, pp. 196–222). New York: Routledge.

Moscovitch, M., & Craik, F. I. M. (1976). Depth of processing, retrieval cues, and uniqueness of encoding as factors in recall. *Journal of Verbal Learning and Verbal Behavior, 15,* 447–458.

Mountcastle, V. B. (1979). An organizing principle for cerebral function: The unit module and the distributed system. In F. O. Schmitt (Ed.), *The neurosciences: Fourth study program.* Cambridge, MA: The MIT Press.

Moyer, R. S. (1973). Comparing objects in memory: Evidence suggesting an internal psychophysics. *Perception & Psychophysics, 13,* 180–184.

Moyer, R. S., & Dumais, S. T. (1978). Mental comparisons. In G. H. Bower (Ed.), *The psychology of learning and motivation* (Vol. 12, pp. 117–156). New York: Academic Press.

Müller, P. U., Cavegn, D., d'Ydewalle, G., & Groner, R. (1993). A comparison of a new limbus tracker, corneal reflection technique, Purkinje eye tracking and electro-oculography. In G. d'Ydewalle & J. Van Rensbergen (Eds.), *Perception and cognition* (pp. 393–401). Amsterdam: North Holland.

Murphy, G. L., & Shapiro, A. M. (1994). Forgetting of verbatim information in discourse. *Memory & Cognition, 22,* 85–94.

Murphy, G. L., & Smith, E. E. (1982). Basic level superiority in picture categorization. *Journal of Verbal Learning and Verbal Behavior, 21,* 1–20.

Murray, B. (1995, April). Merits of reading techniques debated. *APA Monitor,* p. 44.

Muter, P. (1980). Very rapid forgetting. *Memory & Cognition, 8,* 174–179.

Myers, N. A., & Perlmutter, M. (1978). Memory in the years from two to five. In P. A. Ornstein (Ed.), *Memory development in children* (pp. 191–218). Hillsdale, NJ: Erlbaum.

Näätänen, R. (1982). Processing negativity: An evoked potential reflection of selective attention. *Psychological Bulletin, 92,* 605–640.

Näätänen, R. (1985). Selective attention and stimulus processing: Reflections in event-related potentials, magnetoencephalogram, and regional cerebral blood flow. In M. I. Posner & O. S. Marin (Eds.), *Attention and performance XI* (pp. 355–373). Hillsdale, NJ: Erlbaum.

Näätänen, R. (1986). Neurophysiological basis of the echoic memory as suggested by event-related potentials and magnetoencephalogram. In F. Klix & H. Hagendorf (Eds.), *Human memory and cognitive capabilities* (pp. 615–628). Amsterdam: Elsevier.

Nadel, L. (1992). Multiple memory systems: What and why. *Journal of Cognitive Neuroscience, 4,* 179–188.

Nakatani, C. H., & Hirschberg, J. (1994). A corpus-based study of repair cues in spontaneous speech. *Journal of the Acoustical Society of America, 95,* 1603–1616.

Nasby, W. (1994). Moderators of mood-congruent encoding: Self-/other-reference and affirmative/nonaffirmative judgement. *Cognition and Emotion, 8,* 259–278.

Natsoulas, T. (1993a). What is wrong with appendage theory of consciousness. *Philosophical Psychology, 6,* 137–154.

Natsoulas, T. (1993b). The importance of being conscious. *The Journal of Mind and Behavior, 14,* 317–340.

Naveh-Benjamin, M., & Ayres, T. J. (1986). Digit span, reading rate, and linguistic relativity. *Quarterly Journal of Experimental Psychology, 38,* 739–751.

Neale, M. A., & Northcraft, G. B. (1986). Experts, amateurs, and refrigerators: Comparing expert and amateur negotiators in a novel task. *Organizational Behavior and Human Decision Processes, 38,* 305–317.

Needham, D. R., & Begg, I. M. (1991). Problem-oriented training promotes spontaneous analogical transfer: Memory-oriented training promotes memory for training. *Memory & Cognition, 19,* 543–557.

Neisser, U. (1963). The multiplicity of thought. *British Journal of Psychology, 54*, 1–14.

Neisser, U. (1967). *Cognitive psychology.* New York: Appleton.

Neisser, U. (1987). From direct perception to conceptual structure. In U. Neisser (Ed.), *Concepts and conceptual development* (pp. 11–24). New York: Cambridge University Press.

Neisser, U. (1988). What is ordinary memory the memory of? In U. Neisser & E. Winograd (Eds.), *Remembering reconsidered: Ecological and traditional approaches to the study of memory* (pp. 356–373). New York: Cambridge University Press.

Neisser, U. (1994). Multiple systems: A new approach to cognitive theory. *European Journal of Cognitive Psychology, 6*, 225–241.

Neisser, U., & Harsch, N. (1992). Phantom flashbulbs: False recollections of hearing the news about *Challenger.* In E. Winograd & U. Neisser (Eds.), *Affect and accuracy in recall: Studies of "flashbulb" memories* (pp. 9–31). New York: Cambridge University Press.

Nelson, K. (1985). *Making sense: The acquisition of shared meaning.* Orlando, FL: Academic Press.

Nelson, K. (1986). *Event knowledge: Structure and function in development.* Hillsdale, NJ: Erlbaum.

Nelson, T. O. (1977). Repetition and depth of processing. *Journal of Verbal Learning and Verbal Behavior, 16*, 151–171.

Nelson, T. O. (1992a). Metamemory. In L. R. Squire (Ed.), *Encyclopedia of learning and memory* (pp. 412–415). New York: Macmillan.

Nelson, T. O. (Ed.). (1992b). *Metacognition: Core readings.* Boston: Allyn & Bacon.

Nelson, T. O. (1996). Consciousness and metacognition. *American Psychologist, 51*, 102–116.

Nelson, T. O., & Dunlosky, J. (1991). When people's judgments of learning (JOLs) are extremely accurate at predicting subsequent recall: The "Delayed-JOL effect." *Psychological Science, 2*, 267–270.

Nelson, T. O., Dunlosky, J., Graf, A., & Narens, L. (1994). Utilization of metacognitive judgments in the allocation of study during multitrial learning. *Psychological Science, 5*, 207–213.

Nelson, T. O., & Leonesio, R. J. (1988). Allocation of self-paced study, time and the "labor-in-vain effect." *Journal of Experimental Psychology: Learning, Memory, and Cognition, 14*, 676–686.

Nelson, T. O., & Narens, L. (1994). Why investigate metacognition? In J. Metcalfe & A. P. Shimamura (Eds.), *Metacognition: Knowing about knowing* (pp. 1–25). Cambridge, MA: MIT Press.

Newell, A., & Simon, H. A. (1972). *Human problem solving.* Englewood Cliffs, NJ: Prentice-Hall.

Newman, J. E. (1994). Language representation and processing. In G. F. Luger (Ed.), *Cognitive science: The science of intelligent systems* (pp. 457–488). San Diego, CA: Academic Press.

Newstead, S. E., Pollard, P., Evans, J. St. B. T., & Allen, J. L. (1992). The source of belief bias effects in syllogistic reasoning. *Cognition, 45*, 257–284.

Ng, W. K., & Lindsay, R. C. L. (1994). Cross-race facial recognition: Failure of the contact hypothesis. *Journal of Cross-Cultural Psychology, 25*, 217–232.

Nickerson, R. S. (1990). William James on reasoning. *Psychological Science, 1*, 167–171.

Nickerson, R. S., Perkins, D. N., & Smith, E. E. (1985). *The teaching of thinking.* Hillsdale, NJ: Erlbaum.

Nilsson, L. G. (1992). Human learning and memory: A cognitive perspective. In M. R. Rosenzweig (Ed.), *International psychological science* (pp. 75–101). Washington, DC: American Psychological Association.

Nisbett, R. E. (Ed.). (1993). *Rules for reasoning.* Hillsdale, NJ: Erlbaum.

Nisbett, R. E., & Ross, L. (1980). *Human inference: Strategies and shortcomings of social judgment.* Englewood Cliffs, NJ: Prentice-Hall.

Nisbett, R. E., & Wilson, T. D. (1977). Telling more than we can know. Verbal reports on mental processes. *Psychological Review, 84*, 231–259.

Nist, S. L., & Mealey, D. L. (1991). Teacher-directed comprehension strategies. In R. F. Flippo & D. C. Caverly (Eds.), *Teaching reading and study strategies at the college level* (pp. 42–85). Newark, Delaware: International Reading Association.

Nobre, A. C., & McCarthy, G. (1994). Language-related ERPs: Scalp distributions and modulation by word type and semantic priming. *Journal of Cognitive Neuroscience, 6*, 233–255.

Noice, H. (1992). Elaborative memory strategies of professional actors. *Applied Cognitive Psychology, 6*, 417–427.

Noice, H. (1993). Effects of rote versus gist strategy on the verbatim retention of theatrical scripts. *Applied Cognitive Psychology, 7*, 75–84.

Noordman, L. G. M., Vonk, W., & Kempff, H. J. (1992). Causal inferences during the reading of expository texts. *Journal of Memory and Language, 31,* 573–590.

Norman, D. A. (1982). *Learning and memory.* San Francisco: W. H. Freeman.

Northcraft, G. B., & Neale, M. A. (1987). Experts, amateurs, and real estate: An anchoring-and-adjustment perspective on property pricing decisions. *Organizational Behavior and Human Decision Processes, 39,* 84–97.

Novick, L. R. (1988). Analogical transfer, problem similarity, and expertise. *Journal of Experimental Psychology: Learning, Memory, and Cognition, 14,* 510–520.

Novick, L. R. (1992). The role of expertise in solving arithmetic and algebra word problems by analogy. In J. I. D. Campbell (Ed.), *The nature and origins of mathematical skills* (pp. 155–188). Amsterdam: North-Holland.

Novick, L. R., & Coté, N. (1992). The nature of expertise in anagram solution. *Proceedings of the Fourteenth Annual Conference of the Cognitive Science Society* (pp. 450–455). Hillsdale, NJ: Erlbaum.

Oakhill, J. V., & Johnson-Laird, P. N. (1985). Rationality, memory, and the search for counterexamples. *Cognition, 20,* 79–94.

Oaksford, M., & Chater, N. (1994). A rational analysis of the selection task as optimal data selection. *Psychological Review, 101,* 608–631.

Obler, L. K., Fein, D., Nicholas, M., & Albert, M. L. (1991). Auditory comprehension and aging: Decline in syntactic processing. *Applied Psycholinguistics, 12,* 433–452.

Oliver, W. (1992). *Personal communication.*

Orasanu, J., & Connolly, T. (1993). The reinvention of decision making. In G. A. Klein, J. Orasanu, R. Calderwood, & C. E. Zsambok (Eds.), *Decision making in action: Models and Methods* (pp. 3–20). Norwood, NJ: Ablex.

Ormerod, T. C., Manktelow, K. I., & Jones, G. V. (1993). Reasoning with three types of conditional: Biases and mental models. *The Quarterly Journal of Experimental Psychology, 46A,* 653–677.

Ormrod, J. E., Ormrod, R. K., Wagner, E. D., & McCallin, R. C. (1988). Reconceptualizing map learning. *American Journal of Psychology, 101,* 425–433.

Osgood, C. E. (1953). *Method and theory in experimental psychology.* New York: Oxford University Press.

Ostergaard, A. L., & Jernigan, T. L. (1993). Are word priming and explicit memory mediated by different brain structures? In P. Graf & M. E. J. Masson (Eds.), *Implicit memory: New directions in cognition, development, and neuropsychology* (pp. 327–349). Hillsdale, NJ: Erlbaum.

Ostrom, T. M. (1994). Foreword. In R. S. Wyer, Jr. & T. K. Srull (Eds.), *Handbook of social cognition* (2nd ed., Vol. 1, pp. vii–xii). Hillsdale, NJ: Erlbaum.

O'Toole, A. J., Deffenbacher, K. A., Valentin, D., & Abdi, H. (1994). Structural aspects of face recognition and the other-race effects. *Memory & Cognition, 22,* 208–224.

Overheard. (1992, July 13). *Newsweek,* p. 15.

Owens, R. E., Jr. (1996). *Language development: An introduction* (4th ed.). Boston: Allyn & Bacon.

Paivio, A. (1978a). On exploring visual knowledge. In B. S. Randhawa and W. E. Coffman (Eds.), *Visual learning, thinking and communication* (pp. 113–132). New York: Academic Press.

Paivio, A. (1978b). Comparisons of mental clocks. *Journal of Experimental Psychology: Human Perception and Performance, 4,* 61–71.

Paivio, A. (1995). Imagery and memory. In M. S. Gazzaniga (Ed.), *The cognitive neurosciences* (pp. 977–986). Cambridge, MA: MIT Press.

Palmer, C. F., Jones, R. K., Hennessy, B. L., Unze, M. G., & Pick, A. D. (1989). How is a trumpet known? The "basic object level" concept and the perception of musical instruments. *American Journal of Psychology, 102,* 17–37.

Palmer, S. E. (1975a). Visual perception and world knowledge: Notes on a model of sensory-cognitive interaction. In D. A. Norman & D. E. Rumelhart (Eds.), *Explorations in cognition* (pp. 279–307). San Francisco: Freeman.

Palmer, S. E. (1975b). The effects of contextual scenes on the identification of objects. *Memory & Cognition, 3,* 519–526.

Palmer, S. E. (1987). PDP: A new paradigm for cognitive theory. [Review of *Parallel distributed processing: Explorations in the microstructure of cognition*]. *Contemporary Psychology, 32,* 925–928.

Palmere, M., Benton, S. L., Glover, J. A., & Ronning, R. (1983). Elaboration and recall of main ideas in prose. *Journal of Educational Psychology, 75,* 898–907.

Parkin, A. J. (1984). Levels of processing, context, and facilitation of pronunciation. *Acta Psychologica, 55,* 19–29.

Pastore, R. E., Li, X. F., & Layer, J. K. (1990). Categorical perception of nonspeech chirps and bleats. *Perception & Psychophysics, 48,* 151–156.

Patel, V. L., Kaufman, D. R., & Magder, S. A. (1996). The acquisition of medical expertise in complex dynamic environments. In K. A. Ericsson (Ed.), *The road to excellence: The acquisition of expert performance in the arts and sciences, sports and games.* Mahwah, NJ: Erlbaum.

Pauker, S. G., & Kopelman, R. I. (1992). Clinical problem-solving. *The New England Journal of Medicine, 326,* 40–43.

Paulos, J. A. (1989). *Innumeracy: Mathematical illiteracy and its consequences.* New York: Hill and Wang.

Paulsen, J. S. (1995). Implicit and explicit memory: Contributions from anesthesia [Review of the book *Memory and awareness in anesthesia*]. *Contemporary Psychology, 40,* 882–883.

Payne, D. G., & Wenger, M. J. (1992). Improving memory through practice. In D. J. Herrmann, H. Weingartner, A. Searleman, & C. McEvoy (Eds.), *Memory improvement: Implications for memory theory* (pp. 187–209). New York: Springer-Verlag.

Payne, J. W., Bettman, J. R., & Johnson, E. J. (1992). Behavioral decision research: A constructive processing perspective. *Annual Review of Psychology, 43,* 87–131.

Payne, J. W., Bettman, J. R., & Johnson, E. J. (1993). *The adaptive decision maker.* New York: Cambridge University Press.

Peal, E., & Lambert, W. E. (1962). The relation of bilingualism to intelligence. *Psychological Monographs, 546.*

Perfect, T. J., & Hanley, J. R. (1992). The tip-of-the-tongue phenomenon: Do experimenter-presented interlopers have any effect? *Cognition, 45,* 55–75.

Perfetti, C. A. (1993). Why inferences might be restricted. *Discourse Processes, 16,* 181–192.

Perfetti, C. A. (1994). Psycholinguistics and reading ability. In M. A. Gernsbacher (Ed.), *Handbook of psycholinguistics* (pp. 849–894). San Diego, CA: Academic Press.

Perfetti, C. A. (1996). *Reading: Universals and particulars across writing systems.* Paper presented at the convention of the Eastern Psychological Association, Philadelphia, PA.

Perfetti, C. A., & Bell, L. (1991). Phonemic activation during the first 40 ms. of word identification: Evidence from backward masking and priming. *Journal of Memory and Language, 30,* 473–486.

Perkins, D. N., Schwartz, S., & Simmons, R. (1991). A view from programming. In M. U. Smith (Ed.), *Toward a unified theory of problem solving* (pp. 45–67). Hillsdale, NJ: Erlbaum.

Perky, C. W. (1910). An experimental study of imagination. *American Journal of Psychology, 21,* 422–452.

Peters, D. P. (1987). The impact of naturally occurring stress on children's memory. In S. J. Ceci, M. P. Toglia, & D. F. Ross (Eds.), *Children's eyewitness memory* (pp. 122–141). New York: Springer-Verlag.

Petersen, S. E., Fox, P. T., Posner, M. I., Mintun, M., & Raichle, M. I. (1989). Positron emission tomographic studies of the processing of single words. *Journal of Cognitive Neuroscience, 1,* 153–170.

Peterson, L. R., & Peterson, M. (1959). Short-term retention of individual verbal items. *Journal of Experimental Psychology, 58,* 193–198.

Peterson, M. A., Kihlstrom, J. F., Rose, P. M., & Glisky, M. L. (1992). Mental images can be ambiguous: Reconstruals and reference-frame reversals. *Memory & Cognition, 20,* 107–123.

Peterson, S. A. (1985). Neurophysiology, cognition, and political thinking. *Political Psychology, 6,* 495–518.

Petitto, L., & Marentette, P. F. (1991). Babbling in the manual mode: Evidence for the ontogeny of language. *Science, 251,* 1493–1499.

Pezdek, K., & Prull, M. (1993). Fallacies in memory for conversations: Reflections on Clarence Thomas, Anita Hill, and the like. *Applied Cognitive Psychology, 7,* 299–310.

Phillips, W. D. (1995). *Personal communication.*

Piattelli-Palmarini, M. (1994). *Inevitable illusions: How the mistakes of reason rule our minds.* New York: Wiley.

Pillemer, D. B., Koff, E., Rhinehart, E. D., & Rierdan, J. (1987). Flashbulb memories of menarche and adult menstrual distress. *Journal of Adolescence, 10,* 187–199.

Pinker, S. (1984). Visual cognition: An introduction. *Cognition, 18,* 1–63.

Pinker, S. (1985). Visual cognition: An introduction. In S. Pinker (Ed.), *Visual cognition* (pp. 1–63). Cambridge, MA: MIT Press.

Pinker, S. (1990). Why the child holded the baby rabbits (a case study in language acquisition). In D. N. Osherson (Ed.), *An invitation to cognitive science* (Vol. 1, pp. 55–81). Cambridge, MA: MIT Press.

Pinker, S. (1993). The central problem for the psycholinguist. In G. Harman (Ed.), *Conceptions of the human mind* (pp. 59–84). Hillsdale, NJ: Erlbaum.

Pinker, S. (1994). *The language instinct.* New York: William Morrow.

Pinker, S., & Mehler, J. (Eds.). (1988). *Connections and symbols.* Cambridge, MA: MIT Press.

Pinker, S., & Prince, A. (1988). On language and connectionism: Analysis of a parallel distributed processing model of language acquisition. *Cognition, 28,* 73–193.

Pisoni, D. B. (1993). Long-term memory in speech perception: Some new findings on talker variability, speaking rate and perceptual learning. *Speech Communication, 13,* 109–125.

Pitz, G. F., & Sachs, N. J. (1984). Judgment and decision: Theory and application. *Annual Review of Psychology, 35,* 139–163.

Platt, R. D., & Griggs, R. A. (1993a). Facilitation in the abstract selection task: The effects of attentional and instructional factors. *The Quarterly Journal of Experimental Psychology, 46A,* 591–613.

Platt, R. D., & Griggs, R. A. (1993b). Darwinian algorithms and the Wason selection task: A factorial analysis of social contract selection task problems. *Cognition, 48,* 163–192.

Platt, R. D., & Griggs, R. A. (1995). Facilitation and matching bias in the abstract selection task. *Thinking and Reasoning, 1,* 55–70.

Plous, S. (1993). *The psychology of judgment and decision making.* New York: McGraw-Hill.

Pollard, P., & Evans, J. St. B. T. (1983). The role of "representativeness" in statistical inference: A critical appraisal. In J. St. B. T. Evans (Ed.), *Thinking and reasoning: Psychological approaches* (pp. 107–134). London: Routledge & Kegan Paul.

Pollard, P., & Evans, J. St. B. T. (1987). Content and context effects in reasoning. *American Journal of Psychology, 100,* 41–60.

Pollatsek, A. (1993). Eye movements in reading. In D. M. Willows, R. S. Kruk, & E. Corcos (Eds.), *Visual processes in reading and reading disabilities* (pp. 191–213). Hillsdale, NJ: Erlbaum.

Pollatsek, A., & Rayner, K. (1989). Reading. In M. I. Posner (Ed.), *Foundations of cognitive science* (pp. 401–436). Cambridge, MA: MIT Press.

Pollina, L. K., Greene, A. L., Tunick, R. H., & Puckett, J. M. (1992). Dimensions of everyday memory in young adulthood. *British Journal of Psychology, 83,* 305–321.

Pollina, L. K., Greene, A. L., Tunick, R. H., & Puckett, J. M. (1993). Dimensions of everyday memory in late adulthood. *Current Psychology: Research & Reviews, 12,* 1–11.

Poon, L. W. (1980). A systems approach for the assessment and treatment of memory problems. In J. M. Ferguson & C. B. Taylor (Eds.), *The comprehensive handbook of behavior medicine* (Vol. 1, pp. 191–212). New York: Spectrum.

Posner, M. I. (1986). Overview. In K. R. Boff, L. Kaufman, & J. P. Thomas (Eds.), *Handbook of perception and human performance* (pp. v-3–v-10). New York: Wiley.

Posner, M. I. (1991). *Interaction of arousal and selection in the posterior attention network.* Unpublished paper, University of Oregon.

Posner, M. I. (1992). Attention as a cognitive and neural system. *Current Directions in Psychological Science, 1,* 11–14.

Posner, M. I. (1994). Attention: The mechanisms of consciousness. *Proceedings of the National Academy of Science, 91,* 7398–7403.

Posner, M. I., Goldsmith, R., & Welton, K. E., Jr. (1967). Perceived distance and the classification of distorted patterns. *Journal of Experimental Psychology, 73,* 28–38.

Posner, M. I., Grossenbacher, P. G., & Compton, P. E. (1991). *Visual attention.* Unpublished paper, University of Oregon.

Posner, M. I., & McLeod, P. (1982). Information processing models—in search of elementary operations. *Annual Review of Psychology, 33,* 477–514.

Posner, M. I., & Raichle, M. E. (1994). *Images of mind.* New York: W. H. Freeman.

Posner, M. I., & Raichle, M. E. (1995). Précis of *Images of mind. Behavioral and Brain Sciences, 18,* 327–383.

Posner, M. I., & Rothbart, M. K. (1991). Attentional mechanisms and conscious experience. In

D. Milner & M. Rugg (Eds.), *The neuropsychology of consciousness*. Orlando, FL: Academic Press.

Posner, M. I., & Rothbart, M. K. (1994). Constructing neuronal theories of mind. In C. Koch & J. L. Davis (Eds.), *Large-scale neuronal theories of the brain* (pp. 183–199). Cambridge, MA: MIT Press.

Postman, L. (1975). Verbal learning and memory. *Annual Review of Psychology, 26,* 291–335.

Potter, M. C., Moryadas, A., Abrahams, I., & Noel, A. (1993). Word perception and misperception in context. *Journal of Experimental Psychology: Learning, Memory, and Cognition, 19,* 3–22.

Poulton, E. C. (1994). *Behavioral decision theory: A new approach*. Cambridge, England: Cambridge University Press.

Powers, S., & López, R. L. (1985). Perceptual, motor and verbal skills of monolingual and bilingual Hispanic children: A discriminant analysis. *Perceptual and Motor Skills, 60,* 999–1002.

Pressley, M., & Afflerbach, P. (1995). *Verbal protocols of reading: The nature of constructively responsive reading*. Hillsdale, NJ: Erlbaum.

Pressley, M., & El-Dinary, P. B. (1992). Memory strategy instruction that promotes good information processing. In D. J. Herrmann, H. Weingartner, A. Searleman, & C. McEvoy (Eds.), *Memory improvement: Implications for memory theory* (pp. 79–100). New York: Springer-Verlag.

Pressley, M., & Ghatala, E. S. (1988). Delusions about performance on multiple-choice comprehension tests. *Reading Research Quarterly, 23,* 454–464.

Pressley, M., & Grossman, L. R. (Eds.). (1994). Recovery of memories of childhood sexual abuse [Special issue]. *Applied Cognitive Psychology, 8* (4).

Pressley, M., Levin, J. R., & Ghatala, E. S. (1984). Memory strategy monitoring in adults and children. *Journal of Verbal Learning and Verbal Behavior, 23,* 270–288.

Pressley, M., Levin, J. R., & Ghatala, E. S. (1988). Strategy-comparison opportunities promote long-term strategy use. *Contemporary Educational Psychology, 13,* 157–168.

Priest, A. G., & Lindsay, R. O. (1992). New light on novice-expert differences in physics problem solving. *British Journal of Psychology, 83,* 389–405.

Pryor, J. B., & Merluzzi, T. V. (1985). The role of expertise in processing social interaction scripts. *Journal of Experimental Social Psychology, 21,* 362–379.

Pylyshyn, Z. W. (1978). Imagery and artificial intelligence. In C. W. Savage (Ed.), *Perception and cognition issues in the foundations of psychology* (Minnesota Studies in the philosophy of science, Vol. 9, pp. 19–56). Minneapolis, MN: University of Minnesota Press.

Pylyshyn, Z. W. (1984). *Computation and cognition*. Cambridge, MA: MIT Press.

Pylyshyn, Z. W. (1989). The role of location indexes in spatial perception: A sketch of the FINST spatial-index model. *Cognition, 32,* 65–97.

Quinn, P. C., Eimas, P. D., & Rosenkrantz, S. L. (1993). Evidence for representations of perceptually similar natural categories by 3-month-old and 4-month-old infants. *Perception, 22,* 463–475.

Raaijmakers, J. G. W., & Shiffrin, R. M. (1992). Models for recall and recognition. *Annual Review of Psychology, 43,* 205–234.

Rabinowitz, J. C., Ackerman, B. P., Craik, F. I. M., & Hinchley, J. L. (1982). Aging and metamemory: The roles of relatedness and imagery. *Journal of Gerontology, 37,* 688–695.

Rachlin, H. (1994). *Behavior and mind: The roots of modern psychology*. New York: Oxford University Press.

Raichle, M. E. (1994). Images of the mind: Studies with modern imaging techniques. *Annual Review of Psychology, 45,* 333–356.

Ransdell, S. E., & Fischler, I. (1987). Memory in a monolingual mode: When are bilinguals at a disadvantage? *Journal of Memory and Language, 26,* 392–405.

Ratcliff, R. (1990). Connectionist models of recognition memory: Constraints imposed by learning and forgetting functions. *Psychological Review, 97,* 285–308.

Ratcliff, R., & McKoon, G. (1978). Priming in item recognition: Evidence for the propositional structure of sentences. *Journal of Verbal Learning and Verbal Behavior, 17,* 403–417.

Ratner, H. H., & Foley, M. A. (1994). A unifying framework for the development of children's memory for activity. In H. W. Reese (Ed.), *Advances in child development and behavior* (Vol. 25, pp. 33–105). New York: Academic Press.

Ratner, N. B., & Gleason, J. B. (1993). An introduction to psycholinguistics: What do language users know? In J. B. Gleason & N. B. Ratner (Eds.), *Psycholinguistics* (pp. 1–41). Fort Worth, TX: Harcourt Brace Jovanovich.

Rayner, K. (Ed.). (1992). *Eye movements and visual cognition* (pp. 66–88). New York: Springer-Verlag.

Rayner, K. (1993). Eye movements in reading: Recent developments. *Current Directions in Psychological Science, 2,* 81–85.

Rayner, K. (1995). Eye movements and cognitive processes in reading, visual search, and scene perception. In J. M. Findlay, R. Walker, & R. W. Kentridge (Eds.), *Eye movement research: Mechanisms, processes and applications* (pp. 3–22). Amsterdam: Elsevier.

Rayner, K., & Sereno, S. (1994). Eye movements in reading: Psycholinguistic studies. In M. A. Gernsbacher (Ed.), *Handbook of psycholinguistics* (pp. 57–81). San Diego, CA: Academic Press.

Read, S. J., & Cesa, I. L. (1991). This reminds me of the time when . . . : Expectation failures in reminding and explanation. *Journal of Experimental Social Psychology, 27,* 1–25.

Reason, J. (1984). Absent-mindedness and cognitive control. In J. E. Harris & P. E. Morris (Eds.), *Everyday memory, actions and absent-mindedness* (pp. 113–132). London: Academic Press.

Reason, J., & Mycielska, K. (1982). *Absent-minded? The psychology of mental lapses and everyday errors.* Englewood Cliffs, NJ: Prentice-Hall.

Rebok, G. W. (1987). *Life-span cognitive development.* New York: Holt, Rinehart and Winston.

Reed, S. K. (1972). Pattern recognition and categorization. *Cognitive Psychology, 3,* 383–407.

Reed, S. K. (1974). Structural descriptions and the limitations of visual images. *Memory & Cognition, 2,* 329–336.

Reed, S. K. (1977). Facilitation of problem solving. In N. J. Castellan, Jr., D. B. Pisoni, & G. R. Potts (Eds.), *Cognitive theory* (Vol. 2, pp. 3–20). Hillsdale, NJ: Erlbaum.

Reed, S. K. (1993a). Imagery and discovery. In B. Roskos-Ewoldson, M. J. Intons-Peterson, & R. E. Anderson (Eds.), *Imagery, creativity, and discovery: A cognitive perspective* (pp. 287–312). Amsterdam: Elsevier.

Reed, S. K. (1993b). A schema-based theory of transfer. In D. K. Detterman & R. J. Sternberg (Eds.), *Transfer on trial: Intelligence, cognition, and instruction* (pp. 39–67). Norwood, NJ: Ablex.

Reed, S. K., Willis, D., & Guarino, J. (1994). Selecting examples for solving word problems. *Journal of Educational Psychology, 86,* 380–388.

Reeder, G. D., McCormick, C. B., & Esselman, E. D. (1987). Self-referent processing and recall of prose. *Journal of Educational Psychology, 79,* 243–248.

Reeves, L. M., & Weisberg, R. W. (1993). On the concrete nature of human thinking: Content and context in analogical transfer. *Educational Psychology, 13,* 245–258.

Reeves, L. M., & Weisberg, R. W. (1994). The role of content and abstract information in analogical transfer. *Psychological Bulletin, 115,* 381–400.

Reicher, G. M. (1969). Perceptual recognition as a function of meaningfulness of stimuli material. *Journal of Experimental Psychology, 81,* 275–280.

Reinitz, M. T., Morrissey, J., & Demb, J. (1994). Role of attention in face encoding. *Journal of Experimental Psychology: Learning, Memory, and Cognition, 20,* 161–168.

Reisberg, D. (Ed.). (1992). *Auditory imagery.* Hillsdale, NJ: Erlbaum.

Remez, R. E. (1994). A guide to research on the perception of speech. In M. A. Gernsbacher (Ed.), *A guide to research on the perception of speech* (pp. 145–172). San Diego, CA: Academic Press.

Reynolds, A. G. (1991). The cognitive consequences of bilingualism. In A. G. Reynolds (Ed.), *Bilingualism, multiculturalism, and second language learning: The McGill Conference in Honour of Wallace E. Lambert* (pp. 145–182). Hillsdale, NJ: Erlbaum.

Reynolds, R. I. (1992). Recognition of expertise in chess players. *American Journal of Psychology, 105,* 409–415.

Rhodes, G., Brennan, S., & Carey, S. (1987). Identification and ratings of caricatures: Implications for mental representations of faces. *Cognitive Psychology, 19,* 473–497.

Ricciardelli, L. A. (1992). Creativity and bilingualism. *Journal of Creative Behavior, 26,* 242–259.

Richards, A., French, C. C., Johnson, W., Naparstek, J., & Williams, J. (1992). Effects of mood manipulation and anxiety on performance of an emotional Stroop task. *British Journal of Psychology, 83,* 479–491.

Richardson-Klavehn, A., & Bjork, R. A. (1988). Measures of memory. *Annual Review of Psychology, 39,* 475–543.

Richman, H. B., & Simon, H. A. (1989). Context effects in letter perception: Comparison of two theories. *Psychological Review, 96,* 417–432.

Rips, L. J. (1994). *The psychology of proof: Deductive reasoning in human thinking.* Cambridge, MA: MIT Press.

Robins, R. W., & Craik, K. H. (1993). Is there a citation bias in the judgment and decision literature? *Organizational Behavior and Human Decision Processes, 54,* 225–244.

Robinson, D. L., & Petersen, S. E. (1986). The neurobiology of attention. In J. E. LeDoux & W. Hirst (Eds.), *Mind and brain: Dialogues in cognitive neuroscience* (pp. 142–171). New York: Cambridge University Press.

Robinson, J. A. (1992). Autobiographical memory. In M. Gruneberg & P. Morris (Eds.), *Aspects of memory* (2nd ed., Vol. 1, pp. 223–251). London: Routledge.

Roediger, H. L., III. (1980). Levels of processing: Criticism and development [Review of *Levels of processing in human memory*]. *Contemporary Psychology, 25,* 20–21.

Roediger, H. L., III. (1990). Implicit memory: Retention without remembering. *American Psychologist, 45,* 1043–1056.

Roediger, H. L., III. (1991). *Remembering, knowing, and reconstructing the past.* Paper presented at the Annual Convention of the American Psychological Association, San Francisco, CA.

Roediger, H. L., III, Guynn, M. J., & Jones, T. C. (1994). Implicit memory: A tutorial review. In G. d'Ydewalle, P. Eelen, & P. Bertelson (Eds.), *International perspectives on psychological science* (Vol. 2, pp. 67–94). Hove, England: Erlbaum.

Roediger, H. L., III, & McDermott, K. B. (1995). Creating false memories: Remembering words not presented in lists. *Journal of Experimental Psychology: Learning, Memory, and Cognition, 21,* 803–814.

Roediger, H. L., III, Weldon, M. S., & Challis, B. H. (1989). Explaining dissociations between implicit and explicit measures of retention: A processing account. In H. L. Roediger, III, & F. I. M. Craik (Eds.), *Varieties of memory and consciousness* (pp. 3–41). Hillsdale, NJ: Erlbaum.

Roediger, H. L., III, Weldon, M. S., Stadler, M. L., & Riegler, G. L. (1992). Direct comparison of two implicit memory tests: Word fragment and word stem completion. *Journal of Experimental Psychology: Learning, Memory, and Cognition, 18,* 1251–1269.

Rogers, D. (1985). Language development. In A. Branthwaite & D. Rogers (Eds.), *Children growing up* (pp. 82–93). Milton Keynes, England: Open University Press.

Rogers, T. B. (1983). Emotion, imagery, and verbal codes: A closer look at an increasingly complex interaction. In J. Yuille (Ed.), *Imagery, memory, and cognition* (pp. 285–305). Hillsdale, NJ: Erlbaum.

Rogers, T. B., Kuiper, N. A., & Kirker, W. S. (1977). Self-reference and the encoding of personal information. *Journal of Personality and Social Psychology, 35,* 677–688.

Rogoff, B. (1984). Introduction: Thinking and learning in social context. In B. Rogoff & J. Lave (Eds.), *Everyday cognition: Its development in social context* (pp. 1–8). Cambridge, MA: Harvard University Press.

Rogoff, B. (1990). *Apprenticeship in thinking: Cognitive development in social context.* New York: Oxford University Press.

Rojahn, K., & Pettigrew, T. F. (1992). Memory for schema-relevant information: A meta-analytic resolution. *British Journal of Social Psychology, 31,* 81–109.

Roland, P. E., Kawashima, R., Gulyás, B., & O'Sullivan, B. (1995). Positron emission tomography in cognitive neuroscience: Methodological constraints, strategies, and examples from learning and memory. In M. Gazzaniga (Ed.), *The cognitive neurosciences* (pp. 781–788). Cambridge, MA: MIT Press.

Rolls, E. T. (1992). Neurophysiological mechanisms underlying face processing within and beyond the temporal cortical visual areas. In V. Bruce, A. Cowey, A. W. Ellis, & D. I. Perrett (Eds.), *Processing the facial image* (pp. 11–21). Oxford, Great Britain: Clarendon Press.

Rosch, E. H. (1973). Natural categories. *Cognitive Psychology, 4,* 328–350.

Rosch, E. H. (1975a). Cognitive reference points. *Cognitive Psychology, 7,* 532–547.

Rosch, E. H. (1975b). The nature of mental codes for color categories. *Journal of Experimental*

Psychology: Human Perception and Performance, 1, 303– 322.

Rosch, E. H. (1977). Human categorization. In N. Warren (Ed.), *Advances in cross-cultural psychology* (Vol. 1). London: Academic Press.

Rosch, E. H. (1988). Coherences and categorization: A historical view. In F. S. Hessel (Ed.), *The development of language and language researchers: Essays in honor of Roger Brown* (pp. 373–392). Hillsdale, NJ: Erlbaum.

Rosch, E. H., & Mervis, C. B. (1975). Family resemblances: Studies in the internal structure of categories. *Cognitive Psychology, 7,* 573–605.

Rosch, E. H., Mervis, C. B., Gray, W. D., Johnson, D. M., & Boyes-Braem, P. (1976). Basic objects in natural categories. *Cognitive Psychology, 8,* 382–439.

Roskos-Ewoldsen, B., Intons-Peterson, M. J., & Anderson, R. E. (Eds.). (1993). *Imagery, creativity, and discovery: A cognitive perspective.* Amsterdam: North-Holland.

Ross, M., & Buehler, R. (1994). Creative remembering. In U. Neisser & R. Fivush (Eds.), *The remembering self: Construction and accuracy in the self-narrative* (pp. 205–235). New York: Cambridge University Press.

Rosser, R. (1994). *Cognitive development: Psychological and biological perspectives.* Boston: Allyn & Bacon.,

Roșu, D., & Natanson, K. (1987, December). Out of the mouths of babes. *Michigan Today, p. 5.*

Rothbart, M., & John, O. P. (1985). Social categorization and behavioral episodes: A cognitive analysis of the effects of intergroup contact. *Journal of Social Issues, 41,* 81–104.

Rovee-Collier, C. K. (1987, April). *Infant memory.* Paper presented at the annual meeting of the Eastern Psychological Association, Crystal City, Virginia.

Rovee-Collier, C. K. (1995). Time windows in cognitive development. *Developmental Psychology, 31,* 147–169.

Rovee-Collier, C. K., & Boller, K. (1995). Current theory and research on infant learning and memory: Application to early intervention. *Infants and Young Children, 7,* 1–12.

Rovee-Collier, C. K., Borza, M. A., Adler, S. A., & Boller, K. (1993). Infants' eyewitness testimony: Effects of postevent information on a prior memory representation. *Memory & Cognition, 21,* 267–279.

Rovee-Collier, C. K., Evancio, S., & Earley, L. A. (1995). The time window hypothesis: Spacing effects. *Infant Behavior and Development, 18,* 69–78.

Rovee-Collier, C. K., Griesler, P. C., & Earley, L. A. (1985). Contextual determinants of retrieval in three-month-old infants. *Learning and Motivation, 16,* 139–157.

Rubin, D. C. (1995). *Memory in oral traditions: The cognitive psychology of epic, ballads, and counting-out rhymes.* New York: Oxford University Press.

Rubin, D. C., & Baddeley, A. D. (1989). Telescoping is not time compression: A model of the dating of autobiographical events. *Memory & Cognition, 17,* 653–661.

Rubin, D. C., & Kozin, M. (1984). Vivid memories. *Cognition, 16,* 81–95.

Rueckl, J. G. (1993). Making new connections [Review of the book *Connectionism and the mind: An introduction to parallel processing in networks*]. *Contemporary Psychology, 38,* 58–59.

Rueckl, J. G. (1995). Ambiguity and connectionist networks: Still settling into a solution—comment on Joordens and Besner (1994). *Journal of Experimental Psychology: Learning, Memory, and Cognition, 21,* 501–508.

Rueckl, J. G., & Kosslyn, S. M. (1992). What good is connectionist modeling? A dialogue. In A. F. Healy, S. M. Kosslyn, & R. M. Shiffrin (Eds.), *From learning theory to connectionist theory: Essays in honor of William K. Estes* (Vol. 1, pp. 249–266). Hillsdale, NJ: Erlbaum.

Rueckl, J. G., & Oden, G. C. (1986). The integration of contextual and featural information during word identification. *Journal of Memory and Language, 25,* 445–460.

Rugg, M. D. (1995). Event-related potential studies of human memory. In M. S. Gazzaniga (Ed.), *The cognitive neurosciences* (pp. 789–801). Cambridge, MA: MIT Press.

Ruiz-Caballero, J. A., & González, P. (1994). Implicit and explicit memory bias in depressed and nondepressed subjects. *Cognition and Emotion, 8,* 555–569.

Rumelhart, D. E., & McClelland, J. L. (1982). An interactive activation model of context effects in letter perception: Part 2. The contextual enhancement effect and some tests and extensions of the model. *Psychological Review, 89,* 60–94.

Rumelhart, D. E., & McClelland, J. L. (1986). On learning the past tenses of English verbs. In J. L. McClelland & D. E. Rumelhart (Eds.), *Parallel distributed processing: Explorations in the microstructure of cognition* (Vol. 2, pp. 216–271). Cambridge, MA: MIT Press.

Rumelhart, D. E., & McClelland, J. L. (1987). Learning the past tenses of English verbs: Implicit rules or parallel distributed processing? In B. MacWhinney (Ed.). *Mechanisms of language acquisition* (pp. 195–248). Hillsdale, NJ: Erlbaum.

Rumelhart, D. E., McClelland, J. L., & the PDP Research Group. (1986). *Parallel distributed processing* (Vol. 1). Cambridge, MA: MIT Press.

Rumelhart, D. E., & Norman, D. A. (1988). Representation in memory. In R. C. Atkinson, R. J. Herrnstein, G. Lindzey, & R. D. Luce (Eds.), *Stevens' handbook of experimental psychology* (2nd ed., Vol. 2, pp. 511–587). New York: Wiley.

Runco, M.A. (Ed.). (1994). *Problem finding, problem solving, and creativity.* Norwood, NJ: Ablex.

Rundus, D. (1971). Analysis of rehearsal processes in free recall. *Journal of Experimental Psychology, 89,* 63–77.

Russ, S. W. (1993). *Affect and creativity: The role of affect and play in the creative process.* Hillsdale, NJ: Erlbaum.

Russell, M. J. (1976). Human olfactory communication. *Nature, 260,* 520–522.

Russell, J. A. (1990). In defense of a prototype approach to emotion concepts. *Journal of Personality and Social Psychology, 60,* 37–47.

Russell, J. A., & Ward, L. M. (1982). Environmental psychology. *Annual Review of Psychology, 33,* 651–688.

Russo, R., & Parkin, A. J. (1993). Age differences in implicit memory: More apparent than real. *Memory & Cognition, 21,* 73–80.

Ryan, C. (1983). Reassessing the automaticity-control distinction: Item recognition as a paradigm case. *Psychological Review, 90,* 171–178.

Rychlak, J. F. (1994). *Logical learning theory: A human teleology and its empirical support.* Lincoln: University of Nebraska Press.

Sachs, J. (1967). Recognition memory for syntactic and semantic aspects of a connected discourse. *Perception & Psychophysics, 2,* 437–442.

Sachs, J. (1993). The emergence of intentional communication. In J. Berko Gleason (Ed.), *The development of language* (3rd ed., pp. 39–64). New York: Macmillan.

Safire, W. (1979, May 27). "I led the pigeons to the flag." *The New York Times Magazine,* pp. 9–10.

Sakitt, B., & Long, G. M. (1979). Spare the rod and spoil the icon. *Journal of Experimental Psychology: Human Perception and Performance, 5,* 19–30.

Salasoo, A., & Pisoni, D. B. (1985). Interaction of knowledge sources in spoken word identification. *Journal of Memory and Language, 24,* 210–231.

Salmon, M. H. (1991). Informal reasoning and informal logic. In J. F. Voss, D. N. Perkins, & J. W. Segal (Eds.), *Informal reasoning and education* (pp. 153–168). Hillsdale, NJ: Erlbaum.

Salthouse, T. A. (1991). *Theoretical perspectives on cognitive aging.* Hillsdale, NJ: Erlbaum.

Salthouse, T. A., & Babcock, R. L. (1991). Decomposing adult age differences in working memory. *Developmental Psychology, 27,* 763–776.

Sams, H., Paavilainen, P., Alho, K., & Näätänen, N. (1985). Auditory frequency discrimination and event-related potentials. *Electroencephalography and Clinical Neurophysiology, 62,* 437–448.

Samuel, A. G. (1981). Phonemic restoration: Insights from a new methodology. *Journal of Experimental Psychology: General, 110,* 474–494.

Samuel, A. G. (1987). Lexical uniqueness effects on phonemic restoration. *Journal of Memory and Language, 26,* 36–56.

Samuel, A. G., & Ressler, W. H. (1986). Attention within auditory word perception: Insights from the phonemic restoration illusion. *Journal of Experimental Psychology: Human Perception and Performance, 12,* 70–79.

Sanbonmatsu, D. M., Shavitt, S., & Gibson, B. D. (1994). Salience, set size, and illusory correlation: Making moderate assumptions about extreme targets. *Journal of Personality and Social Psychology, 66,* 1020–1033.

Sanford, A. J. (1985). *Cognition and cognitive psychology.* New York: Basic Books.

Schacter, D. L. (1990a). Memory. In M. I. Posner (Ed.), *Foundations of cognitive science* (pp. 683–725). Cambridge, MA: MIT Press.

Schacter, D. L. (1990b). Perceptual representation systems and implicit memory: Toward a resolution of the multiple memory systems debate. *Annals of the New York Academy of Sciences, 608,* 543–571.

Schacter, D. L. (1992). Implicit memory. In L. R. Squire (Ed.), *Encyclopedia of learning and memory* (pp. 259–263). New York: Macmillan.

Schacter, D. L. (1995). Memory distortion: History and current status. In D. L. Schacter, J. T. Coyle, G. D. Fishbach, M. M. Mesulam, & L. E. Sullivan (Eds.), *Memory distortion: How minds, brains, and societies reconstruct the past.* Cambridge, MA: Harvard University Press.

Schacter, D. L., Bowers, J., & Booker, J. (1989). Intention, awareness, and implicit memory: The retrieval intentionality criterion. In S. Lewandowsky, J. C. Dunn, & K. Kirsner (Eds.), *Implicit memory: Theoretical issues* (pp. 47–65). Hillsdale, NJ: Erlbaum.

Schacter, D. L., Chiu, C. Y. P., & Ochsner, K. N. (1993). Implicit memory: A selective review. *Annual Review of Neuroscience, 16,* 159–182.

Schacter, D. L., Church, B., & Treadwell, J. (1994). Implicit memory in amnesic patients: Evidence for spared auditory priming. *Psychological Science, 5,* 20–25.

Schacter, D. L., & Cooper, L. A. (1993). Implicit and explicit memory for novel visual objects: Structure and function. *Journal of Experimental Psychology: Learning, Memory, and Cognition, 19,* 995–1009.

Schacter, D. L., Cooper, L. A., Delaney, S. M., Peterson, M. A., & Tharan, M. (1991). Implicit memory for possible and impossible objects: Constraints on the construction of structural descriptions. *Journal of Experimental Psychology: Learning, Memory, and Cognition, 17,* 3–19.

Schacter, D. L., & Nadel, L. (1991). Varieties of spatial memory: A problem for cognitive neuroscience. In R. G. Lister & H. J. Weingartner (Eds.), *Perspectives on cognitive neuroscience* (pp. 165–185). New York: Oxford University Press.

Schacter, D. L., Reiman, E., Uecker, A., Polster, M. R., Yun, L. S., & Cooper, L. A. (1995). Brain regions associated with retrieval of structurally coherent visual information. *Nature, 376,* 587–590.

Schank, R. C., & Abelson, R. P. (1977). *Scripts, plans, goals, and understanding.* Hillsdale, NJ: Erlbaum.

Schiffrin, D. (1994). Making a list. *Discourse Processes, 17,* 377–406.

Schneider, W. (1984). Developmental trends in the metamemory-memory behavior relationship: An integrative review. In D. L. Forrest-Pressley &

T. G. Waller (Eds.), *Cognition, metacognition, and communication.* New York: Academic Press.

Schneider, W. (1993). Variety of working memory as seen in biology and in connectionist/control architectures. *Memory & Cognition, 21,* 184–192.

Schneider, W. (1995). *Advances in cognitive neuroscience: Mapping the brain.* Paper presented at the National Institute on the Teaching of Psychology, St. Petersburg Beach, FL.

Schneider, W., & Graham, D. J. (1992). Introduction to connectionist modeling in education. *Educational Psychologist, 27,* 513–530.

Schneider, W., & Pressley, M. (1989). *Memory development between 2 and 20.* New York: Springer-Verlag.

Schneider, W., & Shiffrin, R. M. (1977). Controlled and automatic information processing: I: Detection, search, and attention. *Psychological Review, 84,* 1–66.

Schneider, W., & Shiffrin, R. M. (1985). Categorization (restructuring) and automatization: Two separable factors. *Psychological Review, 92,* 424–428.

Schoenfeld, A. H. (1982). Some thoughts on problem-solving research and mathematics education. In F. K. Lester & J. Garofalo (Eds.), *Mathematical problem solving: Issues in research* (pp. 27–37). Philadelphia, PA: The Franklin Institute.

Schooler, J. (1992). *Personal communication.*

Schooler, J. W. (1994). Seeking the core: The issues and evidence surrounding recovered accounts of sexual trauma. *Consciousness and Cognition, 3,* 452–469.

Schooler, J. W., Fallshore, M., & Fiore, S. M. (1995). Epilogue: Putting insight into perspective. In R. J. Sternberg & J. E. Davidson (Eds.), *The nature of insight* (pp. 559–587). Cambridge, MA: MIT Press.

Schooler, J. W., Gerhard, D., & Loftus, E. F. (1986). Qualities of the unreal. *Journal of Experimental Psychology: Learning, Memory, and Cognition, 12,* 171–181.

Schooler, J. W., & Melcher, J. (1994). The ineffability of insight. In S. M. Smith, T. B. Ward, & R. A. Finke (Eds.), *The creative cognition approach* (pp. 97–133). Cambridge, MA: MIT Press.

Schooler, J. W., Ohlsson, S., & Brooks, K. (1993). Thoughts beyond words: When language overshadows insight. *Journal of Experimental Psychology: General, 122,* 166–183.

Schraagen, J. M. (1993). How experts solve a novel problem in experimental design. *Cognitive Science, 17,* 285–309.

Schraw, G. (1994). The effect of metacognitive knowledge on local and global monitoring. *Contemporary Educational Psychology, 19,* 143–154.

Schraw, G., & Roedel, T. D. (1994). Test difficulty and judgment bias. *Memory & Cognition, 22,* 63–69.

Schwartz, N. H., & Kulhavy, R. W. (1988). Encoding tactics in the retention of maps. *Contemporary Educational Psychology, 13,* 72–85.

Schwartz, S., & Griffin, T. (1986). *Medical thinking: The psychology of medical judgment and decision making.* New York: Springer-Verlag.

Schwartz, S. H. (1971). Modes of representation and problem solving: Well evolved is half solved. *Journal of Experimental Psychology, 91,* 347–350.

Schweickert, R., & Boruff, B. (1986). Short-term memory capacity: Magic number or magic spell? *Journal of Experimental Psychology: Learning, Memory, and Cognition, 12,* 419–425.

Scott, S. (1973). *The relation of divergent thinking to bilingualism: Cause or effect?* Unpublished manuscript. Department of Psychology, McGill University.

Seamon, J. G., & Travis, Q. B. (1993). An ecological study of professors' memory for student names and faces: A replication and extension. *Memory, 1,* 186–191.

Searle, J. R. (1990a). Minds, brains, and programs. In J. L. Garfield (Ed.), *Foundations of cognitive science: The essential readings* (pp. 189–208). New York: Paragon.

Searle, J. R. (1990b, January). Is the brain's mind a computer program? *Scientific American,* 26–31.

Searle, J. R. (1992). *The rediscovery of the mind.* Cambridge, MA: MIT Press.

Searleman, A., & Herrmann, D. (1994). *Memory from a broader perspective.* New York: McGraw-Hill.

Sebel, P. S., Bonke, B., & Winograd, E. (Eds.). (1993). *Memory and awareness in anesthesia.* Englewood Cliffs, NJ: Prentice-Hall.

Sebrechts, M. M., Marsh, R. L., & Seamon, J. G. (1989). Secondary memory and very rapid forgetting. *Memory & Cognition, 17,* 693–700.

Segal, S. J. (1971). Processing of the stimulus in imagery and perception. In S. J. Segal (Ed.), *Imagery: Current cognitive approaches.* New York: Academic Press.

Segal, S. J., & Fusella, V. (1970). Influence of imaged pictures and sounds on detection of visual and auditory signals. *Journal of Experimental Psychology, 83,* 458–464.

Segal, S. J., & Gordon, P. (1969). The Perkey effect revisited: Paradoxical threshold or signal detection error. *Perceptual and Motor Skills, 28,* 791–797.

Seidenberg, M. S. (1993). A connectionist modeling approach to word recognition and dyslexia. *Psychological Science, 4,* 299–304.

Seidenberg, M. S. (1995). Visual word recognition: An overview. In J. L. Miller & P. D. Eimas (Eds.), *Speech, language, and communication* (pp. 137–179). San Diego, CA: Academic Press.

Seidenberg, M. S., & McClelland, J. L. (1989). A distributed, developmental model of word recognition and naming. *Psychological Review, 96,* 523–568.

Seifert, C. M. (1990). Content-based inferences in text. *The Psychology of Learning and Motivation, 25,* 103–122.

Seifert, C. M., McKoon, G., Abelson, R. P., & Ratcliff, R. (1986). Memory connections between thematically similar episodes. *Journal of Experimental Psychology: Learning, Memory, and Cognition, 12,* 220–231.

Seifert, C. M., Robertson, S. P., & Black, J. B. (1985). Types of inferences generated during reading. *Journal of Memory and Language, 24,* 405–422.

Selinker, L., & Gass, S. M. (1994). *Second language acquisition: An introductory course.* Hillsdale, NJ: Erlbaum.

Sellen, A. J. (1994). Detection of everyday errors. *Applied Psychology: An International Review, 43,* 475–498.

Sergent, J., & Signoret, J. L. (1992). Functional and anatomical decomposition of face processing: Evidence from prosopagnosia and PET study of normal subjects. In V. Bruce, A. Cowey, A. W. Ellis, & D. I. Perrett (Eds.), *Processing the facial image* (pp. 55–62). Oxford, Great Britain: Clarendon Press.

Shafir, E. B., Smith, E. E., & Osherson, D. N. (1990). Typicality and reasoning fallacies. *Memory & Cognition, 18,* 229–239.

Shah, P., & Carpenter, P. A. (1995). Conceptual limitations in comprehending line graphs. *Journal of Experimental Psychology: General, 124,* 43–61.

Shallice, T., & Warrington, E. K. (1970). Independent functioning of verbal memory stores: A neuropsychological study. *Quarterly Journal of Experimental Psychology, 22,* 261–273.

Shapiro, K. L. (1994). The attentional blink: The brain's "eyeblink." *Current Directions in Psychological Science, 3,* 86–89.

Shapiro, P. N., & Penrod, S. D. (1986). Meta-analysis of facial identification studies. *Psychological Bulletin, 100,* 139–156.

Shatz, M. & Gelman, R. (1973). The development of communication skills: Modifications in the speech of young children as a function of listener. *Monographs of the Society for Research in Child Development, 38* (2, Serial No. 152).

Shepard, R. N. (1978). Externalization of mental images and the act of creation. In B. S. Randhawa & W. E. Coffman (Eds.), *Visual learning, thinking, and communication* (pp. 133–190). New York: Academic Press.

Shepard, R. N. (1981). Psychophysical complementarity. In M. Kubovy & J. R. Pomerantz (Eds.), *Perceptual organization* (pp. 279–342). Hillsdale, NJ: Erlbaum.

Shepard, R. N., & Chipman, S. (1970). Second-order isomorphism of internal representation: Shapes of states. *Cognitive Psychology, 1,* 1–17.

Shepard, R. N., & Metzler, J. (1971). Mental rotation of three-dimensional objects. *Science, 171,* 701–703.

Sherman, J. W., & Hamilton, D. L. (1994). On the formation of interitem associative links in person memory. *Journal of Experimental Social Psychology, 30,* 203–217.

Sherman, M. A. (1976). Adjectival negation and the comprehension of multiply negated sentences. *Journal of Verbal Learning and Verbal Behavior, 15,* 143–157.

Sherry, D. F., & Schacter, D. L. (1987). The evolution of multiple memory systems. *Psychological Review, 94,* 439–454.

Shiffrin, R. M. (1993). Short-term memory: A brief commentary. *Memory & Cognition, 21,* 193–197.

Shiffrin, R. M., & Schneider, W. (1977). Controlled and automatic human information processing: II. Perceptual learning, automatic attending, and a general theory. *Psychological Review, 84,* 127–190.

Shiffrin, R. M., & Schneider, W. (1984). Automatic and controlled processing revisited. *Psychological Review, 91,* 269–276.

Shiloh, S. (1994). Heuristics and biases in health decision making: Their expression in genetic counseling. In L. Heath, R. S. Tindale, J. Edwards, E. J. Posavac, F. B. Bryant, E. Henderson-King, Y. Suarez-Balcazar, & J. Myers (Eds.), *Applications of heuristics and biases to social issues* (pp. 13–30). New York: Plenum.

Shin, H. J., & Nosofsky, R. M. (1992). Similarity-scaling studies of dot-pattern classification and recognition. *Journal of Experimental Psychology: General,* 278–304.

Shoben, E. J. (1984). Semantic and episodic memory. In R. S. Wyer, Jr., & T. K. Srull (Eds.), *Handbook of social cognition* (Vol. 2, pp. 213–231). Hillsdale, NJ: Erlbaum.

Shoben, E. J. (1988). The representation of knowledge. In M. McTear (Ed.), *Understanding cognitive science* (pp. 102–119). New York: Wiley.

Shoben, E. J. (1992). Semantic memory. In L. R. Squire (Ed.), *Encyclopedia of learning and memory* (pp. 581–585). New York: Macmillan.

Shoben, E. J., Wescourt, K. T., & Smith, E. E. (1978). Sentence verification, sentence recognition, and the semantic/episodic distinction. *Journal of Experimental Psychology: Human Learning and Memory, 4,* 304–317.

Siegler, R. S. (1989). Mechanisms of cognitive development. *Annual Review of Psychology, 40,* 353–379.

Simon, H. A. (1974). How big is a chunk? *Science, 183,* 482–488.

Simon, H. A. (1981). Cognitive science: The newest science of the artificial. In D. A. Norman (Ed.), *Perspectives on cognitive science* (pp. 13–25). Hillsdale, NJ: Erlbaum.

Simon, H. A. (1990). Invariants of human behavior. *Annual Review of Psychology, 41,* 1–19.

Simon, H. A. (1992a). What is an "explanation" of behavior? *Psychological Science, 3,* 150–161.

Simon, H. A. (1992b). *Why the mind needs an eye: The uses of mental imagery.* Paper presented at the Convention of the American Psychological Association, Washington, DC.

Simon, H. A. (1995). Technology is not the problem. In P. Baumgartner & S. Payr (Eds.), *Speaking minds: Interviews with twenty eminent cognitive scientists* (pp. 231–248). Princeton, NJ: Princeton University Press.

Simon, H. A., & Chase, W. G. (1973). Skill in chess. *American Scientist, 61,* 394–403.

Simon, H. A., & Hayes, J. R. (1976). The understanding process: Problem isomorphs. *Cognitive Psychology, 8,* 165–190.

Simpson, G. B. (1984). Lexical ambiguity and its role in models of word recognition. *Psychological Bulletin, 96,* 316–340.

Simpson, G. B. (1994). Context and the processing of ambiguous words. In M. A. Gernsbacher (Ed.), *Handbook of psycholinguistics* (pp. 359–374). San Diego, CA: Academic Press.

Simpson, G. B., & Burgess, C. (1985). Activation and selection processes in the recognition of ambiguous words. *Journal of Experimental Psychology: Human Perception and Performance, 11,* 28–39.

Singer, M. (1990). *Psychology of language: An introduction to sentence and discourse processes.* Hillsdale, NJ: Erlbaum.

Singer, M., Graesser, A. C., & Trabasso, T. (1994). Minimal or global inference during reading. *Journal of Memory and Language, 33,* 421–441.

Slamecka, N. J., & Graf, P. (1978). The generation effect: Dilineation of a phenomenon. *Journal of Experimental Psychology: Human Learning and Memory, 4,* 592–604.

Slobin, D. I. (1966). Grammatical transformations and sentence comprehension in childhood and adulthood. *Journal of Verbal Learning and Verbal Behavior, 5,* 219–227.

Slobin, D. I. (1979). *Psycholinguistics* (2nd ed.). Glenview, IL: Scott, Foresman.

Slovic, P. (1992). Perception of risk: Reflections on the psychometric paradigm. In S. Krimsky & D. Golding (Eds.), *Social theories of risk* (pp. 117–152). New York: Praeger.

Slovic, P., & Fischhoff, B. (1977). On the psychology of experimental surprises. *Journal of Experimental Psychology: Human Perception and Performance, 3,* 544–551.

Slovic, P., Fischhoff, B., & Lichtenstein, S. (1982). Facts versus fears: Understanding perceived risk. In D. Kahneman, P. Slovic, & A. Tversky (Eds.), *Judgment under uncertainty: Heuristics and biases* (pp. 463–489). New York: Cambridge University Press.

Slovic, P., Fischhoff, B., & Lichtenstein, S. (1988). Response mode, framing, and information-processing effects in risk assessment. In D. E. Bell, H. Raiffa, & A. Tversky (Eds.), *Decision making: Descriptive, normative, and prescriptive interactions* (pp. 152–166). Cambridge: Cambridge University Press.

Slovic, P., Kunreuther, H., & White, G. F. (1974). Decision processes, rationality and adjustment to natural hazards. In G. F. White (Ed.), *Natural hazards, local, national and global.* New York: Oxford University Press.

Small, M. Y. (1990). *Cognitive development.* San Diego, CA: Harcourt Brace Jovanovich.

Smith, A. D. (1980). Age differences in encoding, storage, and retrieval. In L. W. Poon, J. L. Fozard, L. S. Cermak, D. Arenberg, & L. W. Thompson (Eds.), *New directions in memory and aging* (pp. 23–46). Hillsdale, NJ: Erlbaum.

Smith, A. D. (1996). Memory. In J. E. Birren & K. W. Schaie (Eds.), *Handbook of the psychology of aging* (4th ed.). San Diego, CA: Academic Press.

Smith, E. E. (1978). Theories of semantic memory. In W. K. Estes (Ed.), *Handbook of learning and cognitive processes* (Vol. 6). Hillsdale, NJ: Erlbaum.

Smith, E. E. (1989). Concepts and induction. In M. I. Posner (Ed.), *Foundations of cognitive science* (pp. 501–526). Cambridge, MA: MIT Press.

Smith, E. E., Langston, C., & Nisbett, R. E. (1993). *The case for rules in reasoning* (pp. 361–401). Hillsdale, NJ: Erlbaum.

Smith, E. E., Shoben, E. J., & Rips, L. J. (1974). Structure and process in semantic memory: A featural model for semantic decisions. *Psychological Review, 81,* 214–241.

Smith, E. E., & Swinney, D. A. (1992). The role of schemas in reading text: A real-time examination. *Discourse Processes, 15,* 303–316.

Smith, E. R. (1991). Illusory correlation in a simulated exemplar-based memory. *Journal of Experimental Social Psychology, 27,* 107–123.

Smith, J. F., & Kida, T. (1991). Heuristics and biases: Expertise and task realism in auditing. *Psychological Bulletin, 109,* 472–489.

Smith, M. U. (1991). A view from biology. In M. U. Smith (Ed.), *Toward a unified theory of problem solving: Views from the content domains* (pp. 1–19). Hillsdale, NJ: Erlbaum.

Smith, S. M. (1988). Environmental context-dependent memory. In G. M. Davies & D. M. Thomson (Eds.), *Memory in context: Context in memory* (pp. 13–34). Chichester, England: Wiley.

Smith, S. M. (1995a). Getting into and out of mental ruts: A theory of fixation, incubation, and insight. In R. J. Sternberg & J. E. Davidson (Eds.), *The nature of insight* (pp. 229–251). Cambridge, MA: MIT Press.

Smith, S. M. (1995b). Fixation, incubation, and insight in memory and creative thinking. In S. M.

Smith, T. B. Ward, & R. A. Finke (Eds.), *The creative cognition approach* (pp. 135–156). Cambridge, MA: MIT Press.

Smith, S. M., Glenberg, A., & Bjork, R. A. (1978). Environmental context and human memory. *Memory & Cognition, 6,* 342–353.

Smith, S. M., Ward, T. B., & Schumacher, J. S. (1993). Constraining effects of examples in a creative generation task. *Memory & Cognition, 21,* 837–845.

Smith, V. L., & Clark, H. H. (1993). On the course of answering questions. *Journal of Memory and Language, 32,* 25–38.

Smyth, M. M., Collins, A. F., Morris, P. E., & Levy, P. (1994). *Cognition in action* (2nd ed.). Hove, Great Britain: Erlbaum.

Smyth, M. M., Morris, P. E., Levy, P., & Ellis, A. W. (1987). *Cognition in action.* Hillsdale, NJ: Erlbaum.

Snodgrass, J. G. (1987). How many memory systems are there really?: Some evidence from the picture fragment completion task. In C. Izawa (Ed.), *Current issues in cognitive processes* (pp. 135–173). Hillsdale, NJ: Lawrence Erlbaum.

Snow, C. E. (1993). Bilingualism and second language acquisition. In J. B. Berko-Gleason & N. B. Ratner (Eds.), *Psycholinguistics* (pp. 391–416). Fort Worth, TX: Harcourt Brace Jovanovich.

Snow, C. E., & Hoefnagel-Hohle, M. (1978). The critical period for language acquisition. *Child Development, 4,* 1114–1128.

Snow, C. E., Perlmann, R. Y., & Gleason, J. Berko. (1990). Developmental perspectives on politeness: Sources of children's knowledge. *Journal of Pragmatics, 14,* 289–305.

Snyder, A. Z., Abdullaev, Y. G., Posner, M. I., & Raichle, M. E. (1995). Scalp electrical potentials reflect regional cerebral blood flow responses during processing of written words. *Proceedings of the National Academy of Science, 92,* 1689–1693.

Spelke, E., Hirst, W., & Neisser, U. (1976). Skills of divided attention. *Cognition, 4,* 215–230.

Sperling, G. (1960). The information available in brief visual presentations. *Psychological Monographs, 74,* 1–29.

Sperry, R. W. (1993). The impact and promise of the cognitive revolution. *American Psychologist, 48,* 878–885.

Spilich, G. J., Vesonder, G. T., Chiesi, H. L., & Voss, J. F. (1979). Text processing of domain-related information for individuals with high and low domain knowledge. *Journal of Verbal Learning and Verbal Behavior, 18,* 275–290.

Spoehr, K. T., & Lehmkuhle, S. W. (1982). *Visual information processing.* San Francisco: Freeman.

Sporer, S. L. (1991). Deep—deeper—deepest? Encoding strategies and the recognition of human faces. *Journal of Experimental Psychology: Learning, Memory, and Cognition, 17,* 323–333.

Squire, L. R. (1987). *Memory and brain.* New York: Oxford University Press.

Squire, L. R. (1992). *Encyclopedia of learning and memory.* New York: Macmillan.

Squire, L. R., Knowlton, B., & Musen, G. (1993). The structure and organization of memory. *Annual Review of Psychology, 44,* 453–495.

Sroufe, L. A., Cooper, R. G., & DeHart, G. B. (1992). *Child development: Its nature and course* (2nd ed.). New York: McGraw-Hill.

Standing, L. (1973). Learning 10,000 pictures. *Quarterly Journal of Experimental Psychology, 25,* 207–222.

Stanovich, K. E., & West, R. F. (1981). The effect of sentence processing on ongoing word recognition: Tests of a two-process theory. *Journal of Experimental Psychology: Human Perception and Performance, 7,* 658–672.

Stanovich, K. E., & West, R. F. (1983). On priming by a sentence context. *Journal of Experimental Psychology: General, 112,* 1–36.

Stemberger, J. P. (1991). Speaking of language, . . . [Review of the book *Speaking: From intention to articulation*]. *Contemporary Psychology, 36,* 119–120.

Sternberg, R. J., & Davidson, J. E. (Eds.). (1995). *The nature of insight.* Cambridge, MA: MIT Press.

Sternberg, R. J., & Lubart, T. I. (1995). *Defying the crowd: Cultivating creativity in a culture of conformity.* New York: Free Press.

Sternberg, R. J., & Powell, J. S. (1983). Comprehending verbal comprehension. *American Psychologist, 38,* 878–893.

Stevens, A., & Coupe, P. (1978). Distortions in judged spatial relations. *Cognitive Psychology, 10,* 422–437.

Stillings, N. A., Feinstein, M. H., Garfield, J. L., Rissland, E. L., Rosenbaum, D. A., Weisler, S. E., & Baker-Ward, L. (1987). *Cognitive science: An introduction.* Cambridge, MA: MIT Press.

Stillings, N. A., Weisler, S. E., Chase, C. H., Feinstein, M. H., Garfield, J. L., & Rissland, E. L. (1995).

Cognitive science: An introduction (2nd ed.). Cambridge, MA: MIT Press.

Stine, E. L., Cheung, H., & Henderson, D. H. (1995). Adult age differences in the on-line processing of new concepts in discourse. *Aging and Cognition, 2,* 1–18.

Stine, E. L., Wingfield, A., & Poon, L. W. (1989). Speech comprehension and memory through adulthood: The roles of time and strategy. In L. W. Poon, D. C. Rubin, & B. A. Wilson (Eds.), *Everyday cognition in adulthood and later life* (pp. 195–221). New York: Cambridge University Press.

Stroop, J. R. (1935). Studies of interference in serial verbal reactions. *Journal of Experimental Psychology, 18,* 643–662.

Suarez-Balcazar, Y., Balcazar, F. E., & Fawcett, S. B. (1992). Problem identification in social intervention research. In F. B. Bryant, J. Edwards, R. S. Tindale, E. J. Posavac, L. Heath, E. Henderson, & Y. Suarez-Balcazar (Eds.), *Methodological issues in applied social psychology* (pp. 25–42). New York: Plenum.

Sugg, M. J., & McDonald, J. E. (1994). Time course of inhibition in color-response and word-response versions of the Stroop task. *Journal of Experimental Psychology: Human Perception and Performance, 20,* 647–675.

Suh, S., & Trabasso, T. (1993). Inferences during reading: Converging evidence from discourse analysis, talk-aloud protocols, and recognition priming. *Journal of Memory and Language, 32,* 279–300.

Suzuki-Slakter, N. S. (1988). Elaboration and metamemory during adolescence. *Contemporary Educational Psychology, 13,* 206–220.

Svartik, J. (1966). *On voice in the English verb.* The Hague: Mouton.

Svenson, O., & Benson, L., III. (1993). Framing and time pressure in decision making. In O. Svenson & A. J. Maule (Eds.), *Time pressure and stress in human judgment and decision making* (pp. 133–144). New York: Plenum.

Sweller, J., & Levine, M. (1982). Effects of goal specificity on means-end analysis and learning. *Journal of Experimental Psychology: Learning, Memory, and Cognition, 8,* 463–474.

Tahta, S., Wood, M., & Loewenthal, K. (1981). Age changes in the ability to replicate foreign pronunciation and intonation. *Language and Speech, 24,* 363–372.

Tanaka, J. W., & Farah, M. J. (1993). Parts and wholes in face recognition. *Quarterly Journal of Experimental Psychology, 46A,* 225–245.

Tanaka, J. W., & Taylor, M. (1991). Object categories and expertise: Is the basic level in the eye of the beholder? *Cognitive Psychology, 23,* 457–482.

Taplin, J. E. (1971). Reasoning with conditional sentences. *Journal of Verbal Learning and Verbal Behavior, 10,* 219–225.

Tarone, E. E., Gass, S. M., & Cohen, A. D. (Eds.). (1994). *Research methodology in second-language acquisition.* Hillsdale, NJ: Erlbaum.

Tartter, V. C. (1986). *Language processes.* New York: Holt, Rinehart and Winston.

Taylor, H. A., & Tversky, B. (1992). Spatial mental models derived from survey and route descriptions. *Journal of Memory and Language, 31,* 261–292.

Taylor, I. A., & Taylor, M. M. (1983). *The psychology of reading.* New York: Academic Press.

Taylor, I. A., & Taylor, M. M. (1990). *Psycholinguistics: Learning and using language.* Englewood Cliffs, NJ: Prentice-Hall.

Thapar, A., & Greene, R. L. (1993). Evidence against a short-term-store account of long-term recency effects. *Memory & Cognition, 21,* 329–337.

Thomas, J. C. (1974). An analysis of behavior in the Hobbits-Orcs program. *Cognitive Psychology, 6,* 257–269.

Thomas, J. C. (1989). Problem solving by human-machine interaction. In K. J. Gilhooly (Ed.), *Human and machine problem solving* (pp. 317–362). New York: Plenum.

Thomas, M. H., & Wang, A. Y. (1996). Learning by the keyword mnemonic: Looking for long-term benefits. *Journal of Experimental Psychology: Applied.*

Thompson, C. P., Skowronski, J. J., & Betz, A. L. (1993). The use of partial temporal information in dating personal events. *Memory & Cognition, 21,* 352–360.

Thompson, C. P., Skowronski, J. J., Larsen, S. F., & Betz, A. L. (1996). *Autobiographical memory: Remembering what and remembering when.* Mahwah, NJ: Erlbaum.

Thompson, R. F. (1993). *The brain: A neuroscience primer* (2nd ed.). New York: Freeman.

Thompson, W. B., & Mason, S. E. (1996). Instability of individual differences in the association between confidence judgments and memory performance. *Memory & Cognition, 24,* 226–234.

Thomson, J. R., & Chapman, R. S. (1977). Who is "Daddy" revisited: The status of two-year-olds' overextended words in use and comprehension. *Journal of Child Language, 4,* 359–375.

Thorndyke, P. W. (1981). Distance estimation from cognitive maps. *Cognitive Psychology, 13,* 526–550.

Thorndyke, P. W. (1984). Applications of schema theory in cognitive research. In J. R. Anderson & S. M. Kosslyn (Eds.), *Tutorials in learning and memory* (pp. 167–192). San Francisco: W. H. Freeman.

Thorndyke, P. W., & Goldin, S. E. (1983). Spatial learning and reasoning skill. In H. L. Pick, Jr. & L. P. Acredolo (Eds.), *Spatial orientation* (pp. 195–217). New York: Plenum.

Tiitinen, H., Sinkkonen, J., Reinikainen, K., Alho, K., Lavikainen, J., & Näätänen, R. (1993). Selective attention enhances the auditory 40-Hz transient response in humans. *Nature, 364,* 59–60.

Titcomb, A. L., & Reyna, V. F. (1995). Memory interference and misinformation effects. In F. N. Dempster & C. J. Brainerd (Eds.), *Interference and inhibition in cognition* (pp. 263–294). San Diego, CA: Academic Press.

Tomasello, M., Conti-Ramsden, G., & Ewert, B. (1990). Young children's conversations with the mothers and fathers: Differences in breakdown and repair. *Journal of Child Language, 17,* 115–130.

Toms, M., Morris, N., & Foley, P. (1994). Characteristics of visual interference with visuospatial working memory. *British Journal of Psychology, 85,* 131–144.

Toms, M., Morris, N., & Ward, D. (1993). Working memory and conditional reasoning. *The Quarterly Journal of Experimental Psychology, 46A,* 679–699.

Trabasso, T., & Suh, S. (1993). Understanding text: Achieving explanatory coherence through online inferences and mental operations in working memory. *Discourse Processes, 16,* 3–34.

Trabasso, T., Suh, S., Payton, P., & Jain, R. (1995). Explanatory inferences and other strategies during comprehension and their effect on recall. In R. F. Lorch & E. J. O'Brien (Eds.), *Sources of coherence in reading* (pp. 219–239). Hillsdale, NJ: Erlbaum.

Trafimow, D., & Wyer, R. S., Jr. (1993). Cognitive representation of mundane social events. *Journal of Personality and Social Psychology, 64,* 365–376.

Trahan, D. E., Larrabee, G. J., & Levin, H. S. (1986). Age-related differences in recognition memory for pictures. *Experimental Aging Research, 12,* 147–150.

Treisman, A. (1960). Contextual cues in selective listening. *Quarterly Journal of Experimental Psychology, 12,* 242–248.

Treisman, A. (1964). Monitoring and storage of irrelevant messages and selective attention. *Journal of Verbal Learning and Verbal Behavior, 3,* 449–459.

Treisman, A. (1986, November). Features and objects in visual processing. *Scientific American, 255*(5), pp. 114B–125.

Treisman, A. (1990). Visual coding of features and objects: Some evidence from behavioral studies. In National Research Council (Ed.), *Advances in the modularity of vision: Selections from a symposium on frontiers of visual science* (pp. 39–61). Washington, DC: National Academy Press.

Treisman, A. (1991). Search, similarity, and integration of features between and within dimensions. *Journal of Experimental Psychology: Human Perception and Performance, 17,* 652–676.

Treisman, A. (1992). Perceiving and re-perceiving objects. *American Psychologist, 47,* 862–875.

Treisman, A. (1993). The perception of features and objects. In A. Baddeley & L. Weiskrantz (Eds.), *Attention: Selection, awareness, and control* (pp. 5–35. Oxford, Great Britain: Clarendon.

Treisman, A., & Gelade, G. (1980). A feature-integration theory of attention. *Cognitive Psychology, 12,* 97–136.

Treisman, A., & Sato, S. (1990). Conjunction search revisited. *Journal of Experimental Psychology: Human Perception and Performance, 16,* 459–478.

Treisman, A., & Schmidt, H. (1982). Illusory conjunction in the perception of objects. *Cognitive Psychology, 14,* 107–141.

Treisman, A., & Souther, J. (1985). Search asymmetry: A diagnostic for preattentive processing of separable features. *Journal of Experimental Psychology: General, 114,* 285–310.

Treisman, A., & Souther, J. (1986). Illusory words: The roles of attention and of top-down constraints in conjoining letters to form words. *Journal of*

Experimental Psychology: Human Perception and Performance, 12, 3–17.

Treisman, A., Vieira, A., & Hayes, A. (1992). Automaticity and preattentive processing. *American Journal of Psychology, 105,* 341–362.

Trolier, T. K., & Hamilton, D. L. (1986). Variables influencing judgments of correlational relations. *Journal of Personality and Social Psychology, 50,* 879–888.

Tulving, E. (1972). Episodic and semantic memory. In E. Tulving & W. Donaldson (Eds.), *Organization of memory.* New York: Academic Press.

Tulving, E. (1983). *Elements of episodic memory.* New York: Oxford University Press.

Tulving, E. (1984). Precis, Elements of episodic memory. *The Behavioral and Brain Sciences, 7,* 223–268.

Tulving, E. (1985). How many memory systems are there? *American Psychologist, 40,* 385–398.

Tulving, E. (1986). What kind of a hypothesis is the distinction between episodic and semantic memory? *Journal of Experimental Psychology: Learning, Memory, and Cognition, 12,* 307–311.

Tulving, E. (1987). Multiple memory systems and consciousness. *Human Neurobiology, 6,* 67–80.

Tulving, E. (1989, July–August). Remembering and knowing the past. *American Scientist, 77,* 361–367.

Tulving, E. (1991). Memory research is not a zero-sum game. *American Psychologist, 46,* 41–42.

Tulving, E. (1993a). Varieties of consciousness and levels of awareness in memory. In A. Baddeley & L. Weiskrantz (Eds.), *Attention: Selection, awareness, and control* (pp. 283–299). Oxford, England: Clarendon Press.

Tulving, E. (1993b). What is episodic memory? *Current Directions in Psychological Science, 2,* 67–80.

Tulving, E. (1993c). Human memory. In P. Andersen, Ø. Hvalby, O. Paulsen, & B. Hökfelt (Eds.), *Memory concepts—1993: Basic and clinical aspects* (pp. 27–45). Amsterdam: Excerpta Medica.

Tulving, E., Kapur, S., Craik, F. I. M., Moscovitch, M., & Houle, S. (1994). Hemispheric encoding/retrieval asymmetry in episodic memory: Positron emission tomography findings. *Proceedings of the National Academy of Science, 91,* 2016–2020.

Tulving, E., & Kroll, N. (1995). Novelty assessment in the brain and long-term memory encoding. *Psychonomic Bulletin & Review, 2,* 387–390.

Tulving, E., & Schacter, D. L. (1990). Priming and human memory systems. *Science, 247,* 301–306.

Turcotte, P. (1993, Summer). Mixed-language couples and their children. *Canadian Social Trends,* pp. 15–17.

Turner, S. R. (1994). *The creative process: A computer model of storytelling and creativity.* Hillsdale, NJ: Erlbaum.

Tversky, A., & Fox, C. R. (1995). Weighing risk and uncertainty. *Psychological Review, 102,* 269–283.

Tversky, A., & Kahneman, D. (1971). Belief in the law of small numbers. *Psychological Bulletin, 76,* 105–110.

Tversky, A., & Kahneman, D. (1973). Availability: A heuristic for judging frequency and probability. *Cognitive Psychology, 5,* 207–232.

Tversky, A., & Kahneman, D. (1974). Judgment under uncertainty: Heuristics and biases. *Science, 185,* 1124–1131.

Tversky, A., & Kahneman, D. (1981). The framing of decisions and the psychology of choice. *Science, 211,* 453–458.

Tversky, A., & Kahneman, D. (1982). Judgment under uncertainty: Heuristics and biases. In D. Kahneman, P. Slovic, & A. Tversky (Eds.), *Judgment under uncertainty: Heuristics and biases* (pp. 3–20). New York: Cambridge University Press.

Tversky, A., & Kahneman, D. (1983). Extensional versus intuitive reasoning: The conjunction fallacy in probability judgment. *Psychological Review, 90,* 293–315.

Tversky, B. (1981). Distortions in memory for maps. *Cognitive Psychology, 13,* 407–433.

Tversky, B. (1991a). Distortions in memory for visual displays. In S. R. Ellis, M. Kaiser, & A. Grunewald (Eds.), *Spatial instruments and spatial displays* (pp. 61–75). Hillsdale, NJ: Erlbaum.

Tversky, B. (1991b). Spatial mental models. *The Psychology of Learning and Motivation, 27,* 109–145.

Tversky, B., & Hemenway, K. (1984). Objects, parts, and categories. *Journal of Experimental Psychology: General, 113,* 169–193.

Tversky, B., & Schiano, D. J. (1989). Perceptual and conceptual factors in distortions in memory for graphs and maps. *Journal of Experimental Psychology: General, 118,* 387–398.

Ucros, C. G. (1989). Mood state-dependent memory: A meta-analysis. *Cognition and Emotion, 3,* 139–167.

Underwood, B. J., Boruch, R. F., & Malmi, R. A. (1978). Composition of episodic memory. *Journal of Experimental Psychology: General, 107*, 393–419.

Underwood, N. R., & McConkie, G. W. (1985). Perceptual span for letter distinctions during reading. *Reading Research Quarterly, 20*, 153–162.

Usher, J. A., & Neisser, U. (1993). Childhood amnesia and the beginnings of memory for four early life events. *Journal of Experimental Psychology: General, 122*, 155–165.

Valian, V. (1985). Saying what we mean, more or less [Review of the book *Speech and situation: A psychological conception of situated speaking*]. *Contemporary Psychology, 30*, 140–141.

van den Broek, P. (1994). Comprehension and memory of narrative texts. In M. A. Gernsbacher (Ed.), *Handbook of psycholinguistics* (pp. 539–588). San Diego, CA: Academic Press.

van der Heijden, A. H. C. (1981). *Short-term visual information forgetting*. London: Routledge & Kegan Paul.

Van Oostendorp, H. (1991). Inferences and integrations made by readers of script-based texts. *Journal of Research in Reading, 14*, 3–20.

Van Orden, G. C. (1987). A rows is a rose: Spelling, sound and reading. *Memory & Cognition, 15*, 181–198.

Van Orden, G. C., Pennington, B. F., & Stone, G. O. (1990). Word identification in reading and the promise of subsymbolic psycholinguistics. *Psychological Review, 97*, 488–522.

Van Selst, M., & Jolicoeur, P. (1994). Can mental rotation occur before the dual-task bottleneck? *Journal of Experimental Psychology: Human Perception and Performance, 20*, 905–921.

van Zomeren, A. H., & Brouwer, W. H. (1994). *Clinical neuropsychology of attention*. New York: Oxford University Press.

VanderStoep, S. W., & Seifert, C. M. (1994). Problem solving, transfer, and thinking. In P. R. Pintrich, D. R. Brown, & C. E. Weinstein (Eds.), *Student motivation, cognition, and learning: Essays in honor of Wilbert J. McKeachie* (pp. 27–49). Hillsdale, NJ: Erlbaum.

Vecera, S. P., & Farah, M. J. (1994). Does visual attention select objects or locations? *Journal of Experimental Psychology: General, 123*, 146–160.

Vellutino, F. R. (1991). Introduction to three studies on reading acquisition: Convergent findings on theoretical foundations of code-oriented versus whole-language approaches to reading instruction. *Journal of Educational Psychology, 83*, 437–443.

Vicente, K. J., & de Groot, A. D. (1990). The memory recall paradigm: Straightening out the historical record. *American Psychologist, 45*, 285–287.

Vosniadou, S., & Ortony, A. (Eds.). (1989). *Similarity and analogical reasoning*. New York: Cambridge University Press.

Voss, J. F., Wolfe, C. R., Lawrence, J. A., & Engle, R. A. (1991). From representation to decision: An analysis of problem solving in international relations. In R. J. Sternberg & P. A. Frensch (Eds.), *Complex problem solving: Principles and mechanisms* (pp. 119–158). Hillsdale, NJ: Erlbaum.

Wagner, R. K., & Torgesen, J. K. (1987). The nature of phonological processing and its causal role in the acquisition of reading skills. *Psychological Bulletin, 101*, 192–212.

Wakefield, J. F. (1992). *Creative thinking: Problem-solving and the arts orientation*. Norwood, NJ: Ablex.

Waldrop, M. M. (1987). The workings of working memory. *Science, 237*, 1564–1567.

Waldrop, M. M. (1993). Cognitive neuroscience: A world with a future. *Science, 261*, 1805–1806.

Walker, W. R., Vogl, R. J., & Thompson, C. P. (1997). Autobiographical memory: Pleasantness and unpleasantness fade with time. *Applied Cognitive Psychology*, in press.

Walker-Andrews, A. S. (1986). Intermodal perception of expressive behaviors: Relation of eye and voice? *Developmental Psychology, 22*, 373–377.

Wallace, B., & Fisher, L. E. (1983). *Consciousness and behavior*. Boston: Allyn & Bacon.

Walsh, D. A., & Thompson, L. W. (1978). Age differences in visual sensory memory. *Journal of Gerontology, 33*, 383–387.

Walton, G. E., Bower, N. J., & Bower, T. G. R. (1992). Recognition of familiar faces by newborns. *Infant Behavior and Development, 15*, 265–269.

Wang, A. Y., & Thomas, M. H. (1995). Effect of keywords on long-term retention: Help or hindrance? *Journal of Educational Psychology, 87*, 468–475.

Wang, A. Y., Thomas, M. H., & Ouellette, J. A. (1992). Keyword mnemonic and retention of second-language vocabulary words. *Journal of Educational Psychology, 84,* 520–528.

Wardlaw, K. A., & Kroll, N. E. A. (1976). Autonomic responses to shock-associated words in a nonattended message: A failure to replicate. *Journal of Experimental Psychology: Human Perception and Performance, 2,* 357–360.

Warren, D. H. (1994). Self-localization on plan and oblique maps. *Environment and Behavior, 26,* 71–98.

Warren, D. H. (1995). From maps to cityscapes: Reactions to modes of spatial representation. In W. Pape & F. Burwick (Eds.), *Reflecting senses: Perception and appearance in literature, culture, and the arts* (pp. 33–52). Berlin: Walter de Gruyter.

Warren, D. H., Scott, T. E., & Medley, C. (1992). Finding locations in the environment: The map as mediator. *Perception, 21,* 671–689.

Warren, R. M. (1970). Perceptual restoration of missing speech sounds. *Science, 167,* 392–393.

Warren, R. M. (1984). Perceptual restoration of obliterated sounds. *Psychological Bulletin, 96,* 371–383.

Warren, R. M., & Warren, R. P. (1970, December). Auditory illusions and confusions. *Scientific American, 223*(6), 30–36.

Warrington, E. K., & Weiskrantz, L. (1970). Amnesic syndrome: Consolidation or retrieval? *Nature, 228,* 629–630.

Wason, P. C. (1968). Reasoning about a rule. *Quarterly Journal of Experimental Psychology, 20,* 273–281.

Wason, P. C., & Johnson-Laird, P. N. (1972). *Psychology of reasoning: Structure and content.* Cambridge, MA: Harvard University Press.

Waterstreet, M. (1995, August). *Making connections in learning and memory class.* Paper presented at the annual meeting of the American Psychological Association, Washington, DC.

Waugh, N. C., & Norman, D. A. (1965). Primary memory. *Psychological Review, 72,* 89–104.

Weatherford, D. L. (1985). Representing and manipulating spatial information from different environments: Models to neighborhoods. In R. Cohen (Ed.), *The development of spatial cognition* (pp. 41–70). Hillsdale, NJ: Erlbaum.

Weaver, C. A., III. (1993). Do you need a "flash" to form a flashbulb memory? *Journal of Experimental Psychology: General, 122,* 39–46.

Weber, E. U., Böckenholt, U., Hilton, D. J., & Wallace, B. (1993). Determinants of diagnostic hypothesis generation: Effects of information, base rates, and experience. *Journal of Experimental Psychology: Learning, Memory, and Cognition, 19,* 1131–1164.

Weber, R. J. (1992). *Forks, phonographs, and hot air balloons.* New York: Oxford University Press.

Weber, R. J., & Perkins, D. N. (Eds.). (1992). *Inventive minds: Creativity in technology.* New York: Oxford University Press.

Weed, K., Ryan, E. B., & Day, J. (1990). Metamemory and attributions as mediators of strategy use and recall. *Journal of Educational Psychology, 82,* 849–855.

Wegner, D. M. (1989). *White bears and other unwanted thoughts.* New York: Viking.

Wegner, D. M. (1992). You can't always think what you want: Problems in the suppression of unwanted thoughts. *Advances in Experimental Social Psychology, 25,* 193–225.

Wegner, D. M. (1994). Ironic processes of mental control. *Psychological Review, 101,* 34–52.

Wegner, D. M. (1996). *Personal communication.*

Wegner, D. M., Schneider, D. J., Carter, S. R. III, & White, T. L. (1987). Paradoxical effects of thought suppression. *Journal of Personality and Social Psychology, 53,* 5–13.

Weingardt, K. R., Loftus, E. F., & Lindsay, D. S. (1995). Misinformation revisited: New evidence on the suggestibility of memory. *Memory & Cognition, 23,* 72–82.

Weinstein, C. E., Duffy, M., Underwood, V. L., & MacDonald, J. E. (1979). *Whose learning strategies deficit . . . the elderly's or the researcher's?* Paper presented at the annual meeting of the American Psychological Association, New York.

Weisberg, R. W. (1993). *Creativity: Beyond the myth of genius.* New York: Freeman.

Weist, R. M. (1985). Cross-linguistic perspective on cognitive development. In T. M. Schlechter & M. P. Toglia (Eds.), *New directions in cognitive science* (pp. 191–216). Norwood, NJ: Ablex.

Weldon, M. S., & Roediger, H. L., III. (1987). Altering retrieval demands reverses the picture superiority effect. *Memory & Cognition, 15,* 269–280.

Well, A. D., Pollatsek, A., & Boyce, S. J. (1990). Understanding the effects of sample size on the variability of the mean. *Organizational Behavior and Human Decision Processes, 47,* 289–312.

Wellman, H. M. (1985). A child's theory of mind: The development of conceptions of cognition. In S. R. Yussen (Ed.), *The growth of reflection in children* (pp. 169–203). New York: Academic Press.

Wellman, H. M. (1988). The early development of memory strategies. In F. W. Weinert & M. Perlmutter (Eds.), *Memory development: Universal changes and individual differences* (pp. 3–29). Hillsdale, NJ: Erlbaum.

Wellman, H. M., & Gelman, S. A. (1992). Cognitive development: Foundational theories of core domains. *Annual Review of Psychology, 43,* 337–375.

Wells, G. L., & Hryciw, B. (1984). Memory for faces: Encoding and retrieval operations. *Memory & Cognition, 12,* 338–344.

Werker, J. F. (1994). Cross-language speech perception: Development change does not involve loss. In J. C. Goodman & H. C. Nusbaum (Eds.), *The development of speech perception: The transition from speech sounds to spoken words* (pp. 93–120). Cambridge, MA: MIT Press.

Werker, J. F., & Tees, R. C. (1984). Cross-language speech perception: Evidence for perceptual reorganization during the first year of life. *Infant Behavior and Development, 7,* 49–63.

Wheeler, D. (1970). Processes in word recognition. *Cognitive Psychology, 1,* 59–85.

Whitbourne, S. K., & Powers, C. B. (1996). Psychological perspectives on the normal aging process. In L. L. Carstensen, B. A. Edelstein, & L. Dornbrand (Eds.), *Practical handbook of clinical gerontology.* Beverly Hills, CA: Sage.

Wickelgren, W. A. (1965). Acoustic similarity and intrusion errors in short-term memory. *Journal of Experimental Psychology, 70,* 102–108.

Wickelgren, W. A. (1973). The long and the short of memory. *Psychological Bulletin, 80,* 425–438.

Wickens, D. D., Dalezman, R. E., & Eggemeier, F. T. (1976). Multiple encoding of word attributes in memory. *Memory & Cognition, 4,* 307–310.

Willows, D. M., Kruk, R. S., & Corcos, E. (Eds.). (1993). *Visual processes in reading and reading disabilities.* Hillsdale, NJ: Erlbaum.

Wilson, B. A. (1984). Memory therapy in practice. In B. A. Wilson & N. Moffat (Eds.), *Clinical management of memory problems* (pp. 89–111). Rockville, MD: Aspen.

Wilson, T. D. (1994). The proper protocol: Validity and completeness of verbal reports. *Psychological Science, 5,* 249–252.

Wingfield, A. (1993). Sentence processing. In J. B. Gleason & N. B. Ratner (Eds.), *Psycholinguistics* (pp. 199–235). Fort Worth, TX: Harcourt Brace.

Winograd, E. (1992). Naturalistic approaches to the study of memory. In P. Morris & M. Gruneberg (Eds.), *Theoretical aspects of memory* (2nd ed., Vol. 2, pp. 273–295). New York: Routledge.

Winograd, E. (1993). Memory in the laboratory and everyday memory: The case for both. In J. M. Puckett & H. W. Reese (Eds.), *Mechanisms of everyday cognition* (pp. 55–70). Hillsdale, NJ: Erlbaum.

Wittgenstein, L. (1953). *Philosophical investigations.* New York: Macmillan.

Wittrock, M. C. (1974). Learning as a generative process. *Educational Psychologist, 11,* 87–95.

Wolfe, J. M. (1992). The parallel guidance of visual attention. *Current Directions in Psychological Science, 1,* 124–128.

Wolff, A. S., Mitchell, D. H., & Frey, P. W. (1984). Perceptual skill in the game of Othello. *Journal of Psychology, 118,* 7–16.

Wolford, G., Taylor, H. A., & Beck, J. R. (1990). The conjunction fallacy? *Memory & Cognition, 18,* 47–53.

Woltz, D. J. (1988). An investigation of the role of working memory in procedural skill acquisition. *Journal of Experimental Psychology: General, 117,* 319–331.

Wood, N., & Cowan, N. (1995). The cocktail party phenomenon revisited: How frequent are attention shifts to one's name in an irrelevant auditory channel? *Journal of Experimental Psychology: Learning, Memory, and Cognition, 21,* 255–260.

Wurtz, R. H., Goldberg, M. E., & Robinson, D. L. (1982, June). Brain mechanisms of visual attention. *Scientific American, 246,* 124–136.

Wyer, R. S., Jr., & Srull, T. K. (Eds.). (1994). *Handbook of social cognition* (2nd ed.). Hillsdale, NJ: Erlbaum.

Yeni-Komshian, G. H. (1993). Speech perception. In J. B. Gleason & N. B. Ratner (Eds.), *Psycholinguistics* (pp. 89–131). Fort Worth, TX: Harcourt Brace Jovanovich.

Yopp, H. K. (1992). Developing phonemic awareness in young children. *The Reading Teacher, 45,* 696–703.

Yuille, J. C. (1983). The crisis in theories of mental imagery. In J. C. Yuille (Ed.), *Imagery, memory and cognition* (pp. 263–284). Hillsdale, NJ: Erlbaum.

Yuille, J. C. (1985). A laboratory-based experimental methodology is inappropriate for the study of mental imagery. *Journal of Mental Imagery, 9,* 137–150.

Yuille, J. C., & Catchpole, M. J. (1977). Imagery and children's associative learning. In A. M. Lesgold, J. W. Pellegrino, S. D. Fokkema, & R. Glaser (Eds.), *Cognitive psychology and instruction.* New York: Plenum.

Yussen, S. R., & Bird, J. E. (1979). The development of metacognitive awareness in memory, communication, and attention. *Journal of Experimental Child Psychology, 19,* 502–508.

Yussen, S. R., & Levy, V. M. (1975). Developmental changes in predicting one's own span of short-term memory. *Journal of Experimental Child Psychology, 19,* 502–508.

Zacks, R. T., & Hasher, L. (1992). Memory in life, lab, and clinic: Implications for memory theory. In D. J. Herrmann, H. Weingartner, A. Searleman, & C. McEvoy (Eds.), *Memory improvement: Implications for memory theory* (pp. 232–248). New York: Springer-Verlag.

Zelinski, E. M., & Gilewski, M. J. (1988). Memory for prose and aging: A meta-analysis. In M. L. Howe & C. J. Brainerd (Eds.), *Cognitive development in adulthood: Progress in cognitive development research* (pp. 133–158). New York: Springer-Verlag.

Photo Credits

Color Figure 3.
Courtesy of Marcus E. Raichle, M.D., Washington University School of Medicine.

Demo 7-6.
Reprinted by permission of Academic Press, Inc.

Figure 12-1.
Courtesy of Carolyn Rovee-Collier.

Demo 2-2.
Gibson, Eleanor J., *Principles of Perceptual Learning and Development,* © 1969, p. 88. Reprinted by permission of Prentice Hall, Englewood Cliffs, New Jersey.

Figure 2-2.
Biederman, Irving, "Higher-level vision" from *Visual Cognition and Action: An Invitation to Cognitive Science,* Vol. II, © 1990. Reprinted by permission.

Figure 2-3.
Cave, C.B., & S.M. Kosslyn (1993). "The role of parts and spatial relations in object identification," from *Perception,* 22, 229-248. Reprinted by permission.

Figure 2-5.
Schacter, D.L. et al. (1991). "Implicit memory for possible and impossible objects: Constraints on the construction of structural descriptions" from *Journal of Experimental Psychology: Learning, Memory and Cognition,* 17, p. 4. Reprinted by permission.

Figure 2-6.
Tanaka, J.W., & M.J. Farrah (1993). "Parts and wholes in face recognition," from *Quarterly Journal of Experimental Psychology,* 46A, 225-245. Reprinted by permission.

Demo 2-6.
Treisman, A.M., & J. Souther (1985). "Search asymmetry: A diagnostic for preventive processing of separalbe features," from *Journal of Experimental Psychology: General,* 114. Reprinted by permission.

Figure 3-1.
Atkinson, R.C., & R.M. Shiffrin (1968). "Human memory: A proposed system and its control processes," from *The Psychology of Learning and Motivation: Advances in Research and Theory,* Vol. II. Reprinted by permission of Academic Press, Inc. and the author.

Table 3-1.
Adapted from Kintsch, W., & H. Buschke (1969). "Homophones and synonyms in short-term memory," from *Journal of Experimental Psychology,* 80, 403-407.

Figure 3-2.
Rundus, D. (1971). "Analysis of rehearsal processes in free recall," from *Journal of Experimental Psychology,* 89, 63-77. Reprinted by permission.

Figure 3-5.
Greenwald, A. & M.R. Banaji (1989). "The self as a memory system: Powerful, but ordinary," from *Journal of Personality and Social Psychology,* 57. Reprinted by permission.

Figure 4-3.
Crowder, R.G. (1982). "Decay of auditory memory in vowel discrimination," from *Journal of Experimental Psychology: Learning, Memory and Cognition,* 8, 153-162. Reprinted by permission.

Figure 4-5.
Naveh-Benjamin, Moshe & Thomas Ayres (1986). "Digit span, reading rate, and linguistic relativity," from *Quarterly Journal of Experimental Psychology,* 38, 739-751. Reprinted by permission.

Figure 4-6.
Brandimonte, M.A. (1992). "Influence of short-term memory codes on visual image processing: Evidence from image transformation tasks," from *Journal of Experimental Psychology: Learning, Memory and Cognition,* 18, 157-165. Reprinted by permission.

Figure 4-7.
Wickens, D.D., R.E. Dalezman, & F.T. Eggemeier (1976). "Multiple encodings of word attributes in memory," from *Memory & Cognition,* 4, 307-310. Reprinted by permission of Psychonomic Society, Inc.

Figure 5-1.
Conway, M.A., G. Cohen, & N. Stanhope (1992). "Very long-term memory for knowledge acquired at school and university," from *Applied Cognitive Psychology,* 6, 467-482. Reprinted by permission.

Demo 5-7.
Roediger, III, H.L. & K.B. McDermott (1995). "Creating false memories: Remembering words not presented in lists," from *Journal of Experimental Psychology: Learning, Memory and Cognition,* 21, 803-814. Reprinted by permission.

Figure 5-4.
Loftus, E.F., H.J. Burns, & D.G. Miller (1978). "Semantic integration of verbal information into visual memory," from *Journal of Experimental Psychology: Human Learning and Memory,* 4.

Demo 6-1 and Figure 6-1.
Shepard, R.N., & J. Metzler (1971). "Mental rotation of three-dimensional objects," from *Science,* 171, 701-703.

Figure 6-2.
Jolicoeur, P., & S.M. Kosslyn (1985). "Demand characteristics in image scanning experiments," from *Journal of Mental Imagery,* 9, figure 2. Reprinted by permission.

Figure 6-3.
Intons-Peterson, M.J., W. Russell, & S. Dressel (1992). "The role of pitch in auditory imagery," from *Journal of Experimental Psychology: Human Perception and Performance,* 18, 233-240. Reprinted by permission.

Figure 6-5.
Paivio, A. (1978). "Comparison of mental clocks," from *Journal of Experimental Psychology: Human Perception and Performance,* 4.

Figure 6-6.
Brooks, L.R. (1968). "Spatial and verbal components of the act of recall," from *Canadian Journal of Psychology,* 22, 349-368. Reprinted by permission.

Figure 6-7.
Craver-Lemley, C., & A. Reeves (1987). "Visual imagery selectively reduces vernier acuity," from *Perception,* 16, 599-614. Reprinted by permission of Pion Limited, London, and the author.

Figure 7-1.
Smith, E.E. (1978). "Theories of semantic memory," from *Handbook of Learning and Cognitive Processes: Linguistic Functions in Cognitive Theory,* 6. Reprinted by permission of Lawrence Erlbaum Associates, Inc.

Figure 7-5.
Lovelace, Eugene A. (1984). "Probability of recalling an item, as a function of experimental condition and rated likelihood of answering the question," from *Journal of Experimental Psychology: Learning, Memory and Cognition,* 10. Reprinted by permission.

Figure 7-6.
Cull, W.L., & E.B. Zechmeister (1994). "The learning ability paradox in adult metamemory research: Where are the metamemory differences between good and poor learners?" from *Memory & Cognition,* 22, 249-257. Reprinted by permission of authors.

Table 7-2.
Murphy, G.L. & A.M. Shapiro (1994). "Forgetting of verbatim information in discourse," from *Memory & Cognition,* 22, 85-94. Reprinted by permission.

Figure 8-3.
Posner, M.I. & M.E. Raichle (1994). *Images of mind,* from *Scientific American Library.* Reprinted by permission.

Demo 9-3 and Figure 9-3.
Clark, H. & D. Wilkes-Gibbs (1986). "Referring as a collaborative process," from *Cognition,* 22, 1-39. Reprinted by permission.

Figure 9-4.
New England Telephone, "Customer Notification: Multilanguage Statement." Used with permission of New England Telephone.

Figure 9-5.
Bahrick, H.P., et al. (1994). "Fifty years of language maintenance and language dominance in bilingual Hispanic immigrants," from *Journal of Experimental Psychology: General,* 123, 264-283. Reprinted by permission.

Figure 10-5.
Amabile, T.M. (1983). Figure excerpt from *The Social Psychology of Creativity.* Copyright © 1983 by Springer-Verlag. Reprinted by permission.

Table 11-3.
Frisch, D. (1993). "Reasons for framing effects," from *Organizational Behavior and Human Decision Processes,* 54, 399-429. Reprinted by permission.

Figure 12-2.
Rovee-Collier, C. & K. Boller (1995). "Current theory and research on infant learning and memory," from *Application to Early Intervention, Infants and Young Children,* 7 (3), 1-12. Reprinted by permission.

Figure 12-5.
Kuhl, et al. (1991). "Linguistic experience alters phonetic perception in infants by six months of age," from *Science,* 255. Reprinted with permission. Copyright © 1991 by the American Association for the Advancement of Science.

Abelson, R. P., 243
Abrahamsen, A., 17
Abrams, R. A., 291
Adams, J. L., 299
Adelson, E. H., 109
Adeyemo, S. A., 351
Adler, J., 369
Adler, T., 146
Afflerbach, P., 311
Agans, R. P., 428
Agnoli, F., 405
Ahn, W. K., 233
Alba, J. W., 242, 245, 246, 254, 255
Albert, M. L., 152
Albertson, S. A., 451
Albrecht, J. E., 300
Alexander, J. M., 457
Allbritton, D. W., 305
Allport, A., 45, 47
Alterman, R., 307
Amabile, T., 376, 377, 378–379
American Psychological Association, 277
Anderson, J. R., 80, 228, 230–233, 354, 358, 363, 364
Anderson, R. E., 160, 221
Anderson, S. J., 243
Andreassen, C., 457
Andrews, F. M., 376, 377
Anes, M., 291
Anglin, J. M., 468
Anthony, T., 153
Antonietti, A., 183
Arbuckle, T. Y., 213
Archibald, R. B., 422
Aretz, A. J., 209
Aristotle, 3
Ashcraft, M. H., 348
Astington, J. W., 454
Atkinson, R. C., 5, 65, 66, 67–75, 104, 108, 115–116, 257
Ayres, T. J., 121

Baars, B. J., 57
Babcock, R. L., 451

Baddeley, A. D., 70, 73, 74, 78, 91, 93, 101, 115–116, 118, 119, 120, 127, 128, 130, 131, 133, 154, 176, 197, 224, 257
Bahrick, A. S., 176
Bahrick, H. P., 137, 138, 154, 176, 334, 335, 336, 337
Bahrick, L. E., 176
Bahrick, P. E., 176
Baillargeon, R., 441
Baird, J. C., 184, 186
Baker-Ward, L., 447
Baldo, S., 183
Bales, J., 426
Banaji, M. R., 83, 85, 168
Banks, W. P., 109, 110
Barber, G., 109
Barber, P., 44
Barclay, C. R., 158
Barnhardt, T. M., 155, 165
Baron, J., 244, 298, 357, 369, 373, 375, 377, 397, 415, 426
Barsalou, L. W., 7, 228, 234, 240, 244, 268
Bartlett, F., 6, 184, 242, 253, 300
Bartsch, K., 454
Bassili, J. N., 148
Bates, E., 17, 461, 462, 465, 467, 470
Batterman, N., 468, 469
Bauer, M. I., 391
Bauer, P. J., 437, 444
Beach, K., 177
Beaton, R. J., 109
Beattie, G., 316, 327
Bechtel, W., 17
Bédard, J., 366
Begg, I., 140, 170, 171, 362
Bell, L., 298
Bell, P. B., 388
Bellezza, F. S., 83, 84, 119, 152, 153, 169, 171, 172, 179
Benson, L. III, 421
Berardi-Coletta, B., 371
Bernardo, A. B. I., 300
Berry, S. L., 310

Berz, W. L., 131
Besner, D., 17, 295, 296, 298
Bevan, K. M., 37
Bialystok, E., 332, 333, 336, 337, 339
Biederman, I., 28, 33, 34
Bieman-Copland, S., 459
Bird, J. E., 454
Birnbaum, M. H., 405
Birren, J. E., 436, 449
Bjork, E. L., 142
Bjork, R. A., 93, 142, 176
Bjorklund, D. F., 447, 456
Black, J. B., 230, 232
Blanc, M. H. A., 334
Blanchard, H. E., 292
Blaney, P. H., 144, 145
Bliss, J. C., 105
Bloom, C. P., 25
Bloom, L. C., 79
Blumstein, S. E., 279, 280
Bly, B., 321, 326
Bock, J. K., 317, 318
Bock, K., 259, 276, 316, 320
Boden, M. A., 373
Bohm, P., 421
Bolger, F., 429
Boller, K., 437, 438, 440
Bookman, L. A., 307
Boruff, B., 120
Bothwell, R. K., 153
Bottoms, B. L., 446
Bourg, T., 188
Bower, G. H., 83, 144, 145, 170, 173, 174, 175, 212, 234, 254, 301
Bowers, K. S., 58
Bowles, C., 428
Bradshaw, J. L., 296
Brandimonte, M. A., 123, 124, 128
Bransford, J. D., 6, 30, 79, 250, 251, 253, 342, 346
Brennan, S. E., 307, 322
Brewer, W. F., 21, 157, 246
Breyer, S., 409
Briere, J., 166

Brigham, T. C., 153
Broadbent, D. E., 49
Bronfenbrenner, U., 168
Brooks, L. R., 196, 197
Brouwer, W. H., 55
Brown, A. L., 442, 454
Brown, A. S., 259, 268
Brown, J., 116, 117, 118
Brown, N. R., 154, 409
Brown, P., 83, 326
Brown, R., 5, 155, 156, 257–258, 259, 470
Brown, R. T., 375
Brown, S. I., 342
Bruce, P. R., 459
Bruce, R. T., 33
Bruce, V., 40, 63
Bruck, M., 154, 299, 444, 445, 446, 475
Bryant, D. J., 219
Buck, C., 166
Buck, D. K., 152
Buehler, R., 155, 160, 165
Burgess, C., 278
Burgess, N., 131
Buschke, H., 70–71, 74, 123
Busey, T. A., 110
Bush, G., 318
Bushnell, I. W. R., 437
Butters, N., 11, 148
Byrne, B., 296
Byrne, R. M. J., 392, 393, 432

Cairns, R. B., 447
Calderwood, R., 432
Calkins, M. W., 4
Camp, C. J., 177
Campbell, L., 409
Campbell, R., 286, 333
Cannon, C. K., 426, 428
Caramazza, A., 298, 334
Carlson, E. R., 403, 426
Carlson, L., 175
Carlson, R. A., 115
Carpenter, P. A., 115, 183, 188, 295
Carrasco, M., 184

Carroll, D. W., 272, 276, 288, 300, 313, 316, 320, 322, 465
Carver, C. S., 83
Castle, J. M., 299
Catchpole, M. J., 449
Catlin, J., 234
Cattell, J., 37
Cave, C. B., 33, 35
Ceci, S. J., 152, 166, 168, 363, 444, 445, 446, 475
Cerella, J., 449
Cernoch, J. M., 437
Cervone, D., 414
Cesa, I. L., 243
Chafe, W., 327
Chambers, D., 201, 202, 203, 207
Chang, T. M., 225
Chapman, G. B., 419
Chapman, J. P., 411
Chapman, L. J., 411
Chapman, R. S., 468
Charness, N., 363, 459
Chase, C. H., 25
Chase, W. G., 277, 364
Chastain, G., 37
Chater, N., 394, 395
Chawarski, M. C., 293
Cheng, P. W., 51, 395
Cherry, C., 46
Chi, M. T. H., 363, 364, 365, 366, 371
Chialant, D., 298
Chipman, S., 195
Chomsky, N., 7, 274–276, 277
Christensen-Szalanski, J. J. J., 409, 428
Church, B. A., 150
Churchland, P. M., 14, 16
Churchland, P. S., 14, 16
Clark, D. M., 60
Clark, E. V., 467, 468
Clark, H. H., 2, 259, 277, 321, 322, 322–324, 325, 326, 461
Clark, M. C., 175
Claxton-Oldfield, S. P., 403
Clemen, R. T., 397
Clement, C. A., 391

Clement, J., 364
Cohen, G., 10, 80, 153, 158, 228, 451
Cohen, J. D., 48, 99
Cohen, M. M., 289
Cohen, M. S., 392, 426, 429
Cohen, N. J., 99
Cohen, R., 217
Cole, R. A., 286, 287
Collins, A. M., 228–230, 233
Coltheart, M., 110, 295, 296, 297
Connolly, T., 429
Conte, J., 166
Conway, A. R. A., 122
Conway, M. A., 137, 138, 154, 157, 168, 243
Coon, V. E., 451
Cooper, L. A., 40, 186, 188, 285, 291
Corballis, M. C., 51
Corbetta, M., 56
Coren, S., 13, 27, 283
Cornoldi, C., 264
Corteen, R. S., 47
Corter, J. E., 238
Cosmides, L., 395
Coté, N., 366
Coupe, P., 213
Courage, M. L., 444
Cowan, N., 8, 46, 106, 109, 110, 111, 113–114, 115–116, 118, 120, 133
Cowey, A., 63
Cox, J. R., 395
Craik, F. I. M., 2, 76, 77, 78, 79, 80, 102, 251, 398, 449, 450, 451, 453
Cranberg, L. D., 152
Crandall, C. S., 398
Craver-Lemly, C., 197, 198, 199–200, 204, 208, 221
Crevier, D., 13, 14
Creyer, E., 428
Crick, F., 97, 98, 102
Crocker, J., 411
Cross, D. R., 458
Crovitz, H. F., 15

Crowder, R. G., 74, 112–113, 115, 122, 167, 290, 292, 297, 298, 313, 450
Cull, W. L., 264, 265
Cummins, D. D., 362, 391
Cunningham, T. F., 122
Cutler, B. L., 162, 163, 181

Daneman, M., 294, 330
Danielewicz, J., 327
Dark, V. J., 47
Darke, S., 122
Darwin, C. J., 111, 112, 113
Davidson, D., 246, 249, 342, 347, 405, 443
Davidson, J. E., 369, 370, 381
Davidsson, P., 396
Davies, G. M., 142, 163
Dawes, R. M., 426
De Groot, A., 364
De Jong, G., 307
De Jong, R., 49
De Jong, T., 364
de Villiers, J. G., 467, 470, 471, 475
de Villiers, P. A., 467, 470, 471, 475
DeCasper, A. J., 437
Deese, J., 317
DeHart, G., 466
Dell, G. S., 17, 315, 319, 320
Dember, W. N., 4
Dempster, F. N., 126, 176
Dennett, D. C., 14
Dent, H., 446
Desimone, R., 42
Desrochers, A., 171
Deutsch, D., 49
Deutsch, J. A., 49
Devolder, P. A., 263
Di Lollo, V., 109, 110
Diaz, R. M., 333
Dietrich, D., 428
Dixon, P., 110
Dixon, R. A., 459
Doctor, E. A., 296
Dodd, B., 286

Donley, R. D., 348
Donnellan, A. M., 122
Dopkins, S., 302
Dostoyevski, F., 59
Dror, I. E., 183, 188
Du Boulay, B., 354
Dumais, S. T., 191
Duncan, E. M., 188
Duncker, K., 369
Dunlosky, J., 262, 264
D'Ydewalle, G., 86

Ebbinghaus, H., 4, 5, 6, 9, 253
Egeth, H., 162
Eimas, P. D., 283, 284, 286, 287, 313, 339, 462
Einhorn, H. J., 426
Einstein, G. O., 170
Eisenberger, R., 379
Eiser, J. R., 17
Elias, J. W., 452
El-Dinary, P. B., 169, 179
Elliott, C. S., 422
Elliott, J. M., 80
Ellis, A., 327
Ellis, A. W., 63
Ellis, H. D., 162
Elman, J., 17
Engle, R. W., 122, 295, 442
Epstein, S., 405
Erber, J. T., 450
Erdelyi, M. H., 60
Ericsson, K. A., 58, 131, 151–152, 153, 181, 363, 364, 381
Ervin-Tripp, S., 325, 472
Estes, W. K., 74, 98
Evans, J. St. B. T., 8, 386, 392, 395, 401, 403, 432
Evans, R. B., 4
Eysenck, M. W., 6, 8, 9, 14, 43, 49, 67, 92, 224, 228, 373

Faigley, L., 327
Falmagne, R. J., 391
Farah, M. J., 11, 41, 42, 55, 198, 204, 205, 207, 221

Farrar, M. J., 443
Farthing, G. W., 57, 63
Favreau, O. E., 188
Feinstein, M. H., 25
Feldman, D. H., 373
Fenson, L., 467
Ferber, R., 320
Ferguson, E. L., 219
Ferguson-Hessler, M. G. M., 364
Fernald, A., 466
Ferreira, F., 291, 316, 317
Fielding-Barnsley, R., 296
Fifer, W. P., 437
Finke, R. A., 183, 184, 202, 203, 204, 373, 374, 375, 377, 381
Finley, G. E., 451
Fischhoff, B., 416, 427, 428
Fischler, B., 67, 170
Fischler, I., 334
Fisher, D. L., 51
Fisher, L. E., 57
Fiske, S. T., 2
Fivush, R., 2, 443
Flavell, E. R., 454
Flavell, J. H., 447, 454, 455, 458
Fletcher, C. R., 274
Flin, R., 446
Flores d'Arcais, G. B., 287
Flower, L. S., 328
Fodor, J. A., 17
Foley, H. J., 13, 27, 63, 283
Foley, M. A., 442, 445, 449
Fong, G. T., 401
Forster, K., 37
Forward, S., 166
Foss, D. J., 278, 301, 315
Foti, R. J., 243
Fournier, J., 177
Fox, C. R., 397
Frankel, A. D., 377
Franklin, N., 217–219
Franks, J. J., 30, 250, 251
Freeman, M., 373
Frensch, P. A., 122
Freud, S., 60
Frick, R. W., 128

Friedman, W. J., 154
Frisch, D., 397, 423, 424, 429
Fromkin, V. A., 315
Fruzzetti, A. E., 162, 163
Fry, P. S., 449
Fusella, V., 198

Galambos, S. J., 333
Galotti, K. M., 386, 390
Ganellen, R. J., 83
Gara, M. A., 144
Gardner, H., 3–4, 6, 9, 10, 11, 24, 57, 184, 205, 358
Gardner, R. C., 332
Garfield, M. H., 25
Gärling, T., 209
Garman, M., 271
Garner, W. R., 31
Garnham, A., 390
Garrett, M. F., 316
Garry, M., 163
Garton, A. F., 466
Garvey, C., 472
Gass, S. M., 333
Gathercole, S. E., 116, 127, 128, 130, 131, 133, 447
Gazdar, G., 271
Gazzaniga, M. S., 13, 24
Gebotys, R. J., 403
Gegenfurtner, K. R., 107
Geiselman, R. E., 140, 141
Gelade, G., 51, 52
Gellatly, A., 351
Gelman, R., 472
Gelman, S. A., 454, 472
Genesee, F., 333
Gernsbacher, M. A., 300, 313, 339
Gero, J. S., 373
Gerrig, R. J., 300, 305, 322
Ghatala, E. S., 308, 309
Gibbs, R. W., 326
Gibson, E., 31, 32
Gigerenzer, G., 396, 402, 425, 426, 429
Gilewski, M. J., 451
Gilhooly, K. J., 356, 357, 377

Gilligan, S. G., 83
Gilmore, G. C., 450
Ginossar, Z., 403
Glaser, R., 363, 364, 365, 366
Glass, A. L., 171
Gleason, J. B., 276, 339, 466
Glenberg, A. M., 308, 311
Glenny, J., 140, 141
Glicksohn, J., 214
Glover, J. A., 175
Gluck, M. A., 238
Glucksberg, S., 278
Golden, R. M., 307
Goldin, S. E., 209
Goldinger, S. D., 283
Goldin-Meadow, S., 333
Goldman, W. P., 136
Goldstein, A. G., 162
Goldstein, E. B., 27, 63
Goleman, D., 373
Golombok, S., 2
Gonsiorek, J. C., 412
González, P., 144
Goodglass, H., 11
Goodman, G. S., 443, 446
Goodsitt, J. V., 462
Gordon, P., 198
Gotlib, I. H., 144
Gowin, D. B., 342
Graber, M., 440–441
Graesser, A. C., 302, 305
Graf, P., 78, 147
Graham, D. J., 2, 16, 17
Green, B. F., 348
Green, B. L., 456
Green, D. P., 422
Green, F. L., 454
Green, G. M., 326
Green, I., 294
Greenberg, J., 426
Greene, J., 306
Greene, R. L., 74, 78, 121, 147, 148, 151
Greeno, J. G., 343, 345, 347, 354, 356, 357, 358, 359
Greenwald, A. G, 60, 83, 85
Gregory, W. L., 413
Griffin, D., 426

Griffin, T., 425
Griffith, P. L., 299
Griggs, R. A., 394, 395, 396
Groninger, L. D., 173
Gross, C. G., 42
Gross, T. F., 456
Grossman, L. R., 166, 181
Gruneberg, M., 154, 175
Guilford, J. P., 374–375
Gunner, M. R., 288

Haaga, D. A. F., 144
Haber, R. N., 110
Hakuta, K., 332, 333, 336, 337, 339
Hale, S., 453
Hall, C., 369
Hall, L. K., 137, 176
Halpern, D. F., 346, 349, 351, 359, 381, 391
Halpin, J. A., 83
Hamers, J. F., 334
Hamilton, D. L., 249, 401, 411, 412, 413
Hamond, N. R., 443
Hanley, J. R., 259
Harder, P., 15
Hardiman, P. T., 365
Hardyck, C. D., 296, 298
Harris, G., 322
Harris, J. F., 442
Harris, R. A., 274
Harris, R. J., 254–255, 316
Harsch, N., 157
Hartley, A. A., 48
Hartman, M., 452
Hasher, L., 93, 177, 178, 228, 242, 245, 246, 254, 255, 452
Hastie, R., 364, 428–429, 432
Hawkins, H., 44, 45
Hawkins, S. A., 428–429
Hayes, D. S., 454
Hayes, J. R., 327, 328, 329, 330, 342, 344, 345, 346, 348
Hayman, C. A. G., 92
Hearnshaw, L. S., 3
Hearst, E., 3, 21

Hegarty, M., 219
Heibeck, T. H., 467
Helstrup, T., 202
Hemenway, K., 239
Hennessey, B. A., 342, 378
Herrmann, D. J., 74, 75, 78, 93, 154, 171, 172, 174, 177, 178, 181, 459
Hershey, D. A., 366
Hertel, P. T., 177
Hertzog, C., 179, 459
Higbee, K. L., 171
Hill, J. W., 105
Hill, R. D., 172
Hineline, P. N., 5
Hinrichs, T. R., 342
Hinsley, D., 359
Hinsz, V. B., 402, 403
Hinton, G. E., 97
Hintzman, D. L., 6, 7, 88
Hirschberg, J., 318
Hirsh-Pasek, K., 466
Hirst, W., 43, 44, 45, 47, 57, 58, 93, 147, 174
Hirtle, S. C., 210, 211
Hitch, G. J., 74, 127, 128, 131
Hochberg, J., 291
Hoefnagel-Hohle, M., 337
Hoffman, J. E., 36
Hoffrage, U., 402, 429
Hogarth, R. M., 426
Hogben, J. H., 109
Hollingworth, H., 143
Holmes, V. M., 278, 316
Holtgrave, D. R., 418
Holyoak, K. J., 6, 115, 360, 395
Horowitz, L. M., 234
Houtz, J. C., 377
Hoving, K. L., 442
Howard, R. W., 78, 99, 102, 105
Howe, M. L., 444, 445
Howes, J. L., 155
Hoyt, S. K., 83, 84
Hryciw, B., 79
Hubbard, T. L., 184, 186
Hubel, D. H., 13, 31
Huber, V. L., 422
Huey, E. B., 290

Hug, K., 396
Huitema, J., 302, 303, 304
Hulicka, I., 449
Hulme, C., 447
Humphreys, M. S., 93
Hunt, E., 10, 346, 363, 453
Hunt, R. R., 80
Huntsman, L. A., 188
Hyman, I. E. Jr., 202

Inhoff, A. W., 292
Intons-Peterson, M. J., 153, 177, 184, 189, 191, 192, 204, 221
Iran-Nejad, A., 292
Irwin, D. E., 110

Jackendoff, R., 279, 280
Jackson, S. L., 395
Jacoby, L. L., 149
Jacquette, D., 14
Jakimik, J., 287
James, W., 4, 5, 9, 15, 43
Janowsky, J. S., 462
Jarvella, R. J., 272–273, 274
Jenkins, F., 163
Jenkins, J. J., 248–249
Jennings, J. M., 453
Jernigan, T. L., 151
Jespersen, O., 333
John, O. P., 401
Johnson, E. J., 419
Johnson, J. S., 336–337
Johnson, M. K., 6, 93, 155, 159, 160, 164, 228, 257
Johnson, R. D., 421
Johnson-Laird, K. F., 73
Johnson-Laird, P. N., 73, 94, 232, 390, 391, 392, 393, 395
Johnston, W. A., 47
Jolicoeur, P., 30, 188, 189
Jones, D. M., 130
Jonides, J., 51, 211
Jordan, K., 188
Jordan, T. R., 37
Jou, J., 316

Jusczyk, P. W., 287, 289
Just, M. A., 115, 188, 295

Kahn, J. H., 60
Kahneman, D., 397, 399, 400, 401, 402, 404, 405, 406, 408, 410, 413, 414, 415, 416–417, 418, 419, 420, 421, 425, 429
Kail, R. V. Jr., 188, 437, 442, 447, 455, 456, 475
Kardash, C. A. M., 254
Kasper, L. F., 171
Katz, A. N., 83, 155, 227
Kaufman, N. J., 311
Kaufmann, G., 202, 351
Kausler, D. H., 436, 450
Keane, M. T., 7, 9, 67, 92, 224, 228, 359
Keil, F. C., 11, 468, 469
Keller, T. A., 114
Kelley, C. M., 259
Kellogg, R. T., 327, 328, 339
Kelly, A. E., 60
Kemper, S., 461
Kendler, H. H., 6
Kent, D., 184
Keren, G., 349, 351, 425
Kerr, N. H., 188
Kida, T., 418
Kiewra, K. A., 177
Kihlstrom, J. F., 17, 60, 84, 85, 140, 151, 155, 165
Kilborn, K., 336
Kintsch, W., 70–71, 74, 123, 131, 153, 274, 286, 300, 301, 307, 364
Kirker, W. S., 82
Kitchin, R. M., 208
Klaczynski, P. A., 396
Klein, G. A., 397, 432
Klein, S. B., 84, 85
Klinger, M. R., 60
Koenig, O., 206, 307
Koestler, A., 351
Koh, K., 360
Komatsu, L. K., 233, 234, 235, 241

Kopelman, R. I., 408
Koriat, A., 78, 161, 259
Kosslyn, S. M., 11, 33, 35, 98, 99, 183, 184, 188, 189, 191, 192, 203, 204, 205, 206, 208, 221, 241, 307, 449
Kounios, J., 227
Kowalski, R. M., 326
Kozielecki, J., 409
Kozin, M., 156
Krajicek, D., 110
Krantz, D. H., 405
Kreutzer, M. A., 454
Kreuz, R. J., 302, 324
Kroll, N., 47, 91
Krueger, L. E., 37
Kuczaj, S. A., 470, 471
Kuhl, P. K., 283, 284, 287, 288, 289, 307, 313, 462–463, 464, 466
Kuhn, D., 396
Kuiper, N. A., 82
Kulhavy, R. W., 209
Kulik, J., 155, 156
Kunda, Z., 17, 401
Kurdek, L. A., 412

La Voie, D., 451
LaBerge, D. L., 4
Labov, W., 321
Lachman, M. E., 449
Lamb, C., 373
Lambert, W. E., 332, 333, 334
Laming, D., 124
Landau, M. J., 30
Lange, G., 457
Langer, E. J., 366
Lansman, M., 346
Larkin, J. H., 364
Lave, J., 140
Lavigne, V. D., 451
Lawson, A. E., 359
Lawson, D. I., 359
Leal, L., 262
Legrenzi, P., 393
Lehman, A. C., 151, 153, 363
Lehmkuhle, S. W., 31

Lehnert, W. G., 232
Leichtman, M., 444, 446
Leonard, L. B., 276
Leonesio, R. J., 263
Lesgold, A., 341
Levelt, W. J. M., 315, 316, 317, 320
Levin, I. P., 421, 422
Levine, M., 356
Levinson, S. C., 326
Levy, C. M., 327, 329
Levy, V. M., 456
Lewandowsky, S., 14, 99
Li, S. C., 99
Liben, L. S., 447
Liberman, A., 288
Liberman, A. M., 299
Liberman, I. Y., 299
Light, L. L., 449, 451, 452, 453, 459, 461, 475
Liker, J. K., 152, 363
Lima, S. D., 453
Lind, H., 421
Linde, C., 321
Lindsay, D. S., 163, 166, 259
Lindsay, R. C. L., 153
Lindsay, R. O., 364
List, J. A., 162
Littman, M. L., 322
Lively, S. E., 287, 291
Locke, J. L., 464
Lockhart, R. S., 77, 78, 79, 102, 147
Loeb, D. F., 276
Loftus, E. F., 60, 110, 162, 163, 164, 166, 168, 228–230, 233, 444
Loftus, G. R., 110
Logie, R. H., 127, 128, 131, 133, 345
Long, G. M., 108, 109
López, R. L., 334
Lorch, R. F., Jr., 290, 311, 313
Lord, C. G., 234
Lord, R. G., 243
Lovelace, E. A., 260, 261, 262, 449, 451, 459
Lowe, R. K., 183

Lu, A. L., 114
Lubart, T. I., 373, 376, 377
Luchins, A. S., 365, 367
Luger, G. F., 10, 13, 16
Lupart, J. L., 449
Lupker, S. J., 16
Lutz, J., 183

MacDonald, M. C., 295
Macfarlane, A., 437
Macias, F. M., 444
MacLeod, C. M., 48, 122, 148, 409
Madigan, S., 4
Maher, M. L., 373
Maier, N. R. F., 58
Maki, R. H., 310
Malpass, R. S., 153
Malt, B. C., 228, 234
Mandler, G., 6, 7, 8
Mandler, J. M., 436, 441, 444, 467
Manis, M., 410
Manketelow, K. I., 386
Mannion, K., 412
Mäntysalo, S., 114
Maratsos, M., 272, 279, 288
Marentette, P. F., 464
Margolis, E., 233
Markman, E. M., 467
Markovitz, H., 392, 395
Marr, D., 33
Marsh, G. R., 459
Marshall, J. C., 13
Marslen-Wilson, W. D., 289, 301
Martin, E., 263
Martin, J. H., 307
Martin, R. C., 128
Martindale, C., 16, 95
Mascolo, M. F., 210, 211
Mason, M., 298
Mason, S. E., 262
Massaro, D. W., 8, 286–287, 289, 405
Masson, M. E. J., 228
Matheny, L., 272, 279

Matlin, M., 13, 27, 63, 143, 144, 179, 283, 387, 466
Mattingly, I., 288
Mayer, J. D., 144, 145, 234
Mayer, R., 421
Mayer, R. E., 342, 346, 348
Mazzoni, G., 262, 264
McCarthy, G., 282
McClelland, A. G. R., 429
McClelland, J. L., 14, 15, 16, 25, 37, 95, 97, 99, 299, 470
McCloskey, M., 99, 157
McConkie, G. W., 291, 292
McDaniel, M. A., 170, 171, 184
McDermott, K. B., 166, 168
McDonald, J. E., 48
McDonough, L., 441, 444, 467
McDowd, J. M., 451
McKeachie, W. J., 179
McKelvie, S. J., 170, 368
McKitrick, L. A., 177
McKoon, G., 87, 91–93, 302, 303, 305
McLaughlin, M. L., 324
McLeod, P., 8
McNamara, T. P., 209, 210
McNeil, B. J., 421
McNeill, D., 257–258, 259
McTear, M. F., 11, 472
Meacham, J. A., 161
Medin, D. L., 233
Mednick, M. T., 375
Mednick, S. A., 375
Mehler, J., 17, 275
Melcher, J., 370, 372
Melkman, R., 78
Mellers, B. A., 397
Melton, A. W., 70
Menard, M. T., 281
Menyuk, P., 464, 465, 466
Merck, Sharp, & Dome Pharmaceuticals, 175
Merluzzi, T. V., 244
Mervis, C. B., 234, 237, 238
Metcalfe, J., 268, 370, 371, 372
Metzler, J., 185, 186, 187–188
Meyer, A. S., 259
Miller, G. A., 7, 58, 119, 271, 435

Miller, J. L., 283, 284, 286, 287, 289, 313, 339, 462
Miller, J. R., 274
Miller, L. C., 472
Miller, P. H., 447
Miller, S. A., 447
Miller, T. P., 327
Millis, K. K., 217, 305
Mills, C. J., 83
Milner, B., 73
Mineka, S., 144
Miner, A. C., 259
Miner, C. S., 122
Mitchell, D. B., 147
Miyake, A., 278, 294
Moar, I., 212
Moely, B. E., 447
Moody, D. B., 289
Moravcsik, J. E., 300
Moray, N., 46, 49
Morris, M. W., 239
Morris, N., 130
Morris, P. E., 160, 161, 168, 175
Morrow, D. G., 301
Moscovitch, M., 79, 251
Mountcastle, V. B., 15
Moyer, R. S., 191, 192, 193
Mudd, S. A., 79
Müller, P. U., 291
Murphy, G. L., 239, 251, 252
Murray, B., 299
Muter, P., 122
Mycielska, K., 161
Myers, N. A., 442

Näätänen, R., 56, 114
Nadel, L., 67
Nakatani, C. H., 318
Nantel, G., 392
Narens, L., 262
Nasby, W., 144
Natanson, K., 473
Natsoulas, T., 57
Naveh-Benjamin, M., 121
Neale, M. A., 419, 421
Needham, D. R., 362
Neisser, U., 7, 8, 14, 107, 111, 157, 158, 234

Nelson, K., 443, 469
Nelson, T. O., 57, 58, 86, 256, 260, 262, 263, 264, 268
Nettleton, N. C., 296
Newell, A., 357, 358
Newman, J. E., 271
Newport, E. L., 336–337
Newsome, G. L. III, 177
Newstead, S. E., 392, 432
Ng, W. K., 153
Nickerson, R. S., 4, 375, 388
Niesser, U., 444
Nilsson, L. G., 74
Nisbett, R., 58, 147, 256, 398, 401, 410, 432
Nobre, A. C., 282
Noice, H., 152
Noordman, L. G. M., 305
Norman, D. A., 67, 217, 233
Northcraft, G. B., 419, 421
Nosofsky, R. M., 30
Novick, L. R., 360–362, 364, 365, 366

Oakhill, J. V., 390, 395
Oaksford, M., 394, 395
Obler, L. K., 277
O'Brien, E. J., 290, 313
Oden, G. C., 37, 38, 289
O'Hara, R., 4
Oliver, W., 33, 173
Olson, M., 428
Olson, M. W., 299
Orasanu, J., 429, 432
Ormerod, T. C., 390
Ormrod, J. E., 208
Ortony, A., 268
Osgood, C. E., 43
Ostergaard, A. L., 151
Ostrom, T. M., 9
O'Toole, A. J., 153
Over, D. E., 386
Owens, R. E., Jr., 465, 470, 475

Paivio, A., 170, 193, 194, 195
Palmer, C. F., 240

Palmer, S. E., 17, 36
Palmere, M., 80, 81
Paris, S. G., 458
Parkin, A. J., 78, 451
Pastore, R. E., 289
Patel, V. L., 366
Pauker, S. G., 408
Paulos, J. A., 399
Paulsen, J. S., 151
Payne, D. G., 176
Payne, J. W., 397, 424
Peal, E., 333, 334
Pennington, N., 151–152, 153
Penrod, S. D., 162, 163, 181
Perfect, T. J., 259
Perfetti, C. A., 291, 295, 297, 298, 302
Perkins, D. N., 344, 373
Perky, C., 197
Perlmutter, M., 442
Peronnet, F., 205
Perrett, D. I., 63
Peters, D. P., 442
Petersen, S. E., 11, 281
Peterson, L., 116, 117, 118
Peterson, M., 116, 117, 118
Peterson, M. A., 203
Peterson, S. A., 425
Petitto, L., 464
Petrinovitch, L. R., 296, 298
Petro, S. J., 177
Pettigrew, T. F., 249, 268
Pezdek, K., 155
Phelps, E., 176
Phillips, W. D., 79, 80, 264, 325
Piaget, J., 7, 184, 242, 436
Piattelli-Palmarini, M., 397, 432
Pierce, S. H., 457
Pillemer, D. B., 155
Pinker, S., 17, 27, 30, 33, 186, 270, 273, 274, 288, 470
Pisoni, D. B., 284, 285
Pitz, G. F., 400
Platt, R. D., 394, 395, 396
Plous, S., 397
Pollard, P., 395, 401, 403
Pollatsek, A., 37, 291, 292
Pollina, L. K., 160, 459
Poon, L. W., 177

Porter, R. H., 437
Posner, M. I., 3, 8, 12, 13, 30, 55, 56, 57, 63, 281, 282
Postman, L., 122
Potter, M. C., 293
Poulton, E. C., 397, 401, 403, 413, 415, 432
Powell, J. S., 293, 294
Powers, C. B., 449
Powers, S., 334
Pressley, M., 166, 170, 179, 181, 263, 308, 309, 311, 457
Presson, J., 44, 45
Priest, A. G., 364
Prince, A., 470
Prull, M., 155
Pryor, J. B., 244
Pylyshyn, Z. W., 17, 185, 206–207, 208

Quinn, P. C., 467
Quinsey, V. L., 426, 428

Raaijmakers, J. G., 97
Rabinowitz, J. C., 459
Rachlin, H., 3, 4
Raderscheidt, A., 56
Raichle, M. E., 12, 13, 55, 56, 63, 281, 282
Ransdell, S., 327, 329, 334
Rastle, K., 295
Ratcliff, R., 92, 302, 303, 305
Ratner, H. H., 442, 445
Ratner, N. B., 276, 339, 466
Raye, C. L., 160
Rayner, K., 37, 290, 291, 292
Read, J. D., 166
Read, S. J., 243
Reason, J., 161
Rebok, G. W., 450
Reder, L., 80, 259
Reed, S. K., 30, 183, 200–201, 207, 359, 360, 363
Reeder, G. D., 83, 85
Reeves, A., 197, 198, 199, 204, 208

Reeves, L. M., 359
Reicher, G. M., 37
Reinitz, M., 44, 54
Reisberg, D., 184, 201, 202, 207, 221
Remez, R. E., 283, 284
Ressler, W. H., 285
Reyna, V. F., 163
Reynolds, A. G., 333
Reynolds, R. I., 363
Rhodes, G., 30
Ricciardelli, L. A., 334
Richards, A., 48
Richardson-Klavehn, A., 93, 142
Richman, H. B., 37
Ridout, J. B., 184
Rips, L. J., 225, 407
Rissland, E. L., 25
Roberts, R. M., 324
Robins, R. W., 398
Robinson, D. L., 11
Robinson, J. A., 154
Roşu, D., 473
Roedel, T. D., 262
Roediger, H. L. III, 77, 147, 148, 149, 150, 151, 166, 168
Rogers, D., 471
Rogers, T. B., 82, 83
Rogers, W., 425
Rogoff, B., 10, 436
Rojahn, K., 249, 268
Roland, P. E., 12
Rolls, E. T., 42
Rosch, E. H., 31, 233, 234, 235, 236, 237, 238–239, 241
Roskos-Ewoldsen, B., 221, 373
Ross, L., 398, 410
Ross, M., 155, 160, 165
Ross, W. T., Jr., 428
Rosser, R., 442
Rothbart, M. K., 55, 281, 401
Rovee-Collier, C., 437, 438, 439, 440
Rubin, D. C., 10, 154, 156, 170, 181
Rueckl, J. G., 37, 38, 94, 99, 278
Rugg, M. D., 12
Ruiz-Caballero, J. A., 144

Rumelhart, D. E., 15, 37, 97, 98, 99, 217, 233, 260, 307, 470
Runco, M. A., 342
Rundus, D., 71–73
Russ, S. W., 373
Russell, J. A., 209, 234, 437
Russo, R., 451
Ryan, C., 51
Rychlak, J. F., 143

Sachs, J., 250, 465
Sachs, N. J., 400
Safire, W., 287
Sai, F., 437
Sais, E., 333
Sakitt, B., 109
Salasoo, A., 285
Salmon, M. H., 396
Salthouse, T. A., 436, 449, 451, 452, 453, 459, 460, 475
Sams, H., 56
Samuel, A. G., 285
Sanbonmatsu, D. M., 413
Sanford, A. J., 8
Sato, S., 51, 54
Savary, F., 395
Schacter, D. L., 39, 40, 90, 98, 145–146, 147, 148, 149, 150, 151, 155, 162, 209
Schaie, K. W., 436, 449
Schank, R. C., 243
Schiano, D. J., 212
Schiffrin, D., 321
Schmidt, H., 53
Schmidt, M. J., 204
Schneider, W., 2, 12, 16, 17, 48, 49, 50, 51, 52, 61, 127, 457, 458
Schoenfeld, A. H., 348
Schooler, J. W., 164, 166, 168, 369, 370, 372, 422
Schraagen, J. M., 364
Schraw, G., 262, 310
Schwanenflugel, P. J., 457
Schwartz, N. H., 209
Schwartz, S., 425
Schwartz, S. H., 353
Schweickert, R., 120

Scott, M. S., 442
Scott, S., 334
Seamon, J. G., 136, 155
Searle, J. R., 14, 57
Searleman, A., 74, 75, 78, 93, 171, 172, 177, 178, 181
Sebel, P. S., 151
Sebrechts, M., 122
Segal, S., 198
Segal, S. J., 198
Seidenberg, M. S., 99, 295, 296, 298, 299, 307
Seifert, C., 245, 304, 305, 359, 362
Selbst, M., 379
Selinker, L., 333
Sellen, A. J., 160, 161
Sereno, S., 291, 292
Sergent, J., 42
Serra, M., 310
Servan-Schreiber, D., 99
Sewell, D. R., 244
Shaffer, L. S., 428
Shafir, E. B., 405
Shah, P., 183
Shallice, T., 73
Shapiro, A. M., 251, 252
Shapiro, K. L., 43
Shapiro, P. N., 162, 163
Shatz, M., 472
Shepard, R. N., 184, 185, 186, 187–188, 195
Sherman, J. W., 249, 401
Sherman, M. A., 277
Sherman, S. J., 155
Sherry, D. F., 90
Shiffrin, R. M., 5, 48, 49, 50, 51, 52, 61, 66, 67–75, 97, 104, 108, 115–116, 117, 118, 257
Shiloh, S., 409, 418
Shimamura, A. P., 268
Shin, H. J., 30
Shoben, E. J., 92, 225, 242
Siegel, A. W., 442
Siegler, R. S., 409, 437
Signoret, J. L., 42
Simon, H. A., 2, 5, 37, 58, 119, 204, 344, 345, 346, 348, 354, 357, 358, 364

Simpson, G. B., 278
Singer, J., 161
Singer, M., 274, 302, 306
Slamecka, N. J., 78
Slobin, D. I., 275–276, 471
Slovic, P., 409, 411, 415, 416, 421, 422, 426, 427, 428
Small, M. Y., 442, 443, 447
Smith, A. D., 450, 452, 453
Smith, A. F., 198
Smith, E. E., 225, 226, 234, 239, 300, 366, 367, 370, 377, 390
Smith, E. R., 411
Smith, J., 152, 153, 181
Smith, J. F., 418
Smith, M. U., 341, 342
Smith, S. M., 142, 368, 381
Smith, V. L., 259
Smyth, M. M., 127, 153, 215, 216, 286, 287, 397
Snodgrass, J. G., 93
Snow, C. E., 336, 337, 472
Snyder, A. Z., 281
Souther, J., 53, 54
Speer, S. R., 301
Spelke, E., 44
Spellman, B. A., 6, 115
Spence, M. J., 437
Sperling, G., 107, 108, 109, 111, 112
Sperry, R. W., 7, 8
Spilich, G. J., 300
Spoehr, K. T., 31
Sporer, S. L., 79
Springston, F., 174
Squire, L. R., 67, 70, 73, 88, 341
Sroufe, L. A., 466
Srull, T. K., 2
Staines, P. J., 388
Stainton, M., 330
Standing, L., 136
Stang, D. J., 143, 144
Stanovich, K. E., 37
Stein, B. S., 346
Stemberger, J. P., 315
Sternberg, R. J., 293, 294, 373, 376, 377, 381
Stevens, A., 213
Stillings, N. A., 15, 25, 356, 357,

358
Stine, E. L., 450, 461
Strawson, C., 298
Stroop, J. R., 48
Suarez-Balcazar, Y., 342
Sugg, M. J., 48
Suh, S., 303
Sutton, S. K., 144
Suzuki-Slakter, N. S., 263
Svartik, J., 277
Svenson, O., 421
Sweller, J., 356
Swinney, D. A., 300
Szsambok, C., E., 432

Tahta, S., 336
Tanaka, J. W., 41, 42, 240
Taplin, J. E., 390
Tarone, E. E., 333
Tartter, V. C., 307, 462
Taylor, H. A., 217
Taylor, I. A., 37, 271, 277, 317, 332, 334
Taylor, M., 240
Taylor, M. M., 37, 271, 277, 317, 332, 334
Taylor, S. E., 2
Tees, R. C., 462
Thagard, P., 17
Thal, D., 462
Thapar, A., 74
Thomas, J. C., 342, 343, 356
Thomas, M., 172
Thompson, C. P., 12, 154
Thompson, L. W., 450
Thompson, R. F., 25, 279
Thompson, W. B., 262
Thomson, J. R., 468
Thorndyke, P. W., 209, 210, 242
Tiitinen, H., 56
Tindale, R. S., 402, 403
Titcomb, A. L., 163
Togeby, O., 15
Tolstoy, L., 59
Tomasello, M., 466
Toms, M., 128, 130, 390
Topolski, R., 292
Tordoff, V., 447

Torgesen, J. K., 296
Trabasso, T., 301, 303
Trafimow, D., 243, 244
Trahan, D. E., 451
Travis, Q. B., 155
Treisman, A., 30, 46, 47, 51, 52, 53, 54, 59, 61
Treyens, J. C., 21, 246
Trolier, T. K., 411
Trope, Y., 403
Tulving, E., 10, 57, 65, 66, 76, 78, 80, 87–93, 151, 168, 201
Turcotte, P., 332
Turner, S. R., 373
Turvey, M. T., 112
Tversky, A., 397, 399, 400, 401, 402, 404, 405, 406, 408, 410, 413, 414, 415, 416–417, 418, 419, 420, 421, 425, 426, 429
Tversky, B., 212, 213, 214, 215, 216, 217, 217–219, 219
Twohig, P. T., 459
Tyler, A., 301

Ucros, C., 145
Underwood, B. J., 92
Underwood, N. R., 291
Usher, J. A., 444

Valian, V., 326
Valsiner, J., 447
van den Broek, P., 301
van der Heijden, A. H. C., 109
van Dijk, T. A., 274
Van Oostendorp, H., 303
Van Orden, G. C., 297, 298
Van Selst, M., 188
van Zomeren, A. H., 55
VanderStoep, S. W., 359, 362
Vecera, S. P., 55
Vellutino, F. R., 296
Vicente, K. J., 364
Vosniadou, S., 268
Voss, J. F., 365

Wagner, R. K., 290, 292, 296, 297, 298, 313
Wahlund, R., 396
Wakefield, J. F., 373
Waldrop, M. M., 11
Walker, W. R., 143
Walker-Andrews, A. S., 464
Wallace, B., 57
Walsh, D. A., 450
Walter, M. I., 342
Walton, G. E., 437
Wang, A., 172
Ward, L. M., 209
Ward, T. B., 381
Wardlaw, K. A., 47
Warren, D. H., 208, 209
Warren, R. M., 284, 285
Warren, R. P., 285
Warrington, E., 73, 148
Wason, P. C., 391, 393, 394
Waters, H. S., 457
Waterstreet, M., 89
Watson, J., 184
Watson, J. B., 5, 9
Waugh, N. C., 67
Weatherford, D. L., 208
Weaver, C. A. III, 157
Weber, E. U., 409
Weber, R. J., 373
Wegner, D. M., 59, 60, 63
Weingardt, K. R., 163
Weinstein, C. E., 452
Weisberg, R. W., 359, 373, 381
Weiskrantz, L., 148
Weisler, S. E., 25
Weldon, M. S., 149, 150, 151
Well, A. D., 401
Wellman, H. M., 158, 447, 454, 455, 457, 472
Wells, G. L., 79
Wenger, M. J., 176
Werker, J. F., 462
West, R. F., 37
Whitbourne, S. K., 449
White, P., 140
Wickelgren, W. A., 70, 123
Wickens, C. D., 209
Wickens, D. D., 124–125, 126
Wiebe, D., 370

Wiesel, T. N., 13, 31
Wilkes-Gibbs, D., 322–324
Willham, C. F., 428
Willows, D. M., 290
Wilson, B. A., 177
Wilson, T. D., 58, 147, 256
Wingfield, A., 270
Winograd, E., 10, 168
Winzenz, D., 169
Wittgenstein, L., 237
Wittrock, M. C., 174
Wolfe, J. M., 54

Wolff, A. S., 364
Wolford, G., 405
Wood, B., 47
Wood, N., 46
Wundt, W., 3–4, 5, 9, 37, 184
Wurtz, R. H., 56
Wyer, R. S., 2, 243, 244

Yeni-Komshian, G. H., 289
Yeomans, J. M., 110

Yopp, H. K., 299
Yuille, J. C., 184, 449
Yussen, S. R., 454, 456

Zacks, R. T., 177, 178, 452
Zechmeister, E. B., 264, 265
Zelinski, E. M., 451
Zeman, B. R., 447
Zimmer, J. W., 175
Zóla, D., 292

Note: New terms appear in boldface print.

Abstract reasoning problems, difficulties with, 391

Abstraction
definition of, 250
schemas and, 250–252

Accuracy. *See also* Theme 2 (efficiency and accuracy)
of autobiographical memory, 155
of long-term memory, 137–153, 155
of metacomprehension, 308–310
of metamemory, 260–262, 456
of problem solving, 366

Acoustic coding, in short-term memory, 73–74, 122–123

ACT* theory, 230–232, 358

Active voice
language comprehension and, 277
selection of, in speech, 317, 318

Actors, expertise of, 152–153

Additive bilingualism, 332

Affirming the antecedent, 387–390

Affirming the consequent, 387–390

Afterimages, and imagery, 204

Aged. *See* Elderly people

AI (artificial intelligence), 13–15, 306–308

Algorithm, 354

Alignment heuristic, 214–217

Alzheimer's disease, 148, 172

Ambiguity
ambiguous sentences, 275
imagery and ambiguous figures, 200–203
language comprehension and, 275, 277–278, 279

Ambiguous sentences, 275

Amnesia, infantile, 444

Amnesic patients, implicit memory of, 148

Analog code, 184–185, 205–206

Analogy approach to problem solving, 358–362

Anchor, definition of, 415

Anchoring and adjustment heuristic, 414–420

Angles, and cognitive maps, 212

Antecedent, in conditional reasoning, 387–389

Anterior attention network, 56

Aphasia, 279–280

Artificial intelligence (AI)
computer simulation, 14–15
definition of, 306
machine metaphor and, 13–14
processing and, 16
pure AI, 14, 306
reading and, 306–308

Association for Advancement of Behavior Therapy, 9

Atkinson-Shiffrin model of memory
current status of, 74–75
description of, 67–69
evidence against, 73–74
neuroscience research and, 73, 74
research on, 70–74

Attention
automatic versus controlled processing and, 49–51
biological basis of, 54–57
bottle-neck theories of, 48
consciousness, 57–60
definition of, 43
dichotic listening, 46–47
divided attention, 44–45, 52
early theories of, 48
elderly and, 452–453
exercises (demonstrations) on, 48, 52, 53, 57

Attention *(cont.)*
feature-integration theory of, 51–54
focused attention, 51–52
problem understanding and, 345–346
selective attention, 45–48
Stroop effect and, 47–48
theories of, 48–54

Auditory sensory memory. *See* Echoic memory

Autobiographical memory
accuracy of, 155
in children, 443–446
definition of, 154
ecological validity and, 167–168
exercises (demonstrations) on, 155, 158, 161, 165
eyewitness testimony, 162–167
and face identification by eyewitnesses, 162–163
false memory controversy, 165–167
flashbulb memory, 155–157
memory for action, 159–162
misinformation effect and, 163–165
and misleading post-event information, 163–165
prospective memory, 160–161
reality monitoring, 159–160
schemas and, 157–159

Automatic processing
attention and, 49–51
definition of, 49
thought suppression and, 59

Availability heuristic, 406–414

Babbling, 464

Background information, and framing effect, 418, 420

Base rate
definition of, 401
representativeness and, 401–403

Base-rate fallacy, 402–403

Basic-level categories, 238

Bayes' theorem, 402

Behaviorism
cognitive approach and, 5, 9
consciousness as inappropriate for study, 57
definition of, 5
insight as inappropriate for study, 369
mental imagery as inappropriate for study, 184
"pure behaviorism," 9

Belief-bias effect, 391–392

Biases
belief-bias effect, 391–392
confirmation bias, 394–396
experimenter expectancy, 189–191
hindsight bias, 426–429
own-race bias, 153

Bilingual, definition of, 332

Bilingualism
additive bilingualism, 332
advantages of, 333–334
definitions concerning, 332
disadvantages of, 334
examples of, 331–332
exercise (demonstration) on, 337
maintenance of first language among immigrants, 334–335
second-language proficiency as function of age of acquisition, 335–337

Bilingualism *(cont.)*
subtractive bilingualism, 332

Blocking-plus-retrieval-failure theory, 470

Bottle-neck theories of attention, 48

Bottom-up processing. *See also* Theme 5 (bottom-up and top-down processing)
definition of, 21
pattern recognition and, 28–36
problem solving and, 363

Brain
aphasia and, 279–280
attention and, 54–57
Broca's area in, 279–280
cerebral cortex, 15–16, 54–57
cognitive neuroscience and, 11–13
imagery and, 204–205
language and, 278–282
lesions of, 11, 56
machine metaphor for, 13–14
semantic memory and, 241
Wernicke's area, 280

Brain lesions, 11, 56

Broca's aphasia, 279–280

Broca's area, 279–280

Categorization, in prototype approach to semantic memory, 237–240

Category size effect, 228

Central executive, 130–131

Cerebral cortex
attention and, 54–57
definition of, 15
parallel distributed processing approach and, 15–16

Characteristic features, 227, 469

Children
autobiographical memory in, 443–446
imagery in, 449
infantile amnesia and, 444
language development in, 435–436, 466–473
long-term memory in, 442–446
memory in, 441–449
memory strategies of, 446–449
metacognition in, 454–458
metamemory in, 454–458
morphology in, 469–470
organizational strategies in, 447–448
pragmatics in, 471–473
problem finding by, 342
rehearsal by, 447
sensory memory in, 442
syntax in, 470–471
vocabulary growth and word usage in, 461, 467–469
working memory in, 442

Chunking, as mnemonic method, 174

Chunks, 119–120

Classical view of concepts, 233–234

Coarticulation, 284

Cognition. *See also* Metacognition; and headings beginning with Cognitive
definition of, 2
reasons for study of, 2–3

Cognitive approach
definition of, 2
emergence of contemporary cognitive psychology, 6–8
history of, 3–8

Cognitive development
exercises (demonstrations) on, 443, 448, 455, 466, 468

Cognitive development (cont.)
language development, 435–436, 460–473
memory in children, 441–449
memory in elderly people, 449–453
memory in infants, 436–441
metacognition in children, 454–458
metacognition in elderly people, 459–460
Cognitive maps
alignment heuristic and, 214–217
angles and, 212
curves and, 211, 212
definition of, 208–209
distance and, 209–211
exercises (demonstrations) on, 211, 216
and number of intervening cities, 210
relative positions and, 213–217
and road-route distance, 210
rotation heuristic and, 213–214
semantic categories and, 210–212
shapes and, 212–213
spatial arrangement and, 213
spatial framework model and, 218–219
symmetry heuristic and, 212
verbal descriptions used to create mental models, 217–219
Cognitive neuroscience
current issues in, 11–13
definition of, 11
echoic memory and, 114
imagery and, 204–205

Cognitive neuroscience (cont.)
language comprehension and, 280–282
memory and, 73, 74, 114
semantic memory and, 241
and Tulving's model of memory, 91–92
Cognitive psychology
artificial intelligence (AI) and, 13–15
cognitive neuroscience and, 11–13
cognitive science and, 10–11
criticisms of, 9–10
current issues in, 9–17
definition of, 2
emergence of contemporary cognitive psychology, 6–8
historical roots of, 3–6
parallel distributed processing approach to, 15–17
themes in, 20–21
Cognitive Psychology (Neisser), 7
"Cognitive revolution," 7
Cognitive science, 10–11
Cognitive unconscious, 60
Collins and Loftus network model, 228–230
Color afterimages, and imagery, 204
Common ground, 322–324
Comprehension. *See* Language comprehension
Computational approach, to pattern recognition, 33–35
Computational metaphor, 13–14
Computer simulation, 14–15, 306, 357–358
Conceptually driven processing, 35. *See also* Top-down processing
Conditional reasoning
belief-bias effect, 391–392

Conditional reasoning (cont.)
confirmation bias in, 394–396
constructing only one model of the premises, 392–393
definition of, 386
difficulties with abstract reasoning problems, 391
difficulties with negative information, 390
failure to transfer knowledge to new task, 396
illicit conversion in, 393
overview of, 387–390
Confidence intervals, 416–418
Confirmation bias, 394–396
Conjugate reinforcement technique, 437–440
Conjunction fallacy, 403, 404–405
Conjunction rule, 405
Connection weights, 98
Connectionism, 15–17, 94, 98. *See also* Parallel distributed processing (PDP) approach
Consciousness
cognitive unconscious, 60
definition of, 57
exercise (demonstration) on, 57
about higher mental processes, 58–59
thought suppression, 57, 59–60
Consensual assessment technique, 376
Consequent, in conditional reasoning, 387–389
Constituents, 272–274
Constructionist view, of inferences, 302–303
Constructive model of memory, 250–251
Constructivist approach to memory, 165

Content addressable, 95

Context

as accuracy determinant
in long-term memory,
140–142

and discovering meaning
of unfamiliar word,
292–294

expertise and, 151–152

pattern recognition and,
36–39

social context of speech,
322–327

speech perception and,
284–286

Control processes, 69

Controlled processing

attention and, 49–51

definition of, 49

thought suppression and,
59

Conversational format, 324–325

Cooing, 464

Correlation

definition of, 144n

illusory correlation and
availability, 411–413

Correlational research, on
Tulving's model of memory,
92

Creativity

approaches to, 373–376

consensual assessment
technique, 376

definition of, 373

divergent production and,
374–375

exercises (demonstrations)
on, 374, 375

incubation and, 377

influences on, 377–379

investment theory of, 376

Remote Associates Test
(RAT), 375–376

social factors influencing,
377–378

Crib speech, 471

Cross-race effect, 153

Curves, and cognitive maps,
211, 212

Data-driven processing, 35. *See
also* Bottom-up processing

Decision making. *See also*
Problem solving and
anchoring and adjustment
heuristic, 414–420

availability heuristic and,
406–414

base-rate fallacy in,
402–403

conjunction fallacy in,
403, 404–405

definition of, 386

errors in, 397–398

exercises (demonstrations)
on, 399, 403, 406, 410,
415, 417– 419, 423, 427

framing effect and, 418,
419, 420–425

hindsight bias and,
426–429

optimists versus
pessimists, 429–430

overconfidence in
decisions, 425–429

representativeness
heuristic and, 398–406

simulation heuristic and,
413–414

Declarative knowledge, 230–232

Deductive reasoning

belief-bias effect, 391–
392

conditional reasoning,
386, 387–390

confirmation bias in,
394–396

constructing only one
model of premises,
392–393

definition of, 386

difficulties with abstract
reasoning problems,
391

Deductive reasoning *(cont.)*

difficulties with negative
information, 390

exercises (demonstrations)
on, 388, 394

failure to transfer
knowledge to new task,
396

illicit conversion in,
393

propositional reasoning,
386, 387–390

syllogism, 386–387

Deep dyslexia, 296

Deep representation, 206

Deep structure, 274–275

Default assignment, 97

Defining features, 227, 469

Demand characteristics, 203

Denying the antecedent, 388,
389–390

Denying the consequent, 388,
389–390, 389n

Depictive representation,
184–185, 205–206

Depth-of-processing approach
to memory, 77. *See also*
Levels-of-processing
approach to memory

Descriptive representation, 186,
206–207

Development of cognition. *See*
Cognitive development

Dichotic listening, 46–47

Direct-access theory, of word
recognition, 295, 296

Directives, 325–327

Discourse

definition of, 300, 320

forming coherent
representation of text,
300–301

inferences in reading,
301–306

metacomprehension,
308–311

producing discourse,
320–321

Discourse *(cont.)*
understanding of, 300–311
Dissociation, 148–149
Distance, and cognitive maps, 209–211
Distinctive features, definition of, 31
Distinctive-features models, 31–33
Distinctiveness, 79–80
Distributed processing, 98
Distribution of practice effect, 176
Divergent production, 374–375
Divided attention, 44–45, 51, 52
Divided-attention tasks, 44, 45
Dual-route hypothesis, of word recognition, 295, 297
Duplex model, 70
Dyslexia, 296

Echo, 111
Echoic memory, 68, 111–114, 450
Ecological validity
autobiographical memory and, 168–169
definition of, 10, 167
Elaboration, 80
Elaborative rehearsal, 77
Elderly people
explanations for age differences in memory, 452–453
long-term memory in, 451–452
memory in, 449–453
metacognition in, 459–460
sensory memory in, 450
working memory in, 450–451
Emotion. *See* headings beginning with Mood
Encoding
definition of, 79

Encoding *(cont.)*
in levels-of-processing approach to memory, 79
Encoding specificity principle, 140–142, 149–150
Episodic memory
compared with semantic memory, 88–92, 224–225
definition of, 88, 224–225
exercise (demonstration) on, 90
and Tulving's model of memory, 88–92
ERP (event-related potential technique), 12, 56–57, 281
Errors in speaking, 317–320
Event-related potential technique (ERP), 12, 56–57, 281
Everyday memory, 154. *See also* Autobiographical memory
Evoked-response potential technique, 12
Exhaustive search, 354
Expanding retrieval practice, 176
Experience. *See* Past experience
Experimenter expectancy, 189–191
Expertise
and accuracy of long-term memory, 151–153
context-specific nature of, 151–152
definition of, 151, 363
knowledge base and, 363–364
novices compared with experts, 153
own-race bias and, 153
problem solving and, 363–366
of professional actors, 152–153
of waiters, 152
Explicit memory measures, 145–151, 451

External memory aids, 177
Eye movements, during reading, 110–111, 291–292
Eyewitness testimony, 162–167

Face perception, 40–42
Face recognition
depth of processing and, 78–79
eyewitness testimony and, 162–163
infant's recognition of mother's face, 437
Fallacies
base-rate fallacy, 402
small-sample fallacy, 401
False memory controversy, 165–167
Familiarity, and availability, 409–410
Family resemblance, 237
Fast mapping, 467
Feature comparison model, of semantic memory, 225–228
Feature inhibition mechanism, 54
Feature-integration theory, 51–54
Feeling of knowing, 259
First language (L1)
definition of, 332
maintenance of, among immigrants, 334–335
First letter technique, as mnemonic method, 174–175
Fixations, 291
Flashbulb memory, 155–157
fMRI (functional magnetic resonance imaging), 12, 204
Focused attention, 51–52
Forgetting. *See* Memory
Framing effect, 418, 419, 420–425
FRUMP, 307
Functional fixedness, 368–369
Functional magnetic resonance imaging (fMRI), 12, 204

General knowledge. *See*
  Metacognition; Schemas;
  Semantic memory
General mechanism approaches
  to speech perception, 289
General Problem Solver (GPS),
  358
Generation effect, 78
Geometrical ions, 33, 34
Geons, 33, 34
Gestalt psychology, 6, 369
Goal state of problem, 342
Government-binding theory,
  276
GPS (General Problem Solver),
  358
Graceful degradation, 98, 260
Graded structure, 234
Grammar
  definition of syntax,
    272
  syntax of children,
    470–471
  transformational
    grammar, 274–276
Graphs, for representing a
  problem, 351, 352

Habituation, 462
Heuristics, *See also* Theme 2
  alignment heuristic,
    214–217
  anchoring and
    adjustment heuristic,
    414–420
  availability heuristic,
    406–414
  in decision making,
    398–420
  definition of, 242, 354,
    397
  means-ends heuristic,
    355–358
  for problem solving,
    354–358
  90°-angle heuristic, 212
  representativeness
    heuristic, 398–406

Heuristics *(cont.)*
  rotation heuristic,
    213–214
  schemas as, 242
  simulation heuristic,
    413–414
  symmetry heuristic, 212
Hierarchical tree diagrams,
  349–351
Hierarchy, as mnemonic
  method, 174, 175
Higher level inferences,
  305–306
Hindsight, 426
Hindsight bias, 426–429
Holistic (processing), 41
Homonyms, 296

Icon, 107
Iconic memory, 68, 70, 107–111
Illicit conversion, 393
Illusory conjunction, 54
Illusory correlation, 411–413
Imagery
  ambiguous figures and,
    200–203
  analog versus
    propositional coding
    for, 184–186, 205–207
  characteristics of mental
    images, 184–207
  in children, 449
  cognitive maps, 208–219
  and color afterimages,
    204
  definition of, 169, 183
  exercises (demonstrations)
    on, 185, 189, 193, 200,
    202
  and experimenter
    expectancy, 189–191
  interference and, 196–200
  mnemonics using,
    169–173
  and neuropsychological
    evidence for similarity
    with perception,
    204–205

Imagery *(cont.)*
  oblique effect and,
    203–204
  psychophysics and, 191
  for representing the
    problem, 351
  rotation and, 185, 186–188
  shape and, 193–196
  size and, 188–193
  stabilized images, 204
  uses of, 183–184
  vision-like processes and,
    203–204
  visual acuity and, 203
Imitation, 441
Immigrants, maintenance of
  first language among,
  334–335
Implicit memory, 148–150
Implicit memory measures,
  145–151, 451
Incidental learning, 246
Incubation, and creativity, 377
Indirect-access hypothesis, of
  word recognition, 295,
  296–297
Indirect speech acts, 326
Infantile amnesia, 444
Infants
  conjugate reinforcement
    technique and,
    437–440
  imitation by, 441
  language development in,
    460–466
  language production in,
    464–465
  magnet effect and,
    463–464
  memory in, 436–441
  nonnutritive sucking by,
    462
  parents' language to,
    465–466
  recognition of mother by,
    437
  and remembering
    location of objects,
    440–441

Infants *(cont.)*
  speech perception in,
    461–464
Inferences
  constructionist view of,
    302–303
  definition of, 253, 301
  factors encouraging,
    303–305
  higher level inferences,
    305–306
  minimalist hypothesis of,
    302
  in reading, 301–306
  schemas and inferences in
    memory, 252–254
**Information-processing
  approach,** definition of, 8
Initial state of problem, 342,
  365–366
Insight problems, 369–372
Intentional communication, 465
Intentional learning, 249
Interference, and imagery,
  196–200
Internal psycophysics, 191
Introspection, definition of, 3
Investment theory of creativity,
  376

Kernel, 275
Keyword method, as mnemonic
  method, 171–172
Knowledge. *See* Metacognition;
  Schemas; Semantic memory;
  and headings beginning with
  Cognitive
Knowledge base, problem
  solving and, 363–364

L1. *See* First language (L1)
Language comprehension
  ambiguity and, 275,
    277–278
  definitions concerning
    language, 271–272

Language comprehension *(cont.)*
  exercises (demonstrations)
    on, 279, 287, 293, 297,
    302, 310
  factors affecting, 276–278
  memory and, 273–274
  metacomprehension,
    308–311
  nature of language,
    271–282
  negatives and, 276–277
  neurolinguistics and,
    278–282
  neuroscience and,
    280–282
  passive voice and, 277
  phrase structure, 272–274
  reading, 290–311
  speech perception,
    283–289
  transformational
    grammar and, 274–276
  understanding discourse,
    300–311
Language development
  in children, 435–436,
    466–473
  exercises (demonstrations)
    on, 466, 468
  in infants, 460–466
  parents' language to
    infants, 465–466
Language production
  bilingualism, 331–337
  in infants, 464–465
  lack of research on, 315
  problem solving and,
    371–372
  speaking, 316–327
  writing, 327–330
Law of large numbers, 401
Learning
  incidental learning, 246
  intentional learning, 249
  situated learning, 359
Lesions of brain, 11, 56
Levels-of-processing approach
  to memory
    current status of, 86

Levels-of-processing approach
  to memory *(cont.)*
    definition of, 76–77
    description of, 76–77
    and effectiveness of deep
      processing, 79–81
    encoding and retrieval in,
      79
    exercise (demonstration)
      on, 76, 84
    face recognition and,
      78–79
    generation effect in, 78
    research on, 78–81
    self-reference effect,
      81–86
Likelihood ratio, 402
Linearization problem, 316
Linguistics. *See* headings
  beginning with Language
Listening, dichotic, 46–47
Lists, for representing the
  problem, 348
Location of objects, infants'
  remembering of, 440–441
Long auditory storage, 113
Long-term memory (LTM)
  accuracy determinants
    for, 137–153, 155
  in Atkinson–Shiffrin
    model, 68, 69
  autobiographical
    memory, 154–168
  in children, 442–446
  context and, 140–143
  definition of, 69
  in elderly people,
    451–452
  exercises (demonstrations)
    on, 138, 143, 146, 155,
    158, 161, 165, 170, 174
  expertise and, 151–153
  explicit versus implicit
    measures of memory,
    145–151
  eyewitness testimony,
    162–167
  flashbulb memory,
    155–157

Long-term memory (LTM) *(cont.)*
    improvement of, 168–179
    Kintsch and Buschke's
       research on, 70–71
    language comprehension
       and, 274
    mood and, 143–145
    permastore and, 137
    prospective memory,
       160–161
    reality monitoring,
       159–160
    retrospective memory,
       160
    semantic coding in, 74
Long-term recency effect, 74
Long-term working memory,
    153

Machine metaphor, for brain,
    13–14
Machine vision, 33
Magnet effect, 463–464
**Magnetic resonance imaging
    (MRI),** 12
Maintenance rehearsal, 77
Matrices, for representing the
    problem, 348–349
Means-ends heuristic, 355–358
Memory
    age differences in,
       452–453
    Atkinson-Shiffrin model
       of, 67–75
    autobiographical
       memory, 154–168,
       443–446
    in children, 441–449
    constructive model of
       memory, 250–251
    constructivist approach
       to, 165
    definition of, 66
    echoic memory, 68,
       111–114, 450
    in elderly people,
       449–453
    episodic memory, 88–92

Memory *(cont.)*
    exercises (demonstrations)
       on, 76, 84, 89, 90, 94,
       105, 106, 107, 116,
       117, 120, 129, 138,
       143, 146, 155, 158,
       161, 165, 170, 174,
       443, 448
    explicit versus implicit
       measures of, 145–151
    eyewitness testimony,
       162–167
    false memory controversy,
       165–167
    iconic memory, 68, 70,
       107–111
    implicit memory, 148–150
    improvement of, 168–179
    in infants, 436–441
    inferences in, 252–254
    Kintsch and Buschke's
       research on, 70–71
    language comprehension
       and, 273–274
    levels-of-processing
       approach to, 75–86
    long-term memory, 68,
       69, 70–71, 73, 136–179,
       442–446, 451–452
    long-term working
       memory, 153
    metamemory, 178–179,
       260–266, 454–458
    neuroscience research on,
       73, 74
    parallel distributed
       processing (PDP)
       approach to, 94–99,
       228
    pragmatic view of,
       251–252
    problem solving and, 364
    procedural memory, 88,
       89
    prospective memory,
       160–161
    reality monitoring,
       159–160
    repisodic memory, 158

Memory *(cont.)*
    repressed memory,
       166–167
    retrospective memory,
       160
    schemas and inferences
       in, 252–254
    schemas and integration
       in, 254–255
    schemas and memory
       abstraction, 250–252
    schemas and memory
       selection, 245–250
    self-reference effect,
       81–86
    semantic memory, 88–93,
       224–241
    sensory memory, 67–68,
       104, 105–114, 442, 450
    short-term memory,
       68–69, 70–71, 73–74,
       115–131
    spatial memory, 208–209
    Tulving's model of, 87–93
    verbatim memory, 251
    visuo-spatial working
       memory, 128–130
    working memory, 116,
       126–131, 230, 294–295,
       442, 450–451
Memory improvement
    exercises (demonstrations)
       on, 170, 174
    external memory aids,
       177
    keyword method of,
       171–172
    metamemory, 178–179
    method of loci, 172–173
    mnemonics using
       imagery, 169–173
    mnemonics using
       organization, 173–176
    multimodal approach to,
       177–178
    practice for, 176–177
    techniques for, 168–179
Memory span, 118–122, 442
Mental imagery. *See* Imagery

Mental models, 10–11, 217–219
Mental representations,
  importance of, 9
Mental set
  definition of, 366
  problem solving and,
    366–368
Meta-analysis technique, 145,
  428, 451–452
Metacognition
  in children, 454–458
  definition of, 256, 454
  in elderly people,
    459–460
  exercises (demonstrations)
    on, 258, 455
  metacomprehension,
    308–311, 458
  metalinguistics, 333–334
  metamemory, 178–179,
    260–266, 454–458
  problem solving and, 366,
    370–371
  tip-of-the-tongue
    phenomenon, 5, 98,
    257–260
Metacomprehension, 308–311,
  458
Metalinguistics, 333
Metamemory
  accuracy of, 260–262, 456
  awareness of factors
    affecting memory, 263
  in children, 454–458
  definition of, 178, 260
  memory improvement
    and, 178–179
  and necessity of effort,
    455–456
  regulating study
    strategies, 263–266
  relationship between
    memory performance
    and, 262–263, 456–458
Method of loci, as mnemonic
  technique, 172–173
MIDAS, 307
Minimalist hypothesis, of
  inferences, 302

Misinformation effect, 163–165
Mnemonics
  chunking, 173, 174
  definition of, 169
  first letter technique,
    174–175
  hierarchy, 173–174, 175
  keyword method, 171–172
  method of loci, 172–173
  narrative technique,
    175–176
  using imagery, 170–173
  using organization,
    174–176
Mood, and long-term memory,
  143–145
Mood congruence, 144
Mood congruity, 144
Mood-state dependence,
  144–145
Morphemes, 271, 469–470
Morphology, 469–470
Motherese, 465–466
Mothers, infants' recognition of,
  437
Moving window technique, 291
**MRI (magnetic resonance
  imaging),** 12
Multilingual, definition of,
  332
Multimodal approach to
  memory improvement,
  177–178

Narrative technique, as
  mnemonic method, 175–
  176
Narratives, 321
Natural language, 306
Negative information,
  difficulties with, 390
Negatives, and language
  comprehension, 276–277
Network models, of semantic
  memory, 228–233
Neural networks, 15–17, 94. *See
  also* Parallel distributed
  processing (PDP) approach

Neurolinguistics
  adults with aphasia,
    279–280
  definition of, 278
  language comprehension
    and, 278–282
Neurons, 12, 15–16
Neuroscience. *See* Cognitive
  neuroscience
NEXUS, 307
Nodes, 16, 98, 229
Noninsight problems, 369–372
Nonnutritive sucking, 462
Novices. *See also* Expertise
  compared with experts,
    153
  problem solving and,
    363–366

Oblique effect, 203–204
Obstacles, 342. *See also*
  Problems
Older adults. *See* Elderly people
Optimists versus pessimists, and
  decision making, 429–430
Organization
  definition of, 174
  mnemonics using,
    174–176
Organizational strategies, in
  children, 447–448
Other-race effect, 153
Outshining hypothesis, 142
Overconfidence in decisions,
  425–429
Overextension, 467–468
Overregularization, 470
Own-race bias, 153

Parallel Distributed Processing
  (McClelland and
  Rumelhart), 15
**Parallel distributed processing
  (PDP) approach**
  characteristics of, 16–17,
    94–98

Parallel distributed processing (PDP) approach *(cont.)*
current status of, 98–99
definition of, 15, 228, 470
exercise (demonstration) on, 94
to memory, 94–99, 228
origins of, 15–16
to pattern recognition, 37
reactions to, 17
Parallel processing, 16, 49
Parents' language, to infants, 465–466
Parsimony principle, 113–114
Partial-report technique, 108
Participatory responses, 305–306
Passive voice
language comprehension and, 277
selection of, in speech, 317, 318
Past experience, and pattern recognition, 39–40
Pattern recognition
computational approach to, 33–35
context and, 36–39
definition of, 28
distinctive-features models and, 31–33
exercises (demonstrations) on, 28, 32, 36
face perception, 40–42
parallel distributed processing and, 37
past experience and, 39–40
prototype models and, 30–31
recognition-by-components theory of, 33–35
template-matching theory of, 29–30
theories of, 29–35
top-down processing and, 35–40

PDP approach. *See* Parallel distributed processing (PDP) approach
Perception
attention, 43–60
definition of, 27
face perception, 40–42
neuropsychological evidence for similarity between imagery and, 204–205
pattern recognition, 28–42
reading and, 291–292
speech perception, 283–289
Perceptual span, 291
Perky effect, 197–198
Permastore, 137
Pessimists and optimists, and decision making, 429–430
PET scan, 11–12, 55–56, 91, 204, 241, 281
Phoneme, 271, 284–285
Phonemic restorations, 284
Phonetic module, 288
Phonics approach, to teaching reading, 299
Phonological loop, 127–128
Phonological store, 127–128
Phonologically mediated hypothesis, of word recognition, 295, 296–297
Phonology, definition of, 335
Phrase structure, 272–274
PI (proactive inhibition, 124–126, 163
Picture superiority effect, 149
Pollyanna Principle, 143–144
Positron emission tomography (PET scan), 11–12, 55–56, 91, 204, 241, 281
Posterior attention network, 55
Practice
divided attention and, 44–45
for memory improvement, 176–177

Pragmatic view of memory, 251–252
Pragmatics
in children, 471–473
common ground, 322–324
conversational format, 324–325
definition of, 272, 322
directives, 325–327
Preschool children. *See* Children
Primacy effect, 72
Priming effect, 235–236, 239–240
Principles of Psychology (James), 4–5, 15
Proactive inhibition (PI), 124–126, 163
Problem finding, 342
Problem isomorphs, 359
Problem solving. *See also* Decision making
accuracy of, 366
analogy approach to, 358–362
approaches to, 354–362, 364–365
and attention to information in problem understanding, 345–346
characteristics of problems, 342
computer simulation and, 357–358
creativity as, 372–379
definition of, 341–342
exercises (demonstrations) on, 344, 345, 350, 352, 355, 360, 365, 367, 374, 375
expertise and, 363–366
functional fixedness and, 368–369
General Problem Solver (GPS), 358
influences on, 363–372
insight and noninsight problems, 369–372

Problem solving (*cont.*)
    language and, 371–372
    memory and, 364
    mental set and, 366–368
    metacognition and, 366,
        370–371
    and representation of
        problems, 346–353,
        364
    requirements for problem
        understanding,
        343–345
    speed of, 366
    understanding the
        problem, 343–353
Problem space, 354
Problem understanding,
    343–353
Problems. *See also* Problem
    finding; Problem solving
    characteristics of, 342
    goal state of, 342
    initial state of, 342,
        365–366
    insight problems, 369–372
    noninsight problems,
        369–372
    obstacles within, 342
    representation of,
        346–353
    source problems, 359
    subproblems, 355
    target problems, 359
    understanding of,
        343–353
Procedural knowledge, 230
Procedural memory, 88, 89
Processing cycles, 301
Production of language. *See*
    Language production
Pronunciation time, and
    memory span, 120–121
Proposition, 230–232
Propositional calculus, 387–389
Propositional code, 185–186,
    206–207
Propositional reasoning, 386,
    387–390
Prosody, 316–317

Prospective memory, 160–161
Prototype approach, to
    semantic memory, 233–241
Prototype models, 30–31
Prototype-matching theory,
    30–31
Prototypes
    characteristics of, 234–
        237
    compared with classical
        view of concepts,
        233–234
    definition of, 30, 233
    exercises (demonstrations)
        of, 234, 236
Prototypicality, 233
Psycholinguistics, definition of,
    271. *See also* headings
    beginning with Language
Psychophysics, 191
*Publication Manual of the
    American Psychological
    Association,* 277
Pure AI, 14, 306

Question wording, and framing
    effect, 419, 420–422

RAT. *See* Remote Associates Test
    (RAT)
Reading
    artificial intelligence and,
        306–308
    basic reading processes,
        290–299
    compared with writing,
        327
    discovering meaning of
        unfamiliar word,
        292–294
    exercises (demonstrations)
        on, 293, 297
    forming coherent
        representation of text,
        300–301
    inferences in, 301–306

Reading (*cont.*)
    metacomprehension and,
        308–311
    participatory responses
        and, 305–306
    perceptual processes in,
        291–292
    phonics approach to
        teaching, 299
    and sound in word
        recognition, 295–299
    teaching of, to children,
        298–299
    understanding discourse,
        300–311
    whole-language approach
        to teaching, 299
    whole-word approach to
        teaching, 298–299
    working memory and,
        294–295
Reading disorders, 296
Reality monitoring, 159–160,
    442
Reasoning. *See* Deductive
    reasoning
Rebound effect, following
    thought suppression, 59–60
Recall
    definition of, 147
    in elderly persons,
        451–452
Recency, and availability,
    408–409
Recency effect, 4, 72, 74,
    117–118
Recoding, 120
Recognition
    definition of, 147
    in elderly people, 451
**Recognition-by-components
    theory,** 33–35
Regressions, 292
Rehearsal
    by children, 447
    definition of, 69
    elaborative rehearsal, 77
    maintenance rehearsal,
        77

Rehearsal *(cont.)*
subvocal rehearsal
process, 128
Relative positions, and cognitive
maps, 213–217
**Release from proactive
inhibition,** 124
Remembering. *See* Memory
improvement
Remote Associates Test (RAT),
375–376
Repetition priming task, 147
Repisodic memory, 158
Replications, definition of, 4
Representation
importance of, 9
and problem solving, 364
Representative, definition of,
398, 400
Representativeness heuristic,
398–406
Repressed memory, 166–167
Retrieval
definition of, 79
in levels-of-processing
approach to memory,
79
Retroactive inhibition, 163
Retrospective memory, 160
Revision of writing, 329–330
Rotation, and imagery, 185,
186–188
Rotation heuristic, 213–214

Saccadic movement, 111,
291–292
Sample size, and
representativeness, 400–401
Schemas
autobiographical memory
and, 157–159
children's use of, 443
conclusions about, 255
and constructive model of
memory, 250–251
definition of, 158, 242
exercises (demonstrations)
on, 242, 243, 247–249

Schemas *(cont.)*
as heuristics, 242
and inferences in
memory, 252–254
and integration in
memory, 254–255
memory abstraction and,
250–252
memory selection and,
245–250
and pragmatic view of
memory, 251–252
scripts and, 243–245
Scripts, 243–245, 443. *See also*
Schemas
Second language (L2)
definition of, 332
proficiency in, as function
of age of acquisition,
335–337
Selective attention, 45–48
Selective-attention tasks, 45–
48
Self-reference effect, 81–86
Semantic categories, and
cognitive maps, 210–212
Semantic coding
in long-term memory, 74
in short-term memory,
124–126
Semantic memory
ACT* theory of, 230–232,
358
Collins and Loftus network
model, 228–230
compared with episodic
memory, 88–93,
224–225
definition of, 88, 224,
272
exercises (demonstrations)
on, 89, 90, 226, 234,
236
feature comparison
model of, 225–228
network models of,
228–233
prototype approach to,
233–241

Semantic memory *(cont.)*
structure of, 224–241
and Tulving's model of
memory, 88–93
Semantics, 272
Sensory memory
in Atkinson-Shiffrin
model, 67–68
in children, 442
compared with short-term
memory, 106–107
definition of, 67–68, 104
in elderly people, 450
exercises (demonstrations)
on, 105, 106, 107
functions of, 105–106
iconic memory, 68, 70,
107–111
Sensory register, 105. *See also*
Sensory memory
Sensory storage, 105. *See also*
Sensory memory
Sentence verification technique,
226, 227
Sentences, generation of,
328–329. *See also* Grammar;
Speaking; Writing; and
headings beginning with
Language
Serial position effect, 71–72,
117–118
Serial processing, 16, 49
Seven as "magical number" for
memory, 119–120
Shapes
cognitive maps and,
212–213
and imagery, 193–196
Short auditory storage, 113
Short-term memory (STM). *See
also* Working memory
acoustic coding in, 73–74,
122–123
in Atkinson-Shiffrin
model, 68–69
characteristics of, 115
code in, 122–126
compared with sensory
memory, 106–107

Short-term memory (STM) *(cont.)*
  definition of, 68, 104
  duration of, 122
  exercises (demonstrations)
    on, 116, 117, 120, 129
  Kintsch and Buschke's
    research on, 70–71
  language comprehension
    and, 273–274
  methodology in classic
    research on, 116–118
  Miller's magical number
    seven, 119–120
  pronunciation time and,
    120–121
  semantic coding in,
    124–126
  size of, 118–122
  visual coding in, 123–124
  working-memory view of,
    126–131
Simulation. *See* Computer
  simulation
Simulation heuristic, 413–414
Single-cell recording technique,
  12–13
Situated learning, 359
Size, and imagery, 188–193
Slips-of-the-tongue, 318–320
Small-sample fallacy, 401
Social factors
  creativity and, 377–378
  in language development,
    465
  speech and, 322–327
Source problems, 359
Spacing effect, 176, 440
Spatial arrangement, and
  cognitive maps, 213
Spatial framework model,
  218–219
Spatial memory, 208–209
Speaking
  active or passive voice
    selected for, 317, 318
  common ground,
    322–324
  conversational format,
    324–325

Speaking *(cont.)*
  directives, 325–327
  errors in, 317–320
  exercises (demonstrations)
    on, 320, 321, 323, 325
  indirect speech acts, 326
  narratives and, 321
  pragmatics of, 322–327
  problem solving and,
    371–372
  producing discourse,
    320–321
  production process in,
    316–317
  slips-of-the-tongue,
    318–320
  social context of, 322–327
Special mechanism approach, to
  speech perception, 288
Speech. *See* Speaking
Speech perception
  characteristics of, 283–288
  context and, 284–286
  definition of, 283
  general mechanism
    approaches to, 289
  in infants, 461–464
  special mechanism
    approach to, 288
  theories of, 288–289
  and variability in phoneme
    pronunciation, 284
  visual cues as aid to,
    286–287
  word boundaries and,
    287–288
  Speed, of problem
    solving, 366
Spoken language. *See* Language
  comprehension; Language
  production
Spontaneous generalization,
  97
Spreading activation, 229
Stabilized images, 204
STM. *See* Short-term memory
  (STM)
Strategies
  definition of, 447

Strategies *(cont.)*
  memory strategies in
    children, 446–449
  organizational strategies
    in children, 447–448
  study strategies, 263–266
Stroop effect, 47–48
Structural features, 69, 360–362
Study strategies, 263–266
Subordinate-level categories,
  238, 240
Subproblems, 355
Subtractive bilingualism, 332
Subvocal rehearsal process, 128
Subvocalizing, 298
Superordinate-level categories,
  238
Surface features, 359–362
Surface representation, 206
Surface structure, 274–275
Syllogism, 386–387
Symbolic distance effect, 191
Symbols, for representing the
  problem, 347–348
Symmetry heuristic, 212
Syntax, 272, 470–471

Target problems, 359
Taxonomic assumption, 467
Telegraphic speech, 471
Template-matching theory,
  29–30
Templates, definition of, 29
Theme 1 (active processes), 20,
  95, 127, 155, 158, 217, 251,
  271, 301, 342, 471
Theme 2 (efficiency and
  accuracy), 20–21, 34, 95, 153,
  155, 158, 179, 209, 215–216,
  251, 254, 261, 307, 317–318,
  328, 337, 369, 388–389, 396,
  397, 437, 442, 461
Theme 3 (positive information),
  21, 52–53, 144, 276–277, 390,
  395, 413
Theme 4 (interrelated
  processes), 21, 66, 160, 271,
  290, 295, 390, 422, 426

Theme 5 (bottom-up and top-down processing), 21, 35–36, 139, 153, 300, 320, 363, 367, 392, 415

Thinking. *See also* Decision making; Deductive reasoning; Problem solving definition of, 386

Thought suppression, 57, 59–60

Time window, 440

Tip-of-the-tongue phenomenon, 5, 98, 257–260

Tongue twisters, 297

Top-down processing. *See also* Theme 5 (bottom-up and top-down processing)
  and anchoring and adjustment heuristic, 415
  belief-bias effect and, 392
  definition of, 21, 35
  encoding specificity principle and, 149–150
  pattern recognition and, 35–40
  problem solving and, 363, 367, 370

Total time hypothesis, 176

Transformational grammar, 274–276

Transformational rules, 275

Tulving's model of memory
  current status of, 93
  description of, 87–91
  exercises (demonstrations) on, 89, 90
  research on, 91–93

Typicality effect, 227, 235

Unconscious, 60

Underextension, 468

Understanding. *See also* Language comprehension
  attention and problem understanding, 345–346
  definition of, 343
  methods for representing the problem, 346–353
  problem understanding, 343–353
  requirements for problem understanding, 343–345

Validity, ecological, 10, 167–168

Verbatim memory, 251

Visual acuity, and imagery, 203

Visual coding, in short-term memory, 123–124

Visual cues, as aid to speech perception, 286–287

Visual imagery. *See* Imagery

Visuo-spatial working memory, 128–130

Waiters, expertise of, 152

Wernicke's aphasia, 280

Wernicke's area, 280

Whole-language approach to teaching reading, 299

Whole-report technique, 107, 108

Whole-word approach, to teaching reading, 298–299

Word boundaries, 287–288

Word superiority effect, 37

Words. *See also* headings beginning with Language

Words *(cont.)*
  discovering meaning of unfamiliar word, 292–294
  role of sound in word recognition, 295–299
  vocabulary growth and word usage in children, 461, 467–469

Working memory. *See also* Short-term memory (STM)
  in ACT* theory, 230
  approach to short-term memory, 116, 126–131
  central executive and, 130–131
  in children, 442
  current research directions for, 131
  definition of, 127
  in elderly people, 450–451
  long-term working memory, 153
  phonological loop and, 127–128
  reading and, 294–295
  visuo-spatial working memory, 128–130

Writing
  cognitive components of, 327–330
  compared with reading, 327
  planning, 328
  revision of, 329–330
  sentence generation, 328–329

Written language
  reading of, 290–311
  understanding discourse, 300–311